THE ROUGH GUIDE TO
SWEDEN

C016907220

ROUGH
GUIDES

Contents

SKÅNE'S STUNNING SCENERY

Introduction to
Sweden

The mere mention of Sweden conjures up resonant images: snow-capped peaks, reindeer wandering in deep green forests and the 24-hour daylight of the midnight sun. But beyond the household names of ABBA, IKEA and Volvo, Sweden is relatively unknown. The largest of the Scandinavian countries, with an area twice that of Britain (and roughly that of California), but a population of just over ten million, Sweden has space for everyone: the countryside boasts pine, spruce and birch forest as far as the eye can see and crystal-clear lakes perfect for a summer afternoon dip – not to mention possibly the purest air you'll ever breathe. The country's south and west coasts, meanwhile, feature some of the most exquisite beaches in Europe – without the crowds.

In general Sweden is a carefree place where life is relaxed. Indeed, the Swedes' **liberal** and open attitude to virtually every aspect of life is certainly one of their most enviable qualities; people are generally left to do their own thing, providing it doesn't impinge on the rights and freedoms of others. In Sweden, rights go hand in hand with duties, and there's a strong sense of civic obligation (count how few times you see people dropping litter, for example), which in turn makes for a well-rounded and stable society. Many of the cornerstones of the Swedish welfare state, such as tremendously generous benefits and health-care perks, which Swedes still hold dear today, were laid down during forty years of unbroken rule by the Social Democrats.

Yet, over the years, foreigners have somehow confused the open Swedish attitude to society, including nudity and sexuality, with sex. Contrary to popular belief, Sweden isn't populated solely with people waiting for any opportunity to tear off their clothes and make passionate love under the midnight sun. It is, though, a country founded on honesty and straight talking – two of Sweden's most refreshing qualities.

GOTHENBURG'S COLOURFUL ROOFS

Where to go

Sweden is principally a land of forests and lakes. Its towns and cities are small by European standards and are mostly located in the southern third of the country, where the majority of Swedes live. Of its cities, serenely beautiful **Stockholm** is supreme. Sitting elegantly on fourteen different islands, where the waters of **Lake Mälaren** meet the Baltic Sea, the city boasts some fantastic architecture, fine museums and by far the best culture and nightlife in the country. The 24,000 islands which comprise the Stockholm **archipelago** are a perfect antidote to the urban bustle, offering endless opportunities to explore unspoilt island villages and to go swimming. On the west coast, **Gothenburg**, the country's second biggest city, is also one of Sweden's

FACT FILE

- Sweden is the **third largest country** in western Europe – behind only France and Spain – stretching 1600km from north to south. If the country were pivoted around on its southernmost point, the top of the country would reach as far south as Naples in Italy.
- There is no translation for the Swedish word **lagom**, one of the most commonly used terms in the language. Roughly speaking, it means "just the right amount, not too much but not too little", a concept that is the very essence of Swedishness.
- More than half of Sweden's land surface is covered with **forest** – mostly coniferous – punctuated by an astonishing **100,000 lakes**.
- Sweden is home to the world's first and largest **hotel** made entirely of ice and snow. *Icehotel* is built in December using blocks of ice cut from the local Torne River. The hotel melts back into the river in May.
- In northern Sweden frozen lakes and rivers are used by drivers looking for a shortcut to their destination. The national road agency marks out "**ice roads**" and decides when the ice is thick enough to support a vehicle.

SWEDEN

most appealing destinations. Gothenburgers have a reputation for being among the friendliest people in Sweden, and the city's network of canals and spacious avenues is reminiscent of Amsterdam, whose architects designed it.

The south is the most cosmopolitan part of the country, owing to the proximity of Denmark and the rest of the European continent. Here you'll find the glorious ancient university seat of **Lund** and, nearby, Sweden's third biggest city, **Malmö**, which heaves with youthful nightlife around its medieval core.

Inland, southern Sweden boasts some handsome lakes, the two largest of which, **Vänern** and **Vättern**, provide splendid backdrops to some beautiful towns, not least the evocative former royal seat and the monastic centre of **Vadstena**, and **Karlstad**, the sunshine capital of Värmland, a rugged province ideal for river-rafting trips. To the east of the mainland lies **Gotland**, justifiably raved about as a haven for summer revelry, especially within the medieval walls of its unspoilt Hanseatic city, **Visby**.

Central and northern Sweden represent the most quintessentially "Swedish-looking" part of the country. In the centre lies **Dalarna**, an area of rolling hills and

MIDSUMMER MAYHEM

An atmosphere akin to Mediterranean joie de vivre takes over Sweden during the **midsummer solstice** (the weekend closest to June 24), when maypoles are erected as giant fertility symbols in gardens and parks across the country. Midsummer is not a time for staying in towns – everyone heads to the countryside and coasts, with Dalarna, the island of Öland and the shores of the Bohuslän coast being just a few of the most popular spots. Aided in no small part by copious quantities of **alcohol**, the population's national characteristics of reserve and restraint dissolve over midsummer weekend. Long trestle tables draped in white cloths and sagging under the weight of multiple varieties of herring, potatoes with dill and gallons of *akvavit* are set up outside, and parties go on through the light night with dancing to the strains of accordions and fiddles.

NORTHERN LIGHTS

Also known by their Latin name, *aurora borealis*, the **northern lights** are visible all across northern Sweden during the dark months of winter. These spectacular displays of green-blue shimmering arcs and waves of light are caused by solar wind, or streams of particles charged by the sun, hitting the atmosphere. The colours are the characteristic hues of different elements when they hit the plasma shield that protects the Earth: blue is nitrogen and yellow-green is oxygen. Although the mechanisms which produce the aurora are not completely understood, the displays are generally more impressive the closer you get to the poles – low temperatures are also rumoured to produce some of the most dramatic performances. **Gällivare** and **Kiruna**, both well inside the Arctic Circle, are arguably the best places in Sweden to catch a glimpse of the aurora, particularly during the coldest winter months from December to February. Although displays can range from just a few minutes to several hours, the night sky must be clear of cloud to see the northern lights from Earth.

villages that's home to **Lake Siljan**, one of Sweden's most beautiful lakes. North of here lies some of the country's most enchanting scenery, home to bears, wolves and reindeer. To the east, the shoreline of the **Bothnian coast** contains the north's biggest cities: **Sundsvall**, **Umeå** and **Luleå** are all enjoyable, lively places in which to break your journey north.

The far north, inside the **Arctic Circle**, is the home of the **Sámi** – Sweden's indigenous people. Known as **Swedish Lapland**, it is also the land of reindeer, elk and bears, of swiftly flowing rivers and coniferous forest, all traversed by endless hiking routes. Sweden's northernmost town, **Kiruna**, makes an excellent base for exploring the region's **national parks** and the world-famous **Icehotel** in nearby Jukkasjärvi. Swedish Lapland is also the place to come to experience the **midnight sun**: in high summer the sun never sets, whilst in midwinter the opposite is true, though you may be lucky enough to see the sky lit up by the multicoloured patterns of the **northern lights**, or *aurora borealis*.

THE WINTER SWEDE AND THE SUMMER SWEDE

Unsurprisingly, the long, dark winters have a tangible effect on the **Swedish psyche**. During the winter months, you'll find that people are generally quieter and more withdrawn, and protect themselves from the rigours of the cold and dark by deliberately socializing indoors, often choosing to light **candles** throughout the home to create a sense of cosiness. You'll even see candles burning in public buildings and shops to brighten up the gloomiest time of year. It's during winter that Seasonal Affective Disorder, or **S.A.D.**, causes widespread depression, affecting roughly one in five people. Although you're unlikely to suffer during a short visit in winter, you're likely to encounter gloomy faces and a general sense of inertia throughout the winter months. S.A.D. is caused by a lack of daylight which leads to an increase in the production of the sleep-related hormone, melatonin, secreted from a gland in the brain. Naturally people do all they can to alleviate the effects of winter; for example, during the period of 24-hour darkness in northern Sweden, the **Winter Swede** creates a semblance of day and night by switching on bright lights during what would be daytime, and using

low-lighting during the evening hours. Once spring arrives, there's a notable bounce in people's step, and the **Summer Swede** prepares to emerge from months of enforced hibernation – you'll see people sitting in lines on park benches in the sunshine, faces tilted to the sky, making the most of the return of the sun. **Festivals** and **revelries** are thick on the ground in spring and summer, and outdoor life is lived to the full, including picnics under the midnight sun, beach parties lasting late into the night and an exodus to the countryside as people take up residence in their forest or lakeside log cabins to enjoy the brief yet intense summer months.

When to go

In general, **May to September** is the best time to visit Sweden – north or south. **Summer** weather in Sweden is similar to that in southern Britain, though there are more hours of sunshine and less rain. By the end of August, the leaves in northern Sweden start to change colour and night frosts are not uncommon; the first snow falls in September. In Stockholm, snow can fall in October but doesn't generally settle; by November, though, the ground is usually covered in a blanket of snow, which will last until the following March or even April, when there can still be snow showers. **Winters** in the south of Sweden are often mild while in the north you're likely to encounter snow until well into May and temperatures can fall to –30C. For more information and a temperature chart, see page 36.

Author picks

Our authors have visited every corner of Sweden – from the sandy beaches of Skåne to the mountains of Swedish Lapland – to bring you some unique travel experiences. These are some of their own, personal favourites.

Classic journeys Walking part of the Kungsleden trail (see page 344) is a great way to see the wilds of Swedish Lapland, while for the less adventurous the views unfolding from the train window on the Inlandsbanan (see page 291) are equally compelling.

Best beaches Sjaustrehammaren beach on the east coast of Gotland (see page 228) is the perfect place for an overall tan, though the turquoise waters of Sandhammaren beach in Skåne (see page 186) are equally sublime.

Back to nature Be it hiking, river-rafting or wild lake swimming, the unspoilt countryside of the province of Värmland (see page 136) is readily accessible and yours to call your own.

Winter wonderland It's hard to beat the sheer range of activities on offer at *Icehotel* in Jukkasjärvi (see page 340) for a chance to explore the snowy north of Sweden.

Island idylls Both the Stockholm and Gothenburg archipelagos (see pages 78 and 128) are perfect for spending long, lazy summer days messing about in boats and swimming.

Amazing views Mountain scenery to blow your mind from the top of Åreskutan at Åre (see page 308) and Nuolja in Abisko (see page 343) or coastal vistas from the top of Högbonden (see page 260).

Favourite place For its combination of handsome towns and villages, gloriously sandy beaches and rolling countryside studded with medieval churches, Gotland (see page 228) is Sweden at its most alluring.

Our author recommendations don't end here. We've flagged up our favourite places – a perfectly sited hotel, an atmospheric café, a special restaurant – throughout the Guide, highlighted with the ★ symbol.

STEAMER IN THE STOCKHOLM ARCHIPELAGO

ABISKO CANYON LANDSCAPE

25

things not to miss

It's not possible to see everything Sweden has to offer in one trip, and we don't suggest you try. What follows is a selective taste of the country's highlights, from snowmobiling to sampling a smörgåsbord; you can browse through to find the very best things to see and experience. All highlights have a page reference to take you straight to the Guide, where you can find out more.

1

1 DOG SLEDDING
See page 341
Dog sledding is a magical way to see northern Sweden in winter.

2 RIVER-RAFTING, VÄRMLAND
See page 143
Build your own raft and glide down the graceful Klarälven River, taking in some of Sweden's scenery.

3 LUND DOMKYRKAN
See page 166
This twelfth-century cathedral is the finest Romanesque building in northern Europe.

4 SWIMMING IN A LAKE
See page 34
Amongst Sweden's 100,000 lakes, you're bound to find one you can call your own.

5 MIDNIGHT SUN
See page 330
From late May to mid-July the sun never sets in northern Sweden.

6 GOTLAND BEACHES
See page 228
Stretches of white sandy beaches and clear, warm waters are perfect places to relax and play in the summer sun.

7 BIRKA
See page 86
Get to grips with Sweden's stirring Viking past on this Stockholm island.

8 SMÖRGÅSBORD
See page 30
Eat until you drop: the *smörgåsbord* is a perfect way to sample Sweden's excellent cuisine.

9 SÁMI CULTURE, LAPLAND
See page 325
Sights such as Jokkmokk market and Fatmomakke village in Lapland are monuments to the thriving culture of Sweden's indigenous population.

10 GOTHENBURG'S KONSTMUSEUM
See page 113
Poseidon stands guard outside Gothenburg's art museum – home to some of Sweden's finest paintings from the turn of the last century.

10

11 ICEHOTEL
See page 340
One of the most unusual structures in Europe, the *Icehotel* is a masterpiece of snow and ice sculpture.

12 GAMMELSTAD, LULEÅ
See page 275
Proudly listed as a UNESCO World Heritage site, Gammelstad is Sweden's largest church town.

13 VISBY
See page 230
Explore the cobbled lanes and medieval church ruins of this Hanseatic walled city.

14 GAMLA STAN, STOCKHOLM
See page 48
Enjoy a *fika* (coffee and cake) in one of the open-air cafés in Stockholm's atmospheric Old Town.

15 STOCKHOLM ARCHIPELAGO
See page 78
No visit to Stockholm is complete without a trip to one of the 24,000 islands that make up the archipelago.

11

12

16

16 INLANDSBANAN
See page 291
A trip on the Inlandsbanan through northern Sweden is one of Europe's great train journeys.

17 VASA WARSHIP, STOCKHOLM
See page 59
After lying in mud for centuries at the bottom of Stockholm harbour, the mighty *Vasa* has been restored to her former glory.

18 CROSSING THE ARCTIC CIRCLE
See page 330
Don't leave Sweden without crossing the magical Arctic Circle, 66° 33' north.

19 HERRING
See page 30
The quintessential Swedish dish, best enjoyed with a cold beer or a shot of *akvavit*.

20 BOHUSLÄN COAST
See page 131
Sweden's most enchanting stretch of coastline with smooth rocky outcrops perfect for sunbathing.

17

POLCIRKELN

Napapiiri

Arctic Circle

Cercle Polaire

Polarkreis

18

19

20

21

22

23

21 KALMAR SLOTT

See page 198

Take a tour around one of Sweden's finest castles, and marvel at its medieval magnificence.

22 JOKKMOKK WINTER MARKET

See page 331

The Jokkmokk winter market sells everything from bearskins to candlesticks.

23 EUROPE'S LAST WILDERNESS

See page 344

Explore the wild, rugged and remote far north on the Kungsleden hiking trail.

24 ORSA ROVDJURSPARK

See page 292

Europe's biggest bear park is the perfect place to see Sweden's greatest predator in its natural habitat.

25 A SAUNA AND A SPLASH

See page 34

The perfect end to a long day, a Swedish sauna traditionally finishes with a roll in the snow or a plunge into cold water.

Tailor-made trips

Sweden is a vast country, and you can't cover all of it in a single trip. Our Grand Tour concentrates on Sweden's main sights, while our other suggested routes focus on two fascinating regions, one in the south, one in the north. Each itinerary will take a packed two weeks to cover; with only a week to spare you can cover part of one, and get a flavour of the whole country or one of the regions that make Sweden special.

GRAND TOUR OF SWEDEN

Two weeks in Sweden and no idea where to start? Our Grand Tour puts you on the right track.

❶ **Stockholm** The vibrant heart of Sweden is one of Europe's saner capitals, with everything from style-conscious bars and restaurants to world-class museums and galleries. See page 44

❷ **Lund** Awash with students and bikes, likeable Lund boasts the country's greatest cathedral set amid its compact, cobbled centre. See page 166

❸ **Malmö** Sweden's gateway to Europe, Malmö is linked by frequent trains to the Danish capital, Copenhagen, and is accordingly cosmopolitan. See page 170

❹ **Gothenburg** Sweden's second city and Scandinavia's biggest port, handsome Gothenburg looks like Amsterdam with its canals and gabled houses. See page 106

❺ **Dalarna** The Swedes think of Dalarna as the most Swedish part of Sweden – all rolling hills, flower meadows and log cabins. See page 282

❻ **Östersund** Charming lakeside town in the centre of the country which makes a perfect break on the long journey north. See page 303

❼ **Jokkmokk** Tucked just inside the Arctic Circle, Jokkmokk has a strong *Sámi* identity and is a good place to learn more about the country's indigenous population. See page 328

❽ **Luleå** The most attractive of Sweden's northern cities, Luleå provides ready access to the fascinating UNESCO-listed church town at Gammelstad. See page 272

❾ **Sundsvall** Grandiose stone architecture immediately sets Sundsvall apart from its neighbours. The biggest city in the north, it has plenty of good restaurants and bars to sample, too. See page 252

THE BEST OF THE NORTH

❶ **Östersund** Go hunting for Sweden's answer to the Loch Ness monster on Lake Storsjön, which provides a magnificent backdrop to this laid-back town. See page 303

You can book these trips with Rough Guides, or we can help you create your own. Whether you're after adventure or a family-friendly holiday, we have a trip for you, with all the activities you enjoy doing and the sights you want to see. All our trips are devised by local experts who get the most out of the destination. Visit **www.roughguides.com/trips** to chat with one of our travel agents.

② Vildmarksvägen For a taste of wild Sweden, take this switchback route through some of central Sweden's most remote and haunting landscapes. See page 317

③ Vilhelmina A handy stop on the way north; make sure you book into one of the sturdy wooden cottages of the church town for an atmospheric night's accommodation. See page 319

④ Arvidsjaur Take a trip on a steam train or visit the traditional *Sámi* dwellings of the Lappstaden right in the town centre. See page 324

⑤ Jokkmokk In addition to a great *Sámi* museum, there's also a delightful alpine flower garden. See page 328

⑥ Abisko The starting point for the 500km Kungsleden hiking trail as well as the best place in Sweden to see the northern lights. See page 343

⑦ Kiruna Gateway to the famous *Icehotel* in nearby Jukkasjärvi; get here before the whole town sinks into the ground. See page 336

⑧ Luleå Visit the UNESCO-listed church town at nearby Gammelstad or ride the boat out into the stunning archipelago. See page 272

⑨ High Coast The most beautiful stretch of the northern Swedish coast lies north of Härnösand and is best seen from the ferries which serve the offshore islands. See page 259

SOUTHERN SWEDEN

① Malmö The perfect gateway to southern Sweden, Malmö enjoys some of the country's warmest weather and features a string of city beaches ideal for topping up your tan. See page 170

② Lund Enjoy the atmosphere in southern Sweden's most attractive city, renowned for its great bars and restaurants which cater to the huge student population. See page 166

③ Kalmar One of southern Sweden's most underrated destinations, Kalmar is home to the fascinating Kronan exhibition. See page 198

④ Gotland *The* Swedish destination, Gotland's charms are legendary: cobbled medieval streets and alleyways, superb sandy beaches and a party atmosphere that lasts all summer long. See page 228

⑤ Karlstad Busy and fun city set on the shores of Sweden's biggest lake – take a

tour of the city by boat or enjoy the beaches. See page 136

⑥ Vadstena With its moated castle and stunning abbey, historically significant Vadstena is Sweden at its most grand and imposing. See page 216

⑦ Gothenburg The Gothenburgers are said to be the friendliest people in the whole of Sweden – pull up a chair in one of the city's many great cafés and strike up a conversation. See page 106

⑧ Varberg People have been coming to Varberg to take the waters for generations – join them and leave your clothes behind. See page 148

CROWDS IN STOCKHOLM CELEBRATING SWEDISH NATIONAL DAY

Basics

Getting there

Given the extremely long distances and journey times involved in reaching Sweden overland, flying will not only save you considerable amounts of time but money too. The main gateways are Stockholm and Gothenburg, as well as Copenhagen in neighbouring Denmark, just a twenty-minute train ride from Malmö.

Air fares are generally cheaper when booked as far in advance as possible. Midweek travel is less expensive than weekend departures.

Flights from North America

The main two airlines operating between **North America** and Sweden are SAS (ⓦflysas.com) and Norwegian (ⓦnorwegian.com). At certain times of year there are also flights with Delta, American Airlines and United, though this situation changes from year to year. Timetables also change frequently, though generally there are direct flights to Stockholm from New York, Chicago and San Francisco. Less expensive tickets can sometimes be found on European airlines routing via their home hub, for example British Airways (ⓦba.com) via London or Icelandair (ⓦicelandair.net) via Keflavík, the latter very often being a source of reasonable fares to Sweden. From **New York**, a return ticket midweek **fare** to Stockholm (8hr) will cost around US$900 in high season, US$500 in low season. From **Chicago** (9hr), prices are roughly US$150 more than from New York; from the **West Coast** (journey time at least 12hr), you'll pay around US$200–300 more.

There are no direct flights **from Canada**, so the best way of reaching Sweden is generally with Icelandair from one of their Canadian gateways such as **Toronto**. Several other airlines also operate flights from Toronto and Vancouver to European cities, with connections on to Stockholm. **Fares** from Toronto (journey time 9–13hr depending on connections) are around Can$1000 in high season, Can$600 in low season. From Vancouver (13–18hr), they're around Can$300 higher.

Flights from the UK and Ireland

Flights for **Stockholm**, **Gothenburg** and **Copenhagen** leave from several **UK airports**; in winter there are also direct flights from London Heathrow to **Kiruna**. Flying to Sweden with Ryanair (ⓦryanair.com) is usually the cheapest way of getting there. Single **fares** can be as low as £15, though in peak season a return price of £90–120 is more realistic, depending on how early the booking is made. The other main **airline** serving Sweden is SAS (ⓦflysas.co.uk), whose return tickets start around £130. The Scandinavian low-cost operator, Norwegian (ⓦnorwegian.com), is also an option; its fares are generally midway between those of Ryanair and SAS. For southern Sweden, try easyJet (ⓦeasyJet.com) who operate into Copenhagen. **From Ireland**, there are services from Dublin only, and fares are roughly the same as from the UK.

Flights from Australia, New Zealand and South Africa

There are no direct flights to Sweden from **Australia**, **New Zealand** or **South Africa** and by far the cheapest option is to find a discounted air fare to London and arrange a flight to Sweden from there. Alternatively, some airlines such as Air China and Thai Airways offer competitive fares to Stockholm via their hubs in Beijing and Bangkok respectively. **Fares** from Sydney to Stockholm start at around $1500; from Perth or Darwin, flights are usually around $200 more. **From New Zealand** reckon on NZ$2000 as a starting point from Auckland, NZ$200 more from Wellington. **From South Africa**, count on around ZAR7500 for the cheapest return from Cape Town.

By train

Getting to Sweden **by train** is much more expensive than flying. There are no through tickets and the total of all the tickets you'll need from the UK is likely to cost around £300–400. Hence, it's worth buying a rail pass instead; a global **InterRail** pass (from £193) or Eurail pass (from US$252) are the best options. **From London**, trains to Sweden go via Brussels, Cologne,

Hamburg and Copenhagen. A typical journey will involve changing trains four or five times and take around 24 hours. For a dependable summary of the options of getting to Sweden by train, check out ⓦseat61.com/sweden.

RAIL CONTACTS

Swedish Railways (SJ) ⓣ 0046 771 75 75 75, ⓦ sj.se. The general agent for Swedish rail tickets.
Voyages-sncf.com ⓣ 0844 848 5848, US ⓣ 1 800 622 8600, Canada ⓣ 1 800 361 7245, ⓦ uk.voyages-scf.com

Package holidays

Don't be put off by the idea of an inclusive **package**, as it can sometimes be the cheapest way of doing things, and a much easier way of reaching remote areas of northern Sweden in winter. City breaks are invariably less expensive than if you arrange the same trip independently. There are also a number of operators (see below) offering **special-interest holidays** to Sweden.

SPECIALIST OPERATORS

Bentours International Australia ⓣ 1800 221712, ⓦ bentours. com.au. The leading Australian specialist to Sweden offering air, ferry and rail tickets and a host of (often upmarket) escorted and independent tours throughout Scandinavia.
Contiki Tours ⓣ 41 22 929 9216 CONTIKI, ⓦ contiki.com. Budget tours of Scandinavia for 18- to 35-year-olds.

Getting around

The public transport system in Sweden is one of Europe's most efficient. There's a comprehensive train network in the south of the country; in the north travelling by train isn't quite so easy, as many loss-making branch lines have been closed. However, it's still possible to reach the main towns in the north by train, and where train services no longer exist, buses generally cover the same routes.

Look out for city and regional **discount cards**, which often give free use of local transport, free museum entry and other discounts.

By train

Other than flying, **train** travel is the quickest and easiest way of covering Sweden's vast expanses. The service is generally excellent and prices are not that high. At holiday times (see page 39)

and between mid-June and mid-August, trains are often heavily booked; it's worth making reservations (often compulsory) as far in advance as you can. The national train operator is SJ (ⓣ0771 75 75 75, ⓦsj.se) which runs an extensive network across the whole of Sweden. For train and connecting bus information visit ⓦresrobot.se. Many station names in Sweden carry the letter C after the name of the city, for example: Stockholm C; this is a "railspeak" abbreviation of Central.

Tickets

Individual train tickets are rarely cost-effective and visitors doing a lot of touring by train may be better off buying a **train pass** such as InterRail. A one-country InterRail pass (ⓦinterrail.eu) for Sweden allows up to eight days' travel in one month and starts at £248. If you do need to buy an **individual ticket**, it's worth knowing that the sooner you buy it the cheaper it will be. The cheapest tickets, limited in number, cost 95kr on most SJ routes (195kr on express trains) and are available up to ninety days before departure. **Reserved seats** on Swedish trains are not marked, so although it may appear that a seat is free it may not be so.

The Inlandsbanan

If you're in Sweden for any length of time, travelling at least part of the summer-only **Inlandsbanan** (Inland Railway; ⓣ0771 53 53 53, ⓦinlandsbanan.se), which runs through central and northern Sweden, is a must. The route takes in some of the country's most unspoilt terrain – kilometre after kilometre of forests, and several lakes (the train usually stops at one or two of them for passengers to take a quick dip), and offers a chance to see real off-the-beaten-track Sweden. For more information, see page 291. The length of the operating season varies from year to year, but trains generally run from some time in June through to August; check the website for the latest details.

By bus

Although bus travel is a little less expensive than going by train, **long-distance buses** are generally less frequent, and so much slower that they aren't a good choice for long journeys. Most long-distance buses are operated by one of two companies, Swebus (ⓣ0850 513 750, ⓦflixbus.se) and Nettbuss (ⓣ0771 15 15 15, ⓦnettbuss.se). Departures on Friday and Sunday cost more than on other days; a standard single ticket from Stockholm to Gothenburg, for example, costs from 209kr.

Regional buses are particularly important in the north, where they carry mail to isolated areas. Several companies operate daily services, and their fares are broadly similar to one another's (usually 250–350kr for a 1–2hr journey). Major routes are listed in the "Destinations" sections within each chapter, and you can pick up a comprehensive timetable at any bus terminal.

By plane

The main players in the Swedish **domestic airline** market are: SAS (Ⓦsas.se), BRA (Ⓦflygbra.se), Norwegian (Ⓦnorwegian.se) and Air Leap (Ⓦairleap. se) . When booked well in advance, one-way fares on most routes begin at around 450kr.

By ferries and boats

In a country with such an extensive coastline and many lakes, it's only natural that domestic **ferry services** in Sweden are many and varied. The main route is between Visby, on the Baltic island of **Gotland**, and Nynäshamn, on the mainland near Stockholm. Departures are very popular in summer and you should try to book ahead.

Many of the various archipelagos off the coast – particularly the **Stockholm archipelago** with its 24,000 islands (see page 78) – have ferry services which link up the main islands in the group. There's also an extensive archipelago off **Luleå** which is worth visiting (see page 272).

By car

As far as road conditions go, **driving** in Sweden is a dream. Traffic jams are rare (in fact in the north of the country yours will often be the only car on the road), roads are well maintained and motorways, where they exist, are toll-free. The only real **hazards** are reindeer (in the north), elk and deer, which wander onto the road without warning. It's difficult enough to see them at dusk, and when it's completely dark all you'll see is two red eyes as the animal leaps out in front of your car. If you hit an elk or deer, not only will you know about it (they're as big as a horse), but you're bound by law to report it to the police.

Rules and regulations

To drive in Sweden, you'll need your own full **licence**; an international driving licence isn't required. **Speed limits** are 110kph on motorways; 70kph, 80kph or 90kph on main roads; and 30kph, 40kph or 50kph

in built-up areas. For cars towing caravans, the limit is 80kph. Fines for speeding are levied on the spot. You must drive with your **headlights** on 24 hours a day. Studded **tyres** for driving on snow and ice are allowed between October 1 and April 30, longer if there's still snow on the ground; when in use they must be fitted to all wheels.

Swedish **drink-driving laws** are among the strictest in Europe, and random breath tests are common-place. Basically, you can't have even one beer and still be under the limit; the blood alcohol level is 0.02 percent. If you're found to be over the limit you'll lose the right to drive in Sweden, face a fine (often) and a prison sentence (not infrequently).

Parking

Be attentive when it comes to **parking**. Under Swedish law you can't park within 10m of a road junction, be it a tiny residential cul-de-sac or a major intersection. Parking is also prohibited within 10m of a pedestrian crossing, and in bus lanes and loading zones. In city centres, parking isn't permitted on one night each week to allow for cleaning (see the rectangular yellow signs with days and times in Swedish, below the "no stopping" sign on every street). In winter the same applies to allow for snow clearance.

Petrol

The cost of **petrol** (*bensin*) is in line with the European average (about 15kr per litre). At filling stations, you either pay at the pump with a credit card or inside at the till – choose the pumps marked "Kassa" for this.

CAR RENTAL AGENCIES

Avis Ⓦavis.com
Europcar Ⓦeuropcar.com
Hertz Ⓦhertz.com
SIXT Ⓦsixt.com

Cycling

Some parts of the country were made for **cycling**: Stockholm, the southern provinces and Gotland in particular are ideal for a leisurely bike ride. Many towns are best explored by bike, and tourist offices, campsites and youth hostels often rent them out from around 150kr a day. There are a lot of cycle paths in towns, which are often shared with pedestrians.

Accommodation

Finding somewhere cheap to stay in Sweden isn't difficult. There's an extensive network of youth hostels (of an exceptionally high standard) and campsites, while hotels and guesthouses are common in towns and cities. Self-catering accommodation is generally restricted to youth hostels and campsites, where cabins are often equipped with kitchens.

Youth hostels

Youth hostels in Sweden (*vandrarhem*) turn up in the unlikeliest of places. There are over three hundred of them dotted across the country, in converted lighthouses, old castles and prisons, historic country manors, schoolrooms and even on boats. Quite simply, they offer some of the best accommodation in the country. Forget any preconceptions about youth hostelling: in Sweden, dormitories are few, and most hostels only rent double rooms.

The majority of hostels are run by STF (**Svenska Turistföreningen**; ❶ 08 463 21 00, ❷ svenskaturistforeningen.se). Apart from the STF hostels there are a number of independently run hostels, usually charging similar prices; we've mentioned the most useful ones in the text, and tourist offices will have details of any other local independent hostels.

Throughout the Guide we give the non-member **prices** for staying in an STF hostel; members pay 50kr less per stay at every hostel in the country. Generally, the rental of linen and towels is not included in the price of a room or bed; we have noted any exceptions in the book.

Fell stations and cabins

Fell stations (*fjällstationer*), or mountain lodges, provide top-notch, hostel-like accommodation along mountain hiking routes; prices vary and are given in the Guide. They're usually better equipped than the average youth hostel: rooms are private rather than dorms, and each fell station has a sauna, a shop and a kitchen.

Mountain cabins (*fjällstugor*), of which there are around ninety in the country, are often no more than simple huts out in the wilds and are wonderful for getting away from it all. Run by the STF, they are generally located at convenient intervals along popular walking routes. Both fell stations and mountain cabins allow you to use a sleeping bag without a sheet underneath.

Hotels and guesthouses

Hotels and **guesthouses** (usually family-run bed and breakfast establishments) needn't be expensive, and although there's little chance of finding any kind of room for under 550kr a night, you can often find good-value hotel rooms in **summer**, especially between mid-June and mid-August, when business people who would otherwise fill the hotels during the week are on holiday. The only parts of the country where summer discounts don't apply are in some of the popular holiday destinations in southern Sweden such as Gotland, where prices can actually go up in summer. Nearly all hotels include a huge self-service buffet breakfast in the price, which will keep you going for much of the day.

Campsites, cabins and self-catering

Practically every town or village has at least one **campsite**, and they are generally of a high standard. To pitch a tent at any of them you'll need the **Camping Key Europe card**, which costs around 150kr and is issued at the first site you visit; contact the Swedish Camping Site Owners' Association (❷ camping.se). It costs around 200kr for two people to pitch a tent at an

---

ACCOMMODATION PRICES

Accommodation **prices** in Sweden vary according to the day of the week and the season. Pricing falls into two main categories: the **higher price** is charged for stays from Sunday to Thursday outside of the summer peak (generally mid-June to mid-Aug); the **lower rate** is charged on Fridays and Saturdays. This lower rate is also applied every day during the summer peak. Remember though that this rule does not apply across the board and there are some places that actually charge higher prices in summer in line with most other countries; this is usually the case with hotels on the west coast. When we give two prices in the Guide, these reflect the difference in price according to season or day, with the **high-season and weekend rate generally given first**.

Single rooms, where available, usually cost between sixty and eighty percent of the price.

official campsite and most sites are open from June to August. For details on camping rough, see page 34.

Many campsites also boast **cabins**, each of which is usually equipped with bunk beds, a kitchen and utensils, but not sheets. Self-catering in cabins is a good way to keep costs down. Cabins start around 500kr per night for a two-bed number. As usual, it's wise to book ahead to secure one. Sweden also has a whole series of cabins for rent in spots other than campsites, often in picturesque locations such as in the middle of the forest, by a lakeshore or on the coast. For information and to make a booking, contact the local tourist office.

Food and drink

From meatballs to marinated herring, cloudberries to cinnamon buns, Swedish food is always tasty. There's no escaping the fact, however, that eating and drinking is going to take up a large slice of your budget in Sweden – though no more so than in any other northern European country.

Eating well and **eating cheaply** needn't be mutually exclusive aims, however the best strategy is to fuel up on breakfast and lunch, both of which offer good-value options. **Breakfast** is often included in the cost of a night's accommodation, and most restaurants have **lunchtime specials** (*dagens rätt*) that time and again are the best-value meals you'll find. When eating out, resist the temptation to order a starter – throughout Sweden portions are generous and most main dishes are large enough to fill even the emptiest stomach.

Note that although **tipping** in Swedish restaurants is not expected, it is customary to round the bill up to the nearest 20kr or so.

Food

Swedish food – based largely on fish, meat and potatoes, and very varied in preparation – is always tasty and well presented and, at its best, is delicious. Unusual specialities generally come from the north of the country and include reindeer, elk meat and wild berries, while herring and salmon come in so many different guises that fish fiends will always be content.

Sweden's various **salmon** dishes are divine either warm or cold, and a mainstay of any Swedish *smörgåsbord* worth its salt. **Herring** is mostly served marinated, but don't let that put you off as it tastes surprisingly good. **Sauces** feature prominently in Swedish cooking, often flavoured with dill or parsley; alternatively, there are many delicious creamy concoctions too.

Wild berries appear in many dishes, especially the lingonberry, which is something like a cranberry, and makes a good accompaniment to **Swedish meatballs**, a combination praised by many a Swede as a delicacy of the country. You'll also be able to taste orange-coloured sweet cloudberries, which grow in the marshes of Lapland and are delicious with ice cream.

One Swedish speciality to keep an eye out for is **surströmming**, which is Baltic herring fermented for months until it's rotten – something of an acquired taste, even to most Swedes.

Vegetarians should have no problems, with plenty of non-meat options available, especially in the bigger towns; elsewhere the choice may be limited to pizzas and salads.

Breakfast

Breakfast (*frukost*) is almost invariably a help-yourself buffet in the best Swedish tradition; you can go up to the serving table as many times as you like and eat until you're fit to explode. Youth hostels charge around 50kr for breakfast; if you stay in a hotel, it'll be included in the price of your accommodation.

Snacks and light meals

For **snacks** and **light meals** you're really looking at the delights dished up by the *gatukök* (street kitchen). A **gatukök** is often no more than a hole in the wall – generally conspicuous by the snaking queue and gaggle of teenagers it attracts – serving sausages, burgers, chips, soft drinks and sometimes pizza slices

---

FIKA: COFFEE AND CAKE

Coffee is to the Swedes what tea is to the British and there's seemingly no part of the day which isn't perfect for a "**fika**": a cup of coffee, accompanied by a pastry or piece of cake. Unsurprisingly, coffee is something the Swedes excel at, and is always freshly brewed, strong and delicious – head for the local *konditori*, a coffee and cake shop of the first order. A coffee costs around 25kr and the price will often buy you more than one cup.

or chicken pieces. Chips with a sausage or burger generally comes to around 75kr.

Self-catering

For the cheapest eating it's hard to beat the supermarkets and market stalls. Of the **supermarket** chains, ICA and Coop have the biggest range of produce but most supermarkets in Sweden are small local affairs selling just the basics and a few other bits and pieces. Alternatively, head for the indoor or outdoor **markets**, which often have fresher produce than the supermarkets, and at lower prices.

Fish is always excellent value, especially salmon. Pork and beef aren't too bad either, but chicken is slightly more expensive. Sweden is a country rich in **cheeses**, all of which are reasonably good value and make great sandwich fillers; the range runs from stronger ripened cheeses such as Västerbotten and Svecia to milder types like Grevé and Herrgårdsost. Prästost, a medium-strong cheese akin to a mature Cheddar, is also a particular favourite here.

Restaurants

Swedes eat their main meal of the day at lunchtime; do likewise and you'll save lots of cash. However, you don't have to restrict yourself to eating out at lunchtime; many restaurants also offer special deals in the evening, and even if they don't you're bound to find something on their menu that will fit your pocket. Remember that Swedish portions are generous and that, accordingly, you may not have room for a starter as well.

Bear in mind that Swedes eat early; lunch will be served from 11am, dinner from 6pm. It's always a good idea to **book a table** to avoid disappointment, particularly during the summer months of June to August when tables can be at a premium. **Smoking** is not allowed in restaurant or pubs.

At **lunchtime**, go for the **dagens rätt** or set dish of the day, which generally costs between 75kr and 125kr and is one way to sample Swedish *husmanskost* (home cooking). You'll also find various pizza and pasta dishes on offer in Italian restaurants, and basic meals in Thai and Chinese restaurants (sometimes a buffet-type spread). Most cafés also offer some sort of *dagens rätt* but their standard of cooking is often not as good as in restaurants.

An **evening meal** in a mid-range restaurant will cost you 150–250kr without alcohol. A three-course meal naturally costs more; expect to pay something in the region of 400–600kr, and add around 75kr for a strong beer, or 300kr for an average bottle of wine. Dishes usually have some sort of salad accompaniment and come with bread.

While you're in Sweden you should sample a **smörgåsbord** – an array of small dishes, both warm and cold. It's available in the larger restaurants and in hotels for around 400–500kr – expensive, but good for a blowout. If you're a traditionalist you should start with *akvavit*, drink beer throughout and finish with coffee. Coffee will be included in the price, but alcohol won't.

Drinks

Drinking in Sweden can be expensive, but there are ways of softening the blow. Either forgo bars and buy your booze in the state-run liquor shops, the Systembolaget (see page 32), or seek out the **happy hours** (usually called After Work in Swedish) offered at many pubs and bars. The timing of happy hours is usually set to coincide with people finishing work, so keep your eyes peeled for signs either in bar windows or on the pavement outside. Drinking outdoors is frowned upon and you're not allowed to take alcohol onto a train or the street for your own consumption (drinking alcohol purchased on trains or in pavement cafés is permitted).

What to drink

Beer is the most common alcoholic drink in Sweden, although it can be expensive. Whether you buy beer in a café, restaurant or a bar, it'll cost roughly the same, on average 55–75kr for half a litre of lager-type brew. Unless you specify otherwise, the beer you get in a bar will be *starköl* (also referred to as *storstark*), with an alcohol content of 5.6 percent by volume. Low-alcohol beers are available for sale in supermarkets.

Wine in restaurants is pricey; a bottle will set you back something like 300kr, and a glass around 75kr. It's also worth trying the **akvavit** or schnapps, which is made from potatoes, served ice-cold in tiny shots and washed down with beer. It comes in dozens of weird and wonderful flavours, from lemon to cumin-and-dill. If you're in Sweden at Christmas, don't go home without having sampled **glögg**: mulled red wine with cloves, cinnamon, sugar and more than a shot of *akvavit*.

Where to drink

You'll find pubs and bars in all towns and some villages. In Stockholm and the larger cities the trend is towards British- and Irish-style pubs, although the atmosphere inside never quite lives up to the original. Elsewhere – particularly in the north of the country – you'll come across more down-to-earth drinking dens. Drink is no cheaper here, and the clientele is predominantly male and usually drunk.

THE SYSTEMBOLAGET

In any Swedish town or city, the **Systembolaget** is the only shop that sells wine, strong beer and spirits. It's run by the state, is only open office hours (generally Mon–Wed & Fri 10am–6pm, Thurs till 7pm, Sat 10am–2pm) and until quite recently kept all its alcohol on display in locked glass cabinets – this is still the case in many smaller stores. Debate over the future of the system rumbles on and Sweden is coming under increasing pressure from the European Commission to liberalize the sale of alcohol and open up the market to free competition.

In the summer, **café-bars** spill out onto the pavement, which is a more suitable environment for children and handy if all you want is a coffee. When you can't find a bar in an out-of-the-way place, head for the local hotel – but be prepared to pay for the privilege. Bar **opening hours** are elastic, and drinking-up time is generally some time after midnight. **Smoking** is banned in all of Sweden's restaurants, bars, cafés and nightclubs.

The media

Stockholm is the centre of the Swedish media world. All national radio and television stations are broadcast from the capital, and the country's four main daily newspapers are also based there. However, every region or city also has its own newspaper, for example *Göteborgsposten* in Gothenburg or *Norrbottens tidning* in Lapland. In remote parts of the country, particularly in the north, these local media really come into their own; in winter, people depend on them for accurate and up-to-date information on everything from local political machinations to snow depths in the vicinity.

Swedish newspapers

The main Swedish papers are *Dagens Nyheter* and *Svenska Dagbladet* and the tabloids, *Expressen* and *Aftonbladet*. You may also come across *Metro*, a free newspaper available at train and tube stations, which has lots of "what's on" information; its listings are in Swedish only, but will be comprehensible enough if you don't speak the language.

TV and radio

Swedish TV won't take up much space on your postcards home. There are two state channels, SVT1 and SVT2, operated by Sveriges Television (SVT), worth watching if only for the wooden continuity

announcers. TV3 is a pretty dire cable station, and Sweden's only terrestrial commercial station is the somewhat downmarket TV4. TV5 is a cheesy cable channel available in most hotels that seems to show nothing but a string of American sitcoms. On all the channels, foreign programmes are in their original language, which makes for easy viewing; SVT1 and SVT2 show a lot of excellent BBC documentaries and comedy programmes.

On the **radio**, you'll find pop and rock music on P3 and classical music on P2 – all operated by state broadcaster, Sveriges Radio (Swedish Radio; ⓦ sr.se for frequencies). You'll also find **news in English** online courtesy of Radio Sweden (Swedish Radio's international arm; ⓦ radiosweden.org).

Festivals

Swedish festivals are for the most part organized around the seasons. Most celebrations are lively events, as Swedes are great party people – once the beer begins to flow. The highlight of the year is the midsummer festival, when the whole country gets involved, and wild parties last well into the early hours. The date of Midsummer's Day varies from year to year but is the Saturday closest to the actual summer solstice.

FEBRUARY

Great Winter Market, Jokkmokk (first Thursday to Sunday of February). Thirty thousand people flock to Jokkmokk for its famous 400-year-old winter market (ⓦ jokkmokksmarknad.se); see page 331.

APRIL

Valborgsmässoafton (April 30). Walpurgis Night. One of the most important festivals in Sweden, heralding the beginning of spring with bonfires and songs.

MAY

Labour Day (May 1). A none-too-thrilling marching day for the workers' parties.

JUNE

Swedish National Day (June 6). In existence since 1983, though a bit of a damp squib even though it's now a public holiday; worthy speeches are delivered in the evening and the king often puts in an appearance at Skansen in Stockholm.

Midsummer (the Fri & Sat between June 20 and June 26). The biggest and best celebration anywhere in Sweden, with festivities centred around the maypole, an old fertility symbol, which is erected at popular gatherings across the country. The maypole is raised in June because it's often still snowing in northern Sweden in May. There's much dancing and drinking into the night – and severe hangovers the next morning. The most famous celebrations in the country are those held in Dalarna, which culminate in the church boat (*kyrkbåtar*) races held on Lake Siljan (see page 288).

JULY

Pajala marknad (second weekend after midsummer). Forty thousand people make their way to Pajala in northern Sweden for this annual market; see page 348.

Musik vid Dellen, Hudiksvall (beginning of July). Ten-day cultural festival, featuring folk music and more (Ⓦ musikviddellen. se); see page 251.

Årets Näck, Hackås (second Thursday in July). Male fiddle players strip naked to play their instruments in the local river at this annual competition (Ⓦ hackas.se/n-cken-1.html); see page 303.

Ystad Opera Festival (most of July). See page 182.

Åre Bike Festival (July). Four-day mountain-bike competition (Ⓦ arebikefestival.com); see page 309.

Gotland chamber music festival (end of July). Week-long music festival held at the church of St Nicolaus in Visby (Ⓦ gotlandchamber.se); see page 234.

AUGUST

Crayfish parties (throughout Aug). Held in the August moonlight across the country to say a wistful farewell to the short Swedish summer. Competitions are often held to establish the season's best and tastiest crayfish.

Malmöfestivalen, Malmö (Aug). Eight days of free music and entertainment (Ⓦ malmofestivalen.se); see page 180.

Medieval Week, Visby (second week of August). Re-enactment of the Danish conquest of Gotland, featuring music, medieval food and jousting; see page 232.

Surströmming (late Aug). In coastal areas of northern Sweden, particularly along the High Coast, parties are held at which people eat *surströmming* (see page 262), a foul-smelling fermented Baltic herring which is something of an acquired taste – though a quintessentially Swedish experience.

SEPTEMBER

Römpäviiko, Pajala (last week of Sept). The "romp week" cultural festival features live music and street stalls; see page 348.

DECEMBER

Nobel Prize Day (Dec 10). Official ceremonies are held in Stockholm as the winners of the annual Nobel Prizes are awarded. Although this is not a public festival, it is a key date in the Swedish calendar.

St Lucia's Day (Dec 13). Led by a girl with a crown of candles, this is a procession of children who sing songs as they bring light into the darkest month. For many Swedes, this is a welcome highlight during the ever-shortening days of December and a chance to look forward to Christmas and the longer nights of January and onwards.

Sports and outdoor activities

Sweden is a wonderful place if you love the great outdoors, with fantastic hiking, fishing and, of course, winter sports opportunities. Best of all you won't find the countryside overcrowded – there's plenty of space to get away from it all, especially in the north. You'll also find Swedish lakes and beaches refreshingly relaxed and always clean.

Skiing and winter pursuits

During the winter months, **skiing** – a sport which began in Scandinavia – is incredibly popular, and in the north of Sweden people even ski to work. The most popular ski resorts are Åre, Idre, Sälen and Riksgränsen; these and many others are packed out during the snow season when prices hit the roof. If you do intend to come to ski, it is essential to book accommodation well in advance or take a package holiday.

In northern Sweden you can ski from the end of October well into April, and at Riksgränsen in Lappland you can ski under the midnight sun from late May to the end of June when the snow finally melts. Riksgränsen is also the place to head for if you're into **snowboarding**.

Kiruna is a good bet as a base for other winter pursuits, whether you fancy **dog sledding**, **snowmobile-riding**, a night in the world's biggest igloo (*Icehotel* at Jukkasjärvi, see page 340) or **ice fishing**. Bear in mind, though, that the area around Kiruna is one of the coldest in the country, and temperatures in the surrounding mountains can sink to –50°C during a really cold snap.

Hiking

Sweden's Right of Public Access, *Allemansrätten*, means you can **walk** freely right across the entire country (see box). A network of more than forty long-distance **footpaths** covers the whole of Sweden, with overnight accommodation available in mountain stations and huts. The most popular route is the **Kungsleden**, the King's Route, which can get rather busy in July at times, but is still enjoyable. The path stretches for 460km between Abisko and Hemavan, passing through some spectacular landscape in the wild and isolated northwest of the country; the trail also takes in Sweden's highest mountain, Kebnekaise (2102m).

Canoeing and rafting

There are almost one hundred thousand lakes and thousands of kilometres of rivers and canals in Sweden. Needless to say, on summer afternoons taking to a **canoe** is a popular pastime; a good area for this is the Stockholm archipelago (see page 78). Another excellent alternative is **rafting** down the Klarälven River in Värmland (see page 143); one of the companies offering rafting tours even allows you to build your own raft before departure.

Saunas and swimming in lakes

Most public swimming pools and hotels, even in the smallest towns, will have a **sauna**. They're generally electric and extra steam is created by tossing water onto the hot elements. The temperature inside ranges from 70°C to 120°C. Traditional wood-burning saunas are often found in the countryside and give off a wonderful smell. Public saunas are always single-sex and nude; you'll often see signs forbidding the wearing of swimming costumes, as these would collect your sweat and allow it to soak into the wooden benches. It's common practice to take a cold shower afterwards or, in winter, roll in the snow to cool off.

Otherwise in the countryside, people often take a dip in a nearby **lake**. As Sweden boasts around 100,000 lakes and one of the lowest population densities in Europe, you needn't worry about stripping off for a spot of skinny-dipping.

Fishing

Sweden is an ideal country for **anglers**. Salmon are regularly caught from opposite the Parliament building right in the centre of Stockholm, because the water is so clean and fishing there is free. Fishing is also free along the coastline and in the larger lakes, including Vänern, Vättern (particularly good for salmon and char) and Mälaren. In the north of the country, Tärnaby (see page 321) offers top-class mountain fishing for char and trout; and nearby Sorsele (see page 322) is good for fly-fishing for trout, char and grayling. For salmon fishing, the river running up through the Torne Valley (see page 347) is one of the best places. In most areas you need a permit for freshwater fishing, so ask at local tourist offices.

Culture and etiquette

In many ways, Sweden is a model country: society is liberal, people are prosperous

---

THE COUNTRYSIDE – SOME GROUND RULES

In Sweden you're entitled by law to walk, jog, camp, cycle, ride or ski on other people's land, provided you don't cause damage to crops, forest plantations or fences; this is the centuries-old **Allemansrätten** or Everyman's Right. It also allows you to pick wild berries, mushrooms and wild flowers (except protected species), fish and swim, where there are no nearby houses. But this right brings with it certain obligations: you shouldn't get close to houses or walk across gardens or on land under seed or crops; pitch a tent on land used for farming; camp close to houses without asking permission; cut down trees or bushes; or break branches or strip the bark off trees. Nor are you allowed to drive off-road (look out for signs saying "*Ej motorfordon*", no motor vehicles, or "*Enskild väg*", private road); nor light a fire if there's a risk of it spreading; nor disturb wildlife.

It's common sense to be wary of frightening reindeer herds in the north of Sweden; if they scatter it can mean several extra days' hard work for the herders. Also avoid tramping over the lichen – the staple diet of reindeer – covering stretches of moorland. As you might expect, any kind of hunting is forbidden without a permit. National parks have special regulations which are posted on huts and at entrances.

and the social and economic position of women is one of the most advanced in the world. As a result, most visitors find Sweden an easy country to visit.

Swedes, in general, are an efficient nation – planning meticulously and booking ahead to ensure they get what they want, when they want. Accordingly, spontaneity and flexibility are not high on the agenda in Sweden, which can sometimes create a mistaken impression of rudeness to the outsider. Honesty and straight-talking are two highly cherished sides of the Swedish character; a promise in Sweden is just that. Haggling over prices is not the done thing. On meeting, friends of both sexes usually hug, rather than kiss, each other. In more formal situations, people shake hands while saying their name.

In line with the liberal reputation Sweden gained during the 1970s as a result of countless soft porn films, **nudity** is widely accepted. In changing rooms, people are uninhibited about their bodies and don't feel the need to cover up with a towel. Nude lake swimming and sunbathing are common practice across the country. If other people are around, show them consideration, but you're unlikely to meet opposition.

Travel essentials

Admission charges

Entry into **museums** is often free. However, where this is not the case expect to pay around 70kr for admission. In winter, there is often a compulsory charge to **check your coat** when entering a bar or restaurant; this is usually around 30kr.

Climate

Summer **weather** in Sweden is similar to that in southern Britain, though there are more hours of sunshine; the average temperature in Stockholm, for example, is the same as that in London. By the end of August, though, northernmost Sweden is usually experiencing its first frosts. Snow can fall any time from around September onwards and in the Stockholm area there is usually – though not always – snow cover from early December to late March. Winters in the far south of the country are mild and often snow-free.

Daylight is just as important as temperatures in Sweden. In December, it doesn't get light in Stockholm until around 9.30am and it's dark by around 3pm. North of the Arctic Circle there's 24-hour darkness from mid-December to mid-January, and the merest glow of light at noon during the months immediately either side. Conversely, at the height of summer there's no part of Sweden which is dark for any length of time; in the far north there's 24-hour daylight and midnight sun from the end of May until the end of June, and April and July are very light months.

Costs

Although often considered the most expensive country in Europe, Sweden is in fact cheaper than all the other Nordic countries and no more expensive than, say, France or Germany. If you don't mind having your main meal of the day at lunchtime – like the Swedes – or having picnics under the midnight sun with goodies bought from the supermarket, travelling by the efficient public transport system and going easy on the nightlife, you'll find Sweden isn't the financial drain you might expect.

You'll find you can exist – camping, self-catering, hitching, no drinking – on a fairly low **budget** (around £40/US$50/€45 a day), though it will be a pretty miserable experience and only sustainable for a limited period of time. Stay in hostels, eat the *dagens rätt* at lunchtime, get out and see the sights and drink the odd beer or two and you'll be looking at doubling your expenditure. Once you start having restaurant meals with wine, taking a few taxis, enjoying coffees and cakes and staying in hotel accommodation, you'll probably spend considerably more (£100–150/US$150–200/€120–170 a day).

Crime and personal safety

Sweden is in general a **safe** country to visit, and this extends to women travelling alone. However, it would be foolish to assume that Stockholm and the bigger cities are free of petty crime, fuelled as elsewhere by a growing number of drug addicts and alcoholics after easy money. Keep tabs on your cash and passport (and don't leave anything valuable in your car when you park it) and you should have little reason to visit the police. If you do, you'll find them courteous, concerned and, perhaps most importantly, usually able to speak English.

As for offences *you* might commit, a big no-no is drinking alcohol in public places (which includes trains). Being drunk in the streets can get you arrested, and drunk driving is treated especially rigorously (see page 28). Drugs offences, too, meet with the same

AVERAGE DAILY TEMPERATURES (°C) AND PRECIPITATION (MM)

	Jan	March	May	June	July	Aug	Oct	Dec
JOKKMOKK								
°C	-17	-8	6	12	14	12	1	-14
mm	30	24	35	48	78	74	41	32
UMEÅ								
°C	-9	-4	7	13	15	14	4	-7
mm	49	41	41	44	53	78	65	56
ÖSTERSUND								
°C	-7	-4	7	12	13	12	4	-6
mm	27	23	35	57	76	60	37	31
STOCKHOLM								
°C	-3	0	11	16	17	16	8	-1
mm	39	26	30	45	72	66	50	46
GOTHENBURG								
°C	-2	1	11	15	16	16	9	0
mm	62	50	51	61	68	77	84	75
VISBY								
°C	-1	0	10	14	16	16	8	1
mm	48	32	29	31	50	50	50	51
LUND								
°C	-1	2	11	15	17	17	9	1
mm	54	44	43	54	66	63	60	65

harsh attitude that prevails throughout the majority of Europe.

Although **racism** is not a major problem in Sweden, it would be wrong to say it doesn't exist. It stems mainly from a small but vocal neo-Nazi movement, VAM (their full name translates as "White Aryan Resistance"), who occasionally daub slogans like "*Behålla Sverige Svenskt*" (Keep Sweden Swedish) on walls in towns and cities and on the Stockholm metro. Although there have been several racist murders and many attacks on darker-skinned foreigners over the past couple of years, it's still the exception rather than the rule. Keep your eyes and ears open and avoid trouble, especially on Friday and Saturday nights when drink can fuel these prejudices.

Electricity

The supply is 220V, although appliances requiring 240V will work perfectly well. Plugs have two round pins. Remember that if you're staying in a cottage out in the wilds, electricity may not be available.

Entry requirements

European Union, American, Canadian, Australian and New Zealand citizens need only a valid **passport** to enter Sweden, and can stay for up to three months. Once the three months are up, EU nationals can apply for a **resident's permit** (*uppehållstillstånd*) to cover longer visits. For further information on where to obtain the permits, contact the Swedish embassy in your home country. Before you depart, look up any new regulations post-Brexit.

SWEDISH EMBASSIES ABROAD

Australia 5 Turrana St, Yarralumla, ACT 2600 Canberra ☎ 02 6270 2700, ⓦ swedenabroad.com.

Canada 377 Dalhousie St, Ottawa, ON K1N 9N8 ☎ 613 244 8200, ⓦ swedenabroad.com.

South Africa I Parioli Complex, 1166 Park St, Pretoria ☎ 012 426 64 00, ⓦ swedenabroad.com.

UK 11 Montagu Place, London W1H 2AL ☎ 020 7917 6400, ⓦ swedenabroad.com.

US 2900 K St NW, Washington, DC 20007 ☎ 202 467 2600, ⓦ swedenabroad.com.

Health

EU nationals can take advantage of Sweden's **health services** under the same terms as residents of the country. For this you'll need a European Health Insurance Card. Check for regulations post-Brexit. Citizens of non-EU countries will be charged for all medical services, although US visitors will find that medical treatment is far less expensive than they are accustomed to at home. Even so it is advisable to take out travel insurance (see opposite). Note that you need a doctor's prescription to get even minor painkillers in Sweden, so bring your own supplies.

There's no **local doctor** system in Sweden. Instead, go to the nearest hospital with your passport (and Health Insurance Card, if applicable) and they'll treat you; the casualty department is called *Akutmottagning* or *Vårdcentral*. The fee for staying in hospital overnight depends on the care you need.

For **dental treatment**, foreign citizens generally have to pay in full for treatment. You can spot a dental surgery by looking out for the sign "*Tandläkare*" or "*Folktandvården*". An emergency dental service is available in most major towns and cities out of hours – look in the windows of the local pharmacy for contact telephone numbers.

In the countryside, be aware of **ticks**, which can spread tick-borne encephalitis and Lyme disease (see box below).

Insurance

Even though EU health-care rights apply in Sweden, you'd do well to take out an insurance policy before travelling to cover against theft, loss and illness or injury. Before paying for a new policy, however, it's worth checking whether you are already covered: some all-risks home insurance policies may cover your possessions when overseas, and many private medical schemes include cover when abroad.

Internet

Almost all accommodation establishments offer free internet access to guests. Elsewhere, you can get online for free at Pressbyrån newsagents and also on most SJ trains.

Kids

Sweden is an exemplary country when it comes to **travelling with children**. Most hotels and youth hostels have family rooms and both men's and women's toilets – including those on trains – usually offer baby-changing areas. There's a host of child-friendly attractions and activities on offer (see box), from Viking museums to river rafting, theme parks to wildlife sanctuaries. Always ask for children's discounts, as many activities, particularly during the summer months, are geared towards families.

MOSQUITOES AND TICKS

Mosquitoes are common throughout Sweden and it's sensible to protect yourself against bites. Although Swedish mosquitoes don't carry diseases, they can torment your every waking moment from the end of June, when the warmer weather causes them to hatch, until around mid-August. They are found in their densest concentrations in the north of the country, where there's swampy ground, and are most active early in the morning and in the late afternoon/early evening.

The best way to **protect yourself** is to wear thick clothing (though not dark colours, which attract them) and apply mosquito **repellent** to any exposed skin. When camping, make a smoky fire of (damp) peat if feasible, as mosquitoes don't like smoke. Don't scratch mosquito bites (*myggbett*); treat them instead with Salubrin or Alsolsprit creams, or something similar, available from local chemists.

Ticks (*fästingar*) are fast becoming a big problem in Sweden due to a succession of milder winters. The country has one of the highest rates of **tick-borne encephalitis** in Europe, a disease which causes fever and nausea, and in a third of cases spreads to the brain; it causes lasting damage in forty percent of people infected. A third of all ticks also carry the bacteria which cause **Lyme disease**, an illness which can lead to inflammation of the brain and nerves. The insects, which burrow painlessly into the skin, are prevalent predominantly on the **east coast and islands** and are active from March to November. Their preferred habitat is warm, slightly moist undergrowth, bushes and meadows with long grass. In addition to **vaccination**, sprays, roll-ons and creams are available in local pharmacies; eating large amounts of garlic is also effective in keeping ticks away, and you should also wear long-sleeved tops and trousers tucked into your socks.

ROUGH GUIDES TRAVEL INSURANCE

Rough Guides has teamed up with WorldNomads.com to offer great travel insurance deals. Policies are available to residents of over 150 countries, with cover for a wide range of adventure sports, 24-hour emergency assistance, high levels of medical and evacuation cover and a stream of travel safety information. Roughguides.com users can take advantage of their policies online 24/7, from anywhere in the world – even if you're already travelling. And since plans often change when you're on the road, you can extend your policy and even claim online. Roughguides.com users who buy travel insurance with WorldNomads.com can also leave a positive footprint and donate to a community development project. For more information go to ⓦroughguides.com/shop.

Laundry

Sweden has very few public laundries. Your only option to wash your clothes on the road is at youth hostels where there is generally a laundry on site for guest use.

LGBTQ travellers

Swedish attitudes to gay men and lesbians are remarkably liberal – on a legal level at least – when compared to most other Western countries, with both the government and the law proudly geared towards the promotion of **gay rights and equality** (the official age of sexual consent is 15 whether you are gay or straight).

In 1995, Sweden introduced its registered-partnership law, despite unanimous opposition in parliament from the right-wing Moderates and Christian Democrats. Ten years on, in July 2005, the Swedish parliament granted lesbians the right to artificial insemination.

Paradoxically, the acceptance of gays and lesbians in society as a whole can at best be described as sporadic, and in fact homosexuality was regarded as a psychological disease in Sweden until 1979. Outside the cities, and particularly in the north of the country where the lumberjack mentality rules supreme, there can still be widespread embarrassment and unease whenever the subject is mentioned in public.

There are very few **gay bars and clubs** in Sweden, though gay community life in general is supported by the state-sponsored Riksförbundet för Sexuellt Likaberättigande, or **RFSL** (National Association for Sexual Equality; Sveavägen 59, Stockholm; ☎08 501 62 900, ⓦrfsl.se), founded in 1950 as one of the first gay rights organizations in the world. The website ⓦqx.se has useful information about gay and lesbian happenings in Sweden, and listings of bars and discos where they do exist.

Living in Sweden

The Swedish Institute (☎08 453 7800, ⓦsi.se) has a whole host of information about various **work and study programmes** across Sweden and sometimes organizes Swedish language courses abroad.

Mail

The Swedish **post office** is a thing of the past. Postal services are instead to be found in local supermarkets and filling stations; look for the blue postal sign outside (a yellow horn and crown on a blue background) which are open longer hours than the traditional post office used to be. You can buy **stamps** (*frimärken*) at most newspaper kiosks, tobacconists, hotels, bookshops and stationers' shops, as well as at supermarkets and petrol stations. Note that **Swedish addresses** are always written with the number after the street name. In multi-floor buildings, the ground floor is always counted as the first floor.

Maps

The most useful map of **Stockholm** can only be bought in the city itself: the *Stockholm Map* (*Stockholmskartan*) is available from any office of the local transport authority, Storstockholms Lokaltrafik. This map has the advantage of showing all bus and metro routes in the capital, and includes a street index. For maps of the whole country, go for Hallwag's *Sverige/Sweden* (1:8,000,000). There are also regional maps produced by Kartförlaget (1:250,00 and 1:400,000), which are excellent.

If you're staying in one area for a long time, or are **hiking** or walking, you'll probably need something more detailed still, with a minimum scale of 1:400,000 – though preferably much larger for serious trekking. The *Fjällkartan* series produced by Lantmäteriverket, which covers the northwestern mountains at a scale of 1:100,000, is good, although unfortunately rather expensive, both in Sweden and abroad.

Money

The Swedish **currency** is the krona (kr; plural kronor). It comes in coins of 1kr, 5kr and 10kr, and notes of 20kr, 50kr, 100kr, 200kr, 500kr and 1000kr. There's no limit on the amount of Swedish and foreign currency you can take into Sweden. At the time of going to print, the exchange rate was around 12kr to £1, 9.5kr to US$1 and 10.5kr to €1.

The cheapest and easiest way of accessing money while you're in Sweden is from ATMs with your **debit card**. There will be a flat transaction fee for withdrawals, which is usually quite small, but no interest payments.

Credit cards are a good backup source of funds, and can be used either in ATMs or over the counter. Mastercard, Visa, American Express and Diners Card are accepted everywhere for goods or cash.

Traveller's cheques are a safe and simple way of carrying your money, although there can be a hefty commission when you come to change them. Some places charge per cheque, others per transaction, so it's common sense to take large denominations with you, or to try to change as much as you feel you can handle in one go.

Banks have standard exchange rates, but commissions can vary enormously. The best place to change money is at the yellow **Forex** offices (Ⓦ forex.se), which offer more kronor for your currency though also charge commission. You'll find Forex branches in Sweden's main cities as well as at major airports and train stations.

Opening hours and public holidays

Shop opening hours are generally from 10am to 6pm on weekdays and 10am to 4pm on Saturdays. In larger towns, department stores remain open until 7pm or longer on weekdays, and some are also open on Sundays between noon and 4pm. **Museums and galleries** operate various opening hours, but are generally closed on Mondays outside the summer months. **Banks** are open on weekdays from 9.30am to 3pm (until 4/5.30pm on Thursdays); in some cities, banks may stay open to 5.30pm every weekday.

Banks, offices and shops are closed on **public holidays** (see page 40). They usually also close or have reduced opening hours on the eve of the holiday.

Phones

In the land of Ericsson, **mobile phones** work virtually everywhere and almost every Swede has at least one. Consequently, public payphones have all but disappeared. Mobile coverage in the south of the country is virtually a hundred percent. In the north there is good coverage along the main roads and the coast, and even the most remote village in Norrland has some kind of network coverage; with international roaming this means you can use your phone virtually wherever you happen to be.

Shopping

Stockholm is undoubtedly the best place in Sweden to shop – it not only has the biggest

---

THE BEST OF SWEDEN FOR KIDS

Beaches Chill out on fine white-sand beaches at Sandhammaren in Skåne (see page 186) or Sjaustrehammaren in Gotland (see page 238).

Viking history Explore Sweden's thrilling Viking past at Birka (see page 86) or at the Foteviken Viking Museum at Skanör (see page 181).

Wildlife Come face to face with bears, wolves and wolverines at Orsa Rovdjurspark (see page 292), get up close to reindeer at Båtsuoj Sámi Center in Lapland (see page 325), see endangered animals at the Norden's Ark wildlife sanctuary on the Bohuslän coast (see page 135), or check out the Kolmårdens Djurpark safari park near Norrköping (see page 227).

Museums In Stockholm, don't miss the Skansen open-air museum (see page 60) and the Vasaméseet's magnificent ancient warship (see page 59); in Gothenburg head for the fun, interactive Universeum science museum (see page 115).

The great outdoors Spend a day canoeing around the Stockholm archipelago (see page 78) or build your own raft and float down the Klarälven River in Värmland (see page 143). In winter, there's everything from dog sledding to snowmobiling at Lapland's *Icehotel* (see page 340).

Theme parks Strap yourself into some white-knuckle rides at Gröna Lunds Tivoli in Stockholm (see page 60) or Liseberg Amusement Park in Gothenburg (see page 115), or visit Pippi Longstocking at Astrid Lindgren's World at Vimmerby (see page 213).

selection of stores in the country but, thanks to competition, prices tend to be a little lower than elsewhere. **Glassware** is generally a good buy and Swedish glass producers are renowned for their innovation and creative designs; in Stockholm try the Åhléns and NK department stores which keep a wide range of glass products. Other items to look out for are locally produced **handicrafts** which can range from hand-woven table runners to wrought-iron candlesticks. Most towns have a handicrafts store selling "*hantverk*". For English-language **books** try the Akademibokhandeln chain found in major towns across the country, or, better, in Stockholm, the Swedish Institute, Slottsbacken 10, which has an unsurpassed stock of English-language books on Sweden and Sweden-related gifts and souvenirs.

Tipping

Leaving **tips** is not common practice in Sweden. In the big cities, however, it is usual to round up a restaurant bill to the nearest sensible denomination, ie 277kr becomes 300kr, but there is no tradition of routinely tipping by ten to fifteen percent as in some countries.

Time

Sweden conforms to **Central European Time** (CET), which is always one hour ahead of Britain and Ireland. For most of the year Sweden is six hours ahead of New York, nine hours behind Sydney and eleven hours behind Auckland. Clocks go forward by one hour in late March and back one hour in late October (on the same days as in Britain and Ireland).

Tourist information

All towns – and some villages – have a **tourist office** from where you can pick up free town plans and information, brochures, timetables and other literature. Most offices have internet access. During the summer they're open until late evening; out of season it's more usual for them to keep shop hours, and in the winter they're normally closed at weekends. You'll find full details of individual offices throughout the Guide. Sweden's **official website** for tourism, Ⓦ visitsweden.com, is extremely comprehensive and worth a browse before leaving home.

Travellers with disabilities

Sweden is, in many ways, a model of awareness in terms of **disabled travel**, with assistance forthcoming from virtually all Swedes, if needed. Wheelchair access is usually available on trains (InterCity trains have wide aisles and large toilets, and often have special carriages with hydraulic lifts), and there are lifts down to the platforms at almost every Stockholm metro station. In every part of the country there'll be some taxis in the form of minivans specially converted for disabled use.

Accommodation suitable for people with disabilities is often available: most hotels have specially adapted rooms, while some chalet villages have cabins with wheelchair access. Any building with three or more storeys must, by law, have a

---

PUBLIC HOLIDAYS IN SWEDEN

New Year's Day	January 1
Epiphany	January 6
Good Friday	March/April
Easter Sunday	March/April
Easter Monday	March/April
Labour Day	May 1
Ascension Day	Fortieth day after Easter Sunday
Whit Sunday	Seventh Sunday after Easter
National Day	June 6
Midsummer's Eve	Always on a Friday
Midsummer's Day	Saturday closest to the summer solstice
All Saints' Day	Closest Saturday to November 1
Christmas Eve	December 24
Christmas Day	December 25
Boxing Day	December 26
New Year's Eve	December 31

MAKING INTERNATIONAL CALLS TO AND FROM SWEDEN

To **call Sweden from abroad**, dial your country's international access code followed by 46 for Sweden, then dial the area code (without its first 0) and the number.

To **call abroad from Sweden**, dial 00 followed by the required country code then the area code (without its first 0) and the number.

lift installed, while all public buildings are legally required to be accessible to people with disabilities and have automatic doors. For more information, contact De Handikappades Riksförbund, (☎ 08685 80 00, ⓦ dhr.se).

Stockholm

RIDDARHUSET

1 Stockholm

"It is not a city at all. It is ridiculous to think of itself as a city. It is simply a rather large village, set in the middle of some forest and some lakes. You wonder what it thinks it is doing there, looking so important." Ingmar Bergman

Without a shadow of a doubt, Stockholm is one of the most beautiful cities in Europe. Built on no fewer than fourteen islands, where the fresh water of Lake Mälaren meets the brackish Baltic Sea, clean air and open space are in plentiful supply here. One third of the area within the city limits is made up of water, while another third comprises parks and woodlands. As a result, the capital is one of Europe's saner cities and a delightful place in which to spend time. Broad boulevards lined with elegant buildings are reflected in the deep blue water, and rows of painted wooden houseboats bob gently alongside the cobbled waterfront. Yet Stockholm is also a high-tech metropolis, with futuristic skyscrapers, a bustling commercial heart and one of the world's hottest start-up scenes.

For most visitors, the first stop is the Old Town, **Gamla Stan**, a medieval jumble of cobbled streets and narrow alleyways huddled together on a triangular-shaped island. Close by is the tiny island of **Skeppsholmen**, home to the city's main modern art gallery and a quirky floating youth hostel. To the north of the Old Town, the district of **Norrmalm** swaps tradition for a thoroughly contemporary feel: this is Stockholm's downtown area, where you'll find shopping malls, huge department stores and conspicuous, showy wealth. The Central Station and the lively park known as **Kungsträdgården** are located here too. Most of Stockholm's **museums and galleries** are spread across this area and two others: to the east, the more residential **Östermalm**, with its mix of grand avenues and smart houses; and to the southeast, the green park island of **Djurgården**. Here the extraordinary seventeenth-century warship, **Vasa**, rescued and preserved after sinking in Stockholm harbour, and **Skansen**, the oldest and best of Europe's open-air museums, both receive loud and deserved acclaim.

To the south of the Old Town, the island of **Södermalm** was traditionally the working-class area of Stockholm but is now a haven for hipsters. Its grids of streets, lined with lofty stone buildings, create an altogether more homely ambience than the grand and formal buildings of the city centre. It's here, in a fashionable area known as **SoFo** (south of Folkungagatan) that you'll find some of the city's most enjoyable bars and restaurants. Crossing the narrow neighbouring island of Långholmen, known for its popular beaches, you'll reach **Kungsholmen**, an island that's fast becoming a rival to its southern neighbour for trendy restaurants and drinking establishments.

Brief history

Swedish stateman **Birger Jarl** founded Stockholm in 1255 in an attempt to secure the burgeoning city of Sigtuna from maritime attack. However, it was vibrant trade with other towns of the Hanseatic League, such as Hamburg, that helped give Stockholm, rather than Sigtuna, its prominent position within the Swedish realm during the fourteenth and fifteenth centuries. Following the breakup of the Kalmar Union with Denmark, Swedish King Gustav Vasa established royal power in Stockholm, enabling the city to grow into the capital of one of Europe's major powers by the seventeenth century. Military defeat by Russia in the Great Northern War (1700–21) put paid to Swedish territorial expansion in northern and eastern Europe, and, instead, Stockholm developed politically and culturally at the centre of a smaller Swedish state.

Highlights

❶ **Gamla Stan** Wander through the narrow streets and alleyways of the Old Town for a taste of medieval Stockholm. See page 48

❷ **Djurgården** Take a stroll through leafy parkland right in the city centre and enjoy some great waterside views. See page 58

❸ **Djurgården ferry** Ride the ferry across Stockholm harbour for some of the best views of the city. See page 66

❹ **Vasamuséet** Fascinating seventeenth-century warship raised from Stockholm harbour and painstakingly restored to her former glory. See page 59

❺ **Fotografiska** Sample work by some of the world's leading photographers at this slick museum by the waterfront. See page 64

❻ **Swimming in Lake Mälaren** Taking a dip in the refreshing waters of Lake Mälaren is a favourite summer activity among Stockholmers. See page 64

HIGHLIGHTS ARE MARKED ON THE MAP ON PAGE 46

1

▲ Bromma Airport   ▲ Arlanda Airport

GREATER STOCKHOLM

0 ——————— 500
metres

● EATING
Blå Porten	10
Brasserie Elverket	6
Ciao Ciao Grande	7
Flippin Burgers	1
Mamas & Tapas	9
Peppar	2
Salt	8
Samuraj	5
Saturnus	3
Supper	4

■ DRINKING, NIGHTLIFE AND LIVE MUSIC
Cirkus	3
Storstad	1
Tranan	2

SVEAVÄGEN
VALLHALLAVÄGEN
Vanadislunden
BIRGER JARLSGATAN
SANKT ERIKSGATAN
SOLNABRON
VANADISVÄGEN
NORRTULLSGATAN
UPPLANDSGATAN
SVEAVÄGEN
DÖBELNSGATAN
TULEGATAN
ROSLAGSGATAN
ODENGATAN
Tekniska Högskolan
N
KARLAVÄGEN
Stadsbiblioteket
MARKVARDSGATAN
BIRGER JARLSGATAN
@
KARLBERGSVÄGEN
ODENPLAN
Odenplan
Observatorie-lunden
KUNGSTENSGATAN
BADMANSGATAN
ENGELBREKTSGATAN
HORNSGATAN
Sankt Eriksplan
ODENGATAN
DALAGATAN
VÄSTMANNAGATAN
DROTTNINGGATAN
SANKT ERIKSPLAN
Vasaparken
KUNGSTENSGATAN
Rådmansgatan
TEGNÉRGATAN
DÖBELNSGATAN
Strindbergmuséet
Tegnér-lunden
Adolf Fredriks kyrka
DAVID BAGARES GATA
BIRGER J
Hospital
TORSGATAN
WALLINGATAN
HOLLÄNDARGATAN
BRUNNSGATAN
KUNGSGATAN
TEGNÉRGATAN
KAMMAKARGATAN
BANHUSGATAN
REGERINGSGATAN
ALSTRÖMERGATAN
ARBETARGATAN
FRIDHEMSGATAN
KUNGSHOLMS STRAND
OLOF PALMES GATA
Norra Bantorget
Konserthuset
Hötorget
JAKOBS-BERGSGATAN
MÄSTER SAMUELSGATAN
Grubbens-parken
FLEMINGGATAN
SCHEELEGATAN
GAMLA BROGATAN
VASAGATAN
NORRMALM
Fridhemsplan
Kronobergs-parken
KUNGSHOLMGATAN
KUNGSGATAN
T-Centralen
SERGELS TORG
HAMNGATAN
IGNE NEWMANS GRÄND
SANKT ERIKSGATAN
KLARABERGSVIADUKTEN
DROTTNINGGATAN
KUNGSHOLMEN
Rådhuset
BERGSGATAN
PIPERSGATAN
T-Centralen
Klara kyrka
@
Kulturhuset
PONTONJÄRGATAN
HANTVERKARGATAN
SCHEELEGATAN
Operan
GUSTAV ADOLFS TORG
NORR MÄLARSTRAND
Central Station
JAKOBSGATAN
HELGEANDS-HOLMEN
Stadshuset
Ferries to Gripsholm, Birka & Drottningholm
Strömsberg
Riksdags-huset
VASABRON
Riddarhuset
Storkyrkan
Lake Mälaren
6
RIDDARHOLMEN
Riddarholms kyrkan
STORA NYGATAN
Gamla Stan
SEE "SÖDERMALM" MAP
Klippbadet
LÅNGHOLMEN
SEE "CENTRAL STOCKHOLM" MAP
SÖDER MÄLARSTRAND
HELENEBORGSGATAN
MÜNCHENBACKEN
Maria Magdalen kyrka
Stads-muséet
HÖGALIDSGATAN
LÅNGHOLMSGATAN
Zinkensdamm
HORNSGATAN
MARIA-TORGET
SANKT PAULSGATAN
Mariatorget
Hornstull
HORNSGATAN
WOLLMAR YXKULLSGATAN
HÖGBERGSGATAN
Zinkensdamm Sports Arena

HIGHLIGHTS
1. Gamla Stan
2. Djurgården
3. Djurgården ferry
4. Vasaméet
5. Fotografiska
6. Swimming in Lake Mälaren

ACCOMMODATION

Af Chapman	14
Ängby Camping	12
Bema	6
Best Western Plus Time	1
Bredäng Camping	13
City Backpackers	7
Connect City	8
Diplomat	11
Gärdet	4
Hellsten	2
Micro	5
M/S Monika	9
Rex	3
Scandic Hasselbacken	15
Stockholm Hostel	10

1

By the nineteenth century Stockholm was still essentially rural, with country lanes, great orchards, grazing cows and even windmills in the centre of the city; the downside was the lack of pavements (until the 1840s) or piped water supply (until 1858), and the presence of open sewers, squalid streets and crowded slums. Having escaped bomb damage during World War II thanks to Swedish neutrality, the mid-twentieth century ushered in a huge **modernization** programme as part of the Social Democratic out-with-the-old-and-in-with-the-new policy: Sweden, and particularly the capital, Stockholm, was to become a place fit for working people to live. Old areas were torn down as "a thousand homes for a thousand Swedes" – as the project had it – were constructed. Today, Stockholm is a bright and elegant place, and with its great expanses of open water right in the centre, it offers a spectacular city panorama unparalleled anywhere in Europe.

Old Stockholm: Gamla Stan and around

Three islands – Riddarholmen, Staden and Helgeandsholmen – make up the **oldest part of Stockholm**, a cluster of seventeenth- and eighteenth-century buildings backed by hairline medieval alleys. It was on these three adjoining polyps of land that Birger Jarl erected the town's first fortifications. Rumours abound as to the derivation of the name "Stockholm", though it's now widely believed to mean "island cleared of trees", since the trees on the island that is now home to Gamla Stan were probably felled to make way for the settlement. Incidentally, the words *holm* (island) and *stock* (log) are still in common use today. You can experience a taste of Stockholm's medieval past at the excellent **Medeltidsmuseet**, at the northern end of the two bridges – Norrbron and Riksbron – which lead across to Gamla Stan. Although strictly speaking only the largest island, Staden, contains **Gamla Stan**, this name is usually attached to the buildings and streets of all three islands.

Once Stockholm's working centre, nowadays Gamla Stan is primarily a tourist hub with many an eminently strollable area, in particular around the **Kungliga Slottet** (royal palace), **Riksdagshuset** (parliament building) and **Storkyrkan** (cathedral). The central spider's web of streets – best approached over the bridges of Norrbron or Riksbron – is a sprawl of monumental buildings and high airy churches which form a protective girdle around the narrow lanes. Some of the impossibly slender alleys lead to steep steps ascending between battered walls, others are covered passageways linking leaning buildings. The tall, dark houses in the centre were mostly owned by wealthy merchants, and are still distinguished by their intricate doorways and portals bearing coats of arms.

The main square of the Old Town is **Stortorget**, an impressive collection of tall pastel-coloured stone buildings with curling gables which saw one of the medieval city's most infamous incidents, the "Stockholm Bloodbath" (see page 357). Now, as then, the streets **Västerlånggatan**, **Österlånggatan**, **Stora Nygatan** and **Lilla Nygatan** run the length of the Old Town, although today their time-worn buildings harbour a succession of souvenir shops and restaurants. Happily, the consumerism here isn't too obtrusive, and in summer buskers and evening strollers clog the narrow alleyways, making it an entertaining place to wander or to stop for a bite to eat. There are few real targets, but take every opportunity to wander up side streets, where you'll find fading coats of arms, covered alleys and worn cobbles at every turn.

Off the western shore of Gamla Stan, the tiny islet of **Riddarholmen** houses not only one of Stockholm's most beautiful churches, **Riddarholmskyrkan**, the burial place for countless Swedish kings and queens over the centuries, but also the Baroque **Riddarhuset** (House of the Nobility), a reminder of the glory days of the Swedish aristocracy.

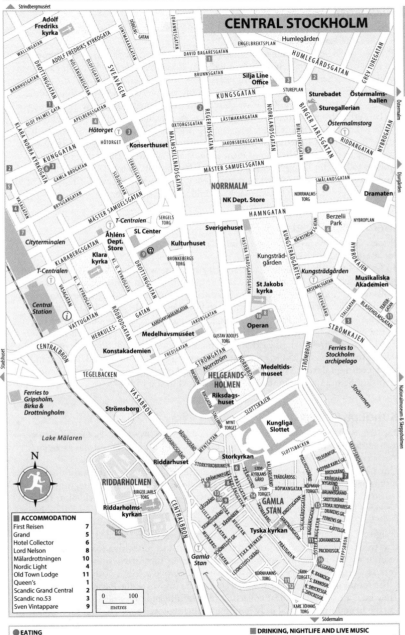

CENTRAL STOCKHOLM

ACCOMMODATION

First Reisen	7
Grand	5
Hotel Collector	6
Lord Nelson	8
Mälardrottningen	10
Nordic Light	4
Old Town Lodge	11
Queen's	1
Scandic Grand Central	2
Scandic no.53	3
Sven Vintappare	9

0 100
metres

EATING

Bakfickan	10	Den Gyldene Freden	16	Prinsen	5
B.A.R.	11	East	1	Sturekatten	4
Bistro Bestick	8	Hermitage	13	Vete-Katten	6
Bistro Ruby		Hötorgshallen	3		
and Grill Ruby	15	K25	2		
Café Panorama	9	KB	7		
Chokladkoppen	14	Le Rouge	12		

DRINKING, NIGHTLIFE AND LIVE MUSIC

The Auld Dub	4	Nalen Stacken	1
Berns	6	Spy Bar	3
End Night Club	8	Stampen	9
Engelen	12	Sturecompagniet	2
Fasching	5	The Secret Garden	11
Icebar by Icehotel	7	Wirströms	10

1

Riksdagshuset

Parliament building • Riksgatan 1 • Late June–late Aug guided tours in English Mon–Fri noon, 1pm, 2pm & 3pm, late Aug–late June Sat & Sun 1.30pm • Free • Gamla Stan T-bana

Perched on Helgeandsholmen, a small oval-shaped island wedged between Norrmalm to the north and Gamla Stan to the south, the **Riksdagshuset**, the Swedish Parliament building, is where Sweden's famous welfare state was shaped and formed during the postwar years of the 1940s and 1950s. The building was completely restored in the 1970s, just seventy years after it was built, and the original, columned facade (viewed to best effect from Norrbron) is rarely used as an entrance today; the main entrance is on Riksgatan, the short street between the bridges of Riksbron and Stallbron. It's the glassy bulge at the back (which you see when coming into Stockholm from the south by train) that is the hub of most activity, and where you're shown round on **guided tours**. This being Sweden, the seating for the 349 members is in healthy, non-adversarial rows, grouped by constituency and not by party, and it has even been known for politicians to breastfeed their children in the chamber.

Medeltidsmuseet

Museum of Medieval Stockholm • Strömparterren 3 • Closed on Mon, Daily noon–5pm, Wed until 8pm • Free • Ⓦ medeltidsmuseet. stockholm.se • T-Centralen T-bana

In front of the Riksdagshuset, accessed by a set of steps leading down from Norrbron, is the **Medeltidsmuseet**, where medieval ruins, tunnels and parts of Stockholm's city walls dating from the 1530s, discovered during excavations under the parliament building, have been incorporated into a walk-through underground exhibition. Reconstructed houses of timber and brick, complete with wax models peering out of the windows, help give a realistic idea of what life was like in sixteenth-century Stockholm. However, it's the extensive remains of the 20m-long *Riddarholm* ship, dating from the early 1520s, which really draws the eye. Built in overlapping clinker-style, common during Viking times, the ship had been equipped with cannons and lead shot before sinking in the Riddarholm canal in the 1520s.

Kungliga Slottet

Royal Palace • Slottsbacken • July & Aug daily 9am–5pm; mid-May–June & Sept daily 10am–5pm; Oct–Dec daily 10am–4pm • A combined ticket for the Apartments, Treasury and Museum Tre Kronor costs 180kr and is only valid for a visit on the specified day • Ⓦ royalcourt.se • Gamla Stan T-bana

Cross Norrbron or Riksbron from the Riksdagshuset and up rears the most distinctive monumental building in Stockholm, the **Kungliga Slottet** – a low, square, brown construction, with two arms that stretch down towards the water. Stockholm's old Tre Kronor (Three Crowns) castle burnt down at the beginning of King Karl XII's reign (1697–1718), leaving his architect, Tessin the Younger (see page 359), a free hand to design a simple and beautiful Baroque structure in its stead. Finished in 1754, the palace is a striking achievement: uniform and sombre outside, but with a magnificent Rococo interior that's a swirl of staterooms and museums. Its sheer size is quite overwhelming and it's worth focusing your explorations on one or two sections of the palace.

The rooms of state used for royal receptions are known as the **Palace Apartments**. They hold a relentlessly linear collection of furniture and tapestries, all too sumptuous to take in and inspirational only in terms of their colossal size. The **Treasury**, on the other hand, is certainly worth a visit for its ranks of jewel-studded crowns. The oldest one was made in 1650 for Karl X, while the two smaller ones belonged to princesses Sofia (1771) and Eugène (1860).

If you're a real palace junkie, check out the **Museum Tre Kronor** at Slottskajen in front of Kungliga Slottet, where you'll find part of the original Tre Kronor castle, its ruins underneath the present building.

Livrustkammaren

Armoury • Slottsbacken 3 • May & June Tues–Sun 10am–5pm; July & Aug Tues–Sun 10am–6pm; Sept–April Tues–Sun 11am–5pm, Thurs until 8pm • Free • Ⓦ livrustkammaren.se

The **Livrustkammaren** is not so much about weapons as ceremony – with suits of armour, costumes and horse-drawn carriages from the sixteenth century onwards. Also on display is the stuffed horse of King Gustav II Adolf, who died in the Battle of Lützen in 1632, and the king's blood- and mud-spattered garments, retrieved after the enemy had stripped him on the battlefield.

Myntkabinett

Royal Coin Cabinet • Closed at the time of writing, set to open in 2020 • Free • Ⓦ myntkabinettet.se • Gamla Stan T-bana

A veritable stash of coins, banknotes and medals from across the centuries, as well as a number of silver hoards from Viking days, the **Myntkabinett** boasts over 600,000 items in its collection and is worth a quick look if money is your thing. The most engaging exhibition is the section devoted to Sweden's own coins, from the very first ones minted during the reign of King Olof Skötkonung (995–1022) to those of today.

Storkyrkan

Trångsund 1 • Jan–Mar & Oct–Dec daily 9am–4pm; April–May & Sept daily 9am–5pm; June–Aug daily 9am–6pm • 60kr • Gamla Stan T-bana

South of Kungliga Slottet, the streets suddenly narrow and darken and you're into Gamla Stan proper. The highest point of the old part of Stockholm is crowned by the **Storkyrkan**, built in 1279, and almost the first building you'll stumble upon. Pedantically speaking, Stockholm has no cathedral, but this rectangular brick church is now accepted as such, and the monarchs of Sweden married and were crowned here.

The Storkyrkan gained its present shape at the end of the fifteenth century following a series of earlier alterations and additions, but was given a Baroque remodelling in the 1730s to better fit in with the new palace taking shape next door. The interior is marvellous: twentieth-century restoration removed the white plaster from its red-brick columns, giving a warm colouring to the rest of the building. Much is made of the fifteenth-century Gothic sculpture of St George and the Dragon (see page 357), certainly an animated piece but easily overshadowed by the royal pews – more like golden billowing thrones – and the monumental black-and-silver altarpiece.

Stortorget

Stortorget, Gamla Stan's main square, one block south of the Storkyrkan along either Trångsund or Källargränd, is a handsome and elegantly proportioned space crowded with eighteenth-century buildings. In 1520, Christian II used the square as an execution site during the "Stockholm Bloodbath" (see page 357), dispatching his opposition en masse with bloody finality. Heading east from the square along Köpmangatan brings you to **Köpmantorget** square, where there's a replica of the George and Dragon statue inside the Storkyrkan.

Tyska kyrkan

German Church • Kindstugatan, just off Västerlånggatan • May–Aug Mon–Sat 11am–5pm, Sun 12.30–5pm; Sept–April Sat & Sun noon–4pm • 40kr • Gamla Stan T-bana

Once belonging to Stockholm's medieval German merchants, the **Tyska kyrkan** served as the meeting place of the Guild of St Gertrude. A copper-roofed red-brick building atop a rise, it was enlarged in the seventeenth century when Baroque decorators got hold of it: the result, a richly fashioned interior with the pulpit dominating the nave,

1

is outstanding. The royal gallery in one corner – designed by Tessin the Elder – adds to the overall elegance of this church, one of Stockholm's most impressive.

Riddarhuset

House of the Nobility • Riddarhustorget 10 • Mon–Fri 11am–noon • 60kr • Ⓦ riddarhuset.se • Gamla Stan T-bana

From the Storkyrkan, it's a five-minute stroll west along Storkyrkobrinken to the handsome, seventeenth-century Baroque **Riddarhuset**. Its Great Hall was used by the Swedish aristocracy for two hundred years for parliamentary debate until a law was passed in 1865 to create Sweden's current two-chamber parliament. The nobility's coats of arms – around two and a half thousand of them – are splattered across the walls. Take a peek at the Chancery downstairs, which stores heraldic bone china by the shelf-load and has racks full of fancy signet rings – essential accessories for the eighteenth-century noble-about-town.

Riddarholmskyrkan

Birger Jarls torg 3 • Mid-May–Sept daily 10am–5pm; Oct–Nov Sat & Sun 10am–4pm • Guided tours in English (summer only) at 11.30am • 50kr including tour; card payments only • Ⓦ royalcourt.se • Gamla Stan T-bana

It's only a matter of seconds to cross the bridge from the Riddarhuset onto **Riddarholmen**, and thus to **Riddarholmskyrkan**. Originally a Franciscan monastery, the church has been the burial place of Swedish royalty for over six centuries. Since Magnus Ladulås was sealed up here in 1290, his successors have rallied round to create a Swedish royal pantheon. Amongst others, you'll find the tombs of Gustav II Adolf (in the green marble sarcophagus), Karl XII, Gustav III and Karl Johan XIV, plus other innumerable and unmemorable descendants. Walk around the back of the church for stunning views of the Stadshuset and Lake Mälaren. In winter, the lake can freeze from here right up to the Västerbron bridge, a couple of kilometres further west, and people skate and take their dogs for walks along the ice.

Skeppsholmen

A 10min walk from Stortorget: cross Strömbron, turn right and cross Skeppsholmbron; you can also take bus #65 from Central Station to Stockholm Östasiatiska museet

Off Gamla Stan's eastern reaches lies the island of **Skeppsholmen**, home to one of Stockholm's best youth hostels. However, it's the eclectic clutch of **museums and galleries**, including the excellent Moderna Muséet, that draw most people here.

Nationalmuseum

National Art Museum • Södra Blasieholmshamnen 2 • Tues–Wed & Sat–Sun 11am–5pm, Thurs 11am–9pm, Fri 11am–7pm • Ⓦ nationalmuseum.se • Kungsträdgården T-bana

As you approach Skeppsholmsbron on the way to Skeppsholmen, you'll pass the striking waterfront **Nationalmuseum**, which contains an impressive collection of Swedish and European fine and applied arts from the late medieval period to the present day, contained on three floors.

Moderna Muséet

Modern Art Museum • Exercisplan 2 • Tues & Fri 10am–8pm, Wed–Thurs 10am–6pm, Sat–Sun 11am–6pm • Free • Ⓦ modernamuseet.se • Kungsträdgården T-bana

On Skeppsholmen itself, Stockholm's **Moderna Muséet** is one of the better modern art collections in Europe, with a comprehensive selection of work by some of the twentieth century's leading artists divided into three periods: 1900–39, 1940–69 and 1970 to

1

the present day. Take a look at Dali's monumental *Enigma of William Tell*, showing the artist at his most conventionally unconventional, and Matisse's striking *Apollo*. Look out also for Picasso's *Guitar Player* and *Spring*, plus a whole host of Warhol, Lichtenstein, Kandinsky, Miró, Magritte and Rauschenberg.

Arkitektur och Designcentrum

Architecture and Design Centre • Exercisplan 4 • Tues & Fri 10am–8pm, Wed–Thurs 10am–6pm, Sat–Sun 11am–6pm • Free • Ⓦ arkdes. se • Kungsträdgården T-bana

Next door to Moderna Muséet is **Arkitektur och Designcentrum**, which serves up a taste of Swedish architecture through the ages in one of the most inspired buildings in the city – there are lots of glass walls and bright, airy exhibition space. The permanent exhibition outlines some of the core themes of pan-Swedish architectural styles, and is housed alongside a number of temporary displays on construction styles.

Östasiatiska Muséet

Museum of Far Eastern Antiquities • Skeppsholmen 41 • Tues 11am–8pm, Wed–Sun 11am–5pm • Free • Ⓦ ostasiatiska.se • Kungsträdgården T-bana

A steep climb up the northern tip of Skeppsholmen brings you to the **Östasiatiska Muséet**. A visit here is half a day well spent: you'll be rewarded by an array of objects displaying incredible craftsmanship, including many from China, the favourite hunting ground of Swedish archeologists. The two main exhibitions, "The Middle Kingdom" and "China before China", tackle five thousand years of imperial Chinese history through a series of engaging artefacts, including just about anything you care to mention in porcelain. There are fifth-century Chinese tomb figurines, intricate ceramics from the seventh century onwards and fine Chinese paintings on paper and silk. Alongside these, take a look at the astounding assembly of sixth-century Buddhas, Indian watercolours, gleaming bronze Krishna figures and a magnificent set of samurai armour, a gift from the Japanese crown prince in the 1920s.

The city centre: Norrmalm

Immediately to the north of Gamla Stan is the commercial heart of modern Stockholm, **Norrmalm**, a compact area full of shops and offices, restaurants, bars and cinemas, always bustling with people and street life. Unfortunately, it also has a high count of ugly modern buildings.

Gustav Adolfs torg

Down on the waterfront, beside Norrbron, is **Gustav Adolfs torg**, more a traffic island than a square these days. A statue of King Gustav II Adolf marks the centre of the square, between the opera house and the Foreign Ministry opposite. Look out, too, for fishermen pulling salmon out of **Strömmen**, the fast-flowing stretch of water that winds its way through the centre of the city. Since the seventeenth century, Stockholmers have had the right to fish this outlet from Lake Mälaren to the Baltic; landing a catch here isn't as difficult as it looks, and there's usually a group of hopefuls on one of the bridges beside the square.

Kungliga Operan

Royal Opera House • Gustav Adolfs torg 2 • Ⓦ operan.se • T-Centralen T-bana

The nineteenth-century **Kungliga Operan** is the proudest, most notable – and ugliest – building on Gustav Adolfs torg. It was here, in an earlier opera house on the same site,

1

that King Gustav III was shot at a masked ball in 1792 by one Captain Ankarström. The story is recorded in Verdi's opera *Un ballo in maschera*, and you'll find Gustav's ball costume, as well as the assassin's pistols and mask, displayed in the Armoury in Gamla Stan (see page 48). The opera's famous restaurant, *Operakällaren* which faces the water, is ruinously expensive, its trendy café, *Bakfickan* (see page 71), less so.

Medelhavsmuséet

Museum of Mediterranean and Near Eastern Antiquities • Fredsgatan 2 • Tues–Fri 11am–8pm, Sat & Sun 11am–5pm • Free • ⓦ varldskulturmuseerna.se/medelhavsmuseet • T-Centralen T-bana

Just off Gustav Adolfs torg, and surrounded by several government ministries, the **Medelhavsmuséet** contains an excellent display on Egypt, including several whopping great mummies; the most attractive pieces, though, are the bronze weapons, tools and domestic objects from the time before the pharaohs. The Cyprus collections are also huge, the largest such assemblage outside the island itself, depicting the island civilization over a period of six thousand years. A couple of rooms examine Islamic culture through pottery, glass and metalwork, as well as decorative elements from architecture, Arabic calligraphy and Persian miniature painting.

St Jakobs kyrka

Västra Trädgårdsgatan 2 • Mon–Wed, Sat & Sun 11am–5pm, Thurs & Fri 11am–6pm • Free • Kungsträdgården T-bana

Though located in a prime position opposite the opera house, **St Jakobs kyrka** is often overlooked by visitors to the city. It stands on the site of an earlier chapel of St James (Jakob in Swedish) and was completed fifty years after the death of its founder, Johan III. Although the church's doors are impressive – check out the south door with its statues of Moses and St James on either side – it's the great, golden pulpit that draws most attention. The date of the building's completion (1642) is stamped high up on the ceiling in gold relief. Organ recitals are occasionally held here, usually on Fridays at 5pm (free).

Kungsträdgården

Isbanan (ice rink) Nov–early March Mon, Wed & Fri 8.30am–6pm, Tues & Thurs 8.30am–8pm, Sat & Sun 10am–6pm • Skate rental 50kr/hr

One block east of St Jakobs kyrka and the opera house, Norrmalm's eastern boundary is marked by the **Kungsträdgården**, the most fashionable and central of the city's numerous parks, reaching northwards from the water as far as Hamngatan. The mouthful of a name literally means "the king's gardens", though if you're expecting perfectly designed flowerbeds and rose gardens you'll be disappointed – it's a pedestrianized paved square, albeit in the form of an elongated rectangle, with a couple of lines of elm and cherry trees, and its days as a royal kitchen garden are long gone. Today the area is Stockholm's main meeting place, especially in summer, when there's almost always something going on: free music, live theatre and other performances take place on the central open-air stage. There are also several popular **cafés**: the outdoors one off Strömgatan at Kungsträdgården's southern edge is popular in spring as a place for winter-weary Stockholmers to lap up the sunshine. In winter, the park is as busy as in summer: the **Isbanan**, an open-air ice rink at the Hamngatan end of the park, rents out skates.

Drottninggatan and around

At the western end of Hamngatan, past the enormous NK department store, lies **Sergels torg**, the ugliest square in modern Stockholm. It's an open-air meeting area and venue for impromptu music performances or demonstrations. From here, the city's two main streets, **Drottninggatan** and **Sveavägen** – the latter with some excellent restaurants and bars – run parallel to the north as far as Odengatan and the Stadsbiblioteket (City Library), passing the market square, **Hötorget**, en route. West of Sergels torg, a short walk along Klarabergsgatan brings you to the **Centralstationen** and

GRETA GARBO IN STOCKHOLM

Greta Garbo (1905–90) began her working life in Hötorget in Stockholm. She toiled as a sales assistant in the hat section of the PUB department store on the square before hitting the big time, acting in no fewer than 27 films. She spent most of her life in the United States, dying in New York in 1990, and it wasn't until 1999 that her ashes were returned to Stockholm after a long legal battle. Garbo is buried in the Skogskyrkogården cemetery in Enskede in the south of Stockholm (take the T-bana green line to the station called Skogskyrkogården to visit).

Cityterminalen, the main hub of Stockholm's transport. The area around here is given over to unabashed consumerism, and there's little to get excited about in the streets surrounding Drottninggatan, just run-of-the-mill shops selling clothing and twee gifts, punctuated by a *McDonald's* and the odd sausage stand.

Kulturhuset Stadsteatern

Sergels torg 3 • Information desk Mon–Fri 11am–7pm, Sat & Sun 11am–5pm • Free, but charges apply for exhibitions • T-Centralen T-bana

Sergel torg's events are centred around the **Kulturhuset**, whose windows overlook the milling concrete square below. Inside this building, devoted to contemporary Swedish culture, are temporary art-and-craft exhibitions and a great kids' play area. As you come in, check with the information desk for details of poetry readings, concerts and theatre performances. Before leaving, make sure you head up to the top floor and the *Café Panorama* (see page 70), where you can take in excellent **views** of central Stockholm.

Klara kyrka

Klara Östra Kyrkogatan 7 • Mon–Fri 8am–5pm, Sat 11am–3pm, 5–7.30pm, Sun 11am–5pm • T-Centralen T-bana

Hemmed in on all sides, with only its spires visible from the streets around, **Klara kyrka** lies just to the south of Klarabergsgatan. The church is particularly delicate, with a light and flowery eighteenth-century painted interior and an impressive golden pulpit. Out in the churchyard, a memorial stone commemorates the eighteenth-century Swedish poet Carl Michael Bellman, whose popular, lengthy ballads are said to have been composed extempore; his unmarked grave is somewhere in the churchyard.

Hötorget

Hötorget T-bana

Stockholm's main market square is the cobbled **Hötorget**, where you'll find a daily open-air fruit, vegetable and flower market (roughly 9am–5pm), as well as the wonderful **Hötorgshallen**, an indoor market boasting a tantalizing array of restaurants and takeaway food options (Mon–Thurs 10am–6pm, Fri 10am–7pm, Sat 10am–4pm). The tall hotel building across the square, PUB, is a former department store where **Greta Garbo** once worked (see box). Hötorget is also home to Stockholm's biggest cinema complex, the Filmstaden Sergel (see page 75); to the east, **Kungsgatan**, running across to Stureplan and Birger Jarlsgatan, has most of the rest of the city's cinemas, interspersed with agreeable little cafés and bars.

Adolf Fredriks kyrka

Holländargatan 14 • Mon 1–6pm, Tues–Sun 10am–4pm • Hötorget T-bana

In secluded gardens on Sveavägen, not far north of Hötorget, sits eighteenth-century **Adolf Fredriks kyrka**, its churchyard popular with lunching office workers. Although the church has a noteworthy past – the French philosopher Descartes was buried in the church's cemetery for eleven years before his body was taken back to France in 1661 – it would have remained unremarkable were it not for one of the most tragic, and still unexplained, events in modern Swedish history: the murder of the former prime minister **Olof Palme** in 1986 (see box, page 56).

1

THE ASSASSINATIONS OF OLOF PALME AND ANNA LINDH

Adolf Fredriks kyrka is of immense significance to modern Swedes, as it is the final resting place of **Olof Palme**; a simple headstone and flowers mark his grave. The then prime minister of Sweden was gunned down in front of his wife on February 28, 1986, while they were on the way home from the Riviera cinema on Sveavägen. As with most Nordic leaders, Palme's fame was his security, and he had no bodyguards with him when he died. A simple **plaque** on the pavement, often respectfully bedecked with flowers, now marks the spot, near the junction with Olof Palmes Gatan, where the prime minister was shot; the assassin escaped up a nearby flight of steps.

Sweden's biggest-ever murder enquiry was launched, and as the years went by, so the allegations of police cover-ups and bungling grew. When **Christer Pettersson**, a small-time criminal, was convicted for the murder in July 1989, most Swedes thought that was the end of the story, but his release just five months later for lack of evidence only served to reopen the bitter debate, with consequent recriminations and resignations within a much-derided police force.

Palme's death sent shock waves through a society unused to political extremism of any kind, and has sadly led to a radical rethink of the open-government policy Sweden had pursued for decades. Although government ministers now rarely go unescorted, Sweden was rocked by the news in September 2003 that a second leading politician had been murdered on home soil; Foreign Minister **Anna Lindh** was fatally stabbed in a Stockholm department store by a man with mental illness who was later arrested and imprisoned (see page 366).

Strindbergsmuséet

Strindberg Museum • Drottninggatan 85 • Tues–Sun noon–4pm, July & Aug from 10am • 75kr • ⓦ strindbergsmuseet.se • Rådmansgatan T-bana

At the northern end of Drottninggatan, you'll come to the intriguing **Strindbergsmuséet** in the "Blue Tower", the last building in which the writer August Strindberg lived in Stockholm between 1908 and 1912. The house is so carefully preserved that you must put plastic bags over your shoes on entering to protect the floors and furnishings. The study is a dark and gloomy place just as Strindberg left it on his death; he always wrote with the Venetian blinds and heavy curtains closed against the sunlight. Upstairs, his library is a musty room with all the books firmly behind glass, which is a great shame as Strindberg was far from a passive reader. He underlined heavily and criticized in the margins as he read, though rather less eruditely than you'd expect – "Lies!", "Crap!", "Idiot!" and "Bloody hell!" tended to be his favourite comments.

Kungsholmen

To the west of the city centre, **Kungsholmen** has a very different feel, with wider, residential streets, larger parks, select shops and Stockholm's Stadshuset (City Hall). Whereas Norrmalm is easy to get to on foot, Kungsholmen is best reached by T-bana (either Rådhuset or Fridhemsplan T-bana stations). Venture further into Kungsholmen and you'll discover a clutch of great bars and restaurants (see pages 69 and 72), and an excellent **beach – Smedsuddsbadet –** at Smedsudden, where you can swim in Lake Mälaren and enjoy fantastic views of the Stadshuset and the Old Town; to get to it, head through the popular **Rålambshovsparken**, or take bus #4 to Västerbroplan, from where it's a five-minute walk.

Stadshuset

City Hall • Hantverkargatan 1 • Guided tours (in English) Daily June–Aug every 30min 9am–4pm; Sept–May hourly 10am–3pm • April–Oct 120kr, Nov–March 90kr • Tower Daily May & Sept 9am–4pm; June–Aug 9am–5pm • 60kr • ⓦ stockholm.se/cityhall • T-Centralen T-bana

Finished in 1923, the **Stadshuset** is one of the landmarks of modern Stockholm and one of the first buildings you'll see when approaching the city from the south by train. Its simple exterior brickwork is no preparation for the intriguing detail inside. If you're a visiting head of state you'll be escorted from your boat up the elegant waterside steps; for lesser mortals, the only way to view the innards is on one of the guided **tours**, which reveal the kitschy Viking-style legislative chamber and impressively echoing Golden Hall. Whilst here, it's worth climbing the steps to the top of the **tower** for a wonderful aerial view of the city centre and Lake Mälaren. The Stadshuset is also the departure point for **ferries** to Drottningholm, Birka, Mariefred and Gripsholm – boats leave from the eastern end of the Stadshusbron bridge.

Östermalm

East of Birger Jarlsgatan – the main thoroughfare that divides Norrmalm from Östermalm – the streets become noticeably broader and grander, forming a uniform grid as far as the circular **Karlaplan**, a handy T-bana and bus interchange full of media types coming off shift from the Swedish Radio and Television buildings at the eastern end of Karlavägen. **Östermalm** was one of the last areas of central Stockholm to be developed; the impressive residences here are as likely to be consulates and embassies as fashionable homes.

Nybroplan

The first place to head for in Östermalm is **Nybroplan**, a square at the water's edge, a ten-minute walk just east along Hamngatan from Sergels torg and marked by the white-stone **Kungliga Dramatiska Teatern**, Stockholm's showpiece Royal Dramatic Theatre, and more commonly known as Dramaten.

Östermalmshallen

Humlegårdsgatan 5 • Mon–Fri 9.30am–7pm, Sat 9.30am–5pm • Östermalmstorg T-bana

From the theatre continue up the hill of Sibyllegatan and you'll reach **Östermalmstorg**, an elegant square that's home to the somewhat ritzy **Östermalmshallen**, a wonderful indoor food market. There are many different items sold here – including reindeer hearts and the wicked-smelling *surströmming* (fermented Baltic herring). Wander round at lunchtime and you'll spot well-heeled ladies and gents sipping Chardonnay and munching on shrimp sandwiches.

Historiska Muséet

Museum of National Antiquities • Narvavägen 13–17 • June–Aug daily 10am–5pm; Sept–May Tues–Sun 11am–5pm, Wed until 8pm • Free • ⓦ historiska.se • Karlaplan T-bana

Covering a period of ten thousand years from the Stone Age to the Middle Ages, the **Historiska Muséet** is the most wide-ranging historical museum in Stockholm, with extensive displays of battles, beliefs and trading patterns, and a breathtaking array of ornately decorated medieval triptychs from across the country.

The Viking Age

The section devoted to Sweden's **Viking** past is particularly engaging and informative in its efforts to portray Scandinavia's former inhabitants not as warriors but as farmers and tradesmen. Exhibits feature a magnificent 2.5m-high "picture stone" from Gotland showing the entry of Viking warriors into Valhalla, as well as Sweden's best-preserved Viking-age boat, dated at around 1000 years old; the boat was discovered near Uppsala alongside a decapitated stallion and a greyhound, which were to accompany the body found in the boat into the afterlife. There's also a lifelike model of the village of Birka (see page 86), complete with an animated film showing daily life.

1

The Gold Room

It's the **Gold Room**, in the basement, with a magnificent 52kg of gold and 200kg of silver including several fifth-century gold collars and other fine pieces of jewellery, that really steals the show. One of the collars is thought to have been worn by a king in the province of Västergötland and features seven rings superimposed on each other, all magnificently adorned with soldered figures.

Millesgården

Carl Milles Väg 2, Lidingö • May–Sept daily 10am–5pm; Oct–April Tues–Sun 11am–5pm • 150kr • Ⓦ millesgarden.se • Take the T-bana to Ropsten, then bus #212 to Torsvikstorg, and walk down Herserudsvägen

Northeast of the city centre, **Lidingö** is a well-to-do commuter island, close to the ferry terminal at Värtahamnen serving Finland, Estonia and Latvia. The island's main attraction is the startling **Millesgården**, the outdoor sculpture collection of **Carl Milles** (1875–1955), one of Sweden's greatest sculptors and art collectors. Phalanxes of gods, angels and beasts sit on terraces carved into the island's steep cliffs, many of the animated, classical figures also perching precariously on soaring pillars, which overlook the distant harbour. A huge *Poseidon* rears over the army of sculptures, the most remarkable of which, *God's Hand*, has a small boy delicately balancing on the outstretched finger of a monumental hand. Those who've been elsewhere in Sweden may find much of the collection familiar, as it includes copies and casts of originals adorning countless provincial towns.

If this collection inspires, it's worth tracking down three other pieces by Milles in the capital: his statue of Gustav Vasa in the Nordiska Muséet on Djurgården (see below); the Orpheus Fountain in Norrmalm's Hötorget; and, out at Nacka Strand (Waxholm boat from Strömkajen), the magnificent *Gud på Himmelsbågen*, a claw-shaped vertical piece of steel topped with the figure of a boy, forming a stunning entrance marker to Stockholm harbour.

Djurgården

You can walk here from the city centre, but it's quite a hike – around 30min from Sergels torg to the Djurgårdsbron bridge across to the island. By public transport, from Östermalm take bus #67 from Karlaplan; from Norrmalm, bus #69 or the Djurgården tram; or from Gamla Stan, the ferry from Slussen (see page 66)

East of Gamla Stan and south of Östermalm, occupying a forested island in Stockholm harbour, **Djurgården** (pronounced "Yoor-gorden") is Stockholm's most enjoyable city park. This finger-shaped island, which served as a royal hunting ground throughout the sixteenth to eighteenth centuries, stretches over 3km in length from Djurgårdsbron bridge in the west (linking it to Strandvägen in Östermalm) to Blockhusudden point in the east. Djurgården is a perfect place to escape the bustle of the capital amongst the groves of pines and spruce, and is also home to some of Stockholm's finest **museums**. You'll need a full day or two to see everything.

Nordiska Muséet

Nordic Museum • Djurgårdsvägen 6 • Daily June–Aug 9am–6pm, Sept–May 10am–5pm, Wed until 10pm • 140kr, free Sept–May Tues 1–5pm • Ⓦ nordiskamuseet.se

The palatial **Nordiska Muséet**, just over Djurgårdsbron from Strandvägen, provides a good grounding in what has made the Swedish nation tick over generations. The displays of trends and traditions are a valiant attempt to represent the last five hundred years of Swedish cultural history and folk art in an accessible fashion, with household furniture, items of clothing and other bits and bobs for perusal. On the ground floor of the

THE ESTONIA FERRY DISASTER

1

The sinking of the **Estonia ferry** in September 1994 was Sweden's worst ever maritime disaster; 852 people lost their lives when the vessel went down in the Baltic Sea en route to Stockholm.

Following the disaster, an official three-nation **investigation** involving Sweden, Finland and Estonia concluded, to great derision from the relatives of those who died on the ferry, that poor design by the original German shipbuilders of the huge hinges which held the bow door in place was to blame for the accident. The shipyard immediately refuted the claim and said that fault lay squarely with the ferry operator, Estline, for shoddy maintenance of the vessel. Following the publication of the official accident report, a number of **conspiracy theories** have surfaced, most alarming being the suggestion that the Russian mafia had weapons on board, and exploded a bomb on the car deck once it became clear that Swedish customs had been tipped off about their illicit cargo and its imminent arrival in Stockholm. The wreck of the *Estonia* now lies on the sea bed southwest of the Finnish Åland islands, covered in a protective layer of concrete to prevent plundering. There's a **memorial** to those who died in the disaster near the Vasamuséet in Djurgården (see below).

cathedral-like interior, you can't fail to spot Carl Milles's phenomenal oak statue of Gustav Vasa (1496–1560), the sixteenth-century king who drove out the Danes (see page 357).

Vasamuséet

Vasa Museum • Galärvarvsvägen 14 • June–Aug daily 8.30am–6pm; Sept–May daily 10am–5pm, Wed until 8pm; guided tours in English hourly June–Aug, less frequently at other times of the year • 150kr • ⓦ vasamuseet.se

Housed in an oddly shaped building close to the Nordiska Muséet, the **Vasamuséet** is without question head and shoulders above Stockholm's other museums. It contains the perfectly preserved seventeenth-century warship, the *Vasa*, which was built on the orders of King Gustav II Adolf, but sank in Stockholm harbour on her maiden voyage in 1628. A victim of engineering miscalculation, the *Vasa*'s hull was too narrow to withstand even the slightest swell which, when coupled with top-heavy rigging, made her a maritime disaster waiting to happen. On August 10 she went down with all hands barely a few hundred metres from her moorings. Preserved in mud for over three hundred years, the ship was raised along with twelve thousand objects in 1961, and now forms the centrepiece of the museum.

Adjacent to the Vasamuséet, three 2.5m-high granite walls now stand in the form of a triangle as a **memorial** to those who died in the *Estonia* ferry disaster in 1994 (see box); the inscription reads simply "their names and their fate, we shall never forget".

The museum

The museum itself is built over part of the old naval dockyard. Impressive though the building is, nothing prepares you for the sheer size of the **ship**: 62m long, the main mast originally 50m above the keel, it sits virtually complete in a cradle of supporting mechanical tackle. Surrounding walkways bring you nose-to-nose with cannon hatches and restored decorative relief, the gilded wooden sculptures on the soaring prow designed to intimidate the enemy and proclaim Swedish might. Carved into the ship's stern, the resplendent figures of two naked cherubs complete with podgy stomachs and rosy cheeks, proudly bearing the Swedish crown between them, are truly remarkable for their fine detail and garish colours.

Adjacent **exhibition halls** and presentations on several levels take care of all the retrieved items, which give an invaluable insight into life on board – everything from combs to wooden barrels for preserving food supplies. There are reconstructions of life on board, detailed models of the *Vasa*, displays relating to contemporary social and political life and a fascinating film of the rescue operation.

1

Skansen

Djurgårdsslätten 49–51 • Daily April 10am–4pm; May–mid-June & Sept 10am–6pm; mid-June–Aug 10am–8pm; Oct–March 10am–3pm • 80–220kr depending on time of year • ⓦ skansen.se

It's **Skansen**, a ten-minute walk south along Djurgårdsvägen from Nordiska Muséet, that most people come to Djurgården for: a vast open-air museum with 150 reconstructed buildings, from a whole town square to windmills, farms and manor houses, laid out on a region-by-region basis. Each section boasts its own daily activities – including traditional handicrafts, games and displays – that anyone can join in. Best of the buildings are the warm and functional *Sámi* dwellings, and the craftsmen's workshops in the old-town quarter. You can also potter around a **zoo** (containing Nordic animals such as brown bears, elk and reindeer, as well as non-native species like monkeys), and an **aquarium** with poisonous snakes and turtles. Partly because of the attention paid to accuracy, and partly due to the admirable lack of commercialization, Skansen manages to avoid the tackiness associated with similar ventures in other countries. Even the snack bars dole out traditional foods and in winter serve up great bowls of warming soup.

Gröna Lunds Tivoli

Lilla Allmänna Gränd 9, immediately opposite Skansen's main gates • Daily late April–Sept roughly noon–10pm • 120kr; an optional all-day *åkband* pass costs 345kr for unlimited rides (275kr after 7pm) or alternatively you can pay per ride • ⓦ gronalund.com

Though Stockholm's main fairground is not a patch on its more famous namesake in Copenhagen, **Gröna Lunds Tivoli** is decidedly cleaner and less seedy. The talk of the place is still the ominous Fritt Fall, a hair-raising vertical drop of around 80m in a matter of seconds, and the Fritt Fall Tilt, which involves being catapulted face-first towards the ground from on high – do lunch later. At night the emphasis shifts as the park becomes the stomping ground for hundreds of Stockholm's teenagers.

ABBA: The Museum

Djurgårdsvägen 68 • Daily May–Aug 9am–8pm; Sept–mid-Dec daily 10am–6pm, Wed & Thurs until 8pm; mid-Dec–mid-Jan daily 10am–7pm • 250kr (no cash accepted; buy online for a small discount and to book a visiting time) • ⓦ abbathemuseum.com

The all-singing, all-dancing **ABBA museum** is a must for lifelong fans of Sweden's most famous band (see page 62), though others may find it pricey and a little underwhelming. Highlights include outfits worn by the fab four, as well as a reconstruction of Polar Studios, where three of the band's last albums were recorded. There's even a piano that, it's said, is hooked up to Benny Andersson's own one. If and when he twinkles the ivories, you'll hear the tunes he's playing. Tickets include entry to the adjacent Swedish Music Hall of Fame, which takes a wider look at the country's best musical exports.

Thielska Galleriet

Thiel Gallery • Sjötullsbacken 6–8 • Tues–Sun noon–5pm, Thurs until 8pm • 130kr • ⓦ thielska-galleriet.se • Bus #69 from Norrmalm

At the far eastern end of Djurgården, known as Blockhusudden, the **Thielska Galleriet** is one of Stockholm's major treasures, a fine example of both Swedish architecture and Nordic art. The house was built by Ferdinand Boberg at the turn of the twentieth century for banker and art connoisseur Ernest Thiel, and turned into an art gallery after he sold it to the state in 1924. Thiel knew many contemporary Nordic artists personally and gathered an impressive collection of paintings over the years, many of which are on show today. There are works by Carl Larsson, Anders Zorn – most notably his portraits and female nudes – Edvard Munch, Bruno Liljefors and August Strindberg, whose paintings of wild Swedish landscapes are displayed. The museum enjoys a dramatic

1

SWEDEN'S FAB FOUR: ABBA

Overturning odds of 20–1, Anni-Frid Lyngstad, Benny Andersson, Björn Ulvæus and Agnetha Fältskog first came to the world's attention as they stormed to victory in April 1974 at the Eurovision Song Contest with *Waterloo*. **ABBA** went on to become the biggest-selling group in the world, second only to Volvo as Sweden's biggest export earner, topping the charts for a decade with hits like *Dancing Queen* (performed to celebrate the marriage of Swedish King Carl Gustaf to German commoner Silvia Sommerlath in 1976), *Mamma Mia* and *Money Money Money*. The winning combination led to a string of number-one hits and even a film, *ABBA The Movie*, released to popular acclaim in 1978.

However, the relentless workload of recording and touring took its toll; frictions within the group surfaced, the two couples – Agnetha and Björn, and Anni-Frid and Benny – divorced, and ABBA called it a day in 1983. News of the split was broken by the Swedish newspaper, *Dagens Nyheter* – Agnetha had casually dropped the bombshell into a conversation and to this day carries the blame for the break-up. Having withdrawn from public life, she now lives as a virtual recluse on the island of Ekerö on Lake Mälaren. Anni-Frid married a German prince, and today lives in Switzerland and spends her time championing environmental causes. After a spell in Henley-on-Thames, near London, during the 1980s, Björn is now back in Stockholm where he partly owns the domestic airline, Nextjet, and writes and produces music with Benny, who has opened his own hotel on Södermalm, *Rival* (see page 68). Together they've worked on a string of musicals including *Chess* and *Mamma Mia*, which uses 27 ABBA songs to tell the tale of the relationship between a mother and her daughter. Fans of the band will not want to miss **Abba: The Museum** (see above).

---

setting at the very tip of Djurgården; indeed the views out over Stockholm harbour and across to the district of Nacka on the southern shore warrant a trip out here.

Södermalm

On foot from Gamla Stan, head south along any of the parallel streets towards Kornhamnstorg or Järntorget squares, and continue past the Slussen T-bana station where Götgatan, Södermalm's main north–south thoroughfare, begins. By public transport, take the T-bana to Slussen, Medborgarplatsen or Mariatorget.

Whatever you do in Stockholm, don't miss the delights of the city's southern island, **Södermalm**, whose craggy cliffs, turrets and towers rise high above the clogged traffic interchange at Slussen. The perched buildings are vaguely forbidding, but venture beyond the main roads skirting the island and a lively and surprisingly green area unfolds, one that has, historically speaking, been working class at heart. After dark, you'll probably end up in one of Söder's bars or restaurants (see pages 70 and 72) in the hip area known as **SoFo**; this is the handful of streets lined with cafés and restaurants which lie "**s**outh of **Fo**lkungagatan" (hence the name), predominantly Åsögatan, Bondegatan and Skånegatan.

Stadsmuséet

Stockholm City Museum • Södermalmstorg • Tues–Fri noon–6pm, Wed until 8pm, Sat & Sun 10am–4pm • Free • ⓦ stadsmuseum. stockholm.se • Slussen T-bana

In Södermalmstorg, right by the Slussen T-bana station, the rewarding **Stadsmuséet** houses collections relating to the city's history as a seaport and industrial centre. The Baroque building, designed by Tessin the Elder and finished by his son in 1685, was once the town hall for this part of Stockholm. Besides the museum, its most engaging offerings – its **walking tours** – can be booked online: amongst them is a tour of Södermalm in the footsteps of Lisbeth Salander and Mikael Blomkvist, the main characters of the Stieg Larsson *Millennium* novels, plus a chance to rediscover 1970s Stockholm with a walking tour devoted to key sites in ABBA's musical history.

SÖDERMALM

● EATING

Barabao	2
Blå Dörren	1
Café String	9
Crêperie Fyra Knop	4
Dionysos	10
Garlic and Shots	7
Kalf & Hansen	3
Koh Phangan	11
Kvarnen	6
Pelikan	14
Snaps	5
Soldaten Svejk	8
Tre Indier	13
Urban Deli	12

■ DRINKING AND NIGHTLIFE

Akkurat	2
Debaser	8
Folk&Friends	5
Gröne Jägaren	9
Kelly's	7
Kvarnen	6
Patricia	1
Pelikan	5
Pet Sounds Bar	10
Sidetrack	4
Södra Teatern	3

■ ACCOMMODATION

Anno 1647	4
Clarion Hotel Stockholm	11
Långholmen	3
Lunda Pensionat	5
Red Boat Mälaren	2
Rival	6
Rygerfjord	1
Scandic Malmen	9
Skanstulls Hostel	10
Tre Små Rum	7
Zinkensdamm	8

▶ Main Line South, also Pendeltåg to Nynäshamn for Ferry to Gotland

1

SWIMMING IN STOCKHOLM

The water in Stockholm is clean and perfect for swimming during the long days of summer. The best **beaches** are all west of the city centre: on Långholmen there's **Långholmens strandbad** to the west of Västerbron bridge, and rocky **Klippbadet** to the east of the bridge; and across on Kungsholmen, **Smedsuddsbadet** (see page 56) has a large grassy area for those who enjoy to sunbathe.

Alternatively, Södermalm is the place to go for **swimming pools;** there are two in fairly close proximity: Forsgrénskabadet in Medborgarplatsen (☎08 508 403 20; Medborgarplatsen T-bana); Erikdalsbadet, Hammarby Slussväg 20, (☎08 508 402 58; Skanstull T-bana), which has an open-air pool. For unofficial **nude** bathing, head out to one of the islands in the archipelago and find your own private spot.

Fotografiska

Photographical Museum • Stora Tullhuset, Stadsgårdshamnen 22 • Daily 9am–11pm, Sat 9am–1am • 165kr • ⓦ fotografiska.eu • Slussen T-bana

A mere five minutes' walk from Slussen along Stadsgårdsleden towards the Viking Line ferry terminal, the **Fotografiska** is housed inside one of the city's former red-brick customs warehouses. Spread across three floors of airy exhibition space, the museum showcases the work of world-renowned photographers both in print and on film. Exhibitions change frequently, though there's every chance that one of the big names will be on display when you visit: star turns have included Robert Mapplethorpe, France's Sarah Moon and Scottish photographer Albert Watson, whose work featured on over two hundred magazine covers, including *Vogue*. For unsurpassed views of the Stockholm waterfront, head up to the museum's top-floor **café** where the vistas are as breathtaking as the photographic work downstairs.

Katarina kyrka

Högbergsgatan 13 • Mon–Sat 11am–5pm, Sun 8.30am–5pm • Medborgarplatsen T-bana

The Renaissance-style **Katarina kyrka** stands on the site where the victims of the so-called "Stockholm Bloodbath" (see page 357) – the betrayed nobility of Sweden who had opposed King Christian II's Danish invasion – were buried in 1520. They were burned as heretics outside the city walls, and it proved a vicious and effective coup, Christian disposing of the opposition in one fell swoop. In 1723, a devastating fire tore through the church, reducing it to ruins, an event that was repeated in 1990 when the building fell victim to another tragic blaze. Painstaking rebuilding work was finally completed five years later when the building reopened.

Mariatorget

Södermalm's main square, **Mariatorget**, is a pleasant leafy space surrounded by grand Art Nouveau buildings on all sides. This is one of the most desirable places for Stockholmers to live, close to the stylish bars and restaurants that are the favourite haunts of Stockholm's young and terminally hip, in particular Benny Andersson's *Rival* hotel and bar (see page 68).

Långholmen

Take the T-bana to Hornstull and then follow signs to the youth hostel, or take bus #4, which crosses Västerbron on its way from Södermalm, Kungsholmen, Norrmalm and Östermalm

True to its name ("long island"), **Långholmen** is a skinny sliver of land that lies off the northwestern tip of Södermalm, crossed by the mighty Västerbron bridge linking Södermalm with Kungsholmen. There are a couple of popular **beaches** here (see box). Leafy and peaceful, Långholmen is a delightful place to take a walk; on the

1

way you'll also get some stunning views of the city towards the Stadhuset and Gamla
Stan.

ARRIVAL AND DEPARTURE   STOCKHOLM

BY PLANE
Arlanda airport Most flights to Stockholm arrive at Arlanda airport (☎010 910 00, ⓦarlanda.se/en), 45km north of Stockholm. Trains operate all day long every 15min from the two dedicated Arlanda Express stations beneath the airport (Arlanda Norra for Terminal 5, Arlanda Södra for the other terminals), and the trip to Centralstationen in Stockholm takes just 20min (295kr one way; ⓦarlandaexpress.com). Cheaper commuter trains take around 40min to get from Arlanda to central Stockholm (160kr one way; ⓦsj.se). The main company operating buses into Stockholm is Flygbussarna, which runs all-day services to Stockholm's long-distance bus station, Cityterminalen, every 10–15min (40min; 99kr single; ⓦflygbussarna.se). Taxis from the airport into town (30–40min) cost around 550kr. If you pick up a rental car and drive into central Stockholm you will be subject to a congestion charge; cameras register vehicles automatically and your credit card will be debited accordingly.

Bromma airport Some domestic flights and all flights with Brussels Airlines arrive at the more central Bromma airport, which is connected to Cityterminalen by Flygbussarna – buses run two to three times per hour (20min; 75kr single).

Ryanair airports Most of Ryanair's Stockholm flights arrive at Skavsta airport, 100km south of the capital close to the town of Nyköping, whilst others come in to Västerås, 100km west of Stockholm; Skavsta and Västerås buses operate in connection with flight arrival and departure times (both routes 1hr 20min; 139kr one way).

BY TRAIN
By train, you'll arrive at Stockholm Centralstationen (the station is also known as Stockholm C, which is an abbreviation of "Central" in railspeak throughout Sweden), a cavernous structure on Vasagatan in the city centre. All branches of the Tunnelbana ("T-bana"), Stockholm's efficient metro system, meet at T-Centralen, the T-bana station directly below the main station.

Destinations Copenhagen (6 daily; 5hr); Gällivare (1 daily; 15hr); Gävle (hourly; 1hr 20min); Gothenburg (hourly; 3–5hr); Karlstad (8 daily; 2hr 30min); Kiruna (1 daily; 16hr); Läggesta (for Mariefred; hourly; 35min); Luleå (2 daily; 13hr 30min); Malmö (hourly; 4hr 20min); Mora (2 daily; 3hr 30min); Narvik (1 daily; 19hr); Nyköping (8 daily; 1hr); Oslo (2 daily; 6hr); Östersund (2 daily; 6hr 30min); Sundsvall (10 daily; 3hr 20min); Umeå (4 daily; 9hr 30min); Uppsala (every 20min; 40min); Västerås (hourly; 1hr).

BY BUS
By bus, your arrival point will be the huge glass structure known as Cityterminalen (☎08 762 59 97), a high-tech terminal adjacent to Centralstationen which handles all bus services. You can get to the northern end of Centralstationen's main hall using a series of escalators and walkways.

Destinations Gävle (3 daily; 2hr 20min); Gothenburg (8 daily; 7hr); Jönköping (9 daily; 5hr); Kalmar (5 daily; 6hr); Norrköping (at least hourly; 2hr 20min); Umeå (2 daily; 9hr 20min).

GETTING AROUND

At first, Stockholm can be a confusing place, winding and twisting its way across islands, over water and through parkland. To get your bearings, the best bet is to walk: it takes about half an hour to cross central Stockholm on foot, from west to east or north to south. Sooner or later though, you'll probably want to use some form of transport.

PUBLIC TRANSPORT
Information Storstockholms Lokaltrafik (SL; ⓦsl. se) operates a comprehensive system of buses and underground trains, which extends well out of the city centre. Its main information office is the SL-Center on the lower level of Stockholm C close to the entrance to the T-bana (daily 7am–9pm). It stocks timetables for the city's bus and T-bana systems and archipelago boats. Up-to-date

---

FERRIES FROM STOCKHOLM
Several **ferries** a day leave central Stockholm bound for Sweden's regional neighbours, including **Finland** and **Estonia**. The Finnish routes in particular are popular with weekending Stockholmers who relish the change of scenery (and the considerably lower alcohol prices onboard). Tallink Silja Line ferries (ⓦtallinksilja.se) run to Helsinki (16hr), Turku (10hr) and Tallinn (16hr) from Värtahamnen, east of the city centre, while Viking Line ferries (ⓦvikingline.se) run to Helsinki and Tallinn from Stadsgården on Södermalm's northern edge.

1

CANOEING IN STOCKHOLM

One of the most fun ways to see Stockholm is from the water. The best place in town to **rent boats** is *Sjöcaféet*, at Galärvarvsvägen 2 (☎08 667 77 01), by the bridge across to Djurgården. It costs 170kr to rent a canoe for an hour, or 400kr/24hr; kayaks cost 140kr/hr or 450kr/24hr. For canoes in the archipelago, try Skärgårdens Kanotcenter at Vegabacken 22 on Vaxholm (☎08 541 377 90, ⬤kanotcenter.com); take bus #670 from Tekniska Högskolan in Stockholm. Alternatively, ask locally on the other islands – corner shops often have a couple of canoes or boats for rent.

information on the public transport system in English can also be obtained on ⬤sl.se.

Travelcards Buying a travelcard, available from Pressbyrån newsagents, SL-Centers and the ticket machines at T-bana stations, will save you time and money. First, buy SL's Access card (20kr), a smartcard onto which you load the travelcard you want: for example, 24hr (130kr), 72hr (260kr) or seven days (335kr); you are then entitled to unlimited travel by bus and T-bana plus the ferries to Djurgården. Note that you can't purchase tickets with cash on the city's buses; you will need to buy a travelcard.

THE TUNNELBANA

The quickest and most useful form of transport is the Tunnelbana (T-bana; ⬤sl.se), Stockholm's metro system, which comprises three main lines (red, green and blue). Station entrances are marked with a blue letter "T" on a white background. From Sunday to Thursday trains operate from around 5am until around midnight, but on Fridays and Saturdays – as well as the evening before a public holiday – there are services all through the night (roughly every 30–40min).

BUSES

Buses Stockholm's buses are often less direct than the metro because of the city's layout – route maps are available from the SL-Center (see above); bus #4 is an excellent way of seeing a lot of the city for very little cost. You can't buy tickets from the driver; get a travelcard instead (see above). Buses are pushchair- and pram-friendly; a special area halfway down the bus is set aside for these.

Night buses These replace the T-bana after midnight, except on Friday and Saturday (and the night before a public holiday), when the T-bana runs all night.

FERRIES AND BOATS

Around Stockholm Ferries link some of the central islands: Djurgården is connected with Slussen (at the

southern end of Gamla Stan) and Skeppsholmen, with services roughly every 20 minutes (32kr one way).

To the archipelago Ferries provide frequent, year-round access to the sprawling archipelago, and sail from outside the *Grand* hotel on Strömkajen (see opposite) near the National museum. For details of services to the archipelago, see page 84.

To Lake Mälaren Boats to Drottningholm, Birka and Mariefred leave from outside the Stadshuset on Kungsholmen. For details of services to Drottningholm see page 85, to Birka see page 86, to Mariefred see page 87.

BIKES, TAXIS AND CARS

Bike rental Available from *Sjöcaféet* at Galärvarvsvägen 2 (☎08 667 77 01), just over the bridge that leads to Djurgården, or from Servicedepån-Cykelstallet at Scheelegatan 15 on Kungsholmen (☎08 651 00 66, ⬤cykelstallet.se); reckon on paying 225kr/day. Another great way to explore the city is by using a LimeBike, a shared bike system available at any time which costs 0.5kr per 30min (⬤citybikes.se).

Taxi ranks Several around the city (including one outside Centralstationen). You can also ring one of the three main operators: Taxi Stockholm (☎08 15 00 00, ⬤taxistockholm.se), Taxi Kurir (☎0771 86 00 00, ⬤taxikurir.se) or Sverige Taxi (☎08 720 80 80, ⬤sverigetaxi.se). The meter will show around 45kr when you get in and will then race upwards at an alarming speed. It's not unheard of for drivers to rip off tourists – try to agree a fixed price wherever possible and be prepared to walk away if the rate seems too high. A short trip across the city centre should cost around 200kr.

By car Be extremely careful when parking: see page 28. For car rental, see page 28 and be aware of the congestion charge in central Stockholm (see page 65).

INFORMATION

Tourist office Stockholm's main tourist office (*turistbyrå*) is on Sergels torg, right next to the Kulturhuset Stadsteatern (Mon–Fri 9am–6pm, Sat 9am–4pm, Sun 10am–4pm; May to Aug Mon–Fri 9am–7pm, Sat 9am–4pm (July–19 Aug 9am–6pm) Sun 10am–4pm; ☎08 508 285 08,

⬤visitstockholm.com), which hands out fistfuls of free brochures.

Listings information *Totally Stockholm* (⬤totallystockholm.com) is good for all kinds of listings. There's also a free Saturday supplement to the *DN* newspaper, *På*

stan – get someone to translate if your Swedish isn't up to it – that details all manner of entertainments, from the latest films to club listings; it's also available in bars and restaurants.

ACCOMMODATION

SEE MAPS PAGES 46, 49 AND 63

Stockholm has plenty of accommodation to suit every taste and pocket, from elegant upmarket **hotels** with waterfront views to **youth hostels** in unusual places – two are on boats and another is in a former prison. From mid-June to mid-August it is always a good idea to **book** your accommodation in advance.

HOTELS AND PENSIONS

Summer in Stockholm means a buyer's market for hotel rooms as business travel declines; double rooms can cost as little as 500kr. The cheapest choices on the whole are found to the north of the Cityterminalen in the streets to the west of Adolf Fredriks kyrka. Don't rule out the more expensive places, however: there are some attractive weekend and summer prices that make a spot of luxury nearer the waterfront a little more affordable. All of the following establishments include breakfast in the price, unless otherwise stated.

GREATER STOCKHOLM

Bema Upplandsgatan 13 ☎ 08 23 26 75, ⓦ hotelbema. se; bus #50/53 from Central Station. A 10min walk from the station in a quiet residential area facing the leafy Tegnérlunden park, this small pension-style hotel has twelve en-suite rooms with beechwood furniture and modern Swedish decor. 900kr/1100kr

Best Western Plus Time Vanadisvägen 12 ☎ 08 545 473 00, ⓦ timehotel.se; Odenplan T-bana. The 144 contemporary, brightly decorated, airy rooms feature wooden floors and French balconies. Self-catering studios are also available. Rooms on the top floor have their own terrace. 1450kr/2115kr

Connect City Ahlströmergatan 41 ☎ 08 420 030 00, ⓦ connecthotels.se; Fridhemsplan T-bana. A bright, airy and modern hotel on Kungsholmen with oak floors and fully tiled bathrooms. True, this hotel is never going to win any prizes for original design but at these prices it really doesn't matter. 699kr/989kr

Diplomat Strandvägen 7C ☎ 08 459 68 00, ⓦ diplomat hotel.com; Östermalmstorg T-bana. One of the city's most famous hotels, this Art Nouveau town house offers individually decorated rooms with elegant furnishings, lovely high ceilings and wonderful views over Stockholm's inner harbour, though the rooms and suites don't come cheap. 3000kr/3200kr

Hellsten Luntmakargatan 68 ☎ 08 661 86 00, ⓦ hellsten.se; Rådmansgatan T-bana. Dating from 1898, the original bourgeois family apartments in this building have been lovingly restored; some still have their tile stoves

whilst others have been individually decorated with antique Asian or African furniture. 1290kr/2090kr

Micro Tegnérlunden 8 ☎ 08 545 455 69, ⓦ hotelmicro. se; Rådmansgatan T-bana. Windowless cabin-style basement rooms with bunk beds and shared facilities, all decked out in bright marine colours, give this budget hotel a strangely maritime feel. Basic, maybe, but certainly a great money-saving option. 595kr

★ M/S Monika Kungsholms Strand 133 ☎ 08 120 921 00, ⓦ msmonika.se; Fridhemsplan/St Eriksplan T-bana. One of Stockholm's more intimate "floatels", this charming wooden boat from 1908 bobs around just off Kungsholmen's north shore. There are just three quirky but compact rooms; the whole boat can be rented out on request. 1300kr

Rex Luntmakargatan 73 ☎ 08 16 00 40, ⓦ rexhotel. se; Rådmansgatan T-bana. The original pine floors and sweeping staircase from 1866 have been lovingly restored to create a sense of style and elegance throughout this tasteful hotel, whose rooms are complemented with granite bathrooms. 1490kr/1890kr

Scandic Hasselbacken Hazeliusbacken 20 ☎ 08 12 13 33 00, ⓦ hasselbacken.com/sv/ Liljevalchs/Gröna Lunds tram stop. One of the only hotels on Djurgården, with a centuries-old restaurant and a handy location near museums and galleries. Rooms are basic for the money but there's a sauna and a gym. 2000kr/2300kr

CENTRAL STOCKHOLM

First Reisen Skeppsbron 12 ☎ 08 22 32 60, ⓦ first hotels.com/reisen; Gamla Stan or Slussen T-bana. One of Stockholm's classic hotels, dating back to the eighteenth century. Rooms are decked out with handsome wood panelling and all have bathtubs (not the norm in Sweden). The more expensive options even have their own Jacuzzis, saunas and balconies overlooking the waterfront. 2195kr/2295kr

Grand Södra Blasieholmshamn 8 ☎ 08 679 35 00, ⓦ grandhotel.se; Kungsträdgården T-bana. Set in a late nineteenth-century waterside building, this is Scandinavia's most refined hotel, providing the last word in luxury. Prices

---

TOP FIVE PLACES TO STAY

Af Chapman see page 69
City Backpackers see page 69
Rival see page 68
Sven Vintappare see page 68
Tre Små Rum see page 68

1

may have fallen in recent years but they're still in a category of their own. **3700kr**

Hotel Collector Storkyrkobrinken 5 ☏ 08 506 401 00, ⊛ thecollectorshotels.se; Gamla Stan T-bana. Traditional hotel in a building dating from the 1470s, with charming rooms tastefully decorated in old-fashioned Swedish style – lots of antique furniture and folk artefacts – though with modern touches such as bathroom underfloor heating. **1990kr/2790kr**

Lord Nelson Västerlånggatan 22 ☏ 08 506 401 20, ⊛ lordnelsonhotel.se; Gamla Stan T-bana. Sister hotel to the *Lady Hamilton*, this is one of the narrowest hotels in Sweden at just 5m wide. It's stuffed full of naval antiques and curiosities including an original letter from Nelson to Lady Hamilton. Rooms are small with ship's teak floorboards and lots of mahogany and brass. **1290kr/2090kr**

Mälardrottningen Riddarholmen ☏ 08 120 902 00, ⊛ malardrottningen.se; Gamla Stan T-bana. Moored off the island of Riddarholmen, this elegant white ship was formerly the gin palace of American millionairess Barbara Hutton. Its cabin-style rooms are a little cramped but make a fun change. **891kr/1084kr**

Nordic Light Vasaplan 7 ☏ 08 505 632 00, ⊛ nordic lighthotel.com; T-Centralen T-bana. Minimalist Nordic design reigns here – standard rooms are individually decorated in shades of white and steely grey, inspired by Lapland's amazing northern lights. Painfully contemporary rather than satisfyingly comfortable, but it's very near the train station. **1460kr/2080kr**

Old Town Lodge Baggensgatan 25 ☏ 08 20 44 55, ⊛ oldtownlodge.se; Gamla Stan T-bana. Set in a handsome old building from the 1600s, this relaxed guesthouse has bright double rooms with shared facilities. There are also some smaller dorm-like doubles, separated from one another by glass walls and curtains. **715kr/690kr**

Queen's Drottninggatan 71A ☏ 08 24 94 60, ⊛ queens hotel.se; Hötorget T-bana. Renovated with a slightly awkward mix of old and new, this central hotel offers individually decorated en-suite rooms that take their decorative cues from the turn of the last century. Surprisingly quiet, given the location in Stockholm's main shopping district. **1500kr/1700kr**

Scandic Grand Central Kungsgatan 70 ☏ 08 512 520 00, ⊛ scandichotels.com; T-Centralen T-bana. As the name suggests, this place is both grand and central, with a winning location near the train station. Standard rooms are modern and elegant, but the "cabins" are very compact. The stylish brasserie is a popular spot among locals seeking pre-theatre drinks. **1495kr**

Scandic no. 53 Kungsgatan 53 ☏ 08 517 365 00, ⊛ scandichotels.se/no53; Hötorget T-bana. Slick, modern hotel with compact rooms, some of which are windowless. There's a patio for use in the summer, and

meals are served in the colourful lounge on the ground floor. **800kr**

★ **Sven Vintappare** Sven Vintappares Gränd 3 ☏ 08 22 41 40, ⊛ hotelsvenvintappare.se; Gamla Stan T-bana. Housed in a charming building from 1607, with just seven rooms, all decorated in Swedish Gustavian style. The bathrooms are to die for, their granite floors and marble walls completing the sense of royal elegance. **1995kr**

SÖDERMALM

Anno 1647 Mariagränd 3 ☏ 08 442 16 80, ⊛ anno1647. se; Slussen T-bana. Located in a seventeenth-century building, with pine floors and period furniture, this hotel is an oasis of elegance and Gustavian charm and has perfect views of the colourful roofs and buildings of Gamla Stan. **1166kr**

Clarion Hotel Stockholm Ringvägen 98 ☏ 08 462 10 00, ⊛ nordicchoicehotels.com; Skanstull T-bana. This reasonably priced business hotel sits in a huge modern block with more than 500 rooms. Rates are decent compared with hotels in Gamla Stan, and there's parking right beneath the building. **980kr**

Lunda Pensionat Lundagatan 31 ☏ 073 086 12 24, ⊛ lundapensionat.se; Zinkensdamm T-bana. This comfortable B&B offers compact hostel and hotel rooms, all with private bathrooms. If you can grab a room with a window, the views of Stockholm make this place a real winner for the money. **695kr**

★ **Rival** Mariatorget 3 ☏ 08 545 789 00, ⊛ rival. se; Mariatorget T-bana. Owned by Benny Andersson of ABBA who designed the hotel in a combination of 1930s and contemporary Swedish style to recapture the former glamour of the building. Some rooms have balconies overlooking the square, and the building includes a bistro and a bakery. **2230kr**

Scandic Malmen Götgatan 49–51 ☏ 08 517 347 00, ⊛ scandichotels.com/malmen; Medborgarplatsen T-bana. Comfortable, if predictable, chain hotel rooms with wooden floors and modern Scandinavian decor, though it's the location close to SoFo that makes this massive hotel worth considering. **1290kr/2490kr**

★ **Tre Små Rum** Högbergsgatan 81 ☏ 08 641 23 71, ⊛ tresmarum.se; Mariatorget T-bana. A clean, comfy option in the heart of Södermalm; the seven simple basement rooms with shared bathrooms are very popular, so book in advance. A help-yourself breakfast from the kitchen fridge is available. **795kr**

Zinkensdamm Zinkens Väg 20 ☏ 08 616 81 10, ⊛ zinkensdamm.com; Zinkensdamm T-bana. Comfortable, well-appointed and homely hotel rooms, all en suite, with tasteful wallpaper and wooden floors located in a separate wing of the youth hostel (see opposite), right on the doorstep of Tantolunden park. **1495kr/1995kr**

HOSTELS

There are some excellent hostels in Stockholm, including the STF-run *Af Chapman* – a grand ship offering stunning city views from its deck. Generally speaking, though, it's the independently run places that tend to be best. The prices we give for STF hostels are for youth-hostel members; non-members pay 50kr more in Stockholm.

STF HOSTELS

★**Af Chapman** Flaggmansvägen 8, Skeppsholmen ☎08 463 22 80, ⊛stfchapman.com; Kungsträdgården T-bana. This smart square-rigged 1888 ship – a landmark in its own right – has views over Gamla Stan that are unsurpassed at the price. One of the quirkiest places to stay in Stockholm, though advance reservations are a must. Make sure you get a room aboard the boat, rather than on dry land. Dorms <u>325kr</u>, doubles <u>750kr</u>

Gärdet Sandhamnsgatan 59A ☎08 463 22 90, ⊛stfturist.se/gardet; Karlaplan T-bana. One of the newer STF hostels, a short metro ride east of the city centre. Accommodation is in one- to four-bed en-suite rooms; there's also a guest kitchen. Doubles <u>745kr</u>

Långholmen Kronohäktet, Långholmsmuren 20 ☎08 720 85 00, ⊛langholmen.com; Hornstull T-bana. On the island of Långholmen, Stockholm's grandest STF hostel is set in the former prison building dating from 1724. The cells are converted into smart private and dormitory rooms, still with their original, extremely small windows. Dorms <u>280kr</u>, doubles <u>670kr</u>

Rygerfjord Södermälarstrand, Kajplats 13 ☎08 840 830, ⊛rygerfjord.se; Slussen T-bana. Near the waterfront in Katerina-Sofia, this basic hotel run by STF has a mix of doubles, singles and family rooms, some with private bathrooms. Doubles <u>560kr</u>

Zinkensdamm Zinkens Väg 20 ☎08 616 81 10, ⊛zinkensdamm.com; Zinkensdamm T-bana. A huge hostel with private rooms and single-sex dorms. It's in a good location for exploring Södermalm, though it's a 30min walk from the city centre. Kitchen and laundry facilities available (also see opposite). Dorms <u>320kr</u>, doubles <u>700kr</u>

INDEPENDENT HOSTELS

★**City Backpackers** Upplandsgatan 2A ☎08 20 69 20, ⊛citybackpackers.se; T-Centralen T-bana. Friendly,
vibrant hostel with a hundred or so beds, a 5min walk from Centralstationen. Skateboards are available for rent and there are regular movie nights and pub crawls. There are also free sauna sessions every night. Some rooms have private facilities. Dorms <u>300kr</u>, doubles <u>820kr</u>

Red Boat Mälaren Södermälarstrand, Kajplats 6, Södermalm ☎08 644 43 85, ⊛theredboat.com; Slussen T-bana. Housed in an old Göta canal steamer (and an adjacent boat), this hostel enjoys a fantastic location overlooking the city hall. Cabins are compact but comfortable and clean. There are no cooking facilities on board due to the risk of fire. Dorms <u>350kr</u>, doubles <u>670kr</u>

Skanstulls Hostel Ringvägen 135 ☎08 643 02 04, ⊛skanstulls.se; Skanstull T-bana. Bright, quirky rooms and dorms at this excellent, laid-back hostel near SoFo's bars and restaurants in Södermalm. There's a stylish kitchen and dining area complete with free tea, coffee and pasta. Dorms <u>285kr</u>, doubles <u>720kr</u>

Stockholm Hostel Ahlströmergatan 15 ☎070 156 55 25, ⊛stockholmhostel.se; Fridhemsplan T-bana. Bright, contemporary design hostel on Kungsholmen. Rooms all have private facilities and their own television – as beds aren't available individually, you'll need to rent the whole room. Two kitchens are available for guests' use. Doubles <u>650kr</u>

CAMPING

With the nearest year-round sites a good half-hour out of the city centre, camping out of season in Stockholm can prove rather inconvenient, though this being Sweden, both sites listed below are well equipped, with modern service buildings providing showers and laundry facilities.

Ängby Camping Blackebergsvägen 20 ☎08 37 04 20, ⊛angbycamping.se; Ängbyplan T-bana; turn left when leaving the station. West of the city on the lakeshore where there are good beaches. Open all year, but phone ahead to book Sept–April. Tents <u>235kr</u>, two-person cabins <u>480kr</u>

Bredäng Camping Stora Sällskapets Väg ☎08 97 70 71, ⊛bredangcamping.se; Bredäng T-bana. Southwest of the city with views over Lake Mälaren. Open all year, though only the campsite's cabins are open between mid-Oct and mid-April. Tents <u>295kr</u>, two-person cabins <u>855kr</u>

EATING
SEE MAPS PAGES 46, 49 AND 63

Eating out in Stockholm needn't be expensive – observe a few rules and you'll manage quite well. If money is tight, switch your main meal of the day to **lunchtime**, when on weekdays almost every café and restaurant offers an excellent-value set menu, known as **dagens rätt**, for 85–115kr. For evening meals, don't assume that Chinese or Italian places will be the least expensive; more often than not they're overpriced and serve food
that's pretty tasteless. You're much better off seeking out one of Stockholm's many **cafés**, Swedish **restaurants** or **food trucks**, where you'll find traditional fare as well as some tasty international dishes. For **self-catering**, try Hötorgshallen food court in Hötorget (see page 55) and the market outside for fruit and vegetables; otherwise, head for the basement supermarket of the Åhléns department store at Sergels torg.

1

CAFÉS AND FOOD COURTS

When it comes to places to snack or *fika* (have a coffee, a chat and some cake), the best advice is to follow the locals. Tourist cafés in Gamla Stan tend to be overpriced and poor quality, though there are a couple of exceptions. At lunchtime it's worth seeking out busy food courts, where yummy international food is served at decent prices.

GREATER STOCKHOLM

★ **Blå Porten** Djurgårdsvägen 64 ☎ 08 663 87 59, ⓦ blaporten.com; bus #69. Glorious café set in a glass-walled building overlooking a courtyard with outdoor seating around an old fountain. The open sandwiches and lunches here are Provençal-influenced and include a wide choice of quiches, pies, salads and soups, including vegetarian options. Mains around 100–150kr. Daily 11am–7pm.

Saturnus Erikbergsgatan 6 ⓦ cafesaturnus.se; Rådmansgatan T-bana. Stockholm's answer to a French patisserie-cum-boulangerie, with a subtle Parisian atmosphere. Excellent range of sandwiches for 50–150kr, salads from 140kr and the biggest and best cinnamon buns in town. Mon–Fri 7am–8pm, Sat & Sun 8am–7pm.

CENTRAL STOCKHOLM

Café Panorama Sergels torg 3 ☎ 08 21 10 35. T-Centralen T-bana. Top-floor café inside the Kulturhuset Stadsteatern (see page 55), with superb views over central Stockholm – try to get one of the window tables. Lunch is dependable and inexpensive. Tues–Fri 11am–8pm, Sat 11am–6pm, Sun 11am–5pm.

Chokladkoppen Stortorget 18 ⓦ chokladkoppen. se; Gamla Stan T-bana. A fabulous, if rather cramped, café overlooking Gamla Stan's main square, specializing in white-chocolate cheesecake and blueberry pie. Also has tasty salmon quiches and light lunch dishes, and is popular with the city's gay lunchgoers. Daily 9am–11pm.

Hötorgshallen Hötorget ⓦ hotorgshallen.se; Hötorget T-bana. Super popular with Stockholm's office workers, this sprawling food court is the place to come for fresh takeaway salads, wraps and kebabs. If you'd prefer a do-it-yourself option, you'll find everything you need here for a picnic. Mon–Thurs 10am–6pm, Fri 10am–7pm, Sat 10am–4pm.

★ **K25** Kungsgatan 25 ⓦ k25.nu/en; Hötorget T-bana. Bustling modern food court stuffed to bursting with cheap and delicious food, from dumplings and burgers to steaming bowls of Vietnamese pho. Expect to pay around 100kr for lunch. Mon–Fri 10am–10pm, Sat 11am–10pm.

★ **Sturekatten** Riddargatan 4 ⓦ sturekatten.se; Östermalmstorg T-bana. With antique tables and chairs seemingly lifted from a grandmother's sitting room, this cosy café has tremendous cakes and pastries as well as filling sandwiches, making it one of the most enjoyable

cafés in Stockholm. Mon–Fri 9am–7pm, Sat 9am–6pm, Sun 10am–6pm.

Vete-Katten Kungsgatan 55 ☎ 08 20 84 05, ⓦ vetekatten.se/en; Hötorget T-bana. Delicious cakes and pastries fill the polished glass cabinets at this long-running *konditori*, which also does a good selection of cheap breakfasts. Mon–Fri 7.30am–8pm, Sat & Sun 9.30am–7pm.

SÖDERMALM

Café String Nytorgsgatan 38 ⓦ cafestring.se; Medborgarplatsen T-bana. Quirky little café with a jumble of mismatched furniture, offering sandwiches, cakes and strong coffee – it's one of the coolest places to *fika* in a very cool part of town. Mon–Thurs 8am–10pm, Fri–Sun 8am–7pm.

RESTAURANTS

Day or night, the main areas for decent eating are: in the city centre, the triangle marked out by Norrmalmstorg, Birger Jarlsgatan and Stureplan; in Östermalm, Grev Turegatan; and in Södermalm, the SoFo district around Folkungagatan, Skånegatan and Bondegatan. In Kungsholmen, restaurants are more spread out, so it helps to know your destination before you set off. Several places in Gamla Stan are also worth checking out, though they tend to be a little expensive. Being organized is always the name of the game in Sweden, and to be sure of a table you should always book ahead.

GREATER STOCKHOLM

Brasserie Elverket Linnégatan 69 ☎ 08 661 25 62, ⓦ brasserieelverket.se; Karlaplan T-bana. Upscale place with lots of dark wood and polished brass, offering a mix of Swedish and French flavours, from classic meatballs to garlic snails (mains around 190–280kr). The bar is handy if you're planning to visit the theatre next door. Mon–Fri 11am–late, Sat 5pm–late.

Ciao Ciao Grande Storgatan 11 ☎ 08 667 64 20, ⓦ www.ciaociaogrande.com; Östermalmstorg T-bana. A safe bet for dependable, tasty and relatively inexpensive Italian food, including really excellent pizzas, in the heart of pricey Östermalm. Pizzas go for 100–155kr, pasta dishes are 150–200kr and meat mains weigh in around 250kr. Mon–Wed 11am–10pm, Thurs & Fri 11am–10.30pm, Sat noon–10.30pm, Sun noon–10.30pm.

Flippin Burgers Observatoriegatan 8 ⓦ facebook.com/ FlippinBurgersSthlm; Odenplan T-bana. Insanely good burgers bring crowds of students to this grungy joint. You can wash down your food with one of several great beers, or a milkshake spiked with Jack Daniels. No bookings are taken, so go early. Mon–Fri 4–10pm, Sat & Sun noon–10pm.

★ **Mamas & Tapas** Scheelegatan 3 ☎ 08 653 53 90, ⓦ tapas.nu; Rådhuset T-bana. Consistently one of Stockholm's best tapas restaurants and *the* place to come for authentic and reasonably priced Spanish cuisine. Tapas from 55kr, paella 120kr and a good-value mixed meat platter including pork, steak, chorizo and vegetables for 195kr. Mon–Fri 5pm–1am, Sat 2pm–1am, Sun 2–9pm.

Peppar Torsgatan 34 ☎08 34 20 52; Sankt Eriksplan T-bana. Attractive Cajun restaurant, with decent-sized portions at fair prices – mains are 150–250kr. Dozens of posters pinned to the walls help create an agreeable, studenty rock-and-roll atmosphere which complements the southern American food perfectly. Mon–Sat 5pm–1am.

Salt Hantverkaregatan 34 ☎08 652 11 00, ⓦsalt barmatsal.se; Rådhuset T-bana. Complete with stuffed elk's head and antlers on the wall, this is the place to come for inspired modern Swedish home cooking (145–225kr per dish), including elk burgers with chips (145kr) and the classic *biff Rydberg* (195kr) with egg yolk and mustard crème. Mon–Thurs 10am–11pm, Fri 10am–midnight, Sat 3–11pm.

Samuraj Kommendörsgatan 40 ☎08 663 68 68, ⓦthefork.se; Karlaplan T-bana. This good and dependable Japanese place is known for its fine food and friendly staff, with mains such as grilled salmon in teriyaki sauce (168kr) at the lower end of the price range (up to around 215kr). Tues–Fri 11am–2.30pm, 4.30–10pm, Sat & Sun 4.30–10pm.

Supper Barnhusgatan 12 ☎08 23 24 24, ⓦsupper.nu/ stockholm; Rådmansgatan T-bana. Stylish and popular South American restaurant, located on a barn. Starters include slow-cooked chuck beef with chocolate and chilli (135kr), while mains include seared tuna with blood grapefruit (280kr). Daily 4pm–late.

CENTRAL STOCKHOLM

Bakfickan Operahuset, Gustav Adolfs torg ☎08 676 58 00, ⓦoperakallaren.se; Kungsträdgården T-bana. A sound choice for Swedish home cooking served around the bar in this charming little place which resembles the snug of a British pub: the butter-fried hake fillet with prawns costs 295kr. Mon–Fri 11.30am–11pm, Sat noon–10pm, Sun 1–9pm.

★ **B.A.R.** Blasieholmsgatan 4A ☎08 611 53 35, ⓦrestaurangbar.se/en; Kungsträdgården T-bana. *The* place to eat fish in Stockholm. Go up to the fish counter and choose the piece you'd like to eat (90–330kr). There are also meat dishes on offer, including a steak tartare (170kr). Mon–Fri 10am–1am, Sat 4pm–1am, Sun 5–9pm.

Bistro Bestick Bryggargatan 8 ☎08 20 31 20, ⓦbistrobestick.se; T-Centralen T-bana. Compact, contemporary Swedish bistro with stark white walls and comfy sofas, serving up delicious home-cooking dishes such as meatballs (185kr) with a focus on local ingredients. Mon–Fri 11am–2pm & 5pm–1am, Sat 4pm–1am.

Bistro Ruby and Grill Ruby Österlånggatan 14 ☎08 20 57 76, ⓦgrillruby.com; Gamla Stan T-bana. *Bistro Ruby* is a long-established French place, tastefully done up in

TOP FIVE PLACES TO EAT
Blå Porten see opposite
Kalf & Hansen see page 72
K25 see opposite
Mamas & Tapas see opposite
Sturekatten see opposite

Parisian style with red walls covered with artwork. Mains cost 175–345kr. Next door, though in the same building, is *Grill Ruby*, which serves up TexMex and American-style charcoal grills of meat and fish (180–500kr) and weekend brunches. Bistro Ruby daily 5pm–late, closed on Sunday; Grill Ruby daily 11.30am–late.

Den Gyldene Freden Österlånggatan 51 ☎08 24 97 60, ⓦgyldenefreden.se; Gamla Stan T-bana. Opened in 1722, Stockholm's oldest restaurant is housed in a combination of vaulted cellars and regular serving rooms whose interiors are pure eighteenth century. Traditional Swedish mains such as pikeperch are around 300kr; better-value home-cooking dishes, such as meatballs, cost from 215kr. Mon–Fri 11.30am–midnight, Sat 1pm–midnight.

East Stureplan 13 ☎08 611 49 59, ⓦeast.se; Östermalmstorg T-bana. Trendy to a T, this is the place for top-quality cuisine from Japan, Korea, Thailand and Vietnam; try the delicious chicken soup with mushrooms, coconut, lime and galangal for 125kr. Mains are 115–355kr. Mon–Sat 11.30am–3am, Sun 5pm–3am.

Hermitage Stora Nygatan 11 ☎08 411 95 00; Gamla Stan T-bana. Long-established and well-respected vegetarian restaurant whose menu often features a few Middle Eastern dishes. Buffet lunches go for 120kr and there's a set dinner for 130kr. Mon–Fri 11am–8pm, Sat & Sun noon–8pm.

KB Smålandsgatan 7 ☎08 679 60 32, ⓦkonstnarsbaren. se; Östermalmstorg T-bana. Excellent Scandinavian food with plenty of seafood in posh 1930s surroundings. Reckon on over 200–300kr for a main course such as fish stew or Norwegian cod; a three-course meal will set you back around 500kr. Mon & Tues 11.30am–11pm, Wed–Fri 11.30am–midnight, Sat noon–midnight.

Le Rouge Brunnsgränd 2–4 ☎08 518 040 00, ⓦlerouge.se; Gamla Stan T-bana. A gloriously OTT Moulin Rouge-style bistro, inspired by nineteenth-century Paris, where everything from the drapes to the sofas are de rigueur bright red. Pan-fried Icelandic salmon is 265kr, while steak from the Scottish highlands is 350kr. Mon–Thurs 11.30am–2pm, 5pm–late Fri 11.30am–1am.

Prinsen Mäster Samuelsgatan 4 ☎08 611 13 31, ⓦrestaurangprinsen.eu/en; Östermalmstorg T-bana. A long-standing haunt of artists, musicians and writers enchanted by its soft lighting, glass panelling and wall etchings. The food is top-notch Swedish home cooking, with the likes of *Wallenbergare*, *biff Rydberg* and herring, all around 190–300kr. Mon 11.30am–11pm, Tues–Fri 11.30am–11.30pm, Sat noon–11.30pm, Sun 1–10pm.

SÖDERMALM

★ **Barabao** Hornsgatan 66 ☎08 643 77 76; Mariatorget T-bana. Decorated with hanging plants, this small, Asian-inspired restaurant serves beautifully soft steamed buns loaded with everything from pork belly to slow-cooked beef with green apple chutney (around 100kr). Veggie options are available too. No reservations. Mon–Thurs 11.30am–2pm & 5–9pm, Fri 11.30am–2pm & 5–10pm, Sat 1–4pm & 6–10pm, Sun noon–6pm.

Blå Dörren Södermalmstorg 6 ☎08 743 07 40, ⓦbla-dorren.se; Slussen T-bana. Unpretentious and popular beer hall-cum-restaurant with vaulted ceilings offering excellent Swedish traditional dishes (150–260kr) such as meatballs, steaks and *pytt i panna*. Great location for both Gamla Stan and Södermalm. Mon 10.30am–11pm, Tues–Thurs 10.30am–midnight, Fri 10.30am–1am, Sat 1pm–1am, Sun 1–11pm.

★ **Crêperie Fyra Knop** Svartensgatan 4 ☎08 640 77 27, ⓦcreperiefyraknop.se; Slussen T-bana, Götgatan exit. Excellent, affordable galettes and crepes for 90–105kr, served in this tiny French-owned and -run restaurant which consists of one intimate little room with rough maroon walls, battered wooden chairs and tables and an ancient Stella Artois advertisement. Daily 5–11pm, Sun noon–11pm.

Dionysos Bondegatan 56 ☎08 641 91 13, ⓦdionysos.se; Medborgarplatsen T-bana. Tasteful Greek restaurant with a homely feel: it's been here since 1974 and is just as good as ever. The food is accomplished: halloumi salad for 145kr, souvlaki for 180kr. Mon–Fri 4pm–midnight, Sat 1pm–midnight, Sun 1–11pm.

Garlic and Shots Folkungagatan 84 ☎08 640 84 46, ⓦgarlicandshots.com; Medborgarplatsen T-bana. A fun American-style diner where every dish is laced with garlic. Mains such as Thai-spiced garlic prawns or deep-fried garlic with halloumi cost around 200–280kr. There's also an extensive choice of vodkas and *akvavits* – and even garlic beer. Daily 5pm–1am.

★ **Kalf & Hansen** Mariatorget 2 ☎08 551 531 51, ⓦkalfochhansen.se; Mariatorget T-bana. This tiny, casual place, overseen by a celebrity chef, specializes in organic fast food with a Nordic twist. Choose between fresh meat, fish and veggie options, served up with seasonal vegetables and bread (around 100kr). Mon–Fri 10am–8pm, Sat 11am–8pm, Sun 11am–5pm.

Koh Phangan Skånegatan 57 ☎08 642 50 40, ⓦkohphangan.se; Medborgarplatsen T-bana. Wacky, tropical-themed Thai restaurant with an interior that's strewn with colourful fairy lights. The soups, salads and noodle dishes are all nicely done, although watered down a little for Swedish tastes. Listen out for the "thunderstorm" that occasionally rumbles through the restaurant. Mon–Fri 4pm–midnight, Sat noon–1am, Sun noon–midnight.

Kvarnen Tjärhovsgatan 4 ⓦkvarnen.com; Medborgarplatsen T-bana. Classic Stockholm beer hall with great Swedish home cooking, including meatballs with lingonberries and gherkins, or *pytt i panna* (both around 175kr). Reindeer is always on the menu, served with mushrooms and a creamy sauce for 200kr. Mon & Tues 11am–1am, Wed–Fri 11am–3am, Sat noon–3am, Sun noon–1am.

★ **Pelikan** Blekingegatan 40 ⓦpelikan.se; Skanstull T-bana. Atmospheric beer hall (from the entrance hall turn right) with excellent traditional food for around 200kr, including *pytt i panna* and meatballs "as big as golf balls". Left of the entrance hall is a smarter restaurant, though still based on home cooking (mains 155–240kr). Mon–Thurs 4pm–midnight, Fri, Sat & Sun noon–1am.

Snaps Götgatan 48 ☎08 640 28 68; Medborgarplatsen T-bana. Good, reasonably priced Swedish food (mains 195–295kr) and an extensive range of schnapps (hence the Swedish name, *snaps*), set in a 300-year-old building. Very popular, especially in summer, when there's outdoor seating in the square. Daily 11am–1am, Fri & Sat until 3am.

Soldaten Svejk Östgötagatan 35 ☎08 641 33 66; Medborgarplatsen T-bana. Lively pub that draws in a lot of students. Simple, Eastern and Central European-inspired menu (schnitzel is always available) with dishes for 100–150kr, and a large selection of Czech beers. Mon–Thurs 5pm–midnight, Fri & Sat 4pm–midnight, Sun 5–11pm.

Tre Indier Åsogatan 92 ☎08 641 03 55; Medborgarplatsen T-bana. A lively Indian restaurant that's slightly tucked away; it's located at the corner of Åsögatan and the tiny street Möregatan. There's an extensive menu and the curry dishes are genuinely tasty and well prepared. Mains go for around 150kr. Mon–Thurs 11am–10pm, Fri 11am–11pm, Sat noon–11pm, Sun noon–10pm.

★ **Urban Deli** Nytorget 4 ☎08 425 500 30; Medborgarplatsen T-bana. Attached to an impressively well-stocked deli, this chic bistro is always busy; there's a handful of tables, plus stools at a long bar. Try the weekend brunch (11.30am–3.30pm), which includes everything from fresh oysters to a classic Swedish fish stew (190kr). Mon, Tues & Sun 8am–11pm, Wed, Thurs & Sat 8am–midnight, Fri 8am–1am.

DRINKING

SEE MAPS PAGES 46, 49 AND 63

As elsewhere in Sweden, the majority of Stockholmers do their drinking and eating together, and all of the places listed below also serve food. **Södermalm** is by far the best area to head for. The scourge of Swedish nightlife – high alcohol prices – has been neutralized in recent years due to increased competition. The tired old stories about

LGBTQ STOCKHOLM

In Stockholm, as the rest of Sweden, the **LGBTQ scene** is small but welcoming and very active. A useful resource is **RFSL** (National Association for Sexual Equality), Sveavägen 59 (☎08 501 629 00, ⓦrfsl.se). The free **newspaper**, QX (ⓦqx.se), available at LGBTQ bars and clubs, is handy for listings.

The best **gay** beach is at Kärsön. Take the metro to Brommaplan T-bana, then any bus towards Drottningholm palace; get off at the stop over the bridge, Brostugan, and walk to the right along the water's edge.

LGBTQ bars and clubs are few and far between: *Patricia* (see page 74) has gay nights, or check out the gay bars listed below.

BARS

The Secret Garden Kornhamnstorg 59 ☎08 599 019 59; Gamla Stan T-bana; map p.49. This is a nice gay bar which is good for a drink at any time and is always busy. They serve good and relatively cheap food. There is also a "secret" garden if you want to relax after dinner. Daily noon–3am, Sun until midnight.

Sidetrack Wollmar Yxkullsgatan 7 ☎08 641 16 88; Mariatorget T-bana; map p.49. Dark, narrow and intimate British-style basement pub popular with gay leather and denim boys. The modern Swedish food here is also worth considering, though try to reserve a table ahead. Wed–Sat 6pm–1am.

drinking requiring a second mortgage are not really true, but cocktails, fine wines and craft beers can all be very costly. **Happy hours** or "After work" sessions throw up some bargains – watch out for signs outside bars and pubs advertising their particular times.

GREATER STOCKHOLM

Storstad Odengatan 41 ☎08 673 38 00, ⓦstorstad. se; Rådmansgatan T-bana. Light and airy lounge and bar with high ceilings that is a firm favourite for Stockholm's media pack and local celebrities. Packed with a credit-card-flashing crowd at weekends. Mon & Tues 4pm–midnight, Wed & Thurs 4pm–1am Fri & Sat 4pm–3am.

Tranan Karlbergsvägen 14 ☎08 527 281 00, ⓦwww. tranan.se; Odenplan T-bana. An atmospheric old workers' beer hall housed in a basement that's been in operation since 1929. One of Stockholm's best and most popular drinking holes, with live music in the basement bar. Mon–Thurs & Sun 11.30am–11pm, Fri & Sat noon–11pm.

CENTRAL STOCKHOLM

The Auld Dub Holländargatan 1 ☎08 679 77 07, ⓦtheaulddub.se; Hötorget T-bana. One of the busiest Irish pubs in town, with a fantastically large selection of foreign beers on tap and by the bottle, plus live music most evenings, often Irish folk. Mon–Thurs & Sun 11am–1am, Fri & Sat 11am–3am.

Berns Berzelii Park, Nybroplan ☎08 566 322 00, ⓦberns.se; Kungsträdgården T-bana. Originally made famous by writer August Strindberg, who picked up character ideas here for his novel, *The Red Room*, this is one of the chicest bars in town, with decor by the British designer Sir Terence Conran. Mon–Thurs 6.30am–1am, Fri 6.30am–2am, Sat 7.30am–2am, Sun 7.30am–1am.

Icebar by Icehotel Vasaplan 4 ☎08 505 635 20, ⓦicebarstockholm.se; T-Centralen T-bana. Aimed squarely at tourists, this hotel bar is built using ice from the Torne River in Swedish Lapland. A "visit" (205kr) lasts 45min and includes a drink from a glass made of ice. Thankfully, gloves are provided. Daily 11.15am–midnight.

Wirströms Stora Nygatan 13 ☎08 21 28 74, ⓦwirstromspub.se; Gamla Stan T-bana. A great favourite among Stockholm's expat community who come here to talk football and sample the large selection of beers and whiskies. There are also a few bar meals such as fish and chips and burgers. Mon noon–midnight, Tues–Fri noon–1am, Sat 11am–1am.

SÖDERMALM

Akkurat Hornsgatan 18 ☎08 644 00 15, ⓦakkurat. se; Slussen T-bana. This famous spot is known for its 280 different whiskies and extensive beer selection on tap and by the bottle, including an impressive array of Belgian varieties. Often has live music at weekends. Mon & Tues 3pm–midnight, Wed & Thurs 3pm–1am, Fri 11am–1am, Sat 3pm–1am, Sun 3pm–midnight.

Folk&Friends Norr Mälarstrand 32 ☎07 632 17 442; Rådhuset T-bana. A cosy gem situated in Kungsholmen by the waterfront with an incredible selection of craft beer. It's super laid back and dogs are allowed which means a lot of friendly faces. Tues–Fri 11am–9pm, Sat noon–9pm, Sun noon–7pm.

Gröne Jägaren Götgatan 64 ☎08 640 96 00, ⓦgronejagaren.com; Medborgarplatsen T-bana. An inordinately popular, and at times, rather drunken bar with some of the cheapest beer in the capital – the clientele is predominantly male and talk here is mainly of women,

1

football and cars. Regular karaoke and pub quizzes. Daily 11am–1am.

Kelly's Folkungagatan 49 ☎ 08 642 60 42, ⓦ kellysbar. se; Medborgarplatsen T-bana. Big, brash and student-friendly rock bar right near Medborgarplatsen, serving what must be some of the city's cheapest beer. If you don't have a coat to hang up (20kr) it's free to get in, too. Daily 11am–3am.

Kvarnen Tjärhovsgatan 4 ☎ 08 643 03 80, ⓦ kvarnen. com; Medborgarplatsen T-bana. This busy beer hall is a favourite haunt of football fans supporting Hammarby, who come here to celebrate their team's every win and defeat. Daily 11am-3am, Sat noon-3am, Sun noon–1am.

Pelikan Blekingegatan 40 ⓦ pelikan.se; Skanstull T-bana. A long-established beer hall that's full of character – and characters – and is one of the city's most satisfying and relaxing places for an evening of drinking. It's a good place to strike up a conversation with local Swedes. Mon–Thurs & Sun 4pm–midnight, Fri & Sat noon–1am.

Pet Sounds Bar Skånegatan 80 ☎ 08 643 82 25, ⓦ psb. bar; Medborgarplatsen T-bana. One of the most popular places in SoFo for a drink, run by the eponymous record store a few doors down; head to the basement bar where there's live music and DJs on Fri and Sat. Tues 5pm–midnight, Wed–Sat 4pm–1am, Sun 4pm–midnight.

NIGHTLIFE
SEE MAPS PAGES 46, 49 AND 63

The **club** scene in Stockholm is surprisingly limited. Cover charges aren't too high at around 150kr, but alcohol isn't cheap: even draft beer is expensive, reaching as much as 90 or 100kr a glass, and cocktails in nightclubs can be ruinously expensive.

CENTRAL STOCKHOLM

Berns Berzelii Park, Nybroplan ☎ 08 566 322 00, ⓦ berns.se; Kungsträdgården T-bana. A Stockholm institution – head downstairs for *Berns* legendary nightclub which has long held the status of the capital's leading dance spot. It's the stunning mix of nineteenth-century Baroque, contemporary design and beautiful people that creates such a buzz. Fri & Sat 10pm–4am.

End Night Club Jakobs torg 10 ⓦ endnightclub.se; Kungsträdgården T-bana. A very cool and huge night club which is open relatively late. Wed, Fri–Sun midnight–5am.

Spy Bar Birger Jarlsgatan 20 ⓦ stureplansgruppen.se/ nattliv/spy-bar/; Östermalmstorg T-bana. *Spy Bar* is one of Sweden's most famous nightclubs. It attracts a mixture of media people and those with a passion for fashion and music. The re-designed old apartment in which it's located helps to create a personal, unforgettable party experience. Thurs–Sat 11pm–5am.

Sturecompagniet Sturegatan 4 ☎ 08 545 076 70, ⓦ sturecompagniet.se; Östermalmstorg T-bana. Long

established as one of Stockholm's leading (and biggest) nightspots, playing house and techno, with three floors of bars; something for everybody, although it can get packed and the queues to get in are always long. Expensive. Thurs–Sat 10pm–3am.

SÖDERMALM

Debaser Hornstulls Strand 9 ☎ 08 462 98 60, ⓦ debaser. se; Hornstull T-bana. Big-name DJs and live bands top the bill at this venue near the waterfront in Hornstull – expect anything from house to hip hop. There's also an American-style bar and a Mexican restaurant. Minimum age 20 on Fri and Sat. Opening times vary.

Patricia Stadsgårdskajen, Slussen ☎ 08 743 05, ⓦ patricia.st; Slussen T-bana. Formerly the royal yacht of Britain's late Queen Mother, today a restaurant-disco-bar with chart and 1980s music. The menu, with a huge variety of imaginative main courses (fajitas and Cajun steaks are always available) is quite simply terrific. Gay night on Sun. Thurs 6pm–midnight, Fri & Sat 6pm–5am, Sun 6pm–5am.

Södra Teatern Mosebacke torg 3 ☎ 08 480 044 01, ⓦ sodrateatern.com; Slussen T-bana. One of the longest-established clubs in town; every night sees a different type of club or event taking place – everything from live music to club nights playing hip hop, indie rock or techno over three dancefloors. Opening times vary.

LIVE MUSIC: ROCK, POP AND JAZZ
SEE MAPS PAGES 46, 49 AND 63

When there's live **rock** and **jazz** music at bars and cafés, it will mostly be provided by local bands, for which you'll pay around 120kr entrance. Most international big names make it to Stockholm, playing at a variety of seated halls and stadiums – tickets for these are, of course, much more expensive. The main **large venue** is the Stockholm Globe Arena in Johanneshov (☎ 0771 31 00 00, ⓦ globen.se; Globen T-bana).

GREATER STOCKHOLM

Cirkus Djurgårdsslätten 43–45 ☎ 08 587 987 00, ⓦ cirkus.se; tram #7. Occasional rock, R&B performances,

classical concerts and theatre take place in the original circular arena dating from 1892 that is still one of the main venues on Stockholm's cultural scene. Opening times vary.

CENTRAL STOCKHOLM

Engelen Kornhamnstorg 59 ☎ 077 182 68 26, ⓦ engelen. se; Gamla Stan T-bana. Great place to see cover bands who perform most nights in various guises: jazz, rock or blues. *Engelen* has a large and loyal clientele, so arrive early to get in. There's also a dancefloor downstairs. Mon–Thurs 11am–1am, Fri 11am–2am, Sat 1pm–3am, Sun 3–10pm.

Fasching Kungsgatan 63, Norrmalm ☎08 20 00 66, ⓦfasching.se; Hötorget T-bana. If you're after local or foreign contemporary jazz, this is the place to come. However, there's also a fair smattering of salsa and soul on offer, too. Can get quite crowded. Mon–Thurs & Sun 6pm–midnight, Fri & Sat 6pm–4am.

Nalen Stacken Regeringsgatan 74 ☎08 505 292 00, ⓦnalen.com; T-Centralen T-bana. Once *the* place to hear music in the city (even the Beatles were booked to play here), now offering rock with a smattering of jazz and swing. Opening times vary.

Stampen Stora Nygatan 5 ⓦstampen.se; Gamla Stan T-bana. Rowdy jazz club, which is best known for swing, dixie and trad, though there's mainstream, blues and 1950s and 1960s rock, too. *Stampen* has been cranking out live music most nights for the past forty years and is still going strong. Tues–Fri 5pm–1am, Sat 2pm–1am, Sun 5pm–1am.

SÖDERMALM

Södra Teatern Mosebacke torg 3 ☎08 480 044 01, ⓦsodrateatern.com; Slussen T-bana. This is one of the best places in the capital for world music, hip hop, rock and pop – if it's happening anywhere, it's happening here. Opening times vary.

THEATRE, CLASSICAL MUSIC AND CINEMA

Stockholm has dozens of **theatres**, but naturally most productions are in Swedish. Reduced-price standby tickets are available from the kiosk in Norrmalmstorg. **Classical music** is always easy to find in the city; **organ music** can be heard at Adolf Fredriks kyrka, Holländargatan 16, Norrmalm; St Jakobs kyrka in Kungsträdgården, Norrmalm; Gustav Vasa kyrka in Odenplan; and Storkyrkan in Gamla Stan on various days.

THEATRES AND CONCERT VENUES

Berwaldhallen Dag Hammarskjöldsväg 3, Östermalm ☎08 784 18 00, ⓦberwaldhallen.se. Concert hall, home to the Swedish Radio Symphony Orchestra and the Swedish Radio Choir.

Dramaten Nybroplan, Östermalm ☎08 667 06 80, ⓦdramaten.se. The Royal Dramatic Theatre stages Swedish and international theatre, as well as opera performances that are less rarefied than those of the main opera house.

Konserthuset Hötorget, Norrmalm ☎08 506 6 77 88, ⓦkonserthuset.se. Stockholm Concert Hall, built in the 1920s to house the Royal Stockholm Philharmonic Orchestra.

Kulturhuset Stadsteatern Sergels torg ☎08 506 202 00, ⓦkulturhusetstadsteatern.se. Has a full range of artistic and cultural events, most of them free; the information desk on the ground floor has free programmes.

Musikaliska Akademien Blasieholmstorg 8, near the Nationalmuseum ☎08 407 18 00, ⓦmusakad.se. The Royal Swedish Academy of Music holds regular concerts.

Operan Gustav Adolfs torg ☎08 791 44 00, ⓦoperan. se. Stockholm's main opera house.

Stockholm Players ⓦstockholmplayers.se. For English-language drama check out Sweden's oldest English-language theatre company, established in the 1920s.

CINEMAS

Cinema-going is an incredibly popular pastime in Stockholm. There are a good number of cinemas the entire length of Kungsgatan between Sveavägen and Birger Jarlsgatan, which are always very lively on Saturday night. Tickets cost around 150kr and films are never dubbed into Swedish.

Filmstaden Sergel Hötorget ☎08 562 600 00, ⓦsf.se. The largest cinema in the city centre.

DIRECTORY

Embassies and consulates Australia, Klarabergsviadukten 63 ☎08 613 29 00, ⓦsweden.embassy.gov.au; Canada, Klarabergsgatan 23 ☎08 453 30 00, ⓦcanadainternational. gc.ca/sweden-suede; Ireland, Hovslagargatan 5 ☎08 545 040 40, ⓦembassyofireland.se; South Africa, Flemingatan 20, fourth floor ☎08 24 39 50, ⓦdirco.gov.za/sweden; UK, Skarpögatan 6–8 ☎08 671 30 00, ⓦukinsweden.fco.gov. uk; US, Dag Hammarskjöldsväg 31 ☎08 783 53 00, ⓦse. usembassy.gov/embassy.

Emergencies Ring ☎112 for police, ambulance or fire services.

Exchange Forex exchange offices at Central Station, Cityterminalen, Vasagatan 16, Stureplan, Terminal 2 & 5, Arlanda airport and Skavsta airport.

Health care CityAkuten, Apelbergsgatan 48 (☎020 15 01 50, ⓦcityakuten.se/CityAkuten), is a walk-in clinic offering on-the-spot treatment for minor ailments.

Laundry Self-service laundry at Västmannagatan 61B (Mon–Fri 8.30am–6.30pm, Sat 9.30am–1pm; ⓦtvattomaten.se).

Left luggage There are lockers at Central Station and the Cityterminalen bus station.

Lost property Klara Östra Kyrkogatan 6 ☎08 600 10 00.

Pharmacy 24hr service at Klarabergsgatan 64 ☎0771 45 04 50.

Police Kungsholmsgatan 43 ☎0771 14 14 00.

Radio English-language programming from Radio Sweden can be heard online at ⓦradiosweden.org.

Day-trips from Stockholm

STOCKHOLM ARCHIPELAGO

Day-trips from Stockholm

Move away from Stockholm, and it's easy to appreciate its unique geographical location. Water surrounds the city and – although you can travel by train and bus – it's worth making the effort to ply the serene waters of Lake Mälaren or the Stockholm archipelago by boat. The archipelago is made up of a staggering 24,000 islands, islets and rocks, as the Swedish mainland slowly splinters into the Baltic Sea; it's a summer paradise for holidaying city-dwellers.

A boat trip inland along Lake Mälaren is also a must, either to the Viking island of **Birka**, where you can see the remains of Sweden's most important medieval trading centre and a dizzying array of ancient finds, or to **Drottningholm**, the seventeenth-century royal residence situated right on the lakeside. Another easy excursion on Lake Mälaren leads to the impressive castle of **Gripsholm** at Mariefred.

Also within easy day-trip reach are the ancient Swedish capital and medieval university town of **Uppsala** and one of the country's oldest settlements, **Sigtuna**, complete with its rune stones and ruined churches.

If you've flown in with Ryanair, consider spending a day in lakeside **Västerås**, with its fascinating mix of the old and new, including a sixth-century royal burial mound, or at handsome **Nyköping** on the Baltic coast which rewards visitors with its laid-back seaside atmosphere and impressive castle.

The Stockholm archipelago

If you arrived in Stockholm by plane, you'll already have had a tantalizing glimpse of the **Stockholm archipelago**. In Swedish the word for archipelago is *skärgård* – literally "garden of skerries" and a pretty accurate description: the array of hundreds upon hundreds of pine-clad islands and islets is the only one of its kind in the world. Most of the little-known islands are flat and are wonderful places for **walking** or **cycling** (ferries to the islands accept bikes onboard); we've picked out the most rewarding islands for strolls and hikes, and have suggested a few trails which are a good way to take in the sweeping sea vistas and unspoilt nature here. The archipelago, though, holds another secret, little known even to most Swedes – many of **ABBA**'s most famous hits were written out here, on the island of Viggsö where the famous foursome owned a couple of summer cottages (see page 81). The easiest and fastest section of the archipelago to reach, and consequently the most popular with day-tripping Stockholmers, the **central archipelago** is the islands at their most stunning: hundreds of rocks, skerries, islets and islands jostle for space in the pristine waters of the Baltic, giving the impression of giant stepping-stones leading back to the mainland.

The islands in the northern stretches of the *skärgård* are far fewer in number. As a result, the appearance of the **northern archipelago** is very different: characterized by open vistas and sea swells rather than narrow sounds and passageways, the islands here are very much at the mercy of the sea and weather. Although sharing more in appearance with the denser central archipelago than its more barren northern counterpart, the **southern archipelago** is generally much quieter in terms of visitor numbers, because it's harder to reach from central Stockholm.

For information about **canoe rental** in the archipelago, see page 66.

MEDIEVAL CHURCH, UPPSALA

Highlights

❶ Gällnö island, Stockholm archipelago
Walk through deep green forest and swim from the shores of an island edged by purple reeds and carpets of wildflowers. See page 81

❷ Birka, Lake Mälaren Get to grips with Viking history in Sweden's oldest town. See page 86

❸ Island beaches, Västerås The chain of islands in Lake Mälaren offer the perfect opportunity to chill out and work on your all-over tan. See page 91

❹ Utter Inn, Västerås A night spent underwater in this mini-oil-rig-cum-hotel in Lake Mälaren is one of Sweden's most unusual accommodation choices. See page 92

❺ Uppsala Potter around the beautiful Linnéträdgården and learn about the fascinating life of the world's leading botanist, Carl von Linné. See page 93

❻ Gamla Uppsala Royal burial mounds and a beautiful medieval church add mystery to this ancient pagan settlement. See page 98

HIGHLIGHTS ARE MARKED ON THE MAP ON PAGE 80

Vaxholm

1hr from Stockholm by boat

Just an hour from the capital, the island of **Vaxholm** is a popular weekend destination for Stockholmers. Its eponymous town has an atmospheric wooden harbour, whose imposing **fortress** (daily: May–mid-June noon–4pm, mid-June–Sept 11am–5pm; 80kr; ⓦvaxholmsfastning.se) once guarded the waterways into the city, superseding the fortifications at Riddarholmen. Having successfully staved off attacks from the Danes and the Russians in the seventeenth and eighteenth centuries, the fortress is now an unremarkable museum of military bits and pieces. Since all boats to and from Stockholm dock at Vaxholm, it's often swarming with visitors, so do yourself a favour – stay on the boat and seek out one of the archipelago's quieter islands, which are quite frankly more worthy of your attention.

2

AROUND STOCKHOLM

SEA OF ÅLAND

BALTIC SEA

HIGHLIGHTS

1. Gällnö island, Stockholm archipelago
2. Birka, Lake Mälaren
3. Island beaches, Västerås
4. Utter Inn, Västerås
5. Uppsala
6. Gamla Uppsala

THANK VIGGSÖ FOR THE MUSIC

The rocky outcrop topped by dense pine forest that lies sandwiched between Grinda and much larger Värmdö to the south holds a big secret. It was here on the island of **Viggsö** that **ABBA** composed *Dancing Queen, Fernando* and several other chart-topping hits; shots of Viggsö were also used in *ABBA: The Movie*. Agnetha and Björn bought a summer cottage here in 1971, closely followed in 1974 by Benny and Anni-Frid; the sound of piano music drifting across the treetops was a sure sign that one or the other couple had sailed their boat out from Stockholm to spend a few days away from the city. The two men would spend days at a time in Björn's yellow wooden outhouse hammering away at a battered upright piano and strumming an old guitar – the restorative calm of Viggsö was at the heart of much of ABBA's music-making.

Grinda

1hr 20min from Stockholm by boat

Grinda is a thickly wooded island typical of the central archipelago, with some sandy beaches. It's particularly popular with families and so can be busy, particularly at weekends. In its favour, Grinda has frequent boat connections, a pleasant **youth hostel** (see page 85), several ad hoc **campsites**, a **restaurant** and a **café** in the centre of the island. To enjoy the sunshine on summer afternoons, head for beaches on the southern side of the island, as the tall trees on the northern side block out the sun. Boats dock at two jetties at the island's southern (Södra Grinda) and northern (Norra Grinda) ends; a walk between the two takes thirty to forty minutes.

Gällnö

1hr 30min–2hr from Stockholm by boat

A beautiful low-lying island covered with thick pine forest, **Gällnö** is the archipelago at its best. Home to just thirty people, a couple of whom farm the land near the jetty, Gällnö has been designated a nature reserve: you can spot deer in the forest or watch eider ducks diving for fish. The **youth hostel** (see page 85) is well signposted from the main village, where there's also a small **shop** selling provisions. From here, there's the choice of two **walks**: either head east through the forest for Gällnönäs, from where you can pick up boats back to Stockholm or further out into the islands, or continue north past the youth hostel, following signs for Brännholmen until you arrive at a small bay popular with yachties. Look for the hut where the toilet is, as one of its walls bears a map and sign on the outside showing the path leading from here to the row-boats – these enable you to cross the narrow sound (around 15m wide) separating Gällnö from its neighbour, Karklö. When you head across, remember to leave one boat on either side of the sound (see page 84).

Karklö

2hr from Stockholm by boat

Karklö is one of the most unspoilt islands in the archipelago and, combined with Gällnö, makes for an excellent day-trip from Stockholm. There are no shops or roads here, only tracks which meander across the island and around farmers' fields, connecting the spot where the rowboats are moored with the main jetty on the other side, where the boats from Stockholm dock. The paths can be difficult to find at times, so it's best to ask directions in the main village, which is close to the rowboat moorings.

Svartsö

2–3hr from Stockholm by boat

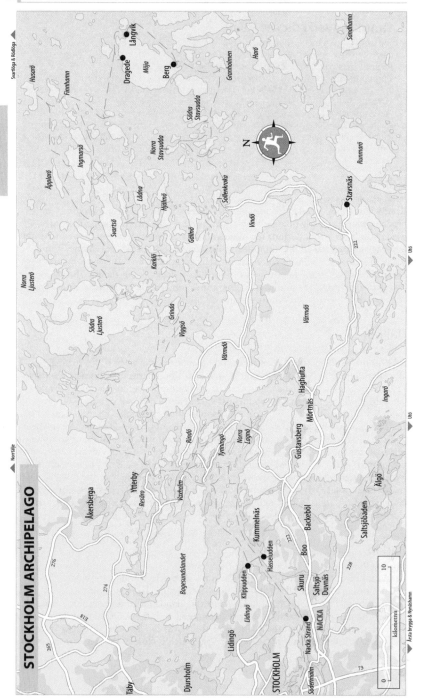

STOCKHOLM ARCHIPELAGO

North of Gällnö, **Svartsö** is busier than its neighbour, though it's never overrun with visitors and there's plenty of space to unwind and sunbathe on the rocky shores – particularly on the western edge of the island. With its fields of grazing sheep, thick virgin forest and crystal-clear lakes, Svartsö has a more pastoral feel than some of the other surrounding islands, where forest predominates, and there are also good roads which make it ideal for cycling or walking.

From the northern jetty, where most boats from Stockholm arrive, there's a pleasant walk, lasting about ninety minutes, across the island to the village of **Alsvik** on the south coast. Head along the road towards the two lakes in the centre of the island, and just before you arrive at the lakes, turn right onto the path that follows the lakeside, passing a few houses on the way. The road then becomes a track heading into the forest. Continue past a couple of hayfields in a forest clearing, and eventually you'll glimpse the sea through the trees at the forest edge; this is an ideal place to sunbathe nude or stop for a picnic. Past a farmhouse and a couple of barns, the track eventually turns into a road again; from here it's another twenty- to thirty-minutes' walk to Alsvik, with its **shop** where you can buy snacks and refreshments – ferry connections back to the capital also depart from here.

Ingmarsö

2hr 30min–3hr from Stockholm by boat

Ingmarsö is an excellent island for walkers. Most boats dock at the northern jetty (Norra Ingmarsö), and from here you can do an enjoyable roundabout **walk** that takes you across the island and on to neighbouring Finnhamn, from where you can catch a boat back. Follow the main road away from the northern jetty, and after about fifteen minutes, turn left at the signpost marked "*Båtdraget*" and "*Femsund*". Before making this turn you may want to continue straight ahead for five minutes to the island's **supermarket** to stock up on provisions, before retracing your steps to the signpost. The road to Femsund eventually turns into a track – marked by blue dots on tree trunks – which strikes out through the forest heading for Kålmårsön. After about an hour, the path skirts a wonderfully isolated lake, where you can swim and sunbathe, before passing through more unspoilt forest and emerging at a small bay filled with yachts. Look carefully here for the continuation of the path – still marked with blue dots – which will take you to row-boat moorings at the narrow sound (around 20m wide) between here and Finnhamn. If you fail to locate the path, follow the coast round to the right for roughly ten to fifteen minutes while facing the yachts in the bay. It takes about two and a half hours to get to the sound from the northern jetty. Row over to Finnhamn, remembering to leave one rowboat on either side of the sound (see page 84).

Finnhamn

2hr from Stockholm by boat

Although only a tiny island, **Finnhamn** is often busy because of its popular **youth hostel** (see page 85). To walk from the rowboat moorings across the sound from Ingmarsö to the main jetty and the youth hostel takes around forty minutes. During summer, the café by the jetty serves up simple snacks and refreshments. If the crowds are too much here, head southeast from Finnhamn's tiny main village for the adjoining islet of Lilla Jolpan, where there are some good bathing opportunities.

Svartlöga and Rödlöga

4hr from Stockholm by boat. For a shorter boat journey, you can get here in 90min from Furusund, a coastal town reached from central Stockholm in about 2hr by a combination of T-bana and bus: from Danderyds sjukhus T-bana, take bus #676X to Norrtälje, and change to the #634 to Furusund

Lying far out in the Baltic towards Finland, Svartlöga and Rödlöga have untouched nature in plenty. **Svartlöga** is the only island in the archipelago whose forest is totally deciduous, and was one of the few to escape Russian incursions in 1719 during the Great Northern War. There are several good rocky beaches on which to relax after the long journey here. Neighbouring **Rödlöga** is a much tinier, red-granite affair, with no roads – just leafy paths, overgrown hedgerows thick with wild roses and wonderful secluded beaches.

Sandhamn

2hr from Stockholm by boat

With its fine harbour, the island of **Sandhamn** has been a destination for seafarers since the eighteenth century and remains so today, attracting yachts of all shapes and sizes. The main village is a haven of narrow alleyways, winding streets and overgrown verandas. If you fancy staying overnight there are a couple of options (see opposite).

Utö

3hr 30min from Stockholm by boat

Far out in the southern reaches of the archipelago, **Utö** is flat and thus ideal for cycling; it's not bad for bathing and picnics either. There are excellent views from the island's windmill on Kvarnbacken hill, ten minutes' walk southwest of the jetty. There's also a youth hostel (see opposite).

ARRIVAL AND DEPARTURE   THE ARCHIPELAGO

By boat Getting to the islands is easy, with Waxholmsbolaget (☎08 600 10 00, ⓦwaxholmsbolaget.se) operating the majority of the passenger-only sailings into the archipelago; its boats leave daily from Strömkajen in front of the *Grand* hotel.
Tickets Tickets are reasonable: Grinda, for example, is 95kr one way, whereas Finnhamn, one of the furthest islands,

is 140kr; pay on the boat. If you're planning to visit several islands, it might be worth buying the Båtluffarbiljett (Island Hopping Pass; 445kr, plus a 20kr fee for the card itself), which gives five days' unlimited travel on all Waxholmbolaget lines. If there's no direct boat to your destination, connections can often be made on the island of Vaxholm.

INFORMATION

Tourist office For timetables and ideas of where to go, drop into the Visit Skärgården information office on Strandvägen at Kajplats 18 (daily 10am–5pm; ☎073 622

61 30, ⓦvisitskargarden.se), where staff can also help with accommodation and eating options.

ACCOMMODATION

There are few **hotels** in the archipelago, but it does have plenty of well-equipped and comfortable **youth hostels**, all of which are open in the summer (May–Sept). It's also

possible to rent **summer cottages** on the islands for 4000–7000kr a week for four people – for more information on prices, contact the tourist office in Stockholm. For

---

DON'T MISS THE BOAT

If you're waiting for the boat out in the archipelago, you must **raise the semaphore flag** on the jetty to indicate that you want to be picked up; torches are kept in the huts on the jetties for the same purpose at night.

In some parts of the archipelago, it's possible to visit a couple of islands on the same trip by taking the ferry to your first port of call, then **rowing across** to a neighbouring island, from where you return to Stockholm by the ferry again – we've detailed these options in the text. For this purpose, there'll be a rowboat either side of the water separating you from your destination. When you use the boats, you have to ensure there's always one left on either side – this entails rowing across, attaching the other boat to yours, rowing back to your starting point, where you leave one boat behind, and then rowing across one last time.

summer stays, you'll need to book well in advance – at least six months before – or you may well find that you've been pipped to the post by holidaying Swedes. It's important to remember that there are very few **restaurants** in the archipelago and opening times fluctuate. It's a much wiser idea to buy some provisions and go self-catering.

GRINDA

Grinda Wärdshus Södra Bryggan ☎08 542 494 91, Ⓦgrindawardshus.se. Youth hostel, hotel and cabin accommodation on the south coast, east of the southern jetty. The hostel and cabins close Nov–April but the hotel stays open all year and can be wonderfully peaceful out of season. Hostel double 600kr, hotel double with private facilities and breakfast 1990kr, two-person cabin 1000kr

GÄLLNÖ

STF Gällnö Vandrarhem Gällnöby ☎08 571 661 17, Ⓦgallno.se. This idyllic hostel is surrounded by low-hanging trees and a pretty garden. The track leading to it is well signposted from the tiny main village. Open mid-May to Sept. Doubles 500kr, two-person cabin 750kr

FINNHAMN

Finnhamn Vandrarhem Finnhamns brygga ☎08 542 462 12, Ⓦfinnhamn.se. A gem of a hostel, set in a dramatically located yellow building complete with waterfront sauna, and perched on rocks looking out to sea. Open all year. Doubles 820kr

SANDHAMN

Sandhamns Värdshus Main village ☎08 571 530 51, Ⓦsandhamns-vardshus.se. An agreeable bed-and-breakfast establishment housed in an attractive timber building by the shore, also serving excellent seafood. It pays to book in advance as there are only half a dozen rooms available – all sharing facilities. 1350kr

Seglarhotellet Main village ☎08 574 504 00, Ⓦsandhamn.com. An exclusive and rather swanky hotel, catering for wealthy yachties and serving excellent seafood; some of the rooms have desirable balconies overlooking the sea. Self-catering apartments also available. Doubles 2590kr, apartments 2790kr

UTÖ

Utö Vandrarhem Gruvbryggan, near where the ferry docks ☎08 504 203 00, Ⓦutovardshus.se. This comfortable hostel has three elegant wooden verandas overlooking the sea plus two self-catering kitchens on site. Open May–Sept. Doubles 650kr

Around Lake Mälaren

Freshwater **Lake Mälaren** dominates the countryside west of Stockholm, and provides the backdrop to some of the capital region's most appealing day-trip destinations. During the summer months, boats sail frequently to **Drottningholm**, home to the Swedish royal family, as well as pretty **Mariefred**, an enchanting little town on the lake's southern shore with a magnificent castle. Sweden's main settlement during the ninth and tenth centuries, the island of **Birka**, is great for anyone interested in Sweden's stirring Viking past. The main city on the lake is **Västerås**, a modern and thoroughly enjoyable place with good sandy beaches and some impressive Viking remains, too.

Drottningholm

Palace April daily 11am–4pm; May–Sept daily 10am–5pm; Oct daily 10am–4pm; Nov–March Sat & Sun 10am–4pm • 140kr, 200kr including the Kina slott • Kina slott May–Sept daily 11am–5pm • Ⓦroyalcourt.se

Even if your time in Stockholm is limited, try to see the architecturally harmonious royal palace of **Drottningholm**, beautifully located on the shores of leafy **Lovön**, an island 11km west of Stockholm's centre that takes less than an hour to reach. **Drottningholm** is perhaps the greatest achievement of the two architects **Tessin**, father and son. Work began in 1662 on the orders of King Karl X's widow, Eleonora, with Tessin the Elder modelling the new palace in a thoroughly French style – giving rise to the stock comparisons with Versailles. Apart from anything else, it's considerably smaller than its French contemporary, utilizing false perspective and trompe l'oeil to bolster the elegant, though rather narrow, interior. On Tessin the Elder's death in 1681, the palace was completed by his son, then already at work on Stockholm's Kungliga Slottet.

Since 1981, the Swedish royal family has lived out at Drottningholm, instead of in the city centre, using it as a permanent home. This move has accelerated efforts to

2

restore parts of the palace to their original appearance, and the monumental **grand staircase** is now once again exactly as envisaged by Tessin the Elder. In the **rooms**, good English notes are available to help you sort out the riot of Rococo decoration, which largely dates from the time when Drottningholm was bestowed as a wedding gift on Princess Louisa Ulrika (a sister of Frederick the Great of Prussia). No hints, however, are needed to spot the influences in the Baroque "French" and the later "English" **gardens** that back onto the palace.

Within the extensive palace grounds is the **Kina slott (Chinese Pavilion)**, a sort of eighteenth-century royal summerhouse. Originally built by King Adolf Fredrik as a birthday gift to Queen Louisa Ulrika in 1753, the structure is Rococo in design and, though it includes some Chinese flourishes which were the height of fashion at the time of construction, it is predominantly European in appearance.

Slottsteater

Court Theatre • Daily May–Sept 11am–4.30pm; Oct noon–3.30pm; Mar, Nov & Dec Sat & Sun noon–3.30pm obligatory guided tours every hour • 110kr • ⓦ dtm.se

Within the palace grounds, the **Slottsteater** dates from 1766, but its heyday was a decade later, when Gustav III imported French plays and theatrical companies, making Drottningholm the centre of Swedish artistic life. Take the guided tour and you'll get a florid but accurate account of the theatre's decoration: money to complete the building ran out in the eighteenth century, meaning that things are not what they seem – painted papier-mâché frontages are *krona*-pinching substitutes for the real thing. The original backdrops and stage machinery are still in place though, and the tour comes complete with a display of eighteenth-century special effects including wind and thunder machines, trapdoors and simulated lightning.

ARRIVAL AND DEPARTURE   DROTTNINGHOLM

By boat Boats sail from Stadshusbron on Kungsholmen to Drottningholm during the summer months (May to early Sept daily 9.30am–6pm, hourly; early Sept to late Oct Sat & Sun 2 daily; 155kr one way, 205kr return), and take just under an hour each way.

By T-bana and bus Take the T-bana to Brommaplan and then any bus from Brommaplan bus terminal (immediately outside the T-bana station). Buses leave from the stop marked for Drottningholm.

Birka

The island of **Björkö** (the name means "island of birches"), in Lake Mälaren, is the site of Sweden's oldest town, **BIRKA**, which was founded around 750AD and is now a UNESCO World Heritage site. For over two centuries, Birka was the most important Viking trading centre in the northern countries, benefiting from its strategic location near the mouth of Lake Mälaren on the portage route to Russia and the Byzantine Empire. Today, a visit here is not only an opportunity to get to grips with Sweden's Viking heritage, thanks to the site's excellent museum, but the boat trip to the island also gives you a chance to explore the tranquil waters of Lake Mälaren.

Brief history

After Birka was founded in the mid-eighth century, tradesmen and merchants were quick to take advantage of the prosperous and rapidly expanding village, and the population soon grew to around one thousand. The future patron saint of Scandinavia, **Ansgar**, came here in 830 as a missionary at the instruction of the Holy Roman Emperor, Louis I, and established a church in an attempt to Christianize the heathen Swedes. They showed little interest and the Frankish monk preached on the island for just over a year before being recalled. Birka reached its peak during the tenth century before sliding into decline: falling water levels in Lake Mälaren, the superior location of the Baltic island of Gotland for handling Russian–Byzantine trade and the emergence of nearby rival Sigtuna all led to its gradual disappearance after 975.

The museum
Open in connection with boat arrivals and departures • Entry included in boat ticket price

Major excavations began on the island in 1990 and the **Birka museum** now recounts the village's history in superb detail. Exhibitions explain how, during Viking times, Björkö was actually two separate islands, with the main settlement located in the northwest corner of the more northern island. As the land rose after the last Ice Age, the narrow channel between the two islands vanished, resulting in today's single kidney-shaped island; remains of jetties have been found where the channel would have been, as well as a rampart which acted as an outer wall for the settlement. Displays of historical artefacts as well as scale models of the harbour and craftsmen's quarters are also available for perusal. The developed nature of Viking society is evident from the finds: scissors, pottery and even keys have all been excavated. Free **guided tours** are available which recount the detail of many of the archeological finds.

The village
In addition to the museum, it's possible to stroll around a reconstruction of a **Viking village** for a taste of how things once looked. In July you can even come face to face with modern-day Vikings, when the staff don period costumes and enact Viking games.

The graveyard
Among Birka's Viking remains, the most striking is the island's **graveyard**, which is the largest Viking-age burial ground in Scandinavia with around four hundred burial mounds, some accompanied by standing stones. Totally surrounding the site of the former village, the graveyard can be found outside the rampart by turning right from where the boat arrives.

ARRIVAL AND INFORMATION **BIRKA**

By boat From Stockholm, Strömma Kanalbolaget sail from Stadshusbron on Kungsholmen (early May to late Sept Mon–Fri 9.30am, Sat & Sun 10am; 2hr; 390kr return including museum entry; ⓦ birkavikingastaden.se). Between July and mid-August Rederi Mälarstaden also operate a boat between Västerås and Birka (Thurs only 9.30am; ⓦ rederimalarstaden.se; 385kr return including museum entry); it's therefore possible to sail between Stockholm and Västerås by changing boats at Birka.

Website For complete information about Birka, check out ⓦ birkavikingastaden.se, where you'll find full details in English about Birka's history as well as practical visitor information, including the latest ferry schedules.

Mariefred

Located on the graceful southern shores of Lake Mälaren, **MARIEFRED** is a tiny, quintessentially Swedish village about an hour west of the city, whose peaceful attractions are bolstered by one of Sweden's finest castles, **Gripsholm**, which you might recognize if you owned any ABBA albums back in the 1970s and 1980s (see below). A couple of minutes up from the quayside and you're strolling through narrow streets where the well-kept wooden houses and little squares have scarcely changed in decades. Other than the castle, the only real sight is the **railway museum**, which offers a rare chance in Sweden to see working steam engines.

Gripsholms slott
Gripsholm Castle • Mid-May–Sept daily 10am–4pm; Oct & Nov Sat & Sun noon–3pm • Guided tours in English mid-May–Sept daily 3pm; 45min • 170kr, guided tours 30kr extra • ⓦ royalcourt.se

Lovely though Mariefred is, it's really only a preface to seeing **Gripsholms slott**, the imposing red-brick castle built on a round island just a short walk south of the centre

2

(walk up the quayside, and you'll see the path to the castle running across the grass by the water's edge). In the late fourteenth century, Bo Johnsson Grip, the Swedish high chancellor, began to build a fortified castle at Mariefred, although the present building owes more to two Gustavs – Gustav Vasa, who started rebuilding in the sixteenth century, and Gustav III, who was responsible for major restructuring a couple of centuries later. Rather than the hybrid that might be expected, the result is rather pleasing – an engaging textbook castle with turrets, great halls, corridors and battlements.

There are optional English-language **guided tours**, on which the key elements of the castle's construction and history are pointed out: there's a vast portrait collection that includes recently commissioned works depicting political and cultural figures as well as assorted royalty and nobility; some fine decorative and architectural work; and, as at Drottningholm, a private **theatre**, built for Gustav III. It's too delicate to be used for performances these days, but in summer, plays and other events are staged out in the castle grounds; more information can be obtained from Mariefred's tourist office (see below). Even ABBA have put in an appearance here – in February 1974 Gripsholm was used as the cover shot for their *Waterloo* album.

Järnvägsmuséet

Railway Museum • Steam trains leave Mariefred roughly hourly in summer: May–mid-July & mid-Aug–Sept Sat & Sun 11am–6pm; mid-July–mid-Aug daily 10am–4pm • 100kr return, includes entrance to the museum • ☎ 0159 210 00, ⓦ oslj.nu

Steam-train fans will love the **Järnvägsmuséet** at the railway station in **Läggesta**, an adjoining small village a few kilometres south of Mariefred. There's an exhibition of old rolling stock and workshops, given added interest by the fact that narrow-gauge **steam trains** still run between Mariefred and Läggesta, a twenty-minute ride away on the Östra Sörmlands Järnväg railway – you'll probably have noticed the narrow-gauge tracks running all the way to the quayside in Mariefred. From Läggesta, it's possible to pick up the regular SJ train back to Stockholm; check for connections at the Mariefred tourist office. Of course, you could always travel to Mariefred from Stockholm by this route too (see below).

ARRIVAL AND INFORMATION

MARIEFRED

By train There's a service from Stockholm to Läggesta (hourly; 35min), from where connecting buses and, at certain times of year, steam trains (see above) shuttle passengers into Mariefred.

By steamboat In summer, you can get to Mariefred from Stockholm on the *S/S Mariefred*, which leaves from Stadshusbron on Kungsholmen (early June & early Sept Sat & Sun 10am; mid-June to end Aug Tues–Sun 10am; 3hr 30min; 210kr one way, 300kr return; ⓦ mariefred.info); buy your ticket on board.

Tourist office Kyrkogatan 13 (June–Aug Mon–Fri 8am–3.30pm, Fri 7.30am–4pm; ☎ 0152 291 00, ⓦ strangnas.se).

ACCOMMODATION

Djurgårdsporten Vandrarhem Djurgårdsgatan 2 ☎ 070 236 31 03, ✉ djurgardsporten@live.se. Basic but centrally located youth hostel; books up early in summer so make sure you reserve well in advance. Dorms **250kr**, doubles **450kr**

Gripsholms Värdhus Kyrkogatan 1 ☎ 0159 347 50, ⓦ gripsholms-vardshus.se. Gloriously opulent rooms full of elegant period furniture in a beautifully restored inn (the oldest in Sweden) overlooking the castle and the lake. Supplements from 800kr per night will upgrade you to one of several luxurious suites. **2490kr**

EATING

Elsas Kantin Storgatan 5 ☎ 0152 189 55, ⓦ elsaskantin. se. Head to this café and deli in the main square for coffee and cakes or for the extensive vegetarian lunchtime buffet, which features a range of different options suitable for vegans. Mon–Fri 11am–2pm, closed on Sat & Sun.

Gripsholms Slottspaviljong ☎ 0159 100 23, ⓦ slottspaviljongen.se. In the park between the castle and the town centre. There's a good selection of salmon and meat dishes at this open-air café, costing around 150–250kr, as well as lunches and snacks. Daily noon–9pm.

Gripsholms Värdshus Kyrkogatan 1 ☎ 0159 347 50, ⓦ gripsholms-vardshus.se. Treat yourself to lunch here and save a fortune over the regular evening prices; whenever you eat, though, the modern Swedish food is

excellent (mains cost 215–315kr) and the restaurant enjoys terrific views over to Gripsholm. Mon, Tues & Sun noon–9pm, Wed–Sat noon–10pm.

Mariefreds Hamnkafé Hamnplanen ☎ 0 76 275 83 81, ⓦ facebook.com/mariefredshamn. This simple café down by the harbour is the best place in town to enjoy freshly baked waffles and cinnamon buns with a cup of coffee. Daily 11am–7pm.

Västerås

Capital of the county of Västmanland and Sweden's sixth biggest city, **VÄSTERÅS** is an immediately likeable mix of old and new. Today, this lakeside conurbation, 100km west of Stockholm, carefully balances its dependence on ABB, the industrial technology giant, with a rich history dating back to Viking times. If you're looking for a place that's lively and cosmopolitan, yet retains cobbled squares, picturesque wooden houses and even a sixth-century royal burial mound, you won't go far wrong here. Västerås also boasts some of Lake Mälaren's best **beaches** (see box), all a short ferry ride from the city centre.

Storatorget and Bondtorget

The city's two main squares are the twin cobbled **Bondtorget** and **Storatorget**. In Storatorget look out for the striking sculpture of a string of cyclists, the *Asea Stream*, which is supposed to portray the original workers of ABB as they made their way to work; today the sculpture is also a reminder of the impressive fact that Västerås has over 300km of bicycle tracks and is a veritable haven for cyclists.

Svartån River

The slender lane from the southwestern corner of Bondtorget leads to the narrow **Svartån river**, which runs right through the centre of the city; the bridge over the river here (known as Apotekarbron) has great views of the old wooden cottages which nestle eave-to-eave along the riverside. Although it may not appear significant (the Svartån is actually much wider further upstream), the river was a decisive factor in making Västerås the headquarters of one of the world's largest engineering companies, **Asea-Brown-Boveri** (ABB), which needed a ready source of water for production; if you arrived by train from Stockholm you'll have passed its metallurgy and distribution centres on approaching the station.

Domkyrkan

Västra Kyrkogatan • Daily 8am–6pm • ⓦ svenskakyrkan.se/uppsala/domkyrkan

North of Storotorget, the brick **Domkyrkan** dates from the thirteenth century, although its two outer aisles are formed from a number of chapels built around the existing church during the following two centuries. The original tower was destroyed by fire, leaving Nicodemus Tessin the Younger (who also built the Kungliga Slottet in Stockholm, see page 50) to design the current structure in 1693. The highly ornate gilded oak triptych above the altar was made in Antwerp, and depicts the suffering and resurrection of Christ. To the right of the altar lies the tomb of Erik XIV, who died an unceremonious death imprisoned in Örbyhus castle in 1577 after eating his favourite pea soup – little did he realize it was laced with arsenic. Local rumour has it that the king's feet had to be cut off in order for his body to fit the coffin, which was built too small. His elegant, black-marble sarcophagus rests on a plinth of reddish sandstone from Öland.

Kyrkbacken

Beyond the cathedral is the most charming district of Västerås, **Kyrkbacken**, a hilly area that stretches just a few hundred metres. Here, steep cobblestone alleys wind between well-preserved old wooden houses where artisans and the petit bourgeoisie lived in the eighteenth century. Thankfully, the area was saved from the great fire of 1714 – which destroyed much of Västerås – and the wholesale restructuring of the 1960s. At the top end of Djäknegatan, the main street of the district, look for a narrow alley called Brunnsgränd, along which is a house bearing the sign "*Mästermansgården*": it was once the abode of the most hated and ostracized man in the district – the town executioner.

Stadshuset

A quick walk south past the restaurants and shops of Vasagatan in the city centre will bring you to the eye-catching modern **Stadshuset** in Fiskatorget – the building is a far cry from the Dominican monastery which once stood on this spot. Although home to the city's administration, the Stadshuset is best known for its 47 bells, the largest of which is known as "the Monk" and can be heard across the city at lunchtimes.

2

Karlsgatan 2: Västerås Konstmuseum and Länsmuseum

Art Museum and County Museum • Karlsgatan 2 • Tues 10am–5pm, Wed 10am–8pm, Thurs & Fri 10am–5pm, Sat & Sun noon–4pm • Free •
Ⓦ karlsgatan2.se, Ⓦ vasteraskonstmuseum.se, Ⓦ vastmanlandslansmuseum.se

The **Karlsgatan 2** building houses two museums: the Västerås Konstmuseum and the Länsmuseum. The **Västerås Konstmuseum**, the town's compact art museum, is rather disappointing. It's worth a quick look for its contemporary collections of Swedish and other Nordic art – but don't expect too much. The **Länsmuseum** unfortunately also lacks direction, containing a ragtag collection of obscure items such as children's dolls and old typewriters, plonked in glass cabinets; you'll glean little about the province's history from this load of junk.

The Anundshög burial mound

To get here, take bus #1 from the centre of town (bus times are at Ⓦ vl.se); buy your bus ticket at the tourist office, at Pressbyrån
newsagents or on the bus with a credit card.

Whilst in Västerås, try not to miss nearby **Anundshög**, the largest royal burial mound in Sweden, just 6km northeast of the city. Dating from the sixth century, the mound – 60m in diameter and 14m high – is said to be the resting place of King Bröt-Anund and his stash of gold. Although unexcavated, the mound is widely thought to contain the remains of a cremation burial and a stone cist. Anundshög was also used for sessions of the local *ting*, or Viking parliament, and several other smaller burial mounds nearby suggest that the site was an important Viking meeting place over several centuries. Beside the main mound lie a large number of **standing stones** arranged end-to-end in the shape of two ships measuring 53m and 50m in diameter. The nearby **rune stone** dates from around 1000 AD though it's not thought to be connected to the

---

VÄSTERÅS BEACHES AND BOAT TRIPS

Boats run from Färjkajen quay in the harbour, southwest of the train station, to a string of small **islands** in Lake Mälaren blessed with great **beaches**.

The closest is **Östra Holmen**, which is noted for its three excellent **nudist beaches** on the southern shore. It's popular with locals who come here to enjoy the wide-open views of Lake Mälaren and to explore the island's undisturbed shoreline – an easy circular walk of around 2km.

Further south, much larger **Ridön** traces its history back to Viking times, and is today a peaceful forested haven, with sheltered coves ideal for **swimming**. A country lane winds across the centre of the island from west to east; there's a small **café** and wooden bell tower at the point where this lane meets the path leading up from the ferry jetty.

Two other uninhabited islands, **Almö-Lindö** and tiny **Skåpholmen**, are perfect for seekers of total solitude. Almö-Lindö, which the boat reaches first, is the better bet since it's larger, has more varied terrain and some good swimming beaches – though no facilities. **Skåpholmen** is a skinny sliver of an island, again with no facilities.

Detailed **ferry times** can be found at Ⓦ rederimalarstaden.se but generally boats sail several times daily between late April and early November.

burial mound. The stone's inscription, when translated, reads "Folkvid erected all these stones for his son, Hedin, brother of Anund. Vred carved the runes."

ARRIVAL AND DEPARTURE

VÄSTERÅS

By plane The airport, served by Ryanair flights from London Stansted, is just 6km east of the city. Taxis (☎018 18 50 00; ⓦtaxivasteras.se) run to the centre (150kr), or take bus #3 – buy your ticket in the arrivals hall.
By train The train station is on Södra Ringvägen.

Destinations Gothenburg (every 2hr; 3hr 40min); Stockholm (hourly; 1hr).
By bus Arriving by bus you'll be dropped at the terminal adjacent to the train station.

INFORMATION

Tourist office Kopparbergsvägen 1 (Mon–Fri 9.30am–5pm, Sat 10am–2pm; ☎021 39 01 00, ⓦvisitvasteras.se). Barely a 2min walk from the train station, with plenty of information plus internet access.
Bike rental Available from SjöEvent at Saltängsvägen 18 (☎070 699 32 40) ⓦsjoevent.se, down by the harbour.

ACCOMMODATION

Arkad Östermalmsgatan 25 ☎021 12 04 80, ⓦhotell arkad.se. Individually designed rooms ranging from contemporary Swedish to nineteenth-century classic. Some include a small kitchen for self-catering and represent great value for money. An excellent relaxation area incorporates a sauna, darts and pool. 850kr/1350kr
Elite Stadshotellet Storatorget ☎0771 788 789, ⓦelite.se. This classic *Jugendstil* hotel opened in 1907 and oozes old-world charm with its sweeping staircases, elaborate chandeliers and elegant rooms where contemporary and antique meet. Superb location in the main square at the heart of everything. 1050kr/1250kr
First Plaza Karlsgatan 9C ☎021 10 10 10. Known locally as the "Skyscraper", this 25-storey glass-and-chrome structure is the last word in Scandinavian chic. Rooms are light and airy, featuring stylish, contemporary Swedish design, and have panoramic views of the city and Lake Mälaren. Check for last-minute summer deals on the website. 1000kr/1160kr
Hem till Gården Slånbärsgatan 13 ☎070 228 75 18, ⓦhemtillgarden.se. Located 3.5km north of Västerås, these three rustic timber houses were once part of a farm.

Today they've been divided up into cosy, self-catering apartments, offering semi-rural accommodation within easy reach of the centre. 1200kr
★ **Hotell Hackspett** Vasaparken ☎021 39 01 00, ⓦvisitvasteras.se. "Hotel Woodpecker" is a fabulous one-room treehouse 13m off the ground in the largest oak tree in Vasaparken, bookable only through the tourist office. Available April–Oct. Per person B&B 1350kr, per person half-board 1600kr
★ **Utter Inn** Lake Mälaren ☎021 39 01 00, ⓦwww. vasterasmalarstaden.se. ⓦvisitvasteras.se. A platform 1km out into Lake Mälaren, not unlike a mini oil rig, whose one and only bedroom is actually underwater. Whilst not for the claustrophobic, it's certainly memorable. Bookable only through the tourist office. Available April–Oct. Per person B&B 1350kr, per person half-board 1600kr
Västerås Vasagatan 22 ☎021 18 03 30, ⓦhotell vasteras.se. Modern if rather cramped rooms in this well-located hotel in town right in the city centre. A worthwhile 100kr extra gets you a superior room with a balcony overlooking one of the main shopping streets. 750kr/995kr

EATING AND DRINKING

Bellman Storatorget 6 ☎021 41 33 55, ⓦbellman. gastrogate.com. The most elegant restaurant in town, with eighteenth-century furniture and linen tablecloths, serving modern Swedish dishes such as butter-fried zander with smoked pancetta (255kr), fillet steak in a green pepper sauce (265kr) and a starter of smoked elk with horseradish and caramelized white turnip (95kr). Mon–Thurs 11am–11pm, Fri 11am–1am, Sat noon–midnight.
Bishops Arms Storatorget, ⓦbishopsarms.com/ vasteras. Enjoyable British-style pub perfectly located in the main square, attached to the *Elite Stadshotellet*, with a large selection of beers and single malt whiskies. Pub food also available and there's outdoor seating in summer. Mon 5–11pm, Tues–Thurs 4pm–midnight, Fri 3pm–1am, Sat noon–1am, Sun 5–10pm.

Boca Storagatan 36 ☎021 21 91 90, ⓦbocavasteras.se. Locals flock to this lounge restaurant for superb tapas (50–125kr), such as grilled goat's cheese, calamari and chorizo. The restaurant is set in a courtyard. Tues–Thurs 5pm–late, Fri 4pm–1am, Sat 5pm–1am.
Brasserie Stadsparken Storagatan 35 ☎021 448 50 80, ⓦbrasseriestadsparken.se. Resembling an enormous glass box, this two-storey brasserie beside the Svartån River is the latest hangout for Västerås foodies. Stylish to a T, it serves a succulent catch of the day (price varies) and a fabulous veal carpaccio with tarragon mayonnaise (110kr), as well as boiled langoustines (four for 160kr). Mon & Tues 11.30am–2pm & 5–11pm, Wed & Thurs 11.30am–2pm & 5pm–late, Fri 11.30am–1am, Sat noon–1am, Sun 1–10pm.

Frank Bistro Storatorget 3 ☎021 13 65 00, ☯frank bistro.com. Serving modern Swedish gourmet dishes, there's no set menu at this trendy little restaurant off the main square; instead, it's whatever the chefs decide to cook up – always inspired and delicious (595kr for three courses). Two sittings 5.30–8.30pm & 9pm–midnight. Tues–Sat 4pm–late.

Kalle på Spången Kungsgatan 2, ☯kallepaspangen. se. Snug and cosy café with tabletop candles serving up great baguettes, pasta salads, lasagne and soup, as well as cakes and a good choice of coffees. It also has a couple of outdoor tables in summer. Mon–Fri 11am–9pm, Sat & Sun 11am–6pm.

Limone Storagatan 4 ☎021 41 75 60, ☯limone ristorante.se. Stylish modern Italian restaurant with high-backed chairs and painted walls, serving top-notch pasta starters from 90kr and regular meat mains – for example, saltimbocca with Parma ham and sage – for 225kr. Mon–Thurs 11am–1.30pm & 5–10pm, Fri 11am–1.30pm & 5–11pm Sat 5–10pm.

Piazza di Spagna Vasagatan 26 ☎021 12 42 10, ☯dispagna.se. The best Italian in town and a very popular place for lunch. Pizzas cost 100–165kr whilst mains, such as fillet of venison in cognac sauce, pepper steak or baked salmon are a bit pricey at 250–315kr. Mon–Tues 11am–10pm, Wed–Thurs 11am–11pm, Fri 11am–midnight, Sat noon–midnight, Sun noon–9pm.

RoseGarden Köpmangatan 12 ☎021 18 82 29, ☯rosegarden.se. *RoseGarden* is Sweden's leading restaurant chain in the Asian food culture. The food buffet always serves ten different dishes prepared and flavoured with natural ingredients. Mon–Thurs 11am–2.30pm, 5.30–9pm, Fri 11am–2.30pm, 5.30–10pm, Sat noon–10pm.

★ **Spicy Hot** Sturegatan 20A ☎021 18 17 40, ☯spicyhot.se. A rather understated interior with simple wooden tables and chairs, but the food here is top-notch: excellent Thai curries and stir fries cost 95kr, and there's a range of vegetarian dishes. Mon–Sat 11am–10pm, Sun noon–9pm.

Varda Vasagatan 14 ☎021 14 81 50, ☯restaurangvarda. se. Chi-chi lounge restaurant with floor-to-ceiling windows and a stylish, contemporary interior that really draws the crowds. Try the zander with chanterelle mushrooms (280kr) or the pork cheek with polenta (245kr). Mon–Thurs 11.30am–2pm, Tues–Thurs 5–11pm, Fri 11.30am–1am, Sat noon–1am.

Uppsala and around

The vibrant university city of **UPPSALA** lies 70km to the north of Stockholm, and boasts some great museums, including the home and gardens of world-renowned botanist Carl von Linné. The city is regarded as the historical and religious centre of the country, and attracts day-trippers seeking a lively alternative to Stockholm as well as travellers looking for a worthwhile stop on the long trek north. A medieval seat of religion and learning, Uppsala clings to the past through its cathedral and university, and a striking succession of related buildings in their vicinity.

Just north of town, the sixth-century burial mounds of **Gamla Uppsala** mark the original site of Uppsala.

Domkyrkan

Domkyrkoplan 2 · Daily 8am–6pm · Free · ☯ uppsaladomkyrka.se

The centre of the medieval town is the great **Domkyrkan**, Scandinavia's largest cathedral. Built as a Gothic boast to the people of Trondheim in Norway that even their mighty church, the Nidarosdom, could be overshadowed, it loses out to its rival only on building materials – local brick rather than imported stone. The echoing interior remains impressive, particularly the French Gothic ambulatory, flanked by tiny chapels and bathed in a golden, decorative glow. One chapel contains a lively set of restored fourteenth-century wall paintings that recount the legend of St Erik, Sweden's patron saint: his coronation, subsequent crusade to Finland, eventual defeat and execution at the hands of the Danes. The relics of Erik are zealously guarded in a chapel off the nave: poke around and you'll also find the tombs of the Reformation rebel Gustav Vasa and his son Johan III, and that of the botanist Linnaeus (see page 96), who lived in Uppsala. Time and fire have led to the rest of the cathedral being rebuilt, scrubbed and painted to the extent that it resembles a museum more than a thirteenth-century place of worship; even the characteristic twin spires are late nineteenth-century additions.

Gustavianum

Akademigatan 3 • Tues–Sun: June–Aug 10am–4pm; Sept–May 11am–4pm • 50kr • ⑩ gustavianum.uu.se

Opposite the west end of the cathedral, the onion-domed **Gustavianum** was built in 1625 as part of the university, and is much touted by the tourist office for the masterpiece of kitsch that is the **Augsburg Art Cabinet** – a treasure chest of black oak containing all manner of knick-knacks presented to Gustav II Adolf by the Lutheran councillors of Augsburg in 1632 – and the world's first ever thermometer from 1745 owned by none other than Anders Celsius, inventor of the temperature scale. Whilst here be sure to make it up to the top floor to see the perfectly preserved **anatomical theatre** from 1660 where convicts' bodies were once carved up in the name of science, until the church stepped in to end the practice. The same building houses a couple of small collections of Egyptian, Classical and Viking antiquities.

The university

Övre Slottsgatan • Mon–Fri 8am–4pm

The current **university** building is the imposing nineteenth-century Renaissance-style edifice opposite Gustavianum. Originally a seminary, today it's used for lectures and

▮ ACCOMMODATION		● EATING				▮ DRINKING AND NIGHTLIFE	
Best Western Svava	4	Amazing Thai	7	Stationen	6	Birger Jarl	5
Centralstation Hotell		Basilico	1	Svenssons Åkanten	4	Bryggeriet Ångkvarn	4
& Vandrarhem	6	Domtrapkällaren	8	Tilltugg	2	Flustret	6
Clarion Gillet	2	Fågelsången	12	Villa Romana	5	Hyllan	2
Grand Hörnan	8	Güntherska				Katalin and all that jazz	1
Radisson Blu Uppsala	5	hovkonditori	10			O'Connors	3
Scandic Uplandia	1	Hambergs fisk	9				
Uppsala City Hostel	3	Ofvandahls	3				
Villa Anna	7	Peppar Peppar	11				

seminars and hosts the graduation ceremonies each May. Among the more famous alumni are Carl von Linné (Linnaeus; see page 96) and Anders Celsius. No one will mind you strolling in for a quick look, but the rest of the building is not open to the public.

Carolina Rediviva

Dag Hammerskjölds väg 1 • Early June–late Aug Mon–Wed & Fri 8.30am–6pm, Thurs 8.30am–7pm, Sat noon–4pm; rest of year Mon–Fri 8.30am–9pm, Sat & Sun 9am–6pm • Free • ⓦ ub.uu.se

From the university, Övre Slottsgatan leads south to the **Carolina Rediviva**, the university library and one of Scandinavia's largest, with around five million books. On April 30 (Valborgsmässoafton) each year the students meet here to celebrate the official first day of spring (usually in the snow), all wearing the traditional student cap that gives them the appearance of disaffected sailors. Take a look in the **manuscript room**, where there's a collection of rare letters and other paraphernalia. The beautiful sixth-century Silver Bible is on permanent display, as is Mozart's original manuscript for *The Magic Flute*.

The castle

Övre Slottsgatan • Guided tours in English mid-June–early Sept Tues–Sun 1pm & 3pm • 120kr

When compared to the glorious building of the university, the **castle** up on the hill, built by Gustav Vasa in the mid-sixteenth century, is a disappointment. Certainly significant chapters of Sweden's history were played out here over the centuries: the Uppsala Assembly of 1593, which established the supremacy of the Lutheran Church, took place in the Hall of State, where also, in 1630, the Parliament resolved to enter the Thirty Years' War. Sadly though, much of the castle was destroyed in the 1702 fire that also did away with three-quarters of the city, and only one side and two towers – the L-shape of today – remain of what was once an opulent rectangular palace. Inside, admission also includes access to the castle's art museum but, quite frankly, it won't make your postcards home.

Linnéträdgården

Linnaeus Garden • Svartbäcksgatan 27 • May–Sept Tues–Sun 11am–5pm (gates close at 8pm) • 80kr including the museum • ⓦ linnaeus.uu.se

The beautiful **Linnéträdgården** contains around 1300 varieties of plants. These are Sweden's oldest botanical gardens, established in 1655 by Olof Rudbeck the Elder, and re-laid out by Linnaeus (see page 96) in 1741 with perennials and annuals either side of the central path; some of the species he introduced and classified still survive here. Incidentally, you can see the garden behind Linnaeus's head on the 100kr note.

The **museum** adjoining the garden was home to Linnaeus and his family from 1743 to 1778, and attempts to evoke his life through a partially restored library, his writing room and even the bed where he breathed his last.

Uppsala Konsert & Kongress

Concert Hall • Vaksala torg 1 • Mon–Fri 10am–6pm, Sat 10am–3pm • Free • ⓦ ukk.se

Uppsala's **Concert Hall**, a mammoth structure of brushed steel and glass, lies a few minutes' walk east of the train and bus stations. With its facade resembling the keys of a giant piano keyboard, it's certainly divided local opinion; many people believe it's little more than a huge carbuncle. Be that as it may, venture inside and take the escalators to the top floor for a superb **view** of the entire city. It hosts Swedish-language theatre as well as musical productions.

2

CARL VON LINNÉ

Born in Småland in 1707, **Carl von Linné**, who styled himself Carolus Linnaeus, is undoubtedly Sweden's most revered scientist. His international reputation was secured by the introduction of his **binomial classification**, a two-part nomenclature that enabled plants and animals to be consistently named and categorized into families; it was Linnaeus who invented the term *homo sapiens*, for example. Only very recently has the basis of his classifications been undermined by genetic methods, resulting in the complete realignment of certain plant families.

Bror Hjorth museum

Norbyvägen 26 • Thurs–Sun noon–4pm, also mid-June–mid-Aug Tues & Wed noon–4pm • Free • ⓦ brorhjorthshus.se • Buses #11 and #7 run here from Storatorget in the city centre (10min)

One of the first sights that greets arrivals on exiting Uppsala train station is an erotic statue of a man with an oversized penis, the work of Uppsala-born sculptor and painter, **Bror Hjorth** (1894–1968). A former professor of drawing at the Swedish Royal Academy of Fine Arts, Hjorth was a modernist with roots in folk art, and is considered one of Sweden's greatest artists. His numerous public art commissions can be seen right across the country – perhaps most strikingly in the church in Jukkasjärvi in Lapland (see page 340). Hjorth's former home and studio in Uppsala, west of the city centre, have now been turned into a **museum** containing the largest and most representative collection of his work in the country.

Linne's Hammarby

May & Sept Fri–Sun 11am–5pm; June–Aug Tues–Sun 11am–5pm (gates close at 8pm) • 80kr including the garden • ⓦ botan.uu.se • Take bus #102 (or less frequently #186) from the bus station and get off at Hammarby vägskäl, from where it's a 1.5km walk; bus times are at ⓦ ul.se

In 1754, Carl von Linné (see box) acquired a country estate at **Hammarby**, 15km southeast of Uppsala, and built a house there. Today, the beautiful homestead, complete with unique wallpaper of botanical engravings, is open to the public and makes a great day-trip. It's surrounded by lush gardens including a collection of Siberian plants and a gene bank for the fruit species of the Lake Mälaren region.

ARRIVAL AND DEPARTURE   UPPSALA

By plane Uppsala can be easily reached from Arlanda airport, Sweden's main airport; trains connect Arlanda C station with Uppsala (daily every 20min; 20min; 164kr) whilst bus #801 also runs to the city (daily every 15–30min; 40min; 85kr).
By train Uppsala's Resecentrum on Kungsgatan, the city's combined bus and train interchange, is the place to catch all

trains to and from the city.
Destinations Arlanda airport (every 20min; 20min); Gällivare (1 daily; 18hr); Gävle (hourly; 40min); Kiruna (1 daily; 19hr 30min); Luleå (1 daily; 16hr 30min); Mora (2 daily; 3hr); Narvik (1 daily; 22hr 30min); Nyköping (3 daily; 2hr); Östersund (24 daily; 6hr 30min); Stockholm (every 20min; 40min); Sundsvall (8 daily; 5hr 30min); Umeå (5 daily; 8hr).

INFORMATION

Tourist office Kungsgatan 59 (Mon–Fri 10am–5pm, Sat 10am–3pm, also July & Aug Sun 11am–3pm; ☎018 727 48

00, ⓦ destinationuppsala.se). Has bundles of leaflets about the city and free internet access.

ACCOMMODATION   SEE MAP PAGE 94

Best Western Svava Bangårdsgatan 24 ☎018 13 00 30, ⓦ bestwestern.se. Modern hotel with all creature comforts, including specially designed rooms for guests with allergies, as well as people with disabilities. Outside the summer period, a free light evening meal is included in the room rate Mon–Thurs & Sun. <u>890kr/1150kr</u>

Centralstation Hotell & Vandrarhem Bangårdsgatan 13 ☎076 185 8485, ⓦ hotellcentralstation.se. Perfectly located for untimely arrivals and departures from the train station opposite, this is a youth hostel and budget hotel is one of the cheapest places to stay in town. The en-suite hotel rooms are small and most don't have a window but the price is hard to beat. If you want a window, be sure to specify when you book. The hostel rooms don't have windows and share facilities. Hostel double ‾550kr‾, hotel double ‾725kr/895kr‾

Clarion Gillet Dragarbrunnsgatan 23 ☎018 68 18 00, ⓦclarionhotelgillet.se. A contemporary beauty with Scandinavian designer rooms and stylish bathrooms with black-and-white tiles, all just a stone's throw from the cathedral. The pool, sauna and gym complex is the best in Uppsala. ‾850kr/1890kr‾

★ **Grand Hörnan** Bangårdsgatan 1 ☎018 13 93 80, ⓦgrandhotellhornan.com. Dating from 1907, this wonderfully elegant place boasts rooms decorated in grand, late nineteenth-century style, many with chandeliers and drapes. Rooms vary in size but the very best are at the front, overlooking the Fyrisån River. ‾1095kr/1495kr‾

Radisson Blu Uppsala Stationsgatan 4 ☎018 474 79 00, ⓦradissonblu.com. The latest designer hotel to grace Uppsala is the eye-catchingly trendy *Radisson Blu*, next to the station, built in the shape of a gently arcing crescent which spans Stationsgatan. As you'd expect from this chain, the invitingly cosy rooms contain the latest Scandinavian chic. ‾1490kr/2490kr‾

Scandic Uplandia Dragarbrunnsgatan 32 ☎018 495 26 00, ⓦscandichotels.com. Bright and airy hotel with Scandinavian colours and designs taking pride of place. Rooms vary in size but the Superior Extra ones are generously proportioned and half as big again as the standard doubles. Impressive hotel gym and sauna suite, too. ‾1030kr/1580kr‾

Uppsala City Hostel St Persgatan 16 ☎018 10 00 08, ⓦuppsalacityhostel.se. Unpretentious, centrally located hostel which has both dorm beds and double rooms – all rooms have windows, unlike at *Centralstation Hotell & Vandrarhem*. There's also access to a well-equipped kitchen. Dorms ‾220kr‾, doubles ‾560kr‾

Villa Anna Odinslund 3 ☎018 580 20 00, ⓦvillaanna. se. Undoubtedly one of the best hotels in Sweden, this intimate place has just eight rooms and three suites, all individually decorated, in an elegant nineteenth-century residence close to the cathedral. The staff's attention to detail is second to none. ‾2600kr/3000kr‾

EATING

SEE MAP PAGE 94

CAFÉS

Fågelsången Munkgatan 3. Plying the masses with caffeine since 1954, this agreeable café is an Uppsala institution, renowned for its terrific selection of pastries and cakes as well as good-value sandwiches: a cheese and ham ciabatta costs just 45kr. Mon–Fri 7.30am–**7pm**, Sat & Sun 9am–6pm.

Güntherska hovkonditori Östra Ågatan 31 ⓦguntherska.se. Gloriously old-fashioned café dating from 1870 which serves simple lunch dishes for around 95kr, and a mouthwatering selection of cakes and pastries under the mellow light of ageing chandeliers. Mon–Sat 10am–7pm, Sun 10am–6pm.

Ofvandahls Sysslomangatan 3–5 ☎018 13 42 04, ⓦofvandahls.se. Near the old part of town, this lively café with antique furniture and fittings first opened in 1878. Don't leave town without trying the famous home-made cakes (*tårtor*) which include a delicious blueberry cake and a mouthwatering Black Forest gateau. Mon–Fri 7.30am–7pm, Sat & Sun 9am–6pm.

RESTAURANTS

★ **Amazing Thai** Dragarbrunnsgatan 46 ☎018 15 30 10, ⓦamazingthai.se. This place is the best Thai in town and has even won awards from the Thai government for its tasty food: stir fries and curries from 145kr or the daily buffet (from 5pm) for a tremendously good value 170kr. Mon–Thurs 11am–10pm, Fri & Sat 11am–11pm, Sun noon–10pm.

★ **Basilico** Svartbäcksgatan 24 ☎0 18 12 50 10, ⓦbasilico.se. Opposite the Linnaeus Garden is the charming ristorante *Basilico*. Here you get authentic Italian food culture and wonderful wine in a lovely environment. Mon–Fri 11am–3pm & 5–10pm, Sat & Sun noon–10pm.

Domtrappkällaren St Eriks Gränd 15 ☎018 13 09 55, ⓦdomtrappkallaren.se. One of the most chi-chi places in town, with an old vaulted roof and a great atmosphere. Mains such as honey-fried hake marinated in citrus juices or venison in red wine sauce with a purée of celery go for 210–325kr; excellent set lunches, too, for a more reasonable 120kr. Mon–Fri 11am–10pm, Sat noon–11pm.

Hambergs Fisk Fyris torg 8 ☎0 18 71 00 50, ⓦhambergs.se. A smartly tiled seafood restaurant which has deservedly earned a reputation over the years as one of the city's best. It serves a good selection of fresh fish caught using environmentally sustainable methods, as well as organic vegetables produced on an island in Östergötland. It's particularly popular at lunchtime, and booking is essential. Reckon on 195–295kr per dish. Tues–Sat 10am–10pm.

Peppar Peppar Suttungs gränd 3 ☎018 13 13 60, ⓦpepparpeppar.se. This cosy red-brick building, once a tractor factory, has mutated into one of Uppsala's finest restaurants, serving modern Swedish-French dishes such as Arctic char with an orange and ginger sauce or slow-cooked lamb rolled in herbs with lemon: mains 225–300kr. Mon–Thurs 5–10pm, Sat 4–11pm, Sun 4–9pm.

Stationen Olof Palmes Plats 6 ☎018 15 35 00, ⓦstationen.se. Located in Uppsala's glorious old station building from 1866, this place is three things in one: a Parisian brasserie, a London pub and a Roman café, serving

2

something for everyone. Mon 10am–11pm, Tues 10am–midnight, Wed & Thurs 10am–1am, Fri 10am–2am, Sat 10am–2am, Sun 10am–11pm.

Svenssons Åkanten St Eriks torg 8 ☏ 018 15 01 50, ⌨ svenssonskrogar.se. The wonderful riverside summer-only (May–Sept) restaurant beside the Saluhallen market hall has great views and is a firm favourite with Uppsala folk. Lots of barbecue dishes such as chicken breast (185kr) as well as lighter salads (175kr). Mon–Fri 11.30am–11pm, Sat & Sun noon–11pm.

Tilltugg Vaksalagatan 24 ☏ 018 12 97 01, ⌨ tilltugg.com. A style-conscious lounge bar with light-grey leather stools and a bar dressed in mosaic tiles. It serves a terrific range of tapas for 30–70kr, ranging from olives to garlic-and-chilli scampi. Mixed tapas plates from 100kr. Mon–Thurs 5–11pm, Fri 4pm–1am, Sat 5pm–1am.

Villa Romana Gamla Torget 4 ☏ 018 12 50 90, ⌨ villaromana.se. A decent Italian restaurant with elegant old wallpaper and a nice wooden floor serving pasta dishes such as linguine with scallops for 155–190kr and meat and fish mains, including rib-eye steak in béarnaise sauce, at 190–285kr. Mon–Thurs 11am–10pm, Fri 11am–11pm Sat noon–11pm, Sun noon–10pm.

DRINKING AND NIGHTLIFE SEE MAP PAGE 94

By evening Uppsala's large student population makes its presence felt and more often than not the city centre is abuzz with life. The most popular places for a drink are all within easy walking distance of each other and are listed below.

Birger Jarl Nedre Slottsgatan 3 ☏ 018 13 50 00, ⌨ birgerjarl.nu. A fun and popular club where the emphasis is on house music. Great for a drink and a favourite hangout for Uppsala's large student population. A good bet, too, for live music. Fri & Sat 11pm–3am.

Bryggeriet Ångkvarn Östra Ågatan 59 ☏ 018 418 02 00, ⌨ bryggerietangkvarn.se. An inordinately popular gastropub and microbrewery which brews its own ales and beers on site. The interior of this converted mill is stylish to a T, too, with rough brick walls and bar. Mon & Tues 4–10pm, Wed & Thurs 4pm–midnight, Sat 3pm–midnight.

Flustret Svandammen 1 ☏ 018 10 04 44, ⌨ flustret.se. This fancy, twin-towered, Tivoli-style building has consistently been one of the busiest drinking holes in town since the 1950s, attracting students and locals alike.

A pub and nightclub rolled into one that really rocks at the weekend. Fri & Sat 10.30pm–3am.

★ **Hyllan** St Eriks torg ☏ 018 15 01 50, ⌨ hyllan.se. The contemporary brick and steel surrounds of this urban loft bar would fit perfectly in New York. Located in the roof space of the Saluhallen, this is Uppsala at its most sophisticated. Opening times vary.

Katalin and all that jazz Roslagsgatan 1 ☏ 018 14 06 80, ⌨ katalin.com. Uppsala's premier spot for live jazz (Fri & Sat nights) located in the converted goods sheds known as Östra Station behind the main train station. Also serves light bar snacks. Tues 4–11pm Wed & Thurs 4pm–midnight, Fri & Sat 1pm–late.

O'Connors Storatorget 1 ☏ 018 14 40 10, ⌨ oconnors.se. A first-floor Irish pub in the main square with over forty different beers on tap and a staggering two hundred whiskey varieties. It's a good place to start the evening – always busy and fun. Mon–Thurs 4pm–3am, Fri 1pm–3am, Sat noon–3am, Sun noon–1am.

Gamla Uppsala

Five kilometres to the north of Uppsala, three huge royal **burial mounds** dating back to the sixth century mark the original site of the town, **GAMLA UPPSALA**. According to legend, they are the final resting places of three ancient kings – Aun, Egil and Adlis. Though the site developed into an important trading and administrative centre, it was originally established as a pagan settlement and a place of ancient sacrificial rites by the Svear tribe. In the eleventh century, the German chronicler, Adam of Bremen, described the cult of the *æsir* (the Norse gods Odin, Thor and Freyr) practised in Uppsala: every ninth year, the deaths of nine people would be demanded at the festival of Fröblot, the victims left hanging from a nearby tree until their corpses rotted. Two centuries later, the great medieval storyteller, Snorri Sturluson of Iceland, depicted Uppsala as the true home of the Ynglinga dynasty (the original royal family in Scandinavia who also worshipped Freyr), a place where grand sacrificial festivals were held in honour of their god.

Gamla Uppsala kyrka

Daily 9am–5pm

The pagan temple where Uppsala's bloody sacrifices took place is now marked by the Christian **Gamla Uppsala kyrka**, which was built over pagan remains when the Swedish kings first accepted baptism in the new faith. Built predominantly of stone, yet characterized by its rear nave wall of stepped red-brick gabling, this is one of the most breathtakingly beautiful churches in Sweden, with an understated simplicity at the very heart of its appeal. Although what survives of the church today is only a remnant of the original cathedral, the relics inside more than compensate for the downscaling. In the **porch** are two impressive collecting chests, one made from an oak log and fitted with iron locks, which dates from the earliest days of the church. Entering the **nave**, look out for the cabinet on the left containing a superb collection of church silver, including a fourteenth-century chalice and a censer from the 1200s. Nearby, in the nave wall, a stone memorial to Anders Celsius, inventor of the temperature scale that bears his name, is a worthy tribute. Outside, if you haven't yet set eyes on a genuine **rune stone** in Sweden, look carefully in the church walls at the back to find a perfectly preserved example from the eleventh century.

The burial mounds

Southeast of the church, the **tinghög** or parliament hill (the only burial mound not fenced in) was once the site of the local *ting* where, until the sixteenth century, a Viking parliament was held to deliberate on all matters affecting Uppsala. Immediately west of here, a path leads around the three main mounds, the first of which, **östhögen** – the east mound – dates from around 550. Following the 1846–47 excavations of Gamla Uppsala, this hill yielded the site's most astonishing artefacts: the cremated remains of a woman – possibly a priestess of the god Freyr – buried in magnificent wool, linen and silk clothing, as well as a necklace bearing a powerful image of a Valkyrie. The adjacent central mound, **mitthögen**, is thought to be around fifty years older than its neighbour but has still to be excavated. Finally, the western **västhögen** has been dated from the late sixth century, and following excavations in 1874 revealed male bone fragments and jewellery commensurate with high status.

Gamla Uppsala museum

April to mid-June & mid-Aug–Sept daily 10am–4pm; mid-June–mid-Aug daily 11am–5pm; Oct–March Mon, Wed, Sat & Sun noon–4pm • 80kr • ⓦ raa.se/gamlauppsala

The finds from the site are proudly displayed at the entrance to the enjoyable **Gamla Uppsala museum**, a brave and successful attempt to portray early Swedish history in a wider non-Viking context. You can gawp at an archeologist's dream – gold fragments, ancient pieces of glass and precious ivory game pieces – as well as amble through exhibitions illustrating the origin of local myths. There's also a full account of Uppsala's golden period, which ended in the thirteenth century.

ARRIVAL AND DEPARTURE   GAMLA UPPSALA

By bus Buses #4, #30 and #1 from Vaksalagatan in Uppsala will drop you at the Gamla Uppsala terminus (buy tickets on the bus with a credit card or in advance from Pressbyrån newsagents), in reality nothing more than a bus stop next to a level crossing opposite the museum. From the bus stop cross the busy Stockholm–Gävle mainline at the level crossing to reach the site; from the Centre paths lead to the church and burial mounds.

EATING

Odinsborg Ärnavägen 4 ⓣ 018 32 35 25. Between the museum and the church and built in Swedish National Romantic style, this café and restaurant serves a Viking spread (365kr) of chicken and ribs which you eat with your fingers – you can even dress in period costume. Lunches available, too. Mon–Sat 10am–6pm, Sun 11am–6pm.

Sigtuna

Forty kilometres south of Uppsala is **SIGTUNA**, a compact little town that dates all the way back to Viking times, with extensive ruined churches and rune stones right in the

2

centre. Apart from its ruins, it looks like any other old Swedish town with cobbled streets and squares. Scratch the surface though, and you'll understand what made Sigtuna so important. Founded in 980 by King Erik Segersäll, Sigtuna grew from a village to become Sweden's first town. Fittingly, it contains **Sweden's oldest street**, Storagatan; the original, laid out during the king's reign, still lies under its modern-day counterpart. Sigtuna also boasts three intriguing **ruined churches** dating from the twelfth century. The Sigtuna district also contains more **rune stones** than any other area in Sweden – around 150 of them have been found to date – and several can be seen close to the ruins of the church of St Lars along Prästgatan.

St Per and St Olof

Two of Sigtuna's most impressive ruins, the churches of St Per and St Olof, lie along Storagatan itself. Much of the west and central towers of **St Per's** still remain from the early 1100s; experts believe it likely that the church functioned as a cathedral until the diocese was moved to nearby Uppsala (see page 93). The unusual formation of the vault in the central tower was influenced by church design then current in England and Normandy. Further east along Storagatan, **St Olof's** has impressively thick walls and a short nave, the latter suggesting that the church was never completed.

Mariakyrkan

Uppsalavägen 4 • Daily 9am–5pm

Close to the church ruins on Olofsgatan is the very much functioning **Mariakyrkan**, constructed of red brick during the mid-thirteenth century to serve the local Dominican monastery. Inside, the walls and ceiling are richly adorned with restored paintings from the fourteenth and fifteenth centuries.

Sigtuna museum

Storagatan 55 • Daily noon–4pm • Free from Oct–April, otherwise 100kr • ⓦ sigtunamuseum.se

On the main road, Storagatan, the **Sigtuna museum** includes material on Sigtuna's role as Sweden's foremost trading centre. Coins bear witness to the fact that this was the first town in the land to mint coins, in 995, plus there's booty from abroad: gold rings and even an eleventh-century clay egg, from Kiev.

ARRIVAL AND INFORMATION   SIGTUNA

By train and bus To reach Sigtuna from Uppsala or Stockholm, take the train to Märsta (every 20min; 20min from both Uppsala or Stockholm), from where buses #570 and #575 run the short distance to the town – the total journey time is around 45min. From Arlanda airport take bus #579 (hourly; 25min).

Tourist office Storagatan 33 Mon–Fri 10am–5pm, Sat 11am–3pm, Sun noon–3pm; ☏ 08 594 806 50, ⓦ destinationsigtuna.se).

ACCOMMODATION

Sigtuna Stadshotell Stora Nygatan 3 ☏ 08 592 501 00, ⓦ sigtunastadshotell.se. Luxurious five-star hotel stuffed full of period fittings from the early 1900s when the hotel first opened, as well as contemporary Scandinavian design furniture. Useful as an alternative to more mainstream hotels at Arlanda airport, just 10km away. **2590kr**

STF Sigtuna Vandrarhem Manfred Björkquists allé 20C ☏ 08 592 583 00, ⓔ vandrarhem@sigtunafolkhogskola. se. Around sixty or so beds are available at this hostel located inside the town's Folkhögskola. All rooms have private facilities and there are good views out over Lake Mälaren, too. Doubles **680kr**

EATING AND DRINKING

Båthuset Strandpromenaden ☏ 08 592 567 80, ⓦ bathuset.com. Set on a floating pontoon in the harbour, this little wooden restaurant dishes up delicious fish and beef mains for around 200–300kr; the menu changes daily,

though the tasty fish and seafood stew is usually available and excellent. Tues–Sat 5–11pm.
Farbror Blå Storatorget 4 ☎08 592 560 50, ⓦfarbrorbla.com. Located next to the town hall, this place serves excellent Swedish home cooking – mains cost 170–345kr. There's also a popular outdoor terrace where people gather to listen to local bands. Mon–Thurs 11am–11pm,

Fri 11am–1am, Sat noon–1am.
Tant Bruns kaffestuga Laurentii gränd 3, ⓦtantbrun-sigtuna.se. This atmospheric old café specializes in home-made bread and is housed in a seventeenth-century building (the oldest wooden structure in Sigtuna), with outdoor seating in summer in a small flower garden. Mon–Fri 10am–5pm, Sat & Sun 10am–6pm.

2

Nyköping

If you're looking for a taste of provincial Sweden before pushing on further south or, alternatively, to Stockholm Skavsta airport, historic **NYKÖPING**, 100km southwest of Stockholm, is perfect. Indeed, since Ryanair established a base in 2003 at Skavsta (7km northwest of the town), the airport has effectively become Nyköping's lifeblood, supplying a steady flow of arriving and departing Ryanair passengers, despite the fact that flight operations have been scaled back somewhat in recent years. Capital of the surrounding pastoral province of Södermanland, Nyköping's underrated charms include an excellent museum in and around the ruins of its thirteenth-century **castle**, and a thriving harbour – a regular target for the Stockholm yachting set – that bustles with life in summer.

St Nicolai kyrka

Storatorget • Mon–Fri 10am–4pm, Sat & Sun 10am–2pm (try the back door if the front one on the square is locked)

On the main square, Storatorget, opposite the tourist office, stands the vast **St Nicolai kyrka** with its white, vaulted ceiling. The building dates from around 1260, although most of what you see is the result of sixteenth-century refurbishment. The pillars here are adorned with dozens of beautiful, heavily moulded silver candle sconces. It's the Baroque pulpit, though, that's the highlight; crafted in Norrköping in 1748, it was modelled on the one in the Storkyrkan in Stockholm. Outside, standing proudly on a nearby rocky outcrop, is the red 1692 **bell tower**, the only wooden building not destroyed in 1719 when the town was attacked from the sea by invading Russian troops who burnt virtually the entire place to the ground.

Nyköpingshus

King's Tower • Daily 10am–5pm, Wed until 8pm • Free • ⓦsormlandsmuseum.se

From Storatorget, it's just a couple of minutes' wander south, down Slottsgatan with the river to your left, to Kungsgatan. Here you'll see the **King's Tower**, the main part of **Nyköpingshus** castle. A late twelfth-century defensive tower, built to protect the trading port at the estuary of the Nyköping river, it was subsequently converted into a **fortress** by King Magnus Ladulås.

In the sixteenth century, Gustav Vasa fortified the castle with gun towers; his son Karl, who became duke of Södermanland, converted the place into one of Sweden's grandest Renaissance palaces. Devastating fires here in 1665 and 1719 reduced all lesser buildings to ash and gutted the castle. With no money forthcoming from the national coffers, it was never rebuilt; only the King's Tower was saved from demolition and became used as a granary. Today, the riverside tower and the adjoining early eighteenth-century house built for the county governor form a **museum complex**. Wandering through the original gatehouse (*porthuset*) beneath Karl's heraldic shield, you reach the extensively restored King's Tower. On the first floor, a stylish job has been done of rebuilding the graceful archways that lead into the Guard Room. The rest of the museum is fairly uninspiring, the best exhibition being a display of medieval shoes and boots.

ARRIVAL AND DEPARTURE

By plane From Skavsta airport, bus #515 runs to the bus station on Västra Kvarngatan, just 500m south of the train station. It's not possible to buy tickets on the bus with cash, so have your credit card ready.
By train The train station on Järnvägsgatan is a 10min walk

NYKÖPING

west of the centre – first head south along Järnvägsgatan, then east on Repslagaregatan, then south again on Brunnsgatan.
Destinations Stockholm (hourly; 1hr); Norrköping (hourly; 40min).

INFORMATION

Tourist office Rådhuset, Storatorget (mid-June to mid-Aug Mon–Fri 9am–6pm, Sat & Sun 10am–4pm; mid-Aug to mid-June Mon–Fri 9am–5pm; ☎0155 24 82 00,

ⓦnykopingsguiden.se). This central and enthusiastic office is housed in the former town hall building and offers internet access.

ACCOMMODATION

Accommodation in Nyköping is remarkably good value and significantly cheaper than Stockholm. There's a good selection of budget options as well as one or two more upmarket choices, and advance booking is not needed.
Clarion Collection Kompaniet Folkungavägen 1 ☎0155 28 80 20, ⓦchoicehotels.se. Near the harbour and overlooking the river, this huge structure of curving red brick is the most stylish and well-appointed hotel in town. The rooms are airy, neutrally decorated and have wooden floors; free evening buffet included. **1200kr/1400kr**
Connect Skavsta General Schybergs väg 23, Skavsta airport ☎0842 00 3000 ⓦconnecthotels.se. Opposite the terminal building, this modern design hotel has both en-suite doubles and simpler "Quick Sleep" budget rooms with bunk beds and shared facilities for around 250kr or less. Regular buses run into Nyköping and Stockholm from opposite the hotel. Doubles **810kr**
★ **Railway Vandrarhem** Södra Bangårdsgatan ☎070

496 92 00, ⓦrailway.nu. This handy hostel is located at the train station and comprises a number of dorms sleeping a maximum of five, and double rooms. The bus to Skavsta airport leaves from right outside the hostel. Dorms **280kr**, doubles **550kr**
Scandic Stora Brunnsgatan 31 ☎0155 29 35 00, ⓦscandichotels.se. Modern, bright and airy Scandinavian design hotel in the heart of Nyköping. All 98 rooms are tastefully appointed with either wooden or carpeted floors and there's also a steam sauna and jacuzzi available to guests. **970kr/1400kr**

CAMPING
Strandstuvikens Camping Strandstuviken ☎0155 978 10, ⓦstrandstuviken.se. Located in a mature pine forest 9km southeast of Nyköping on the Baltic coast. The campsite also has a number of two-berth cabins available to rent. Open May to mid-Sept. Tents **270kr**, cabins **600kr**

EATING AND DRINKING

Most of Nyköping's eating and drinking options are, unsurprisingly, at the harbour. Outside the summer season, though, the scene moves to the town centre where, curiously for a modestly sized town, there's a good range of choice to suit all pockets.
Hamnmagasinet Skeppsbron 1 ☎0155 26 92 92, ⓦhamnmag.se. A classy, brick-walled establishment that stands out as the leading harbourside restaurant, with a large open-air terrace. Plenty of no-nonsense grilled steaks,

burgers and fish dishes for around 180–250kr. May–Aug Mon–Fri 11am–2pm, 5–9pm, Sat & Sun noon–10pm.
Hellmanska Gården Västra Trädgårdsgatan 24 ☎0155 21 05 25, ⓦhellmanskagarden.se. Set in a converted warehouse from the 1700s, with a lovely summer courtyard centred around a beautiful magnolia tree, this place serves great sandwiches, fruit flans, quiches and light lunches as well as fresh bread from its own bakery. Mon–Fri 8am–6pm, Sat 9am–5pm, Sun 11am–4pm.

THE LAST SUPPER

It was in the King's Tower in Nyköpingshus castle (see page 101) in 1317 that the infamous **Nyköping Banquet** took place: one of King Magnus's three sons, Birger, invited his brothers Erik and Valdemar to celebrate Christmas at Nyköping and provided a grand banquet. Once the meal was complete, and the visiting brothers had retired to bed, Birger had them thrown into the castle's dungeon, threw the key into the river and left them to starve to death. In the nineteenth century, a key was caught by a boy fishing in the river; whether the rusting item he found, now on display in the museum, really is the one last touched by Birger, no one knows.

Oliver Twist Fruängsgatan 28 ☎0155 21 63 05, ⓦolivertwist-nyk.se. Close to the bus station, this popular wood-panelled English pub does a good range in food as well as drink: marinated pork fillet with bacon and mushrooms (205kr), pepper steak (240kr) and flounder with prawn sauce (190kr) are all available. Mon–Thurs 11.30am–11pm, Fri 11.30am–midnight, Sat noon–midnight, Sun noon–10pm.

★**Rökeriet** Östra Skeppbron 7 ☎0155 21 38 38, ⓦrestaurangrokeriet.se. In the red warehouse standing beside the roundabout north of the harbour, this fish smokery and fine restaurant with outside seating is a Nyköping institution and renowned for its excellent menu of salmon, mackerel and Baltic herring from 155kr; the succulent Norwegian salmon marinated in lime juice for 210kr is delicious. May–Aug Mon–Fri 4pm–midnight, Sat & Sun noon–11pm.

Skafferiet Västra Storgatan 29 ☎0155 26 99 50, ⓦmickesskafferi.se. Sophisticated bistro serving well-prepared and creative meals such as handmade ravioli filled with Tuscan duck in truffle butter (110kr) or saddle of venison with creamed gnocchi (265kr). This place is widely regarded as the best restaurant in town – and with justification. Mon–Fri 11am–1.30pm & 6–9pm, Sat noon–10pm.

Voyage Brunnsgatan 31 ☎0155 29 35 00, ⓦrestaurang voyage.se. Attached to the *Scandic* hotel, this wonderful retro place, decorated with black-and-white photos of scenes from Southeast Asia, serves excellent modern Swedish food: lobster soup (130kr), saffron risotto with blue mussels (265kr) and cod fillet in beurre blanc (260kr). Mon–Fri 11.30am–1.30pm & Mon–Sun 7–10pm.

2

Gothenburg

GOTHENBURG'S HARBOUR

Gothenburg

Of all the cities in southern Sweden, the grandest is the western port of Gothenburg. Designed by the Dutch in 1621, the country's second largest city boasts splendid Neoclassical architecture, masses of sculpture-strewn parkland and a welcoming and relaxed spirit. The cityscape of broad avenues, elegant squares, trams and canals is not only one of the prettiest in Sweden, but also the backdrop to Scandinavia's biggest seaport, making the city a truly cosmopolitan destination. There is a certain resentment on the west coast that Stockholm wins out in the national glory stakes, but Gothenburg's easier-going atmosphere – and its closer proximity to western Europe – makes it first choice as a place to live for many Swedes. Talk to any Gothenburger and they will soon disparage the more frenetic lives of the "08-ers" – 08 being the telephone code for Stockholm.

At the heart of the city is the historic **old town**: this is the best place to start your sightseeing, although Gothenburg's attractions are by no means restricted to this area. Tucked between the Göta River to the north and the zigzagging Rosenlundskanalen to the south, the old town's tightly gridded streets are lined with impressive facades, interesting food markets and a couple of worthwhile museums, most notably the **Stadsmuseum** and, up by the harbour, the **Maritiman**, a repository of all things nautical. Just across the canal that skirts the southern edges of the old town is **Trädgårdsföreningen** park, in summer full of colourful flowers and picnicking city-dwellers.

Heading further south into the modern centre, **Avenyn** is Gothenburg's showcase boulevard, alive with flashy restaurants and bars. However, it's the roads off Avenyn that are the area's most interesting, with alternative-style café-bars and some of Gothenburg's best museums, including the **Konstmuseum** (Art Museum) further south on **Götaplatsen**. For family entertainment day or night, the classic **Liseberg Amusement Park**, just southeast of the Avenyn district, has been a meeting place for Gothenburgers since the 1920s.

In Vasastan, a small district to the west of Avenyn, crammed with intricately decorated late nineteenth-century apartment buildings and peppered with appealing little cafés, you'll find the **Röhsska Museum** of applied arts. Vasastan stretches west to **Haga**, the old working-class district, now a haven for the trendy and moneyed. Haga Nygatan, the main thoroughfare, leads on to Linnégatan, the arterial road through **Linné**. Fast establishing itself as the most vibrant part of the city, it's home to the most interesting evening haunts, with new cafés, bars and restaurants opening up alongside long-established antique emporiums and sex shops. Further out, the rolling **Slottskogsparken** park is an alluringly pretty place to sunbathe.

Brief history

Founded on its present site in the seventeenth century by Gustav II Adolf, Gothenburg was the Swedes' fifth attempt to create a centre free from Danish influence. The Danes had enjoyed control of Sweden's west coast since the Middle Ages, and extracted extortionate tolls from all vessels entering the country. Sweden's medieval centre of trade had been 40km further up the Göta River than present-day Gothenburg, but to avoid the tolls it was moved to a site north of the present location. It wasn't until Karl XI chose the island of Hisingen, today the site of the city's northern suburbs, as the location for Sweden's trading nucleus that the settlement was first called Gothenburg.

LILLA BOMMEN

Highlights

❶ Nya Älvsborg Hop on a boat in Lilla Bommen harbour for the fascinating trip across the river to Nya Älvsborg fortress. See page 110

❷ Utkiken For breathtaking views of the city and the Göta River, make straight for the top of the Utkiken tower – and enjoy a coffee whilst up there. See page 110

❸ Stora Saluhallen Grab lunch at *KåGes Horna*, a Gothenburg institution, inside the Stora Saluhallen food hall and pick up a few picnic treats from the well-stocked market stores. See page 113

❹ Avenyn Stroll the length of Gothenburg's main boulevard, buzzing Avenyn, and admire the city from the vantage point of Götaplatsen. See page 113

❺ Fürstenberg galleries, Konstmuseum The highlight of the city's grand Konstmuseum, housing paintings by Sweden's finest nineteenth- and early twentieth-century artists. See page 114

❻ Café life in Haga Sip a coffee at the laid-back cafés in Gothenburg's version of Greenwich Village – perfect for people-watching. See page 116

HIGHLIGHTS ARE MARKED ON THE MAPS ON PAGES 108 AND 112

CENTRAL GOTHENBURG

ACCOMMODATION

Barken Viking	2
Clarion Collection Odin	6
Clarion Post	3
Eggers	11
Elite Plaza	10
First Avalon	5
First G	7
Flora	12
Kviberg's Vandrarhem	1
Royal	8
STF Göteborg City	9
Hotel & Vandrarhem	4
Hotel Vanilla	

EATING

Ahlströms Konditori	1
Bar Centro	4
Brogyllen	6
Café du Nord	9
Köttbullekällaren	11
Da Matteo	3
El Barrio	7
Fröken Olssons Kafé	12
Gabriel	
Himalaya	
Kåces Hörna	
Tranquilo	
Vanilj	

DRINKING, NIGHTLIFE AND LIVE MUSIC

7:an	5
Bishops Arms	3
Gretas	2
Irish Embassy	4
John Scott's Palace	1
Nefertiti	8
Sticky Fingers	7
Trädgår'n	6

HIGHLIGHTS

1 Nya Älvsborg
2 Utkiken
3 Stora Saluhallen

Gothenburg City Airport

Göta River

Docks

Lilla Bommen Harbour

Göteborgsoperan

Maritiman

Gullbergskajen

Nils Ericsons Terminalen

Centralstation

Nordstan Shopping Centre

NORDSTADEN

Kronhusbodarna & Kronhuset

Stadsmuseum

Radhuset

Börshuset

Stora Hamnkanalen

Antikhallarna

Domkyrkan

INOM VALLGRAVEN

Copper Mare

Stora Saluhallen

Palm House

Trädgårdsföreningensparken

Heden Bus Terminal

HEDEN

Kungsparken

Kungsportsavenyn

Rosenlundskanalen

Feskekôrka

SEE "SOUTHERN GOTHENBURG" MAP

0   200 metres

SEE MAIN MAP

Harestad
Stannum
Olofstorp
Lerum
Harryda
Landvetter
Jaxviken
Inseros
Mölnlycke
Källered
Lindome
Torslanda
Nordre Älvs Fjord
Dana Fjord
Gothenburg
Askims Fjord
Fredrikshavn & Kiel

Boats to Älvsborg Fortress

Stenpiren

0   5 kilometres

Over the ensuing centuries, the British, Dutch and German traders who settled here left a rich architectural and cultural legacy. The city is graced with terraces of grand **merchants' houses** featuring carved stone, stucco and painted tiles. The influence of the Orient was also strong, reflecting the all-important trade links between Sweden and the Far East, and is still visible in the chinoiserie detail on many buildings. This trade was monopolized for over eighty years during the nineteenth century by the hugely successful **Swedish East India Company**, whose Gothenburg auction house, selling exotic spices, teas and fine cloths, attracted merchants from all over the world.

The old town and the harbour

The **old town** is divided in two by the **Stora Hamnkanalen**, to the north of which is the **harbour**, where the impressive shipyards make for a dramatic backdrop. The streets south of the canal stretch down to Rosenlundskanalen and the excellent Stora Saluhallen. Straddling the Stora Hamnkanalen is the stately main square, **Gustav Adolfs torg**, a good starting point for sightseeing around the old town; you can easily see the whole area in a day.

3

Gustav Adolfs torg

At the centre of **Gustav Adolfs torg**, a copper statue of Gustav II Adolf points ostentatiously to the spot where he reputedly declared: "Here I will build my city." This isn't the original German-made statue of the city founder however: that one was kidnapped on its way to Sweden and, rather than pay the ransom demanded, the Gothenburgers commissioned a new one.

On the western edge of Gustav Adolfs torg stands the **Rådhuset**, which isn't a town hall as the name suggests, but has housed the criminal law courts since 1673. The dull Neoclassical facade is dramatically improved by an extension designed by the ground-breaking Functionalist architect Gunnar Asplund in 1937.

Nordstan

Norra Hamngatan • Mon–Fri 10am–8pm, Sat & Sun 10am–6pm • Ⓦ nordstan.se

Heading north from Gustav Adolfs torg along Östra Hamngatan, you'll pass Sweden's biggest shopping centre, the amorphous **Nordstan**. Packed with glitzy boutiques and branches of just about every Swedish chain store you choose to mention, it's Gothenburg's most ostentatious show of wealth.

Centralstation

If you have time to spare and haven't yet seen the city's impressive **Centralstation**, take a short detour along Burggrevegatan to Drottningtorget. Dating from 1856, this is the oldest train station in the country and its period facade fronts a grand and marvellously preserved interior – take a look at the wooden beam-ends in the ticket hall, each one carved in the likeness of one of the city-council members of the day.

Lilla Bommen harbour

At the riverside **Lilla Bommen harbour** Gothenburg's industrial decline is juxtaposed with its artistic regeneration to dramatic visual effect. To the west, beyond the harbour, redundant shipyard cranes loom across the sky, making a sombre background to the industrially themed bronze and pink-granite sculptures dotted along the waterfront.

Nya Älvsborg

Boat departures early July–late Aug daily 10am, 12.30 & 2pm • 220kr, includes tour • ⓦ alvsborgsfastning.se

Boats leave from Lilla Bommen for the popular excursion to the island fortress of **Nya Älvsborg**, built in the seventeenth century to defend the harbour and the city; the surviving buildings have been turned into a museum and café. On the half-hour guided tours of the square tower, chapel and prison cells (included in the price of the boat trip) you'll hear about violent confrontations with the Danes, and some of the methods used to keep prisoners from swimming away – check out the set of iron shackles weighing over 36kg.

Utkiken

Lookout Point • Lilla Bommen • June–July daily 11am–4pm; Aug–May Mon–Fri 11am–4pm • 40kr

North along the riverbank is **Utkiken**; designed by the Scottish architect Ralph Erskine (who also designed the Sydney Opera House) in the late 1980s, this 86m-high office building resembles a half-used red lipstick. Its top storey offers panoramic views of Gothenburg and the harbour, and there's a café, too.

Maritiman

Packhusplatsen 12 • April–May & Sept–Oct Sat & Sun 11am–4pm; June–Aug daily 10am–6pm • 140kr (June–Aug) 125kr (rest of season) • ⓦ maritiman.se

Walking west along the quay, it's just a couple of minutes to **Maritiman**, the city's engaging maritime museum, which comprises thirteen boats, including the 1915 lightship, *Fladen*, a submarine and a freighter which once sailed regularly from Gothenburg across the North Sea to the east coast of England, each giving a glimpse of how seamen lived and worked on board. The most impressive ship is a monstrous naval destroyer, *Småland*, which saw active service until 1979. There's a rather good café on another of the ships, the ferry *Dan Broström*, with outdoor seating available on the upper deck.

Stadsmuseum

City Museum • Norra Hamngatan 12 • Tues & Thurs–Sun 10am–5pm, Wed until 8pm • 60kr • ⓦ goteborgsstadsmuseum.se

The **Stadsmuseum** is Gothenburg's biggest museum. It is located in the Ostindiska Huset, which housed the offices, goods store and auction house of the enormously influential **Swedish East India Company**. The firm was set up in the early eighteenth century by two Gothenburg-based industrialists, Colin Campbell and Niklas Sahlgren, who were envious of the major maritime nations. The company were granted the sole Swedish rights to trade with China in 1731, on condition that the bounty – tea, silk, porcelain, spices and arrack (an East Indian schnapps used to make Swedish punch) – had to be sold and auctioned in Gothenburg. The Swedish East India Company went on to monopolize all Swedish trade with the Far East for over eighty years. As a result, Chinese influence pervaded Gothenburg society, and wealthy financiers adorned their homes and gardens with Chinese motifs. By 1813, unrest caused by the French Revolution and competition from British and Dutch tea traders meant that profits slid, and the company lost its monopoly. The headquarters, however, remain an imposing reminder of the power and prestige the company – and Gothenburg – once had.

Alongside the historical background on the Swedish East India Company, the museum also contains exhibits on Gothenburg's Viking past, including the impressive remains of the *Äskekärr* longboat, a trading vessel dating from around 900 which was found 30km up the Göta River from present-day Gothenburg. There's also a breathtaking collection of medieval triptychs from churches across western Sweden, as well as a thorough account of the founding of Gothenburg in 1621 and its development through the centuries.

The quayside

Crossing Stora Hamnkanalen from the Stadsmuseum, you'll come to **Lilla Torget**. In itself, the square is nothing to get excited about, but, having nodded at the statue of Jonas Alströmer – the man who introduced the potato to Sweden in the eighteenth century – continue a couple of minutes' walk west to the quayside, **Stenpiren** (Stone Pier). It was from here that hundreds of emigrants said their last goodbyes before sailing off to a "New Sweden" in the United States, in 1638. The granite **Delaware Monument** marking Swedish emigration was carted off to America from Gothenburg in the early part of the nineteenth century, and it wasn't until 1938 that celebrated sculptor Carl Milles cast a replacement in bronze, which stands here looking out to sea.

Domkyrkan

Cathedral • Kungsgatan 37 • Mon–Fri 8am–6pm, Sat & Sun 10am–4pm

A few blocks south of the canal, and left off Västra Hamngatan, is the Neoclassical **Domkyrkan**, built in 1815 – the two previous cathedrals were destroyed by fires in 1721 and 1802. Four giant sandstone columns stand at the portico, and inside, the altarpiece is a picture of gilded opulence. The plain white walls concentrate the eye on the unusual post-Resurrection cross: devoid of a Jesus, and with his gilded grave clothes strewn around, it summons images of an adolescent's bedroom floor. Another quirky feature is the twin glassed-in verandas that run down either side of the cathedral; looking like glamorous trams with net curtains, they were actually designed for the bishop's private conversations.

3

Brunnsparken

Continuing east past the cathedral and north towards Stora Hamnkanalen, the leafy square known as **Brunnsparken** soon comes into view, with Gustav Adolfs torg just across the canal. The sedate house facing the square is now a snazzy bar called *John Scott's Palace* (see page 123), but in 1752 the building was home to Pontus and Gothilda Fürstenberg, the city's leading arts patrons. They opened up the top floor as an art gallery and later donated their entire collection – the biggest batch of Nordic paintings in the country – to the city's Konstmuseum (see page 113). As a tribute to the Fürstenbergs, the museum subsequently made over its top floor into an exact replica of the original gallery.

Along Rosenlundskanalen

Following the zigzagging **Rosenlundskanalen** that marks the southern perimeter of old Gothenburg – a moat during the days when the city was fortified – makes for a fine twenty-minute stroll, past pretty waterside views and a number of interesting diversions. The stretch along **Stora Nygatan** is the most scenic; to one side are Neoclassical buildings all stuccoed in cinnamon and cream, and to the other is the green expanse of Trädgårdsföreningen park (see below).

Trädgårdsföreningen park

The main entrance is just south of the canal, off Kungsportsavenyn • Park May–Sept daily 7am–8pm; Oct–April daily 7am–6pm • Free • Palmhuset June–Aug daily 10am–8pm; Sept–May daily 10am–4pm.

Well-groomed **Trädgårdsföreningen** park contains a number of attractions, the most impressive of which is the 1878 **Palmhuset** (Palm House); designed as a copy of London's Crystal Palace, and looking like a huge English conservatory, it contains a wealth of very un-Swedish plant life, including tropical, Mediterranean and Asian

5 Liseberg Amusement Park, Universeum & Världskulturmuséet

SOUTHERN GOTHENBURG

HIGHLIGHTS

4 Avenyn
5 Furstenberg galleries, Konstmuseum
6 Café life in Haga

ACCOMMODATION
City	1
Gothia Towers	5
Le Mat B&B	2
Maria Eriksson	6
Masthuggsterrassen	4
Scandic Rubinen	3
Slottsskogen	7

DRINKING, NIGHTLIFE AND LIVE MUSIC
John Scott's	12
Noba	7
Notting Hill Pub	10
Odyssea In Loco	6
Peacock Dinner Club	9
Publik	3
Push	2
Pustervik	8
The Rover	4
Studio HPKSM	11
Valand	5
Yaki-Da	1

EATING
28+		Junggrens Café	10
Bord 27	12	Koka	11
Byns Bistro	14	Kometen	1
Café Santo Domingo	5	Lai Wa	6
Cyrano	9	Linnéterrassen	17
Enoteca del Signore	3	Pinchos	18
Familjen	16	Smaka	4
Hemma Hos	8	Solrosen	7
Husaren	15	Tintin	13
	1		

0   200
metres

flowers. Elsewhere in the park is the **Rosarium**, which, with nearly three thousand varieties of rose, provides a myriad of colours throughout the year; in summer it hosts lunchtime concerts and a special children's theatre (details are available at the tourist office).

Just north of the main entrance to the park, across the canal, is **Kungsportsplatsen**, in the centre of which stands a useful landmark, a sculpture known as the "Copper Mare" – though it's immediately obvious if you look from beneath that this is no mare.

Stora Saluhallen

Kungstorget • Mon–Fri 9am–6pm, Sat 9am–4pm • ⓦ facebook.com/storasaluhallen

Continuing west along Rosenlundskanalen from Kungsportsplatsen, one block in from the canal stands **Stora Saluhallen**, a pretty, barrel-roofed indoor food hall built in the 1880s. Full of atmosphere, and busy with shoppers perusing the forty-odd stalls and shops, it's a great place to browse any variety of mouth-watering delicatessen items such as breads, cheeses, cold meats and fish.

Feskekôrka

Fisktorget • Tues–Fri 10am–6pm, Sat 10am–3pm

Five minutes' walk west of Kungsportsplatsen is Gothenburg's oldest food market, the Neo-Gothic **Feskekôrka**, or "Fish Church", whose strong aromas may well hit you long before you reach the door. Despite its undeniably ecclesiastical appearance, the nearest this 1874 building comes to religion is the devotion shown by the fish-lovers who come to buy their dinner here. Inside, every kind of seafood, from cod to crustaceans, lies in gleaming, pungent silver, pink and black mounds, while in a gallery upstairs there's a tiny but excellent fish restaurant (see page 122).

Avenyn and around

Running all the way from Rosenlundskanalen southeast to Götaplatsen is the wide, cobbled length of Kungsportsavenyn. Known more simply as **Avenyn**, this "avenue" teems with life and is Gothenburg's showiest thoroughfare. The ground floor of almost every grand old nineteenth-century home has been converted into a café, bar or restaurant, which the young and beautiful inhabit while sipping overpriced drinks and posing at tables that, from mid-spring to September, spill out onto the street. Avenyn is arguably one of the best places in the city for people-watching, and no visit to Gothenburg is complete without a stroll down it.

At the southern end of the avenue is **Götaplatsen**, modern Gothenburg's main square, centred on a vast statue of *Poseidon* (see box) and flanked to the east and west by the Stadsteatern (Theatre) and Konserthuset (Concert Hall) respectively, and to the south by the fascinating **Konstmuseum**, which contains a fine collection of international art from various periods.

Konstmuseum

Art Museum • Götaplatsen • Tues & Thurs 11am–6pm, Wed 11am–8pm, Fri–Sun 11am–5pm • 60kr • ⓦ konstmuseum.goteborg.se

Götaplatsen's most impressive attraction is the superb **Konstmuseum**, its massive, symmetrical facade reminiscent of the fascist architecture of 1930s Germany. This is one of the city's finest museums, and it's easy to spend half a day absorbing the diverse and extensive collections, the highlights of which are picked out below. A delightful little park, **Näckrosdammen**, lies just behind the museum; with its late-spring rhododendrons and big, duck-filled pond, it's a lovely place for a stroll.

POSEIDON'S SHRINKING PENIS

In the centre of Götaplatsen stands Carl Milles's **Poseidon** – a giant, nude, bronze bodybuilder with a staggeringly ugly face. The size of the figure's flaccid penis at 22cm caused moral outrage when the sculpture first appeared in 1931, and it was subsequently dramatically reduced to its current, rather pathetic proportions, totally out of keeping with a statue that's 7m high. From the front *Poseidon* appears to be squeezing the living daylights out of a massive fish, but if you climb the steps of the Konserthuset and view the statue sideways-on, it becomes clear that Milles won the battle over *Poseidon*'s manhood to stupendous effect, as the fish jutting out from *Poseidon*'s torso looks a lot like an enormous penis.

Hasselblad Center

ⓦ hasselbladfoundation.org

On the ground floor, to the left of the ticket desk, the **Hasselblad Center** contains excellent exhibitions of contemporary photography. Displays are temporary and aim to showcase the work of internationally renowned photographers as well as that of up-and-coming Nordic artists.

European and Swedish collections

The Konstmuseum's collections of European art date from fifteenth to the seventeenth centuries and fill a total of six rooms. Pride of place is taken by Rembrandt's *Knight with Falcon*, although Rubens is also well represented, with works such as *Adoration of the Magi* on display. Elsewhere, you'll find paintings by the celebrated masters of French Impressionism and artists closely linked to them: Monet, Gauguin, Renoir and Cézanne, for example. Look out, in particular, for Van Gogh's *Olive Grove, Saint Rémy* from 1899 which is widely considered to be one of the artist's most powerful works. Collections of Swedish art are dominated by Alexander Roslin who is represented by a portrait of French aristocrats and a group portrait of the well-to-do Grill family.

Fürstenberg Galleries

Highlight of the museum, and the main reason to visit, are the **Fürstenberg Galleries** on the top floor, which celebrate the work of some of Scandinavia's most prolific and revered early twentieth-century artists; well-known works by Carl Larsson, Anders Zorn and Carl Wilhelmson reflect the seasons and landscapes of the Nordic countries, and evoke a vivid picture of Scandinavian life at that time. Paintings to look out for include Larsson's *Lilla Suzanne*, which touchingly depicts the elated face of a baby and is one of his most realistic works; Anders Zorn's *Bathers*, flushed with a pale pink summer glow and exemplifying the painter's feeling for light and the human form; and the sensitive portraits by Ernst Josephson, most notably his full-length portrait of Carl Skånberg – easily mistaken for the young Winston Churchill. The Danish artist Peter Kroyer's marvellous *Hip Hip Hooray* again plays with light, and a couple of works by Hugo Birger also deserve your attention: one depicts the interior of the original Fürstenberg Gallery, while the massive *Scandinavian Artists' Breakfast in Paris*, dominating an entire wall, puts some faces to the artists' names – a pamphlet in the room will help identify them. Also worth a look is an entire room of Larsson's bright, fantastical wall-sized paintings.

Liseberg and around

Southeast of Avenyn is the **Liseberg Amusement Park**, alive both during the day and at night throughout the summer. In its shadow to the south is one of Gothenburg's most engaging museums, **Universeum**, particularly fascinating for children, while the absorbing **Världskulturmuséet** is just next door.

Liseberg Amusement Park

Örgrytevägen 5 • Openings hours vary every day of every month, look carefully on the website; ⓦ liseberg.se • 110kr; all-day ride pass 355kr (pass and entry combined 485kr), or buy tickets as you go – a coupon costs 20kr and each attraction requires 1–4 coupons

Just a few minutes' walk southeast from Götaplatsen, **Liseberg Amusement Park** is a riot of party lights and bubblegum-pink paintwork. Opened in 1923, this is Scandinavia's largest amusement park, and with its flowers, trees, fountains and clusters of lights, it's great fun for adults as well as children, and leagues away from the neon and plastic mini-cities that constitute so many theme parks around the world. The old and the young dance to live bands most evenings, and although the park is louder and more youth-dominated at night (especially on Saturdays), it's all good-humoured. Pride of place at Liseberg goes to its two roller coasters: Kanonen, which reaches its top speed just two seconds after being fired bullet-like from its start point, before plummeting 24m at a ninety-degree angle; and the equally hair-raising Balder, a wooden construction that's twice been voted the best of its kind in the world – travelling at up to 90km per hour, it includes a seventy-degree drop.

Christmas market

If you're around between mid-November and late December, head for Liseberg's enjoyable **Christmas market**, where stalls selling handicrafts and presents are lit by around three million fairy lights. This being Sweden, the commercialism is remarkably low-key, and the pervasive smell of *glögg* (mulled wine), roasted almonds and freshly made waffles adds to the enjoyment. This is also a good place to sample the traditional Swedish *julbord*, a Christmas **smörgåsbord** full of hams, cheeses and heavenly cakes (booking required for the *julbord*, ☎031 40 02 00).

Universeum

Södra Vägen 50 • Daily 10am–6pm • 275kr mid-June–late Aug • ⓦ universeum.se

Just a few steps from Liseberg, the city's science and environment museum, **Universeum**, is well worth an hour or so of your time. Designed by Gothenburg architect Gert Wingårdh, and contained within a splendidly organic building with soaring glass, wood and concrete walls, it couldn't be more in contrast to the fairy lights and pink paint of the amusement park reflected in its vast windows. Water is a major theme (the complex holds the world's largest recirculating water system, processing three million litres a day), and once inside, you can walk some 3km through various different environments – Swedish mountain streams, rainforest, open ocean complete with sharks and stingrays – all of which feel extremely authentic; expect to emerge dripping. There's also an interactive "explora zone" for kids to discover robots, models and all kinds of technological wizardry, plus plenty of information in English and a **café** with good-value meals and organic coffee.

Världskulturmuséet

Museum of World Culture • Södra Vägen 54 • Tues–Sun 11am–5pm, Wed until 8pm• Free • ⓦ www.varldskulturmuseet.se

Next door to Universeum is the unusually interesting **Världskulturmuséet**. A glass and concrete colossus complete with a four-storey glass atrium, the building has been awarded one of Sweden's most prestigious architectural prizes for its innovative design. Through a series of changing exhibitions, the museum aims to reflect the depth, variety and ever-evolving nature of world culture; past displays have ranged from female sexuality in Russia to the native people who live along the Orinoco, and poverty, war and corruption in Afghanistan.

Vasastan

Having explored the city centre, don't miss the opportunity to wander into the **Vasastan** district, where the streets are lined with fine nineteenth-century and National Romantic architecture, and the cafés are cheaper, more laid-back and much more charismatic than those in the centre. The area also boasts Gothenburg's collection of applied arts, the **Röhsska Museum**, and several fine university buildings.

Vasagatan and Engelbrektsgatan

Along **Vasagatan**, the main street through the district, and parallel **Engelbrektsgatan** to the south, you'll come across solid, stately and rangy buildings that epitomize Gothenburg's nineteenth-century commercial wealth and civic pride. White-stuccoed or red-and-cream brick facades are decorated with elaborate ceramic tiles, intricate stone-and-brick animal carvings, shiny metal cupolas and classical windows. With the detail spread gracefully across these six-storey terraces, the overall effect is of restrained grandeur. Many of the houses also have Continental-style wrought-iron balconies; it's easy to imagine high-society gatherings spilling out into the night on warm summer evenings. In contrast, interspersed among all this nineteenth-century swagger are some perfect examples of early twentieth-century National Romantic architecture, with rough-hewn stone and Art Nouveau swirls in plaster and brickwork; look particularly at the low-numbered buildings along Engelbrektsgatan.

Röhsska Museum

Vasagatan 37–39 • Tues & Wed 11am–6pm, Thurs 11am–8pm, Fri, Sat & Sun 11am–5pm • 60kr • ⓦ designmuseum.se

The excellent **Röhsska Museum** is Sweden's main museum of design, fashion and applied arts and an aesthetic Aladdin's cave, with each floor concentrating on different areas of decorative and functional art, from early-dynasty Chinese ceramics to European arts and crafts from the sixteenth and seventeenth centuries. Most arresting is the first floor, which is devoted to twentieth-century decor and features all manner of recognizable designs for domestic furniture and appliances from the 1910s to the twenty-first century – enough to send anyone over the age of 10 on a giddy nostalgia trip.

Haga

The city's oldest working-class suburb is **Haga**; once so run-down that demolition was on the cards, today it's one of Gothenburg's most enjoyable quarters. The transformation took place in the early 1980s, after someone saw potential in the web of artisans' homes known as "governor's houses", distinctive early nineteenth-century buildings constructed with a stone ground floor and two wooden upper storeys. Haga is now a miniature version of Greenwich Village, with well-off and socially aware 20- and 30-somethings hanging out in the style-conscious cafés and shops along its cobbled streets.

Haga Nygatan

There are a couple of good cafés (see page 121) along Haga's main thoroughfare, **Haga Nygatan**, which is really somewhere to come during the day, when there are tables out on the street and the atmosphere is friendly and villagey – if a little self-consciously fashionable. Apart from the boutiques, which sell things like Art Deco light fittings, calming crystals and nineteenth-century Swedish kitchenware, it's worth noting the intervening apartment buildings; these red-brick edifices were originally almshouses

INSIDE THE KONSTMUSEUM

funded by the Dickson family, the city's British industrialist forefathers who played a big part in the success of the East India Company – Robert Dickson's name is still emblazoned on the facades.

Linné

To the west of Haga, the cosmopolitan district of **Linné** is named after the botanist Carl von Linné, who created the system for classifying plants used the world over (see page 96). To get here, turn south off Haga Nygatan into Landsvägsgatan, which joins up with **Linnégatan** – the main thoroughfare. In recent years, so many stylish cafés and restaurants have sprung up along the main drag that Linné is now considered Gothenburg's "second Avenyn", although without the attitude; the street is lined with Dutch-inspired nineteenth-century architecture, tall and elegant buildings interspersed with steep little side roads. However, it's the main roads leading off Linnégatan, prosaically named First Long Street (Första Långgatan), Second Long Street (Andra) and so on up to Fourth (Fjärde), that give the area its real character; the not-very-long Second and Third streets contain a mix of dark antique stores, basement cafés and sex shops.

On the right as you head up Linnégatan away from Järntorget is the forbidding building at no. 9 (at the corner of Fjärde Långgatan and Linnégatan) where King Oscar II had his private **royal apartment** – and his women. Directly opposite is a modern apartment block that's worth a second glance; it replaced a property whose republican owner so hated both the monarchy and the morals of the king that he had a run of colourful ceramic panels depicting the devil installed, facing the royal apartment. Sadly, the Gothenburg propensity for doing away with its own past meant the "devil building", as it was known, has now been demolished, but two of the grotesque panels have been incorporated into the new apartment block.

Slottsskogsparken

Botanical Gardens Daily 9am–dusk; greenhouses May–Aug daily 10am–5pm, Sept–April 10am–4pm • Gardens voluntary 20kr, greenhouses 20kr • ⓦ gotbot.se • Tram #2 • ⓦ vasttrafik.se

Slottsskogsparken is a huge, tranquil expanse of parkland with farm animals and birdlife, including pink flamingoes in summer. On its south side are the impressive **Botaniska Trädgården**, a vast glasshouse akin to London's Kew Gardens, which, at almost two square kilometres, are the biggest in Europe. The gardens hold some sixteen thousand species of plants; highlights are some of Sweden's biggest orchids, the summer flower plantations and the adjoining arboretum.

ARRIVAL AND DEPARTURE
GOTHENBURG

By plane All flights arrive and depart from Landvetter airport (ⓦ swedavia.se), 25km east of the city. Landvetter is connected to Nils Ericsons Terminalen (see below) by bus (daily every 15–20min; 30min; 95kr).

By train All trains arrive at Centralstation, which forms one side of Drottningtorget.

Destinations Copenhagen via Kastrup airport (hourly; 3hr 30min); Kalmar (4 daily; 4hr); Karlstad (2 hourly; 2hr 30min); Luleå (1 daily; 17hr 30min); Malmö (hourly; 3hr); Örebro (2 hourly; 2hr 50min); Oslo (2 daily; 4hr); Stockholm (hourly; 3hr); Umeå (1 daily; 12hr 30min); Västerås (2 hourly; 3hr 40min).

By bus Long-distance buses use Nils Ericsons Terminalen

which is attached to the train station.

Destinations Copenhagen via Kastrup airport (8 daily; 4hr); Malmö (10 daily; 3hr 30min); Oslo (2 hourly; 3hr 30min); Stockholm (2 hourly; 6hr 30min).

By ferry Stena Line (☎0770 57 57 00, ⓦ stenaline.se) operates ferries from Fredrikshavn in Denmark, which dock just a 20min walk from the city centre, close to the Masthuggstorget tram stop on lines #3, #9 and #11; its services from Kiel in Germany put in close to the arching Älvsborgsbron bridge, a couple of kilometres west of the centre – take lines #3 or #9 into town from Jægerdorffsplatsen.

Destinations Fredrikshavn (4–5 daily; 3hr 15min); Kiel (1 daily; 14hr).

THE GÖTEBORG CITY CARD

The **Göteborg City Card** provides unlimited bus and tram travel within the city; free entry to all the city museums and the Liseberg Amusement Park; free sightseeing boat trips and a whole host of other attractions. It also provides free parking in roadside spaces (but not at privately run or multistorey car parks). Buy the card from the tourist offices or online at ⓦ goteborg.com (375kr for 24hr, 535kr for 48hr, 775kr for 72hr).

INFORMATION

Tourist offices The one handiest for those arriving by train or bus is in Nordstan, the indoor shopping centre near Centralstation (Mon–Fri 10am–8pm, Sat & Sun 10am–6pm). The main office, however, is on the canal front at Kungsportsplatsen 2 (May Mon–Fri 10am–6pm, Sat 10am–3pm; June Mon–Fri 10am–6pm; July to late Aug Mon–Fri 10am–8pm; late Aug to Sept Mon–Fri 10am–6pm; ☎031 368 40 00, ⓦ goteborg.com). Both offices provide information, a room-booking service and the useful *Göteborg City Guide* detailing events, music and nightspots in town.

LGBTQ information RFSL Stora Badhusgatan 6 ☎031 788 25 10, ⓦ rfsl.se/goteborg. This friendly office has the latest information on the city's limited gay scene and will know of any special events taking place, too. It also hosts weekly coffee evenings (Wed 6–8pm).

GETTING AROUND

It's easy to walk to almost anywhere of interest in Gothenburg. The streets are wide and pedestrian-friendly, and the canals and the grid system of avenues make orientation simple.

BY TRAM AND BUS

Both are operated by Västtrafik (☎0771 41 43 00, ⓦ vasttrafik.se/en). A free transport map is available at both tourist offices.

By tram Trams are the most convenient form of public transport: a colour-coded system of tram lines serves the city and its outskirts – you can tell at a glance which line a tram is on, as the route colour will appear on the front. Trams run daily every few minutes from 5am to midnight, with a reduced service running after midnight on Fri and Sat nights.

By bus Gothenburg has a fairly extensive bus network, but pedestrianization in the city centre can lead to some odd and lengthy detours. You shouldn't need to use buses much in the centre.

Tickets The best-value tickets to buy are travel passes; these give unlimited travel for 24hr (95kr) or 72hr (190kr) on trams, buses and ferries within the city. Buy them from the travel information offices at Brunnsparken, Drottningtorget and Nils Ericsonsplatsen, or from Pressbyrån newsagents or 7-Eleven supermarkets. It is not possible to buy individual tickets with cash on board buses and trams.

BY BIKE

The city is one of the best in Europe for cycling: most main roads have cycle lanes, and motorists really do seem to give way to those on two wheels. The tourist offices can provide you with the excellent *cykelkarta*, which clearly shows all the cycle routes throughout the city, and out to the archipelago.

Bike rental You can rent a bike from Cykelkungen at Chalmersgatan 19 (☎031 18 43 00, ⓦ cykelkungen.se; 350kr/day) or, alternatively, the *Slottsskogen* hostel (see page 121).

BY TAXI

Taxis can be summoned by calling Taxi Göteborg on ☎031 65 00 00 or Taxi Kurir on ☎031 27 27 27; you can also pick one up at the rank at Centralstation.

ACCOMMODATION SEE MAPS PAGES 108 AND 112

Gothenburg has plenty of good accommodation to choose from, with no shortage of comfortable **hostels**. You should have little trouble finding accommodation whenever you turn up, though in summer it's a good idea to book ahead if you are on a tighter budget, or if you want to stay in the most popular hostels. There are several **campsites**, though none is very central, the closest being just beyond Liseberg Amusement Park.

HOTELS AND PENSIONS

CENTRAL GOTHENBURG

Barken Viking Gullbergskajen ☎031 63 58 00, ⓦ barken viking.com. Characterful and comfortable hotel set on a grand, four-masted sailing ship – built in Denmark in 1906 – moored by the Opera House. It features cosy rooms full of maritime furnishings and beautiful wood panelling. **1295kr**

★ **Clarion Collection Odin** Odinsgatan 6 ☎031 745 22 00, ✉ cc.odin@choice.se. Unique in Gothenburg, this hotel offers designer studios with kitchenettes rather than regular hotel rooms. The superior rooms boast a fully fitted kitchen, dining area and workspace – a real home from home near the train station. **1225kr/1640kr**

Clarion Post Drottningtorget 10 ☎031 61 90 50 ⓦ clarionpost.se. Gothenburg's grand former central post office has been extended and converted into a stunning design hotel, complete with a swimming pool on the top

3

floor. Rooms contain the latest style-conscious Scandinavian fittings and furnishings. 1480kr/1800kr

★ **Eggers** Drottningtorget ☎031 333 44 40, ⓦhotel eggers.se. Dating from 1820, this place was used for secret wartime discussions between British and Nazi military negotiators; it's also said to be haunted. It has individually furnished bedrooms and many original features including stuccoed ceilings and cut-glass chandeliers. 1520kr/2090kr

Elite Plaza Västra Hamngatan 3 ☎031 720 40 00, ⓦelite.se. The magnificent facade of this opulent hotel, which dates from 1889, hides a stunning blend of contemporary and classic decor, with majestic vaulted ceilings and mosaic floors complemented by striking modern paintings. Worth pushing the boat out for. 1430kr/1880kr

★ **First Avalon** Kungstorget 9 ☎031 751 02 00, ⓦavalonhotel.se. Gothenburg's best design hotel, stuffed full of pop art, mosaic pillars and lime-green and orange drapes – there's even a pool on the roof. Rooms, though stylish to a T, can be a little on the cramped side. 1190kr/1660kr

First G Nils Ericsonsplatsen 4 ☎031 63 72 00, ⓦfirst hotels.se. This hotel, curiously suspended over part of the railway station, is the last word in contemporary Nordic design. The rooms are full of natural fibres and materials, and the predominantly green and brown decor creates a wonderfully calming atmosphere. 1260kr/1800kr

★ **Flora** Grönsakstorget 2 ☎031 13 86 16, ⓦhotelflora. se. Stylish designer rooms with wooden floors, flat-screen TVs and the latest Scandinavian chic at this highly praised family-run hotel. The loft rooms are particularly cosy, featuring velux windows in the roof. 1350kr/1480kr

Royal Drottninggatan 67 ☎031 700 11 70, ⓦhotel-royal.com. The oldest hotel in Gothenburg, dating from 1852, oozes grandeur and charm, from the Art Nouveau marble staircase to the individually decorated rooms. Service is personal and friendly. 1695kr/1895kr

★ **Hotel Vanilla** Kyrkogatan 38 ☎031 711 62 20, ⓦhotelvanilj.se. All 32 rooms in this small and friendly hotel, housed in a former snuff factory from the 1800s, are a delight: contemporary and elegant but with a touch of old-fashioned charm. Not surprisingly, they get snapped up fast. 1210kr

SOUTHERN GOTHENBURG

City Lorensbergsgatan 6 ☎031 708 40 00, ⓦcity hotelgbg.se. This hotel has an excellent location in a street parallel to Avenyn. The rooms are nothing special but they're all perfectly comfortable – bright and airy with high ceilings. Share facilities and you can save a further 200kr. 895kr

Gothia Towers Mässansgata 24 ☎031 750 88 10, ⓦgothiatowers.com. Inside the trio of mirrored towers just opposite Liseberg is a subtle, well-designed, contemporary hotel, with wonderful uninterrupted views over the city from the upper floors. 1440kr/1640kr

Le Mat B&B Kristinelundsgatan 13 ☎031 20 48 00, ⓦlemat.se. An eco-friendly, cooperative hotel with 28 modern rooms sharing facilities, decorated in warm colours of grey and turquoise; locally sourced produce is served for breakfast. The budget rooms cost 100kr less but don't have windows. 650kr/750kr

Maria Eriksson Chalmersgatan 27A ☎031 20 70 30, ⓦhotellmariaeriksson.se. Just ten comfortable rooms decorated in modern Scandinavian style, well positioned on a road running parallel with Avenyn. Rooms with shared facilities cost 100kr less. Breakfast is not included. 1000kr

Scandic Rubinen Kungportsavenyn 24 ☎031 751 54 00, ⓦscandic.se. It's hard to get more central than this hotel, which enjoys a perfect location on Avenyn. The good-sized rooms have wooden floors and are decorated in warm reds, oranges and maroons. Smaller "Cabin" rooms don't have windows, though cost several hundred kronor less than the standard ones. 1170kr/1600kr

HOSTELS

Kvibergs Vandrarhem Lilla Regementsvägen 35 ☎031 43 50 55, ⓦvandrarhem.com; tram #7 or #11 from Centralstation. Just 10min by tram from Centralstation, this hostel offers a little taste of the countryside. No dorm beds, but cosy single and double rooms, which cost a little less Sept–June. Doubles 625kr

Masthuggsterrassen Masthuggsterrassen 10H ☎031 42 48 20, ⓦmastenvandrarhem.se; tram #3, #9 or #11 from Centralstation. Up the steps from Masthuggstorget and a couple of minutes' walk from the terminal for the Stena Line ferry from Denmark, this hostel has decent-sized double rooms and an on-site kitchen for self-catering. Add an extra 195kr for sheet hire and breakfast. Doubles 500kr

THE GOTHENBURG PACKAGE

Summer reductions mean that even the better hotels can prove surprisingly affordable, and most places also take part in the **Gothenburg Package**, a scheme coordinated by the tourist office. This is a real bargain as it offers daily, year-round accommodation in a double room, breakfast and a Göteborg City Card (see page 119), all from 775kr per person per night; there's generally a fifty-percent discount for children. To take advantage of the Gothenburg Package, contact the tourist office (see page 119) or book online at ⓦgoteborg.com.

★**Slottskogen** Vegagatan 21 ☎031 42 65 20, ⓦsov. nu; tram #1 or #2 from Centralstation to Olivedalsgatan. Superbly appointed and well-designed hostel with 165 beds, a TV in every room and washbasin in most. On-site sauna, solarium and billiards available. Dorms 195kr, doubles 540kr

STF Göteborg City Hotell & Vandrarhem Drottninggatan 63 5 ☎031 756 98 00, ✉goteborgcity@ stfturist.se. A massive hostel from STF with over a hundred rooms, in an enviably central location. However, rooms are extremely cramped, and bathrooms (all rooms have private facilities) are inadequately small. Linen and towels are included in the room rate. 1045kr

CAMPING

Cabins are worth considering, especially if there are more than two of you. Facilities are invariably squeaky clean and in good working order – and there's usually a well-equipped kitchen too – but you'll have to pay extra for bedding.

Askim Strand ☎031 400 100, Marholmsvägen 124 ⓦliseberg.se; bus #80 from Nils Ericson terminalen to Askimsbadet, direction Snipen. Set beside sandy beaches 12km from the centre, this campsite also has comfortable two-bed cabins. Open late April–late Aug. Tents 375kr, cabins 1250kr

Timmerbyn Olbergsgatan 9 ☎031 400 100, ⓦliseberg. se; tram #5 from Centralstation to Welandergatan, direction Torp. This site offers two-bed cabins set among forest and lakes 4km from the centre, close to Liseberg Amusement Park. There are huge discounts, around 500kr, outside June–Aug. Cabins 1400kr

EATING

SEE MAPS PAGES 108 AND 112

Gothenburg has a multitude of eating places, catering for every budget and for most tastes; among the best to try are the pan-European restaurants which draw on Swedish staples such as good breads, exceptional herring and salmon and, in summer, glorious soft fruits.

CAFÉS AND KONDITORI

During the past few years, café life has really come into its own in Gothenburg, the profusion of new places throughout the city adding to the more traditional *konditori*. Cafés also offer a wide range of light meals and are fast becoming the best places to go for good food at reasonable prices.

CENTRAL GOTHENBURG

Ahlströms Konditori Korsgatan 2 ☎031 13 48 93, ⓦahlstromskonditori.se. Dating from 1901, this traditional café/bakery is very much of the old school, as are many of its patrons. The original features have been watered down by modernization, but it's still a great place for a coffee. Mon–Fri 7.30am–7pm, Sat 9.30am–5.30pm, Sun 10.30am–4.30pm.

Bar Centro Kyrkogatan 31 ☎031 711 00 27, ⓦbar centro.se. This narrow and compact little café is making a big name for itself in coffee circles – it's widely regarded as serving the best cappuccino in the city. There aren't many tables inside, but in good weather you can sit outside. Mon–Fri 6am–6pm, Sat & Sun 8am–5pm.

Brogyllen Västra Hamngatan 2 ☎031 13 87 13, ⓦbrogyllen.se. High ceilings and chandeliers add an old-world charm to this pleasant *konditori* which is one of the best places in town for watching the world go by – large windows look out on the canal. Mon–Thurs 7am–8pm, Fri 7am–7pm, Sat 8am–5pm, Sun 9am–5pm.

Da Matteo Södra Larmgatan 14 ☎031 380 33 10, ⓦdamatteo.se. In the Victoriapassagen arcade, this homely café is a perfect example of Gothenburg's foray into cool little Italian-style coffee houses. There's a smart brick-walled and tiled interior, plus outdoor seating. Mon–Fri 8.30am–5pm, Sat 9am–6pm, Sun 10am–5pm.

Fröken Olssons Kafé Östra Larmgatan 14 ☎031 13 81 93, ⓦfrokenolsson.se. Ecological coffee, lactose-free drinks, vegetarian and vegan meals are the speciality at this right-on café decked out in orange tiles. Look out also for the truly enormous cakes on silver cake trays. Daily 10am–6pm.

★**Vanilj** Kyrkogatan 38 ☎031 13 40 54, ⓦkafevanilj. se. A light and airy modern café with wooden floors, serving up great *kanelbullar* (cinnamon buns) as well as a wide range of pies, salads and breads. Outdoor seating in summer in the rear courtyard. Mon–Fri 7.30am–7pm, Sat 11am–5pm.

SOUTHERN GOTHENBURG

Café Santo Domingo Andra Långgatan 4 ☎031 18 84 83, ⓦcafesantodomingo.se. Sharing premises with the bohemian Dirty Records (where you can buy secondhand LPs), this popular café only serves fair-trade Dominican Arabica coffee. The staff recommend you drink their coffee without milk to appreciate the true flavour of the beans. Wed–Fri 10am–6pm, Sat 10am–4pm.

Husaren Haga Nygatan 28 ☎031 13 63 78, ⓦcafehusaren.se. *The* place to sample Sweden's famous *kanelbullar* (cinnamon buns) which are served here as big as a dinner plate, costing just 35kr. There's also a good selection of cakes, sandwiches and other light snacks. Mon–Thurs 8am–8pm, Fri-Sun 8am–7pm.

Junggrens Café Avenyn 37 ☎031 16 17 51. This atmospheric and convivial place, with chandeliers and wall-paintings of old Gothenburg, has been here since 1898 and is hard to beat for its prime location at the top of Avenyn. Serves a good-value breakfast daily until 10am (50kr). Mon–Fri 8am–9pm, Sat & Sun 9am–9pm.

Tintin Engelbrektsgatan 22 ☎031 18 07 70, ⓦtintin. coffee. One of the very few cafés in Gothenburg open

3

3

around the clock, this busy place is popular with a younger crowd and dishes up mounds of food and coffee at low prices. Open 24hr.

RESTAURANTS

If you want to avoid paying over the odds, it's generally best to steer clear of Avenyn itself and to eat your main meal at lunchtime, when you can fill up on the *dagens rätt* (set dish of the day) for 85–125kr. Some of the best deals are to be found in the Haga and Linné districts.

CENTRAL GOTHENBURG

Café du Nord Köttbullekällaren Kungstorget 3 ☎ 031 13 37 74, ⓦ cafedunord.se. Come here for the best meatballs in town: four of them with mashed potato and lingonberries costs just 115kr. Also serves tuna or Greek salads and sandwiches from 95kr. Mon–Thurs 8am–9pm, Fri & Sat 8am–10pm, Sun 11am–8pm.

El Barrio Magasinsgatan 8 ☎ 031 13 30 00, ⓦ elbarrio. nu. A colourful and cosy South American streetfood bar. Super tasty food and lovely presentation. A menu will go for 250kr. Mon & Thurs 4–10pm, Tues–Wed & Fri-Sat 4pm–3am.

Gabriel Feskekôrka fish hall, Fisktorget 4 ☎ 031 13 90 51, ⓦ restauranggabriel.se. Excellent upstairs fish restaurant serving up Swedish classics such as gravadlax with dill potatoes (175kr), an open prawn sandwich with mushrooms and mashed potatoes (190kr) and a delicious fish soup à la Gabriel for 175kr. Tues–Thurs 11am–5pm, Fri 11am–6pm, Sat 11am–3pm.

★ **Himalaya** Smedjegatan 1C ☎ 0 31 774 11 45, ⓦ restauranghimalaya.com. The food concepts are based on traditional and exotic Nepalese and South Asian flavours. Two courses cost 249kr and three courses cost 299kr. Mon–Fri 11am–2pm, Mon–Thurs 4–10pm, Fri 4–11pm & Sat 1–11pm, Sun 1–10pm.

KåGes Hörna Stora Saluhallen, Kungstorget ☎ 031 13 04 50, ⓦ kages.se. An atmospheric old diner located inside the Saluhallen and accessed through the door closest to the *Avalon* hotel, serving home-cooked classics such as salmon burgers, meatballs and apple pie at fantastic prices – mains around 80kr. Mon–Fri 11am–5.30pm, Sat 11am–4pm.

★ **Tranquilo** Kungstorget 14 ☎ 031 13 45 55, ⓦ tranquilo.se. Latin American food is the order of the day at this funky restaurant with live DJs playing salsa sounds at weekends. Try the braised pork with artichoke purée (215kr) or the burger with mango (185kr). Mon–Thurs 11.30am–late, Fri 11.30am–3am, Sat noon–3am.

SOUTHERN GOTHENBURG

28+ Götabergsgatan 28 ☎ 031 20 21 61, ⓦ 28plus.se. Very fine French-style gourmet restaurant, whose name refers to the fat percentage of its renowned cheese, also sold in the shop near the entrance. Mains such as the delicious

grilled turbot with pea purée cost around 285kr. Tues–Sat 6pm–late.

Bord 27 Haga Kyrkogatan 14 ☎ 031 10 90 50, ⓦ bord27. se. Gothenburgers seemingly can't get enough of this stylish bistro. There's a frequently changing menu of innovative, modern dishes made with local Swedish ingredients such as kale, celeriac, salmon and venison. Starters cost around 115kr, mains 200kr. Daily 5pm–late.

Byns Bistro Tredje Långgatan 13 ☎ 031 24 20 03, ⓦ bynsbistro.nu. A snug interior complete with armchairs, open fire and bookshelves is the cosy setting for this great restaurant serving Swedish classics such as elk meatballs (170kr), venison burgers (150kr) and fish roe on sourdough bread with dill, red onion and cream (140kr). Mon–Fri 11.30am–2pm & 5pm–midnight, Sat 1pm–midnight.

Cyrano Prinsgatan 7 ☎ 031 14 31 10, ⓦ cyrano.se. A superb Provençal-style bistro serving French classics: escargots (from 95kr), *moules marinières* (135kr) and frogs' legs in Pernod (135kr). A set three-course menu costs 340kr, or there's the choice of a salad, pizza and dessert for 245kr. Mon–Fri 5–11pm, Sat 2–11pm, Sun 2–9pm.

Enoteca del Signore Vasaplatsen 4 ☎ 031 13 06 02, ⓦ signore.nu. This cool, elegant basement restaurant is a good bet for tasty and well-prepared Italian dishes such as a creamy risotto (150kr), tagliatelle with grilled scampi (165kr) or *saltimbocca* (220kr). There's not a pizza in sight. Mon–Thurs 11am–11pm, Fri 11am–midnight, Sat 1pm–1am, Sun 1–9.30pm.

Familjen Arkivgatan 7 ☎ 031 20 79 79, ⓦ restaurang familjen.se. An unpretentious brasserie decked out with black-and-white photographs of Gothenburgers at play, serving delicious, upmarket Swedish food such as blackened hake with Jerusalem artichoke and blue mussel vinaigrette. Mains cost 190–335kr, or there are set menus from 355kr. Daily 5pm–late, closed on Sunday.

Hemma Hos Haga Nygatan 12 ☎ 031 13 40 90, ⓦ hemmahoshaga.se. Very popular though rather cramped restaurant serving Swedish dishes, such as meatballs with lingonberries and pickled cucumber (155kr), a heavenly open prawn sandwich (130kr) and schnitzel with parsley potatoes (200kr). Mon–Thurs 4–11pm, Fri 3pm–late, Sat noon–late, Sun noon–10pm.

Koka Viktoriagatan 12 ☎ 031 701 79 79, ⓦ restaurang koka.se. An excellent choice for modern Swedish food with more than a hint of the sea, served amid airy surrounds of birchwood. Menus consist of a list of ingredients, such as mackerel, lamb, beetroot and strawberries, from which the expert chefs rustle up some really creative gastronomy. A three-course menu goes for 480kr. Mon–Thurs 6pm–late, Fri & Sat 5pm–late.

Kometen Vasagatan 58 ☎ 031 13 79 88, ⓦ restaurang kometen.se. Handily located just off Avenyn, this place has been serving Gothenburgers with good-quality home cooking for over 75 years and is justifiably popular: its

SELF-CATERING

Self-catering in Gothenburg will save you a considerable amount of money over eating regularly in cafés and restaurants. There are several great places to buy good, fresh food, particularly succulent, locally caught fish and seafood. Bustling, historic **Stora Saluhallen** at Kungstorget (Mon–Fri 9am–6pm, Sat 9am–4pm; see page 113) is a delightful sensory experience, with a great choice of meats, fish, fruits, vegetables and a huge range of delectable breads. For excellent fresh fish, **Feskekôrka** at Fisktorget (Tues–Fri 10am–6pm, Sat 10am–3pm; see page 113) is an absolute must. The conveniently located Coop Konsum supermarket at Kungsportsavenyn 26–28 (daily 8am–11pm, Fri until 6pm) sells a wide range of fruits, fish and meats, and also has a good deli counter.

Janssons temptation, Wiener schnitzel and herring are all excellent. Mains cost 225–325kr. Mon–Fri 11.30am–9.30pm, Sat noon–2.30am, Sun 1–8pm.

Lai Wa Storgatan 11 ☎031 711 02 39, ⓦlai-wa.se. Established in 1975, this is the best Chinese in town with dependable mains (125kr) such as beef with bamboo shoots and a good number of vegetarian dishes, including stir-fried vegetables with glass noodles in satay sauce. Mon–Fri 3–10pm, Sat noon–10pm, Sun noon–9pm.

Linnéterrassen Linnégatan 32 ☎031 24 08 90, ⓦlinneterrassen.se. Bar food such as fish and chips (150kr), Caesar salad (179kr) and fish gratin (175kr) served in a beautifully restored house with wall-panelling and chandeliers, or on the open-air terrace. When the weather is good, this is one of the most popular places to eat along Linnégatan. Mon–Thurs 5pm–1am, Fri & Sat 5pm–2am.

★ **Pinchos** Övre Majorsgatan 4 ☎073 522 63 34, ⓦpinchos.se. They serve small dishes from all over the world kitchen. A lovely mix of burgers, dumplings and paella, delicious desserts and colorful cocktails. Of course they also have vegetarian and vegan dishes, non-alcoholic drinks and drinks. Tues–Thurs 4–10pm, Fri & Sat 4–11pm, Sun 3–10pm.

★ **Smaka** Vasaplatsen 3 ☎031 13 22 47, ⓦsmaka.se. This elegant restaurant with a striking blue interior is *the* place to sample moderately priced traditional local fare (mains 150–265kr) such as meatballs with lingonberries or herring with Västerbotten cheese. Daily 5pm–late.

Solrosen Kaponjärgatan 4A ☎031 711 66 97, ⓦrestaurangsolrosen.se. Well-prepared veggie and vegan delights are on offer at the oldest vegetarian restaurant in Gothenburg: the set dish of the day costs 95kr, or 90kr for the vegan option, and the salad buffet is an excellent-value 70kr. Mon–Thurs 11.30am–10.30pm, Fri 11.30am–11.30pm, Sat 1–11.30pm.

DRINKING AND NIGHTLIFE

SEE MAPS PAGES 108 AND 112

There's an excellent choice of places to **drink**, and even the hippest bars often serve food and so have a bit of a restaurant atmosphere. Although it's not uncommon for Gothenburgers to drink themselves to oblivion, the atmosphere around the bars is generally non-aggressive. Gothenburg's main **nightclubs** are mostly clustered in the city centre around Vasagatan, Avenyn and Storgatan.

BARS AND PUBS

We've listed some of the city's most popular pubs and bar-restaurants below. The bar scene along Avenyn notwithstanding, the atmosphere is generally a bit low-key in the city centre at night. Having first sampled the delights of Avenyn, head for the area around Järntorget in Haga where there are great places to drink into the early hours.

CENTRAL GOTHENBURG

7:an Kungstorget 7 ☎031 13 60 79. Pronounced *shoo-ann* and meaning simply "number seven", this is one of the city's better beer halls, located close to Stora Saluhallen. The interior is dark, intimate and old-fashioned in feel – a quintessential Gothenburg experience. Mon–Tues & Sun 11am–11.45pm, Wed–Sat 11am–1am.

Bishops Arms Västra Hamngatan 3 ☎031 720 40 45, ⓦbishopsarms.com. Attached to the glamorous *Elite Plaza* hotel (see page 120), this pub is all faux "olde Englishe" inside, but it's nicely done and a cut above similarly styled places around the country. A wide range of beers is on offer. Mon–Thurs 4pm–midnight, Fri 4pm–2am, Sat noon–2am, Sun 4–11pm.

Gretas Drottninggattan 35 ☎031 13 69 49. The one and only gay nightspot in town: gay bar, restaurant and nightclub rolled into one. It hosts occasional drag shows and other live performances, too. If you're aiming to eat here be sure to book well in advance. Fri & Sat 10pm–5am.

Irish Embassy Östra Hamngatan 50b ☎031 13 90 20, ⓦostrahamngatan.irishembassypub.se. For some time, Swedes have been overtaken with a nostalgia for all things old and Irish (or at least a Swedish interpretation of what's old and Irish), this being the most popular exponent. Mon–Thurs 11.30am–3am, Fri 11.30am–5am, Sat noon–5am, Sun noon–1am.

John Scott's Palace Södra Hamngatan 2 ☎031 80 75 50, ⓦjohnscotts.se/palace. The rather splendid former

3

home of the Fürstenbergs and their art gallery (see page 114) is now part of the *John Scott's* chain of bars taking Gothenburg by storm. The ornate interior coupled with an unbeatably central location close to the Centralstation make this a sound choice for a beer or two. Mon & Tues 11.30am–10pm, Wed & Thurs 11.30am–midnight, Fri 11.30am–3am, Sat noon–3am, Sun noon–7pm.

SOUTHERN GOTHENBURG

John Scott's Linnégatan 38 ☎ 031 12 07 77, ⓦ johnscotts. se/linnegatan. In a handy location at the corner of Djupedalsgatan and Linnégatan, this popular outpost of *John Scott's* bears all the hallmarks of the chain: leather-backed books on the bookshelves, coloured glass lampshades and any number of other faux Britannia flourishes – Gothenburgers love it. Mon–Wed noon–11pm, Thurs noon–midnight, Sat noon–1am, Sun noon–midnight.

Noba Viktoriagatan 1A ☎ 031 13 38 54, ⓦ noba.nu. Perch on the benches made of birch trunks and enjoy a drink or two in this bar which serves a wide range of beer from across the Nordic countries both on tap and bottled. Occasional live music, too. Mon 5pm–late, Tues–Thurs 4pm–1am, Fri & Sat 2pm–3am.

Notting Hill Pub Nordhemsgatan 19A ☎ 031 14 47 87, ⓦ nottinghill.se. English pub in a simple and cozy environment. Gets really busy on warm summer evenings. Mon–Thurs 4pm–1am, Fri 4pm–2am, Sat 1pm–2am Sun 1pm–1am.

Publik Andra Långgatan 20 ☎ 031 14 65 20, ⓦ cafepublik.blogspot.com. On a street filled with bars, *Publik* is without a doubt one of the most popular. The good-value food and beer attracts plenty of locals, so you have a good chance of striking up a conversation with some of the regulars. Mon–Fri 11.30am–1am, Sat 1pm–1am.

The Rover Andra Långgatan 12 ☎ 031 775 04 90, ⓦ therover.se. Fun Anglo-Irish pub selling Boddingtons, with other ales, lagers and cider on tap, plus a wide range of bottled beers. Pork, steaks and fish dishes for around 170kr. Mon–Thurs 4pm–late, Fri 3pm–1am, Sat 2pm–1am, Sun 2pm–late.

CLUBS

Odyssea In Loco Viktoriagatan 2A ☎ 031 13 03 02. A suave spot where confident 20- and 30-somethings enjoy a mellow atmosphere. It's also a popular place to eat before the club opens. Sun–Thurs 3pm–late, Fri & Sat 2pm–3am.

Peacock Dinner Club Avenyn 21 ☎ 031 13 88 55, ⓦ peacockdinnerclub.com. The centrepoint of this elegant dining club is an oval gold bar that's home to the DJ. Sofas are arranged around it in the shape of a peacock's tail feathers – perfect for surveying the scene. Wed & Fri 11pm–3am, Sat 1–5am.

Push Kungsportsavenyn 11, ⓔ info@push.se, ⓦ push. se. Still pulling the crowds, this is the place to come for an irresistible mix of pop, rock and party music. Sat night is busiest when the action spills out from inside Stora Teatern onto the outdoor terrace. Fri 10am–3am, Sat 10pm–4am.

Trädgår'n Nya Allén 11 ☎ 031 10 20 80, ⓦ tradgarn. se. One of the city's liveliest haunts, this hip club offers five bars, a casino, a disco playing house and party favourites and show bands. You can also eat here before heading on to the club. Fri & Sat 10pm–3am.

Valand Vasagatan 41 ☎ 031 18 30 93, ⓦ valand.nu. The oldest of the traditional nightclubs in town, with four bars and two dancefloors playing the latest radio hits as well as classic rock tracks. Always crowded. Fri 10pm–3am, Sat 10pm–5am.

Yaki-Da Storgatan 47, ⓔ info@yaki-da.se, ⓦ yaki-da. se. Currently, the most popular club in Gothenburg. Imagine an ornately decorated mansion rambling over four floors with flourishes of Gothic here and there and you've got the picture. Stuffed full of party people who come here to eat and then party the night away. Wed 8pm–3am, Fri & Sat 8pm–4am.

ENTERTAINMENT

Gothenburg's large student community means there are plenty of local **live bands** which tend to play in a cluster of bars in the city centre. The best nights to catch a live performance are Friday and Saturday. **Classical music** concerts are held regularly in the Konserthuset, Götaplatsen (☎ 031 726 53 00, ⓦ gso.se), and occasionally at Stadsteatern, Götaplatsen (☎ 031 708 71 00, ⓦ stadsteatern.goteborg.se); programme details can be obtained from the tourist office. For **opera**, head to the renowned Göteborgsoperan at Christina Nilssons gata at the harbour (☎ 031 13 13 00, ⓦ opera.se).

LIVE MUSIC VENUES

Nefertiti Hvitfeldtsplatsen 6, ⓔ restaurang@nefetriti. se, ⓦ nefertiti.se. The premier place for jazz in Gothenburg with modern jazz, big-band and folk music as well as reggae, blues and soul. Events are advertised online. Times vary.

Pustervik Järntorgsgatan 12 ☎ 031 13 06 80, ⓦ pusterviksbiljetter.com. A popular bar and club off Järntorget where there's a good chance of live music – everything from up-and-coming new bands to big names. Check the website for the latest events and to buy tickets. Mon–Fri 10am–6pm, Sat 11am–3pm.

Sticky Fingers Kaserntorget 7 ☎ 031 701 07 17; ⓦ stickyfingers.nu. This rock club first opened its doors in the late 1980s and has been supporting local talent ever since, hosting live bands several nights a week. Thurs 8pm–2am, Fri 9pm–3am, Sat 9pm–4am.

Studio HPKSM Storgatan 22 ☎ 0709 56 96 24, ⓦ studiohpksm.se. A restaurant with live jazz music where you can enjoy the music until late. Very nice ambiance, which is worth a visit. Mon–Thurs 11.30am–late, Fri 11.30am–1am, Sat 4pm–1am.

CINEMA

There are plenty of cinemas around the city, and English-language films (which make up the majority of what's shown) are always subtitled in Swedish, never dubbed. The most central complexes are Bio Palatset, Kungstorget 2 (☎031 774 22 90, ⓦsf.se), and Filmstaden Bergakungen, at Skånegatan 16B (☎0771 11 12 13, ⓦsf.se). For a great art-house cinema, check out Hagabio at Linnégatan 21 (☎031 42 88 10, ⓦhagabion.se).

DIRECTORY

Dentist Akuttandvården, Odinsgatan 10 ☎010 441 88 00.
Health care Sahlgrenska Hospital at Per Dubbsgatan (☎031 342 10 00). City Akuten, a private clinic at Nordstadstorget 6 (☎031 10 10 10), has doctors on duty 8am–6pm.
Emergency services Ambulance, police and fire brigade are on ☎112.
Exchange Forex exchange offices at Centralstation, Avenyn 22, Nordstan shopping centre and Kungsportsplatsen. More information at ⓦforex.se.

Left luggage Lockers at Centralstation, basement level.
Pharmacy Götgatan 12, in Nordstan shopping centre (Mon–Thurs 7am–10pm, Fri, Sat & Sun 8am–10pm; ☎0771 40 54 05).
Police Stampgatan 28 ☎077 114 14 00.
Swimming The biggest and best pool is Valhallabadet, Valhallagatan 3 (Mon 6.30am–7pm, Tues & Thurs 7am–7pm, Wed & Fri 6.30am–7pm, Sat 7am–3pm, Sun 11am–3pm; ☎031 368 45 31), next to the Scandinavium sports complex.

3

Around Gothenburg

SMÖGEN

Around Gothenburg

The coastline around Gothenburg is one big playground for the city's inhabitants and should be your first stop when moving on from the city. Remarkably, the Gothenburg archipelago, a vast array of forested islands, rocky bluffs and skerries, scattered off the city's western shore, is still little known by visitors. Gothenburgers, however, rave about it – with good reason – and the archipelago is considerably less expensive to reach than the equivalent in Stockholm.

North of Gothenburg, the rugged and picturesque **Bohuslän coast**, which runs all the way to the Norwegian border, attracts countless tourists each summer, the majority of them Scandinavian and German. The most popular spot is the island town of **Marstrand**, with its impressive fortress and richly ornamental ancient buildings, but there are several other worthwhile attractions further up the coast, not least the buzzing summer destination of **Smögen** and the nearby wildlife park, Nordens Ark.

Northeast of the city, the shores of beautiful **Lake Vänern** make a splendid backdrop for the journey to the lake region's main town, **Karlstad**, a thoroughly likeable place and the perfect jumping-off point for **river-rafting** trips through the rural province of **Värmland**.

4

The Gothenburg archipelago

On a fine day, Gothenburgers make for the **coastal islands**, where bathing in the sea and sun is a real pleasure and it's hard to imagine you're so close to a city; regular boats leave for the archipelago from Saltholmen, at the end of tram line #11.

Saltholmen

Around 5km west of the city centre is **SALTHOLMEN**, at the tip of Gothenburg's most westerly peninsula, the jumping-off point for boats to the islands. Outcrops of smooth rocks provide a multitude of hidden sun-worshipping areas, where **nude bathing** is quite the norm. The zone around to your left, on the south side of the peninsula, has become a recognized gay bathing area. Climbing to Saltholmen's highest point, the views are quite idyllic, with boats flecking the water and the offshore islands stretching out into the distance. There's a delightful little outdoor **café** at Saltholmen too.

Brännö

It's a short hop from Saltholmen to one of the archipelago's most popular destinations, **BRÄNNÖ**, a compact island measuring barely a couple of square kilometres, mainly given over to summerhouses converted from fishermen's shacks, and crowded with Gothenburgers through high season. This pastoral island is known for its strong **folk music** traditions and throughout the summer months, on Thursday evenings, there's dancing and music at the jetty in Husvik at the southern end of the island; it's an easy 1km walk here from the main ferry jetty, Rödsten.

Styrsö

Located in the middle of the archipelago, **STYRSÖ** has just three hamlets (Tången, Bratten and Skäret) where most of its residents live all year. The main settlement,

A BOAT BUS DRIFTING ALONG THE CANAL, KARLSTAD

Highlights

❶ Vrångö Chill undisturbed and work on your overall tan on this idyllic island on the furthest reaches of the Gothenburg archipelago. See page 131

❷ Marstrand Rub shoulders with the summer yachting crowd and watch the sun set over one of western Sweden's most attractive towns. See page 131

❸ Fiskebäckskil This picture-perfect fishing village is just one of the highlights of the appealing Bohuslän coast. See page 133

❹ Karlstad Jump onboard one of the city's *båtbussar* (boat buses) and explore this shimmering lakeside town as it should be seen – from the water. See page 136

❺ Mårbacka Get to know one of the Swedes' most loved writers, Nobel Prize winner Selma Lagerlöf, at her former home in central Värmland. See page 142

❻ Rafting on the Klarälven River, Värmland Build your own raft and glide down one of Sweden's most enchanting rivers. See page 143

HIGHLIGHTS ARE MARKED ON THE MAP ON PAGE 130

AROUND GOTHENBURG

0 kilometres 50

HIGHLIGHTS

1 Vrångö
2 Marstrand
3 Fiskebäckskil
4 Karlstad
5 Mårbacka
6 Rafting on the Klarälven river, Värmland

N

NORWAY

OSLO

Mora
Nusnäs
Rättvik
Lake Siljan
Leksand

Malung

Likenäs
6

Klarälven River

Stöllet

Torsby
Ekshärad
Hagfors

Sunne
5 Mårbacka
Arvika
Filipstad

Halden
Strömstad
Sandefjord & Langesund (Norway)

4 Karlstad
Örebro
Stockholm

Säffle
Hallsberg

DALSLAND
Lake Vänern

Sydkoster
Nordkoster
Ed
Sjötorp
Göta Canal

BOHUS -LÄN
Mellerud
Mariestad
Karlsborg

Nordens Ark
Läckö
Källby Husaby
Smögen
Uddevalla
Lysekil
3
Fiskebäckskil
Vänersborg
ROUTE 44
Lidköping
Skövde

Göta River
Trollhättan Canal
Trollhättan
ROUTE 48
Norrköping

Lake Vättern

VÄSTERGÖTLAND
ÖSTER-GÖTLAND

Marstrand
2
Landvetter
ROUTE 40

Gothenburg Archipelago
Brännö
Asperö
Vargö
Styrsö
Vrångö
Dönsö
1
Borås
Jönköping

Frederikshavn Kiel
Gothenburg
Helsingborg, Malmö & Copenhagen

Bratten, is contained in a series of narrow alleyways, clustered around the church. The main reason to come here is to visit the island's family-friendly beach, **Brattenbadet**, a five-minute walk north of the ferry jetty.

Vrångö

If you're looking for unspoilt nature aplenty, a beguiling shoreline punctuated with skerries and islets and a perfect place to get away from it all, the furthest of the main islands, candle-shaped **VRÅNGÖ**, is sure to please. Its one small village lies on the island's west coast, opposite where the ferry from Saltholmen puts in. From the jetty, turn left for the undulating walking path that leads around the island's southernmost point to the village. On the way you'll pass a perfect lagoon with a great beach and a spit of flat stone forming one side. Beyond here are countless creeks and bays where you can sunbathe naked, should you choose, undisturbed. The path continues north of the village, cutting through a nature reserve, on its way back to the ferry quay on the eastern shore.

ARRIVAL AND INFORMATION   GOTHENBURG ARCHIPELAGO

By boat Ferries run every hour or two from Saltholmen to Brännö (20min), Styrsö (30min) and Vrångö (50min); detailed timetables can be found at ⓦstyrsobolaget.se. Travel cards are valid on board the boats – simply flash your card at the card reader as you board – no extra ticket is needed, and bikes go free.

Useful websites Information for the main islands can be found at ⓦbranno.nu, ⓦstyrso.nu and ⓦvrango.com.

ACCOMMODATION AND EATING

Brännö Värdshus Brännö ⓦbrannovardshus.se. This inn, next door to the *Pensionat Baggen*, has mains at around 185–260kr, or a three-course set menu for 475kr. The salmon marinated in juniper and fennel (200kr) is spectacular. Open for lunch & dinner.

Pensionat Baggen Brännö ☎031 97 38 80, ⓦbrannovardshus.se. Located in the middle of the island (ask for directions), this cosy guesthouse has simple double rooms with shared facilities. 1350kr/1190kr

The Bohuslän coast

A chain of **islands** linked by a thread of bridges and short ferry crossings make up the enchanting region of **Bohuslän** where, despite the summer crowds, it's still easy enough to find a private spot to swim. Sailing is also a popular pastime among the many Swedes who have summer cottages here, and all the way along the coast you'll see yachts gliding through the water.

Marstrand

About 50km northwest of Gothenburg, the island town of **MARSTRAND** buzzes with activity in the summer, as holiday-makers come to sail, bathe or take one of the highly entertaining historical tours around its impressive **castle**, Carlstens fästning. With ornate wooden buildings lining the bustling **harbour**, Marstrand is a delightful place to visit and, as an easy day-trip from Gothenburg, it shouldn't be missed.

Brief history

The town's colourful **history** – as so often in western Sweden – mainly revolves around fish. Founded under Norwegian rule in the thirteenth century, it achieved remarkable prosperity through herring fishing during the following century, when the ruling king, Håkon of Norway, obtained permission from the pope to allow fishing in the town even on holy days. Rich herring pickings, however, eventually led to greed and corruption, and Marstrand became known as the most immoral town in Scandinavia. The murder of a cleric in 1586 was seen as an omen: soon after, the whole town

> ## CHURCHES IN BOHUSLÄN
> One feature of the Bohuslän landscape you can't fail to miss is the large number of **churches**. The region has a long tradition of religious observance, fuelled in the early nineteenth century by the dogmatic Calvinist clergyman Henric Schartau, who believed that closed curtains were a sign of sin within – even today, many island homes still have curtainless windows. The churches, dating from the 1840s up to the early twentieth century, are mostly white, simple affairs, and look like windmills without sails. Once you've seen the inside of one you've mostly seen them all, but the few that are exquisite or unusual have been highlighted in the guide. Each church is usually open between 10am and 3pm, but the clergyman invariably lives next door and will be happy to unlock the building at other times.

burned to the ground and the herring mysteriously disappeared from its waters. The fish – and Marstrand's prosperity – partially returned in the 1770s, but the town fell behind Gothenburg in importance, and by the 1820s, the old herring salting-houses had been converted into bathhouses as Marstrand reinvented itself as a fashionable bathing resort.

St Maria kyrka
Late June–early Aug daily 1–5pm

On leaving the ferry, head up Hospitalsgatan and turn right into Kyrkogatan and after a couple of minutes, you'll arrive at a small square, surrounded by beautiful wooden houses painted in pastel hues; the locals play *boules* here beneath the shade of a huge, ancient beech tree. Across the square is the squat, white **St Maria kyrka**, whose interior is simple and unremarkable. From here, all the streets, lined with wooden villas, climb steeply to the castle.

Carlstens fästning
Kungsgatan • Daily early–mid-June & mid–late Aug 11am–5pm; mid-June–mid-Aug 10.30am–6.30pm; rest of year 11am–2pm • 95kr including guided tour • For English-language tours, book ahead on ☎ 0303 611 67 • ⓦ carlsten.se

Carlstens fästning is an imposing sweep of stone walls solidly wedged into the rough rock above. You could easily spend half a day clambering around the castle walls and down the weather-smoothed rocks to the sea, where there are always plenty of places to bathe in private. Informal **tours** of the castle take 45 minutes, and relate the story of Carlstens' most noted prisoner-resident, **Lasse-Maja**, a thief who got rich by dressing as a woman to seduce and rob wealthy farmers. A sort of Swedish Robin Hood, Maja was known for giving his spoils to the poor. Some tours include climbing the 100m-high towers, built in 1658. The views from the top are stunning, but the steep, spiral climb is quite exhausting.

ARRIVAL AND DEPARTURE · MARSTRAND

By bus and ferry Bus #MarsEx leaves Nils Ericson Terminalen in Gothenburg for Marstrand hourly (from early morning until late evening; 50min), terminating on the island of Koön at the stop for the foot passenger ferry over to Marstrand (every 15min; 2min; 41kr return).

By car Take the E6 north out of Gothenburg, and then Route 168 west, leading right to the ferry stop; cars are not permitted on Marstrand, so you must park at the ferry quay on the island of Koön and travel across to Marstrand as a foot passenger.

INFORMATION

Tourist office Hamngatan 33 (late June–mid-Aug daily 10am–6pm; late Aug daily 11am–5pm; ☎ 0303 600 87, ⓦ marstrand.se). Close to the harbour where the ferry docks.

ACCOMMODATION

Grand Rådhusgatan 2 ☎ 0303 603 22, ⓦ grand marstrand.se. Built in 1892 and the former residence of King Oscar II (who spent summers here in room 24), the *Grand* is a real classic. Expertly refurbished with period

furniture from the early 1900s, this glorious hotel more than lives up to its name. Open weekends only out of the summer season. **2195kr**
Hotel Nautic Långgatan 6 ☎ 0303 610 30, ⓦ nautichotell.

com. Although rooms at this mid-range hotel are rather modest in size and decor, it's the lovely setting, surrounded by water and sailing boats, which is the real attraction. Just 100kr more gets you a room with a balcony. **1790kr**

EATING AND DRINKING

★ Bröderna Arvidssons Fisk Hamngatan by Paradisparken ☎ 0303 600 40, ⓦ facebook.com/br.arvidsons.anno.1942. Those in the market for cheap eats are well catered for at this very good smoked fish stall, which serves fresh fish and seafood plus fish and chips, as well as burgers, sausages and ice cream. Mon–Thurs 10am–9pm, Fri & Sat 10am–late, Sun 10am–5pm.

Lasse-Maja Krog Hamngatan 31 ☎ 0303 611 22, ⓦ lassemajaskrog.se. Named after Marstrand's infamous prisoner (see opposite), this spot is very popular with locals and tourists alike for its wide-ranging meat and fish menu. Fishy main courses cost from 200kr and starters from 150kr; try the stunning tuna carpaccio with avocado, lime and chilli. Daily 12am–late.

Marstrands Wärdshus Hamngatan 23 ☎ 0303 603 69, ⓦ marstrandswardshus.se. This long-established favourite is very popular for its large, sunny quayside terrace with basic wooden tables, where you can eat deliciously fresh seafood such as open prawn sandwiches (200kr) and succulent fish dishes priced daily. Mon–Thurs noon–1am, Fri & Sat noon–2am, Sun noon–midnight.

Tenan Rådhusgatan 2 ☎ 0303 603 22, ⓦ grand marstrand.se/matochdryck.asp. Inside the *Grand* hotel, this charming option has been serving the house speciality of garlic-fried crayfish gratin (295kr) for decades. Otherwise reckon on around 265–355kr for dishes such as baked hake and sirloin steak. Daily 6.30pm–late.

Fiskebäckskil

4

FISKEBÄCKSKIL, 50km north of Marstrand, is one of the most attractive villages along the entire length of the Bohuslän coast. Peppered with imposing old wooden houses perched high up on rocky rises, many with fancily carved porches and intricate glazed verandas, it also boasts several attractions that are well worth exploring.

Carl Wilhelmson's house

Carl Wilhelmsons väg 1 • Open one day a year; contact tourist office in Sotenäs for exact details ☎ 0523 66 55 50 • 60kr

Fiskebäckskil's most famous son is the artist **Carl Wilhelmson** (1866–1928), who was born near the marina. He made his name nationally with his powerful, evocative portraits and landscapes, which beautifully reflect west-coast Swedish life at the end of the nineteenth century. In 1912, he had a strikingly elegant cottage built close to his birthplace, with splendid views over the waters towards Lysekil, its double-height windows letting the famous Nordic light flood in.

The house is open only one day a year to the public. Inside, reproductions of his work line the walls (the originals are mostly in Gothenburg's Konstmuseum or the Nationalmuseum in Stockholm), the subjects often being the scenery just outside these windows.

Fiskebäckskils kyrka

Fiskebäckskil church • Fiskebäckskilsvägen • Openings hours vary.

Not far from Carl Wilhelmson's house, close to the marina, the **Fiskebäckskils kyrka** dates from 1772 and its interior has an opulent yet almost domestic feel. There are chandeliers, gold-plated sconces, etched-glass mirrors with hand-carved wood frames and fresh flowers at the ends of each pew. The luxuriance of the decor is thanks to donations from Bohuslän's richest eighteenth-century landowner, Margaretha Huitfeldt, who also paid for the wrought-iron and sheet-metal spire, crowned with a gold-plated weathercock. The wooden, barrel-vaulted ceiling is worth a glance, too: it's covered in eighteenth-century murals, the oddest aspect of which is the scattering of angels' heads. Outside, in the graveyard close to the main door, is Wilhelmson's rather plain grave, his likeness carved into the granite tombstone. More unusual is the grave in the far corner, where an English officer and a German soldier, who died in the Great North Sea Battle of 1916, were buried together.

ARRIVAL AND DEPARTURE   FISKEBÄCKSKIL

By bus and train From Marstrand, take bus #MarsEx to Kungälvsmotet then bus #841 to Bökenäs skola, where you change again for the #845 to Fiskebäckskil – although this sounds rather complicated, it's actually quite straightforward as the buses connect with each other. The journey is generally possible several times a day but since timings change you should always check ⓦ vasttrafik.se before setting out. From Gothenburg, the easiest way to get here is to first take the train to Uddevalla and then connect onto the #845 bus at the train station.

By car From the E6, the easiest approach is via Herrestad and Route 161 southwest via Bökenäs.

ACCOMMODATION AND EATING

Brygghuset Fiskebäckskilsvägen 28 ☎ 0523 222 22, ⓦ brygghusetkrog.se. Located on the marina below the church, this is the place for a really exceptional fish supper: the pan-fried redfish with chorizo and yellow beetroot is sensational. Mains cost 295–320kr. Fri 6pm–late, Sat noon–late, Sun noon–5pm.

Gullmarsstrand Strandvägen 2 ☎ 0523 66 77 88, ⓦ gullmarsstrand.se. Located right on the water, next to the Lysekil ferry, this fine, stylish hotel, decked out in minimalist Nordic furnishings, has plenty of light, airy rooms looking out over the sea. Its restaurant, *Restaurant G*, is excellent; the menu changes frequently but there's an emphasis on fresh fish and seafood such as redfish and cod. Reckon on around 300kr for a main dish. Daily noon–2pm & 6pm–late. <u>1895kr/2250kr</u>

Lysekil

The largest coastal town in this area is **LYSEKIL**, at the tip of a peninsula with the Gullmarsfjorden twisting to the east and the Skagerrak to the west. While the journey into town by Route 162 does not reveal it as immediately attractive, Lysekil does have plenty to recommend it.

Lysekils kyrka

Övre Kyrkogatan 2 • Daily June–Aug 11am–7pm; Sept–May 11am–4pm

Walk up any set of steps from the waterfront and you'll reach the **Lysekils kyrka**, the town's most imposing landmark and visible for miles around. It's hewn from the surrounding pink granite, with beaten copper doors and windows painted by early twentieth-century artist Albert Eldh.

Havets Hus

Strandvägen 9 • Daily end Aug–Dec 10am–4pm • 140kr • ⓦ havetshus.se

From the quay, it's a five-minute walk through the village to **Havets Hus**, an amazing museum of marine life featuring no fewer than forty aquaria. The chief attraction, though, is an 8m-long underwater tunnel, containing 140,000 litres of saltwater and home to dozens of enormous fish, including sharks, that swim around you. Renovated in 2018.

The beach and the waterfront

From Havets Hus, continue west along the shore and you'll reach the best **beach** in town, **Pinnevik**, in about ten minutes. From here, a walking trail heads west across to the rocky headland, **Stångehuvud**, made of the local pink granite, *Bohusgraniten*, where it's also possible to sunbathe and swim; maps are available at the tourist office.

En route to Havets Hus from the quay, the villas along the main road – **Södra Hamngatan** – with their intricately carved eaves, porticoes and windows, are worth a look, too. Lysekil was a popular bathing resort in the nineteenth century, and these ornate houses are a reminder of the time when the rich and neurotic came to take the waters. The fanciest of the houses belonged to **Carl Curman**, a self-styled health guru (a bronze bust of him stands behind it, at the water's edge). In his day, in the late nineteenth century, Curman managed to convince his patients that sunbathing on the exposed rock was dangerous, persuading them that it was in the interests of their health to pay to use the bathhouse, which he conveniently owned. Today, the classic old bathhouse from 1864, by the marina, is a popular place for segregated **nude bathing** (free).

ARRIVAL AND INFORMATION

LYSEKIL

By bus Express bus #840 comes here from Gothenburg (hourly; 1hr 50min).
By ferry From Fiskebäckskil, an hourly passenger ferry runs all day (15min; 41kr) and sails to Lysekil from Östersidans färjeläge at the end of Kaptensgatan.
By car From Fiskebäckskil drive towards Bökenäs for 10km, then take Route 161 and the regular all-day free car ferry

between Finnsbo and Skår (10min) across to the town. From Gothenburg take the E6 north as far as the Gläborgmotet turnoff, from where Route 162 leads to Lysekil.
Tourist office On the quay at Rosvikstorg 9 (late June to early Aug Mon–Fri 11am–5pm, Sat & Sun 11am–3pm; ☏ 0523 130 50, ⊚ visitlysekil.com).

ACCOMMODATION

Grand Hotel Kungsgatan 36 ☏ 0523 61 10 00, ⊚ grandhotellysekil.se. An attractive place, facing the town's appealing park, this grand old double-fronted hotel dates from 1890 and is full of period charm. It also enjoys an enviable central location, just a stone's throw from the Gullmarsfjorden. 1290kr/1690kr
Strand Vandrarhem Strandvägen 1 ☏ 0523 797 51, ⊚ strandflickorna.se. A rather upmarket hostel pleasingly placed on the waterfront next to Havets Hus. Rooms all

have private facilities, free broadband access and television. Breakfast is not included and you must make up your own bed on arrival. Doubles 875kr
★ **Strandflickornas Havshotell** Turistgatan 13 ☏ 0523 797 50, ⊚ strandflickorna.se. This hotel is set in an archetypal red-and-white house from 1905, with a cosy interior full of period furnishings. Also has two luxury waterfront rooms, built on stilts over the sea, which are perfect for a special occasion (3095kr and 3495kr). 1295kr/1595kr

EATING

Café Kungsgatan Kungsgatan 32 ☏ 040 12 12 14. Located up in the town centre, this is the best option for light meals such as quiche, potato salad with accompaniments, various other salads and a good variety of sandwiches. Also serves an excellent weekday lunch buffet for 90kr. Mon–Fri 8am–6pm, Sat 9am–5pm, Sun 10am–4pm.
Pråmen ☏ 0523 134 52, ⊚ pramen.nu. For a good-value fish supper and a beer, this pontoon restaurant-bar floating in the marina off Södra Hamngatan is a pleasant spot, with

views back towards Fiskebäckskil. Dishes cost 195–245kr; the fish and seafood stew with cod and salmon is especially delicious. Late June–Sept daily noon–late.
Rosvik Rosviksgatan 6 ☏ 0523 100 54, ⊚ restaurangrosvik. se. Set just back from the waterfront, this pleasant restaurant is run by mother and daughters and serves up a good array of frequently changing local produce with an emphasis on freshly caught fish (160–220kr). Mon–Thurs 11.30am–5pm, Fri 11.30am–8pm, Sat noon–8pm, Sun noon–4pm.

Nordens Ark

Åby Säteri 5 • Daily mid-March–mid-June & mid-Aug–Sept 10am–5pm; mid-June–mid-Aug 10am–7pm; Sept–mid-March 10am–4pm • 250kr • ⊚ nordensark.se • From Lysekil, head back along Route 162 and turn left (west)

A twenty-minute drive north from Lysekil is **Nordens Ark**, a wildlife sanctuary on the Åby fjord. Don't be put off by the yeti-sized puffin plonked at the entrance: this non-profit-making place is a wildlife sanctuary for endangered animals, where animal welfare takes priority over human voyeurism. Red pandas, lynxes, snow leopards and arctic foxes are among the rare creatures being bred and reared in a mountainous landscape of dense forest and grassy clearings that's kept as close as possible to the animals' natural habitat. The enclosures are so large, and the paths and bridges across the site so discreet, that it's a good idea to bring a pair of binoculars with you.

En route to the sanctuary from Lysekil you'll pass a couple of notable churches, in particular the one at **Brastad**, an 1870s Gothic building with an oddly haphazard appearance: every farm in the neighbourhood donated a lump of its own granite towards the construction, but none of the bits matched.

Smögen

Fifteen kilometres west of Nordens Ark along the coast, the old fishing village and island of **SMÖGEN** is one of the most picturesque and enjoyable destinations in the whole of Bohuslän. The village is an attractive mix of shops and boutiques in old seafront wooden houses, fronted by a quay running for several hundred metres that's famous across

Sweden and known as the **Smögenbryggan**. Smögen first hit the big time in the late 1960s as tourists began to discover its unassuming charms. Then, during the 1970s, it became the number-one summer destination for Swedish teens and 20-somethings who came here to party all night long in the countless bars that once lined the jetty. Things are quieter now and Smögen, though still busy, is once again regaining its dignity.

When it comes to **beaches**, most people take the boat (every 30min; 10min; 100kr return; ⓦhallofarjan.se) from the harbour to the tiny, low-lying island of **Hållö**, which is also a nature reserve; the smooth, flat rocks that make up the entire island are perfect for sunbathing and swimming.

ARRIVAL AND INFORMATION
SMÖGEN

By bus It's a straightforward journey from Lysekil to Smögen (1hr 15min), involving a change of buses (the #850 from Lysekil, then the #862 from Hallinden to Smögen). From Gothenburg, take bus #841 to Torp Terminalen, where you change for the #860 to Smögen.

By car From Lysekil, you'll have to return on Route 162, then take Route 171, as there is no crossing over Åbyfjorden. Smögen is linked to the mainland and its neighbour, Kungshamn, by bridge. From Gothenburg take the E6 north as far as the Gläborgmotet turnoff, from where Route 162 leads towards Lysekil; at the junction of Routes 162 and 171, take the latter for Smögen.

Tourist office In the ICA car park beside the Smögenbron bridge (late June to mid-Aug Mon–Fri 11am–7pm; ☏ 0523 66 55 50, ⓦvastsverige.com/sotenas).

ACCOMMODATION

Makrillvikens Makrillgatan ☏ 0523 315 65, ⓦmakrillviken.se. Located in a former wooden bathhouse set amid rocky outcrops of granite, this youth hostel has sea views and a sauna right on the waterfront. Another 100kr or so gets private facilities. Doubles **700kr**

Smögens Hafvsbad Hotellgatan 26 ☏ 0523 66 84 50, ⓦsmogenshafvsbad.se. Set in an attractive fin-de-siècle house bordered by granite boulders, this elegant hotel also boasts a spa, a lounge and a good restaurant and bar with superb sea views. **1690kr**

EATING

The Barn Kyrkogatan 11 ☏ 031 352 4949, ⓦsurfersinn.se. Located one street away from the waterfront, this is one of the most popular restaurants in the village – a loud but thoroughly enjoyable place, particularly on a balmy summer evening. It's renowned for its excellent and wide range of burgers and fries (140kr). Tues–Thurs 5–11pm, Fri 11am–midnight, Sat 1pm–midnight, Sun 1–11pm.

The Barn Smögen Sillgatan 10. By far the best café in the village, serving American-style eats, such as breakfast pancakes, bagels, chocolate cupcakes and peanut butter sandwiches, though its speciality is a great variety of milkshakes. Fri 5.30–11pm, Sat 12.30–11pm, Sun noon–4pm.

Lagergrens Madenvägen 12 ☏ 0762115492, ⓦlagergrens.com. Laid-back establishment, good for a drink and simpler mains like Caesar salad, chicken breast or fresh cod; reckon on around 250kr per main dish. June–Aug daily 9am–late.

Värmland

Inland from the Bohuslän coast, the landscape is dominated by the largest lake in Western Europe, **Vänern**. Sitting proudly on the lake's northern shores, the provincial capital of Värmland, **Karlstad**, makes an agreeable destination after seeing the highlights of the Swedish west coast; both Route 45 and the rail network lead here from Gothenburg. The city provides ready access to an extensive area of sweeping forests and fertile farmland, crossed by lazy **rivers** – once used to float timber into Vänern these are now an excellent way of seeing this most peaceful part of western Sweden.

Karlstad

Resting elegantly on the northern shore of Lake Vänern, **KARLSTAD** is named after King Karl IX, who granted the place its town charter in 1584. Since then, the town has been

beset by several disasters: devastating **fires** ripped through the centre in 1616 and 1729, but it was in 1865, when fire broke out in a bakery on the corner of Östra Torggatan and Drottninggatan, that Karlstad suffered its worst calamity; virtually the entire town, including the cathedral, burned to the ground – of the 241 buildings that made up the town, only seven survived. Sweden had not experienced such a catastrophe in living memory, and a national emergency fund was immediately set up to help pay for reconstruction. Building began apace, with an emphasis on wide streets and large open squares to act as firebreaks. The result is an elegant and thoroughly likeable town that's the perfect base from which to tour the surrounding country and lakeside.

Storatorget

It's best to start your wanderings around Karlstad in the large and airy market square, Storatorget. The Neoclassical **Rådhuset**, on the square's western side, was the object of much local admiration upon its completion in 1867, just two years after the great fire; local worthies were particularly pleased with the two stone Värmland eagles that adorn the building's roof, no doubt hoping the birds would help ward off another devastating blaze.

LAKE VÄNERN

Covering a whopping 5600 square kilometres (four times the size of Greater London), **Lake Vänern** totally dominates the map of Sweden, stretching 140km in length from Trollhättan, northeast of Gothenburg, up to Karlstad. Travelling along the lake you could be forgiven for thinking you're on the coast: the endless vistas of water and sky really do resemble those of the sea. Indeed, such is its size that the Swedish Met Office even produces a shipping forecast for the lake.

Vänern was created after the last Ice Age about ten thousand years ago. Very slowly, as the land began to rise following the retreat of the ice, islands formed in the extensive waters that once covered this part of southern Sweden. With further landrise, today's familiar pattern of forest and lake gradually took shape. Consequently, Vänern – and neighbouring Lake Vättern – contain several species of marine life left over from the Ice Age and not normally found in freshwater lakes.

In front of the Rådhuset, the rather austere **Peace Monument**, unveiled in 1955, commemorates the peaceful dissolution of the union between Sweden and Norway in 1905, which was negotiated in the town; when translated, the inscription reads, "feuds feed folk hatred, peace promotes people's understanding."

Svenska Migrationscentret

Swedish Migration Centre • Residenstorget 1 (ring the doorbell to gain entry) • Sept–May Mon–Fri 10am–4pm, Tues until 7pm • 40kr • ⓦ migrationcenter.se

Housed on the ground floor of the elegant Residenset (provincial governor's residence) just west of Storatorget, the **Svenska Migrationscentret** charts Swedish emigration to America, in particular that of the people of Värmland. During the latter half of the nineteenth century, one third of the province's population left for a fresh start in the New World as a result of grinding poverty and poor prospects at home. In addition to the changing exhibitions, there's a research centre with documentation on all those who made the journey.

Domkyrkan

Östra Kyrkogatan 4 • Mid-June–mid-Aug Mon–Fri 9am–7pm, Sat 10am–4pm, Sun 10am–6pm; mid-Aug–mid-June Mon–Wed & Fri 9am–4pm, Thurs, Sat & Sun 9am–7pm

Across Östra Torggatan from Storatorget, the **Domkyrkan** was consecrated in 1730, although only its arches and walls survived the flames of 1865. Its most interesting features are the altar, made from Gotland limestone with a cross of Orrefors crystal, and the font, also crystal.

Östra bron and around

Continuing east along Kungsgatan and over the narrow Pråmkanalen into Hagatorget square, the road swings left and changes its name to Nygatan ahead of the longest arched **stone bridge** in Sweden, **Östra bron**. Completed in 1811, this massive construction is made up of twelve arches and spans 168m across the eastern branch of the Klarälven River. It's claimed the bridge's builder, Anders Jacobsson, threw himself off the bridge and drowned, afraid his life's achievement would collapse; his name is engraved on a memorial stone tablet in the centre of the bridge. On sunny days, the nearby wooded island of **Gubbholmen**, reached by crossing Östra bron and turning right, is a popular place for soaking up the rays and an ideal place for a picnic.

Heading back towards town, retrace your footsteps across the bridge and turn right into Tage Erlandergatan. Carry on until you reach the old bathhouse, **Gamla Badhuset**, on Norra Strandgatan, which functioned as a spa and swimming baths until 1978; the building's exterior is worth a quick glance for its impressive red stonework.

Biskopsgården

At the junction of Norra Strandgatan and Västra Torggatan is the bishop's residence, **Biskopsgården**, dating from 1781 and, as such, one of the handful of buildings in Karlstad not destroyed in the great fire. A two-storey yellow wooden building with a mansard roof, it owes its survival to the massive elm trees on its south side which formed a natural firebreak, and to the sterling fire-fighting efforts of the bishop of the time, which gave rise to the local saying, "the bishop swore and doused the flames whilst the governor wept and prayed." The only other houses that survived are in the Almen district of town, next to the river at Älvgatan; though their facades are all nineteenth century, their oldest parts date from the century before.

Värmlands Museum

Sandgrundsudden • Mon, Tues & Thurs 10am–6pm, Wed & Fri 10am–8pm, Sat & Sun 11am–4pm • 100kr • ⓦ varmlandsmuseum.se

From Biskopsgården, a two-minute stroll north along Västra Torggatan leads to Sandgrundsudden point and the **Värmlands Museum**, a comprehensive account of the province's life and times, with engaging displays devoted to the discovery of iron during the 1500s which helped to secure Värmland's economic lifeline for several centuries. The museum also houses a sizeable collection of local art.

Sandgrund Lars Lerin

Västra Torggatan 28 • Tues–Sun 11am–4pm • 80kr • ⓦ sandgrund.org

Diagonally opposite the Värmlands Museum at the northern end of Västra Torggatan, **Sandgrund Lars Lerin** is an art exhibition dedicated to one of Scandinavia's leading watercolourists, Värmland-born Lars Lerin. The artist's work is characterized by his use of bold mêlées of colour, and includes paintings from his visits to the Arctic and Antarctica as well as countries such as India, Iran, Scotland and Iceland. Look out especially for his painting of the harbourside in the Faroese capital, Tórshavn, which is particularly pleasing. Today, Lerin has returned to his native Värmland and resides in Hammarö, just south of Karlstad, beside the shores of Lake Vänern.

Mariebergsskogen

Treffenbergsvägen • Mariebergsskogen Daily 7am–10pm • Free • Lillskogen Daily 9am–4pm • Free • Naturum Värmland daily 11am–5pm • Free • ⓦ mariebergsskogen.se • Bus #12 or the båtbussen (see box) in summer

Originally based on the Skansen open-air museum in Stockholm, **Mariebergsskogen**, 2km southwest of the centre, was established in 1920 when a number of old wooden buildings from across Värmland, including a smoking house, windmill and storehouse, were relocated here. Today, as well as the original open-air museum, the **Lillskogen** section contains a children's animal park with rabbits, cows, pigs and goats.

It's the **Naturum Värmland** nature centre, built right on the water's edge overlooking Mariebergsviken bay, that really makes a trip here worthwhile. The centre was designed to accentuate the closeness to nature: glass exterior walls offering cinemascopic views out over the surrounding trees and the lake help create the impression that you really are out in the wilds. Aimed predominantly at children, it provides a fascinating insight into local flora and fauna as well as the different landscapes found in the province, from marshland to dense forest. For grown-ups, it's the excellent and informative short film (in Swedish only) about the province's wildlife that's the real highlight.

The beaches

Bus #1 hourly from Storatorget

The Karlstad region is renowned throughout Sweden for its relatively long hours of sunshine, something the locals make the most of during the summer months. The **sandy beach** by the campsites at Bomstad, 7km west of the city along the E18, extends for several kilometres and is known as the Värmland Riviera. It benefits from the sheltered waters of Kattfjorden, one of Vänern's northern bays, and the shallow waters here heat up quickly during the long summer days, making swimming deliciously enjoyable. Adjoining to the east, **Skutberget** offers smooth **rocks** which gently slope down to the lake. There's also an unofficial – though popular – **nudist beach** here, at the western end of the beach by *First Camp Karlstad Skutberget*.

KARLSTAD'S BOAT BUSES

Between June and August every summer, a flotilla of gleaming wooden boat buses – **båtbussar** – ply the waters around Karlstad and make a great way of seeing the city. Though routes vary slightly from year to year, the most popular is the hour-long trip from Residenset, just west of Storatorget, via the Pråmkanalen and the harbour area, to Mariebergsskogen (see opposite). Tickets cost just 26kr (a 24hr ticket costs 75kr) and can be bought on board. Timetables are at ⓦkarlstadsbuss.se.

ARRIVAL AND DEPARTURE

KARLSTAD

By plane bmi Regional operates 1–2 daily flights to Karlstad airport (ⓦksdarprt.se) from Frankfurt, providing direct access to Värmland and avoiding transit via Stockholm Arlanda. Information can be found online at ⓦbmiregional.com; to buy connecting tickets with Lufthansa see ⓦlufthansa.com. In connection with flights, a bus operates to and from Karlstad bus station (77kr single) when booked in advance on ☎0771 32 32 00.

By train From Gothenburg, there are two ways to reach Karlstad: regular direct services run up the western shore, covering the journey in around 2hr 30min; alternatively, a limited service (mid-Aug to mid-June only; operating days vary) runs around the eastern shore via Laxå, taking 3hr. The Värmland capital is also served by international trains between Stockholm and Oslo (it's roughly halfway between the two), as well as the more frequent services to and from Stockholm. The train station is on Hamngatan.

Destinations Gothenburg (2 hourly; 2hr 30min–3hr); Oslo (3 daily; 2hr 20min); Stockholm (2 hourly; 2hr 30min); Sunne (2 hourly; 50min).

By bus The bus station is located at the western end of Drottninggatan.

INFORMATION

Tourist office In the library at Västra Torggatan 26 (Mon–Fri 8am–5pm; ☎054 540 00 00, ⓦvisitkarlstad.se). A good place to pick up general information about the city as well as rafting trips on the Klarälven River (see page 143); it also has timetables for buses throughout Värmland (also available at ⓦvarmlandstrafik.se), to help you plan trips elsewhere in the province.

ACCOMMODATION

SEE MAP PAGE 138

Carlstad City Hostel Järnvägsgatan 8 ☎054 21 65 60, ⓦcarlstadcity.se. Perfectly located just around the corner from the train station, this combined budget hotel and hostel is a real find. Choose a hostel room over a regular double (the only difference is that room decor is simpler; both rooms have private facilities) and save 50kr, another 30kr if you make your own bed. Linen costs 75kr extra. Check-in is 4–8pm. **550kr**

Clarion Collection Drott Järnvägsgatan 1 ☎054 10 10 10, ⓦdrotthotel.se. Just 50m from the train station, this is a smart, elegant hotel dating from 1909 and full of old-fashioned charm, wooden floors and period furniture. The daily evening buffet is free to residents. **990kr/1375kr**

Clarion Plaza Västra Torggatan 2 ☎054 10 02 00, ⓦchoicehotels.se. Large, modern, plush four-star hotel very much with the business traveller in mind; there's modern Nordic decor and a fantastic sauna offering panoramic views over the city. **970kr/1560kr**

★ **Elite Stadshotellet** Kungsgatan 22 ☎054 29 30 00, ⓦwww.elite.se. Built in 1870 and beautifully located next to the river, this is Karlstad's best hotel. Whilst the interior with its sweeping staircases and chandeliers conjures up sumptuous old-style elegance, the rooms are a masterclass in modern Swedish design. **1125kr/1305kr**

Freden Fredsgatan 1A ☎054 21 65 82, ⓦfredenhotel.com. Cheap and cheerful place close to the bus and train stations. Rooms all share facilities, though they do have washbasins. Breakfast is not included in the room rates. Hostel-style double rooms with bunks are also available for 560kr. **650kr/700kr**

Savoy Västra Torggatan 1A ☎054 15 66 40, ⓦwww.savoy-karlstad.se. Modern chain hotel with comfortable rooms featuring wooden floors and light decor. What the rooms lack in character is more than compensated for by the fantastic weekend and summer prices, which make this central hotel a sound choice. **875kr/1250kr**

Scandic Karlstad City Drottninggatan 4 ☎054 770 55 00, ⓦscandichotels.com. One of the most stylish hotels in town, with Nordic minimalist decor and warm wooden floors representing Swedish design at its best. Superior rooms 608–620 have their own balcony and cost around 200kr extra – well worth it. **1005kr/1490kr**

Solsta Drottninggatan 13 ☎054 15 68 45, ⓦsolstahotell.se. A good, central budget option on the city's main shopping street with cable TV and a fridge in all rooms and access to a microwave and kettle for self-catering. **895kr/995kr**

STF Karlstad Vandrarhem Kasernhöjden 19 ☎054 56 68 40, ✉karlstad.vandrarhem@swipnet.se; bus #6. The town's elegant STF youth hostel, with top-quality beds and televisions in all rooms, is set in a grand former military building located 1km from the centre. Dorms **290kr**, doubles **690kr**

CAMPING

First Camp Karlstad Skutberget Skutberget ☏054 53 51 20, ⓦfirstcamp.se/karlstad; bus #1 runs from Storatorget. A 7km drive west out of the town along the E18, located beyond IKEA, beside Lake Vänern. Also has cabins. Open all year. Tents <u>250kr</u>, cabins <u>490kr</u>

Karlstad Swecamp Bomstad-Baden Bomstad-Baden ☏054 53 50 68, ⓦbomstadbaden.se; bus #1 runs from Storatorget. Beautifully situated on the shore of Lake Vänern, with a wide range of cabins. Open all year. Tents <u>320kr</u>, cabins <u>490kr</u>

EATING AND DRINKING

SEE MAP PAGE 138

RESTAURANTS

Brasseriet Kungsgatan 18 ☏054 21 95 95, ⓦbrasseriet-restaurant.business.site. This is the best of the row of restaurants which line the northern side of the main square, Storatorget, with outdoor seating in summer. *Brasseriet* is a chic brasserie with lots of steel decor inside, but also a lovely, cosy terrace. They serve sophisticated dishes such as grilled beef and salad (285kr) and excellent fresh fish (prices vary). All ingredients are locally sourced. Mon 11.30am–2pm & 8pm–1am, Tues–Thurs 11.30am–1am, Fri 11am–2am, Sat noon–2am.

Fontana di Trevi Järnvägsgatan 8 ☏054 21 05 00, ⓦditrevi.se. Karlstad's best Italian restaurant, with suspended brass lanterns and a beamed ceiling that create an intimate and romantic atmosphere. Pizzas cost from 105kr; mains include an excellent breast of chicken stuffed with Parma ham and mozzarella for 185kr. Mon & Tues 11.30am–10pm, Fri 11.30am–11pm, Sat noon–11pm, Sun noon–10pm.

Frost Östra Torggatan ☏054 18 06 40, ⓦrestaurang frost.se. No-nonsense food at no-nonsense prices at this popular brasserie serving up the likes of seafood pasta (190kr), Greek salad with feta (160kr) and a delicious rice noodle salad (170kr). Mon–Thurs 11am–10pm, Fri 11am–midnight, Sat noon–midnight.

Olssons Elektriska Drottninggatan 21 ☏054 15 64 54, ⓦolssonselektriska.se. If there's a prize for style among Karlstad's restaurants, this first-floor place above the main shopping street wins hands down: you're greeted by glass, chrome and white tiles seemingly wherever you look. The tapas (from 145kr per dish) are top notch, too. Mon–Thurs 11.30am–8pm, Fri 11.30am–10pm, Sat noon–10pm.

★ **Tom-Yam** Drottninggatan 35 ☏054 18 51 00, ⓦtomyamkarlstad.se. Authentic Thai food is served up here by a friendly Swedish guy and his Thai wife: chicken dishes (including an exceptional massaman curry) go for 180kr, pork dishes such as a salad with red onion, chilli, lime and Thai basil are 185kr, beef dishes cost 190kr and fish/prawns are 200kr, lunch buffet for only 85kr. Wed & Thurs 11.30am–10pm, Fri 11.30am–11pm, Sat noon–11pm.

BARS AND PUBS

Bishops Arms Kungsgatan 22, ⓦbishopsarms.com/karlstad. Classic British-style pub enjoying a great location overlooking the river, with outdoor seating in summer and a wide range of beers. It's also a popular spot for a bite to eat, serving pub meals such as burgers and steaks. Mon–Thurs 4pm–midnight, Fri & Sat 4pm–1am, Sun 4pm–11pm.

Harry's Kungsgatan 16 ☏054 10 20 20, ⓦharrys.se/restauranger/karlstad. There's a wooden Native American figure to welcome guests, and half-built brick walls and chandeliers at every turn at *Harry's*, one of Karlstad's most popular drinking spots. It also serves a range of burgers and other bar snacks. Mon & Tues 4–10pm, Wed & Thurs 4–11pm, Fri 3pm–2am, Sat noon–2am.

Leprechaun Östra Torggatan 4 ☏054 18 25 50, ⓦtheleprechaun.se. Small and dark, Karlstad's best Irish pub is a firm favourite, particularly for its Irish jam evenings and whiskey-tasting sessions which make use of the pub's impressive array of bottles. Mon & Tues 5–11pm, Wed 5pm–midnight, Thurs 4pm–midnight, Fri 3pm–1am, Sat 2pm–1am.

Selma Lagerlöf's house at Mårbacka

40km north of Karlstad • Early–late June and early–late Aug daily 10am–4pm; late June–early Aug daily 11am–4.30pm • 105kr including guided tour • ⓦ marbacka.com

Selma Lagerlöf (1858–1940) was the first female winner of the Nobel Prize for Literature, in 1909, and is arguably Sweden's best-known author of her generation and familiar to every Swede. Her fantastical prose was seen as a revolt against the social realism of late nineteenth-century writing; commissioned to write a geography book for Swedish children, Lagerlöf came up with *The Wonderful Adventures of Nils*, a saga of myth and legend infused with affection for the Swedish countryside, which became compulsory reading at every school in the country. Lagerlöf never married, but had a long-term relationship with another woman, though this wasn't generally acknowledged until their love letters were published some fifty years after Lagerlöf's death.

RAFTING ON THE KLARÄLVEN RIVER

Between June and August, two companies operate **trips** along the Klarälven River on sixteen-square-metre **timber rafts**, each of which holds two people; book ahead no matter which company you choose. Their prices are roughly the same, but with Vildmark i Värmland you build the raft yourself, supervised by a member of staff, using the 3m-long logs and the rope provided; no other materials are allowed. Once you're under way, you'll find the water flows at around 2km/hr, which gives you time to swim, fish and study the countryside and animals (beavers and elk are plentiful). At night, you sleep in a tent either on the raft (which is moored) or on the riverbank. Each company will give you details of where to meet and assemble when you book; departure points vary depending on the length of the tour – full details are on the websites.

Sverigeflotten Transtrand 22, Branäs ☎ 0706 212191, ⓦ sverigeflotten.com. 1 day 960kr (overnight 1360kr), 2 days 1800kr, 3 days 2500kr, 6 days 3000kr; tents, kitchen equipment and canoes can be hired for an extra charge. Start on Sat & Sun for an additional fee of 500kr.

Vildmark i Värmland Röbjörkeby 7, Torsby ☎ 0560 140 40, ⓦ vildmark.se. 4 days 2750kr, 7 days 3310kr. Rates include tent and canoe; there's an extra charge for kitchen equipment.

Her house at **MÅRBACKA**, complete with portico supporting a wonderfully long balcony, was completely rebuilt after Lagerlöf won the Nobel Prize. Upstairs is her **study**, much as she left it, along with a panelled library and an extensive collection of her work.

ARRIVAL AND DEPARTURE   MÅRBACKA

By train and taxi From Karlstad take the train to Sunne. You can rent a taxi via ⓦ rome2rio.com, at Sunne train station, which will take you the 10km to Mårbacka for around 250kr.
By train and bus Alternatively, from Sunne bus station, bus #215 runs to Mårbacka on Tues and Fri at 1.20pm but

must be prebooked on ☎ 0771 32 32 00. Timetables are at ⓦ varmlandstrafik.se.
By car From Karlstad take Route 62 north towards Ekshärad and then the signed left turn for Mårbacka just before the village of Ransäter.

Northern Värmland: Ekshärad

To explore northern Värmland – home to bears, wolves and lynx – pretty **EKSHÄRAD** makes a perfect base. Whilst here, check out the ornately decorated eighteenth- and nineteenth-century wrought-iron crosses in the church graveyard beside the main crossroad.

Ekshärad is a good spot for getting out onto the **Klarälven River**, a 500km-long waterway that begins over the border in Norway near Lake Femunden, entering Sweden at Långflon in the north of Värmland at slightly over half of its course. The Klarälven was one of the last Swedish rivers where timber was floated downstream to sawmills; the practice only ceased here in 1991.

ARRIVAL AND DEPARTURE   EKSHÄRAD

By bus From Karlstad bus station take bus #600 (Mon–Fri 2 daily, Sat & Sun 1 daily; 1hr 50min; ⓦ varmlandstrafik.se).
By car From Karlstad take Route 62 north.

ACCOMMODATION AND EATING

Byns Camping Ekshärad ☎ 076 8354939, ⓦ byns camping.se. British-run riverside campsite located on the other side of the river from the village centre; take the second right after the bridge. Cabins are available as well as tent sites. Also has kayak rental. Open late May–Aug. Tents 180kr, cabins 325kr
Wärdshuset Pilgrimen Klarälvsvägen 35 ☎ 0563 405

90, ⓦ wardshusetpilgrimen.com. Accommodation at this pleasant inn is located at the rear of the main building, with dorm beds as well as simple double rooms. The restaurant in the main building serves a range of meat and fish dishes for around 150kr, and has a weekday lunch buffet between noon and 3pm. Daily noon–10pm. Dorms 250kr, doubles 300kr

The southwest

ALES STENAR

5 The southwest

The southwestern provinces of Halland and Skåne were on the frontiers
of Swedish–Danish conflicts for more than three hundred years. In the
fourteenth to seventeenth centuries, the flatlands and fishing ports
south of Gothenburg were constantly traded between the two countries,
and the presence of several fortresses still bears witness to the area's
status as a buffer in medieval times. Today, for the visitor, the southwest
is one of Sweden's most appealing regions, known for its gently rolling
landscapes and laid-back coastal towns. The attractive coastline south of
Varberg is characterized by seemingly endless wide, sandy bays backed
by gently shelving beaches, which makes it a popular destination for
holidaying Swedes.

Halland, a finger of land facing Denmark, has a coastline of smooth, sandy beaches and
bare, granite outcrops, punctuated by a number of small, distinctive towns. The most
charismatic of these is the old bathing resort of **Varberg**, dominated by its tremendous
thirteenth-century fortress; also notable is the small, beautifully intact medieval core
of **Falkenberg**, while the regional capital, **Halmstad**, is popular for its extensive beaches
and nightlife.

Further south, in the ancient province of **Skåne**, the coastline softens into curving
beaches backed by gently undulating fields. This was one of the first parts of the
country to be settled, and the scene of some of the bloodiest battles during the
medieval conflict with Denmark. Although Skåne was finally ceded to Sweden in the
late seventeenth century, Danish influence died hard and is still evident in the thick
Skåne accent – often incomprehensible to other Swedes and the butt of many a joke –
and in the province's architecture. Today Skåne is known as the breadbasket of Sweden
and its landscapes are those of slabs of yellow rape, crimson poppies and lush green
fields contrasting with charming white churches and black windmills.

In the north of the province, **Båstad** is renowned for glamorous living through
its close links to the country's tennis elite. One of Sweden's best areas for **walking**
and **cycling**, the **Bjäre peninsula** lies to the west of Båstad and comprises forested
hill ranges, spectacular rock formations and dramatic cliffs. To the south, both
Helsingborg, with its laid-back, cosmopolitan atmosphere, and bustling **Malmö**,
Sweden's third city, have undergone some dramatic changes in recent years:
Helsingborg's harbour has been transformed by an influx of stylish bars, while Malmö
has seen the most significant development in recent Swedish history – the completion
of the 16km-long **bridge** linking the city to Copenhagen, and thus Sweden to the rest
of Europe via the Öresund Strait.

Just north of Malmö, the university town of **Lund**, with its wealth of classic
architecture, has a distinctive bohemian atmosphere that contrasts with Malmö's
more down-to-earth heritage, whilst east from Malmö, you'll encounter the pretty
medieval town of **Ystad** on the south coast, and then the splendid countryside
of **Österlen**. Here, pastoral scenery is studded with Viking monuments –
such as the "Swedish Stonehenge" at **Ales Stenar** – and the southwest's most
alluring beaches.

This is one of the easiest regions of Sweden to **get around**; trains run to all the main
towns, and services are frequent; we've given details under each town account. The west
coast can be busy in the Swedish holiday season of mid-June to mid-August, so it pays
to book **accommodation** well in advance.

Highlights

❶ Varberg Fästning Stay in one of the old prison cells in the splendid youth hostel set within the fortress, which dominates the landscape of the west coast. See page 148

❷ Hallands Väderö A boat trip to this unspoilt island off the Bjäre peninsula offers a chance to commune with nature – and spot seals. See page 160

❸ Helsingborg Do as the locals do and ride the boat to-and-fro to Denmark as many times as you like and enjoy a delicious lunch or drink onboard at the same time. See page 161

❹ Domkyrkan, Lund Beneath the finest Romanesque cathedral in Northern Europe lies the eerie crypt where Finn the Giant is said to have been turned to stone. See page 166

❺ Lilla torg, Malmö This beautiful cobbled square in the city centre is a fine place to down a beer or two and rest your feet and mind. See page 174

❻ Sandhammaren beach, Skåne Visit the miles of seamless, fine sands beneath the hot skies of Sweden's southern coast. See page 186

HIGHLIGHTS ARE MARKED ON THE MAP ON PAGE 148

5 Varberg

More atmospheric than any other town in Halland, the fashionable little nineteenth-century bathing resort of **VARBERG** boasts surprisingly varied sights – its imposing fortress the most striking – a laid-back atmosphere and plenty of good places to eat. The rocky coastline becomes sandier heading south, and there are plenty of opportunities for bathing and windsurfing. All of Varberg's sights are concentrated along or near the seafront, although in summer the main square, Stortorget, throngs with **markets** and pavement cafés.

Varbergs Fästning

Varberg fortress • Jan 1st–May 31st: Tues–Thurs 10am–4pm; June 1st–June 30th: Mon–Fri 10am–4pm; July–Aug 11th: Daily 10am–6pm; Aug 13th–Dec 30th: Wed–Fri 10am–4pm; all year Sat–Sun and public holidays noon–4pm • Guided tours in English late June–mid-Aug daily 11am–4pm on the hour • Fortress 100kr including guided tour, museum 100kr, combined ticket 180kr • ⓦ museumhalland.se

The thirteenth-century moated **fortress**, set on a rocky promontory, is Varberg's most prominent attraction. It was home to the Swedish king Magnus Eriksson, who signed important peace treaties with Denmark here in 1343, aimed at preventing further incursions into Swedish territory. The great bastions were added for protection by the

VARBERG'S NUDIST BEACHES

In keeping with Varberg's long tradition as a bathing resort, the town has three **separate-sex nudist beaches**, barely a ten-minute walk from the town centre. Take the signed Strandpromenaden footpath along the shore to reach the first of them: **Skarpe Nord** for women only; next comes another women-only beach, the coarsely named **Kärringhålan**, or "Old Crone's Gap"; then, five minutes beyond here, **Goda Hopp** ("High Hopes") is the men's nudist beach. All beaches consist of smooth rocks and patches of grass rather than sand, and steps lead into the sea for easy swimming.

Danish king Christian IV in the seventeenth century; ironically, they were completed just in time for him to see the fortress fall permanently to Sweden in 1645.

The entrance is on the fortress's seaward side, either through the great archways towards the central courtyard or by a side route. **Tours** in English will take you into the dungeons and among the impressive cocoa-coloured buildings that make up the inner courtyard, and you can even stay in a private **youth hostel** in the fortress, which has been carefully preserved to retain most of its original features (see page 150).

The museum

It's the fortress's **museum** that deserves most of your attention. The most unnerving exhibit is the **Bocksten Man**, a murder victim who was garrotted, drowned, impaled (three stakes were thrust through his body, in the belief this would stop his spirit seeking out his murderers) and thrown into a local bog around 1350, where he remained until 1936 when a farmer dug him up while planting crops. His entire garb preserved by the acidity of the bog, the Bocksten Man sports the Western world's most complete medieval costume, including a cloak, a hood, shoes and stockings. In addition to the skeleton, an unnerving Madame Tussaud-like figure with thick, ringleted blond hair now forms the centrepiece of the exhibition and provides a truly arresting idea of what the Bocksten Man really looked like. An engaging film with English subtitles runs through the carbon-14 dating procedure used to establish the man's age.

Elsewhere in the museum check out the sensitive work of Richard Bergh, Nils Kreuger and Karl Nordström, the so-called **Varberg School**. These three artists linked up in the last years of the nineteenth century and developed a plein-air style that reflected the moods and atmosphere of Halland and Varberg in particular.

The prison

Overlooking the sea, and painted custard and cream, the 1850 **fortress prison** seems like a soft option next to the looming fortress in whose shadow it lies. The first Swedish prison built after the American practice of having cells for individual inmates was begun, it housed lifers until 1931, when the last one ended his days here.

Kallbadhuset

Cold-water Bathhouse • Otto Torells gata 7 • Wed 1–8pm, Sat & Sun 9am–5pm • 70kr • ⓦ kallbadhuset.se

A couple of fine remnants from Varberg's time as a spa resort lie within a minute of the fortress. Just to the north, overlooking the harbour, is the splendid 1903-built **Kallbadhuset**. Beautifully renovated to its original splendour, this dainty bathhouse has single-sex nude bathing areas and is topped at each corner by Moorish cupolas. After bathing here, upper-class ladies would take their repose in the grand **Societetshuset**, a wedding-dress-like confection of cream-and-green carved wood, set in its own small park on the side of the fortress facing the town.

5

SURFING IN VARBERG

From **Apelviken bay**, 2km south of the centre along the Strandpromenaden footpath, it's easy to go wind-, kite- and wave **surfing**. Surfers Paradise at Södergatan 22 (☎ 0340 67 70 55, ⓦ surfers.se) rents out all sorts of boards and equipment to get you out onto the water. They're open from June to Aug (Mon–Fri 1–6pm, Sat 10am–2pm, Sun noon–4pm). There's also a good sandy beach at Apelviken for easy access to the sea.

ARRIVAL AND DEPARTURE   VARBERG

By train Regular trains run up and down the coast between Gothenburg and Copenhagen, all calling at Varberg. From the train station, turn right down Vallgatan, and you'll find the town centre off to the left and the fortress to the right.
Destinations Copenhagen (hourly; 3hr); Gothenburg (hourly; 40min); Malmö (hourly; 2hr 15min).

By ferry Varberg is a handy entry point to southern Sweden: a twice-daily Stena Line ferry sails between here and Grenå in Denmark (4hr).

INFORMATION

Tourist office Västra Vallgatan 39 (May 7th–31st: Tues–Fri noon–5pm, Sat 10am–2pm; June 1st–20th: Mon–Fri 10am–5pm, Sat 10am–2pm; June 24th–Aug 4th: Mon–Fri 10am–6pm, Sat 10am–3pm, Sun 11am–3pm; Aug 5th–Aug 31st: Mon–Fri 10am–5pm, Sat 10am–2pm; Sept 1st–15th: Tues–Fri noon–5pm, Sat 10am–2pm; Sept 16th–May closed; ☎ 0340 868 00, ⓦ visitvarberg.se). This office, just off the main square, has free town maps and internet access.

ACCOMMODATION

★ **Best Western Varberg Stadshotell** Kungsgatan 24–26 ☎ 0340 69 01 00, ⓦ varbergsstadshotell.com. Top-quality luxury rooms at this central hotel in the main square. However, it's the beautifully appointed Asian-style spa on the top floor with saunas and vitality pool for water massage that makes a stay here worthwhile. 1495kr/1695kr

Clarion Collection Fregatten Hamnplan ☎ 0340 67 70 00, ⓦ nordicchoicehotels.se. Varberg's twin-turreted former cold-storage warehouse has been converted into a swanky hotel overlooking the harbour with well-appointed, modern rooms. An evening buffet is included in the room rate. 1500kr/1730kr

Gästis Borgmästaregatan 1 ☎ 0340 180 50, ⓦ hotell gastis.nu. The rooms at Varberg's oldest hotel, dating from 1786, are located in three separate buildings and are individually decorated, mixing old and new styles. There's a well-appointed spa with a steam bath and cold plunge pool, too. 1450kr

Havanna Krabbes väg 4 ☎ 0340 100 50, ⓦ hotel lhavanna.se. It may sound odd, but this hotel is an attempt to create something of the atmosphere of Cuba in Varberg. It is stuffed full of Cuban posters, paintings and curios, and owner Lasse Diding has done a commendable job, though the piped Latin salsa music is likely to pale if you stay several nights. All rooms, though on the small side, have balconies facing west. 1570kr/1945kr

Okéns Bed & Breakfast Västra Vallgatan 25 ☎ 0340 808 15, ⓦ okens.se. A good-value, family-run establishment with sixteen individually decorated, homely rooms, some with four-poster beds. After leaving Florida, the owners wanted to create a hotel with old-world charm – they have succeeded. 1325kr/1375kr

Varbergs Fästning Off Strandgatan ☎ 0340 868 28, ⓦ fastningensvandrarhem.se. Sleep in the original cells of the former fortress prison, complete with spyhole in the door, though only nos. 7, 13 & 19 have windows. Regular doubles are also available next door. Dorms 295kr, doubles 590kr

CAMPING

Apelviken Sanatorievägen 4 ☎ 0340 64 13 00, ⓦ apelviken.se. Varberg's main campsite enjoys a perfect location looking out over the sea and is an easy 2km walk south of the fortress along Strandpromenaden. It also has cabins for rent. Tents 180kr, cabins 500kr

EATING AND DRINKING

There are plenty of good places to **eat** in Varberg, mostly along Kungsgatan, which runs north of the main square. It's a good idea to book a table since the town is a popular holiday spot in the summer.

Café Mignon Drottninggatan 23, ⓦ cafemignon.se. This delightful café is located in Varberg's former pharmacy and boasts an ornately decorated glass ceiling. A good choice of sandwiches and cakes, including home-baked scones. Also serves a daily breakfast (from 85kr). Mon–Fri 7am–8pm, Sat 7am–6pm, Sun 9am–6pm.

★ **Grappa** Brunnsparken ☎ 0340 179 20, ⓦ grappa restaurang.se. This intimate, candlelit restaurant is the place to come for Mediterranean food in Varberg: the entrecôte with ragout, broccoli and chilli mayonnaise (335kr) and the cornfed chicken with mushrooms in a cream sauce (290kr) are both excellent. Mon–Thurs 4pm–late, Fri & Sat 4pm–3am.

Harry's Kungsgatan 18 ⓦharrys.se/restauranger/ varberg. The most popular place to drink in town, with a large open-air terrace, live music in summer and regular happy hours. There's also a choice of burgers and other light meals. Mon–Thurs 5pm–late, Fri 3pm–3am, Sat 11.30am–3am, Sun noon–9pm.

Invito Norrgatan 13 ☎0340 892 88, ⓦinvitovarberg.se. This restaurant serves top notch Italian lunch and dinner. The great Italian ambiance and the delicious pizzas (129kr) make this place popular among the locals. Mon–Thurs 11.30am– 10pm, Fri & Sat 11.30am–11pm, Sun noon–9pm.

Restaurang Stadt Kungsgatan 24–26 ☎0340 69 01 00, ⓦvarbergsstadshotell.com/restaurang. Top-notch restaurant inside the *Stadshotell* with chandeliers and marble pillars: the food is equally impressive, with a choice of modern Swedish classics such as Arctic char, sirloin steak and grilled scallops. Mains 230–340kr. Mon–Fri 11.30am– 1.30pm & 7–10pm, Sat 7–10pm.

Zorba Västra Vallgatan 37 ☎0340 13 22 0, ⓦzorba-varberg.se. Close to the tourist office on Varberg's main road, this Greek restaurant is worth seeking out for its delicious Hellenic specialities from 170kr, though the interior furniture is uninspiringly flat-pack. Wed–Fri 5pm– late, Sat & Sun 1pm–late.

Falkenberg

It's a fifteen-minute train ride south from Varberg to the decidedly likeable medieval town of **FALKENBERG** (falcons were once used for hunting here, hence the name), with some lively museums and a gloriously long beach. It's a well-preserved little town that really comes alive in July and Aug, when most of the tourists arrive.

Falkenberg has a long-standing reputation as a centre for **fly-fishing** on the Ätran River. A succession of wealthy **English gentlemen** came here throughout the nineteenth century; one such devotee, London lawyer William Wilkinson, went so far as to write a book about the experience, *Days In Falkenberg* (1894). In it, he described the place where the well-to-do visitors stayed as "an ancient inn with a beautiful garden leading down to the river". This building, one of the few here to have escaped the dozen or so town fires which devastated the town over the centuries (most recently in the 1840s), now houses *Annas Bakgård*, the best café in town (see page 153).

The upper-class Englishmen brought considerable wealth with them, and had a tremendous influence on the town. Predictably enough, they made no attempt to adapt to local culture: Falkenbergers had to learn English, and throughout the latter half of the nineteenth century, baby boys here were named Charles instead of the Swedish Karl, while the most popular girl's name was Frances, after Wilkinson's daughter. English influence can be seen even today: near the post office there is a British telephone box donated by Oswaldtwistle in Lancashire.

St Laurentii kyrka

Storgatan 50 • Mon–Fri 10am–6pm

The **old town**, to the west of the curving river, comprises a dense network of low, wooden cottages and cobbled lanes. Nestling among them is the fine twelfth-century **St**

SCULPTURES IN FALKENBERG

Falkenberg is full of quirky **sculptures** that make for amusing viewing. Right outside Falkenberg Museum at Skepparestätet 2 you'll find a diverting piece called *Wall*, which you may not realize is a sculpture at all. Per Kirkeby, a celebrated Danish artist, built the two brick walls here for a major exhibition in 1997, to close off the wide space below the museum building down to the river. A series of entrances and window openings are designed to let shadows fall at striking angles – though predictably, the more conservative locals loathe the piece.

The most fun sculpture in town takes up the whole wall at the corner of Nygatan and Torggatan in the centre: *Drömbanken*, by Walter Bengtsson, is a witty, surrealist explosion of naked women, cats, mutant elks, bare feet and beds.

5

> ## SWIMMING IN FALKENBERG
>
> Just fifteen minutes' walk south from town, **Skrea Strand** is a fine, 2km-long stretch of sandy beach, perfect for swimming. At the northern end, the large bathing and tennis complex of **Klitterbadet** has an indoor 50m saltwater pool plus a shallow children's pool, a vast sauna, jacuzzi and steam rooms. At the southern end of the beach, all the way down past the busy wooden holiday cabins, lie some secluded coves; in early summer the marshy grassland here is full of wild violets and clover.

Laurentii kyrka, its ceiling and interior walls awash with seventeenth- and eighteenth-century paintings. It's hard to believe that this gem of a church was – in the early twentieth century – variously a shooting range, a cinema and a gymnasium; indeed, its secular usage saved it from demolition after the Neo-Gothic church was built at the end of the nineteenth century. When St Laurentii kyrka was reconsecrated in the 1920s, its sixteenth-century font and silverware were traced to, and recovered from, places all over northern Europe.

Fotomuseum Olympia

Olympia Photography Museum • Sandgatan 13A • Tues–Thurs 2–6pm, Sun 2–5pm • 50kr • ⓦ fotomuseet-olympia.com

Falkenberg boasts the rather unusual **Fotomuseum Olympia**, home of the town's first purpose-built cinema which opened in 1912. It has over one thousand cameras and a remarkable collection of cinematic paraphernalia, including some superb local peasant portraits taken in 1898. The oldest pictures on show are English and date back to the 1840s. There's also an impressive section on Sweden's well-loved author Selma Lagerlöf (see page 375), who won the Nobel Prize for Literature in 1909.

Carlsberg Sverige brewery

Årstadvägen 6 • 1hr tours (in Swedish) July only Mon–Fri 10am & 4pm • 200kr • Tours must be booked in advance by phone; minimum twelve people required • ☎ 046 87 57 70 00, ⓦ carlsbergsverige.se

For a completely different experience to the other attractions in Falkenberg, head to the **Carlsberg Sverige brewery** where Sweden's popular beer, Falcon, has been brewed since 1896, and is available for sampling at the end of the tour.

ARRIVAL AND INFORMATION

FALKENBERG

By train Falkenberg's train station is an inconvenient 10min bus ride from the centre; shuttle buses run regularly into town, dropping at Storatorget and the bus station.
Destinations Copenhagen (hourly; 2hr 40min); Gothenburg (hourly; 1hr); Malmö (hourly; 2hr).
Tourist office Holgersgatan 11 (Jan 1st–May 24th:

Mon–Fri 10am–5pm; May 27th–June 20th: Mon–Fri 10am–5pm, Sat 10am–3pm; June 24th–Aug 11th: Mon–Fri 10am–6pm, Sat 10am–3pm, Sun 10am–3pm; Aug 12th–24th Mon–Fri 10am–5pm, Sat 10am–3pm; Aug 26th–Dec 31st Mon–Fri 10am–5pm); ☎ 0346 88 61 00, ⓦ visitfalkenberg.se). Has free internet access.

ACCOMMODATION

Falkenberg Strandbad Havsbadsallén 2A ☎ 0346 71 49 00, ⓦ strandbaden.se. A top-of-the-range luxury hotel decorated in colonial style, with model rhinos and elephants at every turn. If you want total indulgence right on the beach at reasonable prices, look no further. **2805kr**
Grand Hotellgatan 1 ☎ 0346 144 50, ⓦ grandhotel falkenberg.se. This elegant, waterside hotel overlooks the historic Tullbron bridge and enjoys the best location in Falkenberg. The smaller standard rooms cost several

hundred kronor less and are certainly worth considering since the standard is still high. **1150kr/1450kr**
Hwitan Storgatan 24 ☎ 0346 144 50, ⓦ hwitan.com. Overlooking a picturesque open courtyard surrounded by low-built houses dating from 1703, the rooms here are cosy and intimate with period furnishings. **1095kr**
Skrea Camping Strandvägen 55 ☎ 0346 171 07, ⓦ skreacamping.se. A comfortable youth hostel and campsite on the beachfront – get here by following

Strandvägen to the beach. No dorm beds. Open all year. Tents **370kr**, cabins **600kr**

Vesterhavet Motellvägen 3 ☎0346 71 18 80, ⓦhotell vesterhavet.se. This is the place to come if you're looking for self-catering apartments. They are all over forty square metres in size, and some have an outside terrace to boot; all are located in a great spot close to the river. **1460kr**

EATING AND DRINKING

The birthplace of Sia Glass – a popular **ice cream** made by Sweden's oldest family firm, established in 1569 – and **Falcon beer**, Falkenberg caters well to the tastebuds. Although the variety of food on offer isn't huge, the town's restaurants and bars are of a standard to make eating and drinking here a pleasant experience.

★ **Annas Bakgård** Storgatan 42 ⓦfacebook.com/ annasbakgard. This welcoming café is the best in town. Housed in one of Falkenberg's oldest buildings, dating from the 1690s, it features mellow furnishings and a lovely garden. There's a wide range of sandwiches and decadent home-made cakes. Mon–Fri 9am–5pm, Sat 10am–4pm.

★ **Gustaf Bratt** Brogatan 1 ☎0346 103 31, ⓦgustaf bratt.se. Housed in a former grain warehouse from 1860, this popular restaurant has a good range of tasty fish and meat dishes: the grilled zander with cauliflower purée and baked chorizo is excellent (225kr). There's also a set two- or three-course menu for 450kr and 500kr respectively. Mon– Thurs 6pm–late, Fri & Sat 5pm–late, Sun 4pm–late.

Harry's Hotellgatan 1 ⓦharrys.se/restauranger/ falkenberg. Enjoying a prime location in the main square, this was Sweden's first ever *Harry's*, the American-style bar now found across the country. It's always packed with drinkers and in summer there's outside seating, too. Mon– Thurs 11.30am–2pm & 5pm–late, Fri 11.30am–2pm & 4pm–late, Sat 1am–late.

Laxbutiken Heberg, signed at exit 49 off the E6 ☎0346 511 10, ⓦlaxbutiken.se. Fans of salmon really should make the effort to come to this salmon restaurant near the village of Heberg, 9km south of Falkenberg. It serves up an array of superb dishes (115–195kr), with salmon the main ingredient. Lunch is 125kr. Daily 10am–7pm.

Royal Thai Storgatan 25 ☎0346 805 99. A friendly place with a wide variety of good-value Southeast Asian mains: beef or chicken dishes cost around 100kr; add another 20kr for prawns. The lunch buffet is good value at 85kr. Mon– Thurs 11am–10pm, Fri 11am–11pm, Sat noon–11pm, Sun noon–10pm.

Halmstad and around

The principal town in Halland, **HALMSTAD** was once a grand walled city and an important Danish stronghold. Today, although most of the original buildings have disappeared, the town makes a pleasant enough stop on the long haul south from Gothenburg, thanks to the extensive – if rather crowded – **beaches** not far away, and a range of really good places to eat. Halmstad is also perfectly placed for a quick jaunt to the **Mjellby Konstmuseum**, which offers art lovers a chance to appreciate the work of the well-known (in Sweden, at least) Halmstad Group.

Brief history

In 1619, the town's **castle** was used by the Danish king Christian IV to entertain his Swedish counterpart, Gustav II Adolf; records show that there were seven solid days of festivities. The bonhomie, however, didn't last much longer, and Christian was soon building great stone-and-earth fortifications around the city, all surrounded by a moat, with access afforded by four stone gateways. However, it was a fire soon after, rather than the Swedes, that all but destroyed the city; the only buildings to survive were the castle and the church. Undeterred, Christian took the opportunity to create a contemporary Renaissance town with a grid of straight streets; today the main street, **Storgatan**, still contains a number of impressive merchants' houses from that time. After the final defeat of the Danes in 1645, Halmstad lost its military significance, and the walls were torn down. Today, just one of the great gateways, **Norre Port**, remains; the moat has been filled in and a road, Karl XIs vägen, runs directly above where the water would have been.

5

Storgatan and around

Pedestrianized **Storgatan** – the main thoroughfare for restaurants and nightlife – is a charming street, with some creaking old houses built in the years following the 1619 fire; the great stone arch of **Norre Port** marks the street's northern end. Towards its southern end is the large, lively market square, **Stora torg**, centred around Carl Milles's *Europa and the Bull*, a fountain with mermen twisted around it, all with Milles's characteristically muscular bodies, ugly faces and oversized nipples.

St Nikolai kyrka

Kyrkogatan 4 • June–Aug daily 9am–4pm; Sept–May Mon–Fri 9am–4pm, Sat & Sun 9am–4pm

Flanking one side of Stora torg is the grand **St Nikolai kyrka**. Dating from the fourteenth century, its monumental size bears witness to Halmstad's former importance, although the only signs of the town's medieval origins that remain are the splodges of bare rock beneath the plain, brick columns.

Värdshuset Tre Hjärtan

Adjacent to the church at Kyrkogatan 7, the **Värdshuset Tre Hjärtan** (Three Hearts) restaurant is a vast, proud building with a crossbeamed ceiling; its name derives from the three hearts that make up the town's emblem, Christian IV having granted the town the right to use it in gratitude for their loyalty to Denmark. It's worth taking your coffee and cake upstairs, where the beams and ceiling are beautifully hand-painted, and photographs of nineteenth-century Halmstad adorn the walls.

Halmstad Castle and Najaden

Just south of Slottsbron bridge in the town centre, **Halmstad Castle** is a striking, coral-red affair half-hidden by trees. Built around 1615 on the orders of Danish king Christian IV (when Halland was part of Denmark) in Danish Renaissance style, the castle consists of four rows of buildings located around a central courtyard. The castle itself is closed to the public as it contains the private residence of the county governor of Halland, but it is possible to access the courtyard for a closer look.

Moored in front of the castle is **Najaden**, a fully rigged sailing ship built in 1897 and once used for training by the Swedish navy.

Norre Katt park

Norre Katts Gränd • Café June Mon–Thurs & Sun 11am–6pm, Fri & Sat 11am–8pm; July & Aug Mon, Tues & Sun 10am–8pm, Wed–Sat 10am–10pm

At the north end of Storgatan is the splendid **Norre Katt park**, a delightful, shady place that slopes down towards the river and is dotted with mature beech, copper beech and horse-chestnut trees, with great weeping willows by the water. The town's most serene spot is at the park's centre, where there's a lily pond crossed by a bridge, overlooked by a popular **café**, *Rotundan*, housed in an ornate former bandstand.

Hallands Konstmuseum

Tollsgatan • Tues–Sun noon–4pm, Wed till 8pm • Free • Ⓦ hallandskonstmuseum.se

At the northernmost edge of Norre Katt park, by the river, is **Hallands Konstmuseum**, the province's modern art museum. Inside you'll find a changing exhibition of the museum's collection of regional art by local painters such as Roj Friberg and Lotta Antonsson, plus a small section devoted to the work of the Halmstad Group (see below).

Hallandsgården

Galgberget • June–Aug 11am–5pm • Guided tours 2pm daily • Free

A ten-minute walk beyond the Konstmuseum, up on Galgberget (Gallows Hill), is a collection of a dozen or so typically Halland buildings which were moved to the site in 1925 to form a miniature outdoor museum, **Hallandsgården**, including a windmill from Morup and a schoolhouse from Eldsberga. There are sweeping views of the Halmstad coastline and Laholmbukten bay from the top of the tower, located beside the steps up to Hallandsgården.

Martin Luthers kyrka

Östra Lyckan 5 • June–Aug daily 9am–5pm; Sept–May Mon–Fri 9am–3pm

A kilometre east of the centre on Långgatan, one of the main roads out of town, stands the gleaming 1970s **Martin Luthers kyrka**. The first church in Scandinavia to be assembled entirely of steel, this unique creation looks from the outside like a clumsily opened sardine can, with jagged and curled edges, and stained glass. Inside it's just as unusual: all the walls are a rust-orange version of the outer skin. The building is famed for its acoustics, and holds occasional concerts (details from the tourist office).

Mjellby Konstmuseum

Mjällby • Daily July–mid-Aug 8am–5pm; mid-Aug–June noon–5pm • 80kr • Ⓦ mjellbykonstmuseum.se • Take bus #350 and alight at the bus stop called "Mjällby"

Five kilometres north of Halmstad is the **Mjellby Konstmuseum**, containing works by the **Halmstad Group**, a body of six local artists from the 1920s who championed Cubism and Surrealism in Sweden. The group, comprising brothers Eric and Axel Olson, their cousin Waldemar Lorentzon and three others, worked together in an artistic alliance for fifty years. The group's members had studied in Berlin and Paris and were strongly influenced by Magritte and Dalí, producing work that caused considerable controversy from the 1920s to the 1940s and sometimes working collectively on projects – an almost unheard-of practice in Swedish art.

Halmstad's beaches

Bus #10 runs to Tylösand hourly from Österskans in the town centre

Eight kilometres west of the town centre, **Halmstad**'s most popular **beach** is at **Tylösand**, which in July and August becomes packed with bronzing bodies, as do the

5

surrounding bars and restaurants in the evenings. There's a smuggler's cove to wander around at **Tjuvahålan**, signposted directly off the beach, and plenty of excellent spots for bathing, including **Svärjarehålan** around the headland to the east, where a bathing beach has been adapted for the disabled. To reach less crowded areas, walk 45 minutes north from Tjuvahålan to **Frösakull** and **Ringenäs**; the latter is popular for windsurfing.

Östra Stranden and Hagön

Bus #63 runs to both beaches hourly from Österskans in town; get off at the stop called "Hästskon" which has direct beach access to Östra Stranden. For Hagön, leave the bus at the same stop and walk for about 30min south along Sommarvägen, passing Hagöns camping, until the road ends at a small car park. From here follow the footpath across the dunes to the sea

The best beach to the east of town is at **Östra Stranden**, where there is also a large, well-equipped campsite. The long beach – sandy and less crowded than at Tylösand – is excellent for children as the waters are particularly shallow. A little further south is **Hagön**, a secluded **nudist beach** where privacy is afforded by the deep hollows between the dunes, behind which is a nature reserve.

ARRIVAL AND DEPARTURE   HALMSTAD

By train From the train station, follow Bredgatan west to the Nissan River, then walk north along Strandgatan to the bridge across to reach the centre of town; it takes about 15–20min.

Destinations Copenhagen (hourly; 2hr 15min); Falkenberg (hourly; 15min); Gothenburg (hourly; 1hr 15min); Malmö (hourly; 1hr 40min).

By bus All long-distance buses depart from behind the train station. Town buses depart from Österskans beside the theatre, across the river from Stora torg.

INFORMATION

Tourist office Köpmansgatan 20 (late June to mid-Aug Mon–Fri 10am–7pm, Sat 10am–4pm, Sun 10am–2pm; mid-Aug to late June Mon–Fri 10am–6pm, Sat 10am–2pm; ☎035 12 02 00, ⍵destinationhalmstad.se). Has free internet access.

ACCOMMODATION   SEE MAP PAGE 154

Best Western Grand Stationsgatan 44 ☎035 280 81 00, ⍵bestwestern.se. Cosy, traditional and ideally located for the train and bus stations, this hotel dates from 1905 and is full of old-world charm. Rooms are spacious, with parquet floors and a mix of period and contemporary furnishings. <u>1100kr/1170kr</u>

Clarion Collection Norre Park Norra vägen 7 ☎035 21 85 55, ⍵nordicchoicehotels.se/hotel/sverige/halmstad/ clarion-collection-hotel-norre-park/. Overlooking the beautiful Norre Katt park, this hotel is reached through the Norre Port arch. Rooms are elegantly decorated in late-nineteenth-century style: all have high ceilings and potted plants in the window and most have wooden floors. <u>1170kr</u>

Continental Kungsgatan 5 ☎035 17 63 00, ⍵continental-halmstad.se. Just a 2min walk from the train station, this elegant building was built in 1904 in the early *Jugendstil* and National Romantic styles and has a bright, well-preserved interior and classy rooms to match. There's also a spa in the basement and an outdoor Jacuzzi. <u>1290kr/1490kr</u>

Hagöns Camping Östra Stranden ☎046 77 110 12 00, ⍵nordiccamping.se. Located 3km to the east of the town centre, this pleasant campsite sits beside a sandy beach and a nature reserve and has four-berth cabins. Open late April–early Sept. Tents <u>150kr</u>, cabins <u>1200kr</u>

STF Kaptenshamn Vardrarhem Stuvaregatan 8 ☎035 12 04 00, ⍵halmstadvandrarhem.se. Centrally located, this hostel is one of the very few budget options in Halmstad. Rooms are plainly decorated and share facilities; there's also a kitchen on site for self-catering. Breakfast is an extra 70kr. Dorms <u>350kr</u>, doubles <u>1200kr</u>

EATING AND DRINKING   SEE MAP PAGE 154

People congregate in the trendy restaurants, bars and clubs along cobbled, pedestrianized **Storgatan**, many of which have shaded outdoor areas along the street. **Lilla torg**, a block to the west at the top end of the street, also swarms with people on summer evenings.

CAFÉS AND RESTAURANTS

Fribergs Konditori Norra vägen 9 ☎035 12 51 11, ⍵fribergskonditori.se. Traditional coffee house overlooking the park, with pictures of Halmstad adorning the interior. A nice relaxed atmosphere and a good place for a coffee and a slice of cake. Mon–Fri 9am–5pm, Sat 10am–4pm.

Fridolfs Brogatan 26 ☎035 21 16 66, ⍵fridolfs. se. There's a maritime feel to the interior of this cosy neighbourhood restaurant, serving a classic mix of French and Swedish: snails in garlic butter (120kr), wild boar with apple sauce (275kr) or cured blackened salmon with cucumber and horseradish (130kr), for example. Mon–Thurs 6pm–late, Fri–Sun 5.30pm–late.

hummër Storgatan 23 ☎ 035 295 22 95, ⓦ hummeor. se. A ridiculous made-up name for this grill restaurant (not even locals know how to pronounce it), but the food on offer is great: top-quality prime cuts of beef (including a delicious slow-cooked cheek of beef in red wine sauce for 180kr) are the signature dishes. Reckon on around 250–350kr for a meaty main. Mon–Thurs 5.30–10pm, Fri 11.30am–11.30pm, Sat noon–11.30pm.

★ **Pio & Co** Storgatan 37 ☎ 035 21 06 69, ⓦ pio.se. A lovely, intimate place with brick walls, where the speciality (*fiskplanka*) is fish served on wooden planks with clouds of mashed potato (280kr). The menu consists of modern Swedish dishes (245–460kr). Mon–Fri 6pm–late, Sat 5.30pm–late.

Yoss Storgatan 35 ☎ 035 18 76 49, ⓦ restaurangyoss. se. This chi-chi French-Italian bistro has some of the best prices in town: mains go for 139–269kr and include oven-baked chicken in a blue cheese sauce, lamb fillet on a bed of mushrooms and grilled salmon with lobster sauce. Mon–Fri 11am–2.30pm & 5.30–10pm, Sat 11.30am–10.30pm.

BARS AND PUBS

★ **The Bull's Pub** Bankgatan 5 ☎ 035 14 09 21, ⓦ thebullspub.se. Next door to the tourist office, this popular, modern English-style bar, rather than pub, with live music and after-work specials, brings people from across town. Also serves light meals and has outdoor seating in summer. Mon & Tues 11.30am–2pm & 4–11pm, Wed & Thurs 11.30am–2pm & 4–11pm, Fri 11.30am–2am, Sat noon–2am, Sun noon–10pm.

Harry's Storgatan 22 ☎ 035 10 55 95, ⓦ harrys.se/restauranger/halmstad. Massively popular pub attesting to the delight taken by some Swedes in all things American. It also does reasonably priced steaks and burgers, as well as a couple of fish dishes for under 200kr. Mon & Sun 5–11pm, Tues, Wed & Thurs 5–11pm, Fri 4pm–1am, Sat noon–2am.

Pio Storgatan 37 ☎ 035 21 06 69, ⓦ pio.se. A stylish lounge bar-cum-restaurant with a cosy seating area. Even though the restaurant is in the middle of the centre, it is away from the noise. The combination of excellent chef's and bartenders make this place the perfect spot for dinner or an after-work drink. Mon–Fri 6pm–late, Sat 5.30pm–late.

Roots Tyghusgatan 10 ☎ 072 37 33 50 9, ⓦ roots norreport.se. *Roots* has it all: great food, excellent drinks and spectacular live performances. Watch some live artists while eating fancy popcorn (50kr) with a strawberry daiquiri (115kr). This is the perfect place for a night out with friends. Wed & Thurs 6–10pm, Fri 6pm–2am, Sat 7pm–2am.

Båstad

Thirty-five kilometres south of Halmstad, a journey of around fifteen minutes by train, lies **BÅSTAD** (pronounced bow-sta). The northernmost town in the ancient province of **Skåne**, its character is markedly different from other towns along the coast. Cradled by the **Bjäre peninsula** (see page 160), which bulges westwards into the Kattegat (the waters between Sweden and Danish Jutland), Båstad is Sweden's **tennis centre**, where the Swedish Open is played at the beginning of July – the centre court down by the harbour is truly impressive. The town also boasts an extremely beautiful setting, with forested hills on the horizon to the south.

There is a downside, though, which can blunt enthusiasm for the place. Ever since King Gustav V chose to take part in the 1930 national tennis championship

SKÅNE TRAVEL PASS

An amazing money-saver if you're spending any significant time in Skåne is **Jojo Sommar** (summer travel pass; ⓦ jojosommar.se). For 699kr, it allows unlimited journeys between mid-June and mid-Aug on buses and trains throughout Skåne. It comes as a smartcard which you buy at Skånetrafiken information centres throughout the province, Pressbyrån newsagents, 7-Eleven stores or you can buy it with the Skånetrafiken app. Alternatively, a 24hr/72hr **travel pass** valid for the whole of Skåne at any time of year costs 195kr/395kr respectively. Buy this most easily from Skånetrafiken information centres. More information on all tickets is at ⓦ skanetrafiken.se.

5

and Ludvig Nobel (nephew to Alfred of the Nobel Prize) gave financial backing to the tournament, wealthy retired Stockholmers have flocked here, bringing an ostentatious smugness to the town for the annual competition held during the second week of July. The locals themselves, however, are quite down-to-earth, and most view this arrogance as a financial lifeline. Despite all this, Båstad isn't a prohibitively expensive place to stay, and makes a good base from which to explore the peninsula.

Köpmansgatan

The main road through town, running parallel to the shore, is **Köpmansgatan**. The street's architecture is unusual for Sweden, and somewhat reminiscent of provincial France, with shuttered, low-rise shops and houses. Partway along, just inland from the harbour, is Båstad's central main square, **Torget**, where you'll find the tourist office (see below) and the fifteenth-century **Sancta Maria kyrka** (June–Aug Mon–Fri 8am–6pm, Sat & Sun 10am–3pm; Sept–May Mon–Fri 8am–3.30pm, Sat & Sun 10am–3pm), a cool haven on a hot summer's day. The altar painting is striking, depicting Jesus on the cross with a couple of skulls and haphazardly strewn human bones on the ground beneath.

The waterfront

For a feel of old Båstad, take a stroll down the ancient cottage-flanked Agardhsgatan, off Hamngatan and parallel with the seashore. To reach the **beach** head down Tennisvägen, off Köpmansgatan, and through a glamorous residential area until you reach Strandpromenaden, where you can take a lovely evening stroll as the sun sets on the calm waters. West of here, the old 1880s bathhouses have all been converted into restaurants and bars which owe much of their popularity to their proximity to the **tennis courts** where the famous tournament is played. Just a few steps further lies the harbour, thick with boat masts.

Norrvikens Trädgårdar

Norrviken Gardens • May & Sept Wed–Sun 10am–5pm; June–Aug daily 10am–5pm; Oct–Dec Sat & Sun 10am–5pm • Free • ⓦ norrvikenbastad.se

Heading west out of Båstad along the coast road, it's just a couple of kilometres to **Norrvikens Trädgårdar**, a paradise for horticulturists and lovers of symmetry. With the sea as a backdrop, these fine gardens were designed by Rudolf Abelin at the end of the nineteenth century; he is buried in a magnificent hollow of rhododendrons near the entrance. The best walk is the "King's Ravine", ablaze in late spring and early summer with fiery azaleas and more blushing rhododendrons, and leading to a fine Japanese-style garden. At the centre of the grounds there's an open-air theatre with occasional productions (details available at the tourist office in Båstad).

ARRIVAL AND DEPARTURE   BÅSTAD

By train In connection with train arrivals, a bus runs from the train station 2.5km southeast of town into the centre of Båstad, passing the central main square and tourist office. Destinations Copenhagen (hourly; 2hr); Gothenburg (hourly; 1hr 40min); Malmö (hourly; 1hr 30min).

By bus To reach Torekov on the Bjäre peninsula, you need to take a bus (6 daily; 30min) from the bus station off Musterivägen near the ICA supermarket.

INFORMATION

Tourist office Köpmansgatan 1 on the main square (Tues–Fri 10am–5pm, Sat 11am–2pm; ☎ 0431 750 45, ⓦ bastad. com). Has maps and information about the town and the Bjäre peninsula.

TUNNEL VISION: THE HALLANDSÅSEN SCANDAL

A full 23 years after construction started, the **railway tunnel** through the Hallandsåsen ridge south of Båstad – Sweden's longest at 8.7km – finally opened to traffic in December 2015. From the outset the project was plagued by an **environmental scandal**, as toxic sealants began to soak into the groundwater, killing fish and cattle, and causing many site workers to fall ill. Construction was halted in 1997 amid further problems – the drill used to bore into the hillside became stuck and wedged in the rock after boring a mere 18m and the drilling company went bankrupt due to the extra costs incurred in sealing the water leaks.

The tunnel is part of a larger project to upgrade the entire Swedish west-coast line to double track. Though trains now operate 10–15 minutes faster between Gothenburg and Malmö, it's estimated the whole project, including a station in Båstad, has cost over 10 billion kronor.

ACCOMMODATION

Accommodation in Båstad is plentiful, but to find somewhere to stay during the **Swedish Open** in July, you'll need to book months in advance. Unlike the rest of Sweden, **prices** increase dramatically during the summer as a result of the town's sporting endeavours.

Enehall Stationsterrasen 10 ☎0431 750 15, ⓦenehall. se. Rooms are located in nine different houses grouped together on the western edge of town, a 20min walk from the centre. Although simply furnished, all rooms are perfectly comfortable, clean and have private facilities. **1260kr/995kr**

Hjorten Roxmansvägen 23 ☎0431 701 09, ⓦhjorten. net. This homely pension just off the main road, Köpmansgatan, dates from 1910 and is the oldest in town. It represents good value for money, though the decor is a little frilly and fussy. Open June–Aug only. **1350kr/995kr**

Hotel Riviera Beach Rivieravägen 33 ☎0431 785 00, ⓦhotelrivierastrand.se. If you want to lay back and relax as a family, then this might be the perfect hotel for you. Among the amenities are a beach, a pool and a climbing wall. Add amazing scenery, comfortable suites, luxurious drinks and delicious food, and you have a destination where everyone can find something they like. **1500kr**

Pensionat Neptun Havsbadsvägen 18 ☎0431 36 91 30, ⓦpensionatneptun.se. A pleasant, traditional wooden house with two enormous verandas that are just 100m from the beach, offering amazingly good-value accommodation in well-appointed and tastefully decorated doubles. Rooms with shared facilities are 300kr less. **1195kr**

Sigfridsgården Ängelholmsvägen 26 ☎0431 36 69 18, ⓦsigfridsgarden.se. Well-regarded B&B with tastefully decorated, light and airy rooms overlooking a pleasant flower garden, located roughly a 15min walk from the town centre, beyond the Statoil filling station. There's also a small café and art gallery on site. **1290kr/820kr**

★ **Skansen** Kyrkogatan 2 ☎0431 55 81 00, ⓦhotel skansen.se. This beautifully designed hotel, set in a cream bathhouse with stylish annexe villas, includes a great health spa (included in all room rates). Rooms in the tennis pavilion annexe and the neighbouring annexe cost around 100kr less. **2060kr**

CAMPING

Norrvikens Camping Kattviksvägen 347 ☎0431 36 91 70, ⓦcaravanclub.se/norrviken-campinginfo. In a pretty spot right by the sea, this site is a couple of kilometres west of the town centre. Open late March–Sept. Tents **185kr**

EATING AND DRINKING

Fiskekajen Hamnplan, 269 33 ☎0431 - 72444, ⓦfiskekajen.nu. Down at the harbour, this is the place to come to get your fishy fix – they have seemingly everything from cold-smoked salmon on rye bread to a delicious fish and seafood stew; you can always pick something up here for around 100kr. June–Aug daily 11am–10pm.

★ **Pepe's Bodega** Hamngatan 6 ☎ 046 431 789 80, ⓦpepesbodega.se. A very popular place with Båstad's 20-somethings, serving pizzas from 220kr and a delicious summer salad with watermelon, feta and sweet chilli for 165kr. The food is good and, this being Båstad, the bar also stocks champagne and sangria. Daily noon–late.

Sand Kyrkogatan 2 ☎0431 55 81 09, ⓦhotelskansen. se/en/restaurant-sand. Attached to *Hotel Skansen*, with glorious views out over the sea, this is an excellent-quality a la carte restaurant (mains from 245kr) serving up veal, steaks, zander and salmon carpaccio. Mon–Fri 7am–2pm & 6–11pm, Sat & Sun 7am–3pm & 6–11pm.

Sands Bakficka Hamngatan 1 ☎046 431 55 82 11, ⓦhotelskansen.se/en/restaurang-sand/sands-bakficka. A bright and breezy bistro which does a roaring trade during the summer months, dishing up open sandwiches, coffees and cakes. Really nice views out over the sea from here. Daily 11am–4pm.

Solbackens Café & Wåffelbruk Munkgatan 10 ☎0431 702 00, ⓦsolbacken.eu. This Båstad institution first opened its doors in 1907 and has been serving delicious fresh waffles and cream ever since. Seating is arranged on a series of terraces with views out over the sea. June–Aug daily noon–5pm.

5 The Bjäre peninsula

Jutting into the Kattegat directly west of Båstad and deserving a couple of days' exploration, the **Bjäre peninsula**'s natural beauty has a magical quality to it. Its varied scenery includes wide fertile fields where potatoes and strawberries are grown, splintered red-rock cliff formations and remote islands ringed by seals, thick with birds and historical ruins.

Kattvik and around

About 8km west of Båstad, and beyond Norrvikens Trädgårdar is **KATTVIK**. Once a village busy with stone-grinding mills, it is now largely the domain of wealthy, elderly Stockholmers, who snap up the few houses on the market as soon as they are up for sale. Kattvik achieved its moment of fame when Richard Gere chose a cottage here as a venue for a summer romance.

Kajs Fisk & Rökeri

Kaj's fish smokery • Hovshallavägen 19 • Late June–late Aug daily from 9am–5pm • ☎ 0431 36 50 25, ⓦ kajsfiskrokeri.se

A kilometre from Kattvik off the Torekov road (follow the sign "*rökt fisk*") is **Kajs Fisk & Rökeri**, an old farm where fish is smoked in little furnaces fired by sawdust from the nearby clog factory. Here you can have a taste of – and buy – the very best smoked fish in the area; as well as the usual mackerel and salmon, sample *horngädda* (garpike), a scaly fish with bright green bones, and *sjurygg* (lumpsucker), an extraordinarily ugly, seven-crested fish with oily, flavoursome flesh.

Hovs Hallar nature reserve

Continue 7km west along the coast from Kattvik, either by road or by following the Skåneleden walking trail, to reach the **Hovs Hallar nature reserve**, where you can clamber down any of several paths towards the sea. The views are breathtaking – screaming gulls circling overhead and waves crashing onto the unique red-stone cliffs – though it's something of a tourist magnet during the summer.

Torekov

On the peninsula's western coast, **TOREKOV** is just 5km from Hovs Hallar nature reserve. The village is named after a little girl later known as St Thora, who, so the story goes, was drowned by her wicked stepmother; the body was washed ashore and given a Christian burial by a blind man, who then miraculously regained his sight. It's a perfect place to chill; indeed, one odd sight is the daily ritual of elderly men in dressing gowns wandering along the pier – so sought after is the property here, these old boys promenade in bathrobes to set themselves apart from the visitors.

Hallands Väderö

Boat trips April–Oct; departures vary by month, though there's generally a boat every 1–2hr; see website for detailed timetables • 140kr return • Seal safaris April–late June & mid-Aug–Oct Sun 10am; late June– mid-Aug Tues & Thurs 6pm • 175kr • ☎ 0431 36 30 45, ⓦ vaderotrafiken.se

The main reason to venture to Torekov is to take one of the old fishing **boats** which regularly leave from its little harbour for the island nature reserve of **Hallands Väderö**. The island is a scenic mix of trees and bare rocks with isolated fishermen's cottages dotted around its edges, while the skies above are filled with countless birds – gulls, eiders, guillemots and cormorants.

One particularly beautiful spot on Hallands Väderö is at its southernmost tip, where weather-smoothed islets stand out amid the tranquil turquoise waters. If you're lucky, you may be able to make out the colony of seals living on the furthest rocks; there are organized "**seal safaris**" here from Torekov.

On the south of Hallands Väderö is the **English graveyard**, surrounded by mossy, dry-stone walls. It holds the remains of English sailors who were killed here in 1809, when the British fleet was stationed on the island in order to bombard Copenhagen during the Napoleonic Wars. Torekov church would not allow them to be buried on its soil as the sailors' faith was, strangely, considered unknown.

GETTING AROUND	THE BJÄRE PENINSULA

By bus Bus #523 runs through the centre of the peninsula from Båstad to Torekov, and stops at the small hamlets of Hov and Karup on the peninsula's southern coast en route.

By bike The well-known Skåneleden walking trail (🕸 skaneleden.se) runs around the entire perimeter of the peninsula and makes for a great bicycle ride. Bike rental is available in Båstad at Svens Cykelaffär at Tennisvägen 31 (Mon–Fri 9am–5pm, Sat 10am–noon; ☎ 0431 701 26; 100kr/day).

ACCOMMODATION AND EATING

Hotell Hovs Hallar Hovshallavägen 160 ☎ 0431 44 83 70, 🕸 hovshallar.com. Smart, modern hotel overlooking the cliffs by Hovs Hallar nature reserve. Most rooms have their own terrace or balcony and some have sea views; the price includes half-board. The hotel's famed restaurant serves fine à la carte meals from a frequently changing menu (mains around 250–350kr) and lunch specials (195kr). All vegetables are grown by the hotel, and meat and fish are all locally sourced; reservations are recommended at all times. Mon–Fri 11.30am–2.30pm & 6–8pm, Sat & Sun 6–8pm. **2300kr**

Helsingborg

Long gone are the days when the locals of **HELSINGBORG** joked that the most rewarding sight here was Helsingør, the Danish town whose castle – Hamlet's celebrated Elsinore (Kronoborg castle) – is visible, just 4km across the Öresund strait. Bright and pleasing, Helsingborg has a tremendous sense of buoyancy. With its beautifully developed harbour area, an explosion of stylish bars, great cafés and restaurants among the warren of cobbled streets, plus an excellent **museum**, it is one of the best town bases Sweden has to offer.

Brief history

In the past, the links between Helsingborg and Copenhagen were less convivial than they are now. After the Danes fortified the town in the eleventh century, the Swedes conquered and lost it again on six violent occasions, finally winning out in 1710 under Magnus Stenbock's leadership. By this time the Danes had torn down much of the town, and on its final recapture the Swedes contributed to the destruction by razing most of its twelfth-century castle – except for the 5m-thick walled **keep** (*kärnan*), which still dominates the centre. By the early eighteenth century, war and epidemics had reduced the population to just seven hundred, and only with the onset of industrialization in the 1850s did Helsingborg experience a new prosperity. Shipping and the railways turned the town's fortunes round, as is evident from the formidable late nineteenth-century commercial buildings in the centre and some splendid villas to the north, overlooking the Öresund.

Rådhus

The most obvious starting point is on the waterfront, by the bronze **statue** of former Skåne governor, Magnus Stenbock, on his charger. With your back to the Öresund and Denmark, to your left is the **Rådhus**, a heavy-handed, Neo-Gothic pile, complete with turrets and conical towers. The extravagance of provincial nineteenth-century prosperity, and the architect's admiration for medieval Italy, make it worth seeing inside (ask about tours at the tourist office), in particular for the many fabulous **stained-glass**

5

windows, which tell the history of the town. The ones to look out for are those in the entrance hall, depicting Queen Margareta releasing her rival, Albert of Mecklenburg, in Helsingborg in 1395, and the last window in the city-council chamber, showing Jean Baptiste Bernadotte arriving at Helsingborg in 1810, having accepted the Swedish crown. When he greeted General von Essen at the harbour, farce ensued as their elaborate gold jewellery and medals became entangled in the embrace. The original wall and ceiling frescoes in the city-council chamber were deemed too costly to restore and were painted over in 1968, though have now been uncovered.

Dunkers Kulturhus

Kungsgatan 11 • Jan 7th–June 16th: Mon–Fri 8am–8pm, Sat–Sun 10am–5pm; June 17th–Aug 18th Mon–Wed 8am–6pm, Thurs 8am–8pm, Fri 8am–6pm, Sat–Sun 10am–5pm • Free, special exhibitions 70kr • Ⓦ dunkerskulturhus.se

Crossing over the road towards the Kattegat sea from the Magnus Stenbock statue, you'll see the **harbour**, divided in two by the bridge to the pier. To the north of the bridge, a white-brick building contains the exceptional city museum, **Dunkers Kulturhus**. The centre is named after Henry Dunker, a local man and pioneer of galoshes – he developed the process for keeping rubber soft in winter and non-sticky in summer, and his brand, Tretorn, became a world leader until the factories closed in 1979. When he died in 1962, he left 58 million kronor to set up a foundation and this museum is a major recipient.

If you're expecting traditional exhibitions, the museum's dramatic special sound effects and lighting certainly come as a surprise. The history of Helsingborg from Ice

HELSINGBORG

Kallbadhuset & beaches

N

● EATING
Château Café Forêt	5
Ebba's Fik	7
Edelweiss	3
Fahlmans	1
Mommee's	9
Oasen	8
Olsons Skafferi	4
Papadam	6
Redimat	2

■ DRINKING
Bishops Arms	2
Harry's	3
Telegrafen	1

■ ACCOMMODATION
Clarion Grand	3
Comfort Nouveau	9
Elite Marina Plaza	4
Elite Mollberg	2
Kärnan	5
Linnéa	6
Råå Vallar Resort	7
STF Miatorp Vandrarhem	8
Viking	1

Teater

Kärnan   Slottshagen

Terrasstrapporna

Dunkers Kulturhus

Rådhus

Magnus Stenbock

Windmill

Knutpunkten
(ferries, trains & buses)

0   200
metres

Library

Råå, 7 & 8 ▼   9 ▼

Age to present day, with water as the theme, is tremendous fun, though there's no explanation in any language so it's more sensory than educational; the coverage of the town's social, economic and military history has far more explanation in English. There are also some **galleries** showing temporary art exhibitions year round. The museum contains a fine **restaurant**, overlooking the Öresund, and a bistro serving light meals.

The kärnan

The keep • Slottshagsgatan • April, May & Sept Tues–Fri 9am–4pm, Sat & Sun 11am–4pm; June–Aug daily 10am–6pm; Oct–March Tues–Sun 11am–3pm • 50kr

Returning to the bottom of **Stortorget** – the central "square", so elongated that it's more like a boulevard – it's a short stroll upwards to the steps leading to the remains of the medieval **castle**, dominated by the massive castellated bulk of the **kärnan** (keep), surrounded by some fine parkland. The keep and Sancta Maria kyrka (see below) were the sole survivors of the ravages of war, but the former lost its military significance once Sweden finally won the day. It was due for demolition in the mid-nineteenth century, only surviving because seafarers found it a valuable landmark. What cannon fire failed to achieve, however, neglect and the weather succeeded in bringing about: the keep was a ruin when restoration began in 1894. It looks like a huge brick stood on end and is worth climbing today more for the views than the scant historical exhibitions within.

Sancta Maria kyrka

Mariatorget • Mon–Fri 8am–5pm, Sat & Sun 9am–4pm

Resembling a basilica, and Danish Gothic in style, the **Sancta Maria kyrka** squats in its own square by a very French-looking avenue of beech trees. The church was begun in 1300 and completed a century later. Its rather plain facade belies a striking interior, with a clever contrast between the early seventeenth-century Renaissance-style ornamentation of its pulpit and gilded reredos, and the jewel-like contemporary stained-glass windows.

Norra and Södra Storgatan

Walking back to Stortorget from the church, you arrive at **Norra** and **Södra Storgatan** (the streets that meet at the foot of the stairs to the *kärnan*), which comprised Helsingborg's main thoroughfare in medieval times and so are lined with the oldest of the town's merchants' houses. As you head up Norra Storgatan, the 1681 **Henckelska house** is hidden behind a plain stuccoed wall; once you have pushed your way through the trees that have grown over the entrance archway, you'll see a rambling mix of beams and windows, with a fine little topiary garden hidden beyond a passage to the right. The garden was laid out in 1766 for the future wife of King Gustav III, who was to spend one night at the beautiful eighteenth-century **Gamlegård house** opposite.

The windmill

Windmill, cottages and café open May–Aug Mon–Fri noon–6pm, Sat & Sun noon–6pm • Ⓦ mollebacken.com

On Södra Storgatan, take the opening to the left of the old cream brick building at no. 31, opposite the modern Maria Församling House, to find a real historical gem. After a fairly arduous climb of 92 steps, you'll find a handsome nineteenth-century **windmill**, which you're free to enter using a narrow ramp. Around the windmill are a number of exquisite farm cottages, and inside the low (1.2m-high) doors is a treasure trove of items from eighteenth-century peasant interiors: straw beds, cradles, hand-painted grandmother clocks and the like. A further reward for your climb is the fact that one house, built in 1763 and brought to this site in 1909, serves **waffles**: it's *Möllebackens Våffelbruk*. Established in 1912, they still use the original recipes.

5

Kallbadhuset and Helsingborg's beaches

Gröningen Norra 1 • Mon & Thurs 10am–8pm, Tues 9am–8pm, Wed 9am–8pm, Fri 9am–8pm, Sat & Sun 9am–6pm • 60kr

An easy walk of around fifteen minutes from the marina area, along the footpath which follows the coastline north from the end of Båthusgatan, will bring you to Helsingborg's ultra-stylish cold-water bathing house, **Kallbadhuset** (also known locally as Kallis), which stands on stilts above the water. Here, separate-sex nudist bathing areas have direct step access into the sea, and there's also a glass-walled sauna inside with stunning views out over the Kattegat. Beyond the Kallbadhuset, a sandy sweep of **beach** runs north to just beyond the junction with Halalid, which runs east into suburbia. On a sunny day, you could be mistaken for thinking that the entire population of Helsingborg is here, frolicking in the sea and catching rays on the beach; it's inordinately popular.

Alternatively, about 5km south of town, at the foot of Högastensgatan in the district of Råå, you'll find Helsingborg's sandy **naturist beach**, close to *Råå Vallar Resort* campsite (see below). Get here on bus #1 from the town centre.

ARRIVAL AND DEPARTURE
HELSINGBORG

By train All services arrive and depart from the underground platforms of the Knutpunkten travel interchange. Destinations Copenhagen (hourly; 1hr 15min); Gothenburg (hourly; 2hr 10min); Kristianstad (hourly; 1hr 30min);

Malmö (hourly; 40min).

By ferry Scandlines (ⓦscandlines.se) operates from the first floor of the Knutpunkten terminal all day long to and from Helsingør in Denmark (every 15min; 20min).

INFORMATION

Tourist office There is no longer a physical tourist office in Helsingborg. Instead go online to chat to staff and get the latest information about the town: ⓦvisithelsingborg.com. There is free wi-fi available throughout the centre of town.

ACCOMMODATION
SEE MAP PAGE 162

Clarion Grand Stortorget 8–12 ☎042 38 04 00, ⓦnordicchoicehotels.se/hotell/sverige/helsingborg/clarion-grand-hotel-helsingborg. Built in 1926, this is one of Helsingborg's biggest and grandest hotels. The interior is a successful blend of modern and classic design, with good-sized rooms in a superbly central location. **1100kr/1640kr**

Comfort Nouveau Gasverksgatan 11 ☎042 37 19 50, ⓦnordicchoicehotels.se/hotell/sverige/helsingborg/comfort-hotel-helsingborg. This lacks the grandeur of the Stortorget hotels, but is pretty central and has all the comforts of the top hotels, including a swimming pool and a sauna. Serves exceptionally good breakfasts. **990kr/1370kr**

Elite Marina Plaza Kungstorget 6 ☎042 19 21 00, ⓦelite.se. Right at the harbourside, next to Knutpunkten. Taking inspiration from the sun, wind and water, the rooms at this modern and well-equipped hotel are bright, airy and contemporary in design and some have sea views. **1550kr/1740kr**

Elite Mollberg Stortorget 18 ☎042 37 37 00, ⓦelite.se. Every inch a premier hotel, with a grand nineteenth-century facade, though rooms are simpler, smaller and more homely than at its sister hotel, the *Marina Plaza*. **1320kr/1740kr**

Kärnan Järnvägsgatan 17 ☎042 12 08 20, ⓦhotell karnan.se. Opposite the Knutpunkten travel interchange, this comfortable staff-owned hotel prides itself on home-from-home rooms with modern furnishings, and the generous buffet breakfast is arguably the best in town. There's also a small library-cum-bar and sauna. **1195kr**

Linnéa Prästgatan 2–4 ☎042 37 24 00, ⓦhotell-linnea.se. Good-value, central option in an elegant building from 1887, with cosy, agreeable rooms with period furnishings. Special offers on two-night stays over a weekend. **1095kr/1195kr**

STF Miatorp Vandrarhem Planteringsvägen 71 ☎042 13 11 30, ⓦmiatorp.nu; bus #1 or #2. All rooms at this hostel, a 20min walk south of the centre, are modern, clean and en suite. Doubles **940kr**

★ **Viking** Fågelsångsgatan 1 ☎042 14 44 20, ⓦhotell viking.se. This is the place to try first. Very appealing, quiet old hotel with beautifully appointed period rooms in a splendid location close to some of the finest buildings in town. Room 15 has its own private Jacuzzi and costs about 500kr more than a regular double. Excellent service and a cosy atmosphere. **1250kr**

CAMPING

Råå Vallar Resort Kustgatan in the district of Råå, 5km south of town ☎042 18 26 00, ⓦnordiccamping. se; bus #1. This campsite is well located for Helsingborg's nudist beach, which is right next door at the foot of Högastensgatan. There's also a selection of cabins available. Tents **320kr**, cabins **945kr**

BACK AND FORTH TO HELSINGØR

For a taste of what the locals traditionally do for fun, buy a **foot passenger ferry** ticket to Helsingør and hop on the boat to Denmark. Scandlines' ferries run every 20min (38kr single; ⓦscandlines.se), and tickets are available on the first floor in the Knutpunkten terminal. Try to go on the *Aurora* or *Hamlet*, which have better restaurants and bars than the *Tycho Brahe*; you can see in the timetable which ship operates which departure. The idea is to "tura" as it's called in Swedish, that is to go back and forth as many times as you like on the same ticket (you only need a single because you don't get off in Denmark). Good-value lunches, dinners and beer are served on the boats and you can also buy duty-free.

EATING AND DRINKING

SEE MAP PAGE 162

The city has a good range of excellent **restaurants**, including a host of stylish bar-restaurants along the restored harbourfront. These places can seem samey, though, and it's the older restaurants that continue to provide the variety. During the day, there are some great **cafés** and *konditorier*.

CAFÉS

★ **Château Café Forêt** Södra Storgatan 19 ☎ 042 12 90 35, ⓦchforet.se. Resembling a French or Belgian modern café-bistro, this is the place to come for a taste of the Gallic continent, with excellent moules frites (185kr), as well as spinach risotto and baked mackerel. Tues–Sat 6pm–late.

★ **Ebba's Fik** Bruksgatan 20 ☎ 046 42 28 14 40, ⓦebbasfik.se. An amazing jumble of 1950s furnishings, and even a jukebox belting out the likes of Little Richard. Every detail of the era – from crockery to menu board – is here. Excellent egg and bacon fry-ups and delicious home-made Swedish beefburgers too. Mon–Fri 9am–6pm, Sat 9am–4pm.

Fahlmans Stortorget 11 ☎ 046 42 21 22 87, ⓦfahlmans.se. This classic bakery/café has been serving elaborate cakes and pastries since 1914 and is *the* place for decadent apple meringue pie – a meal in itself. Also try the chocolate and marzipan confections or filling sandwiches. Mon–Fri 8am–7pm, Sat 8.30am–4.30pm, Sun 8.30am–4.30pm.

Mommee's Södra Storgatan 28 ☎ 042 303 54 94, ⓦmommees.se. Serving the best lunch in Helsingborg, this lunch spot is inspired by Indian influences. The low priced student buffet (230kr) will make everyone happy. Mon–Fri 11am–3pm.

RESTAURANTS

★ **Edelweiss** Drottninggatan 15 ☎ 042 21 37 37, ⓦrestaurangedelweiss.se. A fun German restaurant-cum-beerhall with a tremendous selection of real German beers, as well as a whole variety of different schnitzels (from 160kr), a mammoth plate of Bavarian sausages, sauerkraut and mashed potato (170kr) and a superb goulash soup (90kr). Mon & Tue 5–9pm, Wed & Thurs 5–10pm, Fri 11.30pm–1am, Sat 4pm–1am, Sun 4–9pm.

Oasen Bruksgatan 25 ☎ 042 12 80 74, ⓦoasenfondue.se. This restaurant mainly serves fondues: meat (250kr), seafood (280kr) and Mexican (260kr). Its speciality is a totally wicked Toblerone fondue (100kr) with Cointreau and brandy into which you dip marshmallows, bananas and other fruit. Tues–Thurs 6pm–midnight, Fri & Sat 5pm–midnight.

Olsons Skafferi Mariagatan 6 ☎ 042 14 07 80, ⓦolsonsskafferi.se. With not a pizza in sight, this great Italian place located in a half-timbered building offers wonderfully prepared fish and meat (both around the 150kr mark) as well as pasta dishes (180–220kr), in a relaxed atmosphere. Mon–Sat 11am–10.30pm.

Papadam Bruksgatan 10 ☎ 042 12 16 00, ⓦpapadam indisk.se. Finally, decent Indian food has made it to Helsingborg. Balti dishes are from 130kr, an excellent lamb curry with spinach is 150kr, plus there's a good choice of Indian beers, including Cobra and Kingfisher. Mon–Thurs 11am–10pm, Fri & Sat 11am–11pm, Sun 1–10pm.

Redimat Badhusgatan 4 ☎ 042 13 02 00, ⓦredimat.se. A cellar restaurant that's taken Helsingborg by storm – locals just love the back-to-basics home cooking they dish up here, including the likes of *raggmunk* (potato pancakes; 90kr), *biff à la Lindström* (meat patties with beetroot and capers; 185kr) and fried zander (235kr). Mon–Wed & Fri 11am–3pm, Thurs 6–9pm, Fri & Sat 6–10pm.

BARS AND PUBS

Bishops Arms Södra Storgatan 2 ☎ 042 37 37 77, ⓦbishopsarms.com/helsingborg. At the top end of Stortorget, this centrally located pub is a firm favourite among Helsingborgers for its relatively genuine British pub feel, and its extensive range of beers, most on tap. Mon–Wed 4pm–midnight, Thurs 4pm–1am, Fri & Sat 4pm–2am, Sun 4–10pm.

Harry's Järnvägsgatan 7 ☎ 042 13 91 91, ⓦharrys.se/restauranger/helsingborg. Very popular place for a drink and rather more stylish than the usual *Harry's*, with soft leather armchairs and chandeliers throughout. There's a nightclub here on Fri & Sat nights from 11pm. Mon–Thurs 4pm–late, Fri 3pm–4am, Sat noon–4am.

Telegrafen Norra Storgatan 14 ☎ 042 18 14 50, ⓦtelegrafenhelsingborg.se. A long-term favourite, this cosy British-style pub with wooden floors and a bar lined with tattered old books can do no wrong – Swedes seem to love the mock-Britannia. Snacks such as burgers and fish and chips are available from 110kr. Daily 11.30am–late.

5

Lund

"There is a very tangible Lund spirit – those with it have … an ironic distance to everything, including themselves and Lund, a barb to deflate pompous self-importance", wrote the Swedish essayist Jan Mårtensson. His compatriot, poet Peter Ortman, for his part once described what he termed "Lund syndrome": "a mix of paranoia, exhibitionism and megalomania". Whatever it is about the place, there is indeed a special spirit to **LUND** – a sense of tolerance (it's more relaxed than other Swedish cities), and a belief that people should be judged by what they do, not by what they have.

A few kilometres inland and 54km south of Helsingborg, Lund's reputation as a glorious old **university city** is well founded. An ocean of bikes is the first image to greet you at the train station, and like Oxford in England – with which Lund is usually aptly compared – there is a bohemian, laidback eccentricity in the air. With a twelfth-century Romanesque **cathedral**, medieval streets lined with a variety of architectural styles and a wealth of cafés and restaurants, Lund is an enchanting little city that could well captivate you for a couple of days; it has a wide range of **museums**, a couple of them excellent, a mix of architectural grandeur, plus the buzz of student life. While Lund does lose much of its atmosphere during the summer months, some places remain open through June to August.

Domkyrkan

Cathedral • Kyrkogatan 6 • Mon–Fri 8am–6pm, Sat 9.30am–5pm, Sun 9.30am–6pm • Free

The obvious place to begin your exploration is the magnificent **Domkyrkan**, Lund's crowning glory. One of the world's finest masterpieces of Romanesque architecture, the cathedral is built of storm-cloud charcoal and white stone, giving it an imposing monochrome appearance. Before going inside, have a look round the back of the building; on the way there, you'll notice the grotesque animal and bird gargoyles over the side entrances, their features blunted by eight centuries of weathering. At the very back, the most beautiful part of the exterior, the three-storey **apse** above the crypt, is revealed, crowned with an exquisite gallery.

The interior

The majestic **interior** is surprisingly unadorned, an elegant mass of watery-grey ribbed stone arches and stone-flagged flooring. The cathedral was built in the twelfth century when Lund became the first independent archbishopric in Scandinavia, laying the foundation for a period of wealth and eminence that lasted until the advent of Protestantism. There are several striking features, such as the elaborately carved fourteenth-century choir stalls depicting Old Testament scenes and the grotesque carvings hidden beneath the seats.

The most vividly coloured feature is just to the left of the entrance, an amazing **astronomical clock** dating from the 1440s, which shows hours, days, weeks and the courses of the sun and moon in the zodiac. Each day at noon and 3pm, the clock also reveals its ecclesiastical Punch-and-Judy show, as two knights pop out and clash swords as many times as the clock strikes, followed by little mechanical doors opening to trumpet-blowing heralds and the Three Wise Men trundling slowly to the Virgin Mary.

The crypt

The dimly lit and dramatic **crypt** beneath the apse has been left almost untouched since the twelfth century, and should not be missed. Here, the thick smattering of what look like tombstones is really comprised of memorial slabs, brought down to the crypt from just above. There is one actual tomb, however – that of **Birger Gunnarsson**, Lund's last archbishop. A short man from a poor family, Gunnarsson chose the principal altar-facing position for his tomb, dictating that his stone effigy above it should be tall and regal.

Two **pillars** here are gripped by stone figures – one of a man, another of a woman and child. Local legend has it that **Finn the Giant** built the cathedral for St Lawrence; in return, unless the saint could guess his name, Finn wanted the sun, the moon or the saint's eyes. Lawrence was just preparing to end his days in blindness when he heard Finn's wife boasting to her baby, "Soon Father Finn will bring some eyes for you to play with." The relieved saint hurried to Finn, declaring the giant's name. The livid Finn, his wife and child rushed to the crypt to pull down the columns, and were instantly turned to stone. Even without the fable, the column-hugging figures are fascinating to view.

Lunds Universitets Historiska Museum

Lund University Historical Museum • Kraftstorg 12 • Tues & Wed noon–5pm, Thurs noon–8pm, Fri & Sat noon–5pm • 50kr • ⓦ luhm.lu.se

Just behind the cathedral, the **Lunds Universitets Historiska Museum** is for the most part rather dull unless you have a specialist interest in ecclesiastical history. The statues from Skåne's churches, in the medieval exhibition, deserve a look though, mainly because of the way they are arranged. The crowd of Jesuses hanging on crosses have an ominous quality worthy of Hitchcock, while in the next room all the Madonnas are paired off with the baby Jesuses.

Kulturen

Tegnerplatsen • May–Aug daily 10am–5pm; Sept–April Tues–Sun noon–5pm • May–Aug 120kr; Sept–April 90kr • ⓦ kulturen.com

5

A few minutes' walk from the Lunds Universitets Historiska Museum is the town's best museum, **Kulturen**. It's easy to spend the best part of a day just wandering around this privately owned open-air museum, a virtual town of perfectly preserved cottages, farms, merchants' houses, gardens and even churches, brought from seven Swedish regions and encompassing as many centuries.

Skissernas Museum

Museum of Sketches • Finngatan 2 • Tues–Sun 11–5pm • 50kr • ⓦ adk.lu.se

A few streets north from the cathedral in airy, revamped premises, the **Skissernas Museum** houses a fascinating collection of around 25,000 preliminary sketches and original maquettes of works of art from around the world. An ever-changing selection of them is displayed: usually one room is full of work by all the major Swedish artists, while in another are sketches by international giants, such as Chagall, Matisse, Léger, Miró and Dufy; the best-known sculptural sketches here are by Picasso and Henry Moore. Outside, the sculptures on display include preliminary versions of pieces found in town squares all over Sweden, including those by Bror Marklund.

Botaniska trädgården

Botanical Garden • Östra Vallgatan 20 • Daily 6am–8pm, mid-May–mid-Sept until 9.30pm; greenhouses 11am–3pm • Free • ⓦ botan.lu.se

An antidote to museum fatigue, the **Botaniska trädgården** is as much a venue for picnicking and chilling out as a botanical experience. The greenhouses and rock gardens are the best areas to view; the rarest sights here are the Far Eastern paper-mulberry trees and the huge tulip trees – part of the same family as magnolias – with masses of flowers in June.

ARRIVAL AND DEPARTURE   LUND

By train Trains arrive at the western edge of the centre. From the train station, the centre is a 2min walk, and everything of interest is within easy reach, with all the sights no more than 10min away.

Destinations Copenhagen (hourly; 45min); Gothenburg (hourly; 2hr 45min); Karlskrona (hourly; 2hr 40min); Kristianstad (hourly; 50min); Malmö (very frequent; 10min); Stockholm (hourly; 4hr 15min).

INFORMATION

Tourist office Botulfsgatan 1A, on the corner of Stortorget (Mon–Fri 10am–6pm, Sat 11am–3pm; June–Aug also Sat 11am–3pm & Sun 11am–3pm; ☎046 35 50 40, ⓦ visitlund.se). Has free internet access as well as maps and copies of the information booklet, *Lund*.

ACCOMMODATION   SEE MAP PAGE 166

Although there are plenty of luxury **hotels** in Lund, budget choices are extremely limited, and Malmö, just 12min away by train, has a much greater range. Lund is, nevertheless, a popular destination, so be sure to **book ahead**, especially for the youth hostel and cheaper options.

Concordia Stålbrogatan 1 ☎046 13 50 50, ⓦ concordia. se. A couple of streets southwest of Stortorget, this former student hostel has been upgraded into a very homely contemporary hotel with airy, modern Swedish designer rooms – though some are rather cramped. There's a sauna too. <u>1095kr</u>

Forenom Aparthotel Lund Laboratoriegatan 10 ☎358 20 198 3420, ⓦ forenom.com/sv/lagenhetshotell/lund/ forenom-aparthotel-lund/. Contemporary apartment

hotel close to the Botanical Garden, offering one-room accommodation in various sizes, complete with kitchens. There is also a communal sitting room, laundry facilities and a sauna. <u>995kr</u>

Grand Bantorget 1 ☎046 280 61 00, ⓦ grandilund.se. This imposing nineteenth-century pink-sandstone edifice straddles an entire side of a small, stately and central square. Top of the range, comfortable and unpretentious with period furnishings and chandeliers, this hotel oozes opulence and is perfect for a special occasion. <u>1595kr/2095kr</u>

Lilla Hotellet Bankgatan 7 ☎046 32 88 88, ⓦ lilla hotelletilund.se. Located in no fewer than five interlinked, low-roofed Lund town houses from the 1850s, painted

5

in subtle pastel shades, rooms here are cosy and nicely appointed, decorated in modern Swedish style and colours. **980kr/1380kr**

The More Kastanjegatan 18 ☎046 271 64 00, ⓦthemorehotel.se. Housed in Lund's former engine sheds, a 20min walk southeast of the train station, these stylish studios (over thirty of them) are a real home-from-home. Though they come in different sizes, each has its own kitchenette, including a dishwasher, ideal for self-catering. Special rates available for extended stays. **1185kr/1385kr**

EATING AND DRINKING

SEE MAP PAGE 166

There are plenty of charming places to **eat and drink** in Lund, many frequented by students, which helps keep prices low, especially for beer. For provisions, the **Saluhallen market** at Mårtenstorget (Mon–Fri 9.30am–6pm, Sat 9am–3pm), sells a range of fish, cheeses and meats, including Lund's own tasty speciality sausage, *knake*.

CAFÉS

Café Ariman Kungsgatan 2 ☎046 13 12 63, ⓦariman. se. Attached to the Nordic Law Department, this classic left-wing coffee house is located in a striking red-brick building. It's frequented by wannabe writers and artists, with goatees, ponytails and blonde dreadlocks predominating. Cheap snacks, coffee and cakes. Mon 11am–midnight, Tues–Thurs 11am–1am, Fri & Sat 11am–3am, Sun 3–11pm.

Mondo Sankt Petri Kyrkogatan 23 ☎046 76 404 47 67. In a quaint, half-timbered house with wood-panelled interior, this pleasant little café serves bagels, baguettes, pasta salads and ciabattas. Does takeaway, too, and is a popular student haunt. Mon–Fri 10am–7.15pm, Sat & Sun 10am–6pm.

Ramklints Konditori Mårtenstorget 10 ☎046 211 06 44, ⓦramklints.se. This is a place to pop in for a takeaway sandwich or a cake rather than somewhere to sit and linger as the interior is rather plain. However, its baked goods are always fresh and tasty. Mon–Fri 7.30am–6.30pm, Sat 10am–6pm, Sun 11.30am–5pm.

RESTAURANTS

Gattostretto Kattesund 6A ☎046 32 07 77, ⓦgattostretto.se. Compact neighbourhood Italian which really draws the crowds: try the three-course set menu for 298kr or delicious *fagottini* filled with pear and gorgonzola (145kr). Mon–Fri 11.30am–late, Sat 11.30am–late.

Gloria's Sankt Petri Kyrkogatan 9 ☎046 15 19 85, ⓦglorias.se. Serving Tex-Mex and Cajun food, this sports bar is very popular, particularly when there's a match on the big screen. Try the pork ribs (160kr), fish and chips (160kr) or the chicken burritos (170kr). Mon & Tues 11.30am–11pm, Wed & Thurs 11.30am–midnight, Fri 11.30am–1am, Sat 12.30pm–1am, Sun 1pm–11pm.

Mae Yai Stora Fiskaregatan 15B ☎046 13 00 93, ⓦmaeyai.com. This plain and simple Thai restaurant is very popular with the town's student population for its decent and generous Asian stir-fries and curries: most dishes are 85kr, 5kr less for takeaways. Mon–Fri 11am–10pm, Sat noon–10pm, Sun 1–10pm.

Matt & Destillat Kyrkogatan 17 ☎046 46 128 00, ⓦmatochdestillat.se/om. A restaurant and a cocktail bar on historic land in the heart of Lund. Famous dishes are prepared with the newest techniques, this will create an experience that you will remember. Mon–Thurs 11.30am–11pm, Fri 11.30am–11pm, Sat noon–1am.

Sankt Michel Vin och Tapasbar Östra Mårtensgatan 13 ☎0729 96 58 15, ⓦvintapasbar.se. Taking inspiration from similar restaurants in Barcelona, this is Lund's very own Spanish tapas bar, with a great selection of mouthwatering morsels such as fried feta, Spanish omelette and calamari; 60kr each, or four for 220kr. Mon–Thurs 5–11pm, Fri & Sat 5pm–midnight.

Stäket Stora Södergatan 6 ☎046 211 93 67, ⓦstaket lund.se. A step-gabled vaulted house built in 1570 is the characterful setting for this Mediterranean restaurant. Fillet of veal in a green pepper sauce (230kr), duck breast in a creamy apple sauce (240kr) or seafood risotto (160kr) are all exceptional. Mon–Thurs 11.30am–10pm, Fri 11.30am–10.30pm, Sat noon–10.30pm, Sun noon–10pm.

★**Stortorget** Stortorget 1 ☎046 13 92 90, ⓦstortorget.net. Housed in a National Romantic building that was formerly a bank, this trendy brasserie specializes in modern Swedish dishes, for example, smoked salmon with lemon mayonnaise (195kr) and a succulent lamb roast with root vegetables (210kr). Mains 155–215kr. Mon–Sat 11.30am–late, Sun noon–1am.

Tegnérs Matsalar Sandgatan 2 ☎046 13 13 33, ⓦtegners.se. Next to the Akademiska Föreningen, the student union, though forget any preconceptions you might have about student cafés being tatty, stale-sandwich bars. Lunch (85kr) is self-service and you eat as much as you like from a delicious spread; there's always a vegetarian option, too. Mon–Fri 11.30am–1.30pm.

Malmö

Founded in the late thirteenth century, **MALMÖ** was once Denmark's second most important city, after Copenhagen. The high density of herring in the sea off the Malmö coast – it was said that the fish could be scooped straight out with a trowel – brought ambitious German merchants flocking; their influence can be seen in the striking fourteenth-century St Petri kyrka in the city centre.

Today, with its attractive medieval centre, a myriad of cobbled and mainly pedestrianized streets full of busy restaurants and bars, Malmö has plenty of style. Beyond its compact centre, it's endowed with the stunning and dramatic skyscraper, the **Turning Torso**, a string of popular **beaches** and some interesting cultural diversions south of the centre around **Möllevångstorget**.

Brief history

Eric of Pomerania gave Malmö its most significant medieval boost, when, in the fifteenth century, he built the castle, endowed it with its own mint and gave Malmö its own flag – the gold-and-red griffin of his own family crest. It wasn't until the Swedish King Karl X marched his armies across the frozen Öresund to within striking distance of Copenhagen in 1658 that the Danes were forced into handing back the counties of Skåne, Blekinge and Bohuslän to the Swedes. For Malmö, too far from its own (uninterested) capital, this meant a period of stagnation, cut off from nearby Copenhagen. Not until the full thrust of industrialization, triggered by the tobacco merchant Frans Suell's enlargement of the harbour in 1775 (his jaunty bronze likeness, on Norra Vallgatan opposite the train station, overlooks his handiwork), did Malmö begin its dramatic commercial recovery. In 1840, boats began regular trips to Copenhagen, and Malmö's great Kockums shipyard was opened; limestone quarrying, too, became big business here in the nineteenth century.

During the last few decades of the twentieth century, Malmö found itself facing commercial crisis after a series of economic miscalculations, which included investing heavily in the shipping industry as it went into decline in the 1970s. But recent years have witnessed a dramatic renaissance, reflected in the upbeat atmosphere pervading the town today. Since the opening of the **Öresund bridge** linking the town to Copenhagen, the city's fortunes have been further improved, with Danes discovering what this gateway to Sweden has to offer, as opposed to the one-way traffic of Swedes to Denmark in the past.

Stortorget

The laying out of **Stortorget**, the proud main square, necessitated the tearing down of much of Malmö's medieval centre in the mid-sixteenth century. Among the elaborate sixteenth- to nineteenth-century buildings, the 1546 **Rådhus** draws the most attention. It's an impressive pageant of architectural fiddling and crowded with statuary: restoration programmes in the last century robbed the building of its original design, and the finicky exterior is now in Dutch Renaissance style. To add to the pomp, the red-and-gold flag of Skåne, of which Malmö is so proud, flaps above the roofs. The cellars, home to the *Rådhuskällaren* restaurant (see page 180), have been used as a tavern for more than four hundred years.

To the south of the town hall, have a look inside the **Apoteket Lejonet** (Lion Pharmacy – Swedish pharmacies are always named after creatures of strength): the outside is gargoyled and balconied, the inside a busy mix of inlaid woods, carvings and etched glass. From here, **Södergatan**, Malmö's main pedestrianized shopping street, leads down towards the canal. At the Stortorget end, there's a jaunty troupe of sculptured bronze musicians.

On the opposite side of the square, the crumbling, step-gabled red-brick building was once the home of the sixteenth-century mayor and master of the Danish mint, **Jörgen Kock**. Danish coins were struck in Malmö on the site of the present Malmöhus castle (see page 174), until irate local Swedes stormed the building and destroyed it in 1534. The cellars of Jörgen's pretty home contain the *Årstiderna* restaurant (see page 179),

EATING

Årstiderna	1
Atmosfär	14
Bastard	3
Bord 13	8
Café Siesta	4
Epicuré Re Gustavo	11
Green Chili	5
Gustav Adolf	10
Hollandia	13
Johan P	7
Kafé Agnez	12
La Soupe	15
Lyran	18
Mando Steakhouse	6
Rådhuskällaren	2
Smak	17
Spot	9
Systrar & Bröder	16

ACCOMMODATION

Astoria	6
Best Western Royal	4
Clarion Collection Temperance	8
Elite Hotel Esplanade	5
Elite Savoy	1
Good Morning Malmö	11
Malmö Camping	7
Mayfair Tunneln	2
Scandic Kramer	3
STF Malmö City Vandrarhem	9
The More	10

DRINKING, NIGHTLIFE AND LIVE MUSIC

Babel	7
Bishops Arms	1
Fagan's	6
The Indian Kitchen	8
Mello Yello	3
Moosehead	4
Paddy's	2
TGI Friday's	5

5

MALMÖ

0   250
metres

Central
Station

CARLSGATAN

SLUSS-
PLAN

HORNSGATAN

Bus Station

Canal

NORRA VALLGATAN

SLUSSGATAN

CENTRALPLAN

PETRI
BRON

DROTTNING
TORGET

ÖSTRA PROMENADEN

EXERCISGATAN

ÖSTRA FÖRSTADSGÅRD

ADELGATAN

ÖSTERGATAN

St Petri kyrka

KATTSUNDSGATAN

NORR GATAN

STORA TRÄDGÅRD

Rådhus

RUNDELSGATAN

STORTORGET

DJÄKNEGATAN

STORA KYARNGGATAN
GATAN

SÖDERGATAN

KALENDEGATAN

SNAPPERUPGATAN

GESVÄRSGATAN

RÖRSJÖGATAN

SKOMAKAREGATAN

BALTZARSGATAN

Moderna
Muséet

Canal

EXERCISGATAN

Palladium

PER
WEIJERSGATAN

STORA NYGATAN

MALMSBORGSG.

STUDENTG.

SÖDRA PROMENADEN

ANDREEGATAN

GUSTAV ADOLFS
TORG

LILLANYGATAN

DROTTNINGGATAN

Canal

AMIRALS
BRON

KUNGSGATAN

Sankt Pauli kyrka

SÖDRA VALLGATAN

KAPSTENGATAN

AMIRALSGATAN

KUNGSGATAN

INDUSTRIGATAN

SÖDRAFÖRSTADSGATAN

GATAN

Malmö
Konserthus

FÖRENINGSGATAN

Sankt Pauli
Norra kyrkogård

DISPONENTGATAN

N

KAMEERGATAN

SANKT KNUTS VÄG

HANTVERKAREGATAN

FÖRENINGSGATAN

AMIRALSGATAN

SORGENFRIVÄGEN

SPÄNGGATAN

7

BERGSGATAN

SPANEHUSVÄGEN

RONNEBYGATAN

FRIISGATAN

SÖDRA FÖRSTADSGATAN

10

FRIISGATAN

NORRA PARKGATAN

KARLSKRONA-
PLAN

KAPELLGATAN

8

Folkets
Park

AMIRALSGATAN

KAMMAKREGATAN

BARKGATAN

FALSTERBOGATAN

NOBELVÄGEN

SÖDRA SKOLGATAN

SLÖJDGATAN

MÖLLEVÅNGS-
TORGET

KRISTIANSTADSGATAN

NOBEL-
TORGET

CARL GUSTAFS VÄG

VSTADSGATAN

SIMRISHAMNSGATAN

18

5

the only entry point for visitors today. In the centre of the square, a **statue of Karl X**, high on his charger, presides over the city he liberated from centuries of Danish rule.

St Petri kyrka

Göran Olsgatan • Daily 10am–6pm

A block east of Stortorget, behind the Rådhus, the dark, forbidding exterior of the Gothic **St Petri kyrka** belies a light and airy interior. The church, which is effectively Malmö's cathedral, has its roots in the fourteenth century, and, although Baltic in inspiration, has ended up owing much to German influences, for it was beneath its unusually lofty and elegantly vaulted roof that the German community came to pray – probably for the continuation of the "sea silver", the herrings that brought them to Malmö in the first place. The ecclesiastical vandalism, brought by the Reformation, of whitewashing over medieval roof murals started early at St Petri; almost the whole interior turned white in 1553. Consequently, your eyes are drawn not to the roof but to the pulpit and a four-tiered altarpiece, both of striking workmanship and elaborate embellishment. The only part of the church left with its original artwork was a side-chapel, the **Krämare** (merchant's).

Lilla torg

Despite the size of Stortorget, it still proved too small to suffice as the town's sole main square, so in the sixteenth century **Lilla torg** was tacked onto its southwest corner, over a patch of marshland. With its half-timbered houses, flowerpots and cobbles, this is where most locals and tourists congregate. During the day, people come to take a leisurely drink in one of the many bars and wander around the summer jewellery stalls. At night, Lilla torg explodes in a frenzy of activity, the venues all merging into a mass of bodies who converge from all over the city and beyond.

Form/Design Center

Lilla torg 9 • Tues–Sat 11am–5pm, Sun noon–4pm • Free • ⓦ formdesigncenter.com

Head under the arch on Lilla torg to get to the **Form/Design Center**. Built into a seventeenth-century grain store, it concentrates on Swedish contemporary design in textiles, ceramics and furniture. It's all well presented, if a little pretentious. The courtyard entrance contains several small trendy boutiques and there's a simple café.

Moderna Muséet

Modern Museum • Gasverksgatan 22 • Tues–Sun 11am–6pm • Free • ⓦ modernamuseet.se/malmo

A few streets removed from the other sights of the old town, the **Moderna Muséet** is well worth a visit if you're interested in contemporary art. The museum is housed in an elaborately designed building, the Rooseum, dating from 1900 and originally the home of Malmö electricity company's steam turbines. The structure has been turned into several galleries, playing host to temporary exhibitions of the museum's rich collection from 1900 onwards, as well as classics of modern art from the likes of Matisse, Picasso and Dalí.

Malmöhus and around

Malmöhusvägen 6 • Daily 10am–5pm • 40kr • ⓦ malmo.se

Take any of the streets running west from Stortorget or Lilla torg and you soon come up against the edge of **Kungsparken**, within striking distance of the fifteenth-century castle of **Malmöhus**. For a more head-on approach, walk west (away from the station) up Citadellsvägen; from here the low castle, with its grassy ramparts and two circular keeps, is straight ahead over the wide moat. It's one of Sweden's least aesthetically pleasing castles, with mean windows and patched-up brickwork, but the inside is worth a peek.

After Sweden's destruction of Denmark's mint here in 1534, the Danish king Christian III built a new fortress two years later. This was only to be of unforeseen benefit to his enemies, who, once back in control of Skåne, used it to repel an attacking Danish army in 1677. For a time a prison (its most notable inmate the Earl of Bothwell, Mary Queen of Scots' third husband), the castle declined in importance once back in Swedish hands, and it was used for grain storage until becoming a museum in 1937.

The museum
Once in the **museum**, pass swiftly through the natural history section, a taxidermal Noah's Ark holding no surprises; the most rewarding part of the museum is upstairs in the so-called **art museum**, part of the historical exhibition, where an ambitious series of furnished rooms covers most modern styles, from the mid-sixteenth-century Renaissance period through Baroque, Rococo, pastel-pale Gustavian and Neoclassical. A stylish interior from the *Jugendstil* (Art Nouveau) period is also impressive, while other rooms have Functionalist and post-Functionalist interiors, with some wacky colour and texture combinations. Other sections of the historical exhibition include a display of medieval skeletons from Malmö's churchyards, showing the signs of infection with contemporary diseases like leprosy and tuberculosis – less gruesome than you might imagine. It's more interesting to head into the castle itself, with its spartan but authentic interiors.

Banérskajen
Just west of Malmöhus, running off Malmöhusvägen, is a tiny walkway, **Banérskajen**, lined with higgledy-piggledy fishing shacks selling fresh and smoked fish – a rare little area of traditional Malmö that contrasts with the lively pace of the rest of the city.

South of the centre
Savvy visitors know that there's much more to Malmö these days than the central areas around Stortorget and Lilla torg. South of the canal, around **Amiralsgatan** and **Fersens väg**, there are some charming enclaves of antique shops, cafés and quirky buildings, as well as the impressive Konsthall art exhibition centre. Slightly further afield, a trip down to the hip multicultural district around **Möllevångstorget** is a great way to see some of Malmö's mix of cultures and its Social Democratic roots – the city has been at the forefront of left-wing politics for the last century, and was central to the creation and development of Sweden's Social Democratic Party.

Södra Förstadsgatan and Davidhallstorg
Heading south from Malmöhus along Slottsgatan, first cross over Regementsgatan and then cut across three blocks east to cobbled **Södra Förstadsgatan**; at no. 4 is a splendid

---

MALMÖ'S PARKS
Malmö is justifiably proud of its beautiful **parks**, a chain of which run southwards from the grounds of Malmöhus, and there's a great deal of pleasure to be had by simply strolling around these lovely green expanses. Free guided tours on their flora and royal history are also available (ask at the tourist office).

Heading south from the castle, the first park you encounter is **Kungsparken**, with its graceful trees and classic sculptures, bordering the canal. Just on the south side of the curving river is **Slottsparken**, with graceful, mature trees and places to picnic; further south is the largest of the parks, **Pildammsparken**, boasting several tranquil lakes.

5

house designed in 1904, its National Romantic facade covered with flower and animal motifs. A little further along the same road at no. 18, the **Victoriateatern** is Sweden's oldest still-operating cinema, dating from 1912; it's all fine Art Nouveau swirls of dark oak and bevelled glass. Two blocks east of the cinema is **Davidhallstorg**, an up-and-coming funky little square that's fast becoming home to any number of enticing neighbourhood restaurants.

Konsthall

Arts Centre · St Johannesgatan 7 · Daily 11am–5pm, Wed 11am–9pm · Free · Ⓦ konsthall.malmo.se

Head south down **Fersens väg** (the southward continuation of Slottsgatan after crossing Regementsgatan) for about ten minutes to reach the **Konsthall**, a single-storey glass and concrete building on St Johannesgatan. The enormous white-painted space shows vast modern works in regular temporary exhibitions, with lots of room to stand back and take in the visual feast.

Folkets park

From the canal, head east along Regementsgatan and turn right into **Amiralsgatan**, from where it's a ten-minute walk south to **Folkets park**, Sweden's oldest existing public park, which was once the pride of the community. Restored with an elegant water feature at the Möllevången exit, Folkets park contains a basic amusement park, and at its centre, a ballroom named the **Moriskan**, an odd, low building with Russian-style golden domes topped with crescents. Both the park and the ballroom are now privately owned, a far cry from the original aims of the park's Social Democratic founders. Severe carved busts of these city fathers are dotted all over the park. The socialist agitator August Palm made the first of his several historic speeches here in 1881, marking the beginning of a 66-year period of unbroken Social Democratic rule in Sweden.

Möllevångstorget

More interesting than the giant twirling teacup fun rides in Folkets park is the multicultural character of the city south from here. Strolling from the park's southeastern exit along Falsterbogatan and then left into Kristianstadsgatan to **Möllevångstorget**, you enter an area populated almost entirely by people of non-Swedish descent, where Arab, Asian and Balkan émigré families predominate. The vast square is a haven of exotic food stores, side by side with shops selling pure junk and more recently established Chinese restaurants and karaoke pubs. On a hot summer afternoon it's easy to forget you're in Sweden at all, the more makeshift and ramshackle atmosphere around the bright fruit and veg stands contrasting with the clean, clinical order of the average Swedish neighbourhood.

It's worth taking a close look at the provocative **sculpture** at the square's centre: four naked, bronze men strain under the colossal weight of a huge chunk of rock bearing carved representations of Malmö's smoking chimneys, while two naked women press their hands into the men's backs in support. It's a poignant image, marrying toil in a city founded on limestone-quarrying with the Social Democratic vision of the working man's struggle.

The Turning Torso

From the western side of Malmöhus, Malmö's most breathtaking sight looms on the northern horizon: the **Turning Torso**. An easy fifteen-minute walk north along Mariedalsvägen, crossing the canal over Varvsbron, brings you to Västra Varvsgatan, which streaks in a straight line to the city's **Västra Hamnen** district, home to the **skyscraper** that bears down on you as you approach. The tallest building in Scandinavia, this sleek, twisting tower of steel curves ninety degrees clockwise as it rises to a height of 190m above the ground. Designed to reshape the city skyline that

THE ÖRESUND BRIDGE

Linking Malmö with Copenhagen in Denmark (and thus Sweden with the rest of continental Europe), the elegant **Öresund bridge** was finally completed in 1999, after a forty-year debate. From Lernacken, a few kilometres south of Malmö, the bridge runs to a 4km-long artificial island off the Danish coast, from where an immersed tunnel carries traffic and trains across to the mainland – a total distance of 16km. The bridge itself has two levels, the upper for a four-lane highway and the lower for two sets of train tracks, and comprises three sections: a central high bridge, spanning 1km, and approach bridges to either side, each over 3km long. In December 2010, **Citytunneln**, a underground rail tunnel, was opened beneath the city, speeding trains directly into the heart of Malmö from Denmark; the journey to Copenhagen is faster and more frequent as a result.

The Öresund bridge has inspired and lent its name to the hit Swedish-Danish TV series *Bron* (in Swedish), The Bridge (in English), based in both Malmö and Copenhagen, and starring acclaimed Swedish actor Sofia Helin as crime investigator Saga Norén. Fans of the series may wish to check out some of the filming locations in Malmö – ask the tourist office for their handout "Getting closer to The Bridge".

had been dominated for decades by the frightfully ugly Kockum shipyard crane, the skyscraper now houses luxury flats and penthouses. Indeed, Västra Hamnen is now famed for its impressive green profile – the whole area is self-sufficient in renewable energy produced from water, wind, sun and compostable waste.

Kallbadhus and Malmö's beaches

Ribersborgs kallbadhus: May–Aug Mon–Fri 9am–9pm, Sat & Sun 9am–6pm; Sept–April Mon, Tues, Thurs & Fri 10am–7pm, Wed 10am–8pm, Sat & Sun 9am–6pm • ☎ 040 26 03 66, ⓦ ribersborgskallbadhus.se • Bus #7 (towards Ön) runs from the centre of town

Separated from the Turning Torso by delightful **Ribersborg park**, Malmö's long stretch of sandy **beaches** runs several kilometres to the old limestone-quarrying area of Limhamn to the southwest. Fringed by dunes and grassland, the beaches are popular with families as the water remains shallow for several metres out to sea. The beaches are numbered according to the jetty which gives access into the water: at jetty #1, the **Ribersborgs kallbadhus** is a cold-water bathhouse offering separate-sex **nude bathing** areas and sauna, whilst the last jetty, #10, denotes Malmö's popular **nudist beach**, which is actually not a beach at all but rather a grassy sunbathing area beside the jetty.

ARRIVAL AND DEPARTURE

MALMÖ

By train Malmö's Centralstation is on two levels; all services to and from Denmark use the underground platforms.
Destinations Copenhagen (every 20min; 35min); Copenhagen airport (every 20min; 20min); Gothenburg (hourly; 3hr); Helsingborg (hourly; 40min); Karlskrona (hourly; 3hr); Lund (very frequent; 10min); Stockholm (hourly;

4hr 30min); Ystad (hourly; 50min).
By bus The main bus terminal is in the square immediately outside the train station. Since the train service is so comprehensive, though, you're unlikely to use buses much, unless heading to Skanör (every 30min; 50min). For regional bus information call Skånetrafiken on ☎ 0771 77 44 33.

INFORMATION

Tourist office Opposite Centralstation at Skeppsbron 2 (Mon–Fri 9am–5pm, Sat & Sun 10am–2pm; ☎ 040 34 12 00, ⓦ malmotown.com). Offers a wealth of free information, including the English-language listings

brochure *Malmö Guide*, and free internet access.
Health care For an on-call doctor call ☎ 1177. The Apoteket Gripen pharmacy is at Bergsgatan 48 (daily 8am–10pm).

GETTING AROUND

By bus Although the city centre is easy to walk around, its central squares and streets all interlinked, you'll need to use the city bus service to reach some of the sights and

places to stay. You cannot buy tickets on the bus so instead get a prepaid travel pass known as a Jojo-kort from the Skånetrafiken desk inside the train station.

5

By taxi Several taxi companies in Malmö operate a fixed-price system within the city and surrounding area, but you should always agree the price before you start your journey. To give a rough idea of costs, a trip across the centre costs around 150–200kr. Taxi 97 ☎ 040 97 97 97, Taxi Kurir ☎ 0771 86 00 00, Taxi Skåne ☎ 046 72 266 03 30.

By boat Canal boat tours, known as Rundan Sightseeing, make a fun way of seeing the city; they leave daily from the canal opposite the *Elite Savoy* hotel (late April to Sept daily 10am–6pm; 50min; 140kr; ⊛ rundan.se). Alternatively, pedal boats let you tour around the canal network at your own pace. They're moored at Amiralsbron (May noon–6pm, June–Aug 11am–9pm, Sept noon–6pm; 180kr/hr; ⊛ cityboats.se).

By bike To strike out to the south of the city or further afield, bike rental is a good idea – the best place is from the Rundan Sightseeing terminal (see opposite) on Norra Vallgatan, where a day's rental is 170kr (mid-April–Sept; book online at ⊛ rundan.se).

ACCOMMODATION

SEE MAP PAGE 172

There are some really good and surprisingly affordable **hotels** in Malmö; the city is eager to attract tourists, and competition between the hotels can be fierce. Most hotels can be booked online at ⊛ malmo.se/hotellbokning, where special deals are sometimes also available.

Astoria Gråbrödersgatan 7 ☎ 040 786 60, ⊛ astoria hotel.se. A few minutes from the train station across the canal, this is a good, comfortable hotel with wooden floors and modern Scandinavian decor, worth checking out for its weekend and summer prices. 900kr/1255kr

★ **Best Western Royal** Norra Vallgatan 94 ☎ 040 664 25 00, ⊛ bwhotelroyal.se. The anonymous chain hotel feel has yet to pervade this winning little place that was previously a long-standing family-run hotel. Exceptionally cosy rooms with modern interiors really are a home from home. 890kr/980kr

Clarion Collection Temperance Engelbrektsgatan 16 ☎ 040 710 20, ⊛ nordicchoicehotels.se. As you would expect from the Choice chain, rooms are first-class, modern and classically Swedish in design, with polished dark wood floors, cosy furnishings and top facilities including a sauna and solarium. Free evening buffet included. 880kr/1880kr

Elite Hotel Esplanade Mäster Johansgatan 15 ☎ 040 24 85 00, ⊛ elite.se/sv/hotell/malmo/hotel-esplanade. Built within Malmö's former Saluhallen indoor market, this is the city's most luxurious hotel, with contemporary chic at every turn: soft lighting in purples and pinks, floral wall patterns and fresh flowers throughout. 926kr/1450kr

Elite Savoy Norra Vallgatan 62 ☎ 040 664 48 00, ⊛ elite.se. This is where Lenin, Bardot and Dietrich all stayed, with a brass plaque to prove it. Now part of the upmarket Elite chain, it's lost its edge but the rooms are big and very comfortable, and the extensive breakfast is an experience in itself. 1215kr/1800kr

Good Morning Malmö Stadiongatan 21 ☎ 040 672 85 70, ⊛ gmorninghotels.se; bus #8. Although a 30–45min walk from the centre, the prices at this simple yet functional place make up for the inconvenience, especially during the summer when prices fall by twenty percent. 760kr/1095kr

Mayfair Tunneln Adelgatan 4 ☎ 040 10 16 20, ⊛ mayfairtunneln.com. Very central luxury place and one of the finest of Malmö's more intimate hotels. Rooms are well furnished in cherry and Gustavian pastels. A sumptuous buffet breakfast is served in the vaulted cellar restaurant. 895kr/1100kr

Scandic Kramer Stortorget 7 ☎ 040 693 54 00, ⊛ scandichotels.com. One of two Scandic hotels in Stortorget, this historic building dating from 1878 is the place to come for old-fashioned elegance. A sweeping staircase leads up from the marble arched foyer to the high-ceilinged, spacious rooms. Breakfast is served in the ornate glass veranda overlooking Stortorget. 866kr/1210kr

STF Malmö City Vandrarhem Rönngatan 1 ☎ 040/611 62 20, ✉ malmo.city@stfturist.se. This hostel, which even boasts its own roof terrace, has plainly decorated, rather small rooms with en-suite facilities and the price includes the breakfast buffet. It's a good 20min walk south from the train station. Check-in is from 3pm. Doubles 900kr

★ **The More** Norra Skolgatan 24 ☎ 040 665 10 00, ⊛ themorehotel.com. Good-value and stylishly decorated studio rooms and small apartments for rent in a renovated and central former chocolate factory, a few blocks from Folkets Park. All seventy-odd rooms have kitchen facilities, sitting areas and private bathroom. 1085kr/2170kr

CAMPING

Malmö Camping Strandgatan 101 in Limhamn ☎ 040 15 51 65, ⊛ firstcamp.se; bus #34. This vast but pleasant campsite is not far from the Öresund bridge; it's located right by the sea and has great views across to Denmark. Also has a number of cottages for rent. Open all year. Tents 340kr, cottages 900kr

EATING AND DRINKING

SEE MAP PAGE 172

Between Malmö's many **eating places** you're bound to find something to whet your appetite. Over recent years the influx of immigrants (and second-generation Swedes) has created a demand for all types of cuisine, not just traditional Swedish. Most of Malmö's restaurants, brasseries and cafés are concentrated in and around its three central squares, with **Lilla torg** attracting the biggest crowds. For cheaper eats and a very un-Swedish atmosphere, head south of the centre to **Möllevångstorget**, the heart of Malmö's immigrant community.

CAFÉS

Café Siesta Hjorttackegatan 1 ☎ 040 611 10 27, ⓦsiesta.nu. A great little café with stark white walls and leather stools serving light Scandinavian lunches such as a tasty seafood soup (195kr) or toast with fish roe and dill (145kr) or more substantial dishes like rack of lamb with Västerbotten cheese (205kr). Tue–Thurs 4–11pm, Fri & Sat 11.30am–1am.

Gustav Adolf Gustav Adolfs torg 43 ☎ 040 611 22 72, ⓦgustavadolf.se. Long established and stylishly renovated with rough brick walls, this is still a popular spot for coffee and cakes and for its Sunday brunch buffet for 185kr. Mon–Thurs & Sun 11am–11pm, Fri & Sat 11am–late.

Hollandia Södra Förstadsgatan 8 ☎ 040 12 48 86, ⓦhollandia.se. The oldest café in Malmö, dating from 1905, a classic *konditori* with marble busts, chandeliers and a window full of breads and pastries. The house speciality is mouthwatering chocolate cake. Mon–Fri 7.45am–7pm, Sat 9am–7pm, Sun 9am–7pm.

Kafé Agnez Agnesgatan 11 ☎ 046 73 733 99 43, ⓦfacebook.com/ekokafeagnez. Known rightly for its glorious courtyard strewn with a bohemian collection of garden furniture, this alternative café is really a haven of peace and quiet. Against a background of tinkling water from the fountain, come here to enjoy fresh salads, vegan cakes and buns and a great selection of coffees. Daily 11.30am–5pm.

Systrar & Bröder Östra Rönneholmsvägen 26 ☎ 040 97 34 70, ⓦsystrarbroder.se. Superb breads, cakes and a full range of ciabattas plus a great-value daily breakfast buffet for just 95kr (weekends 105kr) are on offer at this hip joint with leatherette bench seats and a 1960s ambience. Mon–Fri 7.30am–3pm, Sat 8am–3pm, Sun 9am–3pm.

RESTAURANTS

Årstiderna Frans Suellsgatan 3 ☎ 040 23 09 10, ⓦarstiderna.se. This fine old basement restaurant with rough brick walls and period furniture is *the* place for classic Swedish dishes. Its four-course Swedish menu with whitefish roe, herb-baked reindeer fillet, Allerum cheese and finally cloudberries with ice cream is 650kr. Mon–Thurs 5–11pm, Fri & Sat 5pm–midnight.

Atmosfär Fersens väg 4 ☎ 040 12 50 77, ⓦatmosfar.com. Stylish to a T, this chi-chi brasserie serves a blend of accomplished Swedish and Mediterranean dishes such as crab with fennel, cucumber and apple (115kr), lamb brisket with mint aioli (140kr) and scallops with chilli mayonnaise (130kr). Mon–Fri 11.30am–1.30pm and 5pm–late, Sat 5pm–late.

Bastard Mäster Johansgatan 11 ☎ 040 12 13 18, ⓦbastardrestaurant.se. The place to sample` modern

European home cooking, as interpreted by one of Sweden's top chefs, with plenty of odd off-cuts and unusual ingredients (hence the name), such as ox heart, pig's neck and livers of various origins. The menu changes on a daily basis. Tues–Thurs 5pm–midnight, Fri & Sat 5pm–1am.

Bord 13 Engelbrektsgatan 13 ☎ 042 587 88, ⓦbord13.se. Another in the latest vogue of restaurants where the menu changes on a daily basis, with the chefs rustling up whatever they choose based on the day's locally sourced ingredients. If there is a theme it's Nordic cuisine, where the emphasis is on fresh, local and organic. Tues–Sat 5pm–late.

Epicuré Re Gustavo Gustav Adolfs torg 45 ☎ 040 97 11 00, ⓦepicure.nu. One of the city's most accomplished kitchens, this southern Italian restaurant with a hint of Lombardy thrown in, serves up the likes of saltimbocca (190kr), tagliatelle with salmon and pancetta (160kr) and gnocchi with bacon and taleggio (150kr). Mon–Sat 11.30am–late.

★ **Green Chili** Lilla torg 7 ☎ 040 30 77 44, ⓦgreenchili.se. Stylish Indian brasserie in a half-timbered building from around 1600 with outdoor seating, too: there are lots of balti dishes available for around 165–190kr, plus a good selection of tandoori sizzlers from 165kr. Mon–Thurs 11.30am–5pm & 5–10pm, Fri 11.30am–5pm & 5–11pm, Sat noon–11pm, Sun 4–10pm.

Johan P Hjulhamnsgatan 5 ☎ 040 97 18 18, ⓦjohanp.nu. This place has a good reputation for totally delicious fish dishes and the selection of fresh fish is the best in the city, although it doesn't come cheap: turbot with truffle risotto is 450kr, bouillabaisse is 245kr and a set four-course menu is 695kr. Mon–Fri 11.30am–late, Sat noon–late, Sun 1pm–late.

La Soupe Davidhallstorg 9 ☎ 46 70 814 95 60, ⓦlasoupe.se. Cute little neighbourhood restaurant squeezed into tight premises in popular Davidhallstorg, serving up all variety of tasty, home-made soups, such as gazpacho, creamy seafood and tomato and lentil at superb prices – from 70kr for a bowl. Mon & Tues 11.30am–2.30pm, Wed–Sat 11.30am–9pm.

Lyran Simrishamnsgatan 36A ☎ 076 324 52 28, ⓦlyranmatbar.se. There's no set menu at this restaurant that has set tongues wagging across Malmö. The chefs dish up expertly prepared creations depending on whatever their local suppliers have delivered that morning – always fresh, always creative and generally drawing on local Skåne traditions. Reckon on four courses for around 325–375kr. Tues–Sat 5.30pm–late.

★ **Mando Steakhouse** Skomakaregatan 4 ☎ 040 780 00, ⓦmandosteakhouse.com. All meat at this inordinately popular steakhouse with curious copper-plated interior walls comes from local farms and is grilled over lava stones to give it a special barbecue flavour. Mains cost 110–245kr. Mon, Tues & Sun 11.30am–9.30pm,

5

Wed & Thurs 11.30am–10pm, Friday 11am–11pm, Sat 11.30am–11pm.

Rådhuskällaren Stortorget 1 ☎040 790 20, ⓦradhuskallaren.se. This restaurant is housed in the long vaulted cellars of the gloriously decorated town hall. The emphasis here is on gourmet dishes, such as blackened salmon with fennel and dill (185kr) and duck breast with cherry sauce and a purée of root vegetables (245kr). Mon–Fri 11.30am–2pm & 5–10.30pm, Sat 5–11pm, Sun 3–9pm.

Smak St Johannesgatan 7 ☎040 50 50 35, ⓦsmak.info. Inside the Konsthall building, this relaxed café-restaurant does a good line in vegetarian, organic meat and fish dishes using locally sourced ingredients. It's also a very popular place for weekend brunch. Daily 11am–5pm.

Spot Stora Nygatan 33 ☎040 12 02 03, ⓦrestaurang spotmalmo.se. An extremely popular and chic Italian trattoria with tiled walls and floor serving good Italian fare at sensible prices: ricotta and spinach tortellini (150kr), for example, or pasta with pesto and bacon (120kr). Mon–Thurs 11.30am–9pm, Fri 11.30am–10pm, Sat 11am–10pm, Sun noon–6pm.

NIGHTLIFE AND ENTERTAINMENT

SEE MAP PAGE 172

Gone are the days when the only entertainment in Malmö was watching rich drunks become poor drunks at the blackjack table in the Centralstation bar. Nowadays there are some decent **live music** venues and **discos**, most of which are cheaper to get into than their other European counterparts. For **drinking**, Lilla torg is where Malmöites and tourists alike head in the evenings. The square buzzes with activity, as the smell of beer wafts between the old, beamed houses, and music and chatter fill the air. With a largely 20- and 30-something crowd, the atmosphere is like that of a summer carnival.

BARS, CLUBS AND LIVE MUSIC

Babel Spånggatan 38 ☎ 046 40 57 98 96, ⓦbabel malmo.se. *The* place to hear live music in Malmö with latest appearances advertised online. Club nights, too, are inordinately popular, especially on Wed. Times vary.

Bishops Arms Norra Vallgatan 62 ☎040 664 48 88, ⓦbishopsarms.com. This is a cosy but rather staid pub with a heavy-handed insistence on looking British. However, it does have an impressive range of beers on tap. Mon–Sat 5pm–1am, Sun 5–11pm.

Fagan's Per Weijersgatan 4 ☎040 97 09 90, ⓦfagans. se. Malmö's leading Irish pub with lots of whiskeys and Irish beers available. At happy hour (Mon–Thurs 4–6pm, Fri 3–7pm) the place is absolutely packed. Thurs is quiz night; on Fri and Sat nights there's live music. Mon & Tues 4–11pm, Wed & Thurs 4pm–midnight, Fri 3pm–2am, Sat 2pm–2am.

The Indian Kitchen Södra Skolgatan 30 ☎040 12 60 21, ⓦtheindiankitchen.se. This compact little bar close to Möllevångstorget is always packed with students and food lovers who come here to relax and catch a drink to enjoy the atmosphere. Mon–Fri 11am–1pm, Sat & Sun noon–1am.

Mello Yello Lilla torg 1 ☎040 30 45 25, ⓦmelloyello. se. A popular haunt for the 25-plus age group. Lots of people come here to enjoy a bite to eat as well as a drink and there's a good choice of burgers and steaks. Gets lively as the night progresses. Mon–Fri 1.30pm–1am, Sat & Sun noon–1am; May–Aug Mon–Fri from 1.30pm.

Moosehead Lilla torg 1 ☎040 12 04 23, ⓦlillatorg.nu/ moosehead. With rough brick walls and a gorgeous stucco cornice, this stylish bar is one of Malmö's most fun places to drink, and a firm favourite with the 20-somethings. It's known for its great burgers, too. Mon–Fri 1pm–1am, Sat 11.30am–1am & Sun noon–midnight.

Paddy's Kalendegatan 7 ☎040 786 00, ⓦpaddys.se. This is a laidback place for a drink right in the centre of town, known for its good Guinness. Pub quizzes on Mon, live music on Fri and Sat with soul and funk covers. Mon & Tues 4pm–midnight, Wed & Thurs 4pm–1am, Fri & Sat 4pm–2am.

TGI Fridays Lilla torg 17, ☎046 40 97 80 90, ⓦfridays. se. People start their weekend here with great burgers and drinks. Mon & Tues 11.30am–11pm, Wed & Thurs 11.30am–midnight, Fri & Sat noon–2am.

CONCERT VENUES

Malmö Konserthus Föreningsgatan 35 ☎040 34 35 00, ⓦmalmolive.se. Classical music performances take place here, at the home of the Malmö Symphony Orchestra. Check

THE MALMÖ FESTIVAL

Every August Malmö plays host to the annual **Malmöfestivalen** (ⓦmalmofestivalen.se), one of the biggest in Sweden. Sprawling across the city from the parks around Malmöhus to Stortorget and Gustav Adolfs torg, the festival's grand opening, always on a Friday, is marked by a giant crayfish party in Stortorget, when thousands of people bring their own crayfish and *akvavit* to sing and dance the night away. Over the eight days, there's free music and entertainment across the city. World food is dished up from a multitude of stalls: Pakistani, Somali and Bosnian dishes alongside more traditional elk kebabs and Swedish pancakes.

with the tourist office for programme details. Times vary. **Musikhögskolan** Ystadvägen 25 ☎040 32 54 50. Classical music venue. Check with the tourist office for programme details.

Palladium Södergatan 15 ☎040 10 99 90, ⓦ palladium. nu. A good place to see live music and dance performances, with a variety of Scandinavian R&B and rock bands playing in the original 1920s interior. Times vary.

Skanör and around

Leaving Malmö, it's barely 30km due south along the E6 and then Route 100 to Sweden's most southwesterly point and the adjoining medieval town of **SKANÖR**, site of a tremendous beach and nature reserve, plus a remarkable Viking-style settlement at nearby **Foteviken**.

Skanör was once an important commercial centre and was founded as part of the Hanseatic commercial system. In the early twentieth century, the town became a fashionable bathing resort for wealthy Malmö families. Today, Skanör's simple pleasures lie in wandering through the medieval streets and admiring the pretty half-timbered houses around the main square, Rådhustorget, and along Mellangatan.

Sankt Olofs kyrka

Kyrkogatan 5 • Mon–Fri 8am–4pm

In all probability, Skanör's church, **Sankt Olofs kyrka**, dates from the early 1200s though over the following centuries it was extended and its windows, in particular, are High Gothic. It's also one of very few churches in the south of Sweden to have a crypt. When the herring stocks in the Baltic disappeared in the sixteenth century, the town lost its importance, and so the church was never updated, making it all the more appealing today.

The beaches

There's not much to see in Skanör itself, but its **beaches** are superb: long ribbons of white sand bordering an extensive **bird and nature reserve**. North of the town centre, a 5km-long sandy strand stretches out to a point known as **Svanrevet**, where there's a well-known and popular **nudist beach**; simply take the footpath which leads north from Kyrkogatan out towards the beach. Close by is the splendid **Flommen nature reserve**, dominated by wetland meadows carpeted with blue butterfly iris, and sea-holly sprouting between the sand dunes.

A few kilometres to the south of Skanör is Sweden's oldest nature reserve, **Näbben**, one of twelve on the peninsula here. It's home to a huge population of birds – on a good day in September or October you can spot more than fifty species. You can walk southwards, towards the tip of the peninsula, passing the splendid **Ule näbbe beach** on the way, to Sweden's oldest **lighthouse**, Kolabacken, whose beam was created by burning charcoal. At the very tip of the peninsula is the **Måkläppen spit**, a nature reserve known as a refuge for both grey and harbour seals (closed Feb–Oct).

Foteviken Viking Museum

Museivägen 24, Höllviken • May & early Sept Tues–Fri 10am–4pm; June–Aug daily 10am–4pm • 110kr • ☎040 33 08 00, ⓦ fotevikensmuseum.se

Barely 9km east of Skanör, the **Foteviken Viking Museum**, just outside the village of Höllviken (follow the signs), is reputedly located at a pagan sacrificial site, **Foteviken,** which was a market town and centre for herring fishing during Viking times. Today, the whole area has been transformed into a working **Viking-style village** comprising houses, workshops, a sacrificial temple and shipyard – a virtually self-sufficient settlement with

5

an astonishing ring of authenticity. The idea was to show the way of life here in the twelfth century, but more than this, the place has become a magnet for people from all over Europe who want to live as Vikings, together with a not inconsiderable number of characters sporting wild beards and lots of beads, who firmly believe they *are* Vikings.

The resulting atmosphere is that of a hippy commune in a time warp. Everyone dresses entirely in homespun garments of loose, coarse linen, coloured with dyes made from local grasses and herbs. The villagers' simply crafted footwear is made from leather which they cure themselves, and if you wander into the **cure-houses** you'll see the pelts of locally caught mink – along with elk and wild-boar hides donated by local abattoirs. Dotted around the ever-growing village are ant-hill-like **kilns** and **clay ovens** used to bake bread and fire the bowls from which the villagers eat.

Hidden in among the two dozen or so dwelling houses, look out for the **weavers' cottage** which contains the village's answer to the Bayeux Tapestry: a wall-hanging here depicts the Battle of Foteviken of June 4, 1134, in which King Nils of Denmark is seen trying to reconquer Skåne from the rebellious pretender Erik Emune. And it's worth heading down to the shore where **longships**, based on the designs of excavated wrecks, are built.

ACCOMMODATION	SKANÖR
Hotell Gässlingen Rådhustorget 6 ☎040 45 91 00, ⓦhotel-gasslingen.com. Located a few metres from Skanör's town hall, this is an elegant and charming place to stay with its own swimming pool and fitness centre. Perfect for a taste of luxury close to nature. **1995kr**	**Spelabäcken** Mellangatan 58 ☎040 47 53 00, ⓦspelabacken.se. A pleasant, small hotel which boasts a sauna and solarium but is less ornate than its sister establishment, the *Gässlingen*. It has a perfect location on pretty Mellangatan right at the heart of the town. **1295kr**

EATING

Fiskrögeri Hamngatan ☎040 47 40 50, ⓦrogeriet.se. This simple, elegant restaurant at the harbour serves superb fish dishes, with a remarkable range of smoked and pickled fish; 120kr buys a plate of five varieties of herring. April, May & Sept Thurs & Fri 6–10pm, Sat noon–10pm, Sun noon–8pm; June–Aug Mon–Sat noon–11pm, Sun noon–10pm.	**Skanörs Gästgifvaregård** Mellangatan 13 ☎040 47 56 90, ⓦskanorsgastis.com. This restaurant has a reputation for well-prepared, local produce – including grilled zander and slow-cooked side of pork – served in sizeable portions in a historic setting; mains are 175–275kr. Mon–Fri 11.30am–2pm & 5–9pm, Sat 1–3pm & 5–9pm, Sun 1–8pm.

Ystad

Under an hour by local train from Malmö, the medieval market town of **YSTAD** is exquisitely well preserved and boasts a prettiness that may come as a surprise if you've arrived at the train station down by the murky docks. In the historic centre though, you can marvel at the quaint, cobbled lanes, lined with cross-timbered cottages, and the town's chocolate-box central square, oozing rural charm. With the stunningly beautiful coastal region of Österlen (see page 185) stretching northeast from town all the way to Kristianstad (see page 187), Ystad is a splendid place to base yourself for a day or so. It also offers the option of a quick hop to the Danish island of Bornholm (see page 184). Ystad stages its annual **opera festival** through most of July; you can get information on performances and book tickets at the tourist office.

Stortorget

The best place to start your explorations is the well-proportioned **Stortorget**, a grand old square overlooked by the St Maria kyrka (see opposite), around which twist picturesque streets. West of the church is Mattorget, a small square, away from which leads **Lilla Västergatan**, the main street in the seventeenth and eighteenth centuries; strolling down it today, you'll see the best of the town's Lilliputian cottages.

St Maria kyrka

Stortorget • Daily 10am–4pm

In Stortorget, the thirteenth-century **St Maria kyrka** is a handsome centrepiece, with additions dating from nearly every century since it was built. In the 1880s, these rich decorative features were removed, as they were thought "unsightly", and only the most interesting ones were put back during a restoration programme forty years later. Inside, the Baroque early seventeenth-century pulpit is worth a look for the fearsome face carved beneath it, while opposite is the somewhat chilling medieval crucifix, placed here on the orders of Karl XII to remind the preacher of Christ's suffering. The figure of Christ wears a mop of actual human hair – sacrificed by a local parishioner in the nineteenth century, in an attempt to make it look realistic. Notice also the green box pews to either side of the entrance, which were reserved for women who had not yet been received back into the church after childbirth.

Norra Promenaden

Not far from Stortorget, up Lilla or Stora Norregatan, is **Norreport**, the original northern arched entrance to the town. From here, you can stroll through **Norra Promenaden**, an avenue lined with mature horse-chestnut trees and surrounded by parkland. Here you'll find a white pavilion, built in the 1870s to house a genteel café and a dance hall with a brass band.

Klostret i Ystad

Ystad monastery • St Petri Kyrkoplan • Tues–Fri noon–5pm, Sat & Sun noon–4pm • 50kr • ⓦ klostret.ystad.se

Another short stroll from Stortorget, past Garvaregränd's art-and-craft workshops (one of which, Krukmakaren, is in a fantastically higgledy-piggledy house on the right), then up Klostergatan, brings you to the town's thirteenth-century **monastery**, now a simple **museum**. The collection is pretty standard local history paraphernalia, but

5

given piquancy by its medieval surroundings. After the monks were driven out during the Reformation, the monastery declined and was used, among other things, as a hospital and a distillery, before becoming a museum in the early twentieth century. The museum has a small **café** serving coffee and cake.

Brightly painted low cottages line the streets around here; a brief stroll down the most picturesque of these, **Vädergränd**, off Lilla Östergatan, makes for a worthwhile foray. Look out for no. 4, the 1727 Gamla Handtwerfargården – a grocery in a time warp.

Cineteket

Film Museum • Elis Nilssons väg 14, beyond the eastern end of Regementsgatan • Mon–Thurs 10am–4pm, Sat & Sun 10am–4pm • 60k • ☎ 0411 57 70 57, ⓦ ystad.se

Fans of *Wallander* (see below) may wish to visit **Cineteket** to see inside a real film studio where the BBC *Wallander* films (amongst other productions) were recorded, and to learn about film production techniques. There's also a chance to take part in a three-hour guided tour of locations used in the films.

ARRIVAL AND DEPARTURE   YSTAD

By train From the train station, head west until you reach Hamngatan, where you turn right up the street to reach Stortorget, the main square. Trains connect to Malmö frequently (every 30min; 50min).

By bus Buses from Lund and Kristianstad drop you off at the bus station on St Knuts torg, across the tracks from the train station.

By ferry The ferry terminals for the Danish island of Bornholm (3–5 daily; 1hr 20min; ⓦ faergen.dk) and Swinoujscie in Poland (2 daily; 6hr 30min–9hr; ⓦ polferries. se) are 300m southeast of the train station.

INFORMATION

Tourist office St Knuts torg (mid-June to Aug Mon–Fri 9am–6pm, Sat & Sun 10am–5pm; rest of year Mon–Fri 9am–5pm, Sat 11am–2pm; ☎ 0411 57 76 81, ⓦ visitystadosterlen.se). Has internet access and can supply copies of the *Wallander* walking guide and a 1753 map of Ystad that's still a serviceable guide to the old streets.

Bike rental Bikes – a great way to see the surrounding cycle-friendly landscape – can be rented from Roslin Bicycle, Norra Zinkgatan 2 (Mon–Fri 9.30am–6pm, Sat 9.30am–3pm; ☎ 0411 123 15), just east of the bus and train terminals.

ACCOMMODATION   SEE MAP PAGE 183

★ **Anno 1793 Sekelgården** Långgatan 18 ☎ 0411 739 00, ⓦ sekelgarden.se. The best place to stay in town, this is a small family-run hotel in a merchant's house from 1793, with en-suite rooms in both the main house and the old tannery at the back. **995kr/1395kr**

Beach House Fritidsvägen 9, 2km east of the town centre ☎ 0411 665 66, ⓦ beachhouseystad.se; buses #2 and #5. A great location for this gloriously rambling B&B set right on the beach at Sandskogen. Breakfast is an extra 70kr. **685kr/895kr**

Continental du Sud Hamngatan 13 ☎ 0411 137 00, ⓦ hotelcontinental-ystad.se. Sweden's oldest hotel first opened its doors in 1829 and still has a grand lobby of marble and crystal chandeliers, plus bright, comfortable rooms with parquet floors. The breakfast buffet is a treat. **1550kr/1990kr**

Hotell Bäckagården Dammgatan 36 ☎ 046 70 090 60 58, ⓦ backagarden.nu. A small-scale guesthouse with just eight rooms with private facilities in a beautiful, converted private town house just behind the tourist office. There's a

WALLANDER COUNTRY

Kurt Wallander, the anti-hero of author Henning Mankell's crime novels, is one of Sweden's best-known fictional characters. Millions of people across the world have followed Wallander's investigations as he hurries through Ystad's streets, the location for the novels and the spin-off TV series. With the tourist office's special guide in hand, fans can set off in search of some of the town's most famous fictional sites such as Wallander's apartment on Mariagatan and his favourite café, *Fridolfs*. In line with Mankell's no-nonsense approach to his fame, he specifically requested that there should not be a Wallander theme park in Ystad.

5

THE NIGHT BUGLER OF YSTAD

Staying in Ystad, you'll soon get acquainted with a tradition that harks back to the seventeenth century: from a room in St Maria church watchtower, a night watchman (*tornväktaren*) sounds a **bugle** every fifteen minutes from 9.15pm to 1am. The haunting sound isn't disturbing, though it's audible wherever you stay in the centre. The sounding through the night was to assure the town that the watchman was still awake (until the mid-nineteenth century, he was liable to be executed if he slept on duty); however, the real purpose of this activity was as a safeguard against the outbreak of **fire**. The idea was that if one of the thatched cottages went up in flames, the bugle would sound repeatedly for all to go and help extinguish the blaze. The melancholic bellowing only ceased during World War II, though then the residents complained they couldn't sleep in the unbroken silence. If you look carefully from Stortorget, you can just see the instrument appear at little openings in the tower walls each time it's played.

tranquil garden, and a lovely common sitting room with open fire. **1095kr/1295kr**

Stationen Bed & Breakfast Hamntorget 1A ☏ 046 411 450 90, ⓦ ystadstation.com. A perfect location for the train station and the ferries, this B&B is housed in Ystad's brick station building, right on the platform. It has comfortable, high-ceilinged rooms and there's a kitchen for self-catering, too. Both en-suite and shared-facilities rooms available. **795kr/1295kr**

Ystads Saltsjöbad Saltsjöbadsvägen 6 ☏ 0411 136 30, ⓦ ysb.se. Renowned for its beachside position, just east of

town, this large, 100-year-old spa resort hotel (with endless modern extensions) has a sauna, pool and a restaurant in the original saltwater bathing house which is located right on the beach. **2490kr**

CAMPING

Ystad Camping Österleden 97, 2km east of the town centre ☏ 0411 192 70, ⓦ ystadcamping.se; buses #2 and #5. Next to the *Beach House*, in a beautiful location overlooking a large sandy beach that stretches for around 30km to the southeast. Tents **270kr**, cabins **700kr**

EATING

SEE MAP PAGE 183

Bröderna M Hamngatan 11 ☏ 0411 199199, ⓦ brodernam. se. This is the pizzeria which features in the *Wallander* novels, though today it's a cosy lounge bar and restaurant. Mains such as schnitzel or smoked salmon are around 190kr, burgers and pizzas from 75kr. Mon–Fri 11.15am–1.45pm & 5pm–late, Sat noon–late, Sun 2pm–late.

Bryggeriet Långgatan 20 ☏ 046 411 192 00, ⓦ mollers bryggeri.se. The rough, beamed interior dominated by two copper beer casks creates a welcoming ambience at this restaurant, where there's also a cobbled interior courtyard for alfresco dining. The well-cooked steaks and other meat mains are around the 180–250kr mark, and there are even a couple of vegetarian dishes, too. Mon–Fri 5–9pm, Sat noon–9pm.

Gründens Mat Besökaregränd 3 ⓦ grandensmat.se. Find the door to the courtyard and you'll discover a curiously old-fashioned yet bohemian café set in a half-timbered house with outdoor seating in summer. They bake all their own produce and the café is also licensed. Mon–Wed 11am–4pm, Thurs 11am–late, Fri & Sat 11am–late.

Store Thor Stortorget 18 ☏ 0411 185 10, ⓦ storethor. se. Located in the cellars of the fourteenth-century Rådhuset, with tables in the square in summer. Serves a decent herring platter for 110kr, chicken breast with vegetables for 195kr and lamb wrapped in bacon at 245kr. Daily 11.30am–2pm & 5pm–late.

Thai Corner Stora Östergatan 1B ☏ 0411 55 55 88, ⓦ tc-ystad.se. None-too-authentic Thai restaurant which also does takeaways. The usual array of dishes such as red chicken curry and beef with bamboo shoots cost around 115kr, though the lunch buffet at 90kr is perhaps a better bet, allowing you to choose between a small selection of dishes. Mon–Thurs & Sun 11.30am–9pm, Fri & Sat 11.30am–10pm.

Upp eller ner Stortorget 11 ☏ 0411 788 00, ⓦ uppellerner.se. Justifiably the most popular restaurant in town, packed each evening in summer and serving unusual concoctions such as salmon with salsify poached in elderflower (210kr) as well as more mainstream fish and chips (190kr) and burgers (180kr). Mon–Sat 5pm–late.

The Österlen coast

The landscape of the southeastern corner of Skåne, known as **Österlen**, is like a Mondrian painting: horizons of sunburst-yellow fields of rape running to cobalt-blue summer skies, punctuated only by white cottages, fields of blood-red poppies and

5

the odd black windmill. Along with the vivid beauty of its countryside, Österlen has notably picture-perfect villages, plenty of smooth, sandy beaches, and the Viking ruin of **Ales Stenar**. It's not surprising the area has lured writers and artists to settle here more than anywhere else in Sweden.

Ales Stenar

From Ystad take bus #322 to Kåseberga (20min), from where it's a signed walk of around 200m

Above the harbour of the old fishing village of Kåseberga is **Ales Stenar**, an awe-inspiring Swedish Stonehenge. Believed to have been a Viking meeting place, it consists of 56 **stones** forming a 67m-long boat-shaped edifice, prow and stern denoted by two appreciably larger **monoliths**. The site was hidden for centuries beneath shifting sands, which were cleared in 1958; even now, the bases of the stones are concealed in several metres of sand. It's difficult to imagine how these great stones, not native to the region, might have been transported here. Ales Stenar stands on a windy, flat-topped hill, which most of the tourists snapping away don't bother to climb; once at the top, though (it's a steep ten-minute hike), there's a majestic timelessness about the spot that more than rewards the effort.

Hagestad Nature Reserve and Sandhammaren beach

A signposted drive 5km east of Kåseberga; also accessible on bus #322 from Ystad

For a day in really splendid natural surroundings, it's hard to beat the **Hagestad Nature Reserve**, the best of the three reserves around the village of **Backåkra**. Thousands of pines were planted here in the eighteenth and nineteenth centuries to bind the sandy earth, and, together with oaks and birches, they make up a densely forested area; the clumps of gnarled, stunted oaks are particularly distinctive. It's especially beautiful in midsummer when orchids and heathers colour the forest floor; if you're lucky, you may also see elk, badgers and roe deer, while buzzards and golden orioles are often sighted above. The reserve is also the home of the most glorious **beach** in Skåne, known as **Sandhammaren**: walk along any path towards the sea and you'll soon reach a bright white ribbon of sand – marked "Sandhammaren" on signs – backed by steep dunes and lapped by turquoise waters.

Dag Hammarskjöld museum

Backåkravägen 73 (signposted from Backåkra) • ☎ 0411 52 60 10

In the midst of the nature reserve, uphill on heathland towards Backåkra, is an old farmstead once owned by **Dag Hammarskjöld**, United Nations Secretary-General in the 1950s. His love of the Skåne coast led him to buy the farm and the surrounding sixty acres in order to save it from developers. Killed in a plane crash in Zambia in 1961, Hammarskjöld willed the farm and its contents to STF, which has run the house as a **museum**; it contains amazing pieces of art from all over the world, including an ancient Egyptian painting of the jackal-headed god Anubis, Greek bronzes from 200 BC, works by Picasso and Matisse, and contemporary pieces by the Wakefield sculptor Barbara Hepworth (whose work also stands outside the UN's headquarters in New York at Hammarskjöld's instigation). However, due to extensive renovation work, the museum has been closed for several years and at the time of writing there was no fixed schedule for when it may reopen.

GETTING AROUND	THE ÖSTERLEN COAST

By public transport Getting around this part of the country by public transport needs a bit of forward planning but is perfectly feasible; timetables and journey planners are at ⓦ skanetrafiken.se.

By car With your own wheels, getting around is straightforward; roads are good and with a decent map it's no problem to visit the sites by car.

ACCOMMODATION AND EATING

Löderups Strandbad Södra Strandbadsvägen 40, Löderup ☎0411 52 62 60, ⓦloderupsstrandbad.com. Located just west of Backåkra, this is a beautifully situated year-round campsite, which also has a dozen regular double rooms and cabins. There's an open-air swimming pool on site, plus a café and restaurant at nearby Gökvägen. Doubles **990kr**, cabins **1350kr**

STF Backåkra Vandrarhem Östra Kustvägen 1231, Backåkra ☎0411 52 60 80, ⓦbackakra.se. A well-equipped hostel in an old school house with a bus stop right outside; most rooms have bunk beds, though the doubles have regular beds. You also can rent bikes here. Open mid-May to Sept. Doubles **560kr**

Kristianstad

Eighty kilometres northeast of Ystad, quiet **KRISTIANSTAD** (pronounced "cri-SHAN-sta") is eastern Skåne's most substantial historic centre and a convenient gateway to Sweden's southern coast. With an elegant cathedral, a beautiful little park containing a fine Art Nouveau theatre, and boat trips into the local bird-rich wetlands, Kristianstad can easily detain you for a relaxed day-long visit.

Brief history

Kristianstad dates from 1614, when it was created by Christian IV, Denmark's seventeenth-century "builder-king", during Denmark's 44-year rule here. The earliest and most evocative of the king's Renaissance towns, it was a shining example of Christian's architectural preoccupations, with beautifully proportioned central squares and broad, gridded streets flanking the wide river. Christian nurtured plans to make the fortified town one of Denmark's most important, and it wasn't until the mid-nineteenth century that the fortifications were finally levelled, allowing the town to spill beyond the original perimeter. The late nineteenth century saw the creation of Parisian-style boulevards, pleasant to wander through today, though the many bland buildings erected during the 1960s and 1970s have left the town with a rather dull appearance.

5

Heliga Trefaldighetskyrkan

Holy Trinity church • Västra Storgatan 19 • Daily 8am–5pm

The most obvious starting point for a visit to town is the 1618 **Heliga Trefaldighetskyrkan**, right opposite the train station. The church symbolizes all that was glorious about Christian IV's Renaissance ideas: the grandiose exterior has seven magnificent spiralled gables, and the building's high windows allow light to flood the white interior. Inside, the most striking features are the elaborately carved pew ends: each is over 2m tall, and no two are the same. The gilded Baroque magnificence of the 1630 organ facade is also worth a look.

Stora torg

Diagonally across from the Heliga Trefaldighetskyrkan, the main square, **Stora torg**, contains the late nineteenth-century **Rådhus**, built in imitation of Christian's Renaissance design. Inside the entrance, a bronze copy of the king's 1643 bust is something of a revelation: Christian sports a goatee beard, one earring and a single dreadlock, and exposes a nipple decorated with a flower motif, itself a source of interest for a baby elephant round the royal neck. Opposite the town hall, and in marked contrast to it, the 1920s post office and the old Riksbank have an identical 1920s brick design; while the adjacent 1640s Mayor's House is different again, with a Neoclassical yellow-stuccoed facade.

The square also boasts Palle Pernevi's splintered *Icarus* **fountain**, which depicts the unfortunate Greek lad falling from heaven into what looks like a scaffolded building site. The town's streets are peppered with modern **sculptures**; one of the best is Axel Olsson's bronze *Romeo & Julia* at Östra Storgatan 3, close to Stora torg, depicting an accordion player serenading a woman emerging from an open window.

Regionmuséet

Regional museum • June–Aug daily 11am–5pm; Sept–May Tues–Sun 11am–5pm • Free • W www.regionmuseet.se

Just north of Stora torg, behind the Riksbank, is the **Regionmuséet**. Christian began construction of the building in 1616, and intended to make it a grand palace but, thanks to the bloody Skåne wars, work got no further than the low buildings. As soon as they were built, the stables here were turned into an arsenal containing ammunition for the pro-Danish partisans. Today, the museum is home to permanent exhibitions about the town's military and industrial past. There's also an **art gallery** showing good contemporary exhibitions.

Tivoliparken

Wander down any of the roads heading south and you'll reach **Tivoliparken**, known locally as the "English Park", with avenues of horse-chestnut and copper beech trees. In its centre is a fine Art Nouveau **theatre**, a stylish white building whose designer, Axel Anderberg, also designed the Stockholm Opera.

Vattenriket

Nature centre Daily 10am–5pm • Free • Boat tours Mid-May–mid-Sept daily 1.30pm • 3hr • 195kr • W landskapet.se

From the lakeshore in the park, **boats** operated by Landskapet JO leave for three-hour tours of the nearby marshes and wetlands, a UNESCO World Heritage site known as **Vattenriket** and renowned for its rich vegetation as well as extensive bird and marine life. Departures must be booked in advance through the website. Before boarding the boats, try to check out the bird's-eye tour of Vattenriket shown in the Opteryx flight simulator inside the **Vattenriket Naturum nature centre**, accessed via the wooden footbridge from the southwest corner of Tivoliparken.

5

ARRIVAL AND INFORMATION

By train All train services pull in at Kristianstad C, on Västra Boulevarden.

Destinations Copenhagen via Kastrup airport (hourly; 1hr 45min); Helsingborg (hourly; 1hr 25min); Karlskrona (hourly; 1hr 35min); Malmö (hourly; 1hr 30min).

By bus The SkåneExpressen #4 bus from Ystad (1hr 40min)

KRISTIANSTAD

stops outside the train station.

Tourist office Västra Storgatan 14, a 5min walk from the station (mid-June to mid-Aug Mon–Fri 10am–6.30pm, Sat 10am–3pm, Sun 10am–2pm; mid-Aug to mid-June Mon–Fri 10am–5pm, Sat 10am–2pm; ☎ 044 13 53 35, ⊕ kristianstad.se/en/tourism).

ACCOMMODATION

SEE MAP PAGE 187

Best Western Anno 1937 Västra Storgatan 17 ☎ 044 12 61 50, ⊕ hotelanno.se. A rather cramped hotel over two storeys housed in a building dating from the turn of the last century – with annoyingly low ceilings. Rooms are comfortable, some with wooden beams, but lack any real style. **906kr**

Charlottsborgs Camping & Vandrarhem 3km west of the town centre at Jacobs väg 34 ☎ 044 21 07 67, ⊕ charlottsborgsvandrarhem.se; bus #2. A combined campsite and youth hostel, where campers can use all the hostel facilities including the TV and lounge room. There are cottages for two people, too. Dorms **190kr**, doubles **600kr**, tents **160kr**, cottages **380kr**

First Christian IV Västra Boulevarden 15 ☎ 044 20 38 50, ⊕ firsthotels.com. The most glamorous hotel in town, just south of Stora torg, located in a rather splendid building that was once home to a bank, retaining its original fireplaces and parquet floors; the vaults are now a wine cellar. **790kr/1150kr**

Quality Grand Västra Storgatan 15 ☎ 044 28 48 00, ⊕ choicehotels.se. This modern, modest-looking place offers excellent, friendly service and well-equipped en-suite rooms, with supremely comfortable beds and wooden floors. Rooms are individually decorated with inspiration from Kristianstad's past. **756kr/846kr**

EATING AND DRINKING

SEE MAP PAGE 187

CAFÉS AND RESTAURANTS

Bånken Östra Storgatan 27 ☎ 044 10 20 23, ⊕ bånken pub.com. After a legal wrangle, this restaurant in the old Riksbanken building has been forced to adapt its name (hence the "å"), but the food is just as good: burgers (200kr), tapas (35–80kr) and a filling surf and turf plate, too (360kr). Wed–Thurs 5pm–late, Fri 4pm–3am, Sat 6pm–3am.

Duvander Hesslegatan 6 ⊕ conditoriduvander.se. A classic and central *konditori* with high ceilings and ornate cornices which has been serving cakes and meringues since 1934. It's a popular place for lunch, when people come for pasta salads, sandwiches, soup and quiche. Mon–Fri 7.30am–6pm, Sat 8am–5pm, Sun 10am–5pm.

Fornstugan Tivoli Park. An atmospheric and elaborately carved Hansel-and-Gretel lodge in the middle of the park; the outdoor seating area opens in fine weather, though the whole place closes if it rains. Serves waffles, coffee and cakes. May–Aug daily 10am–8pm.

Kippers Källare Östra Storgatan 9 ☎ 044 10 62 00, ⊕ kippers.se. An atmospheric choice in a vaulted cellar dating from 1615 and once regularly frequented by Danish King Christian IV. It specializes in well-prepared steaks (235–335kr) of various kinds – seemingly everything from venison to lamb. Tues–Sat 6–10pm.

La Finestra Västra Storgatan 39 ☎ 044 20 97 20, ⊕ lafinestraitaliana.se. A compact little Italian place tucked inside the Gallerian shopping mall – it's inordinately popular at lunchtimes, when it's full to bursting. On Saturdays there's an extensive brunch menu; otherwise, it's pizzas for around 120kr and a range of meat dishes from 160kr. Takeaways are available. Wed–Fri 11.30am–9.30pm, Sat & Sun 4–9.30pm.

Steakhouse Nya Boulevarden 6A ☎ 044 12 00 20, ⊕ thesteakhouse.se. This first-floor restaurant overlooking the main square specializes in all kind of barbecued meat dishes such as veal fillets, T-bone steaks and marinated pork (around 250kr). However, there's also a number of main-course salads for 100kr. Mon–Thurs 5–11pm, Sat 4pm–midnight, Sun 5–9pm.

BARS

Harry's Bar Östra Storgatan 9 ☎ 044 10 62 00, ⊕ kippers. se. For a convivial drink, try this place (not belonging to the chain *Harry's*), popular with a 30-something crowd. There's also a variety of bar snacks including a mouthwatering fish burger with fennel coleslaw and caper sauce (155kr). Fri & Sat 8.30pm–3am.

The southeast

VISBY

The southeast

Although a less obvious target than the coastal cities and resorts of the southwest, Sweden's southeast certainly repays a visit. The provinces of Sörmland, Östergötland, Småland and Blekinge boast impressive castles, ancient lakeside sites and numerous glassworks amid the forests of the so-called "Glass Kingdom", while off the east coast, Sweden's largest Baltic islands offer beautifully preserved medieval towns and fairy tale landscapes. Train transport, especially between the towns close to the eastern shore of Lake Vättern and Stockholm, is good; speedy, regular services mean that you could see some places on a day-trip from Stockholm.

Blekinge is something of a poor relation to its neighbours in terms of tourism. Towns here put out an endless stream of glossy brochures touting their attractions, but in truth, even Swedes themselves admit the province remains the forgotten corner of the south – perfect if you're looking for a quiet getaway. The neighbouring province of **Småland** encompasses a varied geography and some stridently different towns. **Kalmar** is a very likeable stop; a glorious historic fortress town, it deserves more time than its tag as a jumping-off point for the island of Öland suggests. Inland, great swathes of dense forest are rescued from monotony by the many **glass factories** that continue the county's traditional industry, famous the world over for its design and quality, though today drowning in its own marketing hyperbole. In **Växjö**, the largest town in the southeast, two superb museums deal with the art of glass-making and the history of Swedish emigration: agricultural reforms that denied peasants access to common land, combined with a series of bad harvests, led to more than a million Swedes – a sixth of the population – emigrating to America between 1860 and 1930. At the northern edge of the province and perched on the southernmost tip of Lake Vättern, **Jönköping** is known as Sweden's Jerusalem for its remarkable number of Free Churches; it's also a great base for exploring the beautiful eastern shore of Vättern.

The idyllic pastoral landscape of **Östergötland** borders the eastern shores of the lake and reaches as far east as the Baltic. One of its highlights, and popular with domestic tourists, is the small lakeside town of **Vadstena**, its medieval streets dwarfed by austere monastic edifices, a Renaissance palace and an imposing abbey, brought into being by the zealous determination of Sweden's first female saint, Birgitta.

Just off the southeast coast lie Sweden's two largest islands, Öland and Gotland: adjacent slithers of land with unusually temperate climates for their latitudes. They were domestic tourist havens for years, but now an increasing number of foreigners are discovering their charms – lots of summer sun, delectable beaches and some impressive historic (and prehistoric) sights. **Öland** – the smaller island and closer to the mainland – has a mix of shady forests and flowering meadows that make it a tranquil spot for a few days' exploration. **Gotland**'s well-known highlight is its Hanseatic medieval capital, **Visby**, a city pervaded by a carnival atmosphere in summer when ferry-loads of young Swedes come to sunbathe and party. The rest of the island, however, is little visited by tourists, and all the more magical for that.

Karlskrona

The only real place of interest in Blekinge is the handsome town of **KARLSKRONA**, the provincial capital, which really is something special and merits, say, a day or so of your

KALMAR SLOTT INTERIORS

Highlights

❶ Karlskrona A riot of Baroque architecture and a rich naval past make this seaside town one of the most enticing in southern Sweden. See page 192

❷ Kalmar Slott Visit the exquisite interior of this sensational, twelfth-century castle that has been beautifully remodelled into a Renaissance palace. See page 198

❸ Kullzénska Caféet, Kalmar Tuck into scrumptious cakes amid the wonderful faded gentility of this eighteenth-century home. See page 202

❹ Utvandrarnas Hus, Växjö The exhibition of the poignant stories of millions of Swedes forced to emigrate to the United States in the nineteenth century is an essential stop on any visit to Småland. See page 208

❺ Vadstena This atmospheric town on the eastern shores of Lake Vättern is home to the massive abbey founded by Sweden's first female saint, Birgitta. See page 216

❻ Visby, Gotland Visit the remarkable walled city of the former Hanseatic League stronghold and take in the party along with the thousands of young Swedes who visit this superb Baltic island every summer. See page 230

❼ Sjaustrehammaren beach, Gotland Get back to nature on this unspoilt sandy beach near Ljugarn, backed by pine forest and open flower meadows. See page 238

HIGHLIGHTS ARE MARKED ON THE MAP ON PAGE 194

time. Set on the largest link in a chain of breezy islands, this fine example of Baroque exuberance is unique in southern Sweden.

Brief history

Karlskrona was founded by Karl XI in 1680 as the new base for the Swedish Baltic fleet (the seas here are ice-free in winter). Architects from across the country had drawn up plans for the town's grid of wide avenues and grand buildings, which were to provide the classical purity and Baroque splendour commensurate with a town destined to become Sweden's second city. Built to accommodate the king's naval parades, Karlskrona's original layout has survived intact, a fact which has earned it a place on UNESCO's World Heritage list, despite the anonymous blocks plonked between the town's splendid churches.

HIGHLIGHTS

1. Karlskrona
2. Kalmar Slott
3. Kullzénska Caféet, Kalmar
4. Utvandrarnas Hus, Växjö
5. Vadstena
6. Visby, Gotland
7. Sjaustrehammaren beach, Gotland

Today, cadets in uniform still career around its streets, many of which are named after Swedish admirals and battleships; the town's biggest museum is, unsurprisingly, dedicated to maritime history (see below).

Stortorget

The centre of Karlskrona today occupies the island of **Trossö**, connected to the mainland by the main road, Österleden (the E22). From Österleden, climb uphill past Hoglands Park, named after an eighteenth-century battle between the Swedish and Russian navies (Hogland is an island in the Gulf of Finland), to the main square, **Stortorget**, at the highest point and geographical centre of the island. It's a vast and beautiful space, dominated by two complementary **churches**; both were designed by Tessin the Younger and are stuccoed in burnt orange with dove-grey stone colonnades.

Trefaldighetskyrkan
Stortorget • June–Aug daily 8am–7pm; Sept–May Mon–Fri 11am–3pm, Sat 9.30am–2pm

The more interesting of Stortorget's churches is the circular, domed **Trefaldighetskyrkan**. Built for the town's German merchant community in 1709, its most remarkable feature is its domed ceiling, painted with hundreds of rosettes. The altar is also distinctive, with golden angelic faces peering out of a gilded meringue of clouds. In the crypt are the remains of two of Karlskrona's most revered men: Count Hans Wachtmeister, responsible for much of the building of the town in the late seventeenth century; and Johan Törnström, the Admiralty sculptor, who made most of the fabulous ship figureheads on show at the Marinmuseum (see below).

Fredrikskyrkan
Stortorget • Mon–Fri 10am–4pm, Sat 9.30am–2pm

Fredrikskyrkan, a few steps away from Trefaldighetskyrkan, is an elegant, light-flooded church with towers, but holds fewer surprises inside. Construction began in 1720 in classic Baroque style according to plans drawn up by Nicodemus Tessin, who also designed Stockholm's cathedral and royal palace. Disaster struck just decades after completion, when large parts of the church were destroyed in a devastating fire which ripped through the roof section. Rebuilding began apace and today's elegant structure stood ready in 1806.

Kungliga Amiralitetskyrkan
Royal Admiralty Church • Amiralitetstorget • Daily 11am–3pm

Down from Stortorget, the leafy square ahead is **Amiralitetstorget**, with the huge, apricot-and-grey-painted wooden bell tower of the **Kungliga Amiralitetskyrkan** at its centre. To see the church itself, head down Vallgatan on the left of the square, passing the symmetrical austerity of the Marine Officers' School; the beautifully proportioned, entirely wooden church is up on the right, just before you reach the harbour. It was built in 1685, and is Sweden's biggest wooden church.

Marinmuseum
Maritime Museum • Stumholmen • June–Aug daily 10am–6pm; May & Sept daily 10am–4pm; Oct–April Tues–Sun 10am–4pm • Free • ⓦ marinmuseum.se

Located on the tiny island of Stumholmen at the foot of Kyrkogatan, Karlskrona's **Marinmuseum** has a facade like a futuristic Greek temple; a portrait of Karl XI, who had the navy moved from Stockholm to Karlskrona in 1680, features in the hallway, a pet lion at his feet gazing up at the king's most unappealing, bloated face. Down a spiral staircase from here is a transparent underwater tunnel offering a view of hundreds of fish in the murky depths. The best room, though, contains the **figureheads** designed and made by the royal sculptor to the navy, Johan Törnström. King Gustav III declared that ships of the line should be named after manly virtues, and so have male figureheads, while frigates have female ones. Among the finest is one made for the ship *Försiktigheten* (*Prudence*; 1784) – a metre-long foot, perfectly proportioned and complete with toenails. The museum's latest addition is the **submarine**, *Neptun*, which operated in Swedish waters during the 1980s; there's a chance to climb onboard and explore the boat's cramped interior.

Blekingemuseum

Borgmästaregatan 21 • June–Aug daily 10am–6pm; Sept–May Tues–Sun 11am–5pm, Wed until 7pm • 80kr • ⓦ blekingemuseum.se

The provincial collections housed within the rather dreary **Blekingemuseum** down at the harbourfront are unlikely to set your pulse racing, especially when compared to Karlskrona's other treasures. Infinitely more appealing than the exhibits on shipbuilding and the like is the pleasant summertime café, housed in the 1705 wooden home built for Count Wachtmeister.

Konsthall

Arts Centre • Borgmästaregatan 17 • Tues–Fri noon–5pm, Sat & Sun noon–4pm • Free • ⓦ karlskrona.se/konsthall

Just behind the Blekingemuseum, housed in the town's striking former cinema, the **Konsthall** is the place to look for temporary exhibitions of modern art as well as occasional dance and music productions.

KARLSKRONA

■ ACCOMMODATION	
Aston	6
Clarion Collection Carlscrona	1
Dragsö Camping	3
First Statt	7
Scandic Karlskrona	4
STF Karlskrona Vandrarhem	2/5

■ DRINKING	
Fox and Anchor	2
Nivå	1

● EATING	
Café Tre G	2
Michelangelo	4
Montmatre	3
Nya Skafferiet	5
Sjörök	1

A BEGGAR'S TALE

Outside the entrance to Kungliga Amiralitetskyrkan, take a look at one of the city's best-known landmarks: the wooden statue of **Rosenbom**, around which hangs a sorrowful tale. Mats Rosenbom, one of the first settlers on Trossö island, lived nearby with his family and earned his keep in the shipyard. However, after a fever killed six of his children and left him and his wife too ill to work, he applied for, and was granted, a beggar's licence. One New Year's Eve, while begging at the homes of leading townspeople, he became somewhat drunk from the festive wine on offer and forgot to raise his hat to thank the wealthy German figurehead carver, Fritz Kolbe. When admonished for this, Rosenbom retorted, "If you want thanks for your crumbs to the poor, you can take my hat off yourself." Enraged, Kolbe struck him between the eyes and sent him away, but the beggar, unable to make it home, froze stiff and died in a snowdrift by the church. Next morning, Kolbe found the beggar and, filled with remorse, carved a figure of Rosenbom which stands at the spot where he died. It's designed so that you have to raise his hat yourself to give some money.

6

ARRIVAL AND DEPARTURE
KARLSKRONA

By train The train station is 200m north of Hoglands Park; it's a 10min stroll to Stortorget. To travel to and from Kalmar by train, change at Emmaboda.
Destinations Copenhagen via Kastrup airport (hourly; 3hr 30min); Emmaboda (hourly; 50min); Kristianstad (hourly; 1hr 30min); Malmö (hourly; 3hr).

By ferry The Stena Line ferry to and from Gdynia (just outside Gdansk; 10hr 30min), sails once daily from Verkövägen 101, 10km from Karlskrona centre. Bus #6 runs from the bus station to the ferry terminal; timetables are at ⓦblekingetrafiken.se.

INFORMATION

Tourist office Stortorget 2, just behind Frederikskyrkan (June & late Aug Mon–Fri 9am–7pm, Sat 9am–4pm; July to mid-Aug Mon–Fri 9am–7pm, Sat & Sun 9am–4pm; May & Sept Mon & Tues 9am–5pm, Wed 10am–5pm, Thurs & Fri 9am–5pm; Oct–April Mon–Tues 9am–5pm, Wed 10am–5pm, Thurs 9am–5pm, Sat 9am–2pm; ☏0455 30 34 90, ⓦvisitkarlskrona.se). Has internet access.

ACCOMMODATION
SEE MAP PAGE 196

Aston Landbrogatan 1 ☏0455 194 70, ⓦhotellaston.se. This comfortable place has been redecorated using modern furniture and classic fittings and the result is simple elegance. Over the years it's been popular with ships' crews whilst their boats were being refitted – photographs of this period adorn the walls. **1195kr**

Clarion Collection Carlscrona Skeppsbrokajen ☏0455 36 15 00, ⓦnordicchoicehotels.se. A great hotel close to the station in a contemporary glass-fronted building. Rooms are well appointed and decked out with specially commissioned maritime and historical wallpapers – a really nice touch. A free evening buffet is served to all guests. **1200kr/1540kr**

First Statt Ronnebygatan 37 ☏0455 555 50, ⓦfirsthotels.se. The Empire-style rooms in this 1890 building on the main shopping street are stylish in the extreme and good value for money. Note this is cheaper than the other First hotel in town. **1040kr/1220kr**

Scandic Karlskrona Skeppsgossegatan 2 ☏0455 37 20 00. Beautifully situated on the edge of Fisktorget overlooking the sea, rooms at this hotel are bright and breezy with minimal decor and lots of bright and breezy oranges and greens on the walls. **1000kr/1175kr**

STF Karlskrona Vandrarhem Nya Skeppsbrogatan 1 and Bredgatan 16 ☏0455 100 20, ⓦkarlskrona vandrarhem.se. Two central locations – the Nya Skeppsbrogatan hostel is the better choice of the two, with more modern rooms, and it's also the only one open all year. Bredgatan operates June–Aug only; check-in and reception is at Nya Skeppsbrogatan. En-suite doubles **495kr**

CAMPING

Dragsö Camping Dragsövägen, Dragsö island ☏0455 153 54, ⓦdragso.se; bus #7 to Saltö, the island before Dragsö, from where it's a 1km walk across the bridge. A pleasant waterside campsite that's about 2.5km from the centre of town. Also has modern cabins for rent. Tents **275kr**, cabins **700kr**

EATING AND DRINKING
SEE MAP PAGE 196

CAFÉS AND RESTAURANTS
Café Tre G Landbrogatan 9 ☏0455 31 03 33. Opposite Hoglands Park, this stylish place – the city's only café open on a Sunday – does a good range of baked potatoes and pasta dishes as well as cakes and sandwiches. Daily 8am–8pm.

Michelangelo Ronnebygatan 29 ☏0455 121 95, ⓦrestaurangmichelangelo.se. Elegant Italian restaurant with copies of Renaissance paintings on the brick walls and a good choice of fine cuisine: meat and fish dishes such as braised veal medallions with Parma ham and sage, are 180–260kr. Mon–Fri 11.30am–2pm & 5–11pm, Sat 4–11pm, Sun 4–10pm.

Montmartre Ronnebygatan 18 ☎ 0455 31 18 33, ⓦ montmartre.se. With rough brick walls and velvet drapes, this candlelit bistro is the cosiest of all the Italian places in town. Huge pizzas cost 70–100kr, pasta is 90–120kr and the house speciality – steak flambéed in cognac served in a pepper sauce – is 240kr. Mon–Fri 4–10.30pm, Sat 1–10.30pm, Sun 1–9.30pm.

Nya Skafferiet Rådhusgatan 9 ☎ 0455 171 78, ⓦ nya skafferiet.se. A really good deli and café combined where you can buy air-dried hams, meats and cheeses for picnics, as well as filled baguettes, croissants, great coffee and the best hot chocolate in town. Excellent lunch buffet, too, with several vegetarian options. Mon & Tues 10am–4pm, Wed & Thurs 10am–5pm, Sat 10am–3pm & 6–10pm.

Sjörök Skeppsbrokajen 4 ☎ 0455 32 42 42, ⓦ sjorok.se. If you want to eat fish in Karlskrona, this is the place to come. Overlooking the marina with floor-to-ceiling windows, this acclaimed seafood restaurant is a great place to enjoy the likes of fried turbot in white wine sauce (285kr), flounder with prawns and horseradish (285kr) or grilled char (245kr). Every evening they also serve a traditional Swedish home-cooking dish for a good-value 145kr. Mon 11.15am–2pm, Tues–Fri 11.15am–2pm & 5–11pm, Sat 5–11pm.

BARS AND PUBS

Fox and Anchor Norra Smedjegatan 1 ☎ 0455 229 10, ⓦ foxandanchor.se. British-style drinking den serving 54 different types of beer and over 200 whisky varieties. There's also some decent grub: burgers, fish and chips and steaks; reckon on around 150kr for something substantial. Mon & Tues 5–11pm, Wed 5pm–midnight, Thurs 5pm–1am, Fri 4pm–2am, Sat 6pm–3am.

★ **Nivå** Stortorget ☎ 0455 103 71, ⓦ niva.nu. Semi-circular glass-fronted bar and steakhouse perfectly situated on the edge of the main square, with great views of the Baroque splendour all around. A good selection of wine, beer and cocktails, plus burgers from 165kr, steaks from 210kr and the odd fish dish. Mon & Tues 5pm–late, Wed & Thurs 5pm–late, Fri 4pm–late, Sat noon–late.

Kalmar

Delightful, breezy **KALMAR**, set on a huddle of islands at the southeastern edge of Småland province, has treasures enough to make it one of southern Sweden's most agreeable towns. Chief among its highlights are the **Länsmuseum**, home to an exhibition on the sunken warship, the *Kronan*, and an exquisite fourteenth-century **castle**, Scandinavia's finest preserved Renaissance palace. The town is also perfectly sited for reaching the Baltic island of Öland (see page 203), which is just 6km away across the connecting bridge, or a short hop on a foot-passenger ferry.

Kalmar Slott

Kungsgatan 1 • May, Sept & Oct daily 10am–4pm; June & Aug daily 10am–6pm; April & Nov Sat & Sun 10am–4pm; guided tours in English June & Sept 11.30am, July & Aug 11.30am, 1.30pm & 3.30pm • 130kr • ⓦ kalmarslott.se

Beautifully set on its own island, just south of Stadsparken, is the castle, **Kalmar Slott**. Unlike many other southern Swedish castles, this one is straight out of a storybook, boasting turrets, ramparts, a moat and drawbridge and a dungeon. The fully furnished interior – reached by crossing an authentically reconstructed wooden **drawbridge** and going through a stone-arched tunnel beyond the grassy ramparts – is great fun for a wander. Among the many highlights are the **King's Chamber** with its coffered ceiling, the **Queen's Suite** and the **Golden Room**. The tour guides will tell you that the castle is rattling with ghosts, but for more tangible evidence of life during the Vasa period, the kitchen fireplace is good enough; it was built to accommodate the simultaneous roasting of three cows. There's a splendidly minimalist **café** just inside the walls, dominated by a wonderfully evocative oil painting of a moody chamber interior.

Brief history

Kalmar Slott's foundations were probably laid in the twelfth century; a century later, it became the best-defended castle in Sweden under King Magnus Ladulås. If the castle doesn't appear to be defending anything in particular today, that's because a devastating fire in the 1640s laid waste to Gamla Stan, after which Kalmar was moved to its present site on Kvarnholmen.

The most significant event to take place within the castle's walls was when the Danish Queen Margareta instigated the **Union of Kalmar** in 1397, which made her ruler over all Scandinavia; given the level of hatred between the Swedes and Danes, the union didn't stand much chance of long-term success. The castle was subject to eleven **sieges** as the two rival nations took power in turn; surprisingly, it remained almost unscathed. By the time Gustav Vasa became king of Sweden in 1523, Kalmar Slott was beginning to show signs of wear and tear, and so the king set about rebuilding it, while his sons, who later became Eric XIV and Johan III, took care of decorating the interior. The result, a fine Renaissance palace, is still preserved in fantastic detail today.

The King's Chamber

The **King's Chamber** (King Eric's bedroom) is the most visually exciting room in the castle – the wall frieze is a riot of vividly painted animals and shows a wild boar attacking Eric and another man saving him. Eric apparently suffered from paranoia, believing his younger brother Johan wanted to kill him. To this end, he had a secret door, which you can see cut into the extravagantly inlaid wall panels, with escape routes to the roof in the event of fraternal attack. Eric's suspicions may have been justified – Johan is widely believed to have poisoned him with arsenic in 1569.

The Queen's Suite

Eric's oak **bed**, originally in the King's Chamber, now resides in the **Queen's Suite**, which is otherwise surprisingly devoid of furniture. It is the only surviving piece of furniture from the castle and was originally stolen from Denmark. It is curiously decorated with carved faces on the posts, but all their noses have been chopped off – the king believed that the nose contained the soul and didn't want the avenging souls of the rightful owners coming to haunt him.

The Golden Room

Adjoining the Queen's Suite is the **Golden Room**, which should have been Johan's bedroom, although sibling hatred meant he didn't sleep here while Eric lived. The room has a magnificent ceiling and a couple of huge and intriguing **portraits**: Gustav Vasa was already an advanced age when his was painted, but he appears young-looking, with unseemly muscular legs – the royal artist had been ordered to seek out the soldier with the best legs and paint those, before attempting a sympathetic portrayal of Vasa's face. The portrait next to his is of Queen Margareta, her ghostly white countenance achieved in real life through the daily application of lead and arsenic. Isolated on another wall is King Eric's portrait, hung much higher up than the others: his family believed that the mental illness from which he supposedly suffered could be caught by looking into his eyes – even images of them.

Konstmuseum

Stadsparken • early June & late Aug Mon–Sun 11am–5pm,Tues, Thurs & Sun noon–5pm, Wed 4–9pm, Sat & Sun 11am–4pm • 50kr • ⓦ kalmarkonstmuseum.se

Having left the castle, wandering back towards the town centre along Slottsvägen will bring you to Kalmar's grotesque **Konstmuseum**, a monstrous cube of a building dressed in black wooden panels plonked unceremoniously in the middle of Stadsparken. The museum's collection has an emphasis on Abstract Expressionist work painted by Swedish artists in the 1940s and 1950s, and also contains several nineteenth- and twentieth-century Swedish nude and landscape paintings, including some fine works by Anders Zorn and Carl Larsson, though exhibitions change regularly. In addition, there are often temporary displays of contemporary art.

Gamla Stan

For a feel of Kalmar's quaint **Gamla Stan**, it's best to head into the small warren of cobbled lanes west of *Slottshotellet*, which overlooks Stadsparken and is only a minute's walk along Slottsvägen from the Konstmuseum. The old wooden cottages, painted egg-yolk yellow and wisteria blue, are at their prettiest on Gamla Kungsgatan and Västerlångatan. These little streets surround the attractive **Gamla kyrkogården** (old churchyard), whose seventeenth- and eighteenth-century gravestones have been restored.

Domkyrkan

Norra Långgatan 33 • Daily June–Aug 9am–8pm; Sept–May 9am–4pm

The elegantly gridded Renaissance New Town is laid out around the grand **Domkyrkan** in Stortorget. Designed in 1660 by Nicodemus Tessin the Elder (as was the nearby Rådhus) after a visit to Rome, this vast and airy church in Italian Renaissance style is today a complete misnomer: Kalmar has no bishop and the church no dome. Inside, the altar, designed by Tessin the Younger, shimmers with gold, as do the *Faith* and *Mercy* sculptures around it. The huge *Deposition* painting above the altar depicts in unusually graphic detail Jesus being taken down from the Cross by men on ladders, his lifeless form hoisted down with ropes. The pulpit is also worth a look; its roof is a three-tiered confection crowned with a statue of Christ surrounded by gnome-like sleeping soldiers, below which angels brandish instruments of torture, while on the "most inferior" level, a quartet of women symbolize such qualities as maternal love and erudition.

Larmtorget

Kalmar is at its most animated during the summer months in and around **Larmtorget**, a five-minute walk west of Stortorget. The square is home to several restaurants all with outdoor seating, and hosts free open-air music concerts every Tuesday and Thursday evening between the end of June and early September – simply turn up and enjoy.

The Kronan Exhibition

Skeppsbrogatan 51 • July & Aug daily 10am–5pm; Sept–June Mon–Fri 10am–4pm, Sat & Sun 11am–4pm • 100kr July & Aug, 80kr Sept–June • ⓦ regalskeppetkronan.se

From Stortorget, it's a few minutes' walk south down Östra Sjögatan and then left into Ölandsgatan to the **Kalmar läns museum**, Kalmar's regional museum. The centrepiece of the museum is the awe-inspiring **Kronan exhibition**, housed in a refurbished steam mill. Built by the seventeenth-century British designer Francis Sheldon, the royal ship *Kronan* was once one of the world's three largest vessels; it had three complete decks and was twice the size of the *Vasa*, which sank off Stockholm in 1628 (see page 59).

The *Kronan* went down, fully manned, in 1676, resulting in the loss of 800 of its 842 crew. Its captain, Admiral Creutz, had received a royal order to attack and recapture the Baltic island of Gotland. Pursued by the Danish, Creutz, who had remarkably little naval experience – just one week at sea – was eager to impress his king and engage in combat. To this end, he ignored pleas from his crew and ordered the *Kronan* to turn and face the enemy. A gale caused the ship to heave, and water gushed into her open gun ports, knocking over a lantern, which ignited the entire gunpowder magazine. Within seconds, an explosion ripped the mammoth vessel apart.

It wasn't until 1980 that the whereabouts of the ship's remains were detected, 26m down off the coast of Öland, using super-sensitive scanning equipment. A salvage operation began, led by the great-great-great-great-grandson of the ship's captain, and 25,000 artefacts have so far been recovered. The wreck site, the size of half a football pitch, is still being explored and yields around one thousand items each year.

The exhibits and reconstruction

On the ground floor you come face to face with a dozen of the ship's mighty bronze cannons, richly decorated with coats of arms. However, up on the first floor, things really take off with a full and imaginative **walk-through reconstruction** of the gun decks and admiral's cabin, while the moments leading up to the disaster have been pieced together brilliantly. The ship's **treasure trove** of gold coins is also displayed, but it's the incredibly preserved **clothing** – hats, jackets, buckled leather shoes and even silk bows and cufflinks – which bring this exceptional show to life. Check out, too, the remarkable twelve pewter flasks dating from the mid-1600s which, when salvaged, still contained their original barley-based *akvavit* with an alcohol content of 41.1 percent.

ARRIVAL AND DEPARTURE   **KALMAR**

By train Kalmar's train station is on Stationsgatan, at the southern end of the new town on the island of Kvarnholmen. Change at Emmaboda for trains to Kristianstad.
Destinations Copenhagen via Kastrup airport (hourly; 3hr 45min); Emmaboda (hourly; 30min); Gothenburg (3 daily; 4hr); Malmö (hourly; 3hr 10min); Växjo (hourly; 1hr 20 min).

By boat Between mid-April and Sept, a passenger-only boat sails from Skeppsbron in Kalmar across to Färjestaden on Öland (30min; 50kr one-way; ⓦ ressel.se).

INFORMATION

Tourist office Ölandskajen 9 (Jan–April & Oct–Dec Mon–Fri 10am–5pm; May & Sept Mon–Fri 9am–5pm, Sat 10am–3pm; June & Aug Mon–Fri 9am–7pm, Sat 10am– 4pm; ☎ 0480 41 77 00, ⓦ kalmar.com). Within spitting distance of the train station, and has internet access.

ACCOMMODATION   SEE MAP PAGE 199

Best Western Kalmarsund Fiskaregatan 5 ☎ 0480 48 03 80, ⓦ bestwestern.com. A chain hotel that's a bit lacking in elegance, but with friendly, efficient service, comfortable en-suite rooms and an altogether contemporary feel. There's a sauna, hot tub and roof garden too. <u>1225kr/1435kr</u>

Calmar Stadshotell Stortorget 14 ☎ 0480 49 69 00, ⓦ profilhotels.se. Dating from 1906, this lovely old building with a stuccoed facade in Art Nouveau style is a tasteful mix of old and new, though sadly many rooms have cheap carpets and unstylish furnishings, detracting from the elegance of the public areas. <u>1495kr</u>

Clarion Collection Packhuset Skeppsbrogatan 26 ☎ 0480 570 00, ⓦ nordicchoicehotels.se. Housed in a former waterfront storehouse, the wooden beams of this rambling old building add to the cosiness of the compact modern rooms, many of which have views out over the harbour. A free evening buffet is included. <u>1630kr/1730kr</u>

Frimurarehotellet Larmtorget 2 ☎ 0480 152 30, ⓦ frimurarehotellet.se. Rather grand hotel, set in a castle-like building from 1878 owned by the Freemasons (hence the name: *frimurare* is Swedish for "freemason")

and offering sumptuous rooms with period furniture. <u>1290kr/1490kr</u>

Slottshotellet Slottsvägen 7 ☎ 0480 882 60, ⓦ slottshotellet.se. The prettiest and most regal of Kalmar's hotels, overlooking the castle across the bridge. The authentic interior is extremely tasteful, with a charming conservatory area and a sauna and solarium for use by guests. <u>1495kr/1595kr</u>

Svanen Rappegatan 1 ☎ 0480 129 28, ⓦ hotellsvanen. se. A combined budget hotel and youth hostel located a pleasant 15min walk north of the centre; it's well equipped, with laundry facilities and a shop for basic provisions. The youth hostel has dorm beds and simple double rooms. Dorms <u>195kr</u>, hotel doubles <u>670kr</u>, hostel doubles <u>540kr</u>

CAMPING

Stensö Camping 3km from the centre at Stensövägen, Stensö island ☎ 0480 888 03, ⓦ stensocamping.se; bus #401, then 1.5km walk. As well as camping, there are cabins with lake views here for rent. Open mid-April to Sept. Tents <u>270kr</u>, cabins <u>995kr</u>

EATING   SEE MAP PAGE 199

Gröna Stugan Larmgatan 1 ☎ 0480 158 58, ⓦ grona stuganikalmar.se. A chic and stylish Mediterranean-oriented restaurant which not only prides itself on personal service – the waiting staff here are experts on every dish on the menu – but which serves some creative dishes, too: tuna with grapefruit and pomegranate salad, for example, is 235kr, or there's an equally delicious lamb steak with mushroom risotto (265kr). Mon–Thurs 11.30am–2pm & 5–10pm, Fri 11.30am–2pm & 5–11pm, Sat 5–11pm.

Källaren Kronan Ölandsgatan 7 ☎ 0480 41 14 00, ⓦ kallarenkronan.com. A wonderfully atmospheric vaulted restaurant in a stone building dating from the 1660s, serving top-class Swedish food, such as poached fillet of halibut in lobster sauce (275kr). The best-value option is a two/three-course set menu for 250kr/300kr respectively. Tues–Fri 6–11pm, Sat noon–11pm, Sun 5–10pm.

Krögers med Bremersons Larmtorget 7 ☎ 0480 265 50, ⓦ krogers.se. This noisy bar-restaurant with its fake stained-glass windows and model ships is one of the most popular places in town. The food isn't exactly adventurous, but neither is it too expensive: burgers for 185kr, fish and chips 175kr and steaks 230kr. There's a good choice of bottled beers too. Mon–Thurs 3pm–2am, Fri–Sat noon–3am, Sun noon–2am.

★ **Kullzénska Caféet** Kaggensgatan 26 ☎ 0480 288 82, ⓦ kullzenska.se. This charming *konditori* occupying the first floor of a house dating from 1771 is easily Kalmar's best café. Its eight interconnecting rooms are awash with mahogany furnishings, Indian carpets and crumbling royal portraits. There's a wide selection of sandwiches, cakes and light lunch dishes – the coffee is particularly good. Mon–Fri 10am–6.30pm, Sat 10am–5pm, Sun noon–4.30pm.

Larmgatan 10 Södra Långgatan 6 ☎ 0480 865 25, ⓦ larmgatan10.se. A very genteel place with roped-back drapes, wall paintings and window flowers, serving a good range of simple home-cooked dishes, such as grilled chicken with gorgonzola sauce (170kr) and fillet of pork with cognac and green pepper sauce (180kr). Mon–Thurs 4–10pm, Fri 4–11pm, Sat noon–11pm, Sun noon–9pm.

★ **Restaurang Athena** Norra Långgatan 12 ☎ 046 480 280 88, ⓦ kalmar.kyparn.se/athena. This consistently excellent Greek restaurant, in a building dating from the late 1600s, serves exceptionally tasty modern Greek specialities such as a mouthwatering moussaka (145kr). Mon–Thurs 11am–9pm, Fri & Sat 11am–10pm, Sun noon –9pm.

Stekhuset Skeppsbron 1 ☎ 0480 42 38 58, ⓦ stekhuset ikalmar.se. Steaks from the farms of Småland, such as a delicious fillet steak wrapped in bacon cooked in red wine sauce, are 245–295kr. There are also a number of fish dishes on the menu, including baked sole and perch for 220kr. Mon–Thurs 5–10pm, Fri 5–11pm, Sat 1–11pm, Sun 1–9pm.

Thai Silk Palace Fiskaregatan 8 ☎0480 281 26, ⓦthaisilk.se. Reached through the passage marked "*Koppartorget*" off Fiskaregatan, this ornate Thai restaurant, decorated with reclining Buddhas and lots of carved wood, has an all-day lunch buffet that's especially good value at 100kr on weekdays and 130kr at weekends. Mon–Thurs

11am–8pm, Fri 11am–9pm, Sat noon–9pm, Sun noon–8pm.

Zorbas Fiskaregatan 7 ☎0480 41 17 44, ⓦzorbaskalmar. se. Forget about the menu – everybody in Kalmar comes here for the all-day buffet, which contains a huge variety of different Greek dishes, including salads and desserts. At 100kr on weekdays and 140kr at weekends, it's one of the best bargains in town, and the quality of the food is a notch above average. Mon–Fri 11am–10pm, Sat & Sun noon–10pm.

6

Öland

Linked to mainland Sweden by a 6km-long bridge, the island of **ÖLAND**, with its unspoilt beaches, mysterious forests, pretty meadows and wooden cottages, has been drawing Swedes in droves for over a century. Although it's a popular destination in summer and holiday traffic can clog the road from the bridge north to the main town **Borgholm**, this long, splinter-shaped island retains a very likeable old-fashioned holiday atmosphere. The bathing opportunities are among the best in Sweden, and the island's attractions include numerous ruined castles, Bronze and Iron Age burial cairns, runic stones and forts, all set amid rich and varied fauna and flora and striking geography. Labyrinthine **walking trails** and **bicycle routes** wend their way past more than four hundred old wooden **windmills**, which give Öland a peculiarly Dutch air.

The island is perfect for **camping**, and while you can pitch your tent anywhere under the rules of *Allemansrätten* (see page 34), there are plenty of official sites. Almost all are open only between May and September, and are scattered the length of the island; for more details, visit ⓦcamping-oland.com.

Brief history

From the mid-sixteenth century until 1801, Öland was a royal hunting ground, ruled with scant regard for its native population. Peasants were forbidden from chopping wood, owning dogs or weapons and selling their produce on the open market. While protected wild animals did their worst to the farmers' fields, Kalmar's tradesmen exploited the restrictions on the islanders' trade to force them to sell at low prices. Danish attacks on Öland (and a ten-month occupation in 1612) made matters worse, with seven hundred farms being destroyed. A succession of disastrous harvests in the mid-nineteenth century was the last straw, causing a quarter of the population to pack their bags for a new life in America. In the twentieth century, mainland Sweden became the new magnet for Öland's young and, by 1970, the island's inhabitants had declined to just twenty thousand, around five thousand less than today's total.

ÖLAND'S GEOLOGY AND FLORA

Öland's **geology** varies dramatically due to the crushing movement of ice during the last Ice Age, and the effects of the subsequent melting process, which took place 10,000 years ago. To the south is a massive **limestone** plain known as **alvaret**; indeed, limestone has been used here for thousands of years to build runic monuments, dry-stone walls and churches. The northern coastline is craggy and irregular, peppered with dramatic-looking **raukar** – stone stacks, weathered by the waves into jagged shapes.

Among the island's **flora** are plants that are rare in the region, such as the delicate rock rose and the cream-coloured wool-butter flower, both native to Southeast Asia and found in southern Öland. Further north are the twisted, misshapen pines and oaks of the romantically named **trollskogen** (trolls' forest).

ARRIVAL AND DEPARTURE
ÖLAND

By bus Buses run regularly from Kalmar on the mainland to Borgholm, though the bus timetable, available at Kalmar's bus station and tourist office (see page 202), is almost impossible to decipher – Ölanders mostly laugh when you refer to it. Bus #101 is a safe bet, however, and runs pretty well every hour from Kalmar bus station to Borgholm, taking about 50min; timetables are online at ⓦ klt.se.

By boat Passenger-only boats cross from Kalmar across to Färjestaden for part of the year (mid-April to Sept; 30min; 50kr one-way); buy tickets onboard with a credit card. Departures vary from month to month – check the timetable at ⓦ ressel.se. Bikes are allowed on the ferry (but not the bridge to Öland). From Färjestaden, buses run to Borgholm (5 daily; 1hr 15min) and elsewhere on Öland; full details are available at ⓦ klt.se. Another boat operates from Oskarshamn to Byxelkrok (mid-June to mid-Aug 2 daily; 2hr 20min; 150kr one-way; ⓦ olandsfarjan.se); this service does take vehicles.

GETTING AROUND

By bus Public transport around Öland is limited to buses heading up Route 136 towards Böda Sand; timetables are at ⓦ klt.se.

By bike Route 136 is safe for cycling, and there are plenty of tracks that lead off the main drag.

Borgholm

As you walk the simple square grid of streets that makes up **BORGHOLM**, Öland's "capital", it becomes clear that tourism is the lifeblood of this small town. But despite being swamped by visitors each July, Borgholm is in no way the tacky resort it could be. Encircled by the flaking, turreted and verandahed villas that were the pride of the town during its first period as a holiday resort in the nineteenth century, most of the centre is a friendly, if bland, network of shops and restaurants lining the roads that lead down to the pleasant harbour.

Borgholms Slott

Sollidenvägen 5 • Daily April & Sept 10am–4pm; May–Aug 10am–6pm • 95kr • ⓦ borgholmsslott.se

The only real attraction in town is **Borgholms Slott**, a colossal stone fortification with rows of huge arches and corridors open to the skies. It's several hundred metres southwest of the centre, reached either through a nature reserve (signposted from the town centre), or from the first exit south off Route 136. Built in the twelfth century, the castle was fortified four hundred years later by King Johan III, and given its present shape – with a tower at each corner – in the seventeenth century. Regularly attacked, it eventually fell into disrepair, and when Borgholm was founded in 1816, the castle was already a ruin.

Sollidens Slottspark

Gardens daily mid-May–mid-Sept 11am–6pm, Sept 11am–4pm • 95kr

Just a few hundred metres to the south of the castle is the present royal family's summer residence, **Solliden**, an Italianate villa built in 1903 to a design specified by the Swedish Queen Victoria (the present king's great-grandmother); a huge, austere red-granite bust of her rises out of the trees at the entrance to the car park. Of Austrian stock, Victoria loathed Sweden, and demanded that the bust face Italy, the country she most loved. The villa itself is not open to the public, but the formal **gardens, Slottsparken**, can be visited. There's a very ordered Italian garden, a colourful Dutch garden and a simple English-style one.

Villagatan

To see what Borgholm looked like before the likes of the *Strand Hotel* were built, head along **Villagatan**, the road to the left of the *Strand* as you face out to sea; it's lined with classic wooden villas, their porches and eaves all fancy fretwork. You can't drive along the street without authorization, though, as this is the route used by the king and queen to reach their summer home.

Blå rör

Just to the north of the town centre is Öland's largest Bronze Age cairn, **Blå rör**, a huge mound of stones excavated when a coffin was discovered in 1849. People have been turning up artefacts from time to time ever since: in the 1920s, burnt bones, indicating a cremation site, were found, along with bronze swords and tweezers – apparently common items in such tombs.

INFORMATION	BORGHOLM

Tourist office Storgatan 1 (June Mon–Fri 9am–5pm, Sat 10am–4pm; July Mon–Fri 9am–6pm, Sat 10am–6pm, Sun 10am–4pm; Aug & Sept Mon–Fri 9am–5pm; Oct–May Mon–Fri 10am–4pm; ☎ 0485 890 00, ⓦ oland.se).

ACCOMMODATION

It's imperative to **book ahead** if you're planning a visit to Öland during the June to August peak summer period, since the island is extremely popular with Swedish holiday-makers. Unlike elsewhere in Sweden, rooms prices go up in summer, so the lower rate is for out of season.

Borgholm Trädgårdsgatan 15–19 ☎ 0485 770 60, ⓦ hotellborgholm.com. A smart central choice with interior decor by Philip Starck amongst others, and some pleasant gardens, too. The beautifully appointed top-floor double rooms with their wooden floors, French balconies and stone finishes are worth splashing out on. 1395kr

Kapelludden Camping Sandgatan 27 ☎ 0485 56 07 70, ⓦ kapelludden.se. A family-oriented campsite (under 25s not allowed unless with children) that's set on a small peninsula 5min walk from the centre. It has a number of overpriced cottages for rent. Open late April to Sept. Tents 355kr, cottages 1500kr

STF Ebbas Vandrarhem Storgatan 12 ☎ 070 990 04 06, ⓦ ebbas.se. This spacious hostel is right in the heart of town and boasts a delightful garden café. Accommodation is in one- to four-bed rooms and it pays to book well ahead in summer. Open May–Sept only. Dorms 340kr, doubles 680kr

Strand Borgholm Villagatan 4 ☎ 0485 888 88, ⓦ strandborgholm.se. Straddling one side of the harbour and blandly styled like a modern seaside hotel, this massive hotel includes a small shopping mall, a disco and nightclub; it's one of the most popular hotels in town, so book early. 1195kr/1095kr

Villa Sol Slottsgatan 30 ☎ 0485 56 25 52, ⓦ villasol.nu. A central and tranquil guesthouse located in a charming pale-yellow house with stripped wooden floors and old tiled fireplaces. The lush gardens provide fresh fruit, made into gorgeous jams for breakfast. 715kr

EATING AND DRINKING

Hotel Borgholm Trädgårdsgatan 15 ☎ 0485 770 60, ⓦ hotellborgholm.com/restaurang. This chi-chi hotel restaurant with walls covered in modern art is the best place in town for fine Swedish/pan-European food. A three-course set menu featuring a seafood soup, steak and a dessert costs 545kr. Tues–Sat 6pm–late.

Mamma Rosa Södra Långgatan 2 ☎0485 129 10. Beside the harbour, a smart pizza and pasta parlour with a varied menu, including a decent selection of traditional Italian meat dishes. Reckon on around 150–200kr per main dish. Daily noon–10pm.

Ölandsglass Slottsgatan 10. A great place for a wide range of local, island-made ice creams and sorbets from Ölandsglass, and a pleasant eating area in the back garden with a vine-covered veranda. June–Aug daily 10am–10pm.

Pubben Storgatan 18 ☎0485 124 15, ⊛pubben.se. A cosy and extremely popular pub run by the friendliest of owners, with old radios and crystal sets for decor. It specializes in whisky but also has lager, stout and bitter. Daily June–Aug 11am–2am; Sept–May 4pm–1am.

Robinson Crusoe Hamnvägen 1 ☎0485 777 58, ⊛robinsoncrusoe.se. Jutting into the harbour waters, this restaurant-cum-bar is a fine place for a drink, and the Swedish home cooking on the menu is certainly tasty, though watch what you order as the prices can be a little inflated – lobster gratin, for example, is 595kr. May–Sept 11am–late.

Northern Öland

Öland's most varied and interesting landscape is to be found towards the north, with no shortage of idyllic villages, dark woods and flowery meadows as you head up from Borgholm along the main road, **Route 136**. Though there aren't many proper hotels north of the Borgholm area, **campsites** are marked off the road every couple of kilometres; most of these high-standard sites are close to a beach.

Föra

At **FÖRA**, a village about 20km north of Borgholm, there's a good example of a typical Öland church, built in the medieval era (the font is the oldest part, dating from 1250). It doubled as a fortress, and was capable of accommodating a considerable garrison in times of war. A couple of kilometres north, a sign to **Knisa Mosse** leads to a peaceful nature reserve, centred on a shimmering lake, and to some Bronze Age burial mounds, though there's not much to see at the burial area itself.

Högby and Löttorp

Continuing north from Föra on Route 136, **HÖGBY**, about 15km further on, has the only remaining tied church houses on the island, relics of the medieval Högby kyrka nearby; there's not a lot to see though. For a filling (though somewhat pricey) dining experience, head for the village of **LÖTTORP**, off Route 136, and follow the signs east for 4km down country lanes to the *Lammet & Grisen* restaurant (see below).

Byrums raukar and the beaches

Close to Öland's northern tip and west off Route 136, following signs for Byrums Sandvik and Raukområde, you come to **Byrums raukar**, a striking sight: solitary limestone pillars formed by the eroding action of the sea, at the edge of a sandy beach.

The best **beaches** are along the east coast. Small lanes run east from the main road to the beaches, and there are many campsites signposted off Route 136. From the hostel at Mellböda (see below), it's just 2km north to one of the island's best sandy beaches, **Böda Sand**. The most popular stretch of sand is a couple of kilometres north at **Lyckesand**, with a **nudist beach** just to the north, the start of which is marked simply by a large boulder in the sea. Take the narrow road heading east from Route 136 to reach the gently curving coastline of Bödabukten bay, which forms Öland's northeastern tip.

ACCOMMODATION AND EATING   NORTHERN ÖLAND

Lammet & Grisen Hornvägen 35, Löttorp ☎0485 203 50. Housed in a building like a Spanish hacienda, this restaurant has a menu tending towards spit-roasted lamb and pork (hence the name). A plate of lamb and pork costs 370kr and includes as much as you can eat from the accompanying buffet. Daily 4.30pm–late.

STF Böda Vandrarhem Mellböda, 50km north of Borgholm ☎0485 220 38, ✉mikael.sten@telia.com. Large and well-equipped STF hostel with a cosy kitchen. Accommodation is in private cabins which have their own toilet facilities. Open mid-May to Aug. Doubles **440kr**

Småland

The thickly forested province of **SMÅLAND** makes up the southeastern wedge of Sweden. Although the scenery is appealing at first, the uniformity of the landscape means it's easy to become blasé about so much natural beauty. Småland is often somewhere people travel through rather than to – from Stockholm to Malmö and the south, or from Gothenburg to the Baltic coast. It does, however, have a few vital spots of interest of its own, alongside opportunities for hiking, trekking, fishing and cycling.

Historically, Småland has had it tough. The simple, rustic charm of the pretty painted cottages belies the intense misery endured by generations of local peasants: in the nineteenth century, subsistence farming failed, and the people were starving; consequently, a fifth of Sweden's population left the country for America – most of them from Småland. While their plight is vividly retold at the House of Emigrants exhibition in **Växjö**, a town which makes an excellent base from which to explore the region, the province's main tourist attractions are its myriad **glass factories**. The bulk of these celebrated glassworks lie within the dense birch and pine forests that, together with a thread of lakes, make up the largely unbroken landscape between Kalmar and Växjö. Consequently, the area is dubbed **Glasriket**, or the "Glass Kingdom", with each glassworks signposted clearly from the spidery main roads.

6

Växjö and around

Founded by St Sigfrid in the eleventh century, **VÄXJÖ** (approximately pronounced "veck-shur"), 120km from Kalmar deep in the heart of Småland, is by far the handiest base hereabouts. Though its centre is fairly bland and quiet, Växjö, whose name derives from *väg sjö*, or "way to the lake", is within easy reach of some beautifully tranquil lake scenery. The town itself offers a couple of great **museums**, and once a year comes to life for the **Karl Oskar-dagar** (second weekend in Aug) – a long weekend of unbridled revelry in honour of the character Karl-Oskar, created by author Wilhem Moberg, who symbolized the struggles of Småland's Swedish peasants in the nineteenth century. In reality, it means Våxjö's youth drink themselves silly through the nights while daytime entertainment fills the streets.

Smålands Museum

Södra Järnvägsgatan 2 • June–Aug daily 10am–5pm; Sept–May Tues–Fri 10am–5pm, Sat & Sun 11am–4pm • 80kr combined ticket with Utvandrarnas Hus • ⓦ smalandsmuseum.se

The best place to kick off your exploration of Våxjö is the **Smålands Museum**, behind the train station, which holds two permanent exhibitions: a history of Småland during the nineteenth and twentieth centuries, with a section dedicated to Våxjö, and the infinitely more interesting "Six Centuries of Swedish Glass". The latter shows sixteenth-century place settings, eighteenth- and nineteenth-century etched glass and stylish Art Nouveau-inspired pieces, with subtle floral motifs. "Trees in Fog", designed in the 1950s by Kosta designer Vicke Lindstrand, illustrates just how derivative so much of the twentieth-century work actually is. Look out, in particular, for the Absolut vodka bottles made in nearby Limmared, which formed the basis of today's design.

Utvandrarnas Hus

House of Emigrants • Wilhelm Mobergs gata 4 • June–Aug daily 10am–5pm; Sept–May Tues–Fri 10am–5pm, Sat & Sun 11am–4pm • 80kr combined ticket with Smålands Museum • ☎ 0470 201 20, ⓦ utvandrarnashus.se

In a plain building directly in front of the Smålands Museum, the inspired **Utvandrarnas Hus** explores the intense hardship faced by the Småland peasant population in the mid-nineteenth century and their ensuing emigration; between 1850 and 1929, one quarter of Småland's population left to begin a new life in America. The museum's **displays**, which include English-language translations and audio narratives, trace the lives of individual emigrants and recount the story of the industry that grew up around emigration fever. Most boats used by the emigrants left from Gothenburg and, until 1915, were British-operated sailings to Hull, from where passengers crossed the Pennines to Liverpool by train to board the transatlantic ships; conditions onboard the ships were usually dire and the emigrants often shared their accommodation with oxen, pigs, calves and sheep. Exhibitions change frequently but there's generally a mock-up of a street in early 1900s Chicago, a popular destination for the emigrants, where all the stores are run by Swedes – everything from a grocer's to a photographer's shop.

The Moberg Room

The museum also contains a section on **women emigrants**, entitled "Not Just Kristina", a reference to a fictitious character in *The Emigrants*, a trilogy by one of Sweden's most celebrated writers, **Wilhelm Moberg**. Upon publication, it became the most-read Swedish history book in the country, and was made into a film starring Max von Sydow and Liv Ullman. On display in the museum is Moberg's writing cabin, which was given to the museum after his death in 1973. Moberg would himself have emigrated, only his father sold a farrow of piglets to pay for his son to go to college in Sweden.

Domkyrkan

Linnégatan 2 • Daily 9am–6pm

In the centre of town, the distinctive **Domkyrkan**, with its unusual twin green towers and apricot-pink facade, is certainly worth a look. The combined impact of regular restorations, the most recent in 1995, together with a catalogue of disasters, such as sixteenth-century fires and a 1775 lightning strike, have left little of note except an organ. There are, however, some brilliant glass ornaments by three of the best-known contemporary Glass Kingdom designers: Göran Wärff's wacky church font of blue

6

IKEA

Among Swedish exports, only Volvo and ABBA spring to mind as readily as the furniture store **IKEA**, the letters standing for the name of its founder – **Ingvar Kamprad** (born 1926) – and his birthplace, Elmaryd, a farm in the Småland parish of Agunnaryd. Outside Sweden, the identity of IKEA's originator, now one of the world's richest men, is played down, and the firm is known for simple, modern design lines and prices that appeal to a mass market. Every item of furniture IKEA produces is assigned a fictional or real Swedish name; the styles of certain items are drawn from particular areas of the country, and are given a relevant name.

Founded in 1943 at Älmhult, a small town 50km southwest of Växjö, as a mail-order company, IKEA began producing furniture based on folk designs, which Kamprad had simplified. In the 1950s, Sweden's existing furniture-makers were sufficiently irritated by what they regarded as an upstart that they tried to pressure IKEA's suppliers into boycotting the company. Kamprad responded by importing furniture from abroad.

In his 1976 book, *Testament of a Furniture Dealer*, Kamprad wrote that from the outset, he wanted to promote "constructive fantasies": to change the world's view of design, rather than produce what people already believed they wanted. Having opened in Denmark in 1969, the company began expanding around the world, though it didn't enter the US market until 1985 or the UK until 1987. In 2006, IKEA opened its most northerly store in the world in Swedish Haparanda, drawing shoppers from across Lapland.

A number of biographies have been published on Kamprad, one of which (*The History of IKEA*) was authorized. They have revealed Kamprad's Nazi sympathies during World War II; in response, he blamed his former political leanings on the folly of youth.

Today, if you pass through Älmhult, you can see the original IKEA store, built in 1958; the street on which it stands is called, appropriately enough, Ikeagatan. Ironically, IKEA's headquarters are no longer in Sweden, but in Leiden in the Netherlands.

---

glass, a stunning triptych altarpiece made entirely of glass designed by Bertil Vallien and the tree of life with Adam and Eve surrounded by glass leaves by Erik Höglund. The cathedral is set in **Linnéparken**, named after Carl von Linné (see page 96), who was educated at the handsome school next door.

ARRIVAL AND INFORMATION   VÄXJÖ

By train The train station is next to the bus station in the middle of town, from where it's a straightforward walk of around 10min to reach the main square.

Destinations Copenhagen via Kastrup airport (hourly; 2hr 40min); Gothenburg (3 daily; 2hr 45min); Jönköping (hourly; 1hr45min); Kalmar (hourly; 1hr 10min); Malmö (hourly; 2hr).

Tourist office Stortorget (June–Aug Mon–Fri 10am–6pm, Sat 10am–4pm; Sept–May Mon–Fri 10am–5pm; ☎0470 73 32 80, ⓦvaxjoco.se). Has internet access.

ACCOMMODATION   SEE MAP PAGE 207

Best Western Royal Corner Liedbergsgatan 11 ☎0470 70 10 00, ⓦbestwestern.se. Smart, comfortable rooms with wooden panels, floors and fittings in keeping with the latest Swedish design trends. Extremely reasonable weekend and summer rates. **800kr/1150kr**

Clarion Collection Cardinal Bäckgatan 10 ☎0470 72 28 00, ⓦnordicchoicehotels.se. This winning hotel, just off the main drag, tastefully combines old and new, plus there's some decent art on the walls. A friendly welcome, too, and a free evening buffet make this hotel hard to beat. **830kr/1300kr**

Elite Stadshotell Kungsgatan 6 ☎0470 134 00, ⓦelite.se. A good central location for this hotel with the usual executive-class hotchpotch of shiny marble, potted palms and terrible carpets, but with a generous buffet breakfast included in the rates and an in-house English pub, the *Bishops Arms*. **1120r/1250kr**

Esplanad Norra Esplanaden 21A ☎0470 225 80, ⓦhotelesplanad.com. A reasonable family-owned central hotel, whose compact rooms are cosy, if lacking in style, and refreshingly free of the staid chain hotel sameness. No frills, but it's appealingly inexpensive and there's always tea and coffee available. **745kr/945kr**

Värend Kungsgatan 27 ☎0470 77 67 00, ⓦhotellvarend.se. Another standard hotel with rather plain rooms but a warm welcome from the family who own and run the place. It also offers good-value triple rooms at 200kr more than the rate for a double. The respectable prices make this

6

exceptionally good value for money. 695kr/850kr
Växjö Vandrarhem Evedals Brunn, 6km northeast of Växjö ☎ 0470 630 70, ⓦ vaxjovandrarhem.se; take Linnégatan north, following signs for Evedal, or bus #7 from Växjö bus station to the end of the route, from where it's a 700m walk. This beautifully maintained hostel is located in an eighteenth-century house, set in parkland beside Helgasjön lake with its own beach. Doubles 550kr

CAMPING

Evedals Camping Evedals Brunn, 6km northeast of Växjö ☎ 0470 630 34, ⓦ evedalscamping.com; take Linnégatan north, following signs for Evedal, or bus #7 from Växjö bus station to the end of the route, from where it's a 700m walk. Located beside Växjö youth hostel (see opposite), this campsite has tent pitches and two-person cabins with cooking facilities, plus a decent shop for stocking up on food. Tents 270kr, cabins 700kr

EATING AND DRINKING

SEE MAP PAGE 207

Växjö is a good place to try traditional **Småland cuisine**, which shows the influence both of the forests and of the poverty associated with the region; look out, in particular for, **foristerband**, a flavoursome, spicy sausage, and **krösamos**, mashed potato with lingonberry sauce.

CAFÉS AND RESTAURANTS

Broqvists Kronobergsgatan 14 ☎ 0470 120 20, ⓦ broqvistkonditori.se. This café just off Stortorget may be nothing special to look at, but it's a Växjö institution nonetheless – somewhere locals come to gossip or read the paper while enjoying a coffee and a slice of cake. Mon–Fri 8am–7pm, Sat 8am–5pm, Sun 9am–5pm.

Gräddhyllan De Luxe Sandgärdsgatan 19 ☎ 0470 74 04 10, ⓦ graddhyllan.info. This charming old wooden house is *the* place for fine dining in Växjö, featuring pork, steak and lamb dishes; the interior is decorated in the style of an old-fashioned dining room. Set menus are available for 490kr, 590kr and 690kr. Wed–Fri 11.30am–2pm & 6pm–late, Sat 6pm–late.

★ **Kafe de Luxe** Sandgärdsgatan 19 ☎ 0470 74 04 09, ⓦ kafedeluxe.se. Alternative, retro café, done out in 1960s style and full of battered old furniture. The best deal here is the lunchtime buffet (145kr), which features a range of salads, fry-ups and dessert. Wed & Thurs 11.30am–1am, Fri 11.30am–3am, Sat 10am–3am, Sun 10am–1am.

★ **PM & Vänner** Storgatan 24 ☎ 0470 759 700, ⓦ pmrestauranger.se. A great bar-bistro and an elegant (evening-only) fine-dining restaurant make up the two

halves of this popular place. Bistro meals such as mackerel or veal ravioli go for 230–375kr or there are bar snacks and tapas from 35kr. A sophisticated three-course affair at the restaurant costs 545kr. Mon & Tues 11.30am–10.30pm, Wed & Thurs 11.30am–11pm, Fri & Sat 11.30am–1am.

Umami Monkey Storgatan 18 ☎ 0470 73 90 00. A funky burger bar serving up what the staff call "fusion burgers" – regular burgers but featuring flavours taken from various world cuisines, for example, a burger with wasabi, ginger, bacon and shiitake mushrooms, or one with grilled halloumi, Portobello mushrooms and pesto. They cost around 120kr. Mon–Thurs 11am–10pm, Fri 11am–midnight, Sat noon–midnight.

Venezia Linnégatan 31 ☎ 0470 461 70. Serving the people of Växjö since 1974, this neighbourhood trattoria buzzes with people enjoying the sensibly priced and tasty pasta dishes (85–150kr), pizzas (80–135kr) and meat mains such as pork with red pesto and potatoes (165kr). Mon 11am–2pm & 4.30–9pm, Tues–Fri 11am–2pm & 4.30–10pm, Sat 4.30–10pm, Sun 4.30–9pm.

PUB

Bishops Arms Kungsgatan 6 ☎ 0470 276 66. Like elsewhere in Sweden, this fake English pub is attached to the town's *Elite* hotel and is an inordinately popular place for a drink. There are sometimes special After Work deals on beer – look out for the signs outside. Mon & Tues 5pm–midnight, Wed & Thurs 5pm–1am, Fri 4pm–2am, Sat 5pm–2am, Sun 5–11pm.

The Glass Kingdom

Glass-making in Sweden was pioneered by King Gustav Vasa, who'd been impressed by the glass he saw on a trip to Italy in the mid-sixteenth century. He initially set up a **glassworks** in Stockholm; however, it was Småland's forests that could provide the vast amounts of fuel needed to feed the furnaces, and so a glass factory was set up in the province in 1742. Called Kosta, after its founders, Anders Koskull, Georg Bogislaus and Stael von Holstein, it is still the largest glassworks in Småland today.

All of the dozen or so glassworks still in operation in Småland give captivating **glass-blowing** demonstrations. Several have permanent exhibitions of either contemporary glasswork or pieces from their history, and all have a shop. **Bus** services to the glassworks, or to points within easy walking distance of them, are extremely limited, and without your own transport it is almost impossible to see more than a couple in

> ## GLASS-MAKING AND -BUYING IN THE GLASS KINGDOM
> The **glass-making process** can be mesmerizing to watch, with a glass plug being fished out of a shimmering, molten lake (at 1200°C) and then turned and blown into a graphite or steel mould. With wine glasses, a foot is added during the few seconds when the temperature is just right – if the glass is too hot, the would-be stem will slide off or sink right through; if too cold, it won't stick. The piece is then annealed – heated and then slowly cooled – for several hours. It all looks deceptively simple and mistakes are rare, but it nevertheless takes years to become a *servitör* (glass-maker's assistant), working up through the ranks of stem-maker and bowl-gatherer.
>
> Glassware is marketed with a vengeance in Småland – take a look at the often absurd hyperbole in the widely available *Kingdom of Crystal* magazine. If you want to buy glassware, don't feel compelled to snap up the first things you see: the same designs appear at most of the glassworks, testimony to the fact that the biggest factories by far, Kosta Boda and Orrefors, are now under the same umbrella ownership, while many of the smaller works have also been swallowed up, even though they retain their own names.

a day (though this will satisfy most people). The **Glassriket Pass** gives free entry to the glassworks and discounts on some glassware products; it's available at the tourist office in Växjö and online (100kr; @glasriket.se).

Kosta Boda glassworks

Glassworks Mon–Fri 9am–3.15pm, Sat & Sun 10am–4pm • 30min tour 40kr, bookable on @ 0478 345 29 or via email at @ info@kostaboda.se • Outlet store Daily 10am–8pm • @ kostaboda.se • Take Route 25 to Lessebo, then follow signs to Kosta, or hop on the direct bus #218 from Växjö; timetables are at @ lanstrafikenkron.se

While each glassworks has its individual design characteristics, **Kosta Boda** is the easiest to reach from Växjö, has extensive displays and gives the best picture of what's available. The Kosta Boda and Åfors glassworks are both operated by the same team. While two of Kosta's most celebrated and hyped designers, Bertil Vallien and Ulrica Hydman-Vallien, have their studios at Åfors, the bigger glassworks is at Kosta.

The **outlet store** here contains some of the most delicate fin-de-siècle glassware, designed by Karl Lindeberg; for contemporary simplicity, Anna Ehrner's bowls and vases are the most elegant. Among the most brilliantly innovative works are those by Göran Wärff – examples of his expressive work can also be found in Växjö's cathedral. Current design trends tend more towards colourful and rather graceless high kitsch; nonetheless, new designer sculptural pieces can go for astoundingly high prices: commercialized designs start at 2500kr, although for a single, traditional *akvavit* glass you're looking at paying something like 200kr.

ACCOMMODATION, EATING AND DRINKING · KOSTA BODA

Glasbaren Stora Vägen 75 @ 0478 348 40. Inside the *Kosta Boda* hotel (see opposite) is this remarkable bar; its entire decor is cobalt-blue glass – from panels on the bar to lights designed to look like icicles. Try the excellent home-made meatballs served with horseradish and lingonberries in a creamy sauce for 170kr. Mon & Tues 4–11pm, Wed & Thurs 4pm–midnight, Fri 3pm–1am, Sat 2pm–1am, Sun 2–11pm.

Kosta Boda Art Stora Vägen 75 @ 0478 348 30, @ kostabodaarthotel.se. No fewer than seven of Kosta's designers helped create this incredibly stylish hotel and as a result it's a glass lover's dream – even the sinks and bedside lamps are made of glass. There's also a spa complex onsite. <u>2790kr</u>

Jönköping

Perched at the southernmost tip of Lake Vättern, northwest of Växjö along Route 30, **JÖNKÖPING** (pronounced "yurn-shurping") makes a pleasant place to break your journey. One of the oldest medieval trading centres in the country, having won its town charter in 1284, the town is today famous for being the home of the **matchstick**, the nineteenth-century manufacture and worldwide distribution of which made Jönköping a wealthy place. It's also remarkable for the sheer number of **Free Churches** – over twenty in the immediate vicinity – leading the town to be dubbed "Sweden's Jerusalem". As the traditional Church watches its congregations diminish, people are turning instead to these independent and fundamentalist churches.

6 Jönköpings läns museum

Jönköping county museum • Dag Hammarskjöldsplats 2 • Mid-June–mid-Aug Mon–Fri 10am–5pm, Sat & Sun 11am–3pm; mid-Aug–mid-June Tues, Thurs & Fri 10am–7pm, Wed 10am–9pm, Sat & Sun 11am–3pm • Free • ⓦ jkpglm.se

Whilst you're in town, have a look inside **Jönköpings läns museum**, on the east side of the canal between lakes Vättern and Munksjön. A mishmash of oddities, with exhibits ranging from posters showing Swedish support for Che Guevara through garden chairs throughout the ages to samovars and doll's houses, the place is like a well-stocked junk shop. The best part is the well-lit collection of paintings and drawings by **John Bauer**, a local artist who enthralled generations of Swedes with his Tolkienesque representations of gnomes and trolls in the *Bland tomtar och troll*, a well-known series of Swedish children's books which were published around Christmas between 1907 and 1915.

Arkivhuset

Mon–Fri 9am–7pm, Sat & Sun 11am–3pm • Free

To the left of the main entrance to the museum, beyond the reference library, you'll find an account of Jönköping's history from 1200 or so onwards in old maps, paintings and models housed in a building known as **Arkivhuset** – worth a look on a rainy day.

ARRIVAL AND INFORMATION   JÖNKÖPING

By train The train station is part of the Resecentrum on the lake's southernmost edge, along with the bus station and the tourist office. For services to Stockholm and Malmö, change trains at Nässjö.

ASTRID LINDGREN – CREATOR OF PIPPI LONGSTOCKING

Some 120km east of Jönköping, and reachable on Routes 31 and 33, is **VIMMERBY**, near where one of Sweden's most popular children's authors, **Astrid Lindgren** (1907–2002), was born. Her most endearing character, **Pippi Longstocking** (in Swedish, Pippi Långstrump), burst upon the world in 1945. Pippi had red hair and long thin legs on which she wore nonmatching stockings. Wealthy and energetic, she could do as she pleased, and her adventures appealed hugely to children everywhere.

Lindgren's eighty books have, in total, sold more than 80 million copies worldwide, and her face has appeared on a Swedish 6kr stamp. Yet her writing wasn't simply about lighthearted adventures: her cleverly conceived tale, *Bröderna Lejonhjärta* ("The Lionheart Brothers"), tries to explain the concept of death to children. In later years, she became a Swedish Brigitte Bardot figure, campaigning on animal-rights issues, and she was also involved with children's rights. Following her death in 2002 in Stockholm, she was buried in the family grave in Vimmerby cemetery.

Today, Vimmerby is home to **Astrid Lindgren's Värld** (June–Aug daily 10am–6pm; 420kr, children under 13 310kr; ⩗alv.se/en), a theme park where actors take on the roles of her most famous characters. Trains to Vimmerby run from Kalmar.

Destinations Nässjö (every 30min; 35min); Växjö (hourly; 1hr 50min).

Tourist office Inside the Resecentrum (July & Aug Mon– Fri 10am–7pm, Sat 10am–4pm, Sun noon–4pm; Sept– June Mon–Fri 10am–5pm, Sat 10am–2pm; ☎0771 21 13 00, ⩗jkpg.com).

ACCOMMODATION
SEE MAP PAGE 212

Clarion Collection Victoria F.E. Elmgrensgatan 5 ☎036 71 28 00, ⩗nordicchoicehotels.se. The best choice in town for style, atmosphere and value for money. Afternoon coffee and cakes and an excellent buffet supper in the appealing atrium dining area are included, and the split-level sauna is the best in town. **950kr/1540kr**

Elite Stora Hotellplan ☎036 10 00 00, ⩗elite.se. Jönköping's most historic hotel, built between 1856 and 1860 in Italian Renaissance Baroque style. Rooms are decorated in Gustavian-style pastels, and bathrooms here have that very unusual Swedish commodity – bathtubs. Some rooms have lake views. **990kr/1400kr**

★ **Familjen Ericsson's City** Västra Storgatan 25 ☎036 71 92 80, ⩗cityhotel.nu. Less than a 5min walk south from the train station, this is a very comfortable choice, though plainer than many other establishments in town. Rooms in the nicer, newer, more modern section of the hotel cost a couple of 100kr more. **655kr/995kr**

Grand Hovrättstorget ☎046 36-14 00 00, ⩗grandhotel jonkoping.se. Built in 1904, this rather elegant building is home to a family-owned hotel offering airy rooms with wooden floors. It's exceptional value for money, and the location is great, too, right on the main shopping street. **700kr/950kr**

STF Jönköping Vandrarhem Odengatan 10, Huskvarna ☎036 14 88 70, ✉148870@hhv.se; bus #1 from the Resecentrum to the stop marked "Esplanaden". The nearest youth hostel is 6km to the east in the neighbouring town of Huskvarna; ask for a room with private facilities for 200kr more. Doubles **745kr**

CAMPING

Villa Björkhagen Friggagatan 31, Rosenlund ☎036 12 28 63, ⩗camping.se/f6; bus #1 from the Resecentrum. Roughly halfway between the town centre and the youth hostel; if you don't come by bus, you can get here by walking east about 3km along the lakeside Strandpromenaden (a continuation of Norra Strandgatan). Has cabins with cooking facilities and private bathroom. Tents **360kr**, cabins **1295kr**

EATING, DRINKING AND NIGHTLIFE
SEE MAP PAGE 212

Jönköping's most popular **eating** and **drinking** area is the harbour pier, though the rest of town has plenty of good, lively spots too. For a local food speciality, go for the **vätternröding** (Lake Vättern char), brought here from the unusually cold and deep Lake Vättern, which can sustain fish normally found in the Baltic Sea.

CAFÉS AND RESTAURANTS

Anna-Gretas Bar & Mat Kapellgatan 19 ☎036 71 25 75, ⩗annagretas.se. The oldest café in town and formerly the staple haunt of market traders, this popular place serves great Spanish food and an impressive range of tapas. Reckon on 40–60kr per item. Mon–Thurs 11.30am–2pm & 5–11pm, Fri 11.30am–2pm & 5pm–midnight, Sat 5pm–midnight.

★**Aqua Dinner & Drinks** Barnarpsgatan 24 ☎ 036 12 00 99, ⓦ aquadinner.se. This restaurant delivers a Scandinavian theme mixed with European influences to produce flavours you won't forget. Mains, cost 170–270kr. Mon–Thurs 11.30am–4pm & 5–11pm, Fri 11.30–late, Sat 11.30–late, Sun noon–8pm.

★**En Italienare & En Grek** Barnarpsgatan 35B ☎ 036 30 77 55, ⓦ italienareochgrek.se. Well-priced, tasty Italian and Greek food (moussaka 170kr, pasta 140–175kr, pizzas from 115kr), good service and an attractive location overlooking the turreted old tram depot in the university district. Also has outside tables in summer. Mon–Thurs 11am–10pm, Fri 11am–11pm, Sat noon–11pm, Sun noon–9pm.

Hemma Smedjegatan 36 ☎ 036 10 01 55, ⓦ restaurang hemma.se. The town's most popular venue for laidback live music, with very friendly service and a relaxing terrace garden. There's also a decent menu of home-cooking dishes served Tues–Thurs evenings for 165kr. Mon–Fri 11.30am–2pm, Wed–Thurs 6pm–late, Fri 4.30pm–late, Sat 6pm–late.

Jungle Thai Trädgårdsgatan 9 ☎ 036 13 28 28, ⓦ jungle thai.com. One of the most popular places in Jönköping, and a good choice, though the elephant heads and plastic greenery are a bit OTT. Thai and other Asian dishes cost 180–260kr. Mon–Thurs 11am–3pm & 5–10pm, Fri 11am–11pm, Sat noon–11pm, Sun 1–9pm.

Mackmakeriet Smedjegatan 26A ☎ 036 19 03 05, ⓦ mackmakeriet.se. The best café in town, friendly and housed in a wonderful eighteenth-century building with an original painted ceiling portraying two young girls sitting by a lake. Delicious fresh-filled baguettes cost around 55kr to take away. Mon–Fri 8.30am–6.30pm, Sat 10am–4pm.

BARS AND PUBS

Bishops Arms Hotellplan ☎ 036 215 50 52, ⓦ bishops arms.com/jonkoping. Attached to the *Elite Stora* hotel, this is a good choice for a drink and is a firm favourite amongst the locals. There's an impressive selection of whiskies and beers and a few bar snacks, too, such as burgers and steaks. Mon & Tues 4–11pm, Wed & Thurs 4pm–midnight, Fri 4pm–1am, Sat noon–1am, Sun noon–10pm.

Harry's Brunnsgatan 13–1 ☎ 036 71 94 80, ⓦ harrys. se/restauranger/jonkoping. *Harry's* trademark half-built brick walls between the tables are well in evidence here. It's an inordinately popular place for a drink and a bite to eat, too; the burgers are especially tasty and juicy. Wed & Thurs 5pm–late, Fri & Sat 5pm–2am.

Gränna

Forty kilometres north of Jönköping, the lakeside town of **GRÄNNA** is associated with the unlikely combination of pears and a gung-ho nineteenth-century Swedish balloonist (see opposite). In late spring, the hills around Gränna are a confetti of pear blossom, Per Brahe having encouraged the planting of pear orchards hereabouts; the Gränna pear is one of the best-known varieties in the country today. Approaching from the south, the beautiful Gränna Valley sweeps down to your left, with the hills to the right, most notably the crest of Grännaberget, which provides a majestic foil to some superb views over **Lake Vättern** and its island, Visingsö. On a hot summer's day, the trip here from Jönköping has something of the atmosphere of the French Riviera, evoked in particular by the winding roads, red-tiled roofs and the profusion of flowers in the old cottage gardens – not to mention the equal profusion of Porsche and Mercedes cars.

Per Brahe, one of Sweden's first counts, built the town in the mid-seventeenth century, using the symmetry, regularity and spaciousness of planning that he had learnt while governor of Finland. The charming main street, **Brahegatan**, was subsequently widened and remodelled, allowing the houses fronting it to have gardens, while the other main roads were designed so Brahe could look straight down them as he stood at the windows of his now-ruined castle, **Brahehus**. The gardens along Brahegatan remain mostly intact, and until the 1920s, there were no additions to the original street layout. Even now, there's very much a village feel to the little town.

Grännaberget café

Grännaberget • May–Aug daily 10am–9pm • ☎ 0390 101 09

True, it's a bit of a climb (243 steep steps, to be precise) but there's a view from *Kaffestugan Grännaberget* which should not be missed: from the sloping main square, walk over to the church then south for 100m to the junction with Parkgränd and the wooden steps in the hillside to your left. Outside seating affords a fabulous vista over the lake. Better still, you can explore inside a range of ancient grass- and thatch-roofed buildings brought from the surrounding areas.

The Grenna Kulturgård: Andrée Expedition Polarcenter ### 6

Mid-May–Aug daily 10am–5pm; Sept–mid-May Mon–Fri 10am–4pm • 70kr • ⓦ grennamuseum.se

Within the Grenna Kulturgård on Brahegatan is the fascinating **Polarcenter**, dedicated to Salomon August Andrée, the Gränna-born **balloonist** who led a doomed attempt to reach the North Pole by balloon in 1897. Born at Brahegatan 37, Andrée was fired by the European obsession of the day to explore and conquer unknown areas; with no real way of directing his balloon, however, his trip was destined for disaster from the start. After a flight lasting only three days, during which time it flew more than 800km in different directions, the balloon made a forced landing on ice just 470km from its departure point. The crew of three attempted to walk to civilization, but the movement of the ice floes meant they made no progress; after six weeks' trekking, they set up camp on a floe drifting rapidly southwards. Sadly, the ice cracked and their shelter collapsed, and with it their hopes. Finally, they died from the effects of cold, starvation and trichinosis, caught after they ate the raw meat of a polar bear they had managed to spear. It would be another 33 years before their frozen bodies and their equipment were discovered by a Norwegian sailing ship. They were reburied in Stockholm at a funeral attended by a crowd of forty thousand.

The museum exhibition poignantly includes a diary kept by one of the crew and film taken by the team, which makes for pitiful viewing: the men are seen with the polar bear they'd hunted, and other sequences show the three hopelessly pulling their sledges across the ice sheets. The museum also covers exploration of the polar region in general, with exhibitions centring on the Arctic and Antarctic historical expeditions, using Andrée as a springboard to a wider picture.

ARRIVAL AND INFORMATION GRÄNNA

By bus Bus #101 runs roughly every 30min from Jönköping to Gränna and takes 1hr.

Tourist office Grenna Kulturgård, Brahegatan 36 (daily June–Aug 10am–6pm; Sept–May 10am–4pm; ☏ 0390 10 38 60, ⓦ grenna.se). Housed in the same building as the museum (see above) and library, with free internet access.

ACCOMMODATION

Strandterrassen ☏ 0390 418 40, ⓦ strandterrassen.se. Gränna's youth hostel is located down at the harbour in two separate buildings at the foot of Hamnvägen. Facilities are shared and there's a kitchen for guest use. Doubles 560kr

★ **Västanå slott** About 5km south of Gränna ☏ 0390 107 00, ⓦ vastanaslott.se; get here by taxi (Gränna Taxi ☏ 0390 121 00; about 200kr). A sensational historic country manor built in 1590 by Count Sten Bielke and owned in the seventeenth century by Per Brahe. This low, white castle now belongs to the von Otters, descendants of Bielke. There are no televisions in the rooms – but the sheer majesty of the antique-strewn furnishings and the fabulous lake views from the magnificent first-floor drawing room are worth the stay alone. Open April–Dec. 1590kr

EATING

Fiket Brahegatan 43 ☏ 0390 100 57. A 1950s-themed café with a rear terrace where you can enjoy the house speciality, *mandelpastej*, a rich almond tart, or their excellent Gränna *knäckebröd*, a crunchy, tasty crispbread made with linseed and sunflower and sesame seeds. Mon–Fri 8.30am–6pm, Sat 8.30am–4pm, Sun 10am–4pm.

Hamnkrogen At the harbour ☏ 042 12 87 55. A very pleasing restaurant specializing in well-prepared fish and meat meals from 180kr, for example baked salmon in hollandaise sauce with chives, or fried char in crayfish sauce with dill. There's outside eating in summer on the sunny terrace overlooking the lake. June–Aug daily noon–late.

Vadstena

With its beautiful lakeside setting, **VADSTENA**, which once served as a royal seat and important monastic centre, is a fine place for a day or two's stay. Sixty kilometres north of Gränna, the town's main attraction is its moated **castle**, designed in the sixteenth century by Gustav Vasa as part of his defensive ring protecting the Swedish heartland around Stockholm. The cobbled, twisting streets, lined with cottages covered in climbing roses, also contain an impressive fourteenth-century abbey, whose existence is the result of the passionate work of **Birgitta**, Sweden's first female saint (see page 218).

While Vadstena boasts numerous ancient sites and buildings, each with an information plate (in English), the two outstanding attractions here are the **castle** and the **abbey**. Vadstena is also made for romantic evening strolls, with wonderful lakeside sunsets and attractive streets of irregularly shaped houses.

Vadstena Slott

May–early June daily noon–4pm; early–late June daily 10am–5pm; July–early Aug daily 10am–5pm; early–late Aug daily noon–4pm; late Aug–mid-Sept daily noon–4pm; mid-Sept–early Oct Mon–Fri noon–4pm • Tours (in English) July–early Aug daily at noon • 90kr, tours 130kr • ⓦ vadstenaslott.com

Those who've visited the castle at Kalmar will be familiar with the antics of Gustav Vasa and his troubled family, whose saga continues at **Vadstena Slott**. With a grand moat and four round towers, each with a diameter of 7m, it was originally built as a fortification to defend against Danish attacks in 1545, but was then prettified to serve as a home to Vasa's mentally ill third son, Magnus. His elder brother, Johan III, was responsible for its lavish decorations, but fire destroyed them all just before their refurbishment was completed, and to save money they simply painted fittings and decor on the walls, including the swagged curtains that can still be seen today. The castle's last resident was Hedvig Eleanor, the widowed queen of Karl X; after she died in the 1770s the castle was regarded as hopelessly unfashionable, and so no royal would consider living there. At the end of the seventeenth century, the building fell into decay and was used as a grain store; the original hand-painted wooden ceilings were chopped up and turned into grain boxes. Today, the interior is crammed with **portraits** mainly of the Vasa family, characterized by some very unhappy and unattractive faces. It's worth joining the regular English-language **tours** to hear all the Vasa family gossip.

Klosterkyrkan

June–Aug Mon–Fri 8am–7pm, Sat & Sun 9am–7pm; Sept–May Mon–Thurs 8am–4pm, Fri 8am–7pm, Sat & Sun 10am–4pm • Free

St Birgitta specified that the **Klosterkyrkan**, easily reached by walking towards the lake from the castle, should be "of plain construction, humble and strong". Wide, grey and sombre, the lakeside abbey, consecrated in 1430, certainly fulfils her criteria from the outside; inside it has been embellished with a celebrated collection of medieval artwork. More memorable than the crypt containing the tombs of various royals is the statue of Birgitta, now devoid of the hands "in a state of ecstasy" – as the description puts it. To the right, the poignant "Door of Grace and Honour" was where each Birgittine nun entered the abbey after being professed – the next time they would use the door would be on the day of their funeral. Birgitta's bones are encased in a red velvet box, decorated with silver and gilt medallions, in a glass case down stone steps in the monks' choir stalls.

The **altarpiece** here is worth a glance, too: another handless Birgitta, looking rather less than ecstatic, is portrayed dictating her revelations to a band of monks, nuns and

6

ST BIRGITTA

Birgitta (1303–73) came to the village of Vadstena as a lady-in-waiting to King Magnus Eriksson and his wife, Blanche of Namur, who lived at Bjälbo Palace. Married at 13, she gave birth to eight children, and had the first of her many visions while living at the palace. Such was the force of her personality, she persuaded her royal employers (to whom she was vaguely related) to give her the palace in order to start a convent and a monastery. To obtain papal approval for the monastery, she set off for Rome in 1349, but the times were against her – the pope was in Avignon, France. She spent the next twelve years in Rome, having more visions, pressing for his return but dying before she could return to Vadstena. She was canonized in 1391, a final vision having already told her this would be the case. Her daughter, Katarina, carried on her work and brought about the building of the monastery and abbey; she too became a saint and her remains lie in the same coffin as her mother's.

acolytes, while around her, representations of hell and purgatory depict finely sculpted faces of woe disappearing into the bloody mouth of what looks like a hippopotamus. Other than Birgitta's, a tomb to note inside the abbey is that of Gustav Vasa's son Magnus. His grand, raised tomb is flanked at each corner by obese, glum-faced cherubs, but the most impressive feature is the remarkably lifelike hands raised in prayer on the likeness of Magnus on the top.

The monastery and nunnery

Although now housing the *Vadstena Klosterhotel* (see opposite), the **monastery** and **nunnery** on either side of the abbey are open for tours. The most interesting part of the nunnery, housed in the thirteenth-century Bjälbo Palace, is the King's Hall, with an elegant lofty ceiling. On its conversion to a convent, Birgitta had the ceiling lowered to what she considered a more appropriate level for the nuns – it remains thus today.

The Hospitalsmuséet

Mental Hospital Museum · Lastköpingsgatan · July–early Aug daily noon–5pm · 90kr

Just beyond the gates of the abbey graveyard, the **Hospitalsmuséet** is based in what was Sweden's oldest mental hospital, dating from 1757. The display of terrifying contraptions used to control and "cure" the inmates includes a spinning chair, which patients were tightly strapped to and spun until they vomited; an iron bath, in which patients were tied and then scalded; and a tub, used until 1880, in which patients were held down among electric eels. The most poignant displays on the first floor are the patients' own excellently drawn pictures, depicting the tortures inflicted on them. Also on display are moving photographs of inmates from the nineteenth century (extensive research having first been carried out to ensure that the people shown have no surviving relatives).

ARRIVAL AND DEPARTURE · VADSTENA

By public transport There are no trains to Vadstena and getting here from Gränna is circuitous. It's easiest (though not fastest) to return to Jönköping and then take the train, via Nässjö, to Motala, from where bus #612 runs to Vadstena. Motala is also easily reached from Örebro and Norrköping. The main bus stop is in the centre of town, between the castle and the abbey; there's a four-weekly service to Stockholm (4hr 30min) with Swebus (w swebus. se).

By car It's a straight run along the E4 and Route 50 north from Gränna.

INFORMATION

Tourist office In the castle (May & Sept Mon–Sat 10am–3pm; June & Aug Mon–Sat 10am–6pm, Sun 10am–4pm; July daily 10am–6pm; Oct–April Wed–Fri 10am–2pm; ☏ 0143 315 70, w visitostergotland.se).

ACCOMMODATION

Pensionat Solgården Strågatan 3 ☎0143 143 50, ⓦpensionatsolgarden.se. The best-value alternative to the pricier hotels, this beautifully maintained villa from 1905 is located in a quiet, central position. Rooms are named after famous artists such as Chagall and Matisse and feature prints of their work; you'll pay 300kr more for private facilities. Open May–Sept. **990kr**

STF Vadstena Vandrarhem Skänningegatan 20 ☎0143 765 60, ⓦvadstenavandrarhem.se. This hostel is close to the lake and barely a 5min stroll from the centre, just up from the abbey. Advance booking is essential outside the mid-June to mid-Aug period. Doubles **560kr**

Vadstena Klosterhotel ☎0143-13 000, ⓦkloster hotel.se. Dating (in parts) from 1369, this hotel is located in the nunnery next to the abbey and has suitably atmospheric public areas. Try for a room in the main building, which is one of the few remaining from the medieval period; disappointingly, room interiors err on the modern and uninspiring side. **1850kr**

EATING AND DRINKING

Gamla Konditoriet Storgatan 18 ☎046 143 311 73. This classic, busy bakery and *konditori* in a fine seventeenth-century house is open every day for traditional cakes and sandwiches. It's also a good choice for a spot of lunch with quiches and salads. Mon–Fri 9am–6pm, Sat 9am–5pm, Sun 11am–5pm.

På Hörnet Skänningegatan 1 ☎0143 131 70. An understated neighbourhood pub that serves great food, including fresh cod, oven-baked salmon and duck breast, all 185–225kr. It's well worth seeking out solely for its heavenly starter of smoked salmon with chilled wild garlic soup, pickled fennel and watermelon (125kr). Tues–Sat 5.30–11pm.

Rådhuskälleren Rådhustorget 5 ☎0143 121 70. Informal restaurant set in the cosy cellars of the sixteenth-century courthouse, with main dishes like fried local char with crayfish sauce (190kr) or chicken fillet with tzatziki and potato wedges (140kr). It's also a pub, particularly popular with locals on Fri and Sat. Mon & Sun noon–9pm, Tues 6–9pm, Wed & Thurs noon–10pm, Fri noon–1am, Sat noon–2am.

Örebro and around

The lively, youthful and handsome town of **ÖREBRO** lies on the shores of the country's fourth largest lake, Hjälmaren, roughly two-thirds of the way between Stockholm and Karlstad and around 110km north of Vadstena. Örebro's development was dictated by its important strategic position: the main route from southwest Sweden to Stockholm, King Erik's Way, ran right through the centre, where a build-up of gravel made the river fordable (Örebro means "gravel bridge"). The heart of Örebro comes as a pleasant surprise, its much-fortified thirteenth-century **castle** forming a magnificent backdrop to the water-lily-studded **Svartån River**. Aside from the town-centre attractions, there are a couple of fun trips you can make by bike, namely to the **Naturens hus** nature centre, just east of town on the shores of Hjälmaren, and to **Tysslingen lake**, a few kilometres west.

Örebro Slott

Örebro Castle • Entry on tours only: June & late Aug daily in English at 1pm; July–late Aug in English at 4pm • 50kr

The town's first defensive fort was built after a band of German merchants settled here in the thirteenth century, attracted by rich iron ore deposits. It was enlarged in

ÖREBRO OPEN ART

Every odd-numbered year, between mid-June and early September, the city's pedestrianized centre is transformed into a huge open-air contemporary art exhibition, **Open Art** (ⓦopenart. se), as designers and artists display their work. Past displays have included a gigantic upside-down teddy bear made of wood and a floating platform for model ducks and seals on the water below the castle; you name it, anything goes – the aim is to provide an urban forum for thought-provoking modern art.

the fourteenth century by King Magnus Eriksson, who lived here; Gustav Vasa's son Karl IX added fortifications and then, following in the footsteps of Vasa's other sons, turned it into a splendid Renaissance castle, raising all the walls to the height of the medieval towers and plastering them in cream-coloured stucco. When the Danes were no longer a threat, the town lost its importance, and **Örebro Slott** fell into disuse and subsequently became a storehouse and a jail.

In the old **prison** on the fourth floor, you can see words scratched into the walls by Russian prisoners of war. Another room was used to hold suspected witches and was well furnished by King Karl as a **torture chamber**; at the time, fear of witchcraft was reaching fever pitch, and over four hundred women lost their heads here having survived attempts to drown them in the nearby river. Naturally, the castle is said to be riddled with ghosts, ranging from that of King Magnus Eriksson's wife Blanche (also known as Blanka in Swedish and said to be in torment for having murdered her son), to Engelbrekt, who had his head lopped off two years after he stormed the castle in 1434 and led a riot on behalf of farmers oppressed by harsh taxes.

The fairy tale exterior you see today is the result of renovation in the 1890s. Influenced by contemporary National Romanticism, the architects carefully restored the castle to reflect both medieval and Renaissance grandeur. The same cannot be said for the interior, where the valiant guides face a real challenge: there's no original furniture left, and many of the rooms are used for conferences, hence the emphasis on the building being a "living castle". Among the few features of interest are some fine doors and floors, dating from as recently as the 1920s, with the inlays depicting historical events

---

BOAT TRIPS AROUND ÖREBRO

Given Örebro's easy access to **Lake Hjälmaren** just east of the town, you might want to consider taking a boat trip around the lake on *M/S Gustav Lagerbjelke*, which operates from late June to mid-August. There are several options available but the most popular is the five-hour **cruise** out into Hjälmaren and through the Hjälmarekanal with its many locks. Transport back to Örebro is by bus and the return ticket costs 370kr. Alternatively, shorter lunch cruises including a dish of salmon with pesto, parmesan and potatoes cost a good-value 270kr. There's more information at ⓦ lagerbjelke.com.

Another option is to rent your own **canoe** or **kayak** and paddle out yourself: both are available from KFUM Örebro Kanotcenter located out of town at Hästhagsvägen (ⓣ 019 26 04 00; 50kr/hr, 200kr/day). Give them a call and they'll help with pick-up and drop-off.

6

---

at Örebro; and, in the main state room, a large **family portrait** of Karl XI and his family, their eyes all popping out as a result of using arsenic to whiten their faces.

St Nicolai kyrka

Storgatan 27 • Mon–Fri 9am–8pm, Sat 10am–6pm

Just a few hundred metres south of the castle, **St Nicolai kyrka**, at the top of the very oblong Stortorget, dates from 1260. Extensive restoration in the 1860s robbed it of most of its medieval character, though renovations have tried to undo the damage. It was here in 1810 that the relatively unknown figure of Jean Baptiste Bernadotte, Napoleon's marshal, was elected successor to the Swedish throne. The descendants of the new King Karl Johan, who never spoke a word of Swedish, are the current royal family. Engelbrekt was also supposed to be buried here after his execution (see page 219), but when his coffin was exhumed in the eighteenth century, it was empty, and his bones have never been recovered.

Konsthall

Arts Centre • Olaigatan 17B • Opening hours summer 11am–5pm • Free • ⓦ orebrokonsthall.se

Just north of the castle is the **Konsthall**, located in a former bank. A surprisingly spacious series of galleries exhibit temporary collections of contemporary international art, spread over the ground floor and in the basement in the old vaults.

Stadsparken

From the Konsthall, it's a pleasant stroll east along the waterside Olaigatan, crossing the Svartån River over Hamnbron bridge, to continue east along Kanalvägen to Örebro's stunning **Stadspark**, one of the most beautiful town parks in the country. Sunbathing locals flock here to picnic amid the park's most exceptional feature – the colour-coded border walks, each section bursting with a rainbow of flowers separated by tone. The park is also known for its profusion of different varieties of magnolia trees which are at their most spectacular around mid-May.

Wadköping

Museum May–Aug daily 11am–5pm; Sept–April Tues–Sun 11am–4pm • Free • Café Daily 10am–5pm • ⓦ orebro.se/wadkoping

At the far end of the park stands an open-air museum, **Wadköping**. An entire village of centuries-old wooden cottages and shops was brought to the site in the 1950s when urban planning was threatening the historic dwellings with demolition. A local man, Bertil Waldén, campaigned to save the better ones, and relocated them here at

6

Wadköping on the banks of the river. The extremely pretty little "high street" is flanked with low eighteenth-century buildings on one side, and on the other with taller houses dating from after the town fire of 1854. Some of the cottages are now lived in again and there's a very good **café**.

Naturens hus

Oljevägen 15 • Daily 11am–5pm • Free

From Wadköping, it's a pleasant cycle ride of around five to ten minutes along the banks of the Svartån River to one of Örebro's best out-of-town destinations: **Naturens hus nature centre**. The building's harmonious design and building materials (stone and glass) blend effortlessly into the natural surroundings and it's a great spot to enjoy views out over the lake, Hjälmaren. Inside you'll find information about the wildlife around the lake as well as a good café.

Tysslingen lake

Tysslingen lake lies a few kilometres west of town, and can be easily reached by bike. In late March, several thousand whooper swans settle here for two or three weeks to feed on their way up to northern Finland and make spectacular viewing from the lakeside (binoculars are essential).

ARRIVAL AND GETTING AROUND   ÖREBRO

By train The train station is in the Resecentrum travel centre on Järnvägsgatan, north of the castle, along with the bus station. From Vadstena, take bus #612 north to Motala and change there for the train to Örebro.

Destinations Falun (hourly; 2hr 20min); Gävle (hourly; 3hr 45min); Gothenburg (two-hourly; 2hr 45min); Motala (2 hourly; 1hr 10min); Stockholm (hourly; 1hr 50 min); Västerås (hourly; 50min).

By bike The town centre is easily seen on foot but if you want to get a flavour of the surrounding countryside, it's a good idea to rent a bike. Mountain bikes and regular cycles are available at Gustavsvik Camping (see opposite).

INFORMATION

Tourist office Inside Örebro Slott (May & Sept daily 11am–3pm; June–Aug daily 10am–5pm; Oct–April daily 11am–3pm; ☎ 019 21 21 21, ⓦ visitorebro.se).

ACCOMMODATION   SEE MAP PAGE 220

Behrn Stortorget 12 ☎ 019 12 00 95, ⓦ behrnhotell. se. A comfortable hotel overlooking the main square with antique furniture in an otherwise thoroughly modern structure. This hotel makes for an agreeable mix of old and new, and breakfast is served in a pleasant atrium. 1020kr/1780kr

Best Western City Kungsgatan 24 ☎ 019 601 42 00, ⓦ cityhotelorebro.se. Rooms at this business-oriented hotel, although perfectly adequate and full of the latest Scandinavian designer touches, are a little on the cramped side. Decor is typically chain-hotel: anonymous white walls, wooden floors and nondescript armchairs. 800kr/1230kr

Clarion Örebro Kungsgatan 14 ☎ 019 670 67 00, ⓦ nordicchoicehotels.se. Well designed and stylish to a T, this place has remarkable weekend and summer discounts on its sumptuous bedrooms and wonderful bathrooms done out with black-and-white chequered tiles. On the top floor there's also a gym, sauna, Jacuzzi and spa. 870r/1350kr

★ **Elite Stora** Drottninggatan 1 ☎ 019 15 69 00, ⓦ elite.se. The oldest hotel in town was built in 1858, and is said to be haunted by the ghost of a young woman who hanged herself over an arranged marriage. Rooms and suites are extremely attractive, especially on the top floor of the annexe. 900kr/1395kr

First Örebro Storgatan 24 ☎ 046 19 611 73 00, ⓦ first hotels.se. Great hotel on the main drag, decked out in maritime colours and designs, and personally decorated in line with the owner's interests – refreshingly different for a chain hotel. Rooms are stylish and airy, making this an excellent choice. 820kr/1300kr

Katrinelund Gästgiveri Katrinelund 470 ☎ 019 44 90 60, ⓦ katrinelund.se. Located 25km east of the centre of the city, this lakeside hotel enjoys sweeping views over Hjälmaren. Attracting a fair few Swedish glitterati (who are wont to jet in by seaplane), this is a place to live it up in luxurious surroundings and give yourself over to some serious pampering. Rooms are elegant enough but it's the proximity to such a vast expanse of open water which makes this hotel rather special. **1800kr**

Livin Järnvägsgatan 22 ☎019 31 02 40, ⓦlivin.se. This hotel combines regular double rooms and simpler budget hostel-style accommodation, though still with private facilities, costing around one third less. Decor is modern and features bold swirls and floral designs. **1170kr**

CAMPING

Gustavsvik Camping Sommarrovägen ☎019 19 69 00, ⓦgustavsvik.se. The nearest campsite is 2km south of the centre at Gustavsvik. On site there's a large open-air swimming complex as well as well-appointed cabins to rent. Open mid-April to early Nov; cabins open year-round. Tents **330kr**, cabins **1095kr**

EATING, DRINKING AND NIGHTLIFE

SEE MAP PAGE 220

6

CAFÉS AND RESTAURANTS

A mano Stallbacken ☎019 32 33 70, ⓦa-mano.se. Off Kungsgatan in a quiet courtyard, this style-conscious Italian place with small square tables facing a long leather bench serves classic Tuscan-inspired mains for around 280kr. The three-course set dinner (500kr) features a delicious fillet of veal with garlic and thyme-scented potatoes in a cassis *jus*. Mon–Sat 6pm–midnight.

★ **Bara Vara** Köpmangatan 24 ☎019 10 78 32, ⓦbaravara.net. This justifiably popular place is where those in the know come for excellent cakes, muffins, ice cream, a good range of speciality coffees and a few light lunch dishes, such as lasagne, quiches and salads. Mon–Fri 10am–8pm, Sat 10am–6pm, Sun noon–6pm.

Bröderna Bar & Bistro Inside Saluhallen food hall, Kungsgatan 15 ☎019 707 04 50, ⓦbrodernaihallen. se/barbistro. Separate from the *Bröderna* fine-dining restaurant at the rear of the food hall, this street-side bistro run by the same team is ideal for a filling burger, salad or tasty seafood soup for around 150–200kr. It's also a popular place for a drink after work and into the early evening. Mon & Tues 11am–2pm, Wed & Thurs 11am–2pm and 5–9pm, Fri 11am–2pm and 5–9pm, Sat noon–3pm and 6–9pm.

Chandani Kungsgatan 4 ☎019 12 55 55, ⓦchandani. se. Upmarket Indian restaurant serving an excellent choice of Indian specialities, such as lamb rogan josh, chicken tandoori sizzlers and butter chicken. Mains are 175–210kr, while starters such as paneer and samosas cost around 90kr. Mon–Thurs 5–10.30pm, Fri 4.30–11pm, Sat 1–11pm, Sun 1–9pm.

Saigon Rudbecksgatan 18 ☎019 10 08 75, ⓦsaigon express.se. This stylish Asian restaurant is boldly decorated in greens and oranges and the food is equally sophisticated: the tiger prawns with Thai basil, pad thai and red curry are all winners. Mains are around 100kr including a soft drink. Daily 11am–9pm.

Sorella Stortorget 11 ☎019 12 21 20, ⓦsorellaorebro. se. On a sunny evening, it's hard to find a table at this open-air restaurant in the main square, which serves feel-good summer food, such as tangy tuna salad, chicken souvlaki and rack of lamb with rosemary for around 250kr. The tables catch the sun all evening and the atmosphere is fun and hedonistic once the beer starts to flow. Booking ahead is advisable. Tues–Fri 5pm–late, Sat noon–late.

★ **Wobbler** Kyrkogatan 2 ☎019 10 07 40, ⓦwobbler. se. Classic Swedish cooking with a modern twist at this bright and airy place with a separate tapas lounge. Elaborate mains (from 180kr) include roast zander from Lake Hjälmaren with a horseradish and crayfish sauce (240kr), while tapas plates cost 185kr per person (minimum two people). Mon–Fri 11am–2.30pm & 5pm–late & Sat 10am–2pm, 5pm–late.

Zao Street Kitchen Inside Saluhallen food hall, Kungsgatan 15 ☎019 10 19 99, ⓦzaostreetkitchen.se. Genuinely tasty Southeast Asian street food featuring any number of rice and stir-fry dishes, including a sensational chicken with lemongrass, galangal, coconut milk and rice (80kr) and grilled chicken with soya, ginger, sour cabbage and black radish (85kr). Mon–Thurs 11am–7pm, Fri–Sat 11am–9pm.

BARS, PUBS AND CLUBS

Bishops Arms Drottninggatan 1 ☎019 15 69 20, ⓦbishopsarms.com/orebro. Hugely popular for outdoor drinking, with a large summer terrace overlooking the castle, this pub serves a limited range of bar meals and is rightly known for an impressive selection of on-tap beers and ales. Mon & Tues 4pm–midnight, Wed & Thurs 4pm–1am, Fri 3pm–2am, Sat 1pm–2am, Sun 4–11pm.

O'Learys Drottninggatan 12 ☎019 12 90 00, ⓦolearys. se/orebro. Sportsbar with a great atmosphere. Fresh burgers and large pints will make this the perfect place to watch a sports match. Mon 4–9pm, Tues–Thurs 4–10pm, Fri 4–midnight, Sat noon–midnight, Sun noon–9pm.

Pitchers sgatan 8 ☎019 25 30 40, ⓦpitchers.se/ restauranger/orebro. A long and narrow sportsbar with big screens showing the latest matches. Extremely busy, and popular with the town's sports followers. In summer there's also a big outdoor terrace overlooking the river. Mon–Thurs 2pm–midnight, Fri & Sat noon–2am, Sun noon–midnight.

Stallyktan Södra Strandgatan 3B ☎019 10 33 23, ⓦstallyktan.se. This excellent, rustic pub is a better choice for a quiet drink and dinner than most of the bigger venues. Wed–Sat 6pm–1am.

Norrköping and around

Although ranking only as Sweden's tenth largest city, enjoyable **NORRKÖPING** punches well above its weight. It's the town's striking industrial heritage that draws people here – the old mills clustered around the Motala River, together with a general youthful air, make for an appealing diversion. The last big mill closed its doors in the early 1990s, but Norrköping retains one of Europe's best-preserved industrial landscapes, with handsome red-brick and stuccoed mills reflecting in the waters of its river. Based here, you could easily visit the **Kolmårdens Djurpark** (see page 227), Sweden's premier zoo and safari park, as a day-trip or head out for the myriad islands and islets that make up the **Östergötland archipelago** (see page 228).

Drottninggatan

Norrköping's north–south central artery, **Drottninggatan** runs ruler-straight from the train station and crosses the **Motala ström**, the small, rushing river that attracted the Dutch industrialist **Louis de Geer** (1587–1652) to the town in the early seventeenth century. He was known as the father of Swedish industry, and his paper mill became the biggest factory in town. Many of Norrköping's buildings, and the trams, are painted in de Geer's colour of choice – a tortilla-chip yellow – which has become synonymous with the town.

Just a few steps down from the station, compact **Carl Johans Park** has 25,000 cacti, formally arranged in thematic patterns and interspersed with brilliantly coloured flowers and palm trees. Glance to the right from here (with the train station behind you) across Slottsgatan, and you'll see the splendid 1906 city **theatre**, with its Art Nouveau curves and double Ionic columns. Over the river, follow the tram lines up cobbled Drottninggatan and after a few hundred metres turn right into Repslagaregatan for **Gamlatorget**, overlooked by a charismatic Carl Milles sculpture of Louis de Geer with a bale of cloth slung over his shoulder.

6

Konstmuseum

Kristinaplatsen • June–Aug Tues–Sun noon–4pm, Wed until 8pm; Sept–May Tues–Sun 11am–5pm, Tues & Thurs until 8pm • Free • Ⓦ norrkopingskonstmuseum.se

At the southernmost tip of Drottninggatan, Norrköping's **Konstmuseum** holds some of the country's best-known modernist works. Founded by a local snuff manufacturer at the turn of the twentieth century, the museum offers a fine, well-balanced progression from seventeenth-century Baroque through to twentieth-century work.

De Geerhallen

To the west of Gamlatorget lies the modern and stylish riverside **De Geerhallen**, a concert hall surrounded by trees and providing a lovely setting for a lunchtime-only restaurant (Mon–Fri 11.30am–1.30pm). It's worth stepping inside for a moment, as the concert hall's apparent modernity belies the fact that this was once one of de Geer's paper factories, though little remains now of its former incarnation.

Arbetets museum

Museum of Work • Daily 9am–5pm, Sept–May Thurs 11am–8pm • Free • Ⓦ arbetetsmuseum.se

West along the river from the De Geerhallen is the exceptionally well-presented **Arbetets museum**, housed in a triangular, yellow-stuccoed factory built in 1917. Known as *Strykjärnet* ("the iron") – though its shape and colour are more reminiscent of a wedge of cheese – the building was described by Carl Milles as Europe's most beautiful factory. The museum has seven floors of exhibitions on living conditions, workers' rights and day-to-day life in the mills. The most poignant exhibit (and the only permanent one) tells the story of Alva Carlsson, who worked in the building for 35 years – a fascinating insight into working-class culture and the role of Swedish women in the first half of the twentieth century.

Stadsmuseum

City Museum • Tues–Fri 11am–5pm, Sat & Sun noon–5pm • Free • Ⓦ norrkopingsstadsmuseum.se

The excellent **Stadsmuseum** is set in an interconnecting (and confusing) network of old industrial properties. The most rewarding of its permanent exhibitions is a street showing various trades from the nineteenth century: there are workshops of a milliner, confectioner, chimney sweep and, in a back yard, a carriage maker. All are cleverly designed and well worth a wander.

Visualiseringscenter

Visualization Centre • Kungsgatan 54 • July–mid-Aug daily 10am–5pm; mid-Aug–June Mon–Wed & Fri 8am–4pm, Thurs 8am–8pm, Sat & Sun 11am–4pm • 115kr for both the exhibition and the cinema • Ⓦ visualiseringscenter.se

Just to the west of Bergsbron, beyond the Arbetetsmuseum, you'll find Norrköping's pride and joy: the **Visualiseringscenter**. The centre's rather worthy aim is to explain, predominantly to younger visitors, how various visual techniques are used in science today, in areas ranging from weather forecasts to postmortems. However, it's the massive dome-shaped **cinema** which really makes a visit here worthwhile, showing a range of breathtaking 3D films.

ARRIVAL AND DEPARTURE
NORRKÖPING

By train The train station is in the Resecentrum on Norra Promenaden, from where it's a 10min stroll uphill towards the town centre and the museum complex.

Destinations Copenhagen via Kastrup airport (6 daily; 3hr 45min); Malmö (hourly; 3hr 10min); Nyköping (hourly; 45min); Stockholm (hourly; 1hr 15min); Västerås (hourly; 1hr 50min).

INFORMATION AND TOURS

Tourist office Källvindsgatan 1 (May, June & late Aug to mid-Sept Mon–Fri 10am–5pm, Sat 10am–2pm; July–late Aug Mon–Fri 10am–6pm, Sat 10am–5pm, Sun 11am–4pm; mid-Sept to April Mon–Thurs 10am–5pm, Fri 10am–3pm, Sat 10am–2pm; ☎011 15 50 00, ⓦexperience.

norrkoping.se). A helpful office 10min walk from the Resecentrum, with internet access.

Tours Staff at the tourist office can give information about routes and times for the 1902 vintage tram, which circles around on a sightseeing tour between late June and early August.

ACCOMMODATION
SEE MAP PAGE 224

Thanks largely to the booming local economy, Norrköping receives a lot of business trade during the week, and has a good array of **hotels** to cater for its often demanding visitors, though there are also a number of cheaper options available.

Best Western Princess Skomakaregatan 8 ☎011 28 58 40, ⓦprincesshotel.se. Located in a quiet street close to the museums and the main drag, this chain hotel is predictably modern, unadventurous and rather plain. Its summer and weekend prices, though, make this one worth considering. 890kr/1100kr

Centric Gamla Rådstugugatan 18–20 ☎011 12 90 30, ⓦcentrichotel.se. An inexpensive, comfortable hotel, 500m south of the train station. The stylish building dates from 1932, and the reception features a striking wall fresco by Gothenburg artist Lars Gillies depicting Norrköping's central areas. 770kr/1095kr

Elite Grand Tyskatorget 2 ☎011 36 41 00, ⓦelite.se. This upmarket hotel from the early twentieth century is certainly the best in town, though it doesn't come cheap. Bang in the centre, its rooms are a stylish blend of classic

and modern, and its staff go the extra mile to create a home-from-home feel. 920kr/1340kr

President Vattengränden 11 ☎011 12 95 20, ⓦprofil hotels.se. Straight out of an IKEA catalogue, the designer rooms here are well equipped, full of the latest furniture and decked out with loud, brash colours; some of the rooms also have their own private Jacuzzi. Tastefully done and extremely central. 1095kr/1380kr

Södra Södra Promenaden 142 ☎011 25 35 00, ⓦsodra hotellet.se. A calm and pleasant alternative to the chain hotels, set in a sympathetically renovated 1920s house in a residential street formerly favoured by textile-mill owners. There's also a sauna and a couple of exercise bikes for guests' use. 895kr/995kr

STF Centralstationens Hotell & Vandrarhem Centralstationen ☎011 10 18 28, ⓦcentralstationens. se. Norrköping's comfortable and centrally located STF hostel is located in the train station building, right beside Platform 1. There's a choice between double rooms with private facilities and rooms with shared bathrooms for around 300kr less. Doubles 840kr

EATING, DRINKING AND NIGHTLIFE
SEE MAP PAGE 224

There's a fair selection of **places to eat and drink** in Norrköping, some of which double as bars. Although in Swedish terms it's only a moderately sized town, the array of food on offer is unmatched for miles around. The nicest place to eat is **Knäppingsborg**, an up-and-coming area of trendy restaurants and bars.

CAFÉS AND RESTAURANTS

Bagarstugan Knäppingsborgsgatan 3 ☎011 470 20 20, ⓦbagarstugan.se. The best of the restaurants in the Knäppingsborg area, serving a good selection of salads and sandwiches, lasagne (95kr) and seafood soup (100kr) during the day, as well as more substantial meals such as red

snapper (190kr) in the evenings. Mon–Thurs 9.30am–9pm, Fri 9.30am–11pm, Sat 9.30am–11pm, Sun 10am–9pm.

Burgers & Bangers Drottninggatan 15 ☎011 10 35 00, ⓦburgersandbangers.se. "Come hungry, Leave Happy" is the motto of Burgers & Bangers. Cosy and snug burger restaurant with great milkshakes and nice beers. Tues–Sat 4pm–late, Sun noon–6.30pm.

Café Kuriosa Hörngatan 6 ☎011 10 36 70, ⓦkafe kuriosa-norrkoping.torget.se A super, central old-fashioned café with a little garden, serving home-made cakes, savoury pies and ice cream. Quiche and salad costs 70kr. Try the fragrant Kuriosa tea, scented with apricots and vanilla. Mon–Thurs 10am–7pm, Fri 10am–6pm, Sat 10am–4pm.

Pappa Grappa Gamla Rådstugugatan 26 ☎011 16 00 16, ⓦpappagrappa.se. There are three restaurants in one here, but the best choice is *Matbaren*, where you'll find simple and well-cooked Italian food at respectable prices: spaghetti *arrabiata* (145kr), lasagne (125kr) and pizzas from 95kr. If the weather's good, though, choose the outside terrace at the rear, *Terrassen*. Mon–Fri 4–10pm, Sat noon–10pm, Sun noon–9pm.

Trädgårn Prästgatan 1 ☎011 10 07 40, ⓦtradgarn uteservering.se. This summer bar and grill is very popular, especially on warm evenings when seemingly the entire town squeezes in; the entrance is beneath an iron sign marked "VIP Paraden". On the menu there's prawn salad (200kr), burgers (165kr), a steak sandwich (255kr) and gravadlax (190kr) as well as champagne, cava and sangria. May–Sept daily 4pm–1am; closed in bad weather.

Urbane Goat St Persgatan 88 ☎011 18 18 85, ⓦurbaneg oat.se. Trendy little bistro which brags that it serves food influenced by the world's great cuisines, though the unadventurous menu of prawn salad, chicken fajitas, burgers and spring rolls with dips suggests otherwise. Be that as it may, locals love it and flock here for a taste of the world in Norrköping. Mon–Tues 4.30–9pm, Wed–Sat 4.30pm–late.

Vila Bråddgatan 9 ☎011 18 18 49, ⓦrestaurangvila. se. It may be a vile concrete block from the outside, but the views from inside this combined lounge bar and restaurant – looking out over the widest expanse of the Motala ström – are great, as is the sophisticated food: fish and seafood stew (140kr), veal fillet with sun-dried tomatoes and prosciutto chips (285kr) and any number of fancy burger creations (from 155kr). Tues & Sun 4–11pm, Wed 4pm–midnight, Thurs 4–11pm, Fri 4pm–1am, Sat 4pm–1am, Sun 4–11pm.

BARS, PUBS AND CLUBS

Bishops Arms Drottninggatan 2 ☎011 36 41 20. One of the most popular pubs in Norrköping, this place has gone from strength to strength since opening in 1994 and boasts the biggest selection of beers and whiskies in town. Outdoor seating in summer. Mon–Thurs 4pm–midnight, Fri 4pm–1am, Sat 3pm–1am, Sun 4–10pm.

Black Lion Inn Gamla Rådstugugatan 11 ☎011 10 41 05, ⓦblacklion.se. This addition to the town's drinking scene has taken Norrköping by storm. Replete with old china plates, model ships, wood panelling and even a battered Union Jack in the window, locals love all the Britannia – even the fish and chips (165kr) served up. Make it your watering hole of choice in town. Mon & Tues 4–10pm, Wed–Thurs 4pm–midnight, Fri 4pm–1am, Sat 2pm–1am, Sun 4–10pm.

Cromwell House Kungsgatan 36 ☎011 18 26 00, ⓦcromwell.se. Dark, faux-English pub full of stained glass and screens showing live matches. Quite good-value grilled meat dishes, including beef tenderloin marinated in Guinness, cost 140–260kr. There's also a busy nightclub here at weekends. Mon 11am–11pm, Tues–Thurs 11am–midnight, Fri 11am–3am, Sat 1pm–3am, Sun 1–10pm.

Highlander Inn Hörngatan 1 ☎011 16 58 90, ⓦhighlanderinn.info. Norrköping's answer to a real Scottish pub is well known for its large selection of beers and whiskies, and is a popular hangout with the locals. It also serves bar meals such as shepherd's pie (125kr) and burgers for 100–200kr. Mon–Thurs noon–10pm, Fri & Sat noon–1am, Sun noon–10pm.

Knäppingen Västgötegatan 19 ☎011 10 74 45, ⓦknappingen.se. This urban-chic gastro pub with its own brewery is hidden away in the industrial quarter, but is well worth seeking out for a glass or two of top-quality beer and what locals claim are the best burgers in town. There's an outdoor beer terrace at the rear, too. Tues–Thurs 4pm–late Fri 4pm–1am, Sat noon–1am.

Around Norrköping: Kolmårdens Djurpark

Kolmården wildlife park • May, June & mid-Aug–late Aug daily 10am–6pm; July–mid-Aug daily 10am–8pm; Sept Fri, Sat & Sun 10am–5pm • 449kr • ⓦ kolmarden.com • Bus #432 or #433 from Norrköping; timetables at ⓦ ostgotatrafiken.se

If you've only got time for one excursion from Norrköping, make it to **Kolmårdens Djurpark**, a safari park, zoo and dolphinarium that is one of Sweden's biggest attractions. Just 28km northeast of Norrköping and accessible by frequent buses, the whole park is understandably popular with children, for whom there's a special section, and if your views on zoos are negative, it's just about possible to be convinced that this one is different. There are no cages; instead, sunken enclosures, rock barriers and moats prevent the animals from feasting on their captors as you glide silently over their heads in a cable car.

Kolmården is also home to the fastest wooden **roller coaster** in the world, Wildfire, travelling at up to 110km per hour, the ride includes a hair-raising drop of 50m at an 83-degree angle – not for the faint-hearted.

Tropicarium

Daily May, June, Aug & Sept 10am–7pm; July 10am–9pm; Oct–April 10am–4pm • 130kr • ⓦ tropicarium.se

The adjacent **Tropicarium** contains Sweden's largest collection of tropical plants and animals, spread out over two square kilometres. The interior really is extremely realistic, even featuring a mock-up of an alligator swamp which receives rain and thunderstorms every hour. The most popular attraction is the shark aquarium, with three different species of shark and hundreds of other tropical fish.

ACCOMMODATION	KOLMÅRDENS DJURPARK
First Camp Kolmården Bodaviken ☎ 011 39 82 50, ⓦ firstcamp.se/kolmarden. Campsite 5km from Kolmårdens Djurpark, with four-bed cabins and the decent *Ettans Café* next door. Tents <u>210kr</u>, cabins <u>1295kr</u>	**Varglyan** Kolmårdens Djurpark ☎ 010 - 708 70 00. Excellent hostel within the safari park, offering five four-bed and four six-bed rooms. Mid-June to mid-Aug only. Four-bed dorms <u>940kr</u>, six-bed <u>1250kr</u>

Around Norrköping: the Östergötland archipelago

Around 50km east of Norrköping, the coastline of **Östergötland** splinters into countless rocks, skerries and small islands. This is a popular summer playground for many families from Norrköping who come here to explore the islands on foot or by kayak, or simply to take a dip in the surprisingly warm waters of the Baltic Sea. From north to south, the archipelago is divided into three main sections centred on the small towns of **ARKÖSUND** (closest to Norrköping), **Tyrislöt** and **Fyrudden** – though, to be honest, the archipelago looks pretty much the same no matter where you are: peaceful, forested islands, sometimes farmed, dotted between smaller islets and rocky outcrops.

The best way of exploring is to take the once-daily *Skärgårdslinjen* passenger **boat** from Arkösund, which calls in at half a dozen different islands and jetties on its way to end-of-the-line Harstena, before returning to Arkösund the same day. Alternatively, you can rent a **kayak** in Arkösund.

ARRIVAL AND GETTING AROUND	OSTERGÖTLAND ARCHIPELAGO
By bus Bus #440 runs from Norrköping bus station to Arkösund (6 daily; 1hr 15 min). **By boat** The *Skärgårdslinjen* departs from Arkösund daily at 10am (early July–early Aug; ⓦ skargardslinjen.com). A	return ticket from Arkösund to Harstena (2hr 30min one-way) costs 500kr. **Kayak rental** You can rent a kayak from Arkö Kayak in Arkösund (☎ 070 269 96 87, ⓦ arkokajak.se).

Gotland

Tales of good times on **GOTLAND** are rife. Wherever you are in Sweden, one mention of this ancient Baltic island 90km from the mainland will elicit a typical Swedish sigh, followed by an anecdote about what a great place it is. You'll hear that the short summer season is an exciting time to visit; that the place is hot, fun and lively. These claims are largely true: the island has a distinctly youthful feel, with young, mobile Stockholmers deserting the capital in summer for a boisterous time on its beaches. The flower-power era still makes its presence felt with a smattering of elderly VW camper vans lurching off the ferries, but shiny Volvos outnumber them fifty to one. During summer, the bars, restaurants and campsites are packed, the streets swarm with revellers and the sands are awash with bodies. It's not everyone's cup of tea: to avoid the hectic summer altogether, travel in late May or September when, depending on your level of bravado, you might still manage to swim in the waters around the island. To experience the setting at its most frenetic, come in August during **Medieval Week** (see page 232), when people put a huge effort into dressing the part.

Brief history

Visby, Gotland's capital, has always been the scene of frenetic activity of some kind. Its temperate climate and position attracted the **Vikings** as early as the sixth century, and the lucrative trade routes they opened, from here through to Byzantium and western Asia, guaranteed the island its prosperity. With the ending of Viking domination, a "golden age" followed, with Gotland's inhabitants maintaining trading posts abroad and signing treaties as equals with European and Asian leaders. However, by the late twelfth century, their autonomy had been undermined by the growing power of the **Hanseatic League**. Under its influence, Visby became one of the great cities of medieval

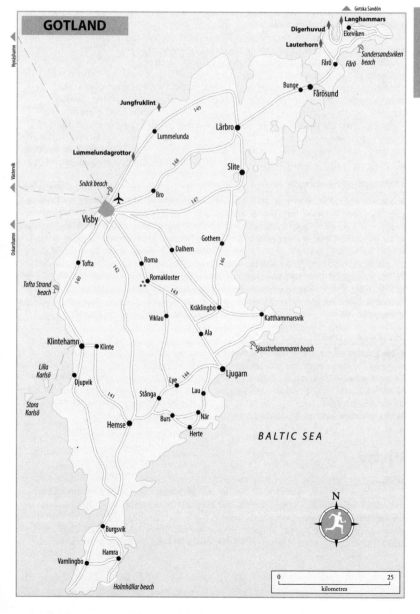

6

Europe, as important as London or Paris, famed for its wealth and strategic power. A contemporary ballad had it that "The Gotlanders weigh their gold with twenty-pound weights. The pigs eat out of silver troughs and the women spin with golden distaffs."

Gotland today

Today, all the revelry which keeps Visby buzzing from late June to the end of August takes place against the spectacular backdrop of its medieval architecture; two hundred or so Hanseatic warehouses are dotted among stone and wooden houses, the whole lot nestled within its ancient walls.

There is a real charm to the **rest of Gotland** – rolling green countryside, forest-lined roads, fine beaches and small fishing villages. Everywhere the rural skyline is dominated by **churches**, the remnants of medieval settlements destroyed in the Danish invasion. Nowhere else in Scandinavia holds such a concentration of medieval churches, and 93 of them are still in use, displaying a unique Baltic Gothic style and providing the most permanent reminder of Gotland's ancient wealth. Churches aside, however, very few people bother to explore the island, perhaps because of Visby's magnetic pull; consequently, the main roads around Gotland are pleasingly free of traffic and minor roads positively deserted – **cycling** is a joy. As you travel, keep an eye out for the waymarkers erected in the 1780s to indicate the distance from Wisby (the old spelling of the town's name), calculated in Swedish miles – one of which is equivalent to 10km.

ARRIVAL AND DEPARTURE   GOTLAND

By plane Flights to Gotland are good value if booked early. SAS (⊕ sas.se) operates from Arlanda airport in Stockholm; BRA (Braathens Regional Airways; ⊕ flygbra. se) has services from Bromma airport in Stockholm and no fewer than a dozen provincial airports, from Malmö in the south to Luleå in the north (full details on the website). The cheapest single tickets, with BRA from Stockholm, are 395kr. In addition to these regional flights, there are flights to Helsinki in Finland with BRA and to Oslo with Norwegian (⊕ norwegian.com).

By ferry Ferries to Gotland are numerous and, in summer, packed, so try to plan well ahead. Two ferry companies serve a total of three mainland ports: Nynäshamn, Oskarshamn and Västervik. Departures vary depending on the ferry company and the time of year, but in general there are 1–5 sailings daily, with the highest frequency between mid-June and mid-Aug. Crossings take about 3hr from Nynäshamn and Oskarshamn, 2hr from Västervik. Prices depend on season; a one-way ticket starts at 90kr. Buy tickets online at ⊕ destinationgotland.se.

GETTING AROUND

By bus It's common for there to be several hours between bus services so always check timetables before setting out; see ⊕ gotland.se/kollektivtrafiken. Unusually, it's still possible in Gotland to buy tickets on board buses with cash, though not credit cards.

By bike For getting around the island, it's hard to resist the temptation to rent a bike, given the flat terrain and empty roads. See page 235 for rental outlets in Visby. Bikes can also easily be rented at various towns to the south of the capital, less so further north. Gotland's buses take limited numbers of bikes; the driver will hang your cycle on the back of the bus outside.

Visby

VISBY is a city made for wandering and lingering over coffees and slices of cake. Whether climbing the **ramparts** of the surrounding walls, or meandering up and down the warren of cobbled, sloping streets, there's plenty to tease the eye. Strolling around the twisting streets and atmospheric walls is not something that palls quickly, but if you need a focus, aim for **Norra Murgatan**, above the cathedral, once one of Visby's quietest areas. The end of the street nearest Norderport enjoys the best view of the walls and city rooftops.

6

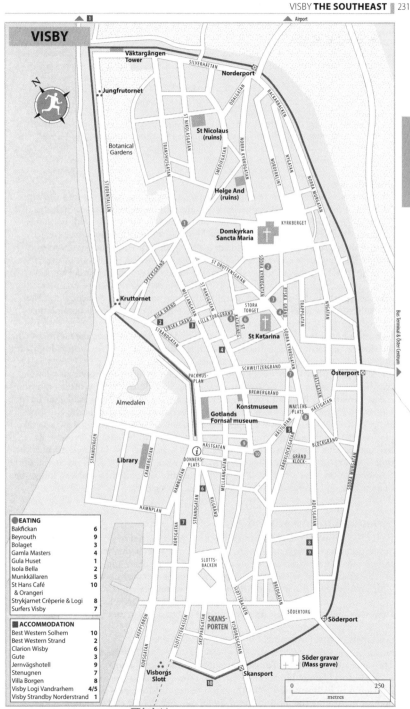

VISBY

Väktargången Tower

SILVERHÄTTAN

Norderport

Jungfrutornet

ST NICOLASGATAN

St Nicolaus (ruins)

Botanical Gardens

TRANSHUSGATAN

STUDENTALLEN

SMEDJEGATAN

ODALGATAN

BÄCKGÄNDET

NORRA KYRKOGATAN

NORRA MURGATAN

NORDERKLINT

NYGATAN

Helge And (ruins)

KYRKBERGET

Domkyrkan Sancta Maria

ST DROTTENSGATAN

SÖDRA KYRKOGATAN

Kruttornet

SPECKSGRAND

RIGA GRÄND

MELLANGATAN

ST HANSGATAN

LÜBSKA GRÄND

STRANDGATAN

LILLA TORGGRÄND

STORA TORGET

FISKA GRÄND

TRAPPGATAN

NYGATAN

KATTHÄ.LHG

St Katarina

SÖDRA KYRKOGATAN

SCHWEITZERGRAND

Österport

PACKHUS- PLAN

BREMERGRÄND

Almedalen

Konstmuseum

Gotlands Fornsal museum

WALLERS PLATS

HÄSTGATAN

HÄSTGATAN

Bus Terminal & Öster Centrum

STRANDVÄGEN

CRAMERGATAN

Library

HÄSTGATAN

DONNERS PLATS

MELLANGATAN

VÅRDKLOCKEGATAN

GRÄND KLOCK-

BLOCKGRAND

SÖDRA KYRGATAN

HAMNGATAN

STRANDGATAN

KILGRÄND

HAMNPLAN

KORSGATAN

ADELSGATAN

SLOTTS- BACKEN

BREDGAIAN

SKEPPSBRON

SLOTTSTERRASSEN

SKEPPARGATAN

SKANS- PORTEN

SLOTTSBACKEN

VISBORGSGATAN

SÖDERTORG

Söderport

KORSGATAN

Visborgs Slott

Skansport

Söder gravar (Mass grave)

0   250
metres

Ferry Terminal

Airport

MEDIEVAL WEEK

During the second week of August, Visby becomes the backdrop for a boisterous reenactment of the conquest of the island by the Danes in 1361. **Medieval Week** (w medeltidsveckan. se) sees music in the streets, medieval food on sale in the restaurants (no potatoes – they hadn't yet been brought to Europe) and on the Sunday a procession reenacting Valdemar's triumphant entry through Söderport to Storatorget. Here, people in the role of burghers are stripped of their wealth, and the procession then moves on to the Maiden's Tower. Locals and visitors alike really get into the spirit of this festival, with a good fifty percent of people dressed up and on the streets. There are also weekly **jousting tournaments** throughout July and early August.

Brief history

Visby is much older than its medieval trappings suggest: its name comes from *vi*, "the sacred place", and *by*, "the settlement", a derivation that reflects its status as a Stone Age sacrificial site. After the Gotlanders had founded their trading houses in the eleventh and twelfth centuries, the Hansa or **Hanseatic League** was created, comprising a group of towns that formed a federation to assert their interests and protect their seaborne commerce. Following the foundation of Lübeck in the 1150s, German merchants began to expand into the eastern Baltic area in order to gain access to the coveted Russian market. A trading agreement between Gotlanders and the League in 1161 gave the islanders the right to trade freely throughout the whole Saxon area, while Germans were able to settle in Visby, which became the League's principal centre and the place where all lines of Baltic trade met. As Visby metamorphosed from Gotlandic village to international city, it was the Germans who led the way in form and architecture, building warehouses up to six storeys high with hoists facing the street, still apparent today.

In 1350, the **Black Death** swept through Gotland, creating ghost towns of whole parishes and leaving more than eight thousand people dead. Eleven years later, during the power struggle between Denmark and Sweden, the Danish King Valdemar III took Gotland by force and advanced on Visby. The burghers and traders of the city, well aware of the wealth here, shut the gates and sat through the slaughter which was taking place outside, only surrendering when it was over. Hostilities and piracy were the hallmarks of the following two centuries. In 1525, an army from Lübeck stormed the much-weakened Visby, torching the northern parts of the town. With the arrival of the Reformation and the weakness of the local economy, the churches could no longer be maintained, and Visby's era of greatness clanged to a close.

Strandgatan and around

Pretty **Packhusplan**, the oldest square in the city, is bisected by curving **Strandgatan**. Strandgatan is the best place to view the impressive **merchants' houses** looming over the narrow streets, with storerooms above the living quarters and cellars below; most notable among these is the clearly signposted **Burmeisterska huset** in Donnerplats, which is attractive and in good condition. One of the most picturesque buildings on the street is the old pharmacy, **Gamla Apoteket**, a lofty old place with gloriously higgledy-piggledy windows; it's at the corner of Strandgatan and Lybska gränd.

Gotlands Fornsal museum

Historical Museum of Gotland • Strandgatan 14 • Daily 10am–6pm • 150kr, 160kr with the Konstmuseum • w gotlandsmuseum.se

The outstanding **Gotlands Fornsal museum** is a must-see for anyone interested in **Viking history**. Housed in a mid-eighteenth century distillery, it comprises five storeys of exhibition halls covering eight thousand years of history, plus a good café and bookstore. Among the most impressive of the displays is the **Hall of Picture Stones**.

Dating mostly from the fifth to seventh centuries, these large, keyhole-shaped stones are richly ornamented. The earlier ones are covered in runic inscriptions and are more intriguing, with vivid depictions of people, animals, ships and houses. Other rooms trace the history of **medieval Visby**; look out for the original trading booth, the sort of place where the burghers of Visby and foreign merchants would have dealt in commodities – furs, lime, wax, honey and tar – brought from all over northern Europe. Gotland's ecclesiastical history is also well covered with an impressive exhibition of ornate wooden carvings of bishops, Mary Magdalene and a truly magnificent triptych dating from the early sixteenth century from Vall church on the island.

6

The Viking Treasury

It's the **Viking Treasury** on the first floor that really steals the show. Gotland's wealth of gold and silver objects is unique; more hoards of Viking-age treasure have been found on the island than anywhere else in the world, clearly a sign of its economic and social importance. On display are hundreds of shiny coins and trinkets – some brought to Gotland from as far afield as Samarkand, Persia and Afghanistan, others from England. In a room off the treasury, the world's largest find of Viking-age silver, the **Spillings Hoard**, is proudly exhibited in a vast glass cabinet. Discovered in a farmer's field in the north of Gotland in 1999, the hoard, which lay buried for 1130 years, is truly breathtaking. It comprises 87kg of silver and bronze, including over 14,000 coins (the earliest dating from 539AD), neck rings, armbands and spiral rings. Elsewhere in the museum, look out for the two skeletons displayed in glass cases. The occupant of one, a 40-year-old man buried in foetal position with two pieces of antler and flint arrows, is, at roughly 8000 years old, one of the oldest human remains found in Sweden.

Gotlands Konstmuseum

St Hansgatan 21 • Mid-June–mid-Aug daily 10am–6pm; mid-Aug–mid-June Tues–Sun 12–4pm • 100kr, 150kr with the Fornsal museum • ⓦ gotlandsmuseum.se

A couple of streets up from the Fornsal museum, **Gotlands Konstmuseum** has some innovative temporary exhibitions of contemporary painting and sculpture, and installations which tease the eye. The permanent collection on the top floor is for the most part much less exciting, given over to twentieth-century Gotlandic art; among the few notable classics is Axel Lindman's 1917 oil of Visby from the beach, showing brilliant dabs of sun before a storm. The eye is also drawn to a stunning picture by William Blair Bruce of his wife, the sculptor Carolina. The painting, from 1891, shows her at work, and the lifelike qualities of the style are remarkable.

The town wall

The oldest of the towers in Visby's **town wall** is the dark, atmospheric **Kruttornet** (Gunpowder Tower), built in the eleventh century to protect the old harbour and offering some grand views of Visby. The wall itself, a 3km circuit enclosing the entire settlement, was built around the end of the thirteenth century for a rather different purpose: it was actually aimed at isolating the city's foreign traders from the locals.

Running north from Kruttornet along the water's edge, **Studentallén** is a popular late-evening haunt and the sunsets are magnificent – brilliant fiery reds, glinting mirrored waters and bobbing sailing boats in the distance. At its northern end is the **Jungfrutornet** (Maiden's Tower), where a local goldsmith's daughter was walled up alive – reputedly for betraying the city to the Danes. Nearby, it's possible to climb onto a section of the city wall via the **Väktargången tower** (free).

At the southern end of the town walls are the fragmentary ruins of **Visborgs Slott**, overlooking the harbour. Built in the fifteenth century by Erik of Pomerania, the castle was blown up by the Danes in the seventeenth century.

Söder gravar

Just outside the wall to the east of Söderport (South Gate), **Söder gravar** is a mass grave, excavated in the twentieth century, of two thousand people; more than half were women, children and invalids who were slaughtered when Danish King Valdemar attacked the town in 1361. There's a cross here, erected by the survivors of the carnage; the inscription reads: "In 1361 on the third day after St James, the Goths fell into the hands of the Danes. Here they lie. Pray for them."

Valdemar's Breach

A section of the wall near Söderport was broken down to allow Valdemar to ride through as conqueror. **Valdemar's Breach** is recognizable by its thirteen crenellations representing, so the story goes, the thirteen knights who rode through with the Danish king. Valdemar soon left, in possession of booty and trade agreements, and Visby continued to prosper while the countryside around it stagnated, its people and wealth destroyed.

The churches

At the height of its power, Visby maintained more **churches** than any other town in Sweden – sixteen in all. Seventeenth- and eighteenth-century builders and decorators found the smaller churches in the city to be an excellent source of free limestone, tiles and fittings, which accounts for the fact that most are ruins today – though one, the Domkyrkan Sancta Maria (see below), is still in use. Considering the number of tourists clambering about them, it's surprising that the smaller church ruins manage to retain a proud yet abandoned look.

Domkyrkan Sancta Maria

Daily mid-June–mid-Aug daily 9am–9pm; mid-Aug–mid-June 9am–5pm

Constructed between 1190 and 1225, the **Domkyrkan Sancta Maria** was built for visiting Germans, becoming the German parish church when they settled in the city. In 1300, a large Gothic chapel was built to the south, the eastern tower was elevated and the nave was raised to create storage space; this was where the burghers kept their money, papers and records. It's been heavily restored, and about the only original fixture left is the thirteenth-century sandstone font inside. Most striking are its **towers**, a square one at the western front end and two slimmer eastern ones, standing sentry over the surrounding buildings. Originally each had spires, but following an eighteenth-century fire, they were crowned with fancy Baroque cupolas, giving them the appearance of inverted ice cream cones. Inside, have a look beneath the pulpit, decorated with a fringe of unusually ugly angels' faces.

St Nicolaus

Best of Visby's church ruins is the great **St Nicolaus**, just down the road from the Domkyrkan. Destroyed in 1525, its part-Gothic, part-Romanesque shell hosts a week-long **chamber music festival** (w gotlandchamber.se), starting at the end of July; tickets cost around 250kr for most events and are available from the tourist office.

St Katarina

One of the loveliest ruins to view at night is **St Katarina** in Storatorget; its Gothic interior is one of the finest in Visby, having belonged to one of the town's first Franciscan monasteries, founded in 1233. This church was built in 1250; at night its glorious arches, lit creamy yellow, frame the blue-black sky.

ARRIVAL AND GETTING AROUND

VISBY

By plane Visby airport is 3km north of town and a 5min ride by taxi into the centre (not more than 185kr). Between mid-June and mid-Aug, Flygbussarna run a bus to and from the airport in connection with flights (w flygbussarna.se; 99kr single).

By ferry Ferries serving Visby all dock at the same terminal, just outside the city walls; for the centre, turn left out of the terminal and keep walking for 5min.

By bike You can rent bikes just outside the ferry terminal from Gotlands Cykeluthyrning, Skeppsbron 2 (from 80kr/ day; w gotlandscykeluthyrning.com) and from Visby Hyrcykel at Östervägen 1 near Österport (100kr/day; w visbyhyrcykel.se).

INFORMATION

Tourist office Donnersplats 1 (May & Sept daily 9am–5pm; June–Aug daily 9am–6pm; Oct–April Mon–Fri 9am–5pm, Sat 10am–4pm; ☎ 0498 20 17 00, w gotland. info). Visby's main tourist office is conveniently en route between the ferries and the old town; it has plentiful maps and information brochures and the informative English-language guide, *The Key to all of Gotland's Churches*, which lists the key features of all the island's churches in alphabetical order.

Tours There are several tours, one of which, the walking tour of the town (mid-June to mid-Aug 2–3 times a week; 100kr), is worth considering, especially if time is short. The tourist office has more information about times and routes.

ACCOMMODATION

SEE MAP PAGE 231

Finding accommodation in Visby should seldom be a problem. There are plenty of **hotels** (though few are particularly cheap), several **campsites** with cabins and a couple of good **hostels**. Unlike most other places in Sweden, prices in Gotland are higher in summer; the lower price we give is for out of season and non-summer weekends.

Best Western Solhem Solhemsgatan 3 ☎ 0498 25 90 00, w solhemhotel.se. Just outside the city walls at Skansporten, this large, comfortable chain hotel has a basement sauna and is quieter than the more central options. Rooms are modern, if uninspiring; they vary in size so ask to see one before you accept. 1800kr/1200kr

Best Western Strand Strandgatan 34 ☎ 0498 25 88 00, w strandhotel.se. A rather glamorous place in a quiet cobbled street in the heart of town, with a sauna, steam bath, indoor pool and a stylish atmosphere. Altogether more luxurious than its sister hotel, the *Solhem*, though not always more expensive. 1400kr/1200kr

★ **Clarion Wisby** Strandgatan 6 ☎ 0498 25 75 00, w nordicchoicehotels.se. Splendid, central hotel in a building dating back to the Middle Ages when it was used as a merchant's storehouse. Rooms are beautifully decorated with wooden panelling, soft lighting and period furniture, and there's a generous pool, too. Recent extensions have been in keeping with the original structure and the rooms are equally appealing, with elegant drapes, sheepskins and sumptuous furnishings. 2300kr/1460kr

Gute Mellangatan 29 ☎ 0498 20 22 60, w hotellgute. se. Very central and reasonably comfortable hotel housed in a building dating from 1887 which once served as Visby's cinema. All rooms are individually decorated, though some are overly flowery and fussy. 1690kr/990kr

Jernvägshotell Adelsgatan 9 ☎ 0498 20 33 06, w gtsab.se. Although train services on Gotland ceased in 1960, the former railway hotel – now a youth hostel – is still in operation. Rooms are modern and comfortable, though they must be booked months in advance. During the summer guests must be aged over 25. Doubles 1000kr

Stenugnen Korsgatan 4–6 ☎ 0498 21 02 11, w stenugnen.nu. Bright and airy rooms abound at this cosy hotel where the decor has a subtle maritime feel. The staff are friendly and personable, and breakfast is served in a sunny glass atrium at the rear. 999kr

Villa Borgen Adelsgatan 11 ☎ 0498 20 33 00, w gtsab. se. Attractive family hotel in the middle of the action, yet with lovely, peaceful gardens. Tastefully decorated en-suite, though rather small, rooms. There's a sauna and solarium too. 2295kr/1190kr.

★ **Visby Logi Vandrarhem** St Hansgatan 31 ☎ 070 752 20 55, w visbylogi.se. Five cosy double rooms decorated in tasteful whites and greys make up this youth hostel in an atmospheric old house dating from the 1600s. Also operates a similar, second site at Hästgatan 14. Rooms are up to 550kr cheaper outside the peak June–Aug period. 950kr

CAMPING

Visby Strandby Norderstrand Österväg 3A ☎ 0498 21 21 57, w visbystrandby.se. This campsite, with cabins to rent, is barely 800m outside the city walls – follow the cycle path that runs through the Botanical Gardens along the seafront. It's imperative to book early as it's extremely popular, though it's not possible to book camping pitches in advance in summer. Tents 280kr, cabins 975kr

EATING, DRINKING AND NIGHTLIFE

SEE MAP PAGE 231

6

CAFÉS

★ Gula Huset Tranhusgatan 2 ☎ 0498 24 96 90. This cosy garden café outside a vine-covered cottage is close to the Botanical Gardens and a favourite amongst locals who flock here on sunny weekends. It's deservedly well known for its delicious cake made with port, cream and fruit (55kr). Sat & Sun noon–5pm.

St Hans Café & Orangeri St Hansplan 2 ☎ 0498 21 07 72. Between May and September this café has outdoor seating in the rear garden amid a series of atmospheric medieval church ruins – for atmosphere it's hard to beat. Terrific cakes, muffins and pies as well as light lunches. Daily 10am–6pm.

Surfers Visby Kyrkogatan 1 ☎ 0498 21 18 00, ⓦ surfersvisby.se. Appealing, characterful, relaxed surf café. If you want to relax, then this might be the perfect spot for you. Tasty Chinese food is served, enjoy the different small dishes form 88kr. Wed–Sun 5pm–late.

RESTAURANTS

Bakfickan Storatorget 1 ☎ 0498 27 18 07, ⓦ bakfickan visby.se. A quiet, relaxed little restaurant with a tiled interior that specializes in some of the best seafood in town. The fried Baltic herring with mashed potato (150kr) is superb, as is the fish soup with aioli (180kr). Starters cost from around 90kr. Mon–Fri 11am–10pm, Sat & Sun noon–10pm.

Beyrouth St Hansgatan 15 ☎ 0498 27 83 80, ⓦ beyrouth.se. A taste of Lebanon on Gotland at this stylish restaurant in the old town. The menu is loaded with meze – try sixteen hot and cold appetizers for 299kr, or order tabbouleh, falafel and lamb sausages individually from 60kr. Mon–Fri 11am–10.30pm, Sat & Sun noon–11pm.

Bolaget Storatorget 6 ☎ 0498 21 50 80, ⓦ bolaget.fr. A delightful, though extremely small French bistro right on the main square with a good range of French classics: slow-cooked veal (235kr), bouillabaisse (210kr) and a delicious warm goat's cheese starter (125kr) are all good bets. Daily 5–10pm.

★ Gamla Masters Stora Kyrkogatan 10 ☎ 0498 21 66 55, ⓦ gamlamasters.se. A justifiably popular bistro decked out with mosaic tiles and serving everything from starters of blackened Norwegian salmon and Gotland wild garlic soup to sophisticated meat and fish dishes (185–295kr). A three-course set menu goes for 525kr. It's a great place, too, for an after-dinner drink. Daily 6pm–2am.

Isola Bella Södra Kyrkogatan 20 ☎ 0498 21 87 87, ⓦ isolabella.se. Great Italian trattoria, with a superb vaulted cellar restaurant to the rear. Beef carpaccio goes for 150kr and there's an excellent prawn risotto at 170kr, while the baked hake with butter sauce at 260kr is truly delicious. Mon–Fri 11.30am–2pm & 5pm–late, Sat & Sun 6pm–late.

Munkkälleren Lilla Torggränd 2 ☎ 0498 27 14 00, ⓦ munkkallaren.se. This vast place in one corner of the main square is massively fashionable, and consequently crowded. There's a choice of burgers (160kr), a couple of fish dishes (205kr) and a couple of grilled meat choices for around 250kr. Mon–Thurs 6pm–2am, Fri & Sat 6pm–3am.

★ Strykjärnet Crêperie & Logi Wallersplats 3 ☎ 0730 870506, ⓦ creperielogi.se. This fantastic low-ceilinged creperie is squeezed into the narrowest of triangular buildings at the corner of Adelgatan and Hästgatan (it's named "the iron" for its shape). A wide range of savoury galletes (including vegetarian options) from around 100kr; sweet crepes from 45kr. Daily 11am–late.

Roma

Bus #11 from Visby; timetable available from the Visby tourist office or at ⓦ gotland.se/kollektivtrafiken

The small settlement of **ROMA**, 15km southeast of Visby on Route 143, actually has nothing to do with Rome, but instead takes its name from "room" or "open space" – this was the original location of ancient Gotland's courthouse. The place looks something of a ghost town as its century-old sugar beet factory, to the right of the main road as you approach from Visby, closed some years back, and the early twentieth-century cottages fronting Route 143 are also deserted (they can't be demolished, though, as they're protected for their rarity value). The church here, dating from 1215, is large and pretty; the three-aisled nave gives it a surprisingly Romanesque appearance, and because of this the church is known as the False Basilica.

Romakloster

Just 1km further down the road from Roma, the Cistercian cloister ruins of **Romakloster**, in the hamlet of the same name, are the real draw of the area; follow the sign left down a long avenue of beech trees. The crumbling Roma

GOTLAND'S BEST BEACHES

Gotland is renowned throughout Sweden for its fine sandy beaches. The coast between **Sjaustrehammaren** and **Ljugarn** on the east coast, backed by pine forest, is the best beach on the entire island, a vast, unsullied stretch of golden sand; the southern section in front of Mullvalds strandskog forest and nature reserve is popular with **naturists**. Get here on bus #41 to Gammelgarn, from where it's a fifteen-minute cycle ride along the road towards Ljugarn, and then follow one of the narrow forest tracks which lead off down left to the shore.

The best of the rest are detailed below; all are marked on the map on page 229.

Holmhällar in the far south is surrounded by wild, unspoilt countryside and limestone *raukar*; take bus #11 from Visby.

Snäck is a 5km cycle ride north of Visby and popular with families who appreciate the gently sloping sands which make paddling particularly easy and safe for kids.

Sundersandsviken on Fårö is a perfectly formed sandy bay; take bus #20 from Visby to the ferry at Fårösund, then a taxi to the beach itself (book on ☎ 0498 20 20 00).

Tofta strand is also suited to families with children, since the water is relatively shallow and warm; take bus #10 south from Visby.

monastery, dating from 1164, lacks both apse and tower, being Romanesque in design; it would once have comprised a church with three wings built around a rectangular cloister. What is left is sturdy stuff – big arches of grey stone blocks so regular they could be breeze blocks. The multitude of spotlights set in the ground here make it very dramatic as a backdrop for night-time **theatre** (Shakespeare performances are staged each summer), though they detract from the site's timeless character by day.

The ruin is not the isolated site one might expect, as it's behind the cream-stucco **manor house**, Kungsgården, built in the 1730s for the county governor. Part of the monastery was in fact destroyed by the Danish crown during the Reformation of the early sixteenth century, and it was further ruined when the governor used materials from it in the building of the house. Temporary art exhibitions are held within the manor house, and there's a **café** (see below).

EATING
ROMA

Drängstugan Romabrunnen pizzeria, restaurang & kvarterskrog Visbyvägen 21 ☎072 498 54 01. This restaurant offers delicious pizzas for just 80kr. Mon–Fri 11am–10pm, Sat & Sun noon–10pm.

Konstnärsgården Ala, 15km southeast of Roma just off Route 143 ☎070 345 38 08. This is a complex of art galleries, though the main reason to come here is to eat at the appealing and popular restaurant round the back, serving filling meals including excellent fish and meat dishes for around 120kr at lunchtime. There's also a café, offering the usual baguettes and cakes. Open mid-May–late Aug daily noon–9pm.

Hemse and around

Bus #10, #11 or #12 from Visby; timetable available from the Visby tourist office or at ⊛ gotland.se/kollektivtrafiken

The so-called "capital" of the south, **HEMSE**, around 50km from Visby along Route 142, is little more than a main street. You can rent **bikes** from Endrells, Ronevägen 4, which is the most convenient outfit in town (☎0498 48 03 33).

Taking Route 144 east from Hemse, signposted for Burs, you'll find the countryside is a glorious mix of meadows, ancient farms and dark, mysterious forest. The village of **BURS**, one of the most charming in the area, is just a couple of kilometres further on; its gorgeous thirteenth-century saddle church, so-called because of its low nave and high tower and chancel, has a fabulously decorated ceiling, medieval stained-glass windows and ornately painted pews. A couple of kilometres further, the sandy **beach** at **Herte** is one of the best on the island.

EATING
HEMSE

Jonassons Bageri & Konditori Storgatan 54, Hemse ☎ 0498 48 00 07. A good local café and bakery serving delicious fresh bread and a limited range of sandwiches and cakes. Mon–Fri 7.30am–5pm, Sat 7.30am–2pm.

Ljugarn

The lively and charming town of **LJUGARN** makes a good base for **Sjaustrehammaren**, Gotland's best beach (see page 237), and is the nearest thing the island has to a resort. You can get here from Roma by heading straight down Route 143 for around 30km. Ljugarn is famous for its *raukar* – tall limestone stacks rising up from the sea. From the main street, it's only 100m to the town **beach**. Alternatively, a delightful cycle or stroll down Strandvägen follows the coastline northeast through woods and clearings carpeted in *blåelden* (viper's bugloss), the electric-blue flowers for which the area is known. The *raukar* along the route stand like ancient hunched men, their feet lapped by the waves.

ACCOMMODATION AND EATING
LJUGARN

Espegards Konditori & Bageri Storvägen 58 ☎ 046 70 247 88 63 ⓦ espegards.se. A visit to this splendid café is a must. It serves some of the best cakes around – try the almond and blueberry tart – and its famously good breads, in particular *gotlandslimpa*, a dark, slightly chewy loaf, have been made here and shipped to the mainland since the 1930s. The place is very popular, so expect a queue in summer. Fri, Sat & Sun 11am–4pm.

Ljugarns Strandcafé & Restaurang Strandvägen 6 ☎ 0498 49 33 78, ⓦ strandcafe.se. Located on the beach itself, this is the loveliest place to eat or drink in town, serving delicious, top-notch Swedish specialities, such as pan-fried salmon with new potatoes and dill mayonnaise (150kr); its large, open-air terrace is beautifully placed for a drink right on the sand. Mid-June–Aug daily 10am–late.

STF Ljugarn Vandrarhem Storgatan 1 ☎ 0498 49 31 84, ✉ ljugarn@gotlandsturist.se. Ljugarn's hostel is located in an atmospheric former customs house from the 1850s right in the centre of the village. There's an on-site kitchen for self-catering. This place fills up quickly so it's essential to book well in advance to secure a bed. Open late May–Aug. Doubles **500kr**

Lummelundagrottan

Daily May–early June 10am–3pm; early–late June 10am–4pm; late June–early July 10am–5pm; early July–mid-Aug 9am–6pm; mid-Aug–late Aug 10am–4pm; Sept 10am–2pm • 140kr • ☎ 0498 27 30 50, ⓦ lummelundagrottan.se • Bus #61 from Visby; timetable available from the Visby tourist office or at ⓦ gotland.se/kollektivtrafiken

The **Lummelundagrottan**, a system of limestone caves, stalagmites and stalactites 13km north of Visby on Route 149, are disappointingly dull despite being marketed

INGMAR BERGMAN

From the mid-1960s until his death in 2007, Sweden's best-known film director and screenwriter, **Ingmar Bergman** lived for much of the time on the island of Fårö, off northernmost Gotland. He was born in Uppsala in 1918, the son of a Lutheran pastor. The combination of his harsh upbringing, his interest in the religious art of old churches and the works of August Strindberg inspired Bergman to constantly consider the spiritual and psychological conflicts of life in his films. The results – he made forty feature films between 1946 and 1983 – are certainly dark, and for many, deeply distressing and/or depressing.

Bergman made his first breakthrough at the Cannes Film Festival in 1944, winning the Grand Prix for his film *Hets* (Persecution), based on his school life. Among his best-known movies are *The Seventh Seal* (1957), starring Max von Sydow, and *Wild Strawberries* (also 1957). The two most prevalent themes in his films were marriage and the motives for marital infidelity, and the divide between sanity and madness. One of his finest films, *Fanny and Alexander* (1982), portrays bourgeois life in Scandinavia at the turn of the twentieth century; it's actually based on the lives of his own maternal grandparents and is the last major film he made. Bergman married five times, divorcing all but the last of his wives, who died in 1995.

as Gotland's most visited tourist attraction. The **cave adventures** here are fun if you enjoy clambering around in the damp, but are not recommended if you suffer from claustrophobia (minimum age 15).

Jungfruklint

Ten kilometres to the north of the caves there's a more interesting natural phenomenon: **Jungfruklint**, the highest of Gotland's coastal *raukar* (see page 203). These remnants of reefs formed over four hundred million years ago, and the fact that the stacks are now well above the tide line is proof that sea levels were once much higher. This particular stack, 11.5m high, is said to look like the Virgin and Child – something you'll need a fair bit of imagination to discern.

6

Bro

Instead of taking the coastal road north from Visby, you could head around 10km inland along Route 148 towards the village of **BRO**, which has one of the island's most beautiful **churches**. Several different stages of construction are evident from the Romanesque and Gothic windows in its tower, but the most unusual aspect is the south wall, with its flat-relief picture stones, carved mostly with animals, which were incorporated from a previous church that once stood on the site.

Fårö

The island of **FÅRÖ** lies off northernmost Gotland; from Visby, take bus #20 to Fårösund, where the ferry departs. Most of Fårö is flat limestone heath, with shallow lakes and stunted pines much in evidence. In winter (and sometimes in summer, too) the wind whips over the Baltic, justifying the existence of the local windmills – and of the sheep shelters, with their steeply pitched reed roofs, modelled on traditional Fårö houses.

For swimming, the best place to head for is the 5km-long arc of white sand at **Sundersandsviken** (see box); alternatively, try **Ekeviken**, on the other side of the isthmus. The rest of the coastline is rocky, spectacularly so at **Lauterhorn** and, particularly, **Langhammars**, where limestone stacks (*raukar*) are grouped together on the beach. At Lauterhorn you can follow the signs for **Digerhuvud**, a long line of stacks leading to the tiny fishing hamlet of Helgumannen, which is no more than a dozen shacks on the beach, now used as holiday homes.

The Bothnian coast

LULEÅ

The Bothnian coast

Sweden's east coast, bordering the Gulf of Bothnia (Bottenhavet), forms a corridor of land that is quite unlike the rest of the north of the country; the forest, so apparent in other parts of the north, has been felled here to make room for settlements. The entire coastline is dotted with towns and villages that reveal a faded history; some, like Gävle and Hudiksvall, still have their share of old wooden houses, though sadly much was lost during the Russian incursions of the eighteenth century. However, it is cities like Sundsvall, Umeå and Luleå that are more typical of the region: modern, bright and airy metropolises that rank as some of northern Sweden's liveliest and most likeable destinations.

All along the coast you'll find traces of the religious fervour that swept the north in centuries past; **Skellefteå** and particularly **Luleå** (included on the UNESCO World Heritage List) both boast excellently preserved **kyrkstäder** or church towns – clusters of old wooden cottages dating from the early eighteenth century, where villagers from outlying districts would spend the night after making the lengthy journey to church in the nearest town. Working your way up the coast, perhaps on the long train ride to Swedish Lapland, it's worth breaking your trip at one or two of these places.

The highlight of the Bothnian coast is undoubtedly the stretch known as the **Höga Kusten**, or the High Coast (see page 259), north of Härnösand: for peace and quiet, this is easily the most idyllic part of the Swedish east coast. Its indented coastline is best seen from the sea, with shimmering fjords that reach deep inland, tall cliffs and a string of pine-clad islands that make it possible to island-hop up this section of coast. The weather here may not be as reliable as further south, but you're guaranteed clean beaches (which you'll often have to yourself), crystal-clear waters and some of the finest countryside for walking.

GETTING AROUND
THE BOTHNIAN COAST

Unlike southern Sweden, travel anywhere in the north of the country requires careful planning. Many **trains** only operate once or twice daily and **bus** services to destinations off the beaten track can be skeletal – particularly between mid-June and mid-August when, arguably, the need for transport is greatest. Before setting off, make sure you check all travel details thoroughly: two good places to start are the SJ and Resrobot websites, ⓦ sj.se and ⓦ resrobot.se.

By train Following the completion of a section of track north of Härnösand (the Botniabanan railway), the train route to northern Sweden now hugs the coast from Gävle all the way up to Umeå before looping inland to reach Luleå. From Sundsvall trains run inland to Östersund via Ånge where you can connect with services operating on the Inlandsbanan through central and northern parts of the country.

By bus From Umeå bus services run north to major towns along the coast, bound for all points north to Haparanda. There are also several bus services running inland from Umeå and Skellefteå, which can whisk you up into the mountains of Swedish Lapland, should you wish to head inland.

By ferry Along the High Coast, island-hopping north of Härnösand via Högbonden, Ulvön and Trysunda (see page 260 onwards) is a wonderful way to make your way north and to take in one of northern Sweden's most beautiful regions at the same time. Ferry tickets here are good value; see page 260 for details. Once again, though, you'll need to carefully check departure times to make sure you're not left stranded either on the islands or the mainland; the general pattern of services is given in the text.

Gävle and around

It's only ninety minutes north by train from Stockholm to **GÄVLE** (pronounced "yerv-luh", and confusingly similar to a much-used Swedish swear word),

A LOCAL ELK BULL

Highlights

①Stone architecture, Sundsvall Admire the grand avenues of this vibrant northern city, lined with elegant turn-of-the-twentieth-century stone buildings. See page 252

②Högbonden, High Coast A night in the former lighthouse on this unspoilt island, complete with shore-side sauna, is unbeatable. See page 260

③Elk farm, Bjurholm Come face to face with the elusive "King of the Forest" at this fascinating farm outside Umeå. See page 266

④Pite Havsbad, Piteå Northern Sweden's premier beach resort is renowned for long hours of sunshine and warm waters, while in winter it's the departure point for icebreaker tours. See page 271

⑤Gammelstad, Luleå Over four hundred gnarled wooden cottages make up Sweden's most extensive church town, offering an insight into the country's religious past. See page 275

⑥Luleå archipelago Take a boat trip to one of the dozens of pine-clad islands at the very top of the Gulf of Bothnia. See page 276

HIGHLIGHTS ARE MARKED ON THE MAP ON PAGE 244

Gällivare
Gällivare & Kiruna
Torne Valley

Ammarnäs
Arjeplog
Kukkolaforsen
Boden
Haparanda
Tornio
Älsybyn
Gammelstad
Luleå
NORRBOTTEN
Arvidsjaur
45
E4
5
6

Storuman
Piteå
Pite Havsbad
4

Jörn
95

Skellefteå
Bastuträsk
Lycksele
Burträsk
365
VÄSTERBOTTEN
Östersund
E12
45
92
Bjurholm **3**
Vännäs
Åsele
ÅNGERMANLAND
Umeå
Vaasa
Mellansel
90
E4
Långsele
335
Sollefteå
Örnsköldsvik
Ange & Bräcke
Kramfors
Ångerman River
High Coast bridge
Höga Kusten (High Coast)
2
FINLAND
MEDELPAD
E14
Härnösand
Sundsvall **1**
GULF OF BOTHNIA
N

HÄLSINGLAND
Östersund & Trondheim
Sveg
84
Hudiksvall
Hornslandet Peninsula
Bollnäs
Söderhamn
83
Dalarna
Folun
Gothenburg
80
Gävle
68
E4
GÄSTRIKLAND
Åland Islands

Uppsala, Stockholm & Arlanda airport

HIGHLIGHTS
1 Stone architecture, Sundsvall
2 Högbonden, High Coast
3 Elk farm, Bjurholm
4 Pite Havsbad, Piteå
5 Gammelstad, Luleå
6 Luleå archipelago

0   100
kilometres

THE BOTHNIAN COAST

capital of the province of Gästrikland. Gävle is also the southernmost city of **Norrland**, the region – comprising almost two-thirds of Sweden – which represents wilderness territory in the minds of most Swedes. To all intents and purposes, Norrland, Sweden's main reservoir of natural resources with vast forests and large ore deposits, means everything north of Uppsala; crossing into here from Svealand (which together with Götland makes up the southern third of the country) is – as far as the Swedish psyche is concerned – like leaving civilization behind.

Although Gävle is one of the bigger towns in Norrland, you can comfortably see everything in a day. Your first point of call should be **Gamla Gefle**, the old town district. Nearby, the **Heliga Trefaldighets kyrka** is a riot of seventeenth-century woodcarving and makes a pleasant stop en route to Gävle's city park, **Boulognerskogen**, a vast expanse of forested parkland ideal for a picnic or a leisurely stroll.

Brief history

Gävle's town charter was granted as long ago as 1446, a fact that's at variance with the modernity of the centre's large squares, broad avenues and proud monumental buildings. The city was almost completely rebuilt after a devastating fire in 1869 and its docks and warehouses reflect the heady success of its late nineteenth-century industry, when Gävle was one of Sweden's main ports for the export of locally produced iron ore and timber. Today, the city is more famous as the home of **Gevalia coffee** ("Gevalia" being the old Latinized name for the town), which you'll no doubt taste during your time in Sweden and certainly smell in the air in Gävle.

Gamla Gefle and around

It's only a ten-minute walk from the train station, across the Gavleån River, to the district of **Gamla Gefle**, which escaped much of the fire damage and today passes itself off as the authentic old town. Unfortunately, though it's the most interesting part of the city, it doesn't amount to much. The few remaining narrow cobbled streets – notably Övre Bergsgatan, Bergsgränd and Nedre Bergsgränd – boast pastel-coloured wooden cottages, window boxes overflowing with flowers in summer and old black lanterns. It's all very attractive and quaint and the jumbled lanes now house the odd craft shop and a café or two.

Joe Hill-Gården

Nedre Bergsgatan 28 • June–Aug Sat noon–4pm; other times by arrangement • Free • ☎ 026 65 26 41, ⓦ joehill.se

For a glimpse of social conditions in Gävle a century ago, visit the **Joe Hill-Gården**, the birthplace of one Johan Emanuel Hägglund in 1879. He emigrated to the United States in 1902, changed his name to Joe Hill and became a working-class hero – his songs and speeches became rallying cries to comrades in the International Workers of the World, a Utah-based syndicalist organization, which runs the museum today. Its collection of pictures and belongings is given piquancy by the inclusion of the telegram announcing Joe Hill's execution in 1915 – he was framed for murder in Salt Lake City – and his last will and testament.

Länsmuséet Gävleborg

Södra Strandgatan 20 • Tues–Fri 11am–6pm, Sat & Sun noon–4pm • Free • ⓦ lansmuseetgavleborg.se

Reopening after renovation work, the county museum, **Länsmuséet Gävleborg**, contains displays of artwork by some of the great Swedish artists from the seventeenth century to the present day, including Gunnar Cyrén, Nils Kreuger and Carl Larsson. Also on display is the work of a local artist, Johan-Erik Olsson (popularly known as

"Lim-Johan"), whose vivid imagination and naive technique produced some strange childlike paintings.

Gävle Slott

Follow the river west from the **Länsmuséet Gävleborg** to the double bridges of Rådmansbron and Kungsbron and you'll come to **Gävle Slott**, the seventeenth-century residence of the provincial governor, which lost its ramparts and towers years ago and now lurks behind a row of trees like some minor country house. However, it's not open to the public.

North of the river

The modern city lies north of the river, its broad streets and avenues designed to prevent fires from spreading. A slice through the middle of the centre is comprised of parks, tree-lined spaces and fountains, running north from the spire-like **Rådhus** to the beautiful nineteenth-century **theatre** designed by Axel Nyström. All the main banks, shops and stores are in the grid of streets on either side of Norra Kungsgatan and Norra Rådmansgatan; the **Resecentrum** is about 700m to the east.

EATING
Brända Bocken	3
Brasserie Absint	2
Church Street Saloon	5
Helt Enkelt	4
Konditori Lido	6
Matildas	7
Österns Pärla	1

DRINKING
| O'Learys | 1 |

ACCOMMODATION
Alderhomen	1
Aveny Bed & Breakfast	7
Boulogne	4
Clarion Winn	2
Elite Grand	3
Furuviks Havscamping & Skogscamping	5
Gamla Gefle Vandrarhem	6

THE CHRISTMAS GOAT OF GÄVLE

As odd as it may sound, Christmas and Gävle are synonymous in most Swedes' minds with a giant **straw goat**. At 13m high and 7m long, the yule goat (a traditional symbol of the festive period in Sweden) has been erected in Slottstorget every year during Advent since the late 1960s, and was originally intended to attract shoppers into the city centre. The **Gävlebocken**, as it's known in Swedish, can be viewed via webcam at ⓦ visitgavle.se/gavlebocken from the first Sunday in Advent – an attempt, perhaps, to protect it from local saboteurs who have repeatedly set it on fire over the years.

The warehouses

From the train station, look across the tracks and you'll see the beginnings of an industrial area. Off Norra Skeppsbron, just by the river, are three parallel streets of old dock-side **warehouses** – a reminder of the days when ships unloaded coffee and spices in the centre of Gävle. To get to them, use the subway to head under the railway tracks, and walk east to the riverside. Today, with company names emblazoned on the red, wooden fronts of the empty buildings, the area feels more like a Hollywood movie set than a Swedish town. Continue to the far eastern end of the warehouses and the heady smell of roasting coffee becomes ever stronger: Gevalia has its production centre here right next to the harbour at Nyhamn, north off Norra Skeppsbron.

Heliga Trefaldighets kyrka

Kyrkogatan 1 • Mon–Sat 11am–4pm & Sun 10am–2pm

From the Rådhus, it's a short walk west to the **Heliga Trefaldighets kyrka**, the Church of the Holy Trinity, a seventeenth-century masterpiece of woodcarved decoration: check out the pulpit, towering altarpiece and screen, all the superb work of the German craftsman, Ewardt Friis.

Boulognerskogen park

West of the city centre and a twenty-minute stroll down picturesque Kungsbäcksvägen, a narrow street lined with brightly painted wooden houses, you'll come to the rambling nineteenth-century park, **Boulognerskogen**. It's a good place for a picnic and a spot of sunbathing or a visit to the music pavilions, open-air **café** or the sculpture, by Carl Milles, of five angels playing musical instruments.

Sveriges Järnvägsmuseum

Swedish Railway Museum • Rälsgatan 1 • closed for renovation until the end of 2020 • 120kr mid-June–mid-Aug, rest of year 80kr • ⓦ jarnvagsmuseet.se • Bus #3 from the Rådhuset (bus times at ⓦ x-trafik.se)

On a rainy day (or even a fine one) you may find yourself contemplating the **Sveriges Järnvägsmuseum**, 2km south of the centre. Located in what used to be Gävle's engine shed, it's a train enthusiast's paradise, stuffed to the gills with really old locomotives and information on SJ's pride and joy, the X2000 series of trains. The highlight is the hunting coach dating from 1859; one of the world's oldest railway carriages, it once belonged to King Karl XV.

Furuvik amusement park

Daily late May–mid-June & mid–late Aug 10am–5pm; mid-June–mid-Aug 10am–7pm • Entry is 259kr plus a further 199kr for an *åkband* ticket covering unlimited rides on the attractions • ⓦ furuvik.se • Trains run hourly (7min)

The most popular attraction outside Gävle is the **Furuvik amusement park**, handily located just a seven-minute train ride away. The place boasts a zoo with chimpanzees and orangutans, fairground, parks and playgrounds.

7

Beaches

Bus #95 towards Harkskär leaves from the Rådhus and runs to Engeltofta and Engesberg and on to Bönan; bus #501 runs to Rullsand (bus times at @ resrobot.se) • *MS Drottning Silvia* departs from Södra Skeppsbron, behind the Resecentrum, and sails to Limön, via Engeltofta if required (summer up to 3 daily; 40min; 50kr; @ gavle.se/limobaten)

Northeast of Gävle, the beaches at **Engeltofta** and **Engesberg** are within easy striking distance without your own transport. Just north at **Bönan**, an old lighthouse marks a good spot for swimming. Other enjoyable beaches are on the island of **Limön**, connected by a summer ferry; the ferry calls at Engeltofta on the way, if required, and terminates at Furuvik, on the mainland east of Gävle. Another 15km or so east of Furuvik, at **Rullsand**, there's a vast stretch of sandy coastline, part of which is designated as a naturist beach.

ARRIVAL AND DEPARTURE GÄVLE

By train Travel by train to and from Gävle is much more convenient than by bus, as services are not only more frequent but also faster. The train station shares space with the bus station in the Resecentrum on Centralplan.

Destinations Falun (2 hourly; 1hr); Hudiksvall (2 hourly; 1hr 15min); Kiruna (1 daily; 16hr); Luleå (1 daily; 10hr 20min); Örebro (2 hourly; 3hr 40min); Östersund (3 daily; 3hr 30min); Stockholm (hourly; 1hr 30min); Sundsvall (hourly; 2hr 15min); Umeå (4 daily; 5hr); Uppsala (hourly; 45min).

INFORMATION

Tourist office Inside the Stadshuset, Drottninggatan 22 (mid-June to mid-Aug Mon–Fri 10am–5pm; mid-Aug to mid-June Mon–Fri 11am–3pm; ☎ 026 17 71 17, @ visitgavle.se). A 10min walk from the Resecentrum.

ACCOMMODATION SEE MAP PAGE 246

Alderholmen Norra Skeppsbron 3C ☎ 072 51 15 115, @ hotellalderholmen.se. A compact little hotel with just eight smart rooms, all with wooden floors and private facilities overlooking the river. A hot drink and a sandwich are provided free of charge every evening. **820kr**
Aveny Bed & Breakfast Södra Kungsgatan 31 ☎ 046 26 61 55 90, @ hotelaveny.eu. A small and comfortable family-run hotel south of the river, whose thirty-odd brightly painted rooms are hung with wall paintings and have nice wooden floors. There's a small buffet provided free to guests Mon–Thurs. **1075kr**
Boulogne Byggmästargatan 1 ☎ 026 12 63 52, @ hotel lboulogne.com. Cosy, basic hotel, with just seven plainly decorated rooms, and breakfast brought to your room on a tray; room prices here are among the lowest in town. Freshly brewed coffee available every evening. Close to Boulognerskogen park. **750kr/795kr**
Clarion Winn Norra Slottsgatan 9 ☎ 026 64 70 00, @ clarionwinngavle.se. A smart hotel with 200 rooms plus its own pool, sauna and sunbeds. Rooms have tasteful, neutral decor and wooden floors. The extensive breakfast buffet is outstanding. **850kr/1590kr**

Elite Grand Kyrkogatan 28 ☎ 026 400 73 00, @ elite. se. "Grand" certainly sums up this elegant hotel, housed in a sumptuously decorated building dating from 1901, overlooking the river a stone's throw from the train station. Rooms, as you might expect, offer totally luxury amid decor from the turn of the last century. **1160kr/1600kr**
Gamla Gefle Vandrarhem Södra Rådmansgatan 1 ☎ 026 62 17 45, @ geflevandrarhem.se. Rooms at this cosy hostel, beautifully located in the cobbled old town, are a little on the small side but the location is great. It's worth timing your arrival carefully as reception is not staffed from 10am to 5pm. Dorms **240kr**, doubles **520kr**

CAMPING

Furuviks Havscamping & Skogscamping Södra Kungsvägen, Furuvik ☎ 046 10 708 70 00, @ camping. se/x12; bus #501 (roughly every 30min). Gävle's campsite, complete with open-air swimming pool, is located by the amusement park, off Östnäsvägen, out at Furuvik (see above), Also has cabins for rent. Open late May to late Aug. Tents **180kr**, cabins **600kr**

EATING AND DRINKING SEE MAP PAGE 246

CAFÉS AND RESTAURANTS
Brända Bocken Stortorget ☎ 026 12 45 45, @ branda bocken.se. Young and fashionable, with a classic menu featuring smoked salmon with lemon hollandaise (245kr), rack of lamb (245kr) and Caesar salad (155kr), as well as

a range of burgers from 170kr. There's outdoor seating in summer, plus an upstairs terrace. Mon–Fri 11am–late, Sat noon–late.
Brasserie Absint Norra Slottsgatan 9 ☎ 026 64 70 00, @ nordicchoicehotels.com. A delightful French

brasserie with lots of mirrors and black tiling, attached to the *Clarion Winn* hotel. A wide range of dishes range from grilled venison with potato gratin (255kr) to loin of cod with smoked pork and potato purée (265kr). There's also a set three-course menu for 505kr. Mon & Tues 4pm–midnight, Wed–Sat 4pm–1am, Sun 5–10pm.

★ **Church Street Saloon** Kyrkogatan 11 ☎ 026 12 62 11, ⍟ churchstreetsaloon.se. A fun American saloon diner complete with riding boots, bridles and saddles and an American flag in the window. Plenty of Wild West grills on the plates and can-can dancing on the tables at weekends. Meaty mains from around 250kr. Mon–Fri 5pm–midnight, Sat 11.45am–midnight.

Helt Enkelt Norra Kungsgatan 3 ☎ 026 12 06 04, ⍟ heltenkelt.org. Modern Swedish mains with a hint of the Mediterranean dominate the menu at this stylish restaurant: chicken fillet stuffed with feta (189kr), moules frites (189kr) and the house burgers (185kr) are all worth trying. Mon, Tues, Wed & Sun 4–11pm, Thurs, Fri & Sat 4pm–2am.

Konditori Lido Södra Kungsgatan 10 ☎ 026 61 19 42, ⍟ konditorilido.se. Undisputedly the best café in town, and especially popular for its extensive salad buffet which is available weekdays 9am–4pm. The café also brags that it was here that the idea for the Gävlebocken straw goat

(see page 247) was born. Mon–Fri 7am–6pm, Sat 8am–5pm, Sun 10am–5pm.

Matildas Timmermansgatan 22 ☎ 026 62 53 49, ⍟ matildas.nu. Long-established neighbourhood restaurant which has earned the reputation for serving the best food in Gävle. All produce is locally sourced and the menu is classic modern Swedish: Matildas classic fillet of beef from Swedish farms (320kr), belly of pork with cauliflower and caramel cream (230kr) and a delicious starter of browned white asparagus and pork (170kr). Tues–Sat 5pm–late.

Österns Pärla Ruddammsgatan 23 ☎ 026 51 39 68, ⍟ osternsparla.nu. A stylish Asian restaurant with brushed metal interior walls decorated with bamboo poles. A good selection of Thai, Chinese, Japanese and vegetarian options, such as spicy Szechuan chicken (145kr). Mon–Thurs 11am–9.30pm, Fri 11am–10.30pm, Sat 12.30–10.30pm, Sun 1–9.30pm.

PUB
O'Learys Drottninggatan 6, ☎ 046 12 42 00, ⍟ olearys. se/gavle. Sports bar with a great atmosphere. Fresh burgers and pints will make this the perfect place to watch sports matches. You can also play bowling, too. Mon 3–10pm, Tues–Thurs 4–10pm, Fri 2pm–midnight, Sat 11am–midnight, Sun 11am–10pm.

Hudiksvall and around

North of Gävle, **HUDIKSVALL**, the provincial capital of Hälsingland, makes for a leisurely stop en route to the bigger towns and tourist centres further north. Its wood-panelled architecture and convenience for visiting the natural beauty of the nearby **Hornslandet peninsula**, jutting out into the Gulf of Bothnia, are the main draws. Train services are frequent along this stretch of coast.

Brief history
Granted town status in 1582 by King Johan III and accordingly the second oldest town in Norrland, Hudiksvall has seen its fair share of excitement over the years. The original settlement was built around what had been the bay of Lillfjärden, at the mouth of the Hornån River, but when the harbour began to silt up it was decided in the early 1640s to move the town to its current location: the old bay is now a lake.

THE DECORATED FARMHOUSES OF HÄLSINGLAND
The province of Hälsingland, located between Gävle and Sundsvall, is known throughout Sweden for its one thousand or so ornately decorated **farmhouses**, seven of which are on UNESCO's World Heritage List. The buildings were constructed during the 1800s by well-to-do farmers who developed a rich tradition of handpainting to adorn their substantial timber homes. The paintings represent a fusion of folk art and the styles favoured by the landed gentry of the time, namely Rococo and Baroque. One particular characteristic of the buildings is the provision of a separate room or outbuilding known as the **herrstuga**, which was only used for special festivities.

Around fifty farmhouses, including two of the UNESCO-listed structures, are open to the public. There are full details online at ⍟ halsingland.se/en/farmhouses-of-halsingland.

The town has suffered no fewer than ten **fires**, the worst occurring in 1721 when Russian forces swept down the entire length of the Bothnian coast, burning and looting as they went. Hudiksvall, at that time an important commercial and shipping centre, bore the brunt of the onslaught. A further blaze, east of Rådhustorget, in 1792 led to a rethink of the town's layout, and so the street plan which exists today was conceived.

St Jakobs kyrka

June–Aug daily 10am–4pm; Sept–May Mon–Thurs 11am–3pm

Still pockmarked with cannonball holes today, **St Jakobs kyrka**, dating from 1672, was the only building to remain standing after the harrying events of 1721 during the Great Northern War between Sweden and Russia. Although the white stone exterior topped with an onion dome is elegant enough, it's the interior that really impresses; nineteenth-century renovators opted for brown marble hand-painted wall decoration, delicately lit by candle-bearing chandeliers – unusually ornate for the Swedish Orthodox church.

Möljen

Turn right out of the train station and cross the narrow canal, Strömmingssundet ("Herring Sound"), and you'll soon see the small old **harbour** on the right; this area is known as **Möljen**. Here the wharfside is flanked by a line of red wooden fishermen's cottages and storehouses, all leaning into the water; it's a popular place for locals to while away a couple of hours in the summer sunshine, dangling their feet into the water. The back of the warehouses hides a run of handicraft studios.

Fiskarstan

More impressive and much larger than Möljen, **Fiskarstan** (Fishermen's Town), beyond the *First Hotel Statt* down Storgatan, contains neat examples of the so-called "Imperial" wood-panel architecture of the late eighteenth and nineteenth centuries. It was in these tightly knit blocks of streets, lined with beautiful wooden houses and fenced-in plots of land, that the fishermen used to live during the winter. Take a peek inside some of the little courtyards – all window boxes, flowers and cobblestones.

Hälsinglands Museum

Storgatan 31 • Mon & Sat noon–4pm, Tues–Fri 10am–4pm • Free • ⓦ halsinglandsmuseum.se

The history of the buildings in Fiskarstan is put into context in the excellent **Hälsinglands Museum**, which traces the development of Hudiksvall as a harbour town since its foundation. The museum's real showstoppers, however, are the ornately decorated **Malsta rune stone**, from around 1000 AD, ornately engraved with the letter-less Helsinge runic script (ask at the museum reception for a translation of the inscription), the expertly executed Post-Impressionist works by local artist, **John Sten**

HÄLSINGLAND'S GAUGUIN: JOHN STEN

If you're visiting the Hälsinglands Museum, be sure to see the paintings by **John Sten** (1879–1922) on the first floor: born near Hudiksvall, he moved to Paris at the age of 30, where he was greatly influenced by Post-Impressionist master Paul Gauguin. Tragically, Sten died of dysentery at the age of 42 in Bali; like many artists of his day he travelled extensively in Southeast Asia collecting impressions and designs, and became one of the first to work with Cubism, from which his work extends towards a more decorative, fanciful style.

> **MUSIK VID DELLEN**
>
> Undoubtedly the best time to visit Hudiksvall is during the beginning of July, when the town hosts the **Musik vid Dellen**, a multifarious cultural ten-day festival, including folk music and other traditional events, held in churches and farms in the surrounding countryside. For more information, contact the tourist office or see ⓦ musikviddellen.se.

(see box), and the quite breathtaking collection of **medieval church art** kept in a dimly lit room, just behind the café on the ground floor. From altar screens to intricately carved wooden figures of Sweden's saints, this astounding array of outstanding craftsmanship is sure to impress; the centrepiece is the early sixteenth-century figure of the Madonna and Child by renowned local artist Haaken Gulleson, from the village of Fläcka in Hälsingland; his style is easy to spot – heavy eyelids, ruddy cheeks and a benign expression.

ARRIVAL AND DEPARTURE   HUDIKSVALL

By train The train station is opposite the bus station on Stationsgatan, from where it's a 2min walk to the town centre.

Destinations Gävle (hourly; 1hr 15min); Stockholm (hourly; 2hr 40min); Sundsvall (2 hourly; 1hr); Uppsala (hourly; 2hr).

INFORMATION

Tourist office Storgatan 33 (mid-May to mid-June & mid-Aug to mid-Sept Mon–Fri 10am–5pm; mid-June to mid-Aug Mon–Fri 10am–6pm, also July Sat & Sun 10am–3pm; mid-Sept to mid-May Mon–Fri noon–4pm; ☎ 0650 191 00, ⓦ hudiksvall.se/turism).

ACCOMMODATION

Malnbadens Camping & Vandrarhem Malnvägen 34, Malnbaden, 3km from town ☎ 0650 132 60, ⓦ malnbadenscamping.com; bus #5 runs hourly in summer (10am–6pm); at other times you'll have to get here by taxi. In addition to the campsite there are youth hostel rooms and cottages (790kr) for rent for two people. Open April–Nov. Doubles **620kr**, tents **220kr**

Quality Statt Storgatan 36 ☎ 0650 150 60, ⓦ nordic choicehotels.se. The swishest hotel in town, dating from 1878 and still retaining many of the original features and flourishes. It was here that the barons of the timber industry made merry, coining the phrase "*Glada Hudik*" ("Happy Hudiksvall"), after the town's lively social life. **1020kr/1530kr**

Temperance Håstagatan 16 ☎ 0650 311 07, ⓦ hotell temperance.se. For atmospheric hotel accommodation in a grand old building dating from 1904, this place has just six doubles with private facilities plus simpler hostel-style rooms sharing facilities. **720kr**

EATING AND DRINKING

The Bell Bankgränd 1 ☎ 046 650 40 22 61, ⓦ thebell hudik.se. Hudiksvall's one and only bar is opposite the fishermen's warehouses at Möljen. There's a wide selection of British ales, lager and cider, plus live music and quiz nights. Mon–Thurs 4–11pm, Fri & Sat 4pm–1am.

Dackås Konditori Storgatan 34 ☎ 0650 123 29, ⓦ dackas.se. For a snack, try this Hudiksvall institution that's been here since the 1950s and is now decked out as a modern lounge-style café. It offers a range of baked potatoes, quiches and pancakes, plus coffee and cakes. Mon–Fri 7am–6pm, Sat 9am–3pm.

★ **Hot Chili** Hamngatan 5 ☎ 0650 757 50, ⓦ hotchili. se. Try this superb option near the bus and train stations for authentically spicy Asian stir-fries, rustled up before your eyes by chefs in the open kitchen for just 99kr (takeaway also available); it's arguably the best and most popular place in town for lunch. Mon, Tues, Wed & Sun 11am–9pm, Fri 11am–10pm, Sat noon–10pm.

Old Texas Saloon Hamngatan 5 ☎ 0650 121 50, ⓦ texas saloon.se. With cacti and life-size models of cowboys and Indians, the Wild West has truly arrived in Hudiksvall at this fun restaurant serving juicy steaks (from 247kr) and burgers (from 135kr). Mon–Fri 4–10pm, Sat & Sun noon–10pm.

The Hornslandet peninsula

For a day-trip from Hudiksvall, head southeast out to the beautiful and unspoilt **Hornslandet peninsula**, renowned for its quaint fishing villages of red wooden cottages and sandy **beaches**. This egg-shaped chunk of land is the geological result of continuous land rise since the last Ice Age; as recently as the Viking era, the Arnösund sound, which once separated Hornslandet from the mainland, was easily navigable, and it remained an important channel for seafarers until the tenth century. Today, though, the sound has silted up and the peninsula is effectively an extension of the Bothnian coast. This whole area is rich in flora and fauna, as well as being ideal for swimming, fishing and walking; there are two villages to head for in particular: **Hölick** and **Kuggörarna**.

Hölick

Located at the southern tip of the peninsula, **HÖLICK**, the larger of the two villages, traces its history back to the sixteenth century when a small fishing community became established here. Although there are no sights to speak of, the main purpose for coming here is to enjoy the plentiful peace and tranquillity on the very edge of the Gulf of Bothnia; a set of wooden steps leads up from the pilot boat station (*lotsstation*) in the centre of the village onto the rocks from where there are unsurpassed **views** out over the sea. A 7km-long circular **walking path** (allow around two hours) will take you through the surrounding nature reserve to some of the peninsula's finest **beaches**: from the village the path leads southeast out to the Hornslandsudden promontory – there are sandy stretches of coast all the way to the furthest point of the promontory – from where it cuts inland, heading over a series of low hills, back towards Hölick. Heading in the opposite direction and following the road out of Hölick back towards Hudiksvall, you'll come to another popular beach near **Arnöviken**, frequented by **naturists** (details at ⓦ naturistnet.org).

Kuggörarna

Tiny **KUGGÖRARNA**, actually located on a small island, is joined to the rest of the peninsula by a narrow bridge across the dividing sound. Once again, it's for solitude and great sea vistas that most visitors come here, although the hamlet does have a couple of things worth seeking out: the eighteenth-century **chapel** up on the hill above the houses is worth a quick look (you'll find the key hanging by the door), and, just to the north of the cluster of houses, is a well-preserved stone **labyrinth**, a collection of winding walkways delineated by large stones on the ground, used in centuries past by superstitious fishermen to ensure a good catch. There's no accommodation or anywhere to eat in Kuggörarna.

ARRIVAL AND DEPARTURE   HORNSLANDET PENINSULA

By public transport Getting to the Hornslandet peninsula by public transport is only possible in summer: take bus #37 (mid-June to mid-Aug, 2 daily; ⓦ xtrafik.se) which runs from the bus station via Hölick (40min) to Kuggörarna (1hr). **By car** With your own transport, Route 778 leads to Kuggörarna from Hällby, just north of Hudiksvall.

ACCOMMODATION AND EATING

Hölick Havsresort Arnöviken, Hölick 84 (look out for the signs where the road into the village ends) ☏ 0650 56 50 32, ⓦ holick.se. Accommodation in Hölick is restricted to this gem of a resort, which has superb cabins decorated in maritime whites and blues. With a spa and great dining options in the restaurant it is a great place to stay. Open whole year. Cabins **1395kr**

Sundsvall

SUNDSVALL, the capital of the tiny province of Medelpad, is often referred to as "Stone City", for the simple reason that most of its buildings are made of stone – a fact that distinguishes it immediately from other coastal towns here. Having gawped at Sundsvall's imposing architecture, most visitors then make for the city's other main attraction: **Kulturmagasinet**, a superb museum complex located right in the city centre housing the paintings and sculptures of local artist Carl Frisendahl, amongst others. In summer, **Gaffelbyn**, Sundsvall's outdoor craft village, is definitely worth a look, too – try your hand here at baking the northern Swedish flatbread, **tunnbröd**.

Brief history

Once home to a rapidly expanding timber industry, the whole city burned to the ground the day after midsummer in June 1888. A spark from the wood-burning steamboat *Selånger* (promptly dubbed "The Arsonist") set fire to a nearby brewery, and the rest, as they say, is history – so much so that the remark "that hasn't happened since the town burned down" is now an established Sundsvall saying. Nine thousand people lost their homes in the resulting blaze. The work of rebuilding the city began at once, and within ten years a new centre had been constructed, entirely of **stone**. The result is a living document of turn-of-the-twentieth-century urban architecture, designed and crafted by architects who were involved in rebuilding Stockholm's residential areas at the same time. Wide streets and esplanades that would serve as firebreaks in the event of another fire formed the backbone of their work. These thoroughfares are home to 573 residential buildings, all of which went up in four years; the centrepiece is the house that dominates the main square, Storatorget.

The reconstruction, however, was achieved at a price: the workers who had laboured on the city's refurbishment became the victims of their own success. They were shifted from their old homes in the centre and moved out south to a run-down suburb – the glaring contrast between the wealth of the new centre and the poverty of the surrounding districts was only too obvious. When **Nils Holgersson**, a character created by the children's author Selma Lagerlöf (see page 375), looked down on the town from the back of his flying goose, he remarked: "There was something funny about it when you saw it from above, because in the middle there was a group of high stone houses, so impressive that they hardly had their equal in Stockholm."

Around the stone houses was an empty space, and then there was a circle of wooden houses, which were pleasantly scattered in little gardens, but which seemed to carry an awareness of being of lesser value than the stone houses and therefore dared not come too close."

Storatorget

Storatorget, the central square, is a delightfully roomy shopping and commercial centre, home to the city hall and various impromptu exhibitions and displays. The square's limestone and brick buildings are four- and five-storey palatial structures. As you stroll the surrounding streets, you can't help but be amazed by the tremendous amount of open space that surrounds you, even in the heart of the city; Sundsvall is unique among Swedish cities in this respect, yet it's the most densely populated metropolis in northern Sweden. A wide central avenue, **Esplanaden**, runs down the eastern side of the square, cutting Sundsvall's grid of streets in two. The main pedestrian street, **Storgatan**, runs along the northern side of the square.

Kulturmagasinet

Packhusgatan 4 • Mon–Thurs 10am–7pm, Fri 10am–6pm, Sat & Sun 11am–4pm • Free • ⓦ sundsvall.se/kulturmagasinet

Several of the buildings in the centre are worth a second look, not least the sturdy **Kulturmagasinet**, housed within two blocks of late nineteenth-century warehouses, spanned by a glass roof, down by the harbour. The buildings stood empty for twenty years before a decision was taken to turn them into what's now the Kulturmagasinet, comprising museum, library and café. The museum is actually built over an old street, Magasinsgatan, that once held train tracks running between the warehouses to carry loads of coffee and rice. Deserving of a quick look, the first floor of the museum does its best to depict the history of Sundsvall, including the great fire of 1888, and the province of Medelpad. Up on the second and third floors, the art exhibition warrants a few minutes of your time: the works of twentieth-century Swedish artists are on show here, in particular, those of the local artist and sculptor **Carl Frisendahl** (1886–1948) whose early style is heavily influenced by Rodin. At the age of 20, Frisendahl studied in Paris where he met his wife, Marie Barbaud. Forsaking his native Sweden for a studio in Montparnasse, he began painting in the 1920s. His works, which often depict animals and mythological figures in combat, clearly show inspiration from Delacroix and Orthon Friesz.

Gustav Adolfs kyrka

Rådhusgatan 36 • June–Aug daily 11am–4pm; Sept–May Mon–Sat noon–3pm

At the western end of Storgatan you'll come across a soaring red-brick structure from 1894, **Gustav Adolfs kyrka**, which marks the western end of the new town. The church's interior looks like a large Lego set, its pillars, vaults and window frames all constructed from smooth bricks, making an eye-pleasing picture of order.

BOAT TRIPS FROM SUNDSVALL

Boat trips aboard the *M/S Medvind* depart from the eastern end of Hamngatan between May and September, and sail around the nearby island of Alnö, which lies due east of Sundsvall. The boat generally does two enjoyable trips a day (both 3hr 30min), one at lunchtime and one early evening; a buffet lunch or dinner is included in the price (from 295kr). You'll find detailed departure times and more information at ⓦ msmedvind.com.

Norra Berget and Gaffelbyn

Beyond the city's architecture, the most enjoyable diversion is the tiring 3km climb to the heights of **Gaffelbyn** on **Norra Berget**, the hill that overlooks the city to the north; walk up Storgatan, cross over the main bridge and follow the sign to the youth hostel. If you'd prefer to spare your legs, any bus for Norra Berget will take you up there. The view on a clear day is fantastic, giving a fresh perspective on the city's planned structure and the restrictive nature of its location, hemmed in on three sides by hills and the sea. From here you can see straight across to Södra Berget, the southern hill, with its winter ski slopes.

The viewing tower

The best views can be had from the top of the **viewing tower** which has stood on this spot since 1897. Originally made entirely from wood, the tower fell victim over the years to the Swedish winter. By the 1930s it was in such poor condition that during one particularly severe autumn storm, the entire thing blew down; the present concrete replacement, 22m high, dates from 1954.

Norra Bergets Hantverksmuseum

Norra Bergets Handicrafts Museum • Norra Berget • Daily 11am–5pm • 20kr

The **Norra Bergets Hantverksmuseum** is an open-air handicrafts museum with the usual selection of twee wooden huts and assorted activities, though you can often try your hand at baking some *tunnbröd*, the thin bread that's typical of northern Sweden. The idea is to roll out your dough extra thin, brush off as much flour as you can, slip the bread into the oven on a big, wooden pizza-type paddle, and count slowly to five.

ARRIVAL AND DEPARTURE	SUNDSVALL

By plane The airport is 24km north of town on the way to Härnösand. A taxi into town will cost around 250kr.

By train From the train station, it's a 5min walk to the city centre; turn left as you come out of the station, cross the car park then take the underpass beneath Parkgatan.

Destinations Gävle (2 hourly; 2hr 15min); Hudiksvall (2 hourly; 1hr); Luleå (1 daily; 7hr 50 min); Östersund (1 hourly; 2hr 30min); Stockholm (2 hourly; 3hr 30min); Umeå (1 hourly; 3hr).

By bus The bus station is close to the train station at the bottom of Esplanaden. For the twice-weekly Lapplandspilen express bus to Vilhelmina, Storuman and destinations to Klippen contact Lapplandspilen (☎ 0940 150 30, ⓦ lapplandspilen.se).

Destinations Docksta, High Coast (5 daily; 1hr 30min).

INFORMATION

Tourist office Stadshuset, Kyrkogatan 19 (June–Aug Mon–Fri 10am–6pm, Sat 10am–4pm; Aug–May Mon– Fri 10am–6pm, Sat 11am–3pm; ☎ 060 658 58 00, ⓦ visitsundsvall.se).

ACCOMMODATION	SEE MAP PAGE 253

Best Western Baltic Sjögatan 5 ☎ 060 14 04 40, ⓦ baltichotell.com. Centrally located, near the Kulturmagasinet and the harbour, with tastefully decorated rooms featuring carpets and chandeliers in a compact building dating from the 1880s. The smaller economy rooms off reception are excellent value. 900kr/1400kr

Clarion Collection Grand Nybrogatan 13 ☎ 060 64 65 60, ⓦ nordicchoicehotels.se. The sauna and Jacuzzi suite and gym at this central hotel are excellent, and included in the room rate; the rooms, however, are on the small side, though nicely decorated in classic, modern Swedish style with wooden floors and smart furnishings. 970kr/1570kr

Elite Knaust Storgatan 13 ☎ 060 608 00 00, ⓦ elite. se. Dominated by a magnificent marble staircase in the entrance hall, this is the most luxurious option in town.

The mix of old-world opulence and Scandinavian designer chic is a winning combination. The sumptuous loft suites all feature the original beamed roofs. 1250kr/1750kr

First Strand Strandgatan 10 ☎ 060 64 65 60, ⓦ first hotels.se. Handily located close to the train station, with modern rooms which feature either pleasant maritime decor or more contemporary, bolder colours and stripes. Furnishings are modern Nordic and the beds are especially comfortable. 1000kr/1480kr

Lilla Hotellet Rådhusgatan 15 ☎ 06061 35 87, ⓦ lilla-hotellet.se. Built one year after the great fire, this fine old hotel has just nine rooms (all en suite) and lots of charm: high ceilings, period furniture and ornate chandeliers. It's one of the most reasonably priced hotels in town; smaller budget singles cost 150kr less than the standard rooms and

7

are a great bargain. **900kr**

Quality Hotel Esplanaden 29 ☎046 60 16 00 00, ⓦnordicchoicehotels.se/hotell/sverige/sundsvall/quality-hotel-sundsvall. Expertly renovated and stylish to a T, this chain hotel boasts rooms with gorgeous nature paintings on the walls, plus saunas, sunbeds and a good breakfast, too. Prices are reasonable for the opulence. **875kr/1400kr**

Scandic Sundsvall City Trädgårdsgatan 31–33 ☎060 64 17 50, ⓦscandichotels.com. Quite a sizeable pile with over 140 rooms – all en suite and some with baths. Worth trying, especially if the cheaper hotels are full, though breakfast is an extra 85kr. **890kr/1380kr**

Sidsjö Paviljongvägen 9B ☎060 12 51 25, ⓦsidsjohotell.se. Just 2km from the city centre and eminently walkable, this hotel is (as its name suggests) located beside a lake.

Though there's a lingering institutional feel to the place – it was a former mental asylum – the rooms, both en suite and sharing facilities, are comfortable enough and exceptional value. **750kr**

Sundsvall City Vandrarhem Sjögatan 11 ☎ 046 60 785 62 00, ⓦsundsvallcityhostel.se. Good-quality, central youth hostel with a mix of doubles featuring regular beds as well as bunks, plus dorms where facilities are in the room itself rather than down the corridor. Dorms **300kr**, doubles **820kr**

CAMPING

Sundsvalls Camping Norrstigen 15 ☎060 55 44 75, ⓦsundsvallscamping.se. Sundsvall's campsite is 4km south of town, close to the E4; the tourist office can help with directions. Also has a range of cabins. Open all year. Tents **200kr**, cabins **500kr**

EATING AND DRINKING SEE MAP PAGE 253

Restaurants have mushroomed in Sundsvall over the last couple of few years, and there's a good choice of places to eat and cuisines to choose from, including unusual options such as Vietnamese, Spanish and Indian – something you may want to make the most of if you're heading further north, where culinary options are limited.

CAFÉS

Café Charm Storgatan 34 ⓦcafecharm.se. Very much of the old school, this café is bedecked with chandeliers and has a quiet and refined seating area at the rear. A good choice for coffee and cake, sandwiches, pastries and naughty-but-nice cream concoctions. Mon–Fri 7.30am–7pm, Sat 9.30am–5pm, Sun 11am–5pm.

Konditori Pallas Strandgatan 16 ☎060 61 10 57, ⓦpallas konditori.se. Replete with 1950s furniture and music of the same vintage, this retro café has expertly recreated 1950s Sundsvall and is a real find. Serves a great range of fresh pastries, too. Mon–Fri 7am–5pm, Sat 9am–4pm.

Tant Anci/Fröken Sara Bankgatan 15 ☎060 785 57 00, ⓦtantanci.se. This acclaimed café/restaurant/takeaway serves locally sourced, organic treats. The popular vegetarian burger dish (190kr) with hummus, almonds, eggplant and soybeans is genuinely tasty. The tortellini filled with pesto and Padano cheese (98kr) are also delicious. Mon–Thurs 11am–9pm, Fri 11am–8pm, Sat 11am–6pm, Sun noon–4pm.

RESTAURANTS

★ **Bite Line** Köpmangatan 20 ☎060 61 00 29, ⓦbiteline.se. Fun American pizza joint serving genuine deep-pan pizzas from 85kr. Also has salad options for 100kr, and there's an eat-as-much-as-you-can taco buffet every evening until 9pm. Football matches are shown live on the big screen. Mon & Tues 10.30am–10pm, Wed–Fri 10.30am–11pm, Sat noon–11pm, Sun noon–10pm.

Indian Palace Torggatan 12 ☎060 61 40 90, ⓦindian palacesundsvall.se. One of the country's best Indian restaurants: the food here is tasty and well-presented – it's as close as you'll come in Sweden to the Indian restaurants you're familiar with from home. Come here at lunchtime (Mon–Fri 11am–3pm) for the fantastic buffet which features several curries and accompanying side dishes for just 85kr. Mon–Fri 11am–9.30pm, Sat & Sun noon–10pm.

Invito Storgatan 6–8 ☎060 15 39 00, ⓦsundsvall. invitobar.se. Wonderful modern Italian cuisine is served up in this smart and elegant brasserie: fish and meat mains, such as steak with truffle butter or zander in white wine sauce, go for 170–300kr, or there's a really excellent home-made spaghetti carbonara for 195kr. Mon–Thurs 11am–2pm & 5–11pm, Fri 11am–2pm & 4pm–late, Sat 5pm–late.

Ming Palace Esplanaden 10 ☎060 61 53 00. The best Chinese restaurant in Sundsvall, which has been successfully feeding the masses for years with an impressive range of dishes (from 110kr). Takeaway service also available. Tues–Thurs 11am–10pm, Fri 11am–10.30pm, Sat 1–10.30pm, Sun 1–10pm.

Norrlandskällaren Storgatan 18 ☎060 17 40 40, ⓦnorrlandskallaren.nu. Feeding the masses since 1985, this basement restaurant is the place to come for traditional Swedish fare: Arctic char with dill, gravadlax and lobster soup. Mains are 160–280kr. Mon–Thurs 11am–9pm, Fri & Sat 11am–10pm, Sun noon–9pm.

Pizzeria La Spezia Sjögatan 6 ☎046 60 61 12 23. If money's tight, look no further than this long-established pizzeria serving a wide range of decent bargain-basement pizzas from 55kr. It has a handy takeaway service, too. Mon–Fri 11am–9.40pm, Sat & Sun noon–9.40pm.

Saffran Nybrogatan 25 ☎060 17 11 07, ⓦsaffran.nu. An authentic and much-praised Spanish restaurant whose menu features a wide range of tasty tapas dishes, such as potatoes in a spicy cayenne pepper sauce, octopus with chilli and paprika and fried Serrano ham with Manchego cheese – reckon on 50–90kr per dish. Mon–Thurs 5–10pm, Fri & Sat 4–11pm.

The Sea Street Sjögatan 9 ☎060 17 30 31, ⓦseastreet sushibar.se. Genuine Japanese sushi restaurant which has taken Sundsvall by storm and is exceptional value for money. Mix and match: six pieces for 60kr, nine for 79kr and fifteen for 145kr. Mon–Fri 11am–8pm, Sat noon–8pm, Sun 1–8pm.

BARS AND PUBS

Bishops Arms Storgatan 13 ☎060 608 00 11, ⓦbishops arms.com/sundsvall. Yet another Swedish attempt to create a traditional British wood-panelled pub in Norrland. The result is not bad though, and it's a fine place to sample a wide selection of British ales and beers. Mon & Sun 4–11pm, Tues, Wed &Thurs 4pm–midnight, Fri 4pm–1am, Sat 1pm–1am, Sun 4pm–11pm.

Estreet Esplanaden 14 ☎060 890 07 01, ⓦestreet.nu. A popular bar that's big on live music (Mon is jazz night) and karaoke. The sumptuous interior, with lots of comfy sofas and high-backed leather chairs, makes this a mellow place to spend the evening. Mon–Thurs 4–11pm, Fri & Sat 4pm–3am, Sun 4pm–2am.

O'Leary's Storgatan 40 ☎046 60 61 10 10, ⓦolearys. se/sundsvall. A popular pub spilling over three floors with large video screens showing various sports, and live entertainment several nights a week; there's even a bowling alley on the top floor. Tues–Thurs 5–11pm, Fri & Sat 5pm–1am, Thurs 2pm–1am, Sun 4pm–midnight.

Udda Tapas Esplanaden 17 ☎073 098 66 07, ⓦuddasundsvall.se. Despite the name, this trendy drinking establishment is more bar than restaurant. The decor is big on urban chic; seating is either at small round tables beside the tiled bar or on sofas in front of it. Outdoor seating at the rear, too. Mon & Tues 5pm–late, Wed 5pm–2am, Thurs 5pm–late, Fri & Sat 5pm–3am.

Härnösand

An hour's trip along the coast from Sundsvall, **HÄRNÖSAND** is full of architectural delights, including a number of old wooden cottages dating from the 1730s, and is definitely worth a stop on the way north. The town's highlights are the architectural treasures around the harmonious main square, **Storatorget**, and winding **Östanbäcksgatan** with its eighteenth-century wooden houses painted in gentle pastel shades. A short walk from the town centre, the extensive open-air museum at **Murberget** showcases vernacular architecture from around the country. Härnösand also marks the beginning of the stunningly beautiful region of **Ångermanland** – one of the few areas in Sweden where the indented, soaring coastline resembles the fjordlands of neighbouring Norway.

Brief history

Härnösand was founded at the mouth of the Ångerman River by King Johan III in 1585. In 1647, the town was selected as the capital of the second most northerly diocese in Sweden and, accordingly, the new bishop decreed that the old stone church, which already stood in the town, be enlarged into a cathedral. The town has since had more than its fair share of disasters: in 1710, flames tore through it after drunken churchgoers accidentally set fire to a boathouse; just four years later, Härnösand fell victim to a second great fire, started by a group of school students. Newly rebuilt, the town was razed by a third blaze in 1721, during the Great Northern War, when invading Russian forces burnt every house to the ground, bar one.

Storatorget

For a provincial place, Härnösand reeks of grandeur and self-importance, each of its proud civic buildings a marker of the confidence the town exudes. The main square, **Storatorget**, was once declared by local worthies as the most beautiful in Sweden and it's easy to see why: its western edge is proudly given over to the governor's residence, built in Neoclassical style by the court architect, Olof Tempelman, using local brick.

Konsthall

Arts Centre • Storatorget 2 • Tues–Fri 11am–3pm, Sat noon–3pm • Free

Inside the Neo-Renaissance former provincial government building, on the southwestern edge of Storatorget, you'll find both the town's tourist office (see below) and the **Konsthall**, whose small collection of contemporary Swedish art is worth a quick glance on your way in and out of the tourist office.

Domkyrkan

Franzéngatan 14 • Daily 10am–4pm

From Storatorget take a stroll up Västra Kyrkogatan to the heights of the Neoclassical **Domkyrkan**, the smallest cathedral in the country. Dating from the 1840s, it incorporates elements from earlier churches on the site; the Baroque altar is from the eighteenth century, as are the VIP boxes in the nave.

Östanbäcksgatan

From the Domkyrkan, turn right and follow the road round and back down the hill until you come to the narrow old street of **Östanbäcksgatan**, with its pretty painted wooden houses from the 1730s. This is one of the oldest parts of town, Östanbäcken, where the houses were among the first to be built after the Russian incursions.

Nybrogatan

To see more of the town's architectural splendour, take a walk up the hilly main street, **Nybrogatan**, to its junction with Storgatan: the Neoclassical dark orange **Rådhuset** here, complete with white circular portico, originally served as a school and home to the diocesan governors. Further up the hill, at the corner of Brunnshusgatan, the headquarters of the Provincial Administration Board (Länsstyrelsen) is particularly beautiful, housed in a Neo-Baroque and Art Nouveau building with a pastel yellow facade. From the top of Nybrogatan, there are good **views** back over the town and the water.

Murberget

Daily 11am–5pm • Free • ⓦ murberget.se • Buses #2 and #52 run from Nybrogatan in front of the Rådhuset; alternatively, it's a 30min walk from the town centre – from the train station, head north along Stationsgatan (turning into Varvsallén), passing through the docks on the way to the museum

The impressive **open-air museum** at **Murberget** is the second biggest in Sweden after Skansen (see page 60). The first building to take up its location here was a bell tower, which was moved from the village of Ullånger on the High Coast to its current position in 1913. There are around eighty other buildings, most notably traditional Ångermanland farmhouses and the old Murberget church, once a popular venue for local weddings. Look out for the **Rysstugan**, the one and only wooden building to escape the devastating fire caused by the Russians in 1721. The nineteenth-century **Spjute Inn** is still home to a restaurant, and also contains a skittle alley dating from 1910, where you can have a game.

ARRIVAL AND INFORMATION   HÄRNÖSAND

By public transport Buses and trains operate from the Resecentrum on Järnvägsgatan, a 5min walk from the centre.

Tourist office Storatorget 2 (Tues–Fri 10am–4.30pm; ☎0611 881 40, ⓦ harnosand.se/turism).

ACCOMMODATION

First Stadt Härnösand Skeppsbron 9 ☎ 0611 55 44 40, ⓦ firsthotels.se. The biggest and plushest of the town's hotels, with a perfect waterside location and well-appointed, if rather staid, rooms decked out in predictable Scandinavian chain-hotel style. There is, however, a decent buffet breakfast available. 860kr/1340kr

★ **Östanbäcken Logi** Östanbäcksgatan 14 ☎ 0611 55 60 00, ⓦ ostanbackenlogi.com. These cute red-and-white wooden cottages hidden in a charming garden off Östanbäcksgatan are a real find. Pine interiors, en-suite bathrooms and fully fitted kitchens make them the number one place to stay in Härnösand. Bed linen is an extra 50kr. 850kr

Royal Strandgatan 12 ☎ 0611 204 55, ⓦ hotelroyal.se. Perfectly located for the Resecentrum, this nineteenth-century pile with just 24 comfortable rooms has wonderful high ceilings and generously proportioned windows. It's also the cheapest hotel in Härnösand. 850kr/950kr

Sälstens Camping Sälsten ☎ 0611 181 50, ⓦ camping.se/y21. This waterfront campsite also has a small selection of four-bed cabins. It's around 2km northeast of the town centre; to get there, take Storgatan off Nybrogatan and follow the road as it swings eastwards along the coast. Open mid-May to Aug. Tents 200kr, cabins 500kr

STF Härnösand Vandrarhem Franzéngatan 14 ☎ 0611 243 00. Centrally located beside the cathedral in a charming building dating from 1844, the town's youth hostel is modern, clean and a great money saver; all rooms have private facilities. It's open year-round, though reception is only staffed between 3pm and 6pm. Dorms 200kr, doubles 500kr

EATING AND DRINKING

First Hotel Stadt Skeppsbron 9 ☎ 0611 55 44 43. The best option in Härnösand is this bistro inside the *First Stadt*, up on the first floor. It offers great views of the quayside and serves a range of locally sourced produce including several tasty fish dishes. Reckon on around 200kr for a main dish. Mon & Tues 11am–2pm & 5–10pm, Wed & Thurs 11am–2pm & 5–11pm, Fri 11am–2pm & 5pm–late, Sat 5pm –late.

New China Restaurant Storgatan 34 ☎ 0611 136 06, ⓦ newchinarestaurant.se. A run-of-the-mill Asian restaurant with a decent range of predictable Chinese mains (from 95kr) as well as better Indonesian (from 125kr), Thai and Indian (from 105kr) ones. It's one of the most popular places in town for lunch. Mon–Thurs 11am–9pm, Fri 11am–10pm, Sat noon–10pm, Sun noon–9pm.

Östanbäckens Pizzeria Östanbäcksgatan 1 ☎ 0611 50 05 52, ⓦ ostanbackens.nu. This neighbourhood pizzeria and grill restaurant is a good bet for tasty pizzas from 60kr, and also offers a few meat dishes such as schnitzel (from 70kr). Daily 11am–9pm.

Rutiga Dukens Café Västra Kyrkogatan 1 ☎ 0611 174 77. A snug and cosy café below the cathedral that's a great place for a cup of coffee and good home-baked pastries. Also has good-value weekday lunch specials which are worth seeking out. Mon–Fri 7am–6pm, Sat 10am–4pm, Sun 11am–4pm.

Höga Kusten – the High Coast

A UNESCO World Heritage Site, **HÖGA KUSTEN**, or the High Coast (ⓦ hogakusten.com), is the highlight of any trip up the Bothnian coast. This stretch of striking coastline north of Härnösand is elementally beautiful: rolling mountains and verdant valleys plunge precipitously into the Gulf of Bothnia, and the rugged shoreline of sheer cliffs and craggy outcrops gives way to gently undulating pebble coves. The dramatic landscape of Höga Kusten is the result of the isostatic uplift that has occurred since the last Ice Age; as the ice melted, the land, no longer weighed down by ice up to 3km thick, rose by 286m. There's nowhere in the world where the uplift has been so great as in this part of Sweden, and, in fact, it is still rising at a rate of 8mm every year.

Off Höga Kusten are dozens of islands, some no more than a few metres square in size, others much larger and covered with dense pine forest. It was on these islands that the tradition of preparing the foul-smelling **surströmming** is thought to have begun (see page 262). A trip here is a must for anyone travelling up or down the Bothnian coast; from out at sea, you'll get the best view possible of the coastal cliffs which (as the very name High Coast suggests) are the tallest in the country. The islands themselves are havens of peace and tranquillity, offering the chance to get away from it all. Among the most beautiful in the chain are, from south to north: **Högbonden**, **Ulvön** and **Trysunda**. Each of these islands can be visited using a combination of buses and boats; before setting off, make sure you've understood the boat timetables (available at tourist offices), which are in Swedish only and can be confusing.

GETTING AROUND   THE HIGH COAST

By boat The boats that serve the islands operate only in summer, except for the *M/F Ulvön*, which sails for Ulvön all year round. For the latest bus and ferry times, check out ⓦmfulvon.se or ⓦresrobot.se. All boats accept bicycles but not cars.

By car Travelling between Härnösand and Örnsköldsvik along the E4 will involve crossing over the Ångerman River

via the stunning High Coast bridge (no tolls). One of the longest suspension bridges in the world, with a span of 1210m, it has dramatically shortened the journey by cutting out a lengthy detour upriver to the old bridge between Lunde and Klockestrand. Reaching a height of 180m above the water, the bridge is only 70m shorter than San Francisco's Golden Gate Bridge, which it closely resembles.

Högbonden

After a mere ten-minute boat ride from Bönhamn on the mainland, the steep sides of the tiny island of **HÖGBONDEN** rise up in front of you. Although the island can feel a little overcrowded with day-trippers in peak season (July to mid-August), at its best it's a wonderfully deserted, peaceful haven. There are no shops – so bring any provisions you'll need with you – and no hotels on the island; in fact the only building here is a former lighthouse, now converted into a **youth hostel** (see below). It's situated on a rocky plateau at the island's highest point, where the pine and spruce trees, so prominent elsewhere on the island, have been unable to get a foothold; Högbonden's flora also includes rowan, sallow, aspen and birch trees, as well as various mosses that compete for space with wild blueberries.

You'll only get to know the special charm of Högbonden if you stay a couple of nights and take time to explore: a narrow gorge runs north–south across the island, and there are also forested hillsides and a shoreline where eider ducks glide by with their young. The **views** out across the Gulf of Bothnia are stunning; on a sunny day you could easily imagine you're in the middle of the Mediterranean.

Wood-burning sauna

At any time, you can head for the traditional **wood-burning sauna** down by the sea, two minutes' walk from the jetty (it's signposted "bastu" off the island's one and only path); you'll need to book your slot with the youth hostel staff, who keep the sauna's key. Afterwards, you can take a quick skinny-dip in the cool waters of the Gulf of Bothnia. The sunsets, seen from the boardwalk in front of the sauna, are truly idyllic.

ARRIVAL AND DEPARTURE   HÖGBONDEN

By boat from Bnham *M/S Högbonden* makes the 10min trip out to Högbonden from the mainland village of Bönhamn (mid-May to early Oct up to 4 daily; 150kr return; ☎0613 105 50, ⓦhkship.se). To get to Bönhamn on public transport from Härnösand, take the 11.10am bus to

Ullånger, where you change for a connection to Nordingrå and once there, change again for Bönhamn (check times at ⓦdintur.se). To reach Bönhamn by car, turn off the E4 at Gallsäter onto the minor road leading there via Nordingrå.

ACCOMMODATION

★**Högbonden Fyr & Vandrarhem** In the former lighthouse ☎0613 230 05, ⓦhogbondenfyr.se. To add to the novelty of sleeping in a converted lighthouse, this hostel's clifftop vantage point affords sweeping sea views. The main building houses a kitchen, two bathrooms and

several small rooms (with creaking floorboards) located over three floors. Two more rooms are in the building in the garden. Breakfast is not included. Open mid-May to early Oct. Doubles **800kr**

SURSTRÖMMING

Mention the word **surströmming** to most Swedes and they'll turn up their noses in disgust. It's best translated as "fermented Baltic herring" – though to the non-connoisseur, the description "rotten" would seem more appropriate. The tradition of eating the foul-smelling stuff began on Ulvön sometime during the sixteenth century when salt was very expensive; as a result just a little was used in preserving the fish, a decision which inadvertently allowed it to ferment.

The number of **salthouses** producing the herring has dwindled from several hundred early in the twentieth century to around twenty to thirty now. Today, *surströmming* is made in flat tins containing a weak salt solution. Over the course of the four- to ten-week fermentation process, the tins blow up into the shape of a soccer ball under the pressure of the gases produced inside. Restaurants refuse to open the tins on the premises because of the lingering stink that's exuded, not unlike an open sewer; the unpleasant job has to be done outside in the fresh air.

The **season** for eating *surströmming* begins on the third Thursday in August, ending around two to three weeks later, when supplies run out. The fish can be accompanied with the yellow, almond-shaped variety of northern Swedish potatoes and washed down with beer or *akvavit*; alternatively, it's put into a sandwich, perhaps with onion or tomato, all rolled up in a piece of *tunnbröd*, the thin unleavened bread traditional in this part of the country. There's more information at Ⓦ surstromming.se.

Ulvön

ULVÖN, 20km northeast of Högbonden and 12km southwest of Trysunda, is really two islands, Norra and Södra Ulvön, their combined area making it the largest in the High Coast archipelago. The southern island is uninhabited, separated from its northern neighbour by a narrow channel, Ulvösund, which provides a well-protected harbour. During the seventeenth and eighteenth centuries, Ulvön became home to the High Coast's biggest fishing community, as fishermen from Gävle came here to exploit the rich fishing grounds off the island; in subsequent centuries, though, many islanders moved to the mainland, especially after World War II, when the industry started to decline. Today, there are only around fifty permanent residents.

Ulvön is famous for its production of **surströmming**, fermented Baltic herring (see box); two of the firms involved, Söderbergs Fisk and Ruben Madsen, are based in the main village of Ulvöhamn (see below) and it's possible to buy the locally produced stuff in the island's shop.

Ulvöhamn

All boats to the island dock at the main village, **ULVÖHAMN**, a picturesque one-street affair with red-and-white cottages and tiny boathouses on stilts snuggling up eave to eave. Walking along the waterfront, you'll pass the pretty **fishermen's chapel**, dating from 1622 and now the oldest wooden building in Ångermanland (mid-June to mid–Aug daily noon–3pm; free); inside, its walls are covered with flamboyant eighteenth-century murals. The chapel was established by Gävle fishermen, who began summer fishing forays up the Baltic coast in the sixteenth century. Its detached bell tower was once used to signal that it was time to assemble for the daily fishing trip.

The beaches

To get to Ulvön's **beaches**, follow the sign marked "Strandpromenad Söder" from the tourist office (see opposite); it's about twenty minutes on foot past small sandy coves to the harbour entrance and a promontory of red rocks, Rödharen, beyond which lie several pebbly stretches.

ARRIVAL AND DEPARTURE

By boat from Docksta The *M/S Kusttrafik* departs from the mainland village of Docksta at 10.15am (June–Aug daily; 150kr one-way, 225kr day return; ☎0613 105 50, ⓦhkship.se), arriving in Ulvöhamn, on Ulvön, at 11.30am, heading back to the mainland at 3pm. If you are coming from Härnösand, take the 8am bus to Docksta (50min) to connect with the boat.

ULVÖN

By boat from Köpmanholmen There are also sailings on the *M/F Ulvön* to Ulvöhamn from Köpmanholmen, 24km south of Örnsköldsvik on the mainland (year-round; 100kr single, 150kr return) – handy if you are coming from north. Timetables change according to the time of year but can be found at ⓦmfulvon.se. Boats sometimes go via Trysunda.

INFORMATION

Tourist office In a tiny wooden hut beside the fishermen's chapel (mid-June to mid-Aug daily 11am–5pm; ☎0660 22 40 93, ⓦulvon.info). You can rent bikes here and pick up information about the Ulvöregatta, an annual gathering for ostentatious yachting types that takes place in mid-July.

ACCOMMODATION

Ulvö Hotell Hamngatan 1 ☎0660 22 40 09, ⓦulvo hotell.se. Just to the right of the quay as you come off the boat, the island's only hotel has cosy, modern rooms decorated in stylish floral swirls and bold colours with good views of the sea (those in the annexe cost a little less). Open May–Sept. __1195kr__

Ulvö Lakeside Resort By the village shop ☎076 774 00 09, ⓦulvon.com. Ten snug log cabins located a 10min walk up the hill behind the harbour, where there's also an outdoor pool. All the cabins have their own kitchen and private bathroom with shower. Bedding and towels are extra. Sun–Thurs __1125kr__, Fri & Sat __1375kr__

EATING AND DRINKING

If you are self-catering, the village **shop**, at the southern end of Ulvöhamn's main street, has a decent array of provisions. Out of season, you'll have no choice but to cook for yourself since all eating places close down for the winter. There's a pleasant **pub** and café below the hotel that buzzes in summer.

Almagränd Near the tourist office ☎0660 22 41 32. The place to come for burgers, pizzas and other grilled dishes costing in the range of 150kr. The menu may be less than stimulating but the waterfront location is a fine spot to dine and enjoy fantastic views over the harbour. Mid-June–mid-Aug daily 11am–late.

Café Måsen Near the tourist office. A charming garden café where you can sit outside among the wild flowers and herbs and enjoy home-baked bread, sublime cakes, salads, sandwiches and pasta. June–Aug daily 10am–6pm.

Ulvö Skärgårdshotell Hamngatan 1 ☎0660 22 40 09, ⓦulvohotell.se. This excellent hotel restaurant offers adventurous main courses (180–345kr) such as duck leg confit and Merguez lamb sausages as well as a mouthwatering fish and seafood buffet for 225kr which includes cold and warm smoked salmon, whitefish, eel and prawns – plus a dessert. Daily noon–3pm & 6–9.30pm.

Trysunda

The charming fishing village of **TRYSUNDA**, on the tiny island of the same name, is the best preserved in Ångermanland, hemmed in around a narrow U-shaped harbour, with forty or so red-and-white houses right on the waterfront. The village's wooden **chapel**, which is usually unlocked, is one of the oldest on the Bothnian coast, dating from around 1655. Like the church on neighbouring Ulvön, the interior is decorated with colourful murals.

Trysunda is crisscrossed with walking paths, leading through the forests of dwarf pine that cover the island, many of which have become gnarled and twisted under the force of the wind. The island's gently sloping rocks make it ideal for bathing, and you'll find plenty of secluded spots where you can do so. There's a **sandy beach** at **Björnviken**, a bay on the eastern part of the island, and some smooth rocks on the north coast, just to the east of **Bockviken**. An easily walked path from the village will take you to both beaches and around the entire island in an hour or two. To continue east from Björnviken, don't be tempted to strike off round the headland, as the rocks there are impassable; instead, stay on the path, which cuts inland, and follow the signs for Storviken.

Skrubban

As you approach or leave the island, you might be lucky enough to catch a glimpse of elk on the neighbouring island, the volcanic and uninhabited **Skrubban**. Although the island has been a nature reserve since 1940, every year some hunting is allowed to control the animal population and prevent unnecessary suffering from starvation, a practice followed elsewhere in Sweden, too.

ARRIVAL AND DEPARTURE   TRYSUNDA

By boat from Köpmanholmen The *M/F Ulvön* runs to Trysunda from Köpmanholmen, 24km south of Örnsköldsvik on the mainland (year round; 80kr one-way, 120kr return); all boat times are at ⓦ mfulvon.se.

By boat from Ulvön There are several boats from Ulvön; the exact number of departures varies with the time of year. Check timetables at ⓦ mfulvon.se.

ACCOMMODATION AND EATING

If you're self-catering, the village **shop** stocks the bare necessities, including fresh and smoked fish, and the dreaded *surströmming* (see page 262).
Kajen Köpmanholmsvägen 2 ☎00660 22 34 96, ⓦ restaurangkajen.se. Down at the harbour, this simple little restaurant serves a good-value lunch on weekdays (75kr; 11am–2pm), as well as a range of Swedish classics, such as *pytt i panna* (90kr), salmon (140kr) and fried schnitzel (120kr). Mon–Thurs 8am–6pm, Fri 8am–7pm,

Sat & Sun noon–7pm.
Trysunda Vandrarhem Köpmanholmsvägen 2 ☎0660 22 34 96, ⓦ restaurangkajen.se/vandrarhem. Located right by the harbour inside the red building which functions as the service centre for the marina, this hostel has 36 beds in rather cramped double rooms sharing facilities. There's also a kitchen, dining room, sauna and washing machine on site. Open May–Sept. Doubles **500kr**

Umeå and around

UMEÅ is the biggest city in the north of Sweden, with a current population of 122,000 people, which means that an astonishing one in ten of the residents of Norrland live here. Demographically speaking, it's probably Sweden's youngest city, a notion borne out by taking a stroll around the airy modern centre: you'll form the impression that anyone who's not in a pushchair is pushing one, and that the cafés and city parks are full of teenagers. Indeed, one in five people are in their twenties, figures that are partly due to the presence of Norrland University. Its youthfulness may well be responsible for the fact that Umeå is the one of the few towns or cities in northern Sweden where there's an air of dynamism: new restaurants and bars are opening all the time, there's a thriving cultural scene and the **Botniabanan** high-speed rail link to Stockholm means the capital can be reached in just over six hours.

The sound of the **rapids** along the Ume River gives the city its name: **uma** means "roar". With its fast-flowing river – a feature few other Swedish coastal cities enjoy – and wide, stylish boulevards, Umeå is an appealing metropolis. It would be no bad idea to spend a couple of days here, sampling some of its bars and restaurants – the variety of which you won't find anywhere else in Norrland. An added attraction is the nearby **elk farm** at Bjurholm, which makes a great day-trip from the city.

Gammlia

Gammliavägen • ⓦ vbm.se • Local bus #2 or #7, or a 20min walk from the train or bus stations

Most visitors to Umeå want to see **Gammlia**, the city's excellent museum complex which is home to a terrific collection of exhibitions on everything from *Sámi* life to skiing and merits a good half-day's exploration. In summer, the open-air section even has people dressed in period costume going about their daily tasks much as their predecessors did several centuries ago.

Friluftsmuseum

Late June–late Aug daily 10am–5pm, Wed till 8pm • Free

Gammlia grew out of the **Friluftsmuseum**, an open-air cluster of twenty regional buildings, including a windmill, church, two threshing floors, a smokehouse for pork and a couple of squat *Sámi* structures, the oldest of which is the seventeenth-century gatehouse you pass on the way in. The grounds are home to the customary farmyard animals – cows, pigs, geese and the like – and the *Sámi* section also has the occasional reindeer tethered close by. The guides dressed in period costume are very willing to tell you about life in their mock town, and at the bakery there are demonstrations of how to make the thin unleavened bread, *tunnbröd*, which used to be baked in people's homes. You can also take a ride through the grounds in a horse-drawn carriage (free), an experience that's bound to entertain kids.

Västerbottens Museum

Daily 10am–5pm, Wed till 8pm • Free

The indoor **Västerbottens Museum** houses Gammlia's main collection: three exhibitions that canter through the county's past, from prehistoric times (the section on this period contains the oldest ski in the world, over five thousand years old) to the Industrial Revolution. It's all good stuff, well laid out and complemented by an array of videos and recordings; a useful English guidebook is available at reception.

7

Fiske och Sjöfartsmuseum

Fishing and Maritime Museum • Daily 10am–5pm, Wed till 9pm • Free

UMEÅ

N

■ ACCOMMODATION	
Aveny	2
Clarion Collection Uman	8
Comfort Winn	4
Elite Mimer	5
First Camp Umeå	1
Pilen	9
Scandic Plaza	6
STF Umeå Vandrarhem	3
U&Me Hotel	7

● EATING	
Angelini	5
Gandhi	2
Great Eastern	1
Hunger och Törst	13
Kafé Station	12
Köksbaren	3
Konditori Mekka	4
Lottas Krog	6
Nya Konditoriet	8
Rex Bar och Grill	10
Rost Mat	9
Sjöbris	11
TC	7

■ DRINKING	
Bishops Arms	3
Gotthards Bar	4
O'Leary's	1
Runt Hörnet	2

Bus station

Train station

Guitars: The Museum

Radhus

Cinema

Stadskyrkan

Umeälven

Döbelns-
park

Bildmuséet

0 — 200 metres

UMEÅ: CITY OF BIRCH TREES

Umeå is sometimes referred to as the "**City of Birch Trees**", after the trees that were planted along every street following a devastating fire in 1888. Most of the city was burnt to the ground in the blaze, and two-thirds of the town's three thousand inhabitants lost their homes. In the rebuilding which soon began apace, two wide esplanades – one of which is Rådhusesplanaden – were constructed to act as fire breaks and help prevent such a disaster happening again. A decree was then handed down stating that the birch was the most suitable tree to add life to the town's reconstructed streets; even today, the city council places ads for free trees in the local papers and provides free birch saplings every spring to anyone who wants them.

The **Fiske och Sjöfartsmuseum** tries its best to be a regional maritime museum: the tug, *Egil*, which once operated in the Ume River, is squeezed into a small hall together with several fishing and rowing boats. The museum also has a brief display about seal hunting in the region.

Guitars: The Museum

Vasagatan 18–20 • Mon–Fri noon–6pm, Sat noon–4pm • Tours (45min) at noon, 1pm & 3pm • 150kr • ⓦ guitarsthemuseum.com

Undoubtedly Umeå's most quirky museum and one that is surprisingly engaging, **Guitars: The Museum** showcases around five hundred guitars and other musical paraphernalia housed in a rambling old school from the 1920s. The collection belongs to twin brothers, Samuel and Michael Åhdén, who hail from nearby Vännäsby, and contains rare guitars once played by the likes of Paul McCartney, Jimi Hendrix and George Harrison. However, the pièce de résistance is an electric guitar made for ABBA to mark their fortieth anniversary. In the shape of a glittery, silver star, the guitar has been signed by all four members of the band and is an exact copy of the one they played on stage in Brighton 1974 when they won the Eurovision Song Context with *Waterloo*. You're free to wander around at your leisure to peruse the exhibits, though there are also free daily guided tours.

Bildmuséet

Östra Strandgatan 30B • Tues–Thurs 10am–5pm, Fri 10am–9pm, Sat & Sun 10am–5pm • Free • ⓦ bildmuseet.umu.se • Bus #1, #5, #6 or #8, or a 15min walk from the city centre

Umeå university's art museum, the **Bildmuséet**, houses thought-provoking displays of contemporary Swedish and international art, photojournalism and visual design. It's located on part of the university campus, an easy walk along the Umeå River from the city centre.

Umedalens Skulpturpark

Umedalen, 2km west of the centre • Always open • Free • ⓦ umedalenskulptur.org • Bus #1 or #61 from Vasaplan; get off at the "Löftets gränd" stop

Occupying the grounds of Umeå's former mental hospital out at Umedalen, a couple of kilometres west of the centre, this acclaimed **sculpture park** is a riot of modern form in all shapes and sizes. The permanent exhibition contains pieces from, amongst others, Miroslaw Balka, Tony Cragg and Antony Gormley, alongside work from visiting international sculptors.

Älgens hus elk farm

Västra Nyliden 23, Bjurholm • Mid-June–mid-Aug Tues–Sun noon–6pm; mid-Aug–mid-June by advance booking on ☎ 0932 500 00 • 140kr • ⓦ algenshus.se • Buses run from Umeå daily (every 2–3hr; 1hr; ⓦ resrobot.se)

Umeå is ideally placed for a jaunt to the **Älgens hus elk farm** in **BJURHOLM**, a small village 65km west of the city. Driving around Sweden you may well have caught the briefest glimpse of the "King of the Forest", Europe's largest land animal, as tall as a horse but with antlers. The farm, though, provides an excellent opportunity to come face to face with these cumbersome-looking beasts and to learn all about their behaviour from the knowledgeable staff, who also make cheese from elk milk – a rare and inordinately expensive delicacy. Incidentally, elk love bananas, so you may wish to pack a few for your visit.

ARRIVAL AND DEPARTURE   UMEÅ

By plane Umeå's busy airport is 6km south of the city, with direct domestic flights to and from Stockholm (Bromma and Arlanda), Gothenburg, Kiruna, Luleå, Östersund and Visby, as well as international flights to Helsinki in Finland; it's linked with the centre by airport buses (45kr) and taxis (175kr).

By train Trains calling at Umeå pull in at the northern end of the city centre on Järnvägsallén.

Destinations Arlanda airport (3 daily; 6hr day train, 8hr night train); Gävle (3 daily; 5hr day train, 6hr 30min night train); Kiruna (1 daily; 8hr); Luleå (2 daily; 4hr 30min); Narvik (1 daily; 11hr); Stockholm (3 daily; 6hr 20min day train, 8hr 30min night train); Uppsala (3 daily; 5hr 45min day train, 7hr 30min night train).

By bus The bus station shares premises with the train station.

Destinations Haparanda/Tornio, Finland (5 daily; 6hr 30min); Luleå (6 daily; 4hr 30min); Skellefteå (hourly; 2hr); Storuman (Mon–Fri 5 daily, Sat & Sun 2 daily; 3hr 20min); Sundsvall (2 daily; 3hr 50 min); Tärnaby/Hemavan (Mon–Fri 3 daily, Sat & Sun 1 daily; 5hr).

By ferry Wasaline ferries operate at least one daily return service to Vaasa in Finland year round (4hr 30min; ⓦ wasaline.com). The ferries dock at Holmsund, 20km south of Umeå, and there is a connecting bus from Umeå to the port – see the website for details.

INFORMATION

Tourist office Rådhusesplanaden 6A (Mon–Fri 10am–6pm, Sat 11am–3pm; ☎ 090 16 16 16, ⓦ visitumea.se).

ACCOMMODATION   SEE MAP PAGE 265

Aveny Rådhusesplanaden 14 ☎ 090 13 41 00, ⓦ profil hotels.se/hotelaveny. The city's outstanding design hotel deserves a stay in its own right: an orgy of marine blues, organic greens and golden hues at every turn. The beds are sumptuous beyond belief – in short, come here for serious pampering. **995kr/1595kr**

Clarion Collection Uman Storgatan 52 ☎ 090 12 72 20, ⓦ nordicchoicehotels.se. Located in the grand former home of the city's chief medical officer, this cosy place, decked out with a medical theme, really is a home from home. An evening buffet for all guests is included in the price. **1000kr/1700kr**

Comfort Winn Skolgatan 64 ☎ 090 71 11 00, ⓦ choice hotels.se. Smart and comfortable, though lacking character and with rather cramped rooms and a bizarre apricot and purple colour scheme. The breakfast is good, and served in a glass atrium flooded with natural light. **750kr/1490kr**

Elite Mimer Kungsgatan 75 ☎ 090 203 94 00, ⓦ elite. se. The stone staircase sweeping up from reception sets the scene for this elegant, opulent hotel, housed in a former school. High ceilings and ornate cornicing in the rooms add a touch of old-world style to the urban chic of the breakfast room and other communal areas. **900kr/1500kr**

Pilen Pilgatan 5 ☎ 090 14 14 60, ⓦ hotellpilen.se. One of Umeå's smaller, cheaper hotels, with just twenty or so smartly renovated rooms, whose cosy interiors have been

redesigned to reflect the style of the building which dates from the turn of the last century. **895kr/1095kr**

Scandic Plaza Storgatan 40 ☎ 090 205 63 00, ⓦ scandichotels.se/plazaumea. For a treat, head for this very smart place which is popular with business travellers, with rooms decorated in the latest Scandinavian designs. There are superb views from the fourteenth-floor sauna suite, which is worth a stay here in itself. **900kr/1900kr**

STF Umeå Vandrarhem Västra Esplanaden 10 ☎ 090 77 16 50, ⓦ umeavandrarhem.com. This centrally located hostel, just 450m from the station, is one of Sweden's best, with 28 bright and airy en-suite rooms and good catering facilities. Bed linen/towel (70kr) and breakfast (also 70kr) are extra. Dorms **230kr**, doubles **550kr**

U&Me Hotel Storgatan 46 ⓦ umehotel.se. An innovative self-service hotel (no staff and no telephone number) where you check in yourself at a machine inside the Väven shopping complex and receive your key and receipt there. The hotel is located in a high-rise block beside Väven, and all rooms, which come in different sizes and offer stylish, modern decor, enjoy exceptional rooms out over the city and the Umeå River. **630kr/1190kr**

CAMPING

First Camp Umeå Nydalasjön 2, Nydala ☎ 090 70 26 00, ⓦ firstcamp.se/umea; bus #2, #6, #7 or #9, get off at

7

Nydala and walk for around 5min towards Nydalabadet, which is signposted. Umeå's campsite is located 5km from

town on the shore of a lake, and has a whole variety of cabins. Open year round. Tents **200kr**, cabins **750kr**

EATING AND DRINKING

SEE MAP PAGE 265

Eating and drinking opportunities are varied and generally of a high standard in Umeå, partly because of the size of the city and partly due to the large student population. The city buzzes at night, with plenty of stylish and friendly **bars** to choose from, most of them British-style pubs or brasseries. The city centre is most lively during termtime when students are around. Many of the popular eating and drinking places, though, are closed on Sunday.

CAFÉS

Kafé Station Östra Rådhusgatan 2L ☎090 14 19 90, ⓦkafestation.com. Handily located next to the Filmstaden cinema, this café, with its rough brick walls and tiled floor, is a firm favourite with all Umeåites. It serves a wide selection of sandwiches as well as great coffee and cheesecake. Mon–Sat 10am–7pm, Sun 11am–8pm.

Konditori Mekka Rådhusesplanaden 15 ☎090 77 44 04, ⓦmekka.se. Close to the train station, this long-established café is known for its delicious baked goods, especially its mouthwatering blueberry, carrot and squidgy *kladdkaka* cakes. Also has a good array of sandwiches, handy for last-minute purchases before boarding the train. Sun–Tues 11.30am–8.30pm, Wed–Sat 11.30am–10.30pm, Sun 10am–6pm.

Nya Konditoriet Kungsgatan 57 ☎090 77 14 04, ⓦnyakonditoriet.se. Known to its regulars simply as *NK*, this long-established café, replete with ornate chandeliers, is a city institution – it's been providing the folk of Umeå with coffee and fine pastries and cakes (all baked on the premises) since 1927. You'll find the seating area upstairs; the ground floor is used for over-the-counter sales. Mon–Fri 8.30am–7pm, Sat 8.30am–6pm, Sun noon–5pm.

RESTAURANTS

★ **Angelini** Rådhusesplanaden 14 ☎090 17 14 85, ⓦangelini.se. Style is high on the agenda at this Italian-American restaurant with mosaic walls and wooden floors. Burgers (185kr), fillet of beef (235kr) and spaghetti with clams (195kr) are all good bets on the tasty menu. Daily 5–11pm.

Gandhi Järnvägstorget 18 ☎090 12 50 75, ⓦgandhi. se. Reasonably tasty Indian food, including tandoori specialities, at sensible prices, from 150kr. The lunchtime buffet is good value at 85kr on weekdays (11am–1.30pm), 100kr on Sat (noon–3pm). Mon 6.30am–1.30pm, Tues–Thurs 6.30am–1.30pm, 5–10.30pm, Fri 6.30am–1.30pm, 5–11.30pm, Sat 7.30–11am, 5–11.30pm, Sun 7.30–11am.

Great Eastern Magasinsgatan 17 ☎090 13 88 38, ⓦgreateastern.se. The best Chinese restaurant in

Norrland. There's a very popular lunch buffet (90kr), and in the evening chicken and beef dishes from 105kr as well as a Mongolian barbecue for 170kr. It also has a few Thai mains from around 100kr and Japanese options from 70kr. Mon–Thurs 11am–9pm, Fri 11am–10pm, Sat noon–10pm, Sun 1–9pm.

Hunger och Törst Vasagatan 1 ☎090 77 10 00, ⓦhungerochtorst.se. Housed within a sturdy stone basement, this arty restaurant serves inventive modern Swedish fare. The menu changes every Tues depending on what ingredients are available from the restaurant's local suppliers. Tues–Sat 5pm–midnight.

Köksbaren Rådhusesplanaden 17 ☎090 13 56 60, ⓦkoksbaren.com. This bright and breezy bistro opposite the train station is the place to come for upmarket northern Swedish dishes: the fried perch with roe or the fish and crab burger with oyster mayonnaise are both excellent choices. Mains cost around 200–325kr. Mon–Thurs 11am–11pm, Fri 11am–late, Sat 4pm–late.

Lottas Krog Nygatan 22 ☎090 12 95 51, ⓦlottas. nu. Upmarket pub food served in one of the town's most popular eating places. The extensive menu is a mix of Swedish and world food: Mexican fajitas (200kr), steak and chips (240kr) and pasta carbonara (170kr). Also has some twenty different beers on tap, including Boddingtons. Mon 3–11pm, Tues 3pm–midnight, Wed & Thurs 3pm–1am, Fri 2pm–1am, Sat noon–1am.

★ **Rex Bar och Grill** Rådhustorget ☎090 12 60 50, ⓦrexumea.com. Umeå's very own Swedish-French bistro, serving Swedish classics with a French twist such as reindeer fillet with chervil (325kr) or pan-fried zander (295kr); three courses cost 550kr. Choose to sit in the brasserie or the more upmarket dining room. Mon & Tues 11am–2pm & 5–11pm, Wed & Thurs 11am–2pm & 5pm–midnight, Fri 11am–2pm & 3pm–2am, Sat noon–2am.

Rost Mat Skolgatan 49 ☎090 13 58 00, ⓦrost.nu. This superb and justifiably popular vegetarian restaurant serves organic food, all freshly prepared, and even makes its own cheeses. A hummus sandwich costs 95kr, apple salad 110kr and a cheese platter with lentils and bulgur wheat is a good-value 95kr. Mon–Fri 8am–7pm, Sat 11am–4pm.

Sjöbris Kajen 10 ☎090 77 71 23, ⓦsjobris.nu. An excellent restaurant on board an elegant old white steamer built in 1915. On the menu are well-prepared fish dishes such as a huge plate of prawns (175kr), grilled meats (from 225kr) and a whole range of pizzas and burgers. There's a quayside terrace, too, and live music Tues–Thurs. May–Sept daily 11am–late.

TC Vasaplan ☎090 15 63 21, ⓦumeafolkethus.se/tc. Short for Teatercafé, this place is a firm favourite among all age groups. It serves a wide range of food including starters from 115kr, steaks from 275kr, grilled salmon at 245kr and a heart salad with feta cheese for 115kr. There's outdoor seating in summer. Mon 11am–1.30pm, Tues 11am–1.30pm & 5–10pm, Wed & Thurs 11am–1.30pm & 5–10pm, Fri 11am–1.30pm & 4pm–late, Sat 4.30–11pm.

BARS

Bishops Arms Renmarkstorget 8 ☎ 090 10 09 90, ⓦ bishopsarms.com/umea. Umeå's attempt at an English-style pub and consequently one of the most popular places to be seen and to do the seeing in – always packed. There's outdoor seating in summer, and for those chilly evenings, blankets and free-standing gas heaters. Mon 4pm–midnight, Tues–Thurs 3pm–1am, Fri 2pm–2am, Sat 11am–2am, Sun noon–midnight.

Gotthards Bar Storgatan 46 ☎ 090 690 33 00, ⓦ gotthardskrog.se. Tucked away on the ground floor of the *Stora Hotell*, this adorable little bar is old-fashioned maritime in style: dozens of clear bottles each containing a paper message hang in racks above the bar, whilst elsewhere the decor is a mix of blues and heavy purple velvet, finished off by model ships in the windows. A perfect place for a gin on a cold and dark winter's evening. Mon, Tues & Sun 7–11.30am, 5–10.30pm, Wed–Sat 7–11.30am, 5–11pm.

O'Leary's Skolgatan 64D ☎ 090 12 55 55, ⓦ olearys. se. A vast and popular pub spilling over three floors with large video screens showing various sports, and live entertainment several nights a week; there's even a bowling alley on the top floor. Happy hour Wed, Fri & Sat 10–11.30pm, when it's standing room only. Mon & Tues 10am–midnight, Wed, Fri & Sat 10am–2am, Thurs 10am–1am, Sun 11am–midnight.

Runt Hörnet Kungsgatan 50 ☎ 046 90 12 55 66, ⓦ hornetumea.se. Lovers of urban retro-chic will fall for this bar, which occupies a prime location at the corner of Kungsgatan and Renmarkstorget, perfect for watching the world go by through the floor-to-ceiling windows. Comfy armchairs and an elegant white-tiled bar encourage you to linger. Tues 5–10pm, Wed &Thurs 5–11pm, Fri 3pm–2am, Sat 5pm–2am.

Skellefteå

There used to be a religious fervour about the town **SKELLEFTEÅ**, 140km northeast of Umeå. In 1324, an edict in the name of King Magnus Eriksson invited "all those who believed in Jesus Christ or wanted to turn to him" to settle between the Skellefte and Ume rivers. Many heeded the call, and parishes mushroomed on the banks of the Skellefte River. By the end of the eighteenth century, a devout township was centred around the town's monumental church, which stood out in stark contrast to the surrounding plains and wide river. Nowadays, more material occupations, including computer and electronics industries and the mining of gold and silver, support the town.

There's little to see in the town centre, and you would fare better concentrating on nearby **Bonnstan**, comprising an engaging collection of battered log cottages gathered together to form the **kyrkstad** (church town) next to the Neoclassical **church**, which houses one of Norrland's proudest exhibits – the **medieval carving** of the Virgin of Skellefteå. Skellefteå is also well placed for jaunts into the Swedish interior, with good bus connections to Arvidsjaur and Arjeplog.

Bonnstan

Skellefteå's church and **church town** (see box), known as **Bonnstan**, are within easy striking distance of the centre: walk west along Nygatan and keep going for about fifteen minutes. An evocative sight, the church town, or *kyrkstad*, comprises five long rows of weather-beaten log houses, with battered wooden shutters. The houses are protected by law: any renovations, including the installation of electricity, are forbidden, making this the most genuine example of all Sweden's church towns. You can take a look, but bear in mind that these are privately owned summerhouses today.

Landskyrka

Kyrkvägen, Nordanå • Daily 10am–4pm

Next to the cottages is the **landskyrka**, a proud white Neoclassical church which so enthused Leopold von Buch, a traveller who visited here in the nineteenth

SWEDEN'S CHURCH TOWNS

After the break with the Catholic Church in 1527, the Swedish clergy were determined to teach their parishioners the Lutheran fundamentals, with the result that, by 1681, church services had become compulsory. There was one problem with this requirement, though – the population in the north was spread over considerable distances, making weekly attendance impossible. The clergy and the parishes agreed a compromise: it was decreed that those living within 10km of the church should attend every Sunday; those between 10km and 20km away, every fortnight; and those 20–30km away, every three weeks. The scheme worked, and within a decade, **church towns** (*kyrkstäder*) had appeared throughout the region to provide the travelling faithful with somewhere to spend the night after a day of praying and listening to powerful sermons.

Of Sweden's original 71 church towns, only eighteen are left today, found predominantly in the provinces of **Västerbotten** and **Norrbotten**. Each *kyrkstad* consists of rows of simple wooden houses grouped tightly around the church. The biggest and most impressive, at **Gammelstad** near Luleå (see page 275), is included on the UNESCO World Heritage List. Today, the church towns are no longer used in the traditional way, though people still live in the old houses, especially in summer, and sometimes even rent them out to tourists.

7

century, that he was moved to describe it as "the largest and most beautiful building in the entire north of Sweden, rising like a Palmyra's temple out of the desert". Its domed roof is supported by four mighty pillars along each of the walls; inside, there's an outstanding series of medieval sculptures. Look out too for the 800-year-old **Virgin of Skellefteå**, a walnut **woodcarving** immediately behind the altar on the right – it's one of the few remaining Romanesque images of the Virgin in the world.

Kyrkholmen

Near the church, on the Skellefte River, the islet of **Kyrkholmen**, reached by a small wooden bridge, is a pretty place to sit and while away an hour or two. It's home to an outdoor **café** that specializes in waffles with cloudberry jam (open mid-June to mid-Aug).

Lejonströmsbron

From the church you have two walking routes back to the centre: either follow Strandpromenaden along the river's northern bank, interrupted by barbecue sites and grassy stretches; or cross **Lejonströmsbron**, one of the oldest and longest wooden bridges in Sweden, beneath the hill where the church stands. Dating from 1737, the bridge was the scene of mass slaughter when Russian and Swedish forces clashed there during the marvellously named War of the Hats, which started in 1741. Once on the south side of the river, you can stroll back to Parksbron, past the occasional boat and silent fisherman.

ARRIVAL AND INFORMATION   SKELLEFTEÅ

By bus The bus station is at the top of the central modern paved square, Torget.

Destinations Arjeplog (2 daily; 3hr 15min); Arvidsjaur (3 daily; 2hr); Luleå (2 hourly; 2hr 45min); Umeå (hourly; 2hr).

Tourist office Trädgårdsgatan 7 (end June to early Aug Mon–Fri 10am–6pm, Sat 10am–4pm, Sun noon–4pm; early Aug to end June Mon–Fri 10am–6pm, Sat 11am–3pm; ☏ 0910 45 25 10, ☻ destinationskelleftea.se).

ACCOMMODATION

Best Western Malmia Torget 2 ☏ 0910 73 25 00, ☻ malmia.se. A good central location in the main square for this modern hotel offering everything you'd expect from a chain hotel – creature comforts but with few flourishes; rooms are sadly rather plain and uninspiring. 890kr/1100kr

Quality Skellefteå Stadshotell Stationsgatan 8–10 ☎ 0910 71 10 60, ⓦ skellefteastadshotell.se. Skellefteå's pride and joy: a modern, business-oriented hotel with smart Nordic-style rooms and a superlative gym and sauna. It's streets ahead of any other establishment in town. 880kr/1400kr

Skellefteå Camping About 1.5km north of the centre on Mossgatan, just off the E4 ☎ 0910 73 55 00, ⓦ skelleftea.se/skellefteacamping. This campsite is hugely popular with holidaying Norwegian families, so it pays to book well in advance. As well as camping, you can rent two-bed cabins. The site also has a heated outdoor swimming pool, wave machine and Jacuzzi. Tents 360kr, cabins 870kr

STF Skellefteå Vandrarhem Brännavägen 25 ☎ 0910 72 57 00, ⓦ stiftsgarden.se/boende/vandrarhem. It's well worth seeking out this hostel, housed in a rustic red building by the banks of the Skellefte River, a 30min walk from the centre. Head west along Nygatan (which later becomes Brännavägen) until the junction with Kyrkvägen, where the hostel is on the corner. Bedding is an extra 70kr and breakfast is 100kr. Booking in advance is recommended. Doubles 480kr

Victoria Trädgårdsgatan 8 ☎ 0910 174 70, ⓦ hotel victoria.se. This family-run establishment, on the top floor of one of the buildings on the south side of the main square, is generally the cheapest of the central hotels. Rooms are adequate if rather unexceptional. 875kr/1300kr

EATING AND DRINKING

Lilla Mari Köpmangatan 13J ☎ 0910 391 92. Popular café set in an old-fashioned low-ceilinged wooden cottage in a small courtyard next to Nygatan 33K; for atmosphere it's unbeatable, feeling not unlike a grandmother's parlour. Outdoor seating in summer. Mon–Wed 10am–6pm, Thurs–Fri 10am–8pm, Sat 9am–4pm, Sun noon–4pm.

New GR Krog & Pub Kanalgatan 51 ☎ 0910 77 95 35, ⓦ newgrkrog.se. This popular place is an excellent choice for burgers, salads and steaks of various varieties (from 275kr). There's also a decent bar here. Mon–Thurs 4pm–late, Fri 4–11pm, Sat 3–11pm.

Nygatan 57 Nygatan 57 ☎ 0910 134 44, ⓦ nygatan57.

se. First-floor restaurant with smart floral wallpaper and white tablecloths, serving locally sourced specialities such as Arctic char and cod, as well as dependable dishes such as Caesar salad: mains are rather expensive, though, at around 300kr. Mon–Thurs 5–10pm, Fri noon–3pm, 5–11pm, Sat 5–11pm.

Old Williams Pub Trädgårdsgatan 13–15 ☎ 0910 73 91 61, ⓦ tatung.se/skelleftea/oldwilliams.html. One of Skellefteå's top drinking spots is this faux-English pub in the main square. It's located up on the first floor, with entry via the *Tatung* Chinese restaurant. Mon–Thurs 5pm–midnight, Fri 4pm–2am, Sat 3pm–2am, Sun 3pm–midnight.

Pite Havsbad

From Skellefteå it's 70km north along the E4 highway to the superb sandy **beaches** of **PITE HAVSBAD**, northern Sweden's main beach resort. Renowned for its long hours of summer sunshine, relatively warm water temperatures and sweeping strands of golden sand, it's a great place to unwind. There's even an official **nudist beach:** turn left along the beach and look out for a large rock marked "Naturist Bad".

Äventyrsbadet

Water park · Mid-June–late Aug daily 10am–8pm; late Aug–late June Mon–Thurs 4–8pm, Fri 2–8pm, Sat & Sun 10am–6pm · 105kr · ☎ 0911 327 00, ⓦ pitehavsbad.se/aktiviteter/aventyrsbad

In the **Äventyrsbadet** water park, you'll find open-air pools with water slides and – indoors – a fun pool, Jacuzzis, saunas, steam room, a sun terrace and yet more water slides.

ARRIVAL AND DEPARTURE   PITE HAVSBAD

By bus Buses between Umeå and Luleå call in at Pite Havsbad; for timetables, consult ⓦ resrobot.se.

Destinations Luleå (6 daily; 1hr 30min); Umeå (6 daily; 3hr 30min).

ACCOMMODATION

Hotell Pite Havsbad ☎ 0911 327 00, ⓦ pite-havsbad. se. A choice of superbly appointed, modern rooms, many with sweeping sea views; alternatively, next door there are

four-bed cabins right on the beach. Doubles 750kr/1270kr, cabins 700kr/1190kr

7

Luleå and around

Lively and friendly, the town of **LULEÅ**, 65km from Pite Havsbad up the E4, is immediately likeable, and if you're heading north for the wilds of the Torne valley, Gällivare and Kiruna, or to the sparsely populated regions of Swedish Lapland, Luleå represents your last chance to enjoy a decent range of restaurants and bars. The town has an important **university**, and is also the hi-tech centre of the north, specializing in metallurgy. For tourists, though, the main appeal is likely to be the UNESCO World Heritage-listed church town (see page 275) of **Gammelstad**, 11km northwest of town.

If you're visiting Luleå in summer, taking a boat out into the **archipelago** (see page 276) makes a wonderful day-trip – departures are daily and there's a whole array of islands in the Gulf of Bothnia to choose from: beaches, walking trails and plenty of peace and solitude are the main draws.

Brief history

When Luleå was founded in 1621 it had at its centre a church town and medieval church. Numerous trading ships would load and unload their goods at its tiny harbour, reflecting the importance of trade with Stockholm even in those days. The harbour soon proved too small, thanks to the growth in business, and so, by royal command, the settlement was moved to its present site in 1649; only the church and church town, today part of Luleå's Gammelstad, remained in situ.

Up until the end of the eighteenth century, Luleå was still little more than a handful of houses and storage huts; indeed Carl von Linné, Sweden's famous botanist, who passed through here in 1732 on his journey to Swedish Lapland, described Luleå as a village. Though the town had started to become something of a shipbuilding centre in the nineteenth century, it wasn't until the construction in 1888 of the Malmbanan, the railway built to transport iron ore from the Gulf of Bothnia for wintertime export at the ice-free Norwegian port of Narvik, that Luleå's fortunes really started to flourish. Luleå was at one end of the line, and its port was vital for lucrative iron exports (the main ironfields were – and are – around Kiruna and Gällivare).

Domkyrkan

Rådhustorget • Late June–mid-Aug Mon–Fri 10am–6pm; mid-Aug–late June Mon–Fri 10am–3pm • Free

LULEÅ

■ ACCOMMODATION	
Amber	4
City Sleep	2
Comfort Arctic	6
Elite Luleå	3
First Camp Luleå	7
Gammelstads Gästhem	1
Park	5

● EATING	
Baan Thai	5
Bistro Bar Brygga	1
Cook's Krog	4
Corsica	6
Hemma Gastronomi	2
Roasters	3

■ DRINKING	
Bishops Arms	1

ICEBREAKER TOURS

If you're visiting Pite Havsbad in winter, don't miss the fabulous **icebreaker tours** onboard the *Arctic Explorer*, which was built in Finland in 1963. After retiring from official service, the boat now sails from Piteå out into the frozen expanses of the Gulf of Bothnia on a two-hour excursion through the icefield (Feb–early March Sat 11am; 2hr; 795kr; minimum 10 people required for tour to operate; advance booking essential on ☎ 0911 327 00). There's also the unmissable opportunity to don a survival suit and float off the stern of the ship amid the ice blocks the ship has just broken.

Just to the south of **Storgatan**, the main street, lies Luleå's main square, **Rådhustorget**, with the **Domkyrkan** in the corner. The medieval incarnation of the cathedral disappeared centuries ago and the present one, built in 1893 on the same spot as its predecessor, is a modern barrage of copper chandeliers hanging like Christmas decorations. Unusually for northern Sweden, it's built of brick, in late-Gothic style, to the design of the architect Adolf Emil Melander. The interior was completely renewed in 1938 when the original wooden walls and fittings were removed, revealing the brickwork underneath which was then painted white.

Kulturens Hus

House of Culture • Skeppsbrogatan 17 • Mon–Fri 10am–6pm, Sat 11am–4pm • ⓦ kulturenshus.com • Free

Northeast of the Domkyrkan, **Kulturens Hus** is not only home to the tourist office and the city library but also to the **Konsthall art exhibition hall** which is sometimes worth a look, with interesting displays of changing work from modern Swedish artists and sculptors.

Lapland Heartwork

Smedjegatan 13 • Mon–Fri 10am–6pm, Sat 11am–4pm • ⓦ laplandheartwork.se

There's local art and **handicrafts** on sale at **Lapland Heartwork**, a treasure trove of a store that sells everything from handmade coat hooks in the shape of rams' horns to the seemingly obligatory "*Välkommen*" sign which no Swedish summer cottage is complete without. It's all produced by local artists, and this is a great place to pick up a souvenir or two without paying over the odds.

Norrbottens Museum

Storgatan 2 • Tues, Thurs & Fri 10am–4pm, Wed 10am–8pm, Sat & Sun 11am–4pm; closed Mon in winter • Free • ⓦ norrbottensmuseum.se

From the main square, walk 300m west along Köpmangatan, and you'll come to the **Norrbottens Museum**. Although most of the collection is an informative if rather dull resumé of county history and the effects of the 1809 war with Russia – when northern Sweden's borders were redrawn following the loss of Finland – the museum is worth a look mainly for the **films** that are available for viewing in the small cinema upstairs. In particular try to see the superb hour-long *Herdswoman* (in Swedish with English subtitles), about three generations of *Sámi* women from Nordmaling near Umeå and their groundbreaking court case in 2006 to establish traditional indigenous grazing rights for their reindeer herds; ask for the film at reception as it's not always available in the cinema. The museum also has a pleasant **café**.

The beaches

When the weather's good, it's worth heading to the oddly named **Gültzauudden**, a wooded promontory that has a great **beach**; it was named after the German shipbuilder, Christian Gültzau, who helped to make Luleå a shipbuilding centre.

It's easily reachable on foot from the centre: head north from the cathedral along Rådstugatan, which later changes its name to Norra Strandgatan and veers northwest past the Norrbotten theatre to the junction with Fagerlindsvägen. Turn right and follow the road down to the beach.

Another good bet on a warm day is the long sandy beach at **Lulviksbadet**, just south of the airport, which also has a naturist section. To get here take the airport bus all the way to the airport and then walk south for a further fifteen minutes, following the main road, until you come to the beach on your left-hand side.

ARRIVAL AND DEPARTURE   LULEÅ

By plane The busy airport lies 10km west of the city, with buses (50kr) and taxis (180kr) linking it with Luleå. There are flights to and from Gothenburg, Pajala, Östersund, Sundsvall, Stockholm Arlanda and Umeå, as well as Tromsø in Norway and Oulu in Finland.

By train Train services from the station on Prästgatan are few and far between so it pays to check timetables thoroughly in advance rather than just turn up hoping to jump on a train. Destinations Arlanda airport (1 daily; 12hr 8min); Gällivare (4 daily; 2hr 30min); Gävle (1 daily; 10hr 20min);

Gothenburg (1 daily; 16hr 20min); Kiruna (5 daily; 3hr 40); Narvik (2 daily; 7hr 30 min); Stockholm (1 daily; 12hr 30min); Umeå (2 daily; 4hr); Uppsala (1 daily; 11hr 40min).

By bus The bus station is located at the eastern end of Storgatan. Buses from here provide the most direct way of accessing villages in Swedish Lapland from Luleå. Destinations Arvidsjaur (Mon–Fri 3 daily, Sat 1 daily, Sun 2 daily; 3hr); Haparanda (hourly; 2hr 15min); Jokkmokk (Mon–Fri 3 daily, Sat 1 daily, Sun 2 daily; 3hr); Pajala (Mon–Fri & Sun 2 daily, Sat 1 daily; 3hr 30min).

INFORMATION

Tourist office Kulturens Hus, Skeppsbrogatan 17 (mid-June to mid-Aug Mon–Fri 9am–6pm, Sat 10am–4pm, Sun

11am–3pm; mid-Aug to mid-June Mon–Fri 10am–5pm; ☎ 0920 45 70 00, �� visitlulea.se).

ACCOMMODATION   SEE MAP PAGE 272

Amber Stationsgatan 67 ☎ 0920 102 00, ⓦ amber-hotell.se. A small and cosy family-run place in an old timber building close to the train station. The sixteen rooms are airy with high ceilings and large windows, and each is individually decorated in a modern style. 980kr/1130kr

City Sleep Skeppsbrogatan 18 ☎ 0920 42 00 02, ⓦ citysleep.se. Unbeatable value from this basement budget hotel whose thirty-odd rooms are small and windowless but clean and functional. Bathroom and kitchen facilities are shared. No breakfast is served and bedding costs an extra 50kr. 595kr

Comfort Arctic Sandviksgatan 80 ☎ 0920 109 80, ⓦ nordicchoicehotels.se. This smart little hotel, very handy for the train station, has cosy rooms with wooden floors and chic Nordic decor in bold reds and greens. Contemporary in feel, though still rather homely. 1200kr/1400kr

Elite Luleå Storgatan 15 ☎ 0920 27 40 00, ⓦ elite.se. Over a hundred years old, this grand old place is the most elegant of all the city's hotels, with old-fashioned rooms kitted out with curtains and large armchairs, and a huge breakfast buffet. 1150kr/1520kr

Gammelstads Gästhem Gamla Bodenvägen 11, Gammelstad ☎ 070 50 67 00, ⓦ gammelstadsgasthem. se. There's still an institutionalized feel to Luleå's STF hostel out in Gammelstad, located in a former old people's home. However, all rooms have private bathrooms (some share showers) and there are good self-catering facilities. Doubles 675kr

Park Kungsgatan 10 ☎ 0920 21 11 49, ⓦ parkhotell.se. This homely little place is amongst the cheapest of Luleå's hotels. It has just fourteen smartly renovated rooms, all with private facilities, and there's also access to a fully fitted kitchen for self-catering. 790kr/1490kr

CAMPING

First Camp Luleå Arcusvägen 110, Karlsvik ☎ 0920 603 00, ⓦ firstcamp.se/lulea; bus #8 from Smedjegatan in the city centre (every 1–2hr; 20min). This campsite boasts a superb waterside location with views back towards Luleå, though it's right next to the E4 and can be noisy at night. Also has cabins for rent. Tents 200kr, cabins 600kr

EATING AND DRINKING   SEE MAP PAGE 272

While Luleå often has a busy feel in summer, the city is much livelier when the university is in session. The most interesting **places to eat** are all found along Storgatan. Several of the restaurants listed below are also popular places to head to for a **drink**.

CAFÉS AND RESTAURANTS

Baan Thai Kungsgatan 22 ☎ 0920 23 18 18, ⓦ baanthai lulea.se. A less than authentic Thai menu, with chicken, beef and pork dishes for 120kr and rice and noodle mains from 105kr, served in a kitsch pink interior with hideous mosaic pillars; still a rare find, though, in the north. Weekday lunch buffet for 80kr. Mon–Fri 10.30am–10pm, Sat 11am–10pm, Sun 1–9pm.

Bistro Bar Brygga Skeppsbrogatan ☎ 0920 22 00 00, Ⓦ bistrobarbrygga.se. Known colloquially as *BBB*, this floating pontoon and boat comprise Luleå's most enjoyable outdoor restaurant, offering lots of summer grill dishes such as burger and fries (185kr) and Angus beef with tomato salad (280kr) as well as moules frites (250kr). Mid-May–early Sept Mon–Thurs 5pm–late, Fri & Sat 5pm–3am.

Cook's Krog Storgatan 17 ☎ 0920 20 10 25, Ⓦ cooks krog.se. Intimate and cosy, this is the best place in Luleå for steak and reindeer cooked over a charcoal grill, though it's not cheap – mains tend to be in the 250–300kr bracket. The five-course set Northern Swedish speciality menu at 695kr, which includes reindeer and whitefish roe, is definitely worth considering. Generally closed mid-June to mid-Aug. Mon–Thurs 6–10pm, Fri & Sat 5–10pm.

Corsica Nygatan 14 ☎ 0920 158 40, Ⓦ restaurangcorsica. com. A none-too-authentic French bistro, though with some good-value items on the menu: pasta dishes are just 100kr, salads go for 90kr, whilst a choice of steaks can be had for 200kr. Arguably though, pasta with reindeer (*renskav à la Laponia*) is the safest bet. Mon–Fri 11am–11pm, Sat & Sun noon–11pm.

Hemma Gastronomi Norra Strandgatan 1 ☎ 0920 22 00 02, Ⓦ hemmagastronomi.se. A great little bistro and deli all rolled into one. At lunchtimes it offers a range of Swedish home-cooking dishes, and in the evening it serves up generous tapas made from northern Swedish ingredients, such as salads, herring dishes and charcuterie. Mon–Sat 10am–late.

Roasters Storgatan 43 ☎ 0920 888 40, Ⓦ roasters.se. Perfectly located on the main drag, this is one of the best cafés in Luleå, with magnificent espressos, cappuccinos and lattes. Also has a good selection of sandwiches, light snacks, quiches and salads. Very popular outdoor seating area in summer. Mon & Tues 10.30am–9pm, Wed–Sat 10.30am–11pm, Sun noon–9pm.

PUB

Bishops Arms Storgatan 15 ☎ 0920 27 40 30, Ⓦ bishopsarms.com/lulea. Attached to the *Elite Luleå*, this pseudo-English pub with its bookshelves of battered old novels is undoubtedly the most popular place for a drink in town and is always busy with hotel guests and locals alike. Mon, Wed & Thurs 4pm–midnight, Tues & Sun 4–11pm, Fri 4pm–2am, Sat 1pm–2am.

7

Around Luleå: Gammelstad church town

The original settlement of Luleå, **GAMMELSTAD**, lies 11km northwest of the present city. It's one of the most significant places of historical interest north of Uppsala, and is included on UNESCO's World Heritage List. When Luleå was moved to the coast in 1649 (see page 272), a handful of the more religious among the townsfolk stayed behind to tend the church, and the attached **church town** – the largest in Sweden – remained in use. It comprises over four hundred timber **cottages**, which can only be occupied by people born in Gammelstad; even people from Luleå must marry a local to gain the right to live here.

Visningsstugan

Show cottage • Framlänningsvägen close to the junction of Skolgränd • Early May–mid-June Sat & Sun noon–4pm; mid-June–mid-Aug Mon–Fri 9am–3pm, Sat & Sun noon–4pm • Free

Although Gammelstad's cottages are privately owned and therefore not open to the public, it is possible to enter one of them, no. 253/254, below the church, and known as the "**visningsstugan**" or "show cottage". Inside you'll see a narrow box bed which is typical of the cramped sleeping conditions in the church town.

Nederluleå kyrka

Sockenvägen • Mid-June–mid-Aug daily 9am–5pm; mid-Aug–mid-June Mon–Fri 10am–2pm • Free

The **Nederluleå kyrka** was completed at the end of the fifteenth century; originally intended to be a cathedral, it's one of the largest churches in Norrland, and among the most impressive in the whole of Sweden. On the outside are decorative brick and plaster gables, and above the south door there's an opening through which boiling oil was poured over unwelcome visitors. The high altar, made in Antwerp, is adorned with finely carved biblical scenes; the decorated choir stalls and ornate triptych are other medieval originals. Have a close look at the sumptuous 1712 pulpit, too, a splendid example of Baroque extravagance, its details trimmed with gilt cherubs and red-and-gold bunches of grapes, made by local craftsman Nils Fluur.

Friluftmuséet Hägnan

Hägnan Open Air Museum • Gamla Hamngatan 21 • Mid-June–mid-Aug daily 11am–5pm • Free • ⓦ lulea.se/gammelstad

Down the hill from the church and the cottages is **Friluftmuséet Hägnan**, an open-air heritage park, whose main exhibits are several old farmstead buildings from the eighteenth century, including a bakery, smithy and stables. During summer, it plays host to displays of rural skills, such as sheep-rearing, the making of traditional wooden roof slates and the baking of northern Sweden's unleavened bread, *tunnbröd*. There's also a **café** serving light snacks, beautifully located beside an ancient pine tree.

By bus Gammelstad, 11km northwest of the modern city centre, is readily reached by bus from Luleå: bus #9 (every 1–2hr; 20min) leaves from Smedjegatan in the town centre.
Tourist office Right by Nederluleå kyrka at Kyrktorget 1 (June–Aug daily 10am–6pm; Sept–May Mon–Fri noon–4pm, Sat & Sun 11am–3pm; ☎0920 45 70 10, ⓦ lulea.se/gammelstad). The staff organize guided walks around the village (June–Aug daily at 11am, 1pm & 3pm; 80kr) and have brochures telling you all about the historical significance of the place.

The Luleå archipelago

Luleå's **archipelago** is the only one in the world surrounded by brackish water (the Atlantic Ocean off the Norwegian port of Narvik contains ten times more salt than this part of the Gulf of Bothnia). Made up of over 1700 islands and skerries, most of which are uninhabited and unexploited, it's well worth a visit. The islands are renowned for rich bird-life and a profusion of wild berries: lingonberries, blueberries and raspberries are very common, with Arctic raspberries, cloudberries, wild strawberries and sea buckthorn also found in large numbers.

The **islands** mentioned below are among the most **popular** destinations in the archipelago; they're also the most accessible, being served by once-daily passenger boats from Luleå. With a few notable exceptions, the islands are relatively small – no more than a couple of square kilometres in size – and are therefore ideal for short **walks**. Few are inhabited year-round and there are therefore barely any facilities – you should take all provisions with you and shouldn't count on being able to buy anything once you leave the boat. Although it's perfectly feasible to take a tent and camp on the islands, other **accommodation** is severely limited (we have listed where cabins exist) and most visitors to the islands are day-trippers.

Brändöskär

The wildest and most beautiful of all the islands, **Brändöskär**, is located far out in the Gulf of Bothnia and is consequently exposed to the weather and can often be very windy. Its best features are some terrific upland scenery with plentiful mosses and areas of heathland interspersed with smooth rocks along the coast, ideal for sunbathing. At the island's southern point there's a wooden **fishermen's chapel** dating from 1774 whose altarpiece depicts an impressive fishing catch; ask locally for the key if the chapel is locked.

Hindersön

People have lived and worked on **Hindersön**, one of the bigger islands here, since the sixteenth century. Then, fishing, farming and catching seals were the main occupations; today, this is the only island north of Arholma in the Stockholm archipelago which is still farmed. Much of the island is covered with spruce forest, though, if you look carefully, you may also find wild strawberries, Arctic raspberries, the rare Siberian primrose and ghost orchid; ospreys (*fiskgjuse* in Swedish) also nest on the island.

Kluntarna

Kluntarna has a little of everything – small fishing villages, dense pine forest and thousands of seabirds such as black guillemots and cormorants as well as waders like the greater ringed plover – and is a good choice, especially if you've only time to visit one island. Visitors are requested to show special respect for the delicate environment since the entire island is a protected nature reserve.

Rödkallen

Far out in the outer archipelago, south of Luleå, is **Rödkallen**. Site of an important lighthouse which once guarded the difficult southern approaches to Luleå, this tiny island offers fantastic sea and sky views; parts of it have been declared a nature reserve and the barren, rocky landscape is the result of its exposure to the elements.

Sandön

Klubbviken, a bay on the island of **Sandön**, is the place to come for good sandy beaches, and has the added advantage of regular boat connections to Luleå. Walking paths crisscross the island, taking in some terrific pine moorland scenery.

ARRIVAL AND DEPARTURE   THE LULEÅ ARCHIPELAGO

By boat Boats leave Södra Hamnen for the various islands in the archipelago from late June to mid-Aug, with a reduced service running from mid-Aug to mid-Sept; routes and times vary from year to year but the latest timetable can be found at ⓦ lulea.se/skargard or by contacting the tourist office in Luleå (see page 274). All of the islands listed above are within a 2hr sail of Luleå. A single ticket to Klubbviken is 50kr, 100kr to any of the other islands.

ACCOMMODATION

BRÄNDÖSKÄR

Cottages There are five simple four-bed cottages for rent on Brandöskär, without water and electricity, located on the island's southeast coast at Persögrundet beside the main jetty. There's also a sauna close by which is available to guests. Book via the Luleå tourist office. **490kr**

HINDERSÖN

Jopikgården ☎ 0920 600 12, ⓦ jopik.nu. Choose between individually decorated doubles, decked out in rustic colours, with private facilities in a beautifully restored farmhouse, or, in a separate building across the yard simpler hostel-style rooms with shared bathrooms. **650kr**

KLUNTARNA

Tärnan/Måsen/Truten Located in the main bay, Storviken, three very simple cottages for rent which can be reserved though Luleå tourist office. None has water or electricity; *Tärnan* and *Måsen* sleep four, *Truten* can sleep ten. There's a sauna here for your use as well. *Tärnan/Måsen* **490kr**, *Truten* **1090kr**

SANDÖN

Klubbviken Havsbad ☎ 0920 25 86 05, ⓦ klubbviken. se. There's the choice of four two-berth cabins perched on a hillock overlooking the sea, or, better, thirteen snug two-berth cabins with smart white interiors, right by the water's edge (sharing facilities). **495kr**

Haparanda and around

Right by the Finnish border, at the very northern end of the Gulf of Bothnia, **HAPARANDA** is hard to like. The signpost near the bus station reinforces the fact that the town is a very long way from anywhere: Stockholm, 1100km away; the North Cape in Norway, 800km; and Timbuktu 8386km. Viewed from the south, Haparanda is at the end of a very long road to nowhere. However, turn the map upside down, look a little wider and it's easy to see why IKEA took a strategic risk in late 2006 and opened its most northerly store in the world in Haparanda – a town of barely 10,000 people. The gamble paid off and shoppers from the whole of northern Scandinavia, even from

---

TWO COUNTRIES: ONE TOWN

The inhabitants of Swedish **Haparanda** and Finnish **Tornio** – two towns from different countries that have joined together to create a borderless "**Eurocity**" – are bilingual and use both the euro and the Swedish krona; roughly half of the children in Haparanda have either a Finnish mother or father. Services are also shared between the two towns: everything from central heating to post delivery is centrally coordinated. If a fire breaks out in Tornio, for example, Swedish fire crews from Haparanda will cross the border to help put out the flames. The shared **tourist office** (see opposite) has two phone lines, one dealing with calls from Sweden, the other with enquiries from Finland; staff switch effortlessly from one language to another depending on which line is ringing.

To get to Tornio simply head towards the "Finland" signs on the bridge; there are no border formalities, and so you can simply walk over the bridge to Finland and wander back whenever you like. It's worth remembering that **Finnish time** is one hour ahead of Swedish time and that Haparanda and Tornio have different names in Swedish (Haparanda and Torneå) and Finnish (Haaparanta and Tornio).

7

as far afield as Murmansk in Russia, now travel here to get their hands on those famous flat-packs. Other companies have followed the retailer's lead and set up business here, giving the local economy a long overdue kickstart. Other than the IKEA store, there are only two real sights in town: the train station, and the church.

Brief history

The key to Haparanda's late coming of age is the neighbouring Finnish town of **Tornio**. Finland was part of Sweden from 1105 until 1809, with Tornio an important trading centre, serving markets across northern Scandinavia. Things began to unravel when Russia attacked and occupied Finland in 1807; the Treaty of Hamina followed, forcing Sweden to cede Finland to Russia in 1809 – thereby losing Tornio. It was decided that Tornio had to be replaced, and so in 1821, the trading centre of Haparanda was founded on the Swedish side of the new border, which ran along the Torne River. However, the new town was never more than a minor upstart compared to its neighbour across the water. With both Sweden and Finland now members of the European Union, Haparanda and Tornio have declared themselves a **Eurocity** – one city made up of two towns from different countries (see box).

The train station

The disused **train station**, a grand-looking structure built in 1918, was the result of the town's aspirations to be a major trading centre after World War I and still dominates the suburban streets of southern Haparanda from its location at the junction of Stationsgatan and Järnvägsgatan. Constructed from red brick and complete with stone tower and lantern, it provided Sweden's only rail link to Finland until 1992 when it became another victim of SJ closures. From the platforms, you'll be able to discern two widths of track – Finnish trains run on the wider, Russian, gauge in front of the station; the Swedish tracks are behind the station building. The track between Haparanda and Luleå has now been upgraded and electrified which, in theory at least, will make it possible to once again operate trains via this route to Tornio in Finland, though it's likely to be some time yet before services resume. Until then, the empty sidings, overgrown with weeds and bushes, give the place a strangely forlorn air.

Haparanda kyrka

Smedjegatan 5 • Mid-June–mid-Aug daily 7am–7pm

After the train station, the only other place worthy of some attention is the copper-coloured **Haparanda kyrka**, a monstrous construction that looks like a cross between an aircraft hangar and an apartment building. When the church was finished in 1963, its design caused a public outcry: it won the prize for being the ugliest church in Sweden.

ARRIVAL AND DEPARTURE   HAPARANDA

By bus Haparanda is the terminus for the services that run up the Bothnian coast from Umeå and Luleå, as well as for services coming from neighbouring Finland. Arriving by bus, you'll be dropped at the bus station (Resecentrum) on Krannigatan, just beyond the northern end of Haparanda's main street, Stationsgatan, which runs parallel to the Torne River (the buildings you can see here across the river are in Finland). From here it's a 10min walk south along Storgatan to the main square, Torget.

Destinations Luleå (6 daily; 2hr 30min); Pajala (Mon–Fri 2 daily, Sun 1 daily; 3hr 30min); Umeå (6 daily; 6hr 30min).

INFORMATION

Tourist office Inside the Resecentrum, Krannigatan 5 (Mon–Fri 9am–2pm; ☎ 0922 262 00, ⓦ haparandatornio.com/ en-home). It holds information about both Haparanda and Tornio, and can also help with general queries about Finland.

ACCOMMODATION

Haparanda Stadshotell Torget 7 ☎ 0922 614 90, ⓦ haparandastadshotell.se. Perfectly located in the main square, this is an elegant and sumptuous hotel dating from 1900 with wooden floors and opulent chandeliers. Rooms are well appointed with period furniture and some rooms even have their own private sauna. There are also cheaper, simpler budget rooms available for around half the price. **1250kr/1600kr**

River Motell & Vandrarhem Strandgatan 18 ☎ 0922 611 71, ⓦ rivermotell.se. The cheapest beds in town are at this smart two-storey riverside place, affording good views to Finland – some rooms have a private terrace or balcony facing the river. Rooms have private facilities and bed linen costs an extra 65kr should you require it. There's a good kitchen, too, for self-catering. Dorms **200kr**, doubles **500kr**

EATING

As far as eating, drinking and nightlife go, you're better off in **Tornio** in every respect. Friday nights there are wild, the streets full of people trying to negotiate the return leg over the bridge; meanwhile, Haparanda sleeps undisturbed. It used to be the case that Tornio was much cheaper than Haparanda, but prices are now roughly the same, although drinking is still a little less expensive in Finland.

HAPPARANDA

Hassans Pizzeria Storgatan 88 ☎ 0922 104 40. For eating without trekking over to Finland, this place has a range of pizzas for around 60kr; true, the interior is nothing to write home about but the low prices keep the locals happy. Mon–Fri 10.30am–8pm, Sat & Sun noon–8pm.
IKEA Norrskensvägen 5 ☎ 0775 70 05 00. Though the thought of eating inside a flat-pack furniture store may not immediately appeal, it's clear that the price and quality of what's on offer in the in-store restaurant are streets ahead of any other option in town; eight meatballs and mash costs just 30kr. Daily 9.30am–5.30pm.
Leilani Köpmansgatan 15 ☎ 0922 107 17, ⓦ restaurang leilani.com. Long-established Asian restaurant serving a selection of Thai dishes such as curries and stir-fries as well as dependable Chinese mains and rather uninspiring pizzas, all from 80kr. Mon 10.30am–8pm, Tues–Thurs 10.30am–9pm, Fri 10.30am–10pm, Sat noon–10pm, Sun noon–9pm.

TORNIO

Umpitunneli Hallituskatu 15 ☎ 358 40 126 02 00, ⓦ umpitunneli.fi. Across in Tornio, your best bet is this riverside restaurant, bar and nightclub all rolled into one – it's always packed. Arctic char or grilled chicken costs around €17 and a half-litre of beer €5. Don't expect people to speak much English. Finnish time: Mon–Thurs 3–10pm, Fri 3pm–4am, Sat 1pm–4am, Sun 1–8pm.

7

Central Sweden

LAKE SILJAN

Central Sweden

In many ways, the long wedge of land that comprises central Sweden – the sparsely populated provinces of Dalarna, Härjedalen and Jämtland – encompasses all that is most typical of the country. This vast area of land is really one great forest, broken only by the odd village or town. Rural and underpopulated, it epitomizes the image most people have of Sweden: lakes, log cabins, pine forests and wide, open skies. Until just one or two generations ago, Swedes across the country lived in this sort of setting, taking their cue from the people of these central lands and forest, who were the first to rise against the Danes in the sixteenth century.

Dalarna, centred around **Lake Siljan**, is an intensely picturesque – and touristy – region, its inhabitants maintaining a cultural heritage (echoed in contemporary handicrafts and traditions) that goes back to the Middle Ages. You won't need to brave the crowds of visitors for too long, as even a quick tour around one or two of the more accessible places here gives an impression of the whole: red cottages with a white door and window frames, sweeping green countryside, water that's bluer than blue and a riot of summer festivals. Dalarna is *the* place to spend midsummer, particularly **Midsummer's Eve**, when the whole region erupts in a frenzy of celebration.

The privately owned **Inlandsbanan**, the great Inland Railway, cuts right through central Sweden and links many of the towns and villages covered in this chapter. Running from **Mora** in Dalarna to Gällivare, above the Arctic Circle, it ranks with the best of European train journeys, covering an enthralling 1067km in two days; the second half of the journey, north of Östersund (where you have to change trains), is covered in the Swedish Lapland chapter (see page 312). Buses connect the rail line with the mountain villages that lie alongside the Norwegian border, where the surrounding Swedish *fjäll*, or mountains, offer some spectacular and compelling hiking, notably around **Ljungdalen** in the remote province of **Härjedalen**. Marking the halfway point of the line, **Östersund**, the only town of any size along it and the capital of the province of **Jämtland**, is situated by the side of Storsjön, the great lake that's reputed to be home to the country's own Loch Ness monster, Storsjöodjuret. From here trains head in all directions: west into Norway through Sweden's premier **ski** resort, **Åre**; south to Dalarna and Stockholm; east to Sundsvall on the Bothnian coast; and north into the wild terrain of Swedish Lapland.

Dalarna

A sizeable province, **DALARNA** takes in not only the area around **Lake Siljan** but also the ski resorts of **Sälen** and **Idre**, close to the Norwegian border. The area holds a special misty-eyed place in the Swedish psyche and should certainly be seen, although not to the exclusion of places further north. Tiny countryside villages and rolling meadows sweet with the smell of summer flowers make up most of Dalarna, a rural idyll given a handsome backdrop by the land to the northwest of Lake Siljan, which rises slowly to meet the chain of mountains that forms the border with Norway. One small lakeside town can look pretty much like another, so if time is short, restrict yourself to visiting just one or two: **Leksand** and **Mora** are the best options, and the latter is also the starting point for Sweden's most beautiful train journey, along the **Inlandsbanan** to the Arctic Circle.

Highlights

❶ Boat trip, Lake Siljan Take a trip on the serene waters of Lake Siljan and enjoy unparalleled views of the rolling Dalarna countryside. See page 287

❷ Riding the Inlandsbanan A chance to see Sweden's vast forests and fast-flowing rivers close up without leaving the comfort of your train seat. See page 291

❸ Orsa Rovdjurspark, Dalarna Northern Europe's largest bear park offers a unique chance to see these shy animals at close quarters. See page 292

❹ Hiking Get back to nature and experience the wild side of central Sweden in the beautiful mountains around Grövelsjön or in the remote Härjedalen region. See page 295

❺ Årets Näck, Hackås This fun riverside competition featuring naked male fiddle players has its roots in Swedish folklore. See page 303

❻ Monster spotting, Östersund Go hunting for Sweden's version of the Loch Ness monster in this appealing lakeside town. See page 305

HIGHLIGHTS ARE MARKED ON THE MAP ON PAGE 284

> **SWEDEN'S RED HOUSES**
>
> As you travel around Sweden, you can't help but notice that virtually every timber structure is painted deep red. Many outsiders mistakenly see this lack of individuality and expression as stifling social democratic conformity. It is actually more a question of practicality combined with age-old tradition. In a climate as severe as Sweden's, wood needs special protection from the elements: the red paint used for generations on structures across the country, produced in Falun, contains a natural copper preservative. Known as **Falu rödfärg**, this paint is Sweden's aesthetically more pleasing answer to pebbledash.

North of Mora, the province becomes more mountainous and less populous, the only place of note here being **Orsa**, with its fascinating **bear park**. There's no need to worry about **accommodation** in the province: you'll find numerous hotels, hostels and campsites around.

Falun and around

About 220km northwest of Stockholm and 90km west of Gävle, **FALUN** is essentially an industrial town – a pleasant one at that – known for **copper mining**, which began here in the eleventh century. Falun grew in importance during the seventeenth and eighteenth centuries, when its mines produced two-thirds of the world's copper ore. Commensurate with its status as what was then the second-largest town in Sweden, Falun acquired grand buildings and an air of prosperity. In 1761, two fires wiped out virtually all of central Falun, but the few old, wooden houses that survive are worth seeking out to gain an idea of the cramped conditions mine workers had to live in; you'll find these buildings in the districts of **Elsborg** (southwest of the centre), Gamla Herrgården and Östanfors (both north of the centre). Today, the mines, which closed in 1992, can be visited on hour-long guided tours. Falun is also handily placed for a jaunt to nearby **Sundborn**, the former home of well-known artist Carl Larsson, whose back-to-basics paintings have had more than a passing influence on IKEA's designs over the years.

8

Falu Gruva

Falun Mine • Guided tours May–Sept several tours daily depending on demand, no fixed times • Museum Oct 1st–Apr 30th Sat & Sun 10am–3pm, May 1st–June Mon–Fri 10am–4pm, June 15th–Aug 18th Mon–Sun 10am–3.30pm, Aug 19th–Sept 30 Mon–Fri 10am–4pm, Sat & Sun 10am–3pm; Oct–April Tues–Fri 11am–4pm, Sat & Sun 11am–3pm • English commentary available • 230kr tour & museum, 110kr museum only • ⓦ falugruva.se • From the centre of Falun, walk around 1km along Bergshauptmansgatan to the far end

By far the most interesting attraction in Falun is its **copper mines**. Mandatory **guided tours**, lasting around an hour, are organized on the site, beginning with an elevator ride 55m down to a network of old mine roads and drifts. The temperature down below is only 5°C, so make sure you bring warm clothing; try also to wear old shoes, as your footwear is likely to come out tinged red.

The mine museum

The site has a worthy **museum**, recounting the history of Falun's copper production. Conditions below ground in the mines were appalling, said by the botanist Carl von Linné to be as dreadful as hell itself. One of the most dangerous aspects of eighteenth-century copper mining was the presence everywhere in the mines of **vitriol** gases, which are strong preservatives. It's recorded that the body of a young man known as *Fet Mats* (Fat Mats) was found in the mines in 1719; though he'd died 49 years previously in an accident, his corpse was so well preserved when discovered that his erstwhile fiancée, by then an old woman, recognized him immediately.

Stora Stöten

While you're at the mine, be sure not to miss peering into the **Great Pit** (Stora Stöten), just nearby, which is 100m deep and 300–400m wide. It suddenly appeared on Midsummer's Day in 1687, when the entire pit caved in – the result of extensive mining and the unsystematic driving of galleries and shafts.

Dalarnas Museum

Stigaregatan 2–4 • Tues–Fri 10am–5pm, Sat & Sun noon–5pm • Free • ⓦ dalarnasmuseum.se

In Falun's centre, the riverside **Dalarnas Museum** makes for a worthwhile visit. It contains sections on the province's folk art, the Dala horse, dresses and music, as well as a reconstruction, on the ground floor, of the dark, heavily wood-panelled study where the author Selma Lagerlöf (see page 375) worked when she moved to Villavägen 34 in Falun in 1897. Copies of Lagerlöf's books, including her most famous work *Nils Holgerssons underbara resa genom Sverige* ("The Wonderful Adventures of Nils"), are displayed on the bookshelves, and you can also see a number of black-and-white photographs of her and her home. Look out, too, for the curious black-and-white photographs of the bin Laden family, who visited Falun in 1971 on a family holiday to Sweden when Osama was a teenager.

Carl Larssongården

Obligatory guided tours May–Sept daily 10am–5pm (at least 1 daily in English); advance booking essential • 45min • 220kr • ⓦ carllarsson.se • Bus #237 (hourly; 15min) from Falun bus station

"It was here I experienced the unspeakably delightful feeling of seclusion from all the world's noise and din". Carl Larsson's words on living in Sundborn

Ideally placed for an easy day trip from Falun, the village of **SUNDBORN**, just 13km to the northeast, was once home to artist Carl Larsson. The delightful **Carl Larssongården** – one of Sweden's most visited tourist attractions – was at first the summer dwelling of Carl and his wife Karin, later becoming their permanent home. The artist's own murals and portraits of his children form part of the decor, as do the embroidery and tapestries of his wife. At the start of the twentieth century, when the Larssons had done the place up, the house represented a decorative style for Sweden, its bright, warm interior quite unlike the dark and sober colours used until that time. The artist is buried in the churchyard just outside. Guided tours are obligatory and can be booked online.

ARRIVAL AND DEPARTURE — FALUN

By train Falun is easily reached by train from Stockholm, Arlanda airport and Uppsala, and there are also useful through services from Gävle and Örebro. The train station is southeast of the centre.

Destinations Arlanda airport (2 hourly; 2hr 15min); Gävle (2 hourly; 1hr); Stockholm (2 hourly; 2hr 40min); Örebro (2 hourly; 2hr 30min); Uppsala (2 hourly; 2hr).

By bus The bus station is adjacent to the train station and is known as Knutpunkten.

INFORMATION

Tourist office Opposite the *First Grand* hotel at Trotzgatan 10–12 (Mon–Fri 10am–5pm, Sat 10am–2pm, Sun 11am– 2pm; mid-Aug to mid-June closed Sun; ☏ 0771 62 62 62, ⓦ visitsodradalarna.se).

ACCOMMODATION

Clarion Collection Bergmästaren Bergskolegränd 7 ☏ 023 70 17 00, ⓦ nordicchoicehotels.se. For a homely feel, with elegant furniture and rooms decorated in soft pastel shades, try this place between the train station and the main square, which has a superb sauna suite complete with Jacuzzi and gym. A free evening buffet dinner is included in the room rate. 970kr/1350kr

Falun Trotzgatan 16 ☏ 023 291 80, ⓦ hotelfalun.nu.

Falun's hotel has a good central location, and all double rooms have private facilities. Rooms have been recently redecorated and feature soft, autumnal colours. Youth hostel members receive a discount because the hotel is associated with STF. 1365kr/1990kr

First Grand Falun Trotzgatan 9–11 ☏ 023 79 48 80, ⓦ firsthotels.se. The swankiest hotel in town is the central *First Grand*, whose rooms are sumptuous to say the least.

However, it's the generously sized pool, spa and gym which really make a stay here worth the money. **880kr/1160kr**
Lugnets Camping Lugnetvägen 5 ☎023 654 00, ⓦ lugnetscamping.se. The nearest campsite is up at Lugnet by the National Ski Stadium, 1.5km from the town centre. Choose between cabins with full self-catering facilities or much smaller, simpler ones. Tents **185kr**, small cabins **395kr**, self-catering cabins **695kr**

STF Falu Vandrarhem Vandrarvägen 3 ☎046 23 105 60, ⓦ stffalun.se; bus #11 or #243 from the centre to Koppartorget or Hosjö, and get off at "Koppartorget". Falun's hostel is located 4km from the centre in the Haraldsbo part of town. Rooms are located in three separate single-storey brick buildings which each have a guest kitchen. Dorms **265kr**, doubles **600kr**

EATING AND DRINKING

★ **Banken** Åsgatan 41 ☎023 71 19 11, ⓦ bankenfalun. se. This trendy bistro, with a grand stuccoed ceiling, takes its name from the former bank that once stood here. Changing modern Swedish dishes make up the menu (mains 165–285kr), although there are always burgers (175kr), steaks (325kr) and pasta dishes (165kr) available, too. Mon–Wed 11.30am–10pm, Thurs & Fri 11.30am–11pm, Sat 1–11pm.

Bishops Arms Vattugränd 6. ☎046 23 193 00, ⓦ bishopsarms.com/falun. One of *the* places to be seen, this fake English pub has wooden beams and plenty of brass ornaments, and serves a range of bar meals such as burgers and steaks as well as a good selection of beer on tap. Mon & Sun 4–10pm, Tues 4–11pm, Wed & Thurs 4–11.45pm, Fri 3pm–2am, Sat 1pm–2am & Sun 4–10pm.

The Kings Arms Falugatan 3 ☎023 71 13 44. A bit of a drinkers' den, attracting a crowd of regular locals who know every face that walks through the door. Serves bar meals such as burgers (135kr), fish and chips (145kr), chicken

fillet (175kr) and pytt i panna (120kr). Mon, Tues & Thurs 11am–10pm, Wed 11am–10pm, Fri 11am–2am, Sat noon–2am, Sun noon–9pm.

Rådhuskällaren Slaggatan 2 ☎023 71 13 22, ⓦ radhuskallarenfalun.se. Located under the Rådhus, this is an atmospheric place to indulge, whether in a succulent fillet of venison with artichoke and caramelized salsify (260kr) or a bowl of creamy seafood tagliatelle (150kr.) In summer there's a pleasant outdoor terrace up above the street at the rear. Mon & Tues 11am–2pm, Wed & Thurs 11am–2pm & 5–11pm, Fri 11am–2pm & 4pm–2am, Sat 5pm–2am.

Smak Tapas Deli & Mera Åsgatan 31 ☎023 702 20 75, ⓦ smakochmera.se. A venture for Falun and a real treat, this deli-cum-restaurant serves a tempting range of fish and meat dishes such as hake and pork chops, as well as an excellent goulash soup. Prices are respectable, too – lunch is under 100kr. Daily 11am–11pm.

8

Around Lake Siljan

Things have changed since Baedeker, writing in 1889, observed that "Lake Siljan owes much of its interest to the inhabitants of its banks, who have preserved many of their primitive characteristics. In their idea of cleanliness they are somewhat behind the age." Today it's not the people who draw your attention but the setting. **Lake Siljan**, created millions of years ago when a meteorite crashed into the earth, is what many people come to Sweden for, its gently rolling surroundings, traditions and local handicrafts weaving a subtle spell on the visitor. There's a lush feel to much of the region, the charm of the forest heightened by its proximity to the lake, all of which adds a pleasing dimension to the low-profile towns and villages that interrupt the rural scenery. Only **Mora** stands out as being bigger and busier, with the hustle and bustle of holiday-makers and countless caravans crowding the place in summer.

MUSIK VID SILJAN

Should you be around during the first week or so of July, don't miss **Musik vid Siljan**, nine days of musical performances in lakeside churches, the stunning former limestone quarry, Dalhalla, and at various locations out in the surrounding forest. The range of music covered is exceptionally wide, including chamber music, jazz, traditional folk songs and dance band music, with proceedings starting in the early morning and carrying on until late evening every day. Full details at ⓦ musikvidsiljan.se.

Leksand

Perhaps the most traditional of the Dalarna villages is **LEKSAND**, about 50km northwest of Falun. There's little to do here other than take it easy, but it's certainly worth making the effort to reach at **midsummer**, when it stages festivals recalling age-old dances performed around the **maypole** (Sweden's maypoles are erected in June – in May the trees here are still bare and the ground can be covered with snow), and featuring *kyrkbåtar* boat races (see box).

Leksands kyrka

Kyrkallén 27 • Daily 9.30am–3.30pm

A relaxing stroll along the riverside brings you to **Leksands kyrka**, one of Sweden's biggest village churches; it has existed in its present form since 1715, although the oldest parts of the building date back to the thirteenth century. The church enjoys one of the most stunning locations of any in the land, its peaceful churchyard lined with whispering spruce trees and looking out over the lake to the distant shore.

Hembygdsgård

Homestead Museum • Kyrkallén 3 • No set hours • Free

Next door to the church is the region's best open-air **Hembygdsgård** – about a dozen old timber buildings grouped around a maypole, ranging from simple square huts used to store hay during the long winter months to a magnificent *parstuga*, which forms the centrepiece of the collection. Built in 1793, this two-storey dwelling, constructed of thick circular logs, is notable because buildings of the period were rarely more than one storey in height, since timber was expensive. From directly behind the museum a narrow track leads down to the lake, where there's a reconstruction of a church boathouse used to house the *kyrkbåtar* for which Dalarna is known throughout Sweden.

Lake cruises

May–Sept: timetables vary – check sailing times at ⓦ wasanet.nu • 2hr cruise 125kr, trip to Mora 250kr

Whilst in Leksand, it's worth taking one of the summer **cruises** on Lake Siljan aboard the lovely old steamship *M/S Gustaf Wasa*, built in Stockholm in 1876, which depart from the quay near the homestead museum; take the track down to the reconstructed boathouse (see above) and turn left following the lakeside to the bridge and the quay. Excursions include a two-hour cruise on the lake, and a boat trip to Mora, returning by train.

ARRIVAL AND INFORMATION

By train Trains run between Mora and Borlänge via Leksand in both directions (every 2hr or so). The journey from Mora takes 40min, from Borlänge 30min.

Tourist office Norsgatan 27E (late June to mid-Aug Mon–Fri 9am–6pm, Sat 10am–4pm, July also Sun 10am–4pm; mid-Aug to late June Tues–Fri noon–5pm; ☎0248 79 72 00, ⓦsiljan.se). The office is a 10min walk from the train station up Villagatan towards the centre of town, then left along Sparbanksgatan and right into Norsgatan which becomes Kyrkallén.

MIDSUMMER KYRKBÅTAR RACES

Dalarna's **midsummer celebrations** are the most famous in Sweden, and culminate in the **church boat (kyrkbåtar) races**, a waterborne procession of sleek wooden longboats, which the locals once rowed to church on Sundays. The races start on Midsummer's Day in **Siljansnäs** – take the roughly hourly bus #84 from Leksand – and continue for ten days at different locations around the lake; the races hit Leksand on the first Saturday in July. Leksand's tourist office will have details of the arrangements for each summer's races.

ACCOMMODATION

★ **Korstäppens Herrgård** Hjortnäsvägen 33 ☎0247 123 10, ⓦkorstappan.se. This wonderful old manor house is tastefully decked out in traditional Dalarna colours. Its sitting and dining rooms look out over the lake, whose lapping waters can be reached by a path behind the hotel. **1250kr**

Leksand Strand Siljansvägen 61 ☎0247 138 00, ⓦleksandstrand.se. This lovely lakeside campsite, a 20min walk from the tourist office along Tällbergsvägen, has a sandy beach along Lake Siljan as well as its own swimming pool. There are also cabins for rent. Tents **200kr**, cabins **595kr**

Moskogen Insjövägen 50 ☎0247 146 00, ⓦmoskogen.

com. Instead of traditional hotel rooms, this place offers accommodation in comfortable rooms inside log cabins which come fully equipped with running water, private bathroom, kitchenette and fridge. A buffet breakfast is included in the price. **1260kr**

STF Leksand Vandrarhem Parkgattu 6 ☎046 24 76 48 00, ⓦvandrarhemleksand.se; ask the hostel for details of public transport options. Leksand's cosy STF hostel is one of the oldest in Sweden, located around 2.5km from the train station, over the river. Accommodation is in small wooden cabins as well as in regular rooms in the main building. Open April–Oct. Doubles **500kr**

EATING AND DRINKING

Bosporen Torget 1 ☎0247 132 80, ⓦbosporen.com. Feeding the folk of Leksand for over thirty years, this is the village's main restaurant, located in the tiny pedestrianized main square, serving pizzas from 110kr as well as meat and fish dishes such as pork schnitzel (240kr) and plaice (185kr). Be careful what you order though because prices have shot up in recent years and do not always represent good value for money. Mon–Thurs 3–10pm, Fri 3pm–midnight, Sat noon–midnight, Sun noon–10pm.

Pizzeria Napoli Norsgatan 17 ☎0247 150 75,

ⓦnapolileksand.se. Leksand's one and only Italian restaurant is justifiably popular with locals and visitors alike. The menu is heavy on pub grub such as pizza (around 179kr). Sun–Thurs 11am–9pm, Fri & Sat 11am–10pm.

Siljans Konditori Sparbanksgatan 5 ⓦsiljanskonditori. se. The summer terrace is a wonderful place from which to watch the world go by while sipping a cup of coffee. They serve up sandwiches with fantastic home-made bread, and salads and quiches. Mon–Fri 8.30am–6pm, Sat 9am–5pm, Sun 10am–5pm.

Tällberg

If you believe the tourist blurb, then **TÄLLBERG**, all lakeside log cabins amid rolling hills, *is* Dalarna. Situated on a promontory in the lake 10km north of Leksand, this folksy hillside village, whose wooden cottages are draped with flowers in summer, first became famous in 1850 when the Danish writer Hans Christian Andersen paid it a visit; on his return to Copenhagen, he wrote that everyone should experience Tällberg's peace and tranquillity, and marvel at its wonderful lake views. Ever since, hordes of tourists have flooded into the tiny village to see what all the fuss was about – prepare yourself for the crowds that unfortunately take the shine off what is otherwise quite a pretty little place. Tällberg today is also a prime destination for wealthy middle-aged Swedes, who come to enjoy the good life for a few days, savour the delicious food dished up by the village's hotels, and admire the fantastic views out over Lake Siljan. To escape the crowds, walk down the steep hill of Sjögattu, past the campsite, to the calm lapping water of the lake and a small sandy beach; keep going through the trees to find a couple of more secluded spots.

ARRIVAL AND DEPARTURE   TÄLLBERG

By train Tällberg is on the main train line round Lake Siljan, with services running between Mora and Borlänge every

2hr or so; Mora is a 30min journey, Borlänge is 45min. The station is a 10–15min walk from the village.

ACCOMMODATION

★ **Siljansgården** Sjögattu 36 ☎0247 500 40, ⓦsiljansgarden.com. For accommodation, avoid the expensive hotels and head down Sjögattu to this wonderful old wooden farm building with a cobbled courtyard and a fountain, and rooms that are comparable to those in hostels. **600kr**

Tällbergs Camping Sjögattu 38 ☎0247 513 10, ⓦtallbergscamping.se. Head down to the lakeshore and turn left to find this delightful lakeside campsite; note there are no cabins here and facilities are basic but clean. Tents **175kr**

8

Mora and around

At the northwestern corner of the lake, 60km from Leksand, **MORA** is the best place to head for hereabouts. An appealing, laid-back town, its main draws are two excellent museums, one dedicated to the painter Anders Zorn, and the other to the Vasaloppet ski race. It's also handy for onward trains on the Inlandsbanan (see box) and for moving on to the ski resorts of Idre (see page 294) and Sälen (see page 293).

Zornmuséet and Zorngården

Vasagatan 36 • Museum Daily June–Aug 9am–5pm; Sept–May 11am–4pm • House Daily June–Aug 9.30am–4pm; Sept–May guided tours at 1pm, 2pm & 3pm • Museum 100kr, house 70kr, combined ticket 160kr • ⓦ zorn.se

The main attraction in Mora is the outstanding **Zornmuséet**, showcasing the work of Sweden's best-known painter, **Anders Zorn** (1860–1920), who moved here in 1896. Most successful as a portrait painter, he worked in both oil and watercolour and spent periods living in both St Ives in Britain and Paris. Zorn even went to the United States to paint American Presidents Cleveland, Theodore Roosevelt and Taft. At the museum, look out for his larger-than-life self-portrait dressed in wolfskin from 1915 and the especially pleasing *Midnatt* (Midnight) from 1891, which depicts a woman rowing on Lake Siljan, her hands blue from the cold night air. The artist's remarkable silver collection, containing four hundred pieces ranging from tankards to teaspoons, is also on display.

Across the lawn of the Zornmuséet is Anders Zorn's home, **Zorngården**, where the artist and his wife Emma lived during the early twentieth century. What really makes the place unusual is the cavernous 10m-high hall with a steeply V-shaped roof, entirely constructed from wood and decked out in traditional Dalarna designs and patterns, where the couple lived out their roles as darlings of local society.

Vasaloppsmuséet

Ski Museum • Vasaloppets Hus, Vasagatan • Mon–Wed & Fri 8am–noon & 1–5pm, Thurs 8am–noon & 1–3pm • Free • ⓦ vasaloppet.se/en/about-us/the-vasaloppet-museum

East of the Zorn Museum, on the other side of Vasagatan, the **Vasaloppsmuséet** covers the history of the ski race, **Vasaloppet**, held on the first Sunday in March. The event commemorates King Gustav Vasa's return to Mora after he escaped from the Danes on skis; two men from Mora caught up with him and persuaded him to come back to their town, where they gave him refuge. The longest cross-country ski race in the world, the competition was the idea of a local newspaper editor, who organized the first event in 1922; it was won by a 22-year-old from Västerbotten who took seven and a half hours to complete the course. Today, professionals take barely four hours to cover the 90km. Although the Vasaloppet enjoys royal patronage (the current Swedish king has skied it), it does have a somewhat chequered past, since women were forbidden from taking part until 1981. Whilst at the museum, make sure you watch the half-hour **film** (with English subtitles) about the race – the impressive aerial shots really help to convey the massive scale of the competition.

THE DALA HORSE

No matter where you travel in Sweden, you'll come across small wooden figurines known as **Dala horses** (*dalahästar*). Their bright red colour, stumpy legs and garish floral decorations are, for many foreigners, high kitsch and rather ugly; the Swedes, however, adore bright colours (the redder the better) and love the little horses – it's virtually an unwritten rule that every household in the country should have a couple on display. Two brothers from the town of **Nusnäs**, **Nils** and **Jannes Olsson**, began carving the horses in the family baking shed in 1928, when they were just teenagers. Though they were simply interested in selling their work to help their cash-strapped parents make ends meet, somehow the wooden horses started catching on – Swedes are at a loss to explain why – and soon they were appearing across the country as a symbol of rural life.

THE INLANDSBANAN

Stretching over 1000km from Mora to Gällivare, north of the Arctic Circle, the privately operated **Inlandsbanan**, the Inland Railway, is a great way of travelling off the beaten track through central and northern Sweden; onboard guides provide commentaries and information about places along the route to ensure you get the most out of the journey. State-owned until 1992, it's now run as a private venture, supported by the fifteen municipalities that the route passes through.

INLANDSBANAN PRACTICALITIES

Trains run on the Inlandsbanan for a few months in the summer, generally between late June and late August, though the exact operating season varies year to year, so check the latest timetable at ⓦ inlandsbanan.se. To give an idea of **prices**, Mora–Östersund is 600kr, a seat reservation is an extra 50kr and a bike costs 100kr; InterRail cards are valid. **Timetables** are only approximate, and the train will stop whenever the driver feels like it – perhaps for a spot of wild-strawberry picking or to watch a beaver damming a stream. Generally there's one daily train north from Mora at around 2.45pm, with a connecting train running from Gothenburg via Kristinehamn (the original starting point of the line) from July to mid-August. Done in one go, the journey from Mora to Gällivare lasts two days, with an overnight stop in Östersund. It's a much better idea, though, to take it at a more relaxed pace, with a couple of stops along the route (you can break your journey as many times as you like on one ticket).

If you're planning using the Inlandsbanan a lot, consider investing in the **Inland Railway Card** (Inlandsbanekort; 1995kr), which gives unlimited travel for two weeks.

8

Grannas A. Olssons Hemslöjd

Nusnäs • Mid-June–mid-Aug Mon–Fri 9am–6pm; mid-Aug–mid-June Mon–Fri 9am–4pm • Free • ⓦ grannas.com • Bus #324 from Mora to Nusnäs (every 1–2hr; 20min)

Whilst in Mora you might want to consider a visit to **NUSNÄS**, just east of town on the lakeside, where you'll find **Grannas A. Olssons Hemslöjd**, the **workshop** of the Olsson brothers, creators of Sweden's much-loved **Dala horses** (see box). Skilled craftsmen carve the horses out of wood from the pine forests around Lake Siljan and then hand-paint and varnish them.

ARRIVAL AND DEPARTURE   MORA

By train For the centre of town, you should leave the train at Morastrand station (which consists of little more than a platform), one stop after the main Mora station on trains coming from the south; the Inlandsbanan (see box) begins at Morastrand before calling at Mora station.

Destinations Gothenburg (July to mid-Aug 1 daily; 6hr 30min); Leksand (2 hourly; 45min); Östersund (summer

1 daily; 5hr 45min); Stockholm (2 daily; 3hr 45min); Sveg (summer 1 daily; 2hr 45min); Uppsala (2 daily; 3hr).
By bus The bus station is at Moragatan, close to Morastrand and just off the main Strandgatan.

Destinations Idre (2 daily; 2hr 30min); Orsa (hourly; 30min); Östersund (2 daily; 5hr 20min); Sälen (1 daily; 2hr); Sveg (2 daily; 2hr).

INFORMATION

Tourist office Köpmannagatan 3A (late June to mid-Aug Mon–Fri 9am–6pm, Sat 10am–4pm, July also Sun 10am–4pm; mid-Aug to late June Mon–Fri noon–5pm, Sat 10am–2pm; ☎ 046 77 162 62 62, ⓦ siljan.se). Has all

the usual literature, including a map of the Vasaloppsleden hiking route, which you can follow north from Mora to Sälen (see page 293).

ACCOMMODATION

Although Mora sees a sizeable influx of tourists for the Vasaloppet ski race (see opposite) and during the summer season, there's a surprising lack of choice in terms of places to **stay**. Hence, it pays to book ahead, for mid-June to mid-August in particular.

Kung Gösta Kristinebergsgatan 1 ☎ 0250 150 70, ⓦ kunggosta.se. Close to the main train station, this is a modern hotel with identikit rooms in three price ranges: economy, standard and comfort – though to be honest there's not a lot to choose between them, and you may as well plump for the cheapest option and save yourself some kroner. The hotel has an excellent swimming pool and a refurbished gym, too. 945kr/1380kr

Mora Hotell & Spa Strandgatan 12 ☎ 0250 59 26 50, ⓦ morahotell.se. Mora's biggest and best hotel, opposite Morastrand station, with both modern and old-fashioned rooms hung with Zorn pictures. There's also a first-class sauna suite and gym with pool and Jacuzzi. Prices are rather steep for such a provincial location. 1245kr/1645kr

Mora Parken Parkvägen 1 ☎ 0250 276 00, ⓦ mora parken.se. A comfortable modern hotel catering for families

with children; there's a playground nearby as well as a lake for swimming. It also has a selection of cottages for rent. It's a 10min walk from the centre along Hantverkaregatan, which begins near the bus station. Doubles 995kr/1295kr, cottages from 330kr

STF Mora Målkullan Vandrarhem Björnramsgatan 2 ☎ 046 250 381 96, ⓦ malkullan.se. A comfortable hostel in the heart of Mora at the finishing line for the Vasaloppet race, with double rooms as well as dorm beds located in two separate buildings; there are some rooms with private facilities. Dorms 250k, doubles 520kr

EATING AND DRINKING

China House Moragatan 1, ☎ 0250 152 40, ⓦ mora china.se. The food here isn't overly authentic but this is the only Chinese restaurant for miles around. There are both Chinese and Thai dishes on the menu, with mains starting at 150kr (three-course set menu 180kr). Alternatively there are steaks, from 250kr. Mon–Thurs 11am–10pm, Fri 11am–11pm, Sat noon–11pm, Sun noon–10pm.

★ **Vasagatan 32** Vasagatan 32 ☎ 0250 102 27, ⓦ restaurangvasagatan32.se. With walls decorated with black-and-white photos of the Vasaloppet, this bright and airy restaurant is a breath of fresh air. Well-prepared classic

dishes such as pan-fried salmon and Arctic char go for 125–200kr; lunch is in the form of a buffet, with a choice of a couple of main dishes for 90kr. Mon–Thurs 11am–10pm, Fri & Sat noon–11pm, Sun noon–9pm.

Wasastugan Tingsnäsvägen 6 ☎ 0250 177 92, ⓦ wasastugan.nu. Set within a huge log building between the main train station and the Vasaloppsmuséet, this restaurant-pub serves up Cajun dishes, such as blackened salmon (220kr), chicken fajitas (170kr) and a massive barbecue burger (180kr) that really hits the spot. Mon–Thurs & Sun 11am–11pm, Fri & Sat 11am–2am.

Orsa and the bear park

An uneventful little place barely 20km from Mora, **ORSA**'s draw is its location beside Lake Orsasjön, a northerly adjunct of Lake Siljan – right in the heart of Sweden's **bear country** – and its fascinating bear and predator park. It's reckoned that there are a good few hundred brown bears roaming the dense forests around town, though few sightings are made in the wild.

Orsa Rovdjurspark

Bear and Predator Park · Orsa Grönklitt, 16km from Orsa · Daily mid-June–mid-Aug 10am–5pm; mid-Aug– mid-June 10am–3pm · 285kr · ⓦ orsarovdjurspark.se · Bus #342 from Orsa bus station (1–2 daily); from Mora, take #141 to Orsa and then change

The **Orsa Rovdjurspark** is the biggest **bear park** in Europe. The bears here aren't tamed or caged, but wander around the 325 thousand square metres of the forested park at will, much as they would in the wild. It's the human visitors who are confined, having to clamber up viewing platforms and along covered walkways.

The bears are fascinating to watch: they're gentle and vegetarian for the most part (though occasionally they're fed the odd dead reindeer or elk that's been killed on the roads). Trying hard not to be upstaged by the bears are a few lynx, wolves and wolverines, the other three Swedish predators – although you'll be lucky to spot the wolverines in particular; in fact, it's a good idea to bring along a pair of binoculars to help you pick out any rustlings in the undergrowth.

Ever-expanding, the park features a **Polar World** section, where you'll find a small number of polar bears, though how at ease they are with the mild Swedish summer is an open question. The park also has some snow leopards, Siberian tigers, Kamchatka bears from eastern Russia and a pair of Eurasian eagle owls, the largest owl in the world, and found throughout Sweden's forests.

ARRIVAL AND INFORMATION   ORSA

By train Orsa's train station for Inlandsbanan arrivals and departures is right in the centre of town on Järnvägsgatan, opposite the bus station. Trains to and from Mora (July to mid-Aug 1 daily) take 20min.

By bus There are frequent buses to Mora (1–2 hourly; 25min). **Tourist office** Dalagatan 1, Orsa (late June to mid-Aug Mon–Fri 9am–6pm, Sat 10am–4pm, July also Sun 10am–

4pm; mid-Aug to late June Tues–Fri noon–5pm; ☎0248 79 72 00, ⓦsiljan.se). Near the train and bus stations, this office can help with local accommodation.

ACCOMMODATION AND EATING

Orsa Grönklitt ☎0250 462 00, ⓦorsagronklitt.se. Should you want to stay up at the bear park itself there's a well-equipped hostel with double rooms and also a number of cabins for rent. **310kr**
STF Orsa Vandrarhem Gillevägen 3 ☎0250 421 70, ⓦorsavandrarhem.se. A beautifully located hostel, 1km west of the centre by the side of Orsasjön lake; some rooms have private facilities and some also have showers. There

are two fully fitted kitchens for guest use, and in summer breakfast is also available for 75kr. Doubles **550kr**
Ugglan & Björnen Next door to the hostel at Grönklitt ☎0250 462 31, ⓦdalasmaker.se/ugglan-bjornen. There are filling Swedish meals available on site here; reindeer fillet is 345kr or burger and fries is 175kr, though, arguably the generous lunch buffet is the best deal. Daily 11am–9pm.

Northwestern Dalarna

The area to the northwest of Mora offers travellers approaching from the south a first taste of what northern Sweden is really all about. The villages in this remote part of Dalarna are few and far between, separated by great swathes of coniferous forest which thrive on the poor sandy soils of the hills and mountains which predominate here. On its way to the Norwegian border, **Route 70**, the main artery through this part of the province, slowly climbs up the eastern side of the Österdalälven River valley. After the tiny village of Åsen, the road leaves the river behind and strikes further inland towards the mountains which mark the border between Sweden and Norway. Buses to Särna, Idre and Grövelsjön follow this route, whereas services to Sälen only travel as far as Älvdalen before heading west towards Route 297.

It is predominantly to ski (in winter) or to hike (in summer) that most visitors come to this part of Dalarna. Indeed, **Sälen** and **Idre** are two of Sweden's most popular **ski resorts** and, in season, the slopes and cross-country trails here are busy with Swedes from further south, where snowfall is less certain. In summer, though, **Grövelsjön** makes a better destination than its sleepy neighbours, thanks to some superb hiking trails through the mountains which begin here.

Sälen

Considered as one entity, **SÄLEN** and the surrounding resorts of Lindvallen, Högfjället, Tandådalen, Hundfjället, Rörbäcksnäs and Stöten constitute the biggest **ski centre** in the Nordic area, with over a hundred pistes and guaranteed snow from November to May. It isn't unreasonable to lump all these places together, as each of the minor resorts, despite having its own ski slope, is dependent on Sälen for shops (not least its Systembolaget) and services. Novice skiers can take advantage of Sälen's special lifts,

> ### HIKING AROUND SÄLEN
> The route taken by skiers on the first Sunday in March during the annual Vasaloppet race (see page 290), the 90km-long **Vasaloppsleden** from Sälen to **Mora**, is equally rewarding to explore on foot. The path starts just outside Sälen, in **Berga**, and first runs uphill to Smågan, then downhill all the way to Mora via Mångsbodarna, Risberg, Evertsberg, Oxberg, Hökberg and Eldris. For **accommodation**, there are eight **cabins** along the route, each equipped with a stove and unmade beds.
> Another hike to consider is the little-known **southern Kungsleden**, which starts at the *Högfjällshotellet* in the resort of **Högfjället**, a few kilometres west of Sälen, and leads to **Drevdagen**, a 30min drive west of Idre off Route 70 (bus #395 runs once daily Mon–Fri between Idre and Drevdagen), where it continues to Grövelsjön and all the way north to **Storlien**. There's no accommodation on the Högfjället–Drevdagen stretch.

nursery slopes and qualified tuition; there are also plenty of intermediate runs through the densely forested hillsides and, for advanced skiers, twenty testing runs as well as an off-piste area. To get the best value for money, it's really worth buying a package rather than trying to book individual nights at local hotels; prices are high and in season they're packed to capacity.

During the **summer**, Sälen specializes in assorted **outdoor activities** – fishing, canoeing and beaver safaris are all available, and the hills, lakes and rivers around the town will keep you busy for several days. There's also some fantastic hiking to be had in the immediate vicinity (see box).

ARRIVAL AND INFORMATION SÄLEN

By bus Bus #133 heads from Mora to Sälen (generally 1 daily Mon–Fri; 2hr; see ⓦdalatrafik.se for times). The bus calls at each resort in turn, terminating at Stöten.
Tourist office Inside the Centrumhuset building on the straggly main street that runs through the village (late April to late June & mid-Aug to Nov Mon–Fri 9am–5pm, Sat 10am–2pm; ☎046 0771 62 62 62, ⓦvisitdalarna.se/en/malungsalen).

ACCOMMODATION

Högfjällshotellet Högfjället ☎0280 870 00, ⓦhogis.se; bus (3 daily) from Sälen. A wonderfully situated hotel just inside the tree line at Högfjället, a few kilometres west of Sälen. It has a restaurant and a bar with fantastic panoramic views, a superb sauna suite in the basement and a swimming pool with whirlpool and jet streams. Only open during the ski season. **1995kr**

STF Sälen Vandrarhem Gräsheden, near Stöten ☎0280 820 40, ⓦsalensvandrarhem.se; bus from Sälen. With undisturbed mountain views, this great hostel is really out in the wilds; the bus from Sälen to Stöten will drop you close by, though you need to reserve ahead before heading out. Breakfast can be ordered in advance and there's a kitchen, laundry room and sauna. Doubles **590kr**

Idre and around

IDRE is one of Sweden's main **ski resorts** and home to the country's southernmost community of reindeer-herding *Sámi*. However, if you're expecting wooden huts and reindeer herders dressed in traditional dress, you'll be disappointed – the remaining six herding families live in conventional houses in the area around Idre, and dress like everyone else. Idre is a tiny one-street affair; if you come in summer, stay in the village rather than up the hill at Idrefjäll, which will be completely void of life. The main street, where the bus drops you, is where you'll find everything of any significance, including a supermarket and bank.

The continental climate here – Idre is located at one of the wider points of the Scandinavian peninsula, and thus isn't prone to the warming influence of the Atlantic – means that the **summers** are relatively dry; consequently, Idre, like its fellow ski resort, Sälen (see page 293), offers plenty of seasonal **outdoor activities**. Its tourist office can help arrange fishing trips, horseriding, mountain biking, tennis, climbing and golf. There are some good sandy beaches along the western shore of **Idresjön**, a lake that's a kilometre east of town; you can rent canoes through the tourist office. Staff can also advise on local hiking routes: nearby Grövelsjön (see box) has some of the best hiking anywhere in central Sweden.

Idre's ski slopes are up the mountain at **IDREFJÄLL**, one of the most reliable places for snow in the entire country, with particularly cold winters. Although not quite on the scale of Sälen, Idre's ski resort manages to be Sweden's third largest and one of the most important in the Nordic area. In winter the place is buzzing – not only with skiers but also with reindeer, who wander down the main street hoping to lick the salt off the roads.

Njupeskär waterfall

There's no public transport from Idre; by car, take the main road to Särna, then turn right following signs for Mörkret and later for Njupeskärsvattenfall

DAY-HIKES FROM GRÖVELSJÖN

Grövelsjön *fjällstation* makes an ideal base for **hikes** (summer only) out into the surrounding countryside, with a variety of routes available, some lasting a day, others several days.

Among the established **day-hikes** is the clearly marked route (16km round-trip) from the *fjällstation* up to **Storvätteshågnen** (1183m), with fantastic views over the surrounding peaks and across the border into Norway.

Another worthwhile hike starts with a short walk from the *fjällstation* to Sjöstugan on **Lake Grövelsjön** (roughly 1.5km away), from where you take the morning boat to the northern (Norwegian) end of the lake. You can return along the lakeshore to the *fjällstation* (9km) by way of the Linné path, following in the footsteps of the famous botanist who walked this route in 1734. It's possible to do the whole route in the opposite direction, heading out along the Linné path in the morning and returning by boat in the late afternoon; ask at the *fjällstation* for details of boat departure times.

A third option is to strike out along the path leading northwest from Sjöstugan, heading for the Norwegian border and **Salsfjellet** (1281m) on the other side of it (16km round-trip). There's no need to take your passport as the border is all but invisible; people wander back and forth across it quite freely.

With your own transport, it's an easy day-trip from Idre to see the stunning waterfall, **Njupeskär**, near the village of Särna, 30km away. The waterfall is Sweden's highest, with a drop of 125m. In winter it's particularly popular with **ice climbers**, as the waterfall freezes completely. An easy, circular **walking route** is clearly signposted from the car park to the waterfall and back, making for a good two-hour hike.

8

ARRIVAL AND INFORMATION   IDRE AND AROUND

By bus Bus #104 from Mora follows the densely forested valley of the Österdalälven on its 2hr 30min journey to Idre (Mon–Fri 5 daily, Sat & Sun 2 daily, less frequent in summer; timetables are at ⓦdalatrafik.se). There are 2 daily buses from Idre up to the ski slopes at Idrefjäll (20min).

Tourist office Framgårdsvägen 1 (mid-June to mid-Aug daily 10am–6pm; mid-Aug to mid-June Mon–Fri 9am–5pm; ☎0253 59 82 00, ⓦvisitdalarna.se/en/visitidre). The office is located in a turf-roofed building off the main street, Byvägen, near the entrance to Idre when approaching from Mora.

ACCOMMODATION AND EATING

Pernilla Wiberg Idrefjäll ☎0253 59 30 00, ⓦpernilla wiberghotel.se. Idrefjäll's main hotel is named after one of Sweden's most successful downhill skiers. The hotel has access to the surrounding ski slopes and lifts, and boasts a state-of-the-art sauna suite and modern, well-appointed rooms. Big summer discounts. 720kr/1580kr

Restaurang Lodjuret Framgårdsvägen 1 ☎0253 200 12. This restaurant next to the tourist office has a range of tasty home-cooking specials as well as pizzas and pasta dishes for around 175kr. Daily 11am–10pm.

Sporthotellet Högstvägen 7 2, Idre ☎046 72 564 19 74, ⓦsporthotelletidre.se. Small, comfortable hotel a 10min walk north of Idre's main road. Its rooms are rather small and basic but they're clean and come with private facilities. There's also a guest kitchen on site. 1050kr

Grövelsjön

Surrounded by nature reserves and national parks, **GRÖVELSJÖN**, 45km northwest of Idre and reachable by bus #104 from Mora via Idre, is where the road ends and the mountains and wilderness really start. The area is renowned throughout Sweden for its stark, beautiful mountain scenery and great hiking (see box); in summer, the pasture around here is home to hundreds of grazing reindeer.

ACCOMMODATION   GRÖVELSJÖN

STF Grövelsjön fjällstation ☎46-101902430, ⓦgrovelsjon.se. This is virtually the only building here, with a variety of rooms with private facilities and prices depending on the season; it boasts a restaurant, kitchen, sauna, massage room and solarium. Open all year. Doubles 690kr

Härjedalen

From Mora and Orsa, the Inlandsbanan trundles through the northern reaches of Dalarna before crossing the provincial border into **Härjedalen**, a sparsely populated fell region stretching north and west to the Norwegian border, and containing some of the best scenery anywhere in Sweden. The region belonged to Norway until 1645, and the influence of the Norwegian language is still evident today in the local dialect. From the comfort of the Inlandsbanan, you'll be treated to a succession of breathtaking vistas of vast forested hill and mountainsides (Härjedalen boasts more than thirty mountains of over 1000m) – these are some of the emptiest tracts of land in the whole country, also home to the country's largest population of bears.

Although the sleepy provincial capital, **Sveg**, holds little of appeal, it's from here that **buses** head northwest to the remote mountain villages of **Funäsdalen** and Tänndalen; both have easy access to excellent and little-frequented **hiking trails** through austere terrain that's home to a handful of shaggy musk oxen which have wandered over the border from Norway. Nearby, across the lonely **Flatruet plateau**, with its ancient rock paintings, tiny **Ljungdalen** is the starting point for treks to Sweden's southernmost glacier, **Helags**, on the icy slopes of Helagsfjället (1797m).

Sveg

Around three hours and 140km north of Mora by the Inlandsbanan, **SVEG** is the first place of any significance after Lake Siljan. With a population of just 2600, the town is far and away the biggest in Härjedalen – though that's not saying much. Even on a Friday night in the height of summer you'll be hard pushed to find anyone on the streets. But though there's not an awful lot to do or see, Sveg's a pretty enough place: the wide streets are lined with grand old wooden houses, and the beautiful Ljusnan River runs through the centre of town.

The train station

There are a couple of diversions worthy of attention, the first of which is ideally located for arrivals by both train and bus: on permanent display inside the **train station** building on Järnvägsgatan (which is also used as the bus station) is a free **exhibition** of the life and times of the Inlandsbanan, in old photos and maps. Unfortunately the text and captions are only in Swedish but it's pretty evident that without the railway Sveg probably wouldn't be here at all. The Inlandsbanan has been the town's lifeblood since 1909, when the line to Orsa was opened by King Gustaf V and Queen Viktoria; today it not only brings visitors to the region during the short summer months, but also provides a means of transporting timber and peat pellets to southern Sweden – the countryside around Sveg is made up of vast tracts of uninhabited marshland, and the peat is extracted and turned into heating pellets at Härjedalen's biggest factory, on the outskirts of town.

Svegs kyrka

Vallarvägen • No set opening hours

From the station, your next port of call should be the parish church, **Svegs kyrka**. A church has stood on this spot since the latter part of the eleventh century when Sveg was also the site of an ancient Viking *ting*, or parliament. In 1273 a border treaty between Sweden and Norway was hammered out here, when the church was part of the bishopric of Trondheim. Sadly, though, the glory days are long gone. The present building dates only from 1847 and contains few of the fittings which once made its predecessors so grand; it's predominantly the woven textiles inside that catch the eye today.

HÄRJULF HORNBREAKER

Härjedalen got its name from the unfortunate **Härjulf Hornbreaker**, a servant to the Norwegian king, who mistakenly killed two of the king's men and was banished from the court. He fled to Uppsala, where he sought protection from King Amund, but after falling in love with Amund's cousin, Helga, and arousing the king's fury he was forced to make another hasty exit. It was then he came across a desolate valley in which he settled and which he named after himself: Härjulf's dale, or Härjedalen, as it's known today.

The wooden bear

In front of the church, beside the main crossroads in town, looms the world's largest **wooden bear**, a mammoth and weirdly ominous structure reaching 13m in height; it's meant as a reminder to passers-by that this is bear country – it's thought there are around 1200 animals in Härjedalen and neighbouring Jämtland.

Kulturcentrum Mankell

Ljusnegatan 1 • Mon–Fri 9am–3.30pm • 40kr • ⊚ henningmankell.com/placcs/svcg

The **Kulturcentrum Mankell**, inside the Folkets Hus, is a simple museum dedicated to Sveg's most famous son, Henning Mankell, who was one of Sweden's best-known novelists, particularly for his *Wallander* crime novels (see page 184). Translated into everything from Faroese to Chinese, a collection of Mankell's books is available inside for persual. Mankell died of cancer at the age of 67 in October 2015.

The Ljusnan River

At the western end of Fjällvägen, a pleasant **walk** of twenty to thirty minutes takes you across the road and train bridge on Brogatan to the south bank of the **Ljusnan River**, ideal for a picnic and a bit of skinny-dipping. Once over the bridge, just beyond the point where the railway line veers left and leaves the road, head right over a little stream into the forest, all the time walking back towards the river's edge. Hidden from the road by the trees is a wonderful sweet-smelling open flower meadow, but don't forget your mosquito repellent – the marshland and countless small lakes around Sveg are ideal breeding grounds for the insect.

ARRIVAL AND INFORMATION   SVEG

By train The train station is on Järnvägsgatan, 10–15min walk from the centre.
Destinations Åsarna (summer 4 daily; 1hr 30min); Mora (summer 1 daily; 5hr 14min); Östersund (summer 1 daily; 4hr).
By bus The bus station is next to the train station on Järnvägsgatan.
Destinations Åsarna (2 daily; 1hr 30min); Mora (2 daily;

2hr); Östersund (2 daily; 3hr).
Tourist office In the Folkets Hus building, Ljusnegatan 1 (Mon–Sat 8am–4pm; ☎046 70 622 05 00, ⊚visitsveg. com). To get here from the train station, walk east along Gränsgatan for around 10min. The office has leaflets about local hiking routes, which are useful for their maps even if you don't understand Swedish.

ACCOMMODATION

Härjedalen Vallarvägen 11 ☎0680 103 38, ⊚hotell harjedalen.se. Located near the main crossroads, this rambling old place from the late 1800s has comfortable and spacious rooms and has been run by the same family for the past fifty-odd years. 850kr/1150kr
Mysoxen Fjällvägen 12 ☎0680 170 00, ⊚mysoxen. se. West of the main crossroads, this austere place lacks charm and is rather unwelcoming, but in Sveg choices are

limited and you may well find yourself here. It also doubles as the town's hostel. Hostel doubles 570kr, hotel doubles 1070kr/1460kr
Svegs Camping Kyrkgränd 1 ☎0680 130 25, ⊚svegs camping.se. Enjoying a wonderful riverside location, the campsite is just a stone's throw from the tourist office and also has amazing-value two-berth cabins. Open mid-June to mid-Aug. Tents 145kr, cabins 575kr

EATING

Knuten Berggatan 4 ☎0680 130 15, ⊚pizzeriaknuten. se. A rather dreary pizzeria off the main square, serving

standard pizzas (75kr) and salads (85kr), plus a range of steaks for 100kr, fried plaice and schnitzel (both 80kr).

Mon–Thurs & Sun 11am–9pm, Fri & Sat 11am–10pm.
Mysoxen Fjällvägen 12 ☎0680 170 00, ⊛mysoxen.se.
The often empty restaurant inside the hotel churns out fish
dishes and meat dishes from 130kr without much enthusiasm,
though a better deal is a two-course menu for 175kr or three
courses for 215kr. The food is tasty but it's a strange experience
sitting alone in a relatively large restaurant. Mon–Thurs

6.30–9am, 11am–1.30pm & 6–10pm, Fri 6–10pm.
Thaifood in Sveg Parkgatan 15 ☎046 73 056 02 37.
The authentic Thai cuisine expertly prepared here by native
chefs is genuinely delicious (125kr for a main course) and
comes as a real treat in unadventurous little Sveg – meals
are available to take away and eat in. Mon–Fri 11am–
7pm, Sat noon–7pm.

Tännäs

Although Sveg may be shy, retiring and void of major attractions, what it does have
is some blockbuster scenery right on its doorstep. It's worth leaving the Inlandsbanan
at Sveg to travel into the far reaches of Härjedalen and explore one of Sweden's
least visited and most rewarding landscapes, where compelling views of the vast,
uninhabited forest unfold at every turn. The remote outpost of **TÄNNÄS**, at the
junction of Routes 311 and 84, is remarkable for its **church town**, a handful of gnarled
wooden cottages clinging to the south-facing valley-side where, quite unbelievably for
such a high altitude and latitude location, corn was once grown.

ARRIVAL AND DEPARTURE   TÄNNÄS

By bus From Sveg, bus #631 winds its way northwest
towards the tiny village of Lofsdalen, from where a

connecting service continues to Tännäs (generally 3 daily;
2hr; ⊛lanstrafiken-z.se).

ACCOMMODATION

Tännäskröket Karl Johans väg 1, ☎046 684 240 00,
⊛tannaskroket.se. This well-equipped hillside hostel
lies just to the west of the main road junction and enjoys

tremendous views; it's open all year, though advance
booking is required in May to mid-June & Oct–Dec. It also
serves food. Doubles **590r**

Funäsdalen

From Tännäs the bus heads a further 15km west to reach the pretty mountain resort of
FUNÄSDALEN, which is surrounded by kilometres of superb hiking trails. Curling gracefully
around the eastern shore of Funäsdalssjön lake, this appealing little village, barely 30km
from the Norwegian border, enjoys some fantastic views of the surrounding mountains. The
village is best seen from the top of the sheer Funäsdalsberget mountain (977m), which bears
down over the village and is reached by **chairlift** – you can get to the base-station by walking
ten minutes along the road signed to Ljungdalen at the eastern end of the village.

Härjedalens Fjällmuseum

Rörosvägen 30 • Museum December 17th–April 30th daily 10am–5pm, May 2th–June 21st Mon–Fri 10am–4pm, June 22nd–Sept 30th •
150kr • Fornminnesparken Open access • Free • ⊛fjallmuseet.se

The main thing to do in Funäsdalen is visit **Härjedalens Fjällmuseum**, the province's
mountain museum, which has a short slide-show about the province as well as

---

SWEDEN'S BROWN BEARS

It's estimated there are currently over three thousand **brown bears** in Sweden, the highest
number since the 1800s, roaming across an area stretching from the far north as far south
as northern Värmland. Since the early 1940s it's been legal in Sweden to **hunt** bears every
autumn to keep the population in check, and each year around 250 animals are culled.
Although it's rare to spot a bear in the wild, should you be hiking in an area where bears are
present, you're advised to whistle or talk loudly to alert the bear to your presence, particularly
in autumn when they are present in the forests gorging on wild berries ahead of hibernation.

informative explanations of how the mountain farmers of these parts managed to survive in such a remote location; transhumance (the practice of moving animals to higher ground during summer to fatten them on the fresh lush pasture) is given particular prominence.

The adjacent outdoor **Fornminnesparken** homestead museum is the oldest in Sweden, established in 1894 by a local trader. It contains the usual collection of old timber buildings, plus a former customs house from the early nineteenth century used to regulate cross-border trade with Norway.

ARRIVAL AND INFORMATION FUNÄSDALEN

By bus Buses use the village bus station.
Destinations Östersund (Mon–Fri & Sun 2 daily, Sat 1 daily; 3hr 30min); Sveg (2 daily; 2hr 15min).
Tourist office Rörosvägen 30 (mid-June to Sept daily

10am–6pm; Sept to mid-June Mon–Fri 10am–5pm; ☎0684 155 80, ⍟funasfjallen.se). The best place for advice on the dozens of local hiking trails; also has useful information about canoe rental.

ACCOMMODATION AND EATING

Funäsdalen Berg & Hotell ☎0684 214 30, ⍟funasdalenberghotell.se. The top place to stay in the village is this huge black building down by the lakeside on Strandvägen. The comfortable modern rooms have unsurpassed views out over the lake. There are cheaper hostel-style rooms sharing facilities in the same building but with a separate entrance. Hostel doubles 700kr, hotel doubles 990kr

Gamla Veras Rörosvägen 23 ☎0684 215 30, ⍟gamla veras.bertilssons.se. Located opposite the tourist office on

the main road, this is the best place to eat in the village, not only for its delicious smoked rainbow trout (195kr) and good range of pizzas (from 100kr) and burgers (from 130kr), but also for its wonderful views of the lake. Wed–Sat 5pm–late.

Norrbyns Stugby Vallarvägen 25 ☎0684 212 05, ⍟norrbynsstugby.nu. Two-person cabins are available at this place with terrific views out over Anåfjället mountain; in winter bookings are by the week only, and should be made well in advance. 575kr

The Flatruet plateau rock paintings

With your own transport, turn right in Mittådalen for another hamlet, Messlingen, where you should leave your vehicle. East of the settlement, a track off to the left leads towards Byggevallen and Ruvallen; from the latter a footpath then leads to the paintings – from the road it's a walk of 5–6km • Bus #620 runs between Funäsdalen and Ljungdalen (mid-June–Sept 1 daily; advance booking essential on ☎0771 82 00 83, timetables at ⍟lanstrafiken-z.se

From Funäsdalen, an unnumbered road – the highest in the country – heads north for the bumpy ascent to the hamlet of Mittådalen and beyond to the **Flatruet plateau** (975m), a bare stretch of desolate, rocky land, punctuated only by electricity poles and herds of grazing reindeer. The plateau is renowned for its 4000-year-old Stone Age **rock paintings** (*hällmålningar* in Swedish) at the foot of the Ruändan mountain at the eastern edge of this extensive upland area. Fashioned from a mix of iron ochre and animal fat and etched into slabs of rock, the twenty or so figures show, in remarkable clarity, elk, reindeer and even bears.

Ljungdalen

On the northern side of the Flatruet plateau the road descends steeply towards **LJUNGDALEN**, a charming village of fifty or so wooden houses hemmed in on three sides by high mountains, occupying an area of flat grassland near the head of the Ljungan River.

Helags glacier

Ljungdalen really comes into its own as a base from which to reach the **Helags glacier**. From the ICA supermarket in the centre of the village, take the road signed for "*Helags/Kläppen*"; the road passes through a small settlement, Kläppen, where you should take Kläppenvägen uphill, following the signs, until you reach the car park, 6km from Ljungdalen. A hiking trail leads from the car park for 12km to the STF mountain cabin at Helags at the foot of the glacier. At an altitude of 1796m, Sweden's southernmost glacier is disappointingly small, only a couple of square kilometres in size.

ARRIVAL AND INFORMATION   LJUNGDALEN

By bus Bus #613 runs from Ljungdalen to Åsarna (Mon–Fri & Sun 1 daily; 1hr 50min; timetables at ⓦ lanstrafiken-z. se). For Östersund change in Åsarna. Bus #620 runs to Funäsdalen during the summer months only (mid-June to Sept 1 daily; advance booking essential on ☎ 0771 82 00 83, timetables at ⓦ lanstrafiken-z.se).

Tourist office In a red-painted wooden house in the centre of the village (late June–Aug Mon–Thurs 10am–5pm, Sun 10am–3pm; ☎ 0687 200 79, ⓦ ljungdalen.com). It has good advice about hiking to Helags and onward travel possibilities.

ACCOMMODATION AND EATING

Restaurang Fjällsippan In the centre of the village ☎ 0687 200 24. The best eating option in the village, serving good pizzas (80kr) and Swedish dishes (around 150kr), as well as home-made cakes. It's also fully licensed. Daily noon–late.
STF Ljungdalen Vandrarhem Dunsjögården, on the main street ☎ 0702104873, ⓦ svenskaturistforeningen. se/anlaggningar/stf-ljungdalen-vandrarhem.   This twelve-room hostel has a swimming pool and sauna nearby, for relaxing those aching muscles after hiking. You can cook here, too. Doubles 500kr

Route 535: the road to Åsarna

Bus #613 runs from Ljungdalen to Åsarna (Mon–Fri & Sun 1 daily; 1hr 50 min; timetables at ⓦ lanstrafiken-z.se)

From Ljungdalen, one of the most beautiful journeys anywhere in northern Sweden unfolds. Although the 110km trip to **Åsarna** certainly requires stamina, it offers a real taste of wild Sweden. The switchback road cuts through some of the most spectacular mountain and lakeside landscapes you'll witness in the north, threading its way around serpentine bends and across narrow isthmuses between the extensive areas of swampland and spruce forest that characterize this forgotten corner of the country. Curiously for such a remote route, it is served by bus, providing a rare insight for anyone without their own transport into life in backwoods Sweden.

As the road passes through the tiny villages, you'll notice how the lumberjack culture is alive and well in these parts. Indeed, the stretch of road between the Härjedalen/ Jämtland border and the village of **Börtnan** (1hr 10min from Ljungdalen) runs through one of the region's most important forestry areas; mountains of timber line the roadside awaiting transport to the nearest railhead.

Jämtland

Stretching from just north of Sveg to the border with Lapland, a distance of around 250km, the province of **JÄMTLAND** is centred around one of Sweden's greatest lakes, **Storsjön**, and its associated watercourses, and is altogether more pastoral than its wilder and more mountainous neighbour to the south, Härjedalen. It was the plentiful supply of fish from the lake coupled with successful cultivation of the rich lands around its shores that enabled the region's first settlers to eke out an existence so far north – Stockholm, for example, is 550km to the south. Although the province can trace its history back to the early Iron Age, Jämtland has only been Swedish since 1645, before which it was part of Norway. The people here have a strong sense of regional identity and, in recent years, have even called (albeit rather half-heartedly) for independence from Sweden. Spend any length of time here and you'll soon encounter the tremendous pride the locals have in their villages, forests and lakes.

Approaching from the south, you'll reach the cross-country skiing centre of **Åsarna** first. Just beyond here, **Hackås** is the location for the wildly entertaining *Årets Näck* competition, which sees a group of naked male fiddle-players compete for the prestigious title. The most enjoyable town in the province is the provincial capital of **Östersund**, situated on Storsjön lake, whose murky waters reputedly hide Sweden's own version of the Loch Ness monster. West of Östersund, **Åre** is Sweden's most popular ski destination for foreign tourists, whilst nearby **Storlien** has some great summer hiking right on its doorstep.

Åsarna

From Sveg, the Inlandsbanan veers eastwards in order to skirt the vast area of marshland north and east of the town. The train line finally swings west at Överhogdal, where the Viking Age tapestries now on display in Östersund were discovered (see opposite), before crossing the provincial border into Jämtland and continuing north to **ÅSARNA**, 109km north of Sveg. Blink and you'll miss the place, a tiny one-street affair that serves as a diminutive service centre for the southern part of Jämtland. There's nothing to recommend an overnight stay – there's not much here other than the train station, a filling station and the **Skicenter**, all lined up along the nameless main road – but the Inlandsbanan makes a stop of an hour here (in the northbound direction only), allowing time enough to check out the **outlet stores** at the Skicenter, which sell all manner of outdoor clothing and equipment.

If you fancy breaking the long journey from Mora to Östersund here, consider taking a stroll past the campsite cabins behind the Skicenter and down to the river; turn right here and follow the age-old Kärleksstigen ("Lover's Lane") along the water's edge – you can cross the river over an old stone bridge, further upstream by the rapids, and return on the opposite bank along a minor road. The smooth, low rocks by the bridge make an ideal spot to fish or catch a few rays of sunshine.

ARRIVAL AND INFORMATION
ÅSARNA

By train Åsarna train station lies beside the one and only main road, Olstavägen, which runs through the village.
Destinations Mora (summer 1 daily; 4hr); Östersund (summer 1 daily; 1hr 20min); Sveg (summer 1 daily; 1hr 45min).
By bus Buses pull up at the Skicenter at Olstavägen 45.

Destinations Ljungdalen (Mon–Fri & Sun 1 daily; 1hr 45min); Östersund (6 daily; 1hr 20min); Sveg (2 daily; 1hr 30min).
Tourist information Åsarna's Skicenter, Olstavägen 45 (daily: June–Aug 8am–10pm; Sept–May 8am–8pm; ☎ 0687 302 30, ⓦ asarnaskicenter.se), has limited amounts of tourist information.

ACCOMMODATION AND EATING

Åsarna Skicenter Olstavägen 45 ☎ 0687 302 30, ⓦ asarnaskicenter.se. Down by the river's edge, accommodation here is spread across several timber buildings behind the Skicenter, and there's also a small bathing pool and a sauna. The restaurant is hard to beat for cheap meals, with breakfast, *dagens rätt* until 6pm and evening meals for 95kr. Restaurant daily until 8pm, June–Aug 10pm. Tents <u>125kr</u>, dorms <u>210kr</u>, doubles <u>520kr</u>

Vemdalen

The road from Åsarna to Funäsdalen is especially worth travelling, crossing the provincial border back into Härjedalen and following the ancient track used by the region's merchant farmers through the **Vemdalsskalet pass**. Bound for **VEMDALEN**, the road descends sharply and offers clear views of another of Härjedalen's mighty peaks: the impressive sugarloaf-shaped **Sånfjället** mountain (1278m) to the southwest. Back in the 1900s the forest and fell terrain around the mountain was declared a national park in an attempt to maintain its delicate ecosystem – with great success, since the park is now a favourite habitat for Härjedalen's bear population.

NUDE MALE FIDDLERS: ÅRETS NÄCK

One of the most intriguing and quintessentially Swedish events you'll witness takes place in **Hackås**, just 35km north of Åsarna, on the second Thursday in July. The **Årets Näck** competition (ⓦ facebook.com/aretsnack) features a succession of naked male fiddle players, who compete for the prestigious title by sitting in the unflatteringly chilly waters of the local river to play their instruments. The roots of this eye-opening spectacle of public nudity are to be found in the mists of Swedish folklore where the *näck*, a long-haired, bearded, naked water sprite, would sit by a river rapid or waterfall and play his fiddle so hauntingly that women and children from miles around would be lured to him, only to drown in his watery home. The event begins around 9pm on the island of Gaveriholmen near Strömbacka mill; Hackås is on the Inlandsbanan and is served by buses to and from Östersund.

The church
No set opening hours
Once through the pass and down into Vemdalen, you'll find a stunning octagonal **wooden church** right by the roadside in the centre of the village. Built in Rococo style in 1763, eight years after its separate onion-domed bell tower, the church supports a deep two-stage roof and a central onion turret. Inside, the work of a couple of local craftsmen is proudly displayed: the pulpit, with its bowing cherrywood panels, was made in Ljungdalen, whilst the altar was carved by a carpenter from Klövsjö.

Östersund

8

Sitting gracefully on the eastern shore of the mighty **Storsjön** (Great Lake) about halfway up Sweden, **ÖSTERSUND** is the only large town along the Inlandsbanan (until Gällivare inside the Arctic Circle, another 750km further north), and is well worth a stop. Östersund's **lakeside** position lends it a seaside-holiday atmosphere, unusual this far inland, and it's an instantly likeable place. In addition to the youthful buzz about town, there's an air of commercialism here, too (lacking in most other inland towns), since Östersund is also a centre for the engineering and electronics industries, as well as the Swedish armed forces, who maintain two regiments here. However, it's for its lake **monster**, the Storsjöodjuret, that Östersund is perhaps best known.

Brief history
King Gustav III gave the town its charter two hundred years ago with one thing in mind: to put an end to the lucrative trade that the region's merchant farmers carried out with neighbouring Norway. Travelling over the mountains, they bartered and sold their goods in Trondheim before returning back to the Storsjön region. Although rival markets in Östersund gradually stemmed the trade, it took another century for the town's growth to really begin, heralded by the arrival of the railway from Sundsvall in 1879.

Jamtli
Museiplan, a 15min walk north from the centre along Kyrkogatan • Late June–late Aug daily 11am–5pm; late Aug–late June Tues–Sun 11am–5pm • 290kr for a 2-day visit • ⓦ jamtli.com
Most visitors head straight for Östersund's top attraction, **Jamtli**, home to the beautiful **Överhogdal Viking tapestries** and an **open-air museum** which expertly – and enjoyably – brings to life Östersund from years past.

The Överhogdal tapestries
The museum's prize exhibits are the awe-inspiring Viking **Överhogdal tapestries**, crowded with brightly coloured pictures of horses, reindeer, elk and dogs, and different types of dwellings. Dating from the ninth and tenth centuries and woven from flax,

most of the tapestries were discovered by accident in an outhouse in 1910. One piece was rescued after being used as a doll's blanket – rumour has it the child had to be pacified with a 2kr reward to hand it over – and another was being used as a cleaning rag in the local church. Be sure, too, to watch the informative ten-minute slideshow explaining the tapestries' history and their likely significance.

The Great Lake Monster exhibition

The museum is the place to get to grips with Östersund's **monster** (see opposite). Ask to see the fascinating film (with English subtitles) about the creature, which contains a series of telling interviews with local people who claim to have seen it; one very Swedish thing leaps out at you – having witnessed something unusual out on the lake, many people took several months, even years, to talk about their experience for fear

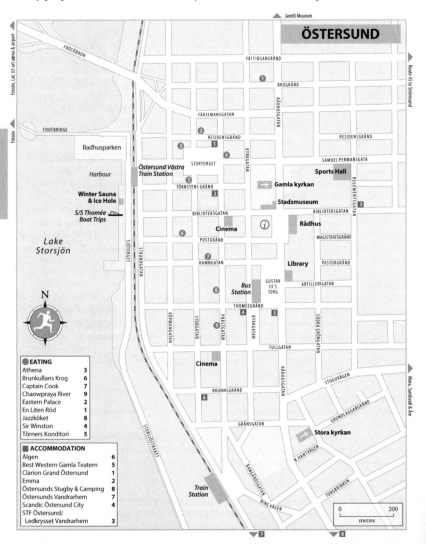

STORSJÖODJURET – THE "GREAT LAKE MONSTER"

The people of Östersund are in no doubt: **Storsjöodjuret** is out there, in their lake. Eyewitness accounts – there are hundreds of people who claim to have seen it – speak of a creature with a head like a dog, long pointed ears and bulging eyes, that sweeps gracefully through the water, sometimes making a hissing or clucking sound, often several hundred metres away from the shore; each summer sees new reports of sightings. Although several explanations have been given that dispel the myth – a floating tree trunk, a row of swimming elk, the wake from a passing boat, a series of rising water bubbles – the monster's existence is taken so seriously that a protection order has been slapped on it, using the provisions of paragraph fourteen of Sweden's Nature Conservation Act. For most people, though, the monster will be at its most tangible not in the lake, but on the web (Ⓦ storsjoodjuret.com).

In 1894, the hunt for this sinister presence began in earnest, when King Oscar II founded a special organization to try to catch it. Norwegian whalers were hired to do so, but the rather unorthodox methods they chose proved unsuccessful: a dead pig gripped in a metal clasp was dangled into the water as bait, and large, specially manufactured pincers were on hand to grip the creature and pull it ashore. Their tackle is on display at Jamtli, together with photographs that claim to be of the creature.

If you fancy a bit of monster-spotting, consider taking a **steamboat cruise** on the lake on board *S/S Thomée*, a creaking 1875 wooden steamship. When we researched this edition of the boat was undergoing renovation work; check Ⓦ visitostersund for the latest details – generally, the boat runs a two-hour trip round the lake leaving from the harbour in town, as well as tours out to the island of **Verkön**, where there's a nineteenth-century castle.

of ridicule. Having seen the film, head downstairs for a further display of monster-catching gear, alongside what's claimed to be a pickled embryo of a similar monster found in the lake in 1895; this quite grotesque thing is kept in a small glass jar on a shelf next to the foot of the stairs.

The open-air museum

The **open-air museum** on the same site is full of people milling around in nineteenth-century costume, farming and milking much as their ancestors did. Everyone else is encouraged to join in – baking, tree felling, grass cutting and so on. The place is ideal for children, and adults would have to be pretty hard-bitten not to enjoy the enthusiastic atmosphere. Intensive work has been done on getting the settings right: the restored and working interiors are authentically gloomy and dirty, and the local store, Lanthandel, among the wooden buildings around the square near the entrance, is suitably old-fashioned. In the woodman's cottage (presided over by a bearded lumberjack, who makes pancakes for the visitors), shoeless and scruffy youngsters snooze contentedly in the wooden cots. Beyond the first cluster of houses is a reconstructed farm, **Lillhärdal**, where life goes on pretty much as it did in 1785, when the land was ploughed using horses, and crops were sown and harvested by hand – even the roaming cattle and the crop varieties are appropriate to the period.

Lat. 63 art arena

Drontvägen 2, Frösön • Opening times vary • Free • Ⓦ lat63.se • Bus #3 or #4 from the town centre to Flygverkstan; buy your ticket by credit card on the bus

Close to the airport and housed in a former hangar for military aircraft, an arts and culture venture, the **Lat. 63 art arena**, showcases changing exhibitions of modern art. Check out the website to see what's on, or check with the tourist office.

Badhusparken

Sauna: mid-Jan–mid-March Tues & Thurs 6–8pm • 150kr • ☎ 063 10 05 20, Ⓦ vinterparken.se

The lakeside **Badhusparken** is an extremely popular sunbathing spot in summer, while in winter it is the place for a quick dip in the invigorating waters of Lake Storsjön – a hole in the ice is kept open here for this purpose (mid-Jan to late March). Once you're out of the water, head straight for the nearby **sauna** or you'll be covered in frost faster than you can say "*Storsjöodjuret*". The park is also the place to rent skates to go long-distance **skating** on the lake (150kr/day), which freezes over each winter.

Frösön

Take the footbridge across the lake from Badhusparken, or the road bridge a little further north, and you'll come to the island of **Frösön**. People have lived here since prehistoric times; the name comes from the original Viking settlement, which was associated with the pagan god of fertility, Frö. There's plenty of good walking on the island, as well as a couple of historical sights. Just over the bridges, in front of the red-brick offices, look for the eleventh-century **rune stone** telling of Austmaður ("East Man"), son of Guðfast, the first Christian missionary to the area. From here, you can clamber up the nearby hill of Öneberget to the fourth-century settlement of **Mjälleborgen**, where a pleasant walking trail of around 4km leads through the area.

Frösö kyrka

June–Aug daily 11am–4pm • Bus #3 the centre; buy your ticket by credit card on the bus

Five kilometres west of the bridges, along the island's main road and up the main hill, is the beautiful **Frösö kyrka**, an eleventh-century church with a detached bell tower. In 1984, archeologists digging under the altar came across a bit of old birch stump surrounded by animal bones – bears, pigs, deer and squirrels – evidence of the cult of ancient gods, who were known as *æsir*. Today, the church is one of the most popular in Sweden for weddings – to tie the knot here at midsummer, you have to book years in advance.

ARRIVAL AND DEPARTURE   ÖSTERSUND

Östersund is a major transport hub: the E14 runs through on its way to the Norwegian border; the Inlandsbanan stops here and other trains run west to Åre and Storlien, east to Sundsvall (a very beautiful run which hugs lakeshore and riverbank the entire way) and south to Stockholm, through some of Sweden's most stunning old-growth forest. Coming from Swedish Lapland, train connections can be made for Östersund in either Sundsvall or Gävle.

By plane The town's airport (ⓦ swedavia.se/ostersund), with flights from Stockholm Arlanda, Gothenburg, Luleå and Umeå, is on Frösön, an island 11km west of town, from where buses (connecting with flights; 90kr) and taxis (415kr) run to the centre.

By train From the train station on Strandgatan, it's a 5min walk north to the town centre.

Destinations Åre (5 daily; 1hr 15min); Arvidsjaur (summer 1 daily; 8hr 30min); Gällivare (summer 1 daily; 12hr 30min); Mora (summer 1 daily; 6hr 15 min); Stockholm (2 daily; 5hr); Storlien (2 daily; 2hr); Sundsvall (2 hourly; 2hr 30min); Sveg (summer 1 daily; 2hr 50min).

By bus The bus station is in the centre of town in Gustav IIIs torg.

Destinations Åsarna (6 daily; 1hr 15min); Funäsdalen (2 daily Mon–Fri & Sun, 1 daily Sat; 3hr 20min); Hackås (hourly; 50min); Mora (2 daily; 5hr 30min); Sveg (3 daily; 2hr 50min).

INFORMATION

Tourist office Rådhusgatan 44 (June 10th–June 23th Mon–Fr 10am–5pm, Sat & Sun 10am–3pm; June 24th–Aug 25th Mon–Fri 9am–6pm, Sat & Sun 10am–3pm; Sept–May Mon–Fri 11am–5pm; ☎ 046 63 701 17 00, ⓦ visitostersund.se). A couple of blocks north of the bus station, opposite the minaret-topped Rådhus.

ACCOMMODATION   SEE MAP PAGE 304

Älgen Storgatan 61 ☎ 063 51 75 25, ⓦ hotelalgen. se. Handy for the train station, this small, central hotel has plain and comfortable en-suite rooms with rather uninspiring modern furnishings. Special emphasis is placed on providing guests with a full breakfast with plentiful fresh fruit and freshly baked bread. <u>1065r/1220kr</u>

Best Western Gamla Teatern Thoméegränd 20 ☎ 063 51 16 00, ⓦ gamlateatern.se. The most atmospheric

hotel in town, housed in a turn-of-the-twentieth-century theatre with sweeping wooden staircases. The Art Nouveau rooms are snug and cosy, and many have delightful pieces of period furniture. Choose carefully, though, because some are rather small. Book early for much reduced prices. <u>625kr/950kr</u>

★ **Clarion Grand Östersund** Prästgatan 16 ☎ 063 55 60 00, ⓦ nordicchoicehotels.se. This business-oriented

GO WEST: PILGRIMS AND VIKINGS

Heading west from Östersund, the **E14** and the **train** line follow the course trudged by medieval **pilgrims** on their way to Nidaros (now Trondheim in Norway) over the border, a twisting route that threads its way through sharp-edged mountains rising high above a bevy of fast-flowing streams and deep, cold lakes. Time and again, the eastern **Vikings** assembled their armies beside the holy Storsjön lake to begin the long march west, most famously in 1030, when King Olaf of Norway collected his mercenaries for the campaign that led to his death at the Battle of Stiklestad.

Today, although the scenery is splendid, the only real attractions en route are the winter skiing and summer walking centres of **Åre** (see page 308) and **Storlien** (see page 309).

hotel is Östersund's finest – the very best rooms have their own marbled hallway, sitting room and sumptuous double beds. The cheaper rooms are less glamorous but still worth the splurge. 930kr/1600kr

Emma Prästgatan 31 ☎ 063 51 78 40, ⓦ hotelemma.com. Eighteen tastefully decorated rooms with high ceilings, wooden floors, old tiled corner stoves and lots of chequers and bold colours, all en suite, in a perfect location on the main drag; reception is not 24hr so be prepared to ring if closed. 750/1395kr

Östersunds Vandrarhem Bangårdsgatan 6 ☎ 063 13 22 32, ⓦ ostersundsvandrarhem.se. Accessed from the far end of the train station car park, this hostel has four beds in rooms sleeping two to four people. Bear in mind that the noise from passing goods trains in the night may disturb your sleep. Dorms 300kr, doubles 400kr

Scandic Östersund City Kyrkgatan 70 ☎ 063 57 57 00, ⓦ hotellostersund.se. A massive modern hotel with 126 rooms that score highly on Scandinavian design and quality, with wooden floors and leather armchairs. The location, too, is unbeatable, right in the heart of the city. 690kr/1120kr

STF Östersund/Ledkrysset Vandrarhem Biblioteksgatan 25 ☎ 063 10 33 10, ⓦ ostersundledkrysset.se. Östersund's smart, central STF hostel is housed in a soaring brick building, and the interior design has been chosen to reflect the natural surroundings of the Swedish mountains, featuring lots of natural woods. Rooms have private facilities or share with just one other. Doubles 600kr

CAMPING

Östersunds Stugby & Camping Krondikesvägen 95C ☎ 063 14 46 15, ⓦ ostersundscamping.se. Located a couple of kilometres south of the town centre, with tent pitches and cottages. Perfect for the fantastic indoor swimming complex, Storsjöbadet. Tents 160kr, cottages 670kr

EATING AND DRINKING

SEE MAP PAGE 304

Athena Stortorget 3 ☎ 063 51 63 44, ⓦ athena ostersund.se. Tucked away in one corner of Stortorget, this rather dingy place serves tasty, authentic pizzas from 80kr, as well as steaks from 270kr. The house speciality is lamb chops marinated in rosemary served with fried mushrooms and Greek salad for 245kr. Mon–Wed 2–9.30pm, Thurs & Fri 2–10pm, Sat noon–10pm, Sun 1–9pm.

Brunkullans Krog Postgränd 5 ☎ 063 10 14 54, ⓦ brunkullanbrasserie.se. This old-fashioned, home-from-home restaurant, with polished lanterns and a heavy wooden interior dating from the 1880s, offers modern Swedish dishes such as grilled salmon and fillet of lamb for around 200kr; the bouillabaisse is delicious and worth every krona (175kr). Tues 5–10pm, Wed & Thurs 5–11pm, Fri & Sat 5pm–1am.

Captain Cook Hamngatan 9 ☎ 046 63 12 60 90, ⓦ captaincook.se. This moderately priced place has a selection of delicious Australian-style specials that really draw in the crowds – try the Bushman sandwich with bacon and coleslaw (145kr) or the elk burger (185kr). Another favourite is fish and chips using Arctic char (170kr). Tues 5–10pm, Wed & Thurs 5–11pm, Fri 6pm–2am, Sat 5pm–2am.

Chaowpraya River Prästgatan 50B ☎ 063 13 00 99. The adventurous interior decor of this Thai restaurant – featuring thatched roofs and more bamboo than you may strictly need – sadly isn't reflected in the food, which is fine but not exceptional. Mains cost from 135kr and starters from 55kr. The lunch buffet is a good-value 80kr. Mon–Fri 11am–10pm, Sat 1–10pm, Sun 3–9pm.

Eastern Palace Storgatan 15 ☎ 063 51 00 15. The town's best Chinese restaurant serves up all the usual dishes from 115kr, against the backdrop of an enormous central aquarium and giant Ming vases. They also have a number of Szechuan mains for 90kr or 125kr, and an evening Mongolian barbecue and Korean buffet at 120kr. Mon–Fri 11am–10pm, Sat noon–10pm, Sun 1–9pm.

En Liten Röd Brogränd 19 ☎ 063 12 63 26, ⓦ enlitenrod.se. A cosy neighbourhood restaurant with a good choice of meat dishes from 265kr and a selection of fondues: chocolate fondue for two people (185kr), cheese fondue for two (245kr) and a delicious seafood fondue for four people (565kr). All fondues, except the meat one, should be ordered one day in advance. Mon–Sat 5–10.30pm.

Jazzköket Prästgatan 44 ☎ 063 10 15 75, ⓦ jazzkoket.

se. Creative brasserie tucked away in a little courtyard, whose signature concept is what it terms a modern Swedish "foodjam" – an innovative mix of local ingredients given a special twist in the kitchen by each individual chef. The results, though pricey (mains are over 250kr), are gastronomically spectacular. Tues–Thurs 5pm–midnight, Fri–Sat 5pm–2am.

Sir Winston Prästgatan 19 ☎063 10 68 00, ✆sirwinston.se. An English-style pub with carpets, wooden wall panels and chandeliers overlooking the main square, serving locally sourced mains such as reindeer in Maderia sauce (290kr), Arctic char (230kr) and steak with potato gratin (295kr). Mon–Thurs 4–10pm, Fri 3pm–midnight, Sat noon–midnight, Sun 4pm–10pm.

★**Törners Konditori** Storgatan 24, ☎046 63 51 87 60. A modern Euro-café rather than a traditional Swedish *konditori*, with a good selection of cakes, pastries, sandwiches and quiches. This is the best and largest café in town, perfect for people-watching. Mon–Fri 8am–5pm, Sat 9am–4pm, Sun 11am–4pm.

Åre

The alpine village of **Åre**, 100km west of Östersund, is Sweden's most prestigious ski resort, with over forty lifts, 114 ski runs and guaranteed snow between December and May. In summer, the village is a quiet, likeable haven for ramblers, sandwiched as it is between the Åresjön lake and a range of craggy hills that's overshadowed by Sweden's seventh highest peak, the mighty **Åreskutan** mountain (1420m).

Kabinbanan

End June–end Aug daily 10am–4pm; Sept Thurs–Sun 10am–4pm • 7min • 135kr return

A cable car, the **Kabinbanan**, whisks you from just behind Storlien's main square up to a **viewing platform** (1274m) and *Stormköket* restaurant (open in connection with the Kabinbanan's operating times), some way up Åreskutan. From the viewing platform it'll take you a further thirty minutes to clamber to the **summit**. Wear sensible shoes and warm clothes, as the low temperatures are intensified by the wind, and it can be decidedly nippy even in summer. From the top the view is stunning – on a clear day you can see over to the border with Norway and a good way back to Östersund. There's a tiny wooden **café**, *Toppstugan*, at the summit (open in connection with the Kabinbanan's operating times), serving coffee and extortionately priced sandwiches. If you're walking back to Åre, bear in mind that even the shortest route (2hr) requires stamina; other, longer, paths lead more circuitously back down to the village. One word of warning: there are phenomenal numbers of **mosquitoes** and other insects up here in July and August, so make sure you are protected by repellent.

Åre Gamla kyrka

In the centre of town, **Åre Gamla kyrka** (use the key hanging on a hook outside the door to get in), just above the campsite, is a marvellous thirteenth-century stone church: inside, the simple blue decoration and the smell of burning candles create a peaceful ambience.

ARRIVAL AND INFORMATION   ÅRE

By train Åre train station is known as Station Åre and is located at St Olafsväg 35.
Destinations Östersund (5 daily; 1hr 15min); Stockholm (1 daily, seasonal; 7hr); Storlien (2 daily; 40min)
By bus Buses pull up right outside the train station. The

only service you're likely to want to take is the twice-daily bus to Östersund (1hr 30min).
Tourist office Station Åre, St Olavsväg 35 (daily 9am–6pm; ☎0647 163 21, ✆visitare.com).

ACCOMMODATION

During the **ski season**, rooms here are like gold dust and prices sky high: book accommodation for this period well in advance through the tourist office or, better still, take a package trip. In summer, some places are closed so it's a good idea to book in advance to be sure you have a bed. The

tourist office can help find a **private room** (from around 300kr per person), almost all of which will have a kitchen, shower and TV.
AGO Mitt i Åre Kabinbanevägen 22 ☎046 647 515 00, wsvenskaturistforeningen.se/anlaggningar/stf-are-

HIKING AND BIKING AROUND ÅRE

A network of tracks crisscrosses the hills around Åre; ask the tourist office for the excellent *Hikebike.se and Sommarguiden* booklets, which will tell you all you need to know. A popular hiking route south of nearby Storlien is the **Jämttriangle**, which takes in fantastic wilderness scenery close to the Norwegian border and involves overnight stays in STF mountain lodges, at Sylarna (☎0647 722 00, ⓦsvenskaturistforeningen.se/anlaggningar/stf-sylarna-fjallstation; doubles 550kr), Blåhammaren (☎0647 722 00, ⓦsvenskaturistforeningen.se/anlaggningar/stf-blahammaren-fjallstation; doubles 850kr) and Storulvån (☎0647 722 00, ⓦsvenskaturistforeningen.se/anlaggningar/stf-storulvan-fjallstation; doubles 550kr).

The mountains around Åre are also a good place to go **mountain biking**; the tourist office can help sort out a bike for you and has information about a series of trails, known collectively as **Åre Bike Park**. In July, the Åre Bike Festival (ⓦarebikefestival.com), a four-day competition, takes place here.

torg-vandrarhem. Perched above the main square, this spacious hostel has around 150 beds but books up fast. It's right in the heart of all the action and a stone's throw away from Kabinbanan. Doubles <u>1890kr</u>

Holiday Club Åre Strand ☎0647 120 00, ⓦholidayclub.se. This swanky lakeside hotel is a whole resort in itself, comprising top-notch Scandinavian-design rooms and apartments as well as a swimming pool, spa and bowling alley. <u>1290kr</u>

EATING AND DRINKING

Broken Torggränd 4 ☎0647 506 33, ⓦbroken-are.com. A small, snug and incredibly popular American bar and grill restaurant, open all year, with fajitas for 150kr, burgers from 130kr and a range of fresh salads, including one with pulled pork, from 115kr. Mon–Fri 4pm–late, Sat & Sun noon–late.

Dahlbom på Torget Årevägen 78 ☎0647 508 20, ⓦdahlbompatorget.se. Smart brasserie offering burgers from 160kr, plus a selection of meat and fish dishes, such as grilled Arctic char, slow-cooked side of pork and lamb meatballs for 170–250kr. The Asian noodle salad with chicken, chilli, peanut sauce and fresh coriander (160kr) is also a good bet. Open ski season only. Mon–Thurs 5pm–late, Fri & Sat noon–late.

★ **Villa Tottebo** Parkvägen 1 ☎0647 506 20, ⓦvillatottebo.se. The best food in town can be found at this restaurant, housed in a former wood-panelled hunting lodge from 1897, opposite the train station. It cooks up gourmet meat and fish dishes (185–330kr), including game meatballs, reindeer with cabbage and apple salad and cod with chorizo and gnocchi. Ski season only. Daily 6–11pm.

Werséns Årevägen 95 ☎0647 505 05, ⓦwersens.se. Extremely popular, this stylish brasserie with white-tiled walls is open all year and serves the likes of reindeer fillet (295kr), home-made sausages (195kr), lamb burger (190kr) and pizza (150kr). Mon–Fri & Sun 5–11pm, Sat noon–11pm and Sun 5–11pm.

Storlien

Just 6km from the Norwegian border and linked to Åre by infrequent train, **tiny STORLIEN** – little more than a couple of streets and a supermarket amid open countryside – is an excellent place to stop if you're into hiking, surrounded as it is by rugged, scenic terrain. The **southern stretch of the Kungsleden** (see page 344) starts here and winds its way south via Sweden's southernmost glacier on the slopes of Helagsfjället, continuing on to Tänndalen and Grövelsjön, terminating on the hills above Sälen. Storlien is also prime berry-picking territory (the rare cloudberry grows here); mushrooms can also be found in great numbers hereabouts, in particular the delicious chanterelle.

ACCOMMODATION AND EATING   STORLIEN

Le Ski Vintergatan 25 ☎0647 701 51, ⓦleski.se. Your best bet for a bite to eat is this restaurant and bar at the station, which has cheapish eats for lunch and dinner; the sliced reindeer with mashed potato for just 150kr is a winner every time, though even better is the slap-up American BBQ every Sat evening (6–9pm). Daily noon–9pm.

STF Storliens Fjällgård Vandrarhem Vackerlidsvägen 7 ☎0647 700 58, ⓦstorliensfjallgard.se. A pleasant mountain lodge with self-catering kitchens and a total of 72 beds in rooms sleeping up to four people. It's a 4km walk across the tracks from the train station to the E14, and then left down the main road. Dorms <u>180kr</u>, doubles <u>600kr</u>

8

Swedish Lapland

THE NORTHERN LIGHTS

9 Swedish Lapland

Swedish Lapland, the heartland of the indigenous *Sámi* people, is Europe's last wilderness, characterized by seemingly endless forests of pine and spruce, thundering rivers that drain the snow-covered fells and peaceful lakeside villages high amongst the hills. The irresistible allure of this vast and sparsely populated region is the opportunity to experience raw nature at first hand. This unsullied corner of the country is a very long way away for many Swedes; in terms of distance, Gothenburg, for example, is closer to Venice than it is to Kiruna. The reputation of the local people for speaking their mind or, alternatively, not speaking at all, has confirmed the region's image within Sweden: remote, austere yet still rather fascinating.

The best way to discover more about *Sámi* culture is to drive the 360km-long **Wilderness Way** (Vildmarksvägen) from **Strömsund**, a notable canoeing centre, over the barren Stekenjokk plateau to isolated **Fatmomakke**, a church town of dozens of traditional wooden *kåtor* (huts) beside the steely waters of Kultsjön lake. The road terminates at **Vilhelmina**, another tiny church town which makes an interesting diversion on the way north. **Storuman** and neighbouring **Sorsele** have handy train and bus connections that are useful access points for a small handful of charming mountain villages close to the Norwegian border, where hiking is the main draw. Back on the main Inlandsbanan train route, **Arvidsjaur** offers a fascinating insight into indigenous culture at its *lappstad*, a diverting collection of religious dwellings and storehuts.

However, it's **Jokkmokk**, just north of the **Arctic Circle**, that is the real centre of *Sámi* life – not least during its Winter Market when thousands of people brave the chill to buy and sell everything from reindeer hides to wellington boots. Moving further north, the iron-ore mining centres of **Gällivare** (where the Inlandsbanan ends) and **Kiruna** share a rugged charm, though it's undoubtedly the world-famous **Icehotel** in nearby **Jukkasjärvi** that is the real winter draw. Beyond, the rugged **national parks** offer a chance to hike and commune with nature like nowhere else: the **Kungsleden trail** runs for 500km from the tiny village of **Abisko** – oddly, yet reassuringly for hikers, the driest place in all of Sweden – to **Hemavan**, northwest of Storuman, through some of the most gorgeous stretches anywhere in the Swedish mountains.

GETTING AROUND

Covering a whopping 110,000 square kilometres – an area only fractionally smaller than the whole of England – Swedish Lapland is inevitably going to make getting from one place to another take up a lot of time.

By train During the short summer months, the Inlandsbanan provides the easiest and most enjoyable form of transport; it generally runs between late June and late August, but the exact operating season varies year to year, so check the latest timetable at ⑩inlandsbanan.se. The train sets off from Östersund (see page 303) around 7.20am every morning in the summer, on its 14hr journey to Gällivare, 100km north of the Arctic Circle, where there are mainline train connections linking most of the major centres and attractions. Slowly snaking its way across the northern hinterland, it often has to stop so that elk and reindeer – and occasionally bears – can be cleared from

the tracks, and it often stops at least once for a bite to eat or a cup of coffee in a wayside café. At the Arctic Circle it stops again, so that everyone can jump off and take some photos.

By car Route 45 (the Inlandsvägen) is the best road north through Swedish Lapland; from Östersund, it sticks close to the train line on its way to Gällivare. It's easy to drive and well surfaced for the most part, although watch out for reindeer with a death wish – once they spot a car hurtling towards them they seem to do their utmost to throw themselves in front of it. You could drive from Östersund to Gällivare in a day if you left very early and put your foot down, but you're better off taking it in stages.

By bus Bus #45 (⑩lanstrafiken-z.se), the daily bus service that runs from Östersund to Gällivare, follows Route 45; it's not as much fun as the train, but is faster and very comfortable.

Highlights

❶ **Vildmarksvägen** By bus or your own car, the Wilderness Way really lives up to its name, offering a taste of nature in the raw, and some great *Sámi* sites, too. See page 317

❷ **Snowmobiling** Scudding across the snowfields of northern Sweden on a snowmobile is one of Lapland's quintessential experiences. See pages 318, 324 and 341

❸ **Lappstaden, Arvidsjaur** The square timber huts and cabins at this *Sámi* church town offer an insight into the life of Sweden's indigenous people. See page 325

❹ **The Arctic Circle, Jokkmokk** The Arctic Circle is undoubtedly the best place to see the

midnight sun, and crossing the magic line gives a real sense of achievement. See page 330

❺ **Icehotel, Jukkasjärvi** Spend a night in a thermal sleeping bag in this awe-inspiring hotel constructed from snow and ice, where the interior temperature hovers at a chilly -5ºC. See page 340

❻ **Northern lights, Abisko** Witness one of the most breathtaking sights in the world in the far north of Swedish Lapland. See page 343

❼ **Kungsleden trail** Don your hiking boots and discover Sweden's longest trail, which winds its way through some of the most haunting scenery the north has to offer. See page 344

HIGHLIGHTS ARE MARKED ON THE MAP ON PAGE 314

9 Strömsund and routes north

At the beginning of its long journey north from Östersund, the Inlandsbanan crosses the Indalsälven River, one of Sweden's greatest natural sources of power, the first sure sign that civilization is slowly being left behind and only the wilds of nature lie ahead. Indeed, it's almost two hours before the train makes the first stop of any significance,

SWEDISH LAPLAND

HIGHLIGHTS

1 Vildmarksvägen
2 Snowmobiling
3 Lappstaden, Arvisjaur
4 The Arctic Circle, Jokkmokk
5 Icehotel, Jukkasjärvi
6 Northern lights, Abisko
7 Kungsleden trail

NORWEGIAN SEA

▭▭▭ Inlandsbanan

0 ——— 60
kilometres

9

LAPLAND, LAPPLAND OR SÁPMI

Whilst Lapland's strong cultural identity is evident in every town and village across the north, it's a much trickier task to try to pin down the region geographically. The word **Lapland** means different things to different people. Mention it to a Swede (the Swedish spelling is **Lappland**) and they'll immediately think of the northern Swedish province of the same name which begins just south of Dorotea, runs up to the Norwegian and Finnish borders in the north, and stretches east towards (but doesn't include) the Bothnian coast. For the original inhabitants of the north, the *Sámi*, the area they call **Sápmi** (the indigenous name for Lapland) extends from Norway through Sweden and Finland to the Russian Kola peninsula, an area where they've traditionally lived a semi-nomadic life, following their reindeer from valley bottom to fell top. Most foreigners have a hazy idea of where Lapland is; for the sake of this Guide, we've assumed Swedish Lapland (the English spelling) to be located within the borders of the administrative province of Lappland but have included all of Route 342 – The Wilderness Way, or Vildmarksvägen – beginning in Strömsund (see opposite), which crosses into Lappland, as well as the Torne Valley, which also lies partly within the province.

at Ulriksfors – the wayside halt for the small waterside town of **Strömsund** – before continuing on to the appealing little town of **Dorotea**. Strömsund is the starting point for Route 342, the **Wilderness Way** (Vildmarksvägen), a circular road looping out towards the Norwegian border; the route passes through stunning scenery more than worthy of its name, rejoining the main road north, the Inlandsvägen, in Vilhelmina.

Strömsund and around

Built on a narrow isthmus of land between Russfjärden lake and the extensive **Ströms Vattudal** network of **waterways** that stretches to the northwest, **STRÖMSUND** is a shy and retiring sort of place. It consists of no more than a couple of parallel streets sporting the odd shop or two, and is of interest mainly as a centre for **canoeing** on the surrounding rivers and lakes. The tourist office can rent out canoes (around 200kr/day).

Stone age rock paintings

Strömsund's other claim to fame is its proximity to the impressive **Stone Age rock paintings** (*hällmålningar* in Swedish) at **Fångsjön**, around 10km southeast along Route 345. The paintings, created by hunter-gatherers around 2500BC, were a plea to their gods for plentiful game.

ARRIVAL AND INFORMATION   STRÖMSUND

By train There's no actual train station in Strömsund, but you can get off the Inlandsbanan at nearby Ulriksfors and walk the 4km into town or take a taxi (☎ 0670 100 63; 200kr).

By bus The Inlandsexpressen bus #45 stops in the town itself.

Tourist office Storgatan 6 (late June–early Aug Mon–Fri 10am–6pm, Sat 10am–3pm; early Aug–late June Mon–Fri 9am–4pm; ☎ 0670 164 00, ⓦ stromsund.se). The office is in the centre of town, and rents bikes for around 150kr/day. It can also provide information – walking routes, details of places to stay and maps – on the road known as the Wilderness Way (see page 317), which starts here.

ACCOMMODATION AND EATING

Annexet Grill Huset Lövbergavägen 1 ☎ 0670 61 40 00. No-nonsense burgers, kebabs and Mexican burritos (all around 85kr) are dished up at this small restaurant on the main road through town. Elegant it certainly isn't but in Strömsund you can't afford to be too choosy. Daily 10am–10pm.

Nordica Ramselevägen 6 ☎ 0670 61 10 00, ⓦ hotel nordica.se. After opening its doors in 1980, the rather unremarkable *Nordica* is still going strong, offering plainly decorated rooms in a sprawling one-storey structure shared with Folkets Hus (the community centre) in the centre of town. Guests also have free use of the sauna. 995kr/1195kr

Strömsunds Camping Strömsvägen 38 ☎ 0670 164 10, ⓦ stromsund.se/stromsundscamping. On the outskirts

9

of town – about 1km out – on the way to Östersund, this peaceful campsite has three heated outdoor pools, and reasonably priced cabins to rent. Open all year round, though outside the June–Aug period check-in is at the tourist office. Tents 200kr, cabins 400kr

A BRIEF LOOK AT THE SÁMI

Among the oldest people in Europe, the **Sámi** – erroneously known to many as "Lapps" – are probably descended from the original prehistoric inhabitants of much of Scandinavia and northern Russia. Today there are around 58,000 *Sámi*, stretched across the whole of the northernmost regions of Norway, Sweden, Finland and Russia; traces of their nomadic culture have even been discovered as far south as Poland. In Sweden itself – though the population is declining – they number around 17,000 (ten percent of the population of northern Sweden), their domain extending over half the country, stretching up from the northern parts of Dalarna.

LANGUAGE

The *Sámi* **language** is a rich one, strongly influenced by their harmonious natural existence. There are no words for certain alien concepts (such as "war"), but there are ninety different terms to express variations in snow conditions. One of the Finno-Ugric group of languages, which also contains Finnish and Hungarian, the *Sámi* language is divided into three dialects which are not mutually comprehensible. In Sweden you'll come across two words for *Sámi*: the politically correct *Sámi* (as used by the *Sámi* themselves), and, more commonly, the Swedish corruption *Same* (plural *Samer*).

REINDEER HERDING

Reindeer, of which there are estimated to be 250,000 in Sweden (the maximum allowed by law is 280,000), have been at the centre of *Sámi* life and culture for thousands of years, with generations of families following the seasonal movements of the animals. Accordingly, the *Sámi* year is divided into eight separate seasons, ranging from early spring, when they traditionally bring the reindeer cows up to the calving areas in the hills, through to winter, when they return to the forests and the pastures.

CHERNOBYL

The *Sámi* were dealt a grievous blow by the **Chernobyl** nuclear disaster of 1986, which led to a fundamental change in *Sámi* living patterns: the fallout contaminated not only the lichen that their reindeer feed on in winter, but also the game, fish, berries and fungi that supplement their own diet. Contamination of reindeer meat meant the collapse of exports of the product to southern Scandinavia, Germany, America and the Far East – and even today the lichen (the reindeer's favourite food) in certain parts of the north is unfit for consumption, a fact which the *Sámi*, perhaps understandably, are keen to play down. Promises of government compensation came late in the day and failed to address the fact that this disaster wasn't just on an economic level for the *Sámi*, their traditional culture being inseparably tied to reindeer herding.

THE SÁMI TODAY

The enduring *Sámi* culture, which once defined much of this land, is now under threat. Centuries of **mistrust** between the *Sámi* and the Swedish population have led to today's often tense standoff; *Sámi* accusing Swede of stealing his land, Swede accusing *Sámi* of scrounging off the state. The escalating problems posed by **tourism** – principally the erosion of grazing land under the pounding feet of hikers – have also made the *Sámi*s traditional existence increasingly uncertain.

However, perhaps as a consequence of Chernobyl, there has been an expansion in *Sámi* culture. Traditional **arts and crafts** have become popular and are widely available in craft shops, and *Sámi* **music** (characterized by the rhythmic sounds of **joik**, a form of throat-singing) is being given a hearing by fans of world music. On balance, it would appear that the *Sámi* are largely managing to retain their culture and identity in modern Sweden.

For more on the *Sámi* in Sweden, visit ⓦsametinget.se.

TRAVELLING THE WILDERNESS WAY BY BUS

The #425 **bus** runs from **Strömsund** to **Gäddede**. There's one daily service and two buses on Fridays (wlanstrafiken-z.se). Travelling on a Friday is best since you can take the first bus, get off wherever you like (just tell the driver to stop), and spend the late afternoon and early evening walking or chilling out by the side of a lake before catching the second bus and continuing on to Gäddede. On weekdays the bus connects in Gäddede with the #472 to Stora Blåsjön and Anakarede, beside the pretty Stora Blåsjön lake.

There's no bus connection from Stora Blåsjön over the **Stekenjokk plateau** to Klimpfjäll, but there are three other options: take a **taxi** from Stora Blåsjön (☎0672 201 53); **hitch** between the two places – there are a lot of German and Dutch camper vans on this stretch of the road who may be able to help out with a lift over the plateau; or **hike** from Ankarede towards Raukasjön lake before heading north up over the Norra Borgafjällen mountains for Slipsiken lake and down into Klimpfjäll – a distance of approximately 40km, best covered over two days.

Once at **Klimpfjäll**, bus #420 runs down to Saxnäs and Vilhelmina (Mon–Fri 2 daily, Sun 1 daily; wtabussen.nu).

Vildmarksvägen: the Wilderness Way

From Strömsund, **Route 342**, the 360km-long **Wilderness Way** (Vildmarksvägen), strikes out northwest towards the mountains at Gäddede, before hugging the Norwegian border and crossing the barren Stekenjokk plateau (876m; only open from early June to mid-Oct). It then swings inland again, joining Route 45 at Vilhelmina. The route ranks as one of the most beautiful and dramatic in Sweden, passing through great swathes of **virgin forest**, tiny forgotten villages and true wilderness. It's also the part of Sweden with the densest population of **bears**. If you're driving, stop wherever you can, turn off the engine and listen to the deep silence, broken only by the calls of the birds and the whisper of the forest.

There are plenty of **lakes** along the way ideal for nude bathing – you can choose whichever one you want to make your own as there'll be nobody else there. One of the most beautiful stretches of rocky beach is just south of the tiny village of Alanäs on the beautiful Flåsjön lake, before you get to Gäddede.

Hällsingsåfallet

If you have your own transport, you should turn left at **Bågede** and follow the minor, very rocky road along the southern shore of **Fågelsjön lake** to reach **Hällsingsåfallet**, an impressive **waterfall**. Sweden's answer to Niagara Falls, it has an 800m-long canyon, into which the falls plummet 43m; the canyon is getting longer every year due to continuing erosion.

Gäddede and Murusjöen lake

The only town along the Wilderness Way is **GÄDDEDE**, whose name means "the spot where the northern pike can no longer go upstream". The name may be cute but the place certainly isn't; give it a miss and instead turn off the main road and follow the road signed "Nordli" for a few kilometres to the long and empty sandy beaches of **Murusjöen lake**, right on the border with Norway (the beach is in Sweden, the water in Norway). You'll be hard pushed to find a more idyllic spot: the silence is total, the deep blue water still and calm, and the mountains in the distance dark and brooding.

Stora Blåsjön and Ankarede

Stora Blåsjön, a lake 50km to the north of Gäddede, is surrounded by blue mountains; the village of **STORA BLÅSJÖN** is where the road starts to climb above the tree line to cross the desolate, boulder-strewn **Stekenjokk plateau** into the province of Lappland. Just outside Stora Blåsjön, look out for the minor road leading to **ANKAREDE**, an age-

9

old meeting place for the local *Sámi*; even today, families from Sweden and Norway get together here at midsummer and again in the autumn. Its old wooden **church** dates from 1896 and is located by the lake, between the two rivers. In addition, there are around twenty circular *Sámi* wooden huts – *kåtor* – close by.

The Stekenjokk plateau is the temporary summer home of several *Sámi* families, who tend their reindeer on the surrounding slopes, including those of the magnificent peak of **Gervenåkko** (1141m) to the east of the road.

Fatmomakke

After dropping into the minuscule village of **Klimpfjäll**, the Wilderness Way continues east. Taking the first turn to the left, after about 12km and then following the signs, you'll reach **FATMOMAKKE**, a fascinating *Sámi* **church town** made up of eighty *kåtor* and twenty cottages, gathered neatly around the church, and twenty log cabins lined up by the side of Kultsjön lake. The first church on the site was built in 1790, but the *Sámi* met together here long before that for special religious celebrations including marriages, christenings and funerals, travelling vast distances on skis, horseback or by boat. The huts are made out of birch wood, with a hole in the roof to let the smoke out, and birch twigs on the floor to sit on. Everything inside is orderly, the fireplace in the middle, the cooking area at the back; there's a strict code of behaviour as well – you must first wait in the entrance before being invited to enter. Look out for the signposted *visningskåta*, the "show hut" to the right of the church up on the hill, and have a peek inside.

Saxnäs

About 20km further east of Fatmomakke, the lakeside hamlet of **SAXNÄS** is as good a place as any to break your journey and enjoy some of the magnificent scenery hereabouts. It's also a good spot for adventure activities, or some pampering at the spa resort (see below).

ACCOMMODATION   SAXNÄS

Kultsjögården Kultsjögården ✆0940 700 44, ⓦkultsjogarden.se. A nicely located hostel with views of the Marsfjällen mountains. Guests have access to a fully fitted kitchen for self-catering or can opt for half-board. Dorms **200kr**, doubles **400kr**, cabins **650kr**

STF Saxnäsgården ✆0940 377 00, ⓦsaxnas.se. A health complex and spa resort combined, this wilderness hotel also has new lakeside cabins for rent, with open fireplaces and a sauna. There's a divine 34°C swimming pool, herbal health baths, massage facilities, saunas, a fitness centre and sports hall, too. It also rents out mountain bikes, canoes, fishing tackle and motorboats and, in winter, arranges dog sledding trips and snowmobile rental. Contact resort for cabins price. Hostel doubles **590kr**, hotel doubles **1200kr**

Dorotea

Avoiding the Wilderness Way detour, it's possible to head directly north from Strömsund both along the Inlandsbanan and the Inlandsvägen to tiny **DOROTEA**, 71km north, a journey of around an hour by rail or road. A textbook example of a linear village, its houses and shops strung out in a long line either side of the main road, Dorotea has a few attractions which merit a stop on the long journey north. For one thing, it has the biggest **bear** population in Sweden; bears regularly wander into town during the night to rummage through rubbish bins for scraps of food.

Last Supper sculpture

Whilst in Dorotea, make sure to see the powerful Björn Martinius group **sculpture** of the Last Supper. Housed in a small chapel in the church graveyard on a low hill just off the main road, the life-size wooden figures sit around three long trestle tables – the very size of the sculpture, filling an entire room, the striking bright colours used to paint the figures, as well as the intense expressions, create a sense of life and motion that's enough to send a shiver down the spine of the most ardent agnostic.

INFORMATION

Tourist office Storgatan 40 (late June–early Aug Mon–Fri 10am–6.30pm, Sat & Sun noon–5.30pm; early Aug–late June Mon–Fri 10am–noon & 1–4pm; ☎0942 140 63, ⓦ

DOROTEA

southlapland.com/en/dorotea). Located at the top of the village, a 10min walk along the main road from the train station. It has good advice on local hiking routes and fishing trips.

ACCOMMODATION AND EATING

Ankis Bar & Pizzeria Storgatan 37 ☎0942 100 68, ⓦankisbar.se. Substantial meaty meals such as Västerbotten schnitzel from 120kr, plus pizzas (from 75kr) and a daily *dagens rätt*. The interior is a little plain and the quality of the food is not great but that doesn't seem to deter the locals. Mon–Fri 10.30am–10pm, Sat & Sun 10.30am–10pm.

Doro Camping Lappland ☎046 073 0807738, ⓦdorocamping.com. Beautifully situated beside the Bergvattenån River, this campsite has two- and four-bed cabins, as well as a number of apartments with a private kitchen and bathroom. There is access to showers and a sauna in the nearby service building. Tents 150kr, cabins

650kr, apartments 500kr

Dorotea Bergsvägen 2 ☎0942 477 80, ⓦfacebook. com/hotelldorotea. Rooms in Dorotea's one and only hotel are bright and clean, though a little lacking in style. There is, however, a decent sauna suite available for guests. 995kr/1195kr

Konditori Dorotea Parkvägen 2, ☎046 942 100 07. A popular café serving the locals for over thirty years and a favourite place for catching up. There's a weekday set lunch as well as a number of open sandwiches and cakes – everything is baked on the premises. Mon–Fri 8am–5pm, Sat 10am–3pm, Sun 11am–3pm.

Vilhelmina

The Inlandsvägen and the Wilderness Way meet up again in the pretty town of **VILHELMINA**, 54km north of Dorotea. Once an important forestry centre, now a quiet, unassuming little place with just one main street, it is named after the wife of King Gustav IV Adolf, Fredrika Dorotea Vilhelmina (as is its southerly neighbour, Dorotea). On the main street the *Sámi* **handicraft store**, Risfjells Sameslöjd, Volgsjövägen 46 (Mon–Fri 10am–5pm, Sat 10am–2pm; ⓦsameslojd.se), is worth a look.

Church town

Hembygdsmuseum • Museigatan 2 • Daily June & Aug 10.30am–3pm; July 10.30am–6pm • 30kr

The principal attraction is the **church town**, nestling between Storgatan and Ljusminnesgatan, whose thirty-odd wooden cottages date back to 1792 when the first church was consecrated. It's since been restored, and the cottages can be rented out via the tourist office (see below). The **Hembygdsmuseum** here contains a mind-numbingly dull display of local history from prehistoric times to the present day, featuring the likes of an old sledge, a mock-up of a former school classroom and a portrait of Queen Fredrika Dorotea V.

ARRIVAL AND INFORMATION

VILHELMINA

By train The town's train station is on Järnvägsgatan. Destinations Arvidsjaur (summer 2 daily; 3hr 15 min); Gällivare (summer 1 daily; 9hr 45min); Jokkmokk (summer 1 daily; 8hr); Östersund (summer 1 daily; 4hr).

By bus The train station also serves as the bus arrival and departure point. Destinations Arvidsjaur (2 daily; 3hr 15 min); Gällivare (1 daily; 7hr 10min); Jokkmokk (1 daily; 5hr 40min); Östersund

(2 daily; 3hr 40min); Umeå (2 daily; 3hr 30min).

Tourist office Tingsgatan 1 (early June–late Aug Mon–Thurs 8am–7pm, Fri 9am–2pm, Sat & Sun 10am–6pm; late Aug–early June Mon–Fri 10am–5pm; ☎0940 398 86, ⓦsouthlapland.com). A 10min walk from the train station: head up Postgatan towards the town centre and then turn left into Volgsjövägen.

ACCOMMODATION

Lilla Granvägen 2 ☎0940 150 59, ⓦlillahotellet. vilhelmina.com. Wonderfully friendly staff are on hand to welcome you to this winning little hotel whose rooms

are decorated in cosy, home-from-home style. The spa in the basement is great for whiling away an hour or two and there's even a masseur on hand. 850kr/1095kr

9

Saiva Camping Baksjön ☎0940 107 60, ⓦsaiva.se. The campsite has two- to six-berth cabins for rent and a great sandy beach; to get there walk down the main street, Volgsjövägen, from the centre and take a left turn after about 10min, just before the Volvo garage. Tents 100kr, cabins 290kr

STF Vilhelmina Kyrkstaden Vardrarhem Storgatan ☎0940 398 87, ⓦsvenskaturistforeningen.se/ anlaggningar/stf-vilhelminakyrkstaden-vandrarhem. Idyllically located in several of Vilhelmina's snug church town cottages, the youth hostel is by far the most atmospheric place to stay, replete with creaking floorboards and low ceilings. Some cottages have their own bathrooms and kitchens. Doubles 540kr

Wilhelmina Volgsjövägen 16 ☎0940 554 20, ⓦhotell wilhelmina.se. Showy, rather rambling hotel where each room (and the sauna) has stunning views out over Volgsjön lake and the distant mountains. In summer, breakfast is served on the open-air terrace, high above the lake. 975kr/1200kr

EATING AND DRINKING

Pizzeria Lilla Fjället Volgsjövägen 50B ☎046 940 105 90. This place serves simple dishes, such as pasta carbonara, margherita pizza and meatballs for 75kr, and is also a popular spot for a drink or two. Mon–Fri 11am–8pm, Sat & Sun noon–8pm.

Quinto Restaurang Volgsjövägen 27 ☎046 940 121 33, ⓦquintorestaurang.wordpress.com. A good choice range of food here, from hamburgers and pizza to pasta and salads. Daily 11am–8pm.

Martin Bergmans fisk Junction of Wilderness Way and Route 45 ☎0940 250 90, ⓦmbergmansfisk. se. Accomplished smokehouse and deli serving top-notch smoked salmon and other seafood. It can be easily reached on foot from town by walking around 3km along the lakeside path, Strandpromenaden. Mon–Wed 9am–5.30pm, Thurs & Fri 9am–7pm, Sat & Sun 9am–5.30pm.

Wilhelmina Volgsjövägen 16 ☎0940 554 20. For something more upmarket, try this hotel's restaurant. It serves traditional northern Swedish dishes such as Arctic char (195kr), or opt for the house speciality – a succulent burger of wild game with chanterelle mushroom, lingonberry mayo and gherkins (185kr). The three-course set menu is 415kr. Mon–Fri 10.30am–9pm, Sat 11.30am–7pm, Sun 11.30am–7pm.

The E12: Blå vägen

The one defining factor that unites the small settlement of **Storuman** with its northwesterly neighbours, **Tärnaby** and **Hemavan**, is the **Blå vägen** (Blue Way) – or E12, as it is less poetically known – running through all three villages. This major artery, one of northern Sweden's better roads, is so named because it follows the course of the great Ume River that flows down from the mountains of southern Lappland to Umeå on the Bothnian coast. Water is omnipresent hereabouts, not only in Storuman, a sleepy little town which sits on the banks of the eponymous lake, best used as an access point to the mountains, but also all the way up to Tärnaby, a small-time skiing centre, and Hemavan, the start of Sweden's longest and best hiking trail, the **Kungsleden**, leading 500km north to Abisko.

Storuman

In 1741, the first settler arrived in what was to become **STORUMAN**, 68km north of Vilhelmina. His first neighbours didn't appear until forty years later and even by World War I, Storuman, then called Luspen (the *Sámi* name for a river which emerges from a lake) numbered barely forty inhabitants working just eight farms. Things changed, though, with the arrival of the railway in the 1920s; today Storuman is an important centre for the generation of hydroelectric power. That said, there's not much to the town: the centre consists of one tiny street that supports a couple of shops and banks. Whilst in Storuman check out the town's emblem, **Wildman**, a giant-sized red figure who stands near the *Toppen* hotel (see opposite) madly brandishing a club, a traditional symbol for Lapland encapsulating strength, riches and determination.

Old railway hotel

Library Mon & Wed 11am–4pm, Tues & Thurs 11am–7pm.

9

Arriving at the train-cum-bus station on Järnvägsgatan, you can't fail to spot the wonderful **old railway hotel** on the opposite side of the street; it was built in association with the Inlandsbanan in 1924, and now houses the local **library**. The wide-planked, tarred exterior in National Romantic style hides an ornate interior, complete with wrought-iron chandeliers and decorative wall painting (similar to folk art styles found in Dalarna), that's well worth a peek.

Utsikten tower

If you find yourself at a loose end whilst waiting for buses or trains, one diversion is the worthwhile short walk signed "*Utsikten*" from the main square, which leads up to a wooden **tower** from where there are fantastic views out over the surrounding lakes and forest towards the mountains which mark the border with Norway; it's around a 2km uphill walk to the platform from the town centre.

ARRIVAL AND DEPARTURE   STORUMAN

Just over an hour by the Inlandsbanan from Vilhelmina, Storuman is a **transport hub** for this part of southern Lapland. From here, **buses** run northwest up the E12, skirting the Tärnafjällen mountains to Tärnaby and Hemavan. In the opposite direction, the road leads down to Umeå via Lycksele, from where there are also train connections to Umeå.

By train The train station is on Järnvägsgatan, along with the bus station.

Destinations Arvidsjaur (summer 1 daily; 2hr 45 min); Gällivare (summer 1 daily; 8hr); Jokkmokk (summer 1

daily; 6hr 20min); Östersund (summer 1 daily; 5hr 45min); Vilhelmina (summer 1 daily; 1hr 40min).

By bus Services from Vilhelmina (ⓦ tabussen.nu) stop behind the train station building. A direct bus, Lapplandspilen (ⓦ lapplandspilen.se), links Storuman with Stockholm.

Destinations Gällivare (2 daily; 55min); Hemavan (3 daily; 2hr); Stockholm (2 weekly; 11hr 45 min); Tärnaby (5 daily; 1hr 30min); Östersund (2 daily; 4hr 45 min); Umeå (6 daily; 3hr 15min); Vilhelmina (3 daily; 55min).

ACCOMMODATION AND EATING

Café Akkan Skolgatan 23 ☎ 046 70 637 95 59. Attached to the library, this is a good place for coffee, cakes and sandwiches. It also serves light lunches, including quiches and salads. Mon, Wed & Fri 10am–4pm, Tues & Thurs 10am–7pm, Sat 11am–3pm.

Restaurang 3:an Järnvägsgatan 15 ☎ 046 951 333 33, ⓦ trean.eu. This restaurant serves a variety of dishes. If you are in the mood for pizza or freshly grilled meat, this might be the right place for you. Mon–Thurs 11am–8pm, Fri 11am–midnight, Sat 1–10pm, Sun 1–7pm.

Storumans Bad & Camping Lokgränd 3 ☎ 0951 143 00, ⓦ storumancamping.se. Lakeside campsite with on-site saunas for guest use, as well as a church built in the style of a *kåta*, a traditional *Sámi* hut. There are also cabins here

for rent. Open late May–early Sept. Tents 160kr, cabins 550kr

Toppen Blå Vägen 238 ☎ 0951 777 00, ⓦ hotelltoppen. se. This hotel is more luxurious and correspondingly expensive than anything else Storuman has to offer, though cheaper, simpler rooms with shared facilities are also available (400kr); kitchens are in the annexe next door. The hotel restaurant serves the finest food in Storuman, using locally sourced produce and featuring a good range of traditional fare such as reindeer and elk. There's also a good lunch menu on weekdays. To get here, walk up Stationsgatan from the station. Restaurant Mon–Fri 11am–late, Sat & Sun noon–late. 850kr/1195kr

Tärnaby and around

TÄRNABY, 125km northwest of Storuman along the E12, is the birthplace of Sweden's greatest skier, **Ingemar Stenmark**. A double Olympic gold medallist, he occasionally spiced up his training here with a spot of tightrope walking and monocycling. It's a pretty place: yellow flower-decked meadows run to the edge of the mountain forests, the trees felled to leave great empty swathes that accommodate World Cup ski slopes. Since there's not much to do in Tärnaby itself, it's a much better idea to explore the surrounding countryside: a popular **walk** leads across the nearby mountain, **Laxfjället**, which affords fantastic views down over the village – it can be reached by chair lift from either of the accommodation options listed below. Another good walk for a sunny day leads to the beach at **Lake Laisan**, though the water is rarely warm enough to swim even

9

in the height of summer; to get there, take the footpath that branches off right from the main Sandviksvägen past the campsite or ask the tourist office for precise directions.

ARRIVAL AND INFORMATION TÄRNABY

By bus The bus station in Tärnaby is at the junction of the main road, the E12, and Granäsvägen. Services from Storuman (1hr 45min) pull in here, in addition to through services to Umeå on the Bothnian coast.

Tourist office Västra Strandvägen 1 (mid-June–mid-Aug Mon–Fri 9am–7pm, Sat & Sun 10am–6pm; mid-Aug to mid-June Mon–Fri 9am–5pm; ☎0954 104 50, ⓦhemavantarnaby.se). This office, on the main road, can supply advice about the excellent local fishing.

ACCOMMODATION AND EATING

Åkerlundska gården Östra Strandvägen 16 ☎0954 104 20, ⓦtarnabyfjallhotell.se. With just ten rooms, this popular hostel books up fast. It's located 2km east of the village, up above the *Fjällhotell*. Self-catering facilities are available. Open all year. Doubles 650kr

Tärnaby Camping Sandviksvägen 4 ☎046 70 547 27 97, ⓦtarnabycamping.se. A riverside campsite which also has dorm beds and cabins. There's even a sauna for rent, handily located beside river rapids for a refreshing dip afterwards. Tents 150kr, dorms 150kr, cabins 400kr

Tärnaby Fjällhotell Östra Strandvägen 16 ☎0954 104 20, ⓦtarnabyfjallhotell.com. Located below the hostel, this smart hotel has been providing weary skiers with comfortable, snug accommodation since the mid-1960s. The sauna has amazing 360-degree views out over the surrounding fells. The hotel restaurant, *Backfickan*, is the best place to find good Swedish home cooking, such as sausages with fries (160kr), local Arctic char (265kr) and sliced reindeer meat (270kr); there's also a tolerable pub here. Restaurant daily 5.30–9pm. 850kr/1200kr

Hemavan

Buses continue from Tärnaby to **HEMAVAN**, 18km northwest, which marks the beginning and the end of the 500km **Kungsleden** trail (see page 344). This tiny, nondescript village, straddling the main road, is totally devoid of attractions. It's purely and simply a service centre which provides accommodation and eating opportunities to hikers starting and ending the trail here. Hemavan can be busy during the peak summer season (mid-June to mid-Aug) and at this time it's therefore wise to book a bed in advance to be sure of somewhere to stay.

ARRIVAL AND DEPARTURE HEMAVAN

By plane The village is reachable from Stockholm on direct flights (5 weekly; 1hr 45min; ⓦflexflight.com).

By bus Bus #31 (3 daily; ⓦtabussen.nu) makes the 2hr drive northwest from Storuman.

ACCOMMODATION AND EATING

Hemavans Fjällcenter Renstigen 1 ☎0954 300 02, ⓦhemavansfjallcenter.se. The hotel-cum-youth hostel here is always busy with hikers, so it's essential to book ahead all year. You'll find a swimming pool, sauna, steam room, Jacuzzi and even a climbing wall on site. The in-house restaurant serves a respectable lunch buffet on weekdays

throughout the year and is also open in the evenings for dinner during the ski season. The bar upstairs also serves pub meals and snacks. Restaurant Mon–Fri 11am–2pm, during winter also Sat & Sun noon–3pm. Hostel doubles 530kr, hotel doubles 1095kr

Sorsele and around

The next major stop on the Inlandsbanan and bus route north of Storuman is **SORSELE**, 76km away – a pint-sized, quiet little town on the **Vindelälven River**. The town became a *cause célèbre* among conservationists in Sweden when activists forced the government to abandon its plans to build a hydroelectric power station, which would have regulated the river's flow. Consequently, the Vindelälven remains in its natural state today – seething with rapids – and is one of only four rivers in the country that hasn't been tampered with in some way or other.

9

The big event here is the **Vindelälvsdraget**, a 400km, four-day dog sled race from Ammarnäs to Vännäsby held in the third week of March. Sorsele is an ideal base for **fly-fishing**: the Vindelälven and the other local river, Laisälven, are teeming with grayling and brown trout, and there are a number of local lakes stocked with char. Ask at the tourist offices for details. If you're looking to get well off the beaten track, Sorsele provides ready access to the *Sámi* mountain village of **Ammarnäs**, which is about as remote as you get by road in this part of Swedish Lapland.

Inlandsbanemuséet

Inlandsbanan museum • Stationsgatan 19, in the same building as the tourist office • June–Aug Mon–Fri 9am–6pm, Sat & Sun 10am–5pm; Sept–May Mon–Fri 9am–4pm • 30kr

Aside from the river, Sorsele's only other attraction is the **Inlandsbanemuséet**, which details the life and times of the Inlandsbanan. The labelling is in Swedish only, though there is an English-language factsheet available, which will help make sense of the evocative black-and-white photographs of German troops travelling up and down the line during World War II; during the height of the conflict, the so-called "horseshoe traffic" (named after the shape of the route) saw 12,000 German soldiers and significant amounts of war material transported every week between Narvik and Trondheim in occupied Norway, travelling via Gällivare, Arvidsjaur and Östersund along the Inlandsbanan in supposedly neutral Sweden.

ARRIVAL AND INFORMATION   SORSELE

By train The train station is beside the main road, Stationsgatan.

Destinations Arvidsjaur (summer 1 daily; 1hr 15min); Gällivare (summer 1 daily; 6hr 30min); Jokkmokk (summer 1 daily; 5hr); Storuman (summer 1 daily; 1hr); Östersund (summer 1 daily; 6hr 45min).

By bus Buses stop outside the train station on Stationsgatan.

Destinations Ammarnäs (2 daily; 1hr 20min); Gällivare (1 daily; 5hr 5min); Östersund (2 daily; 6hr); Storuman (2 daily; 1hr).

Tourist office Stationsgatan 19 (June–Aug Mon–Fri 9am–6pm, Sat & Sun 10am–5pm; Sept–May Mon–Fri 9am–4pm; ☎0952 140 90, ⓦvisitvindelalven.org). The tourist office is at the train station, and has information about local activities such as fishing and canoe rental.

ACCOMMODATION AND EATING

Sorsele Camping/STF Sorsele Vandrarhem Fritidsvägen 1 ☎0952 101 24, ⓦlapplandskatan.nu. The riverside campsite, with four-bed cabins, is also the location for the town's small STF hostel; rooms at the hostel all have bunk beds but no private facilities, plus there's a kitchen for self-catering. Tents 180kr, dorms 250kr, doubles 500kr, cabins 375kr

Sorsele River Hotellgatan 2 ☎0952 121 50, ⓦsorseleriverhotel.se. The only hotel in town is a smart place featuring tasteful rooms with wooden floors and modern furnishings as well as a superb sauna and Jacuzzi suite. The restaurant has a buffet of tasty local fare at lunchtime (until 2pm), and is also open in the evenings for northern Swedish delicacies (95–245kr) such as sliced reindeer and Arctic char. To reach the hotel from the train station, turn left into Stationsgatan, right into Södra Esplanaden, left again into Vindelvägen and finally right into Hotellgatan. Restaurant Mon–Thurs 11am–8pm, Fi 11am–9pm, Sat & Sun noon–8pm. 1195kr

Ammarnäs

The tiny mountain village of **AMMARNÄS**, with a population of around 100, lies ninety minutes' bus ride northwest of Sorsele; the road only reached this remote corner of Sweden in 1939. Set in a wide river valley by the side of the **Gautsträsk lake** and at the foot of the towering **Ammarfjället mountains**, the village offers peace and tranquillity of the first order, and ready access to the Kungsleden trail (see page 344), too. This is **reindeer** country (one-third of the villagers here are reindeer herders), and for hundreds of years the local *Sámi* are known to have migrated with their animals from the coast to the surrounding fells for summer pasture.

9

Brief history

The first settlement began here in 1821 when two *Sámi* brothers, Måns and Abraham Sjulsson, were granted permission to set up home at Övre Gautsträsk. When they failed to keep the terms of their agreement, a new tenant, **Nils Johansson**, took over. He eked out an existence by cultivating the land and is responsible for *Potatisbacken* or **Potato Hill**, adjacent to the church at the eastern end of the village at the junction of Kyrkvägen and Nolsivägen (get here by following Nolsivägen from opposite the *Ammarnäsgården* hotel, signed "*Norra Ammarnäs*"), where the northern Swedish potato (a sweet, yellow variety), is grown – unusual for a location so far north. With the founding of a postal station in 1895, the village changed its name from Gautsträsk (*gaut* is a *Sámi* word meaning "bowl" – an accurate description of its valley-bottom location) to Ammarnäs – the foreland between the Tjulån and Vindelälven rivers. A stone plinth now stands in Nils Johansson's memory across from the church on Strandvägen.

Sámi church town and Samegården

The **Sámi church town**, near the potato hill on Nolsivägen, was built in 1850, and was moved to its present site in 1911. The dozen or so square wooden huts, which are perched on horizontal logs to help keep them dry, are still used today. Three times a year *Sámi* families gather here, much as they have done for centuries, to celebrate important **festivals**: the *Sámi* festival (held on the Sunday before midsummer), Vårböndagshelgen (spring intercession day, on the first Sunday in July) and Höstböndagshelgen (autumn intercession day, on the last Sunday in Sept). The nearby **Samegården** (*Sámi* museum; ring for opening times on ☎0952 602 39) on Strandvägen has a simple display of *Sámi* history and traditions.

Naturum Vindelfjällen

Nature Centre • Tjulträskvägen • Late May–Sept daily 9am–11am & noon–5pm • Free

The **Naturum Vindelfjällen** has information about the local geology, flora and fauna, and an unflattering selection of stuffed animals, including bear, lynx and wolverine. It also shows a 1940s film of bears in the woods along the Vindelälven – just ask them to put it on. Look out also for the model of the surrounding peaks, which will give you an idea of just how isolated Ammarnäs is, locked in on three sides by mountains.

ARRIVAL AND INFORMATION AMMARNÄS

By bus Buses from Sorsele (2 daily; 1hr 30min) will drop you along the main road, Tjulträskvägen.

Tourist office Ammarnäsgården (late May–Sept daily 9am–5pm; ☎046 73 084 70 33, ⍟ammarnas.nu). Has plenty of maps and brochures on the surrounding countryside, and useful information on hiking, and can also help with the renting of dog sleds and snowmobiles in winter, and rides on Icelandic ponies.

ACCOMMODATION AND EATING

Ammarnäsgården Tjulträskvägen 1 ☎0952 600 03, ⍟ammarnasgarden.se. The only hotel in the village, with rather simple en-suite rooms aimed at hikers walking the Kungsleden; the decent sauna and pool complex in the basement makes up for the lack of creature comforts in the rooms. There are also basic youth hostel dorms in a separate building. The hotel's bar and restaurant is the main eating and drinking option in town. Restaurant no fixed opening times. Hostel doubles <u>570kr</u>, hotel doubles <u>1390kr</u>

Ammarnäs Wärdshus Nolsivägen 6 ☎0952 602 00, ⍟ammarnaswardshus.se. Virtually opposite the tourist office, the former village youth hostel now has decent standard hotel rooms alongside the dorms, plus a handful of cottages. There's a sauna and a guest kitchen on site. Dorms <u>290kr</u>, doubles <u>1100kr</u>, cabins <u>580kr</u>

Arvidsjaur and around

An hour and a half by Inlandsbanan and 89km north of Sorsele, **ARVIDSJAUR** was for centuries where the region's **Sámi** gathered to trade and debate. Their presence was of interest to Protestant missionaries, who established the first church here in 1606. The success of this Swedish settlement was secured when silver was discovered in the nearby mountains, and the town flourished as a staging point and supply depot. While these developments unfolded, the *Sámi* continued to assemble on market days and during religious festivals. At the end of the eighteenth century, they built their own church town of simple wooden huts. Today, out of a total population of five thousand, there are still twenty *Sámi* families in Arvisdjaur who make their living from reindeer husbandry, and the town is a good place to get a real hands-on experience of *Sámi* life.

Arvidsjaur is not one of Sweden's more attractive towns – its streets of drab houses strung out either side of the main drag lined with a dozen or so shops make a pretty depressing impression on any first-time visitor. However, although the modern town is decidedly unappealing, it hides one of northern Sweden's top attractions: the traditional *Sámi* site of **Lappstaden**. Arvidsjaur is also the jumping-off point for day-trips to the **Båtsuoj Sámi Center**, 70km away to the northwest, one of the best places in Swedish Lapland to get to grips with *Sámi* culture and traditions.

Lappstaden

Lappstadsgatan, off Storgatan • Always open; tours run mid-June–mid-Aug daily at 6pm • Free, tours 100kr

A good way to find out more about the *Sámi* culture (which manifests itself more and more as you travel north from here) is to visit **Lappstaden**, which lies just off the main drag, Storgatan. Although you probably won't meet any *Sámi* here, you will at least be able to see how they used to live in traditional huts, or *kåtor*. About eighty of these huts in the eighteenth-century *Sámi* **church town** have survived, and are clumped unceremoniously next to a yellow, modern apartment building. The design of these huts – square wooden buildings supporting a pyramid-shaped roof – is typical of the Forest *Sámi* who lived in the surrounding forests, constructing their homes of indigenous timber. Local *Sámi* schoolteacher, Karin Stenberg, made it her life's work to preserve Lappstaden, and the huts are still used today during the last weekend in August as a venue for a special **festival**, Storstämningshelgen.

Båtsuoj Sámi Center

Hedgatan 40, Gasa • Short visit 350kr, half-day trip 690kr, overnight stay 1300kr • ☎ 070 673 10 33 or ☎ 070 642 31 66 • ⓦ batsuoj.se • From Arvidsjaur, head west on Route 45 to the village of Slagnäs, then take the unnumbered minor road 19km north towards Arjeplog. You can reach Slagnäs by Inlandsbanan, from where Båtsuoj staff will collect you if you book in advance

Seventy kilometres west of Arvidsjaur, in the village of **GASA**, the **Båtsuoj Sámi Center** is a good place to get to grips with the everyday life of the *Sámi*. Here, you'll not only come face to face with **reindeer** (*båtsuoj* in *Sámi)* but also meet real reindeer herders. A **short visit** to Båtsuoj of around an hour or so includes a chance to taste dried reindeer meat sitting around the fire in a *kåta*. A longer **half-day-trip** includes dinner of reindeer cooked over an open fire, and the opportunity to learn a bit about the *Sámi* way of life; the *Sámi* will teach you about their religion, show the way to milk a reindeer and demonstrate the tricks of baking their traditional bread. Frozen reindeer meat is also available for purchase. You can **stay overnight** for an extra 410kr per person in a wooden *kåta*, sleeping on a reindeer skin.

ARRIVAL AND DEPARTURE	ARVIDSJAUR
By plane Flights from Stockholm's Arlanda airport land at the modern airport terminal, 15km east of town, which has been designed to resemble a *Sámi* wooden *kåta*. Taxis run from the airport to the centre (☎ 0960 104 00; 300kr).	**By train** The train station is at the junction of Järnvägsgatan and Stationsgatan.
	Destinations Gällivare (summer 1 daily; 5hr); Jokkmokk (summer 1 daily; 3hr 30min); Östersund (summer 1 daily; 8hr).

9

By bus The bus station is in the centre of town at Västlundavägen, just behind the Konsum supermarket.

Destinations Arjeplog (4 daily; 1hr); Gällivare (1 daily; 4hr); Jokkmokk (1 daily; 2hr 15min); Luleå (2 daily; 3hr); Östersund (2 daily; 7hr 30min).

INFORMATION

Tourist office Storgatan 14B (mid-June–mid-Aug Mon–Fri 9.30am–6pm, Sat & Sun 10am–4.30pm; mid-Aug to mid-June Mon–Fri 10am–noon & 1–3pm; ☎0960 175 00, ⓦvisitarvidsjaur.se). A 5min walk from the train station, up Stationsgatan.

Steam train trips Generally available from Arvidsjaur between mid-July and mid-Aug, featuring vintage coaches from the 1930s. The train runs from Arvidsjaur along the Inlandsbanan west to Slagnäs on Fri and Sat (5.45pm; 200kr), stopping at Storavan beach for swimming and a barbecue. Buy tickets on the train. In recent years volunteers have been in short supply, so make sure you check with the tourist office to see whether the trains are still running.

ACCOMMODATION

If you're planning to visit Arvidsjaur during the winter (when the higher price code applies), it's imperative to book well in advance to secure a room, especially in February and March.

Camp Gielas Järnvägsgatan 111 ☎0960 556 00, ⓦarvidsjaur.se/gielas. This campsite sits beside one of the town's dozen or so lakes, Tvättjärn, with its bathing beaches. It has tent pitches and waterside cabins, plus a sports hall, gym, sauna, tennis courts and mini-golf. Tents **250kr**, cabins **570kr**

Lapland Lodge Östra Kyrkogatan 18 ☎0960 137 20, ⓦlaplandlodge.se. A comfortable, brightly decorated bed-and-breakfast place in a former manor house near the church. Lodge rooms have either a shower or a washbasin but shared toilet facilities, while Deluxe rooms in the extension are all en suite. Lodge rooms **690kr**, Deluxe rooms **990kr**

★ **Laponia** Storgatan 45 ☎0960 555 00, ⓦhotell-laponia.se. The sole hotel in town, with 200 comfortable, modern en-suite rooms and a swimming pool. Between Jan and April it's popular with test drivers from Europe's leading car companies, who come to test out their cars; on-demand prices apply at these times. **990kr/1320kr**

Silvercross 45 Fjällströmsvägen 16 ☎070 644 2862, ⓦsilvercross45.se. For inexpensive accommodation this private youth hostel has double rooms with shared facilities but no dorm beds. Most rooms are in the basement and consequently windowless. Reception is unstaffed – ring on arrival to gain access. **600kr**

EATING AND DRINKING

Afrodite Storgatan 10 ☎0960 173 00, ⓦbit.ly/2KT8SVM. You can sit down here to an Arvidsjaur interpretation of Mediterranean food: pizzas from 75kr, meat and fish mains from 170kr and a few Greek dishes such as moussaka from 115kr. Mon–Thurs 11am–9pm, Fri 5–10pm, Sat 4–11pm, Sun 4–9pm.

Tant Svesa Kafe Stationsgatan 20. This welcome café serves coffee and fresh pastries, and also has cheap lunches, sandwiches, pancakes and salads. There's outdoor seating in summer. Mon–Fri 10am–8pm, Sat & Sun noon–4pm.

Arjeplog

Stretching northwest of Arvidsjaur out towards the Norwegian border, the municipality of Arjeplog, roughly the size of Belgium, supports a population of under three thousand   two-thirds of whom live in the lakeside town, **ARJEPLOG**, 85km from Arvidsjaur. Set away from the main inland road and rail routes, it's a tiny, unassuming sort of place, barely one main street leading to what passes as a main square. The surrounding area is one of the most beautiful parts of Sweden, with nearly nine thousand lakes and vast expanses of mountains and virgin forests. The air is clear and crisp, the rivers clean and deep and the winters mighty cold – in 1989 a temperature of -52°C was recorded here. January and February, in particular, are bitter, dark and silent months, but it's during winter that Arjeplog is at its busiest: hundreds of test drivers from across the world descend on the town to put cars through their paces in the freezing conditions, with brakes and road-holding being given a thorough examination on the frozen lakes; the ABS braking system, for example, was developed here.

9

In summer, Arjeplog is a likeable, peaceful little place, where **hiking**, **canoeing** and **fishing** are all popular activities, each offering the chance of blissful isolation, be it by the side of a secluded mountain tarn or in a clearing deep in the pine forest. In late July you can go **cloudberry picking** in the surrounding marshland, and in the autumn you can hunt for lingonberries, blueberries and wild mushrooms.

Silvermuséet

Silver Museum • Torget • June–Aug Mon–Fri 9am–5pm, Sat 10am–2pm; Sept–May Mon–Fri 10am–1pm & 2–4pm, Sat 10am–2pm • 80kr • ⓦ silvermuseet.se

The only sight in town is the **Silvermuséet**, housed in a yellow wooden building in the main square. It's home to fascinating collections of over 700 pieces of *Sámi* silver, including several ornate silver collars that were handed down from mother to daughter; if a mother had several daughters she would divide her chain amongst them. Whilst in the museum, make sure to visit the cinema in the basement, where you can see a **slide show** about the surrounding countryside and nature, and find how people in this remote part of Sweden learnt to adapt to the harsh climate.

Galtispuoda mountain

15km north of Arjeplog; take Route 95 towards Arvidsjaur then turn left where Galtispuoda is signposted

If you're in Arjeplog with your own transport, it's worth making every effort to see the jaw-dropping panoramic vistas from the top of **Galtispuoda mountain** (808m), which lies 15km north of the village. On a clear day from the peak, you can see over 130km in all directions across the surrounding marshland and forest, with views extending even into Norway. From this amazing vantage point, you start to realize just how sparsely populated this remote part of Sweden is: if Stockholm, for example, had the same population density as Arjeplog it would have just fifty inhabitants.

ARRIVAL AND INFORMATION   ARJEPLOG

By bus Daily buses from Arvidsjaur (Mon–Fri 3 daily, Sat & Sun 1 daily; 1hr) arrive and depart from the bus station on Storgatan.

Tourist office In the main square (June–Aug Mon– Fri 9am–5pm, Sat 10am–2pm; Sept–May Mon–Fri 10am–1pm & 2–4pm, Sat 10am–2pm; ☎0961 145 20, ⓦ polcirkeln.nu). The office can help with local hiking trails, fishing and bike rental.

ACCOMMODATION

Bear in mind that in winter (Jan–April), accommodation hereabouts is often booked months in advance by the major car manufacturers, and on-demand prices apply.

Hornavan Västra Skeppsholmen 3 ☎0961 77 71 00, ⓦ hornavanhotell.se. With gorgeous views out over Sweden's deepest lake, Hornavan, this welcoming hotel, perched atop a small hillock, is a great find: rooms are decorated in modern flat-pack style but quite comfortable. __1160kr__

Kraja A 10min walk along Silvervägen ☎0961 315 00, ⓦ silverhatten.se/boende/kraja. This lakeside campsite has snug and well-appointed cabins as well as a number of double rooms; there's also an outdoor swimming pool which is open to non-residents (free). Tents __135kr__, doubles __995kr__, cabins __795kr__

Lyktan/STF Arjeplog Vandrarhem Lugnetvägen 4 ☎0961 612 10, ⓦ hotellyktan-arjeplog.se. This central hotel offers comfortable modern rooms of the highest standard, and also incorporates the palatial STF youth hostel, itself the best-value accommodation in town; every room in the hostel sleeps a maximum of four and has en-suite facilities. Hotel open all year; hostel open May–Oct. Hostel doubles __600kr__, hotel doubles __950kr/1200kr__

EATING AND DRINKING

Hornavan Västra Skeppsholmen 3 ☎0961 77 71 00, ⓦ hornavanhotell.se/restaurang. This hotel restaurant is the place to look for expertly prepared Lapland delicacies, such as reindeer in its various guises, venison meatballs and elk burger. Main courses cost 155–265kr. Thurs–Sat 6–9pm.

Kraja Värdshus At Kraja campsite ☎0961 315 00, ⓦ silverhatten.se/boende/kraja/restaurang. Head to

9

this lakeside restaurant at the campsite for gourmet food such as fillet of elk or saddle of reindeer; reckon around 200kr for a main course. From mid-June to mid-Aug food is served in a *Sámi kåta* in the middle of the campsite. Daily 5–10pm.

Leon's Steakhouse Drottninggatan 4 ☎046 961 614 44, ⓦleonssteakhouse.com. Quite simply the best steak in the area. Mon–Thurs 11am–2.30pm & 4–8pm, Fri 11am–9pm, Sat noon–9pm, Sun noon–9pm.

Pizzeria Verona Drottninggatan 6 ☎046 961 108 00, ⓦpizzeriaverona.nu. Although this place is rather basic to look at, locals swear by the quality of the pizzas. Different mains will set you back a reasonable 80kr per dish. Mon–Fri 11am–10pm, Sat & Sun noon–10pm.

Jokkmokk and around

During his journey in Lapland, the botanist Carl von Linné said, "If not for the mosquitoes, this would be earth's paradise." His comments were made after journeying along the river valley of the Lilla Luleälven during the short summer weeks, when the mosquitoes are at their most active. Along this valley is the town of **JOKKMOKK**, its name deriving from one particular bend (*mokk* in *Sámi*) in the river (*jokk*). The densely forested municipality through which the river runs is the size of Wales and has a tiny population: just three thousand.

The town is a welcome oasis, although not an immediately appealing one; the prettiest part is around Stationsgatan, which links the train station with the main street, Storgatan, where the wooden houses and shops are oddly reminiscent of small-town America. Jokkmokk started life as winter quarters for the *Sámi*, and by the beginning of the seventeenth century had a market and church, which heralded the start of a permanent settlement. Today, as well as being a well-known handicraft centre, Jokkmokk functions as the capital of the *Sámi* and is home to **Samernas Folkhögskola**, the only further education college in Sweden using the *Sámi* language, teaching handicraft-making, reindeer husbandry and ecology.

Ájtte museum

Swedish Mountain & Sámi Museum • Kyrkogatan 3 • Mid-June–mid-Aug daily 9am–6pm; mid-Aug–mid-June Tues–Fri 10am–4pm, Sat noon–4pm • 90kr • ⓦajtte.com

Jokkmokk's fascinating **Ájtte museum** (*ájtte* means storage hut in *Sámi*) is the place to really mug up on the *Sámi*; it's a brief walk east of the centre, off the main street, Storgatan. The displays and exhibitions recount the tough existence of northern Scandinavia's original settlers, and show how things have slowly improved over time – today the modern *Sámi* are more dependent on snow scooters and helicopters to herd their reindeer than on the age-old methods employed by their ancestors. The museum's collection of traditional costumes and silver spoons, which gave the owner prestige and were a symbol of social status, is particularly engaging. There are also impressive displays of stuffed eagles and owls, including an enormous golden eagle.

Fjällträdgård

Alpine Garden • Lappstavägen • June Mon–Fri 11am–5pm; July–mid-Aug Mon–Fri 11am–5pm, Sat & Sun noon–5pm • 50kr • ⓦajtte. com/besoka/jokkmokks-fjalltradgard

Close to the Ájtte museum on Lappstavägen, the **Fjällträdgård** is home to moor-king, mountain avens, glacier crowfoot and other vegetation that's found on the fells around Jokkmokk. There's also a small section of edible plants which the *Sámi* have traditionally used for medicinal purposes.

THE ARCTIC CIRCLE AND THE MIDNIGHT SUN

Just 7km south of Jokkmokk, the Inlandsbanan finally crosses the **Arctic Circle**, the imaginary line drawn around the earth at roughly 66°N, which links the northernmost points along which the sun can be seen on the shortest day of the year. Crossing into the Arctic is occasion enough for a bout of whistle-blowing by the train, as it pulls up to allow everyone to take photos. However, the painted white rocks that curve away over the hilly ground here, a crude delineation of the Circle, are completely inaccurate. Due to the Earth's uneven orbit, the line is creeping northwards at a rate of 14–15m every year; the real Arctic Circle is now around 1km further north than this line. It won't be for another ten to twenty thousand years that the northward movement will stop – by which time the Circle will have reached 68°N – and then start moving slowly south again.

Thanks to the refraction of sunlight in the atmosphere, the **midnight sun** can also be seen south of the Arctic Circle – Arvidsjaur marks the southernmost point in Sweden where this happens – for a few days each year. The further north you travel, the longer the period when the phenomenon is visible, and conversely the longer the polar winter. True midnight sun occurs when the entire sun is above the horizon at midnight. The following is a list of the main towns and the dates when the midnight sun can be seen; remember, though, that even outside these periods, there is still 24-hour daylight in the north of Sweden in summer, since only part of the sun ever dips below the horizon.

Arvidsjaur and Haparanda	June 20/21
Arjeplog	June 12/13 to July 28/29
Jokkmokk	June 8/9 to July 2/3
Gällivare	June 4/5 to July 6/7
Kiruna	May 28/29 to July 11/12
Karesuando	May 26/27 to July 15/16
Treriksröset	May 22/23 to July 17/18

Sámi Duodji

Porjusvägen 4 • July–mid-Aug daily 10am–5.30pm; mid-Aug–June Mon–Fri 1pm–5pm

While you're in town, it's worth popping into **Sámi Duodji**; this *Sámi* handicrafts shop sells a selection of locally produced knives, drinking bowls, leatherware and jewellery and is a good place to pick up a few knick-knacks.

Gamla kyrka

Junction of Hantverkargatan and Köpmangatan, off Stortorget • Not open to the public

The **Gamla kyrka** is a recent copy of the 1753 church on the same site (the original burnt down in 1972). The octagonal design, curiously shaped tower and colours inside the church (not open to the public) represent *Sámi* styles. Outside, notice the space in between the coarsely hewn timbers which was used to store coffins during winter, waiting for the thaw in May when the *Sámi* could go out and dig graves again (temperatures in this part of Sweden regularly plunge to -30°C and below).

ARRIVAL AND DEPARTURE   JOKKMOKK

By train From Arvidsjaur, 161km away, it's a 3hr journey to Jokkmokk on the Inlandsbanan (summer 1 daily). If you're arriving here for the Winter Market, take the train to Murjek (between Boden and Gällivare), from where bus #43 runs west to Jokkmokk.

By bus The Inlandsexpressen bus runs from Arvidsjaur (1 daily; 2hr 15min).

INFORMATION AND ACTIVITIES

Tourist office Stortorget 4 (mid-June–mid-Aug Mon–Fri 9am–6.30pm, Sat & Sun 10am–5pm; mid-Aug to mid-June Mon–Fri 9am–noon & 1–4pm; ☏0971 222 50, ⓦjokkmokk.se/turism). The tourist office has internet access and all sorts of literature useful for planning a hike in the region.

Fishing During the summer, Talvatissjön, the lake behind the *Jokkmokk* hotel (see opposite), is the preferred spot for catching Arctic char and rainbow trout. To fish here you'll need a permit (*fiskekort*), available from the tourist office. There's a barbecue on the lakeside behind the hotel, should you catch anything.

Canoeing It's possible to go canoeing on the unspoilt surrounding lakes and rivers, as well as hiking in the nearby national parks. For more information and canoe bookings, contact Jokkmokkguiderna (☎0971 122 20, ⓦjokkmokkguiderna.com), based in the village of Skabram, 3km west of Jokkmokk. They'll collect you from Jokkmokk once you've made a booking.

ACCOMMODATION

Since accommodation options in Jokkmokk are rather limited, it's a good idea to **book ahead**, particularly during the summer months when the Inlandsbanan is running, as well as during the **Winter Market**, when a reservation is required at least two years in advance (if Jokkmokk is full, try looking for rooms in Arvidsjaur and Gällivare). That said, the tourist office arranges simple dormitory accommodation in the local school during the Winter Market for around 250kr per person, and puts together a list of **private rooms** (500kr per person).

Akerlund Herrevägen 1 ☎0971 100 12, ⓦhotelakerlund. se. Handily situated in the town centre, close to the train station, the simple, brightly decorated en-suite rooms here are clean and tidy, if lacking in character. There's an attractive sauna suite and a very good restaurant on site. **1395kr**

Arctic Camp Jokkmokk Center Notudden, off Route 97 towards Luleå ☎0971 123 70, ⓦarcticcampjokkmokk.

se. Located by the Lule River, 3km southeast of town, this pleasant campsite also has cabins. The best way to get here is to rent a bike from the youth hostel. Tents **195kr**, cabins **460r**

Jokkmokk Solgatan 45 ☎0971 777 00, ⓦhotel jokkmokk.se. In a pretty lakeside location, rooms here are modern and comfortable; ask for one with a lake view. The sauna suite in the basement is one of the best in northern Sweden. **1145kr/1610kr**

STF Jokkmokk Vandrarhem Åsgatan 20 ☎046-703664645, ⓦsvenskaturistforeningen.se/anlaggningar/ stf-jokkmokk-vandrarhem. Jokkmokk's STF hostel, in a wonderful old house surrounded by a pretty garden, has a great central location and cosy double rooms as well as dorms. However, it fills fast so it's wise to book well in advance. Dorms **300kr**, doubles **700kr**

EATING AND DRINKING

Ájtte museum Kyrkogatan 3 ☎0971 170 70, ⓦrestaurangajtte.se. For traditional northern Swedish and *Sámi* home cooking, head for the restaurant inside the museum, where lunch deals go for 85kr; there are also a couple of reindeer dishes on the menu. June–Aug daily 9am–6pm; regular opening hours Mon–Fri 9am–4pm.

City Konditoriet Storgatan 28 ☎0971 106 50. For pastries and a cup of coffee, try this place on Jokkmokk's main street. It also serves up good sandwiches and other light snacks such as quiches and cakes. Mon–Fri 6am–

5pm, Sat 9am–2pm.

Gasskas Porjusvägen 7 ☎ 46 70 365 97 48, ⓦgasskas. se. You'll find some of the best food in the whole of Swedish Lapland at this *Sámi*-run place: slow-cooked reindeer steak, Arctic char and other local delicacies are usually on the changing menu. Reckon on 225kr per main course. Tues–Sat 10am–late.

Kowloon Föreningsgatan 3 ☎0971 100 85. At this cheap and cheerful Chinese restaurant, lunch is 75kr; meals start at 105kr at other times. Curiously for a Chinese restaurant, it

---

JOKKMOKKS MARKNAD: THE GREAT WINTER MARKET

Known simply in Swedish as *Jokkmokks marknad*, the town's 400-year-old **Great Winter Market** (ⓦjokkmokksmarknad.se) traces its origins back to 1602, when King Karl IX decreed that a series of market sites should be set up in the north to help extend Swedish territory and increase taxes to fund his many wars. A chapel, a parsonage and a row of market sheds were built in Jokkmokk, and the rest is history.

Today the market is held on the first Thursday to Sunday of each **February**, when thirty thousand people force their way into town – ten times the normal population. It's the best (and coldest) time of year to be here; there's a Wild West feeling in the air, with lots of drunken stallholders trying to flog reindeer hides and other unwanted knick-knacks to even more drunken passers-by. Held on the frozen Talvatissjön lake behind the *Jokkmokk* hotel (see above), the market's **reindeer races** can be a real spectacle, as man and beast battle it out on a specially marked-out ice track. The reindeer, however, often have other ideas and every now and then veer off with great alacrity into the crowd, sending spectators fleeing for cover.

A smaller **historical market** is held on the proceeding Monday to Wednesday, when people dress in traditional costume and put on various theatrical performances.

9

also serves pizzas – albeit none too authentic ones. Tues–Fri 11am–9pm, Sat 1–9pm, Sun 1–8pm.

Opera Storgatan 36 ☎ 0971 105 05. This is the cheapest place in town for reindeer meat, which is usually available at lunchtime. There are also pizzas, salads and a range of a la carte meat dishes such as schnitzel and *pytt i panna*.

Mon–Thurs 10am–9pm, Fri 10am–1am, Sat & Sun 11am–10pm.

Ravintola Opera Storgatan 36 ☎ 046 971 105 05. This restaurant provides different choices. They provide tasty pizzas, but also healthy salads. Mon–Fri 10am–10pm, Sat & Sun 11am–10pm.

Gällivare

Seven hundred and fifty kilometres north of Östersund, the Inlandsbanan finally reaches its last stop, **GÄLLIVARE**, two and a quarter hours up the line from Jokkmokk. Although the town is not immediately appealing, it is one of the few relatively sizeable ones in this part of northern Sweden, and it's a good idea to spend a day or two here enjoying the relative civilization before striking out in the wilds beyond – Gällivare is a good starting point for walking in the national parks, which fill most of the northwestern corner of the country (see page 334). The town is also one of the most important areas for iron ore in Europe – if you have any interest in seeing a **working mine**, don't wait until Kiruna's tame "tourist tour" (see page 338); instead, take a trip down the more evocative mines here.

Located just north of the 67th parallel, Gällivare has a pretty severe **climate**: as you stroll around the open centre, have a look at the double-glazed windows here, all heavily insulated to protect against the biting Arctic cold. The site the town occupies was once that of a *Sámi* village, and one theory has it that the name Gällivare comes from the *Sámi* for "a crack or gorge *(djelli)* in the mountain *(vare)*". You may also come across the alternative spelling, Gellivare, although the pronunciation is the same – "yell-i-vaar-eh".

Lappkyrkan

Lasarettsgatan 10 • June–Aug daily 10am–4pm

The *Sámi* church, **Lappkyrkan**, down by the river near the train station, is a mid-eighteenth-century construction; it's known as the *Ettöreskyrkan* ("1 öre" church) after the sum Swedes were asked to contribute to the subscription drive that paid for its construction.

Gällivare Museum

Storgatan 16 • Tues, Thurs & Fri 10am–3.30pm, Wed 11am–8pm; late June– early Aug also Sat 11am–2pm • Free

In the town centre, in the same building as the *Vetehatten* café (see page 334), there's a simple **museum** dealing with *Sámi* history and forestry. Keep an eye out, too, for the curious exhibition about a local man, Martin Stenström, who lived his entire life alone in a cabin deep in the forest.

The mines at Malmberget

Iron-ore mine tours Mid-June–mid-Aug daily 9am–noon • 300kr • Copper mine tours Mid-June–mid-Aug Mon, Wed & Fri 2pm • 300kr

Tucked away at **Malmberget**, one of the two hills that overlook the town 5km to the north, the modern **mines** and works are distant, dark blots, towards which the tourist office ferries relays of tourists in summer. There are two separate tours, both running from mid-June to mid-August: one tour explores the underground *LKAB* **iron-ore mine**, the other the open-cast **copper mine** known as *Aitik*, the largest of its kind in Europe (and also Sweden's biggest gold mine – the metal is recovered from the slag produced during the extraction of the copper). The ear-splitting noise produced from the mammoth-sized trucks (they're five times the height of a human being) in the iron-ore mine can be quite disconcerting in the confined darkness.

ARRIVAL AND DEPARTURE

GÄLLIVARE

By train The train station is on Lasarettsgatan.
Destinations Arvidsjaur (mid-June to mid-Aug 1 daily; 5hr); Jokkmokk (mid-June to mid-Aug 1 daily; 1hr 30min);

Kiruna (5 daily; 1hr 10min); Luleå (5 daily; 2hr 20min); Narvik (2 daily; 4hr30min); Östersund (mid-June to mid-Aug 1 daily; 14hr 36 min); Stockholm (1 daily; 14hr 50 min).

INFORMATION

Tourist office Centralplan 4 at the train station (mid-June–mid-Aug Mon–Fri 8am–6.30pm; mid-Aug to mid-June Mon–Fri 9am–5pm; ☎046 (0)970-102 20, ⓦwelcometogallivare.com).
Laponia Visitor Center Centralplan 4 at the train station (mid-June to early Aug daily 10am–6pm; ☎0973

410 10, ⓦlaponia.nu/en/upplev/visitor-centres/laponia-visitor-centre-jiellevarregallivare). For hiking information and the very latest conditions in the national parks. The knowledgeable staff here can help with trail suggestions and accommodation bookings, as well as left luggage.

ACCOMMODATION

SEE MAP PAGE 332

Dundret Per Dundretvägen 1, ☎046 970 145 60 ⓦhotelldundret.se. A small, friendly guesthouse with eight comfortable rooms and shared facilities. There are also larger apartments sleeping up to four people in the adjacent building. Doubles <u>890kr</u>, apartments <u>1200kr</u>
Gällivare Bed & Breakfast Laestadiusvägen 18 ☎046

970 156 56, ⓦbbgallivare.se. This bed and breakfast has bright and airy rooms with a lovely decor. Doubles <u>645kr</u>
Gällivare Camping Kvarnbacksvägen 2 ☎0970 100 10, ⓦgellivarecamping.com. Pleasant campsite in an enviable location close to the centre and right by the river, off Porjusvägen (Route 45 to Jokkmokk). There are also

9

MIDNIGHT SUN TOURS

While in Gällivare do try to take a tour to the top of **Dundret** hill, one of the two peaks dominating the town, to see the **midnight sun** (early June–early Aug daily at 11pm; 200kr return; tickets available from the tourist office). Special taxis run from the train station to the end of the winding road which leads up to the top of the hill. Remember that the sky needs to be free of cloud for you to see the midnight sun properly. Whatever the weather, though, there are free waffles and ice cream available before the return down to Gällivare.

simple cabins with cooking and toilet facilities and youth hostel dorm beds. Open all year. Tents <u>170kr</u>, dorms <u>230kr</u>, cabins <u>700kr</u>

Quality Lapland Lasarettsgatan 1 ☎0970 77 22 90, ⓦqualityhotellapland.se. The best of the bunch in the town centre, with smart, tastefully decorated rooms and a good restaurant; the whole hotel has just been given a makeover and the attention to detail is second to none. <u>1200kr/1900kr</u>

Scandic Gällivare Klockljungsvägen 2 ☎0970 162 00, ⓦscandichotels.se. A modern hotel with sixty smart, Scandinavian-style doubles in a modern block of red brick close to the swimming pool. There's also a decent sauna on site. <u>970kr/1420kr</u>

EATING AND DRINKING   SEE MAP PAGE 332

Alla Tiders Storgatan 18 ☎0970 102 54. Great stylish bar and bistro, serving up a range of quiches, salads and a variety of tasty sandwiches during the day, before turning into a bar three evenings a week. Mon, Tues & Thurs 10am–6pm, Wed 10am–1am, Fri 10am–2pm, Sat 11am–4pm & 9pm–2am.

Husmans Malmbergsvägen 1 ☎0970 170 30. A simple cafeteria-style place with various Swedish home-style dishes on the menu, plus a variety of burgers, sausages, lasagne and schnitzel: oddly, lunch here is served all day. Mains from around 85kr. Mon–Fri 10am–8pm, Sat 12am–8pm.

Manuella Storgatan 9 ☎0970 123 80. One of Gällivare's fast-food outlets, though it tries hard to be an Italian restaurant, serving a range of pizzas (around 85kr), including deep-pan varieties, as well as a couple of steaks (around 150kr). Mon–Fri 10.30am–8.45pm, Sat 1–9pm, Sun 1–8pm.

Nittaya Thai Storgatan 21B ☎0970 176 85. If you're longing for Thai or Indonesian food, make a beeline for this restaurant which keeps the people of Gällivare happy with the likes of nasi goreng and green chicken curry; mains cost around 110kr. Tues–Thurs 10am–9pm, Fri 1–9pm, Sat 1–10pm, Sun 1–8pm.

Strandcaféet Malmbergsvägen 2. Beautifully located campsite café right by the graceful Vassara River, with a small range of open sandwiches, cakes and light lunches of quiches, baked potatoes and salads. June–Aug daily 11am–9pm.

Vetehatten Storgatan 16 ☎0970 666 30, ⓦvetehatten.se. A Gällivare institution, right in the town centre and serving up a selection of sandwiches and gooey cakes. There's outside seating in summer. Mon–Fri 6.30am–5pm.

Swedish Lapland's national parks

It's not a good idea to go **hiking in the national parks** of northern Sweden (ⓦsverigesnationalparker.se) on a whim. Even for experienced walkers, the going can be tough and uncomfortable in parts, downright treacherous in others. The **best time to hike** is from late June to September: during May and early June the ground is still very wet and boggy as a result of the rapid snow melt. Once the snow has gone, wild flowers burst into bloom, making the most of the short summer months. The weather is very changeable – one moment it can be hot and sunny, the next cold and rainy – and snow showers are not uncommon in summer. **Hiking trails** range in difficulty from moderately challenging to a positive assault course.

  Mosquitoes are a real problem: it's difficult to describe the utter misery of being covered in a blanket of insects, your eyes, ears and nose full of the creatures. Yet the beautiful landscape here is one of the last wilderness areas left in Europe – it's one vast expanse of forest and mountains, where roads and human habitation are the exception rather than the norm. **Reindeer** are a common sight, as the parks are their breeding grounds and summer pasture, and **Sámi** settlements are dotted throughout the region – notably at **Ritsem** and **Vaisaluokta**.

9

Four of Swedish Lapland's parks lie about 120km northwest of Gällivare in the tract of Swedish wilderness edging Norway: the low fells, large lakes and moors of **Padjelanta**, **Stora Sjöfallet** (see below) and **Abisko** (see page 343) parks act as the eyebrows to the sheer face of the mountainous **Sarek** park (see page 346). Easy **Muddus** national park lies between Gällivare and Jokkmokk, while **Pieljekaise** national park (see page 346) lies just south of the Arctic Circle, southwest of Jokkmokk. For coverage of the Kungsleden hiking trail, which threads its way through Abisko, Stora Sjöfallet, Sarek and Pieljekaise, see page 344.

Muddus national park

Recommended for novice hikers, **Muddus national park** is a 500-square-kilometre pine-forested and marshland park between Jokkmokk and Gällivare, hemmed in by the Inlandsbanan on one side and the train line from Luleå to Gällivare on the other. Muddus is home to bears, lynx, martens, weasels, hares, elk and (in summer) reindeer; among birds, the whooper swan is one of the most common sights. The terrain here is gently undulating, consisting of bog and forest, though there are clefts and gorges in the southern stretches.

The park's western edges run parallel to Route 45; the easiest approach is to leave the highway at **Liggadammen** (there are also buses here from Gällivare) and then follow the small road to **Skaite**, where an easy **hiking trail** begins; two suggested routes are Skaite–Muddusfallet–Måskoskårså–Skaite (24km) or Skaite–Muttosluobbal–Manson–Skaite (44km). There are **cabins** along both routes (open April–Sept; at other times the keys can be obtained from Jokkmokk and Gällivare tourist offices), and a campsite at Muddus Falls. There are no outlets for buying food or provisions en route.

Padjelanta national park

Padjelanta is the largest of Sweden's national parks; its name comes from *Sámi* and means "the higher country", an apt description for this plateau that lies almost exclusively above the tree line. The **Padjelanta trail** (150km) runs from **Vaisaluokta** through the **Laponia World Heritage Area** (see below) south to **Kvikkjokk**, and is suited to inexperienced walkers – allow at least a week to finish it.

ARRIVAL AND DEPARTURE   PADJELANTA NATIONAL PARK

By bus to Kvikkjokk To get to Kvikkjokk, hop on a bus in Jokkmokk (2 daily; 2hr); all bus times are at ⓦltnbd.se.

By bus and boat to Vaisaluokta To get to Vaisaluokta, take a bus from Gällivare to Ritsem (mid-Feb to Sept 2 daily; 4hr; ⓦltnbd.se), from where a boat takes you across Akkajaure lake to Vaisaluokta (late June–early Sept 2–3 daily; 1hr 20min; 280kr one-way; ⓦstfturist.se/ritsem).

By helicopter There's a helicopter service, operated by

THE LAPONIA WORLD HERITAGE AREA

"It is one of the last and unquestionably largest and best preserved examples of an area of transhumance, involving summer grazing by large reindeer herds", said the UNESCO World Heritage Committee when they established **Laponia** as a **heritage area** in 1996. Covering a vast area of 9400 square kilometres, including the Padjelanta, Sarek and Stora Sjöfallet **national parks**, Laponia is the home and workplace of forest and mountain **Sámi** families from seven different villages, who still tend their reindeer here much as their ancestors did in prehistoric times. The forest *Sámi* move with their herds within the forests, and the mountain *Sámi* follow their animals from the lichen-rich forests, where they spend the winter, up to the tree line by the time spring comes, then on into the mountains for summer; in August they start making their way down. Come September, many animals will be slaughtered either at the **corrals** in Ruokto, on the road between Porjus and Kebnats, or at highland corrals between Ritsem and Sitasjaure.

9

Fiskflyg, between Kvikkjokk, Staloluokta and Ritsem (late June–early Sept daily; 1450kr per person Kvikkjokk– Staloluokta, 1450kr per person Staloluokta–Ritsem; ☎0971 210 40, 🖥 fiskflyg.se).

ACCOMMODATION

In addition to the two accommodation options listed below, simpler **cabins** can be found elsewhere along the Padjelanta trail and wardens have information about the nearest **food** stores.

STF Kvikkjokk fjällstation Kvikkjokk ☎0971 210 22, 🖥 kvikkjokkfjallstation.se. Perched on a rocky outcrop above an impressive set of rapids, this STF mountain lodge enjoys a perfect position – mosquitoes notwithstanding. All rooms have a washbasin but other facilities are shared. Self-catering is possible but there's also an on-site restaurant.

Open March, April & mid-June to Sept. Dorms <u>395kr</u>, doubles <u>1020kr</u>

STF Ritsem fjällstation Ritsem 4 ☎046 10 190 24 51, 🖥 svenskaturistforeningen.se/boende/stf-ritsem. Simple, single-storey STF mountain lodge with eighty-odd beds divided into 26 rooms, sharing facilities and a kitchen. The hostel looks out over Akkajaure lake and is perfectly located for accessing the Padjelanta national park. Open March–early May & mid-June–mid-Sept. Dorms <u>445kr</u>, doubles <u>8900kr</u>

Kiruna and around

Partly because it's the most northerly town in Sweden, and partly due to its proximity to the world-famous **Icehotel** in the nearby village of **Jukkasjärvi**, **KIRUNA**, 200km

THAT SINKING FEELING

9

Due to severe **subsidence** caused by the mines over 1km below the town, Kiruna is sinking. After years of deliberation, in 2012 a location was finally decided for the construction of a **city** – close to the airport at Tuolluvaara. In 2013 the train station was closed and a temporary station 1.5km outside town is now in operation. Over the next few years expect disruption as the old town is torn down and the E10 highway rerouted. The Stadshus and the church will be moved to Kiruna whilst all other buildings will be demolished. Oddly, local people seem unperturbed by the enormity of the task ahead, perhaps because they are painfully aware that without the iron-ore mines on which Kiruna is dependent, the place would cease to exist. The whole operation is expected to take several decades to complete.

north of the Arctic Circle, has become *the* destination in Swedish Lapland, the place that everyone wants to visit. However, don't come here expecting monumental architectural delights, tree-lined avenues and big-city sophistication – it has none of that, at least not for the time being. All that, however, could change when the town ups sticks and moves location for, indeed, that is what is set to happen over the next decade (see box). Ahead of the move, the present town still retains a strangely likeable down-to-earth feel. Although there are a few sights, it's mainly attractive as a base from which to visit this corner of northern Lapland, with rail connections northwest to the start of the Kungsleden trail (see page 344) and Riksgränsen, as well as bus connections into the Torne Valley (see page 347). Sweden's highest mountain, **Kebnekaise** (2102m), is also within easy reach of Kiruna. It's accessed from the tiny village of **Nikkaluokta**, the departure point for ambitious ascents of the peak.

Brief history

When Swedish pioneers first arrived in what is now Kiruna in the early 1600s, they found the *Sámi* already in place (the town's name comes from the *Sámi* word "Giron", meaning "ptarmigan"). Completely ignoring the indigenous population, the Swedes opened their first mine in 1647 at nearby Masugnsbyn ("Blast Furnace Village"), but it wasn't until the beginning of the following century that the **iron-ore** deposits in Kiruna itself were finally discovered. Exploratory drilling began in the 1880s, which nicely coincided with the building of the **Malmbanan**, the iron-ore railway between Luleå and Narvik in Norway; the first train laden with iron ore trundled out from Malmberget in Gällivare in March 1888.

In 1900, the settlers braved their first winter in Kiruna, a year which is now regarded as the town's birthday. Built on a hill to try to keep the temperature up (warm air rises), Kiruna was planned to withstand the coldest snaps of winter – even the streets are curved as protection against the biting polar wind. Sadly, though, much of the wooden architecture of Kiruna's early days, gloriously painted in reds, greens and yellows, was ripped down to make way for today's unprepossessing concrete structures; the town even won an award in the 1960s for its out-with-the-old-in-with-the-new policy.

Kiruna was the hub of the battle for the control of the iron-ore supply during World War II; ore was transported north from here by train to the great harbour at Narvik, over the border in Norway. Much German firepower was expended in an attempt to interrupt the supply to the Allies and wrest control for the Axis. In the process, Narvik suffered grievously, whilst Kiruna – benefiting from supposed Swedish neutrality – made a packet selling to both sides.

Stadshuset

Hjalmar Lundbohmsvägen 31 • Mon–Fri 8am–5pm

Not surprisingly, most sights in Kiruna are firmly wedded to iron in one way or another. The tower of the **Stadshus** is a strident metal pillar, designed by Bror

SUNRISE AND SUNSET IN STOCKHOLM AND KIRUNA

	Stockholm		Kiruna	
	Sunrise	Sunset	Sunrise	Sunset
January	8.47am	2.55pm	24hr darkness	
February	8.01am	4.01pm	8.59am	2.45pm
March	6.48am	5.12pm	7.02am	4.41pm
April	6.17am	7.26pm	5.52am	7.33pm
May	4.52am	8.37pm	3.43am	9.29pm
June	3.47am	9.44pm	24hr daylight	
July	3.40am	10.02pm	24hr daylight	
August	4.35am	9.13pm	3.02am	10.29pm
September	5.46am	7.50pm	5.08am	8.10pm
October	5.54am	5.21pm	5.53am	5.04pm
November	7.08am	3.54pm	7.50am	2.55pm
December	8.19am	2.54pm	10.14am	12.41pm

Marklund and harbouring an intricate latticework clock face and 23 sundry bells that chime raucously; incomprehensibly, the Stadshus won an award in 1964 for being the most beautiful Swedish public building. Inside, there's a tolerable art collection and, in summer, occasional displays of *Sámi* handicrafts.

The mines

Tours: mid-June–mid-Aug 4 daily at 9am, 11am, 1pm & 3pm; early June & late Aug 2 daily at 10am & 2pm • 380kr

The **mines**, ugly brooding reminders of Kiruna's prosperity, still dominate the town, much more depressingly so than in Gällivare; despite its newer central buildings and open parks, Kiruna retains a grubby industrial feel. The tourist office arranges **guided tours** around the mines, on which visitors are bussed down into the *InfoMine*, a closed-off section of the rabbit warren of tunnels comprising a working mine. Inside you'll see facilities such as petrol stations and a workers' canteen, and mining paraphernalia, including trains for transporting ore and equipment, and mills for crushing the ore-bearing rock.

Kiruna kyrka

Gruvvägen 2 • Daily mid-June–mid-Aug 9am–5.45pm; mid-Aug–mid-June 10am–3.30pm

Standing proud in the centre of town, **Kiruna kyrka** causes a few raised eyebrows when people see it for the first time: built in the style of a *Sámi* hut and the size of a small aircraft hangar, it's an origami-like creation of oak beams and rafters. LKAB, the iron-ore company (and the town's main employer) which paid for its construction, was also responsible for the Hjalmar Lundbohmsgården.

Hjalmar Lundbohmsgården

Ingenjörsgatan 1 • Mon–Fri 10am–5pm • 30kr • ⓦ hjalmarsgard.se

The **Hjalmar Lundbohmsgården** is a country house once used by the former managing director of LKAB, who was the town's "founder". Displays consist mostly of early twentieth-century photographs featuring the man himself and his personal study, much as he left it. Try to visit the house in order to get a perspective on the town's history before going down the mine; you'll be all the more aware afterwards how, without the mine, Kiruna would be a one-reindeer town instead of the thriving place it is today – quite a feat when you consider its location on the map (don't be surprised to see snow on the slag heaps in the middle of June).

Kiruna Samegård

9

Brytaregatan 14 • Mon–Fri 7am–noon & 1–4pm • 20kr

For the most rewarding exhibition of *Sámi* culture in town, head for the handicrafts centre, **Kiruna Samegård**. The handicrafts you'll see here may well be familiar by now; what probably won't be is the centre's small but impressive display of *Sámi* art featuring scenes from everyday life in the north. It also has a souvenir shop, where you can pick up a piece of antler or reindeer skin.

ARRIVAL AND DEPARTURE

KIRUNA

By plane Kiruna is served by flights from London Heathrow (winter only) and Stockholm. The airport, 10km away to the east, is linked to town by taxis (350kr) and a shuttle bus (110kr; w horvalls.se/flygbuss.html). Bus #91 also operates between the airport and Narvik in Norway via Abisko; timetables are at w ltnbd.se.

By train The temporary train station is 1.5km west of the city centre; shuttle buses meet all arriving trains and run to the bus station in town, at the corner of Biblioteksgatan and Hjalmar Lundbohmsvägen.

Destinations Abisko (2 daily; 1hr 30min); Jukkasjärvi (Mon–Fri 7 daily, Sat & Sun 2 daily; 35min); Luleå (4 daily; 3hr 30min); Narvik (1 daily; 2hr 50min); Nikkaluokta (2 daily; 1hr 20min); Riksgränsen (2 daily; 2hr 15min); Stockholm (1 daily; 18hr 30min).

INFORMATION

Tourist office In Folkets Hus, on the central square at Lars Janssongatan 17 (Mon–Fri 8.30am–5pm, Sat & Sun 8.30am–4pm; t 0980 188 80, w kirunalapland.se).

ACCOMMODATION

SEE MAP PAGE 336

Arctic Eden Föraregatan 18 t 0980 611 86, w hotel arcticeden.se. A nice combination of wooden floors and brick walls with *Sámi* art and design, this swanky hotel is one of the best places to stay in Kiruna. There's a small pool and sauna suite available for guest use. <u>1400kr</u>

Bishops Arms Föreningsgatan 6 t 046 980 155 00, w bishopsarms.com/Kiruna. A cosy hotel with wooden floors, large double beds and rooms. <u>801kr/1161kr</u>

Gullriset Lägenhetshotell Bromsgatan 12 t 0980 109 37, w lkabfastigheter.se/om-oss/gullriset. A good choice of bright and breezy modern apartments for one to four people, perfect for self-catering. All have private bathrooms and fully fitted kitchens. There's also a sauna on site for guest use. Two-person apartment <u>615kr</u>

Kiruna Hostel Bergmästaregatan 7 t 0980 171 00, w spiskiruna.se. Dorm beds (in rooms sleeping up to ten people) are the best option at this centrally located youth hostel, though there are also double rooms. Boasting its own sauna, it fills quickly and reservations are necessary at any time of year. Dorms <u>335kr</u>, doubles <u>1045kr</u>

Scandic Ferrum Lars Janssongatan 15 t 0980 39 86 00, w scandichotels.com/ferrum. By far the most anonymous place in town, with characterless chain-hotel rooms and indifferent staff, but the palatial sauna suite on the top floor is a wonderful place to relax and watch the midnight sun. <u>1170kr/1400kr</u>

Yellow House Hantverkaregatan 25 t 0980 137 50, w yellowhouse.nu. Budget hotel-cum-youth hostel with dorm beds and double rooms sharing facilities. Linen is not included in the room rate but is available for 60kr extra per stay. Guests also have access to the kitchen and sauna. Dorms <u>170kr</u>, doubles <u>440kr</u>

CAMPING

Camp Ripan Campingvägen 5 t 0980 630 00, w ripan. se. A 20min walk from the centre, this campsite has ninety well-appointed cabins, imaginatively decorated in Nordic colours and designs, plus a heated open-air swimming pool and Jacuzzi, gym and spa. Tents <u>180kr</u>, cabins <u>1330kr</u>

EATING AND DRINKING

SEE MAP PAGE 336

Bishops Arms Föreningsgatan 6 t 0980 155 00, w bishopsarms.com/kiruna. Pubs and bars tend to come and go in Kiruna, but this old favourite has stood the test of time and is still going strong – it's the most popular place in town for a drink. Mon 4–11pm, Tues–Thurs 4pm–midnight, Fri & Sat 4pm–1am, Sun 4–11pm.

Kafé Rost Lars Janssonsgatan 17 t 0980 166 05. This open-plan first-floor café serves up decent sandwiches, including various reindeer concoctions, as well as quiches,

salads and ciabattas. It's also a good place from which to take in Kiruna's goings-on, with an outside terrace in summer. Mon, Wed & Friday 9am–4pm, Tues, Thurs & Sat 9am–3pm.

Landströms Kök & Bar Föreningsgatan 11 t 0980 133 55, w landstroms.net. A good place to tuck into traditional northern home cooking, with dishes such as creamy elk stew with chanterelle mushrooms, fillet of reindeer with blackberry sauce, smoked whitefish with dill

9

cream and baked fillet of Arctic char with herbs – reckon on 210–345kr per main course. Mon–Thurs 6–11pm, Fri & Sat 6pm–1am.

Mommas Lars Janssonsgatan 15 ☎ 0980 39 86 07, ⓦ scandichotels.com/hotels/sweden/kiruna/scandic-ferrum. Inside the *Scandic Ferrum* hotel, this American-style steakhouse serves up good elk burgers (199kr) and steaks (295kr), as well as smoked reindeer heart in a creamy lingonberry sauce (249kr). Mon–Sat 6–11pm.

Safari Geologgatan 4 ☎ 0980 174 60, ⓦ cafesafari.se. This charming café with elegant wallpaper and wooden floors is easily the best choice in town for tea, coffee, sandwiches, salads and baked potatoes. There's outdoor seating in summer, too. Mon–Fri 8am–6pm, Sat 10am–4pm.

Jukkasjärvi village

An obvious destination for any tourist travelling around Kiruna in winter is the tiny village of **JUKKASJÄRVI** (known locally simply as "Jukkas"), 17km east of Kiruna and 200km north of the Arctic Circle, and the location for Swedish Lapland's blockbuster attraction: **Icehotel**. What's effectively the world's largest igloo, *Icehotel* is built every year by the side of the Torne River in late October, from when it stands proudly until temperatures rise definitively above zero in May, when it finally melts away back into the river. Another venture, **Icehotel 365** – three times smaller than the original structure, and made of regular building materials – opened on the same site stays open year-round.

Although *Icehotel* totally dominates tiny Jukkasjärvi from its position at the entrance to the village, it's worth taking a stroll down the main (and only) road, Marknadsvägen, passing a handful of simple dwellings owned by locals – not all of whom are in favour of the changes that the hotel has brought to their village.

Icehotel

Marknadsvägen 63 • Day visits all year around daily 10am–6pm; summer ice-storage tours also available • 349kr entrance, 474kr including a 30min guided tour and lunch at noon or 4pm • ☎ 0980 668 00, ⓦ icehotel.com

The brains behind **Icehotel** belong to Yngve Bergqvist, a southern Swede who moved to Lapland in the 1980s. In 1989, he built an igloo – barely sixty square metres in size – as an art gallery to showcase local *Sámi* crafts and design. Visitors asked to sleep in the igloo, and the concept was born. Today, covering roughly 6000 square metres, *Icehotel* is constructed of thirty thousand tonnes of "snice", as *Icehotel* calls it, a combination of snow and ice (cut from the Torne River); its exact shape and design changes from year to year, though there's always a chapel, in which couples can marry. From the entrance hall there's usually one main walkway filled with ice **sculptures**, from which smaller corridors lead off to the bedrooms and suites (all with electric lights, and beds made out of blocks of compact snow covered with reindeer hides) that make up the bulk of the hotel. Though many visitors stay the night, the hotel is also open for **day visits**.

Staying in the hotel

Icehotel is open the whole year

There are two reception areas: one for cold accommodation (*Icehotel* itself) and another for warm accommodation (double rooms and cabins) – simply follow the direction signs. Staff in the cold reception will dish out warm clothing and general information about how to survive a night in sub-zero temperatures. When it's time to go to bed, you should leave your valuables and most of your clothes in lockers provided close to reception (where there are also heated bathrooms with showers and a sauna) and then make a run for it from here to your room (wearing as little as possible; see page 342) and dive into your sleeping bag as quickly as you can – the temperature inside the hotel is –5°C, while outside it's generally around –20 or –30°C. Guests are provided with specially made, tried-and-tested **sleeping bags** of a type used by the Swedish army, who have used the hotel for Arctic survival training;

ACTIVITIES AT THE ICEHOTEL

There are seemingly countless organized activities from the *Icehotel* and the range varies from year to year; full details are online at ⓦicehotel.com. Generally, though, they include a **dog sledding** trip through the neighbouring forests with a short stop for coffee and cake (90min; 1495kr); an accompanied daytime drive on **snow scooters** down the Torne River and into the wintry forests (3hr; 1195kr); and a night-time **snowmobile** spin to see the **northern lights** (4hr; 1950kr including dinner). In **summer** there are generally organized **fishing and hunting** tours as well as **canoeing**.

the bags are supposed to keep you warm in temperatures down to –35°C. However, as they enclose your entire body and head (bar a small area for your eyes and nose) they are rather claustrophobic. You should take off all the clothes you're still wearing and sleep naked to prevent sweating; stuff your clothes into the bottom of the sleeping bag to keep them warm and place your shoes on the bed with you to stop them freezing. Don't expect to sleep – you won't – it's simply too cold and uncomfortable. In the morning, you can refresh yourself with a sauna and have a hearty breakfast at the restaurant across the road, though you'll soon notice from people's faces that nobody else has slept a wink either.

Icehotel 365

Ever the entrepreneurs, *Icehotel* have now hit on a new idea to satisfy the seemingly bottomless market of visitors who flock to Swedish Lapland every year to experience an Arctic winter: **Icehotel 365**, which offers the chance to sleep in sub-zero temperatures at any time of year – even in the height of summer. Smaller than the original *Icehotel*, *Icehotel 365* is made of regular building materials, though it does also contain snow and ice. Innovative technology has made it possible to store energy captured by a new generation of solar panels which can then be used to cool the structure through the summer months, ensuring a year-round temperature inside of –5°C, just like the original. In many ways, *Icehotel 365* is similar to its predecessor – it's designed with the same arched corridors, it contains ice rooms and suites and even a bar. *Icehotel* says it gives visitors a chance to combine a night in sub-zero temperatures with summer activities like kayaking and hiking. Critics say it's just another attempt to turn Lapland into a theme park and squeeze yet more kronor out of hapless tourists.

The church

Marknadsvägen 3 • Daily 9am–3pm

A traditional sight awaits at the end of the dead-end Marknadsvägen: an old wooden *Sámi* **church**, parts of which date from 1608, making it the oldest surviving church in Lapland. Check out the richly decorated altarpiece by Uppsala artist Bror Hjorth, depicting the revivalist preacher, **Lars Levi Laestadius** (see page 350), alongside the woman who inspired him to rid Lapland of alcohol, Maria of Åsele. The triptych was given to the church in 1958 by the mining company, LKAB, then celebrating its 350th anniversary.

Under the floor are the mummified remains of villagers who died here in the eighteenth century (not on display). The sandy ground and frost are thought to have been responsible for keeping the bodies, including that of a woman dressed in a white wedding dress and high-heeled shoes, so remarkably well preserved. The organ above the door is made from reindeer horn and birch wood; the artwork in the centre of the organ, suspended over the pipes, symbolizes the sun rising over the Lapporten (see page 343), the two U-shaped mountain-tops near Abisko which are one of Lapland's most enduring images.

9

Nutti Sámi Siida

Sámi Homestead museum • Marknadsvägen 84 • Daily 10am–5pm • 150kr

Across the road from the church, the wooden houses of the rather pedestrian **Nutti Sámi Siida** contain the usual suspects: a stuffed reindeer, an old sleigh, a rickety spinning wheel and other equally dull paraphernalia.

ARRIVAL AND DEPARTURE   JUKKASJÄRVI

By bus Bus #501 links Jukkasjärvi with Kiruna (7 daily; 30min; @ltnbd.se).

By dog sled Undoubtedly the best way to arrive in Jukkasjärvi is by dog sled from Kiruna airport; for a hefty

6150kr (price includes up to four people) you can be met at your plane and pulled all the way to your room; you can arrange this via *Icehotel* (see page 340).

ACCOMMODATION

★ **Icehotel** Marknadsvägen 63 ☎0980 668 00, @icehotel.com. Warm and cold accommodation can be booked through the website and you should book well in advance. The dubious pleasure of spending a night in the freezer doesn't come cheap: we've given the higher Thurs–Sun prices (less expensive rates apply Mon–Wed); special prices apply at New Year and over Valentine's Day. The simplest double rooms are known as "ice rooms", and contain little more than a block of snow and ice which serves as a bed; the more stylish "ice suites" are decorated with furniture made of ice and adorned with ice carvings

and ornaments; then there are the top-of-the-range deluxe suites with more sculptures than you can shake an ice pick at. Rooms and suites are divided between the regular *Icehotel* and *Icehotel 365*. Prices are slightly lower for warm accommodation: you can choose between a regular double room, known as *kaamos* (Finnish for twilight or polar night) and beautifully designed in modern Scandinavian style, or a more homely cabin complete with kitchen. *Icehotel* and *Icehotel 365* are open year-round. *Kaamos* <u>2290kr</u>, cabin <u>3390kr</u>, ice room <u>3156kr</u>, ice suite <u>5800kr</u>, deluxe suite <u>8883kr</u>

EATING AND DRINKING

Icebar Inside the Icehotel @icehotel.com/hotel/food-drink/icebar-jukkasjarvi. The *Icebar* is just that: a bar made of transparent blocks of ice with seating in the form of designer chairs and benches made of snow and ice; dress accordingly. Whether it's a cocktail, glass of champagne or a stiff vodka, everything comes in glasses made of ice. The *Icebar 365* is a similar set-up inside the year-round *Icehotel 365*. Generally mid-Nov–March daily 1pm–1am.

Icehotel restaurant Marknadsvägen ☎0980 668 00. You can eat a buffet lunch and a la carte dinner here, with a good selection of tasty northern Swedish specialities in the range of 275–395kr. The set Ice Menu (835kr) consists

of four courses of local delicacies and comes served on an ice platter. June–Aug & Nov–March daily 11.30am–2.30pm & 6–10pm.

Old Homestead Marknadsvägen ☎0980 668 84, @icehotel.com/hotel/food-drink/jukkasjarvi-homestead. Housed in the former village school from 1768, this solid timber structure is a great place for hearty meals such as steaks and chicken breast; mains cost around 225kr. The outdoor terrace, open in summer, has good views of the Torne River. Daily June–Aug 10am–1am; Nov–March 6–10pm.

Nikkaluokta and Kebnekaise

Nikkaluokta, 66km west of Kiruna and reached on the twice-daily bus (#92), is the starting point for treks towards and up Sweden's highest mountain, **Kebnekaise** (2102m). The mountain was first conquered in 1883 by a Frenchman, Charles Robot; today it can be reached in eight to nine hours by anyone in decent physical condition. Two paths lead to the peak: the eastern route goes over Björling glacier, includes some climbing and is only recommended for experts; the western route is much longer and is the one most people opt for.

ACCOMMODATION   KEBNEKAISE

STF Kebnekaise fjällstation Kebnekaise ☎0980 550 00, @stfkebnekaise.com. Known colloquially as simply "Keb", this STF mountain lodge at the foot of the mountain is not accessible by road; instead, a 19km-long trail leads here

from nearby Nikkaluokta. There are self-catering facilities and a restaurant, plus a sauna. Open March, April & mid-June to mid-Sept. Dorms <u>500kr</u>, doubles <u>1000kr</u>

Abisko and around

9

Leaving Kiruna, it's 98km northwest along the E10 to **ABISKO**. Although accessible by both rail and road, it's by **train** that most people arrive at the start of the Kungsleden trail (see page 344). The train line from Luleå, via Kiruna, to Narvik in Norway, known as the **Malmbanan** (see box), is Europe's northernmost line. Even if you don't intend to walk the Kungsleden, there are a couple of attractions right on Abisko's doorstep.

Nuolja mountain chairlift

Mid-June–end Sept daily 9.30am–4pm; also open June & July Tues, Thurs & Sat 10pm–1am for midnight sun • Daytime 195kr return, night-time return 260kr

Departing from directly opposite the *STF Abisko fjällstation*, you can take a **chair lift** 500m up **Nuolja mountain** (1169m), from where there are fantastic views of the surrounding wilderness, including the 70km-long Torneträsk Lake and the spectacular U-shaped mountain-tops of **Lapporten**; the latter have come to represent the gateway to Lapland, and are used as landmarks by the *Sámi* for guiding their reindeer between their summer and winter grazing land.

Aurora Sky Station

Tours: Nov Thurs–Sat 9pm–1am; Dec–March daily 9pm–1am • 745kr, with dinner 1925kr • ⓦ auroraskystation.se

Tucked away in one corner of the **café** at the top of the chair lift, the **Aurora Sky Station** is the best place for miles around to observe the **northern lights**; Abisko lies in a rain shadow and the sky is consequently often free of cloud. Containing all kinds of equipment to measure and hear the lights (they often emit a series of hisses and clicks), it's a perfect introduction for the non-initiated into this most complicated of scientific phenomena, since experts are on hand to explain what you're seeing and hearing. It's possible to combine the tour with a four-course dinner.

Rallarvägen

Nuolja is the starting point for an easy walking path (7km; 2–3hr) leading downhill to nearby **Björkliden**, 9km away by road, comprising nothing more than a few houses gathered around the train station. From here, the **Rallarvägen** (**Navvy Road**) leads to Rombaksbotn, near Narvik, in Norway; the road was built alongside the Malmbanan, then under construction, in order to transport materials needed for the line. Today it provides a walking or mountain-biking route between Abisko and Narvik – though it can be fairly narrow and rough going in parts.

THE MALMBANAN

The **Malmbanan** would never have been built had it not been for the rich deposits of iron ore around Gällivare and Malmberget. The idea to construct the train line, which connects the Bothnian coast with the Atlantic coast (170km), passing through some of the remotest and most inhospitable parts of Europe, was talked about on and off throughout the nineteenth century, when the only means of transporting the ore was by reindeer and sleigh. Finally, in 1884, an English company was awarded the contract to build it; by 1888, the line had reached Gällivare from the Bothnian coast and the company was bankrupt. Ten years passed before the state took over the project; in July 1902, the navvies – who'd been subject to temperatures of -30°C and lower and incredibly harsh conditions – finally shovelled their way through deep snow at Riksgränsen to cross the Norwegian border. A year later the line was officially opened by King Oscar II.

ARRIVAL AND DEPARTURE   ABISKO

By train Arriving by train from Kiruna, get off at Abisko Turiststation (not the first stop, Abisko Ö).
Destinations Gällivare (2 daily; 3hr); Kiruna (2 daily; 1hr

15min); Narvik (2 daily; 1hr 45min); Riksgränsen (2 daily; 1hr); Stockholm (1 daily; 18hr 10min).

ACCOMMODATION

STF Abisko fjällstation ☎ 0980 402 00, ⓦ abisko.nu. A superbly located STF lodge beside the vast Torneträsk lake. There are 300 beds in both private rooms and two-berth

cabins, a great basement sauna suite and a restaurant and bar with views over the lake. Dorms <u>425kr</u>, doubles <u>1175kr</u>

Riksgränsen

From Abisko and Björkliden, the train line and the E10 continue on to **RIKSGRÄNSEN**, 34km from Abisko, a self-contained mountain ski and spa resort 400km north of the Arctic Circle in the shadow of the Norwegian border. The proud claim of Riksgränsen is that plentiful precipitation means there's never any need for artificial snow; you can ski and snowboard until midsummer. Although the minuscule settlement consists of barely a couple of houses supplemented by a top-notch **hotel** it's the chance to explore the only high alpine area in Sweden – sixty peaks over 1350m – that brings trainloads of people here, predominantly during the winter season (mid-Feb to late June). During the summer months, there's some great **fishing** and **hiking** to be had in these parts; the hotel (see below) can supply detailed information as well as rent **mountain bikes** (350kr) for cycling along the Rallarvägen (see page 343) or **canoes** for use on the lake here (350kr). Bear in mind, though, that Riksgränsen is one of the wettest places in the entire country in summer, subject to frequent heavy downpours due to its proximity to the mountains that form the border with Norway.

ARRIVAL AND DEPARTURE   RIKSGRÄNSEN

By train The train station lies immediately to the south of the E10, beside the minor road, Riksgränsvägen, which leads down into the village itself.

Destinations Abisko (2 daily; 50min); Gällivare (2 daily; 3hr 30min); Kiruna (2 daily; 2hr); Narvik (2 daily; 50min); Stockholm (1 daily; 19hr).

ACCOMMODATION

Meteorologen Ski Lodge Riksgränsvägen 13 ☎ 046 980 641 00, ⓦ riksgransen.se. Quality accommodation in a century-old timber building that was once an outpost of the Swedish Met Office. Rooms are nicely appointed and individually decorated, with private facilities. Open all year. <u>1700kr</u>

Riksgränsen Riksgränsvägen 15 ☎ 0980 400 80, ⓦ riksgransen.se. This luxury hotel certainly buzzes in season: it's one of the Swedes' favourite ski destinations. The hotel also boasts a well-appointed spa centre complete with five massage rooms, gym, Jacuzzi and outside hot tubs from where there are breathtaking views over Vassijaure Lake. <u>1990kr</u>

The Kungsleden trail

The **Kungsleden** (literally "King's Trail") is the most famous and popular hiking route in Sweden. A well-signposted, 500km-long path from **Abisko** in the north to **Hemavan**, near Tärnaby (see page 321), it takes in Sweden's highest mountain, **Kebnekaise** (see page 342), en route. If you're looking for splendid isolation, this isn't the trail for you; it's the busiest in the country, though it's the section from Abisko to Kebnekaise that sees most hikers (one of the least busy sections is between Jäkkvik and Adolfström). Most people start the trail at Abisko, but it's equally feasible to begin further south (see page 293).

The ground is easy to walk, with bridges where it's necessary to ford streams; marshy ground has had wooden planks laid down to ease the going, and there are either boat services or rowboats with which to get across several large lakes. The route, which passes through the national parks (see opposite), is traditionally split into the five stages described below. For the distances between the places mentioned on each segment, see the map below on this page; the best map to have of the entire area is Lantmäteriet Kartförlaget's *Norra Norrland* (scale 1:400,000).

9

Stage 1: Abisko to Kebnekaise (6 days; 105km)

From its starting point at *STF Abisko fjällstation*, the Kungsleden winds through the elongated **Abisko national park**, which contains some of the most lush and dense vegetation of the trail, including beech forest lining the valley bottom. From the Alesjaure cabins, perched on a mountain ridge 35km from the start, you'll get a fantastic view over the open countryside below; there's a sauna here, too. The highest point on this segment is the Tjäktja pass (1105m), 50km from the start, from where there are also wonderful views. This section of the trail finishes at **Kebnekaise** *fjällstation*, from where it's possible to leave the main trail and head to Nikkaluokta (see page 342), 19km away (served by buses to Kiruna).

Stage 2: Kebnekaise to Saltoluokta (3 days; 51km)

One of the quietest sections of the trail, this segment takes in beech forest, open fells and deep valleys. First of all you backtrack 14km from **Kebnekaise** *fjällstation* to **Singi**, before heading south again with an unobstructed view of the hills and glaciers of Sarek national park. You then paddle across the river at **Teusajaure** and climb over a plateau into **Stora Sjöfallet national park**, from where you drop steeply through beech forest to **Vakkotavare**. From Vakkotavore a bus runs to the quay at Kebnats, and then a short boat trip brings you to **Saltoluokta** and the start of the next section.

Stage 3: Saltoluokta to Kvikkjokk (4 days; 73km)

This segment involves skirting a tame corner of the inhospitable **Sarek national park**. It crosses two lakes and also passes through a bare landscape edged by pine and beech forests. A long uphill climb of around five to six hours leads first to **Sitojaure**, on a bare high fell. The shallow lake here, which you have to cross, is choppy in the strong wind; take the boat service operated by the cabin caretaker. You then cross the wetlands on the other side of the lake, making use of the wooden planks laid down here, to **Aktse**, where there's a vast field of yellow buttercups in summer. Using the rowboats provided, row across **Lake Laitaure** for Kvikkjokk; as you approach you'll see pine forest.

Stage 4: Kvikkjokk to Ammarnäs (8 days; 166km)

Not recommended for novices, this is one of the most difficult stretches of the trail (distances between cabins can be long, and there are four lakes to cross); it is, however, one of the quietest. From **Kvikkjokk** you take the boat over Saggat Lake and walk to the first cabin at **Tsielejåkk**. It's 55km to the next cabin at **Vuonatjviken**. You then take the boat across Riebnesjaure and walk to Hornavan for another boat across to the village of **Jäkkvik**. It's a short hike of 8km to the next cabin, then on to the village of **Adolfström**, passing through **Pieljekaise national park** en route. Then you get another boat over Iraft Lake and on to the cabins at **Sjnjultje**. From here there's a choice of routes: 34km direct to Ammarnäs, or 24km to Rävfallet and then another 20km into Ammarnäs.

Stage 5: Ammarnäs to Hemavan (4 days; 78km)

This is the easiest part of the trail: you'll pass over low fells and heather-covered moors and through beech forests and wetlands, the horizon lined with impressive fell peaks. The only steep climb is 8km long between **Ammarnäs** and **Aigert**, where there's an imposing waterfall and a traditional steam sauna in the cabin. On the way to the Syter cabin, 48km from Aigert, you'll pass a network of bridges, which cross the various lakes in what is called the Tärnasjö archipelago.

ARRIVAL AND GETTING AROUND

By train You can get to Abisko pretty easily by train; it's just before the Norwegian border on the Kiruna–Narvik run. The Inlandsbanan will get you to Jokkmokk, from where you can get a bus to Kvikkjokk, another point on the trail.

By bus There are several useful bus routes that you can take to link up with the trail, listed below; most of these services are run by Länstrafiken Norrbotten and Länstrafiken Västerbotten (w ltnbd.se and w tabussen.nu).

Services #31 Hemavan to Umeå; #47 Jokkmokk to Kvikkjokk;

THE KUNGSLEDEN TRAIL

#92 Kiruna to Nikkaluokta (19km from Kebnekaise mountain lodge); #93 Gällivare to Ritsem (passes through Vakkotavare and Kebnats for the boat to Saltoluokta); #104 Arjeplog to Jäkkvik; #341 Ammarnäs to Sorsele.

Baggage service The buses operate a *bussgods* service, which allows you to send your pack ahead to your destination or, alternatively, back to your starting point, sparing you the effort of lugging your stuff around; ask about this service at bus stations or on the bus.

ACCOMMODATION

There are basic **cabins** (all open late Feb to April & late June to mid-Sept; advance bookings not possible) along the entire route, and also better-equipped STF *fjällstationer*, or **mountain lodges**, which can be booked ahead.

Stage 1 There are cabins en route at Abiskojaure, Alesjaure, Tjäktja (before the pass), Sälka and Singi. At the end of this section of cabins lies Kebnekaise *fjällstation*.

Stage 2 There are cabins en route at Singi, Kaitumjaure, Teusajaure and Vakkotavare, and a *fjällstation* at Saltoluokta (t 046 10190 23 50, w stfsaltoluokta.com; late Feb to late April & mid-June to mid-Sept; dorms 310kr, doubles 620kr).

Stage 3 There are cabins en route at Sitojaure, Aktse, and Pårte; at Kvikkjokk there's a *fjällstation* (t 0971 210 22,

w kvikkjokkfjallstation.se; March, April & mid-June to Sept; dorms 395kr, doubles 1020kr).

Stage 4 Cabin accommodation en route is at Tsielejåkk, Vuonatjviken, Jäkkvik village, Pieljekaise, Adolfström village, Sjnjultje, Rävfallet and Ammarnäs. The only bookable cabins are at Jäkkvik (*Kyrkans Fjällgård*; Byavägen 4; t 0961 210 39, w kyrkansfjallgardjakkvik.com; 500kr) and Adolfström (*Adolfströms Handelsbod & Stugby*; t 0961 230 41, w adolfstrom.com; 500kr).

Stage 5 Cabins en route are at Aigert, Serve, Tärnasjö, Syter, Viterskalet and Hemavan (see page 322). There are no *fjällstationer* on this stretch of the trail.

The Torne Valley

Along the border with Finland, the lush, gentle slopes of the **TORNE VALLEY** (*Tornedalen* in Swedish) are among the most welcoming sights in northern Sweden. Stretching over 500km from the mouth of the Gulf of Bothnia to Sweden's remote northern tip, the three rivers, Torne, Muonio and Könkämä, mark out the long border between Sweden and Finland. The valley is home to Swedes, Finns and *Sámi*, who speak an archaic Finnish **dialect** known as

BRIDES OF THE ARCTIC CIRCLE

The predominance of heavy labouring jobs in the north of Sweden has produced a **gender imbalance** here – around three men to every woman (a fact which also explains the ridiculously macho behaviour that seems to prevail in these parts). So, to celebrate the village's **400th anniversary** in 1987, the local council in **Pajala** placed advertisements in the national papers inviting women from the south of the country up to Lapland to take part in the birthday festivities. Journalists outside Sweden soon heard of the ads, and articles about the unusual invitation began to appear in newspapers across Europe. Before long, busloads of women from all over the continent were heading for the village. The anniversary festivities proved to be a drunken, debauched bash that tiny Pajala wouldn't forget in a long time, but they did help to redress the gender problem: dozens of East European women lost their hearts to gruff Swedish lumberjacks, and began new lives north of the Arctic Circle. Naturally a succession of winters spent in darkness and in temperatures of −25°C takes its toll and some women left; however, about thirty stayed the course.

9

tornedalsfinska (Torne Valley Finnish, an official minority language), though Swedish is widely understood and is the language of choice for the youth. Refreshingly different from the coast and the heavily wooded inland regions, the area is dotted with small villages, bordered by flower meadows. To either side of Route 99, the main road along the valley, lie open fields providing much-needed grazing land for the farmers' livestock.

Arriving from Gällivare or Kiruna, you can enter the valley by **bus** at its midway point, **Pajala**. From the south, buses also run daily from Haparanda (see page 277).

Pajala

Over time we understood that Pajala didn't actually belong to Sweden… we'd made it by chance. A northerly appendage, desolate swampland where a few people just happened to live, who only partly managed to be Swedish … no roe deer, hedgehogs or nightingales. Just interminable amounts of mosquitoes, Torne Valley Finnish swearwords and Communists.   Mikael Niemi, writing in Popular Music about growing up in Pajala during the 1960s and 1970s

The valley's main village is pretty **PAJALA**, a place that has earned itself a reputation and a half throughout Sweden on two counts: first, the locals' need of women led to the town hitting the headlines across Europe in 1987 (see box); and second, the inordinately successful book, and later film, *Popular Music*, is set here. In order to appreciate the latter claim to fame, you really need to have read the book (one in eight Swedes owns a copy) or seen the film, which played to sell-out audiences in cinemas across the country in 2004. Based around the life of Matti, a teenage boy who dreams of becoming a rock star, the book offers a rare insight into the psyche of the northern Swede and life in the remote Torne Valley. Dotted across town, striking yellow signposts proudly point the way to some of the most infamous locations to feature in the dramatization: Vittulajänkkä, Paskajänkkä and slightly more sedate Strandvägen, all plotted on the free map available from the tourist office.

Having dealt with Pajala the film location, there's little else to do in this unprepossessing town other than rest up for a day or so – take a walk along the riverside, or head off in search of the great grey **owl** (*strix nebulosa*) that sweeps through the nearby forests. The huge wooden **model** of the bird in the bus station will give you an idea of its appearance: lichen grey, with long, slender tail feathers and a white crescent between its black and yellow eyes. Close by, on Torggatan, is the largest **sundial** in the world, a circular affair with a diameter of 38m which tells the real solar time – always 18–25 minutes different from that of a regular watch or clock.

Laestadiuspörtet

Laestadius Museum • Laestadiusvägen 38 Mid-June–mid-Aug Mon–Sat 9am–6pm • 50kr

The solid timber structure known as **Laestadiuspörtet** is where Lars Levi Laestadius (see box) lived whilst rector in Pajala; Laestadius strove throughout his life to rid Lapland of alcohol abuse, though he was rarely popular hereabouts since many workers were

---

RÖMPÄVIIKO AND THE PAJALA MARKET

Taking place in Pajala in the last week in September, the **Römpäviiko** ("romp week") cultural festival, featuring live music and street stalls selling food and handicrafts, is undoubtedly the liveliest time to be in the village. The second weekend after midsummer is another good time to visit, when up to forty thousand people flood into town for the **Pajala market**, one of the biggest in northern Sweden, selling everything from chorizos to reindeer antlers.

LAESTADIUS AND THE DEMON DRINK

No other man has made a greater impression on northern Scandinavia than **Lars Levi Laestadius** (1800–61), the Swedish revivalist preacher who dedicated his life to saving people in three countries from the perils of **alcoholism**. Born in Jäkkvik in 1800 and educated in Kvikkjokk, the young Laestadius soon developed a close relationship with the indigenous *Sámi*, many of whom had turned to drink to escape the harsh reality of their daily lives. It was while the priest was working in Karesuando (1826–49) that he met **Mary of Åsele**, the *Sámi* woman who inspired him to steer people towards a life of total purity.

Following Laestadius's death in Pajala in 1861, the movement continued under the leadership of Juhani Raattamaa before splitting into two opposing branches: a conservative western group in Sweden and Norway, and a more liberal eastern one in Finland. Today tens of thousands of teetotal Swedes, Finns, Norwegians and *Sámi* across the Arctic area of Scandinavia still follow Laestadius's teachings; as well as not drinking, they're not allowed to have flowers or curtains in their homes, nor are they permitted to wear a tie, listen to the radio or watch TV.

paid for their toil in hard liquor. His former home is now a museum dedicated to his life. The spartan interior, including the bedroom where he died in 1861, has been left as it was when he lived here. The guided tour will help make sense of the man and his teachings and throw some light onto his rantings about alcohol and his relationship with the *Sámi*. His **grave** is located in the middle section of the old graveyard next to Pajala kyrka on Kyrkallén.

ARRIVAL AND INFORMATION
PAJALA

By bus The bus station is right in the centre of town. Destinations Gällivare (2 daily; 2hr 20min); Haparanda (2 daily; 3hr); Kiruna (1 daily; 3hr).
Tourist office In the bus station (mid-June–mid–Aug Mon–Fri 9am–7pm, Sat & Sun 11am–5pm; mid-Aug to mid-June Mon–Fri 8am–4pm; ☎0978 100 15, ⓦpajalainswedishlapland.com).

ACCOMMODATION AND EATING

Kahvila Valvet Myntgatan 2 ☎046 73 067 46 00. A friendly café in the town centre with lots of good choices of sandwiches, salads and light lunches, and there's internet access, too. Mon–Fri 7am–5pm, Sat 9am–4pm, Sun 11am–3pm.
Pajala Camping Tannavägen 65 ☎046 73 364 52 78, ⓦpajalacampingroute99.se. This campsite has a beautiful location beside the graceful Torne River. Surrounded by pine forest, cabins come in various sizes and offer differing levels of comfort; the cheapest are two berth ones with cold water and a hotplate. **375kr**

Thai Dan Sai Medborgarvägen 3 ☎046 72 731 30 77, ⓦthaidansai.se. This welcome Thai place serves standards such as green chicken curry and spring rolls to a grateful local clientele. Prices are low too, with mains from 80kr. Tues–Thurs 11am–9pm, Fri 11am–2am, Sat 4pm–2am.
Tre Kronor Tornedalsvägen 11B ☎0978 107 70. This long-standing pizzeria and fast-food place serves pizzas (from 75kr), burgers (75kr) and steaks (from 100kr). It's not exactly fine dining, but at prices like these there are few complaints. Mon–Fri 10.30am–8pm, Sat & Sun noon–9pm.

Karesuando and around

Sweden's northernmost village, **KARESUANDO**, 180km north of Pajala, is a surprisingly likeable little place. This far corner of Sweden is as good a spot as any to take stock of just where you've reached: the North Cape is barely 500km away, you're as far north as the northern tip of Alaska, and the tree line slices through the edge of the village. **Winters** up here can be particularly severe; the first snow falls at the end of September or early October and stays on the ground until late May, when the Muonioälven, the river which curls around the village, also melts. Just a few centimetres beneath the surface, the ground is in the grip of **permafrost** all year round. Summer here is short

9

and sweet – but the region becomes a mosquito paradise in the warmer and lighter months. Karesuando is right in the midst of *Sámi* heartland; reindeer husbandry is of primary importance, particularly in the nearby villages of Övre, Nedre Soppero and Idivuoma, where many herders live.

With your own transport, it's well worth the short drive south along Route 99 towards Pajala for fantastic **views**: some five or ten minutes after leaving the village, take the right turn marked "Kaarevaara" and continue past a small lake, whereupon the road begins to climb up past a TV mast and ends in a small car park. On a clear day you can see for miles across the Swedish and Finnish tundra. The vast tract of land stretching away to the northwest contains **Treriksröset**, the point where Sweden, Finland and Norway meet (see box).

Lars Levi Laestadius museum

Laestadiusvägen, beyond the tourist office • No set hours • Free

The only sight to speak of in Karesuando is the wooden cabin that was once the rectory of **Lars Levi Laestadius**, the village's most famous son (see page 349). Complete with plain wooden pews, it was used as a meeting place while Laestadius was rector in Karesuando, and is now a simple **museum** of his life.

Vita Huset

Village Museum • Laestadiusvägen 113 • Mon–Fri 8am–11am & noon–3pm • 30kr

Along the road to the campsite and worth a quick look is the village **museum**, known as **Vita Huset**, containing a few atmospheric black-and-white photographs from 1944, when Karesuando was inundated by Finns fleeing the approaching German forces – with their cattle. Look for the picture of Olga Raattamaa, known locally as Empress Olga, who once lived in nearby Kummavuopio, and single-handedly saved the lives of dozens of Finns by rowing them across the Könkämä River to safety in neutral Sweden.

ARRIVAL AND INFORMATION   KARESUANDO

By bus You can reach Karesuando from Pajala by bus by changing in nearby Vittangi (1 daily; 3hr 20min for whole journey).

Tourist office In the customs house on the bridge across to Finland (June–Sept daily 8am–4pm; Oct–May Mon–Fri 10am–5pm; ☎ 0981 202 05, ⓦ karesuando.se). This tourist office seems to pick and choose when it opens so don't count on it being open.

TRERIKSRÖSET

Heading north for **Treriksröset** – the **three-nation marker post** where Sweden, Norway and Finland meet – walk over the bridge from Karesuando to Kaaresuvanto in Finland, from where a daily bus leaves at 2.35pm (Finland is an hour ahead of Sweden) for **Kilpisjärvi** (journey time 1hr 40min). From June to mid-September a second daily bus leaves at 4.25pm for Tromsø in Norway, travelling via Kilpisjärvi. From Kilpisjärvi, there are two ways to get to Treriksröset. One of these is a hike of 11km down a track which passes through an area of dwarf woodland before running around a small lake to reach Sweden's northernmost point; don't forget your camera and mosquito repellent. Alternatively, you can shorten the hike to just 3km by taking a **boat ride** from Kilpisjärvi across the lake on *M/S Malla* (late June–early Aug 10am, 2pm & 6pm Finnish time; 45min; €25 return); note that the boat requires at least four passengers to sail.

From Treriksröset, the path continues (14km) towards the **northernmost peak** in Sweden, **Pältsan** (1445m); the going here is rocky in parts. The STF **cabins** (no advance booking; March, April & late June–early Sept; dorm beds 390kr) at the foot of the mountain boast thirty beds and a sauna. There's an easy hike (40km) from the cabins to **Keinovuopio**, where you cross the river to the village of **Peera**, on the main E8 road in Finland; from here you can catch the bus back to Karesuando (daily at approximately 1.45pm, also June–mid-Sept daily at 11.25am; check Finnish bus times at ⓦ matkahuolto.fi).

GETTING TO THE NORTH CAPE

From Karesuando it's a drive of 510km to the **North Cape** in Norway, routing via Enontekiö in Finland and then Kautokeino and Alta in Norway; it will take at least six hours with your own car. By public transport, the easiest option is to walk across to Kaaresuvanto in Finland and pick up the bus for Tromsø which operates from June–mid-September, departing at 4.25pm. Change buses in Skibotn on Norway's E6 highway and then head east towards Alta for connections to the North Cape. Finnish bus timetables are at ⓦ eskelisen.fi, Norwegian ones at ⓦ 177finnmark.no.

ACCOMMODATION AND EATING

Arctic Livs ☎ 0980 203 70. Located between the filling stations, this fast-food place serves burgers and reindeer fry-ups as well as Asian dishes such as lemon chicken rice. A main dish costs around 120kr. Mon–Fri 9am–6pm, Sat 10am–6pm, Sun noon–4pm.

Karesuando Camping Laestadiusvägen 185 ☎ 0981 201 39 or ☎ 070 605 1124, ⓦ karesuando.se/foretag/camping/camping.htm. A 2km walk past the church on the Pajala road, this riverside campsite has regular cabins and a few *Sámi*-style *kåtor*. There's a separate toilet and shower block. Open June–Aug. Tents 140kr, cabins and *kåtor* 500kr

GOLDEN ROOM, STOCKHOLM'S TOWN HALL

Contexts

History

Sweden has one of Europe's longest documented histories, but for
all the upheavals of the Viking times and the warring of the Middle
Ages, the country has, in modern times, seemed to delight in taking
a historical back seat. For a brief period in 1986, when Prime Minister
Olof Palme was shot dead, Sweden was thrust into the limelight.
Since then, the country has regained some of its equilibrium, though
political infighting and domestic disharmony often threatens the one
thing that Swedes have always been proud of, and that other countries
aspire to: the politics of *consensus*, the potential passing of which is
arguably of far greater importance than even the assassination of their
prime minister.

Early civilizations

It was not until around 6000 BC that the **first settlers** roamed north and east into
Sweden, living as nomadic reindeer hunters and herders. By 3000 BC people had
settled in the south of the country and were established as farmers; from 2000 BC
there are indications of a development in burial practices, with **dolmens** and **passage
graves** found throughout the southern Swedish provinces. Traces also remain of the
Boat Axe People, named after their characteristic tool and weapon, shaped like a boat.
The earliest horse riders in Scandinavia, they quickly held sway over the whole of
southern Sweden.

During the **Bronze Age** (1500–500 BC) the Boat Axe People traded furs and amber
for southern European copper and tin – large finds of finished ornaments and weapons
show a comparatively rich culture. This was emphasized by elaborate burial rites, the
dead laid in single graves under mounds of earth and stone.

The deterioration of the Scandinavian climate in the last millennium before Christ
coincided with the advance across Europe of the Celts, which halted the flourishing
trade of the Swedish settlers. With the new millennium, Sweden made its first mark
upon the Classical world. In the *Historia Naturalis*, Pliny the Elder (23–79 AD)
mentioned the "island of Scatinavia" far to the north. Tacitus was more specific: in
98 AD he mentioned a powerful people who were strong in men, weapons and ships,
the *Suinoes* – a reference to the **Svear**, who were to form the nucleus of an emergent
Swedish kingdom by the sixth century.

The Svear settled in the rich land around Lake Mälaren and became rulers of most
of the territory comprising modern Sweden, except the south. They gave Sweden
its modern name: *Sverige* in Swedish or *Svear rik*, the kingdom of the Svear. More
importantly, their first dynastic leaders had a taste for expansion, trading with Gotland
and holding suzerainty over the Åland Islands.

6000BC	98 AD	First century AD	Ninth century AD
First settlers arrive	Tacitus refers to northern tribes as Suinoes	Svear tribe become rulers of land now Sweden	Swedish Vikings travel to Black and Caspian seas

The Viking period

The Vikings – raiders and warriors who dominated the political and economic life of Europe and beyond from the ninth to the eleventh centuries – came from all parts of southern Scandinavia. But there is evidence that the **Swedish Vikings** were among the first to leave home, the impetus being rapid population growth, domestic unrest and a desire for new lands. Sweden being located on the eastern part of the Scandinavian peninsula, the raiders largely turned their attention further eastwards, in the knowledge that the Svear had already reached the Baltic. By the ninth century, the trade routes were well established, with Swedes reaching the Black and Caspian seas and making valuable trading contact with the **Byzantine Empire**. Although more commercially inclined than their Danish and Norwegian counterparts, Swedish Vikings were quick to use force if profits were slow to materialize. From 860 onwards Greek and Muslim records relate a series of raids across the Black Sea against Byzantium, and across the Caspian into northeast Iran.

Domestically, **paganism** was at its height; dynastic leaders would claim descent from Freyr, "God of the World". It was a bloody time: nine **human sacrifices** were offered at the celebrations held every nine years at Uppsala. Adam of Bremen recorded that the great shrine there was adjoined by a sacred grove where "every tree is believed divine because of the death and putrefaction of the victims hanging there".

Viking **law** was based on the **Thing**, an assembly of free men to which the king's power was subject. Each largely autonomous province had its own assembly and its own leaders: where several provinces united, the approval of every *Thing* was needed for any choice of leader. For centuries in Sweden, each newly elected king had to make a formal tour to receive the homage of the individual provinces.

The arrival of Christianity and the early Middle Ages

Christianity was slow to take root in Sweden. Whereas Denmark and Norway had accepted the faith by the turn of the eleventh century, the Swedes remained largely heathen. Missionaries met with limited success: no Swedish king was converted until 1008, when **Olof Skötkonung** was baptized. He was the first known king of both Swedes and Goths (that is, ruler of the two major provinces of Västergötland and Östergötland), and his successors were all Christians. Nevertheless, paganism retained a grip on Swedish affairs, and as late as the 1080s the Svear banished the then king, Inge, when he refused to take part in the pagan celebrations at Uppsala. By the end of the eleventh century, though, the temple at Uppsala had gone and a Christian church was built on its site. In the 1130s, Sigtuna – the original centre of the Swedish Christian faith – was replaced by Uppsala as the main episcopal seat, and in 1164 Stephen, an English monk, was made the first archbishop.

VIKING NAMES

The Vikings were settlers as well as traders and exploiters, and their long-term influence was marked. Embattled Slavs to the east gave them the name **Rus**, and their creeping colonization gave one area in which the Vikings settled its modern name, Russia. Russian names today – Oleg, Igor, Vladimir – can be derived from the Swedish – Helgi, Ingvar, Valdemar.

1008	1157	1229	1323
Baptism of first Swedish king to be converted to Christianity	Swedes lead crusade against heathen Finland	Birger Jarl assumes power in Stockholm	Sweden's eastern frontiers formalized with Russia

The whole of the early Middle Ages in Sweden was characterized by a succession of struggles for control of a growing central power: two families, the Sverkers and the Eriks, waged battle against each other throughout the twelfth century. **King Erik** was the first Sverker king to make his mark: in 1157 he led a crusade to heathen Finland, but was killed in 1160 at Uppsala by a Danish pretender to his throne. Within a hundred years he was to be recognized as patron saint of Sweden, and his remains were interred in the new Uppsala cathedral.

Erik was succeeded by his son **Knut**, whose stable reign lasted until 1196, a period marked by commercial treaties and strengthened defences. Following his death, virtual civil war weakened royal power. As a result, the king's chief ministers, or **jarls**, assumed much of the executive responsibility for running the country, so much so that when Erik Eriksson (last of the Eriks) was deposed in 1229, his administrator **Birger Jarl** assumed power. With papal support for his crusading policies, he confirmed the Swedish grip on the southwest of Finland. He was succeeded by his son, Valdemar, who proved a weak ruler and didn't survive the family feuding after Birger Jarl's death.

In 1275, Valdemar's brother, **Magnus Ladulås**, assumed power. He earned his nickname "Ladulås" ("Barn-lock") from his having prevented the nobility from claiming maintenance at the expense of the peasantry as they travelled from estate to estate. Magnus's reign represented a peak of Swedish royal might that wasn't to be repeated for three hundred years. While he was king, his enemies dissipated; he forbade the nobility to meet without his consent, and began to issue his own authoritative decrees. He also began to reap the benefits of conversion: the clergy became an educated class upon whom the monarch could rely for diplomatic and administrative duties. By the thirteenth century, there were ambitious Swedish clerics in Paris and Bologna, and the first stone churches were appearing in Sweden, the most monumental of which is the early Gothic **cathedral** built at Uppsala.

Meanwhile, the nobility had come to constitute a military class, exempt from taxation on the understanding that they would defend the Crown. In the country, the standard of living was still low, although an increasing population stimulated new cultivation. The forests of Norrland were pushed back, more southern heathland was turned into pasture, and crop rotation was introduced. Noticeable, too, was the increasing **German influence** within Sweden as the Hansa traders spread. Their first merchants settled in Visby and, by the mid-thirteenth century, in Stockholm.

The fourteenth century – towards unity

Magnus died in 1290, power shifting to a cabal of magnates led by **Torgil Knutsson**. As marshal of Sweden, he pursued an energetic foreign policy, conquering western Karelia to gain control of the Gulf of Finland and building the fortress at Viborg, only lost with the collapse of the Swedish Empire in the eighteenth century.

Magnus's son Birger came of age in 1302 and soon quarrelled with his brothers Erik and Valdemar, who had Torgil Knutsson executed. They then rounded on Birger, who was forced to divide up Sweden among the three of them. An unhappy arrangement, it lasted until 1317 when Birger had his brothers arrested and starved to death in prison – an act that prompted a shocked nobility to rise against Birger and force his exile to Denmark. The Swedish nobles restored the principle of elective monarchy by calling on

1323	1350s	1397	1477
Finland becomes part of Sweden	Black Death kills one third of population	Kalmar Union established with Denmark and Norway	Uppsala university founded

the 3-year-old **Magnus** (son of a Swedish duke, and already declared Norwegian king) to take the Swedish crown. During his minority, a treaty was concluded in 1323 with Novgorod in Russia to define the frontiers in eastern and northern Finland. This left virtually the whole of the Scandinavian peninsula (except the Danish provinces in the south) under one ruler.

Yet Sweden was still anything but prosperous. The **Black Death** reached the country in 1350, wiping out whole parishes and killing around a third of the population. Subsequent labour shortages and troubled estates meant that the nobility found it difficult to maintain their positions. German merchants had driven the Swedes from their most lucrative trade routes: even the copper and iron-ore **mining** that began around this time in Bergslagen and Dalarna relied on German capital.

Magnus soon ran into trouble, and was threatened further by the accession of Valdemar Atterdag to the Danish throne in 1340. Squabbles concerning sovereignty over the Danish provinces of Skåne and Blekinge led to Danish incursions into Sweden; in 1361, Valdemar landed on Gotland and sacked **Visby**. The Gotlanders were refused refuge by the Hansa merchants, and massacred outside the city walls.

Magnus was forced to negotiate, and his son **Håkon** – now king of Norway – was married to Valdemar's daughter Margaret. When Magnus was later deposed, power fell into the hands of the magnates who shared out the country. Chief of the ruling nobles was the Steward **Bo Jonsson Grip**, who controlled all Finland and central and southeast Sweden. Yet on his death, the nobility turned to Håkon's wife **Margaret**, already regent in Norway (for her son Olof) and in Denmark since the death of her father, Valdemar. The nobles were anxious for union across Scandinavia, to safeguard those who owned frontier estates and to strengthen the Crown against any further German influence. In 1388 she was proclaimed "First Lady" of Sweden and, in return, confirmed all the privileges of the Swedish nobility. Called upon to choose a male king, Margaret nominated her nephew, **Erik of Pomerania**, who was duly elected king of Sweden in 1396. As he had already been elected to the Danish and Norwegian thrones, Scandinavian unity seemed assured.

The Kalmar Union

Erik was crowned king of Denmark, Norway and Sweden in 1397 at a ceremony in **Kalmar**. Nominally, the three kingdoms were now in union but, despite Erik's kingship, real power remained in the hands of Margaret until her death in 1412.

Erik was at war with the Hanseatic League throughout his reign. He was vilified in popular Swedish history as an evil and grasping ruler, and the taxes he raised went on a war that was never fought on Swedish soil. He spent his time instead directing operations in Denmark, leaving his queen Philippa (sister to Henry V of England) behind. Erik was deposed in 1439 and the nobility turned to **Christopher of Bavaria**, whose early death in 1448 led to the first major breach in the union.

No one candidate could fill the three kingships satisfactorily, and separate elections in Denmark and Sweden signalled a renewal of the infighting that had plagued the previous century. Within Sweden, unionists and nationalists skirmished, the powerful unionist **Oxenstierna** family opposing the claims of the nationalist **Sture** family, until 1470 when **Sten Sture** (the Elder) became "Guardian of the Realm". His victory over

1483	1520	1520	1541
Sweden's first printing press appears	Danes invade, killing nobility and clergy in Stockholm Bloodbath	Gustav Vasa flees on skis to Norway	First edition of the Bible in the vernacular appears

the unionists at the **Battle of Brunkeberg** (1471) – in the centre of what's now modern Stockholm – was complete, gaining symbolic artistic expression in the **statue of St George and the Dragon** that still adorns the Storkyrkan in Stockholm.

Sten Sture's primacy fostered a new cultural atmosphere. The first **university** in Scandinavia was founded in Uppsala in 1477, with Sweden's first printing press appearing six years later. Artistically, German and Dutch influences were predominantly traits seen in the decorative art of the great Swedish medieval churches. Only remote **Dalarna** kept a native folk-art tradition alive.

Belief in the union still existed though, particularly outside Sweden, and successive kings had to fend off almost constant attacks and blockades emanating from Denmark. With the accession of **Christian II** to the Danish throne in 1513, the unionist movement found a leader capable of turning the tide. Under the guise of a crusade to free Sweden's imprisoned archbishop Gustav Trolle, Christian attacked Sweden and killed Sture. After Christian's coronation, Trolle urged the prosecution of his Swedish adversaries (who had been gathered together under the pretext of an amnesty) and they were found guilty of heresy. Eighty-two nobles and clergymen of Stockholm were executed, their bodies burned in what became known as the **Stockholm Bloodbath**. A vicious persecution of Sture's followers throughout Sweden ensued, a move that led to widespread reaction and, ultimately, the downfall of the union.

Gustav Vasa and his sons

Opposition to Christian II was vague and disorganized until the appearance of the young **Gustav Vasa**. Initially unable to stir the locals of the Dalecarlia region into open revolt, he was on his way to Norway, and exile, when he was chased on skis and recalled, the people having had a change of heart. The chase is celebrated still in the **Vasaloppet** race, run each year by thousands of Swedish skiers.

Gustav Vasa's army grew rapidly. In 1521, he was elected regent, and subsequently, with the capture of Stockholm in 1523, king. Christian had been deposed in Denmark and the new Danish king, Frederick I, recognized Sweden's de facto withdrawal from the union. Short of cash, Gustav found it prudent to support the movement for religious reform propagated by Swedish Lutherans. More of a political than a religious **Reformation**, the result was a handover of Church lands to the Crown and the subordination of Church to state. It's a relationship that is still largely in force today, the clergy being civil servants paid by the state.

In 1541, the first edition of the Bible in the vernacular appeared. Suppressing revolt at home, Gustav Vasa strengthened his hand with a centralization of trade and government. On his death in 1560, Sweden was united, prosperous and independent.

Gustav Vasa's heir, his eldest son **Erik**, faced a difficult time, not least because the Vasa lands and wealth had been divided among him and his brothers Johan, Magnus and Karl (an uncharacteristically imprudent action of Gustav before his death). The Danes, too, pressed hard, reasserting their claim to the Swedish throne in the inconclusive **Northern Seven Years War**, which began in 1563. Erik was deposed in 1569 by his brother, who became **Johan III**, his first act being to end the war by the **Peace of Stettin** treaty. At home, Johan ruled more or less with the goodwill of the nobility, but matters

1563	1607	1611	1618
Northern Seven Years War begins	Gothenburg founded to trade with west	Gustav II Adolf becomes king	Thirty Years War breaks out

> ## THE MAKING OF A NATION
>
> The rule of Vasa and his sons made Sweden a **nation**, culturally as well as politically. The courts were filled with and influenced by men of learning; art and sculpture flourished. The **Renaissance** style appeared for the first time in Sweden, with royal castles remodelled – Kalmar being a fine example. Economically, Sweden remained mostly self-sufficient, its few imports being luxuries like cloth, wine and spices. With around eight thousand inhabitants, Stockholm was its most important city, although **Gothenburg** was founded in 1607 to promote trade to the west.

were upset by his Catholic sympathies: he introduced a new Catholic liturgy, familiarly known from its binding as the *Red Book*, which the clergy accepted only under protest. On Johan's death in 1592, his son and heir, Sigismund (who was Catholic king of Poland) agreed to rule Sweden in accordance with Lutheran practice, but failed to do so. When Sigismund returned to Poland, the way was clear for Duke Karl (Johan's brother) to assume the regency, a role he filled until declared King **Karl IX** in 1603.

Karl, the last of Vasa's sons, had ambitions eastwards but was routed by the Poles and staved off by the Russians. He suffered a stroke in 1610 and died the year after. His heir was the 17-year-old Gustav II, better known as **Gustav II Adolf**.

Gustav II Adolf and the rise of the Swedish empire

Sweden became a European power during the reign of **Gustav II Adolf**. Though still a youth he was considered able enough to rule, and proved so by concluding peace treaties with Denmark (1613) and Russia (1617), the latter pact isolating Russia from the Baltic and allowing the Swedes control of the eastern trade routes into Europe.

In 1618, the **Thirty Years War** broke out. It was vital for Gustav that Germany should not become Catholic, given the Polish king's continuing pretensions to the Swedish crown and the possible threat Germany could pose to Sweden's growing influence in the Baltic. In 1629, the Altmark treaty with a defeated Poland gave Gustav control of Livonia and four Prussian seaports, and the income this generated financed his entry into the war in 1630 on the Protestant side. After several convincing victories, Gustav pushed on through Germany, delaying an assault upon undefended Vienna. The decision cost him his life: Gustav was killed at the **Battle of Lützen** in 1632, his body stripped and battered by the enemy's soldiers. The war dragged on until the **Peace of Westphalia** in 1648.

With Gustav away at war for much of his reign, Sweden ran smoothly under the guidance of his friend and chancellor, **Axel Oxenstierna**. Together they founded a new Supreme Court in Stockholm (and did the same for Finland and the conquered Baltic provinces); reorganized the national assembly into four Estates of nobility, clergy, burghers and peasantry (1626); extended the university at Uppsala (and founded one at Åbo – modern Turku in Finland); and fostered the mining and other industries that provided much of the country's wealth. Gustav had many other accomplishments, too: he spoke five languages and designed a new light cannon which assisted in his routs of the enemy.

1632	1658	1662	1741
Gustav II Adolf killed at the Battle of Lützen	Treaty of Roskilde secures southern provinces for Sweden	Work begins on Drottningholm palace	Carl von Linné becomes a professor at Uppsala university

The Caroleans

The Swedish empire reached its territorial peak under the **Caroleans**. Yet the reign of the last of them was to see Sweden crumble. Following Gustav II Adolf's death and the later abdication of his daughter Kristina, **Karl X** succeeded to the throne. War against Poland (1655) led to some early successes and, with Denmark espousing the Polish cause, gave Karl the opportunity to march into Jutland (1657). From there his armies marched across the frozen sea to threaten Copenhagen; the subsequent **Treaty of Roskilde** (1658) broke Denmark and gave the Swedish empire its widest territorial extent.

However, the long regency of his son and heir, **Karl XI**, did little to safeguard Sweden's vulnerable position, so extensive were its borders. On assuming power in 1672, Karl was almost immediately dragged into war: beaten by a smaller Prussian army at Brandenberg in 1675, Sweden was suddenly faced with war against both the Danes and the Dutch. Karl rallied, though, to drive out the Danish invaders, and the war ended in 1679 with the reconquest of Skåne and the restoration of most of Sweden's German provinces.

In 1682, Karl XI became **absolute monarch** and was given full control over legislation and *reduktion* – the resumption of estates previously alienated by the Crown to the nobility. The armed forces were reorganized too: by 1700, the Swedish army had 25,000 soldiers and twelve regiments of cavalry; the naval fleet had expanded to 38 ships and a new base had been built at **Karlskrona** (which was nearer to the likely trouble spots than Stockholm).

Culturally, Sweden began to benefit from the innovations of Gustav II Adolf. *Gymnasia* (grammar schools) continued to expand, and a second university was established at **Lund** in 1668. A national **literature** emerged, helped by the efforts of **George Stiernhielm**, father of modern Swedish poetry. **Olof Rudbeck** (1630–1702) was a Nordic polymath whose scientific reputation lasted longer than his attempt to identify the ancient Goth settlement at Uppsala as Atlantis. Architecturally, this was the age of **Tessin**, both father and son. Tessin the Elder was responsible for the glorious palace at **Drottningholm**, work on which began in 1662, as well as the cathedral at **Kalmar**. His son, Tessin the Younger, succeeded him as royal architect and was to create the new royal palace at Stockholm.

In 1697, the 15-year-old **Karl XII** succeeded to the throne; under him, the empire collapsed. Faced with a defensive alliance of Saxony, Denmark and Russia, there was little the king could have done to avoid eventual defeat. However, he remains a revered figure for his valiant (often suicidal) efforts to take on the rest of Europe. Initial victories against Peter the Great and Saxony led him to march on Russia, where he was defeated and the bulk of his army destroyed. Escaping to Turkey, where he remained as guest and then prisoner for four years, Karl watched the empire disintegrate. With Poland reconquered by Augustus of Saxony, and Finland by Peter the Great, he returned to Sweden only to have England declare war on him.

Eventually, splits in the enemy alliance led Swedish diplomats to attempt peace talks with Russia. Karl, though, was keen to exploit these differences in a more direct fashion. Wanting to strike at Denmark, but lacking a fleet, he besieged Fredrikshald in Norway (then united with Denmark) in 1718 – and was killed by a sniper's bullet. In

1741	1744	1778	1809
Sweden declares war on Russia	Anders Celsius dies	Death of Carl von Linné	Sweden loses Finland to Russia

the vacuum thus created, Russia became the leading Baltic power, receiving Livonia, Estonia, Ingria and most of Karelia from Sweden.

The Age of Freedom

The eighteenth century saw absolutism discredited in Sweden. A new constitution vested power in the Estates, who reduced the new king **Frederick I**'s role to that of nominal head of state. The chancellor wielded the real power, and under **Arvid Horn** the country found a period of stability. His party, nicknamed the "Caps", was opposed by the hawkish "Hats". The latter forced war with Russia in 1741, a disaster in which Sweden lost all of Finland and had its whole east coast burned and bombed. Most of Finland was returned with the agreement that **Adolphus Frederick** (a relation of the crown prince of Russia) would be elected to the Swedish throne on Frederick I's death. This duly occurred in 1751.

During his reign, Adolphus repeatedly tried to reassert royal power, but found that the constitution had been strengthened against him. The Estates' power was such that when Adolphus refused to sign any bills, they simply utilized a stamp bearing his name. The resurrected "Hats" forced entry into the **Seven Years War** in 1757 on the French side, another disastrous venture, as the Prussians were able to repel every Swedish attack.

The aristocratic parties were in a state of constant flux. Although elections of sorts were held to provide delegates for the *Riksdag* (parliament), foreign sympathies, bribery and bickering were hardly conducive to democratic administration. Cabals continued to rule Sweden, the economy was stagnant, and reform delayed. It was, however, an age of **intellectual and scientific advance**, surprising in a country that had lost much of its cultural impetus. **Carl von Linné**, the botanist whose classification of plants is still used, was professor at Uppsala from 1741 to 1778; **Anders Celsius** initiated the use of the centigrade temperature scale; **Carl Scheele** discovered chlorine. A royal decree of 1748 organized Europe's first full-scale **census**, a five-yearly event by 1775. Other fields flourished, too. The mystical works of **Emmanuel Swedenborg**, the philosopher who died in 1772, encouraged new theological sects; and the period encompassed the life of **Carl Michael Bellman** (1740–95), the celebrated Swedish poet whose work did much to identify and foster a popular nationalism.

With the accession of **Gustav III** in 1771, the Crown began to regain the ascendancy. A new constitution was forced upon a divided *Riksdag* and proved a watershed between earlier absolutism and the later aristocratic squabbles. A popular king, Gustav founded hospitals, granted freedom of worship and removed many of the state controls over the economy. His determination to conduct a successful foreign policy led to further conflict with Russia (1788–90) in which, to everyone's surprise, he managed to more than hold his own. But with the French Revolution polarizing opposition throughout Europe, the Swedish nobility began to entertain thoughts of conspiracy against a king whose growing powers they now saw as those of a tyrant. In 1792, at a masked ball in Stockholm Opera House, the king was shot by an assassin hired by the disaffected aristocracy. Gustav died two weeks later and was succeeded by his son **Gustav IV**, with the country being led by a regency during his minority.

The wars waged by revolutionary France were at first studiously avoided in Sweden but, pulled into the conflict by the British, Gustav IV entered the **Napoleonic Wars** in

1814	1860	1867	1896
Norway and Sweden form a union	Emigration to America begins	Famine hits Sweden	Death of Alfred Nobel

1805. However, Napoleon's victory at Austerlitz two years later broke the coalition, and Sweden found itself isolated. Attacked by Russia the following year, Gustav was later arrested and deposed, and his uncle was elected king.

A constitution of 1809 established a liberal monarchy in Sweden, responsible to the elected *Riksdag*. Under this constitution **Karl XIII** was a mere caretaker, his heir a Danish prince who would bring Norway back to Sweden – some compensation for finally losing Finland and the Åland Islands to Russia (1809) after five hundred years of Swedish rule.

On the prince's sudden death, however, Marshal Bernadotte (one of Napoleon's generals) was invited to become heir. Taking the name of **Karl Johan**, he took his chance in 1812 and joined Britain and Russia to fight Napoleon. Following Napoleon's first defeat at the Battle of Leipzig in 1813, Sweden compelled Denmark (France's ally) to exchange Norway for Swedish Pomerania.

By 1814 Sweden and Norway had formed an uneasy union. Norway retained its own government and certain autonomous measures. Sweden decided foreign policy, appointed a viceroy and retained a suspensive (but not absolute) veto over the Norwegian parliament's legislation.

The nineteenth century

Union under Karl Johan, or **Karl XIV** as he became in 1818, could have been disastrous. He spoke no Swedish and just a few years previously had never visited either kingdom. However, under Karl and his successor **Oscar I**, prosperity ensued. Construction of the **Göta Canal** (1832) helped commercially, and liberal measures by both monarchs helped politically. In 1845, daughters were given an equal right of inheritance. A Poor Law was introduced in 1847, restrictive craft guilds reformed, and an Education Act passed.

The 1848 revolutions throughout Europe cooled Oscar's reforming ardour, and his attention turned to reviving **Scandinavianism**. It was still a hope, in certain quarters, that closer cooperation between Denmark and Sweden–Norway could lead to some sort of revived Kalmar Union. Expectations were raised with the **Crimean War** of 1854: Russia as a future threat could be neutralized. But peace was declared too quickly (at least for Sweden) and there was still no real guarantee that Sweden would be sufficiently protected from Russia in the future. With Oscar's death, talk of political union faded.

His son **Karl XV** presided over a reform of the *Riksdag* that put an end to the Swedish system of personal monarchy. The Four Estates were replaced by a representative **two-house parliament** along European lines. This, together with the end of political Scandinavianism (following the Prussian attack on Denmark in 1864 in which Sweden stood by), marked Sweden's entry into modern Europe.

Industrialization was slow to take root in Sweden. No real industrial revolution occurred, and development – mechanization, introduction of railways, etc – was piecemeal. One result was widespread **emigration** amongst the rural poor, who had been hard hit by famine in 1867 and 1868. Between 1860 and 1910 over one million people left for America (in 1860 the Swedish population was only four million). Given huge farms to settle, the emigrants headed for land similar to that they had left behind – to the Midwest, Kansas and Nebraska.

1905	1930s	1940	1943
Norway gains independence from Sweden	Welfare state established	Sweden surrounded by Nazi Germany	Sweden takes in Jews from across Europe

At home, Swedish **trade unionism** emerged to campaign for better conditions. Dealt with severely, the unions formed a confederation (1898) but largely failed to make headway. Even peaceful picketing carried a two-year prison sentence. Hand in hand with the fight for workers' rights went the **temperance movement.** The level of alcohol consumption was alarming, and various abstinence programmes attempted to educate the drinkers and, if necessary, eradicate the stills. Some towns made the selling of spirits a municipal monopoly – not a big step from the state monopoly that exists today.

With the accession of **Oscar II** in 1872, Sweden continued on an even, if uneventful, keel. Keeping out of further European conflict (the Austro-Prussian War, Franco-Prussian War and various Balkan crises), the country's only worry was growing dissatisfaction in Norway with the union. Demanding a separate consular service, and objecting to the Swedish king's veto on constitutional matters, the Norwegians brought things to a head, and in 1905 declared the union invalid. The Karlstad Convention confirmed the break, and Norway became independent for the first time since 1380.

The late nineteenth century was a happier time for Swedish culture. **August Strindberg** enjoyed great critical success, and artists like **Anders Zorn** and **Prince Eugene** made their mark abroad. The historian **Artur Hazelius** founded the Nordic and Skansen museums in Stockholm; and the chemist, industrialist and dynamite inventor **Alfred Nobel** left his fortune to finance the Nobel Prizes. It's an instructive tale: Nobel hoped that the knowledge of his invention would help eradicate war, optimistically believing that humankind would never dare unleash the destructive forces of dynamite.

The two World Wars

Sweden declared strict neutrality on the outbreak of **World War I**, influenced by much sympathy within the country for Germany that stemmed from long-standing cultural, trade and linguistic links. It was a policy agreed with the other Scandinavian monarchs, but a difficult one to pursue. Faced with British demands to enforce a blockade of Germany and with the blacklisting and eventual seizure of Swedish goods at sea, the economy suffered grievously; rationing and inflation mushroomed. The **Russian Revolution** in 1917 brought further problems for Sweden. The Finns immediately declared independence, waging civil war against the Bolsheviks, and Swedish volunteers enlisted in the White Army. But a conflict of interest arose when the Swedish-speaking Åland Islands wanted a return to Swedish rule rather than stay under the victorious Finns. The League of Nations overturned this claim, granting the islands to Finland.

After the war, a liberal–socialist coalition remained in power until 1920, when **Branting** became the first socialist prime minister. By the time of his death in 1924, franchise had been extended to all men and women over 23, and the system of state-controlled alcohol stores (Systembolaget) had been set up. Following the Depression of the late 1920s and early 1930s, conditions began to improve after a Social Democratic government took office for the fourth time in 1932. A **welfare state** was rapidly established, offering unemployment benefits, higher old-age pensions, family allowances and paid holidays. The **Saltsjöbaden Agreement** of 1938 drew up a contract between trade unions and employers to help eliminate strikes and lockouts. With war again looming, all parties agreed that Sweden should remain neutral in any struggle, and so the country's rearmament was negligible, despite Hitler's apparent intentions.

1943	1953	1967
IKEA founded by 17-year-old Ingvar Kamprad	Sweden's Dag Hammarskjöld becomes UN Secretary-General	Sweden changes from left- to right-hand traffic

World War II was slow to affect Sweden. Unlike in 1914, there was little sympathy in the country for Germany, but Sweden again declared neutrality. The Russian invasion of Finland in 1939 brought Sweden into the picture, with the Swedes providing weapons, volunteers and refuge for the Finns. Regular Swedish troops were refused, though, the Swedes fearing intervention from either the Germans (then Russia's ally) or the Allies. Economically, the country remained sound – less dependent on imports than in World War I and with no serious shortages. The position became stickier in 1940 when the Nazis marched into Denmark and Norway, isolating Sweden. Concessions were made – German troop transit allowed, iron-ore exports continued – until 1943–44, when Allied pressure had become more convincing than the failing German war machine.

Sweden became the recipient of countless refugees from the rest of Scandinavia and the Baltic. Instrumental in this process was **Raoul Wallenberg**, who rescued Hungarian Jews from the SS and persuaded the Swedish government to give him diplomatic status in 1944. Anything up to 35,000 Jews in Hungary were sheltered in "neutral houses" (flying the Swedish flag), and fed and clothed by Wallenberg. But when Soviet troops liberated Budapest in 1945, Wallenberg was arrested as a suspected spy and disappeared; he was later reported to have died in prison in Moscow in 1947. However, unconfirmed accounts had him alive in a Soviet prison as late as 1975; in 1989 some of his surviving relatives flew to Moscow in an unsuccessful attempt to discover the truth about his fate.

The end of the war was to engender a serious crisis of conscience in the country. Though physically unscathed, Sweden was now vulnerable to **Cold War** politics. The Finns had agreed to let Soviet troops march unhindered through Finland, and in 1949 this led neighbouring Sweden to refuse to follow the other Scandinavian countries into **NATO**. The country did, however, much to conservative disquiet, return into Stalin's hands most of the Baltic and German refugees who had fought against Russia during the war – their fate is not difficult to guess.

Postwar politics

The wartime coalition quickly gave way to a purely Social Democratic government committed to welfare provision and increased defence expenditure – now non-participation in military alliances did not mean a throwing-down of weapons.

Tax increases and a trade slump lost the Social Democrats seats in the 1948 general election, and by 1951 they needed to enter into a **coalition** with the Agrarian (later the Centre) Party to survive. This coalition lasted until 1957, when disputes over the form of a proposed extension to the pension system brought it down. An inconclusive referendum and the withdrawal of the Centre Party from government forced an election. Although the Centre gained seats and the Conservatives replaced the Liberals as the main opposition party, the Social Democrats retained a (slim) majority.

Sweden regained much of its international moral respect (lost directly after World War II) through the election of **Dag Hammarskjöld** as Secretary-General of the United Nations in 1953. His strong leadership greatly enhanced the prestige (and effectiveness) of the organization, which under his guidance participated in the solution of the 1956

1974	1976	1976	1986
ABBA win Eurovision Song Contest in Brighton, England	Social Democrats lose power after forty years	Swedish King Carl Gustav, marries German commoner	Olof Palme assassinated

Suez crisis and the 1958 Lebanon–Jordan affair. He was killed in an air crash in 1961, towards the end of his second five-year term.

Domestic reform continued unabated throughout the 1950s and 1960s. It was during these years that the country laid the foundations of its much-vaunted social security system, although at the time it didn't always bear close scrutiny. A **National Health Service** gave free hospital treatment, but only allowed for small refunds on doctor's fees and the costs of medicines and dental treatment – hardly as far-reaching as the British system introduced immediately after the war.

The Social Democrats stayed in power until 1976, when a **non-Social Democrat coalition** (Centre–Liberal–Moderate) finally unseated them. In the 44 years since 1932, the socialists had been an integral part of government in Sweden, their role tempered only during periods of war and coalition. It was a remarkable record, made more so by the fact that modern politics in Sweden has never been about ideology so much as detail. Socialists and non-socialists alike share a broad consensus on foreign policy and defence matters, even on the need for the social welfare system. The argument in Sweden has instead been about economics, a manifestation of which is the issue of **nuclear power**. A second non-Socialist coalition, formed in 1979, presided over a referendum on nuclear power (1980); the pro-nuclear lobby secured victory, the result being an immediate expansion of nuclear power generation.

Olof Palme

The Social Democrats regained power in 1982, subsequently devaluing the krona, introducing a freeze on prices and cutting back on public expenditure. They lost their majority in 1985, having to rely on Communist support to get their bills through. Presiding over the party since 1969, and prime minister for nearly as long, was **Olof Palme**. He was assassinated in February 1986 (see page 56), and his death threw Sweden into modern European politics like no other event. Proud of their open society (Palme had been returning home unguarded from the cinema), Swedes were shocked by the gunning down of a respected politician, diplomat and pacifist. The country's social system was placed in the spotlight, and shock turned to anger and then ridicule as the months passed without his killer being caught. Police bungling was criticized and despite the theories – Kurdish extremists, right-wing terror groups – no one was charged with the murder.

Then the police came up with **Christer Pettersson**, who – despite having no apparent motive – was identified by Palme's wife as the man who had fired the shot that night. Despite pleading his innocence, claiming he was elsewhere at the time of the murder, Pettersson was convicted of Palme's murder and jailed. There was great disquiet about the verdict, however, both at home and abroad. Pettersson was eventually acquitted on appeal; it was believed that Palme's wife couldn't possibly be sure that the man who fired the shot was Pettersson, given that she had only seen the murderer once, on the dark night in question, and then only very briefly. The police appear to believe they had the right man all along, but in recent years some convincing evidence of the involvement of the South African secret services has come to light (Palme having been an outspoken critic of apartheid).

1992	1994	1995
Unemployment hits postwar record of fourteen percent	Estonia ferry sinks with loss of 852 lives	Sweden joins European Union

Carlsson and Bildt

Ingvar Carlsson was elected prime minister after Palme's murder, a position confirmed by the **1988 General Election** when the Social Democrats – for the first time in years – scored more seats than the three non-socialist parties combined. However, Carlsson's was a minority government, and with a background of rising inflation and slow economic growth, the government announced an **austerity package** in January 1990. This included a two-year ban on strike action, and a wage, price and rent freeze – strong measures which astounded most Swedes, used to living in a liberal, consensus-style society.

The **General Election of 1991** merely confirmed that the consensus model had finally broken down. A four-party centre-right coalition came to power, led by **Carl Bildt**, which promised tax cuts and economic regeneration, but the recession sweeping western Europe did not pass Sweden by. Unemployment hit a postwar record and in autumn 1992 – as the British pound and Italian lira collapsed on the international money markets – the krona came under severe pressure. In an attempt to steady nerves, Prime Minister Bildt and Carlsson, leader of the Social Democratic opposition, made the astonishing announcement that they would ignore party lines and work together for the good of Sweden – and then proceeded with drastic **public expenditure cuts**.

The fat was trimmed off the welfare state – benefits were cut, healthcare was opened up to private competition, and education was given a painful shake-up. But it was too little, too late. Sweden was gripped by its worst **recession** since the 1930s and unemployment had reached record levels of fourteen percent – the days of a jobless rate of one or two percent were well and truly gone. Poor economic growth coupled with generous welfare benefits, runaway speculation by Swedish firms on foreign real estate and the world recession all contributed to Sweden's economic woes.

The return of the Social Democrats

A feeling of nostalgia for the good old days of Social Democracy swept through the country in September 1994, and Carl Bildt's minority Conservative government was booted out. Swedes voted in massive numbers to return the country's biggest party to power, headed by **Ingvar Carlsson**. He formed a government of whom half the ministers were women.

During 1994, negotiations on Sweden's planned **membership of the European Union** were completed and the issue was put to a referendum, which succeeded in splitting Swedish public opinion right down the middle. The *Ja till EU* lobby argued that little Sweden would have a bigger voice in Europe and would be able to influence pan-European decisions if it joined. *Nej till EU* warned that Sweden would be forced to lower its standards to those of other EU countries, unemployment would rise, drug trafficking would increase, and democracy would be watered down. But in November of that year, the Swedes followed the Austrians and the Finns in voting for membership from 1 January 1995 – by the narrowest of margins, just five percent.

Following membership the krona fell to new lows as money-market fears grew that the minority government wouldn't be able to persuade parliament to approve cuts in state spending. However, the cuts were duly introduced – the welfare state was trimmed back further and new taxes were announced to try to rein in the spiralling

2002	2003	2003
Sámi officially recognized as minority language	Foreign Minister Anna Lindh murdered	Referendum vote rejects membership of the euro

POLITICAL ASSASSINATION

In September 2003, as Swedes prepared to hold a public referendum on adopting the **euro**, the nation was thrown into shock by the **murder** of the former foreign minister, **Anna Lindh**, one of Sweden's most popular politicians, who was tipped to become the country's first female prime minister. Lindh was stabbed repeatedly by a man with a history of psychiatric problems whilst she was out shopping; she later died of massive internal bleeding. **Mijailo Mijailovic**, born in Sweden to Serbian parents, is now serving a life sentence for her murder.

debt. Unemployment benefit was cut to 75 percent of previous earnings, benefits for sick leave were reduced, and lower state pension payments also came into force; a new tax was also slapped on newspapers. To try to keep public support on his side, Finance Minister **Göran Persson** reduced the tax on food from a staggering 21 percent to just twelve percent.

Just when everything appeared under control, Carlsson resigned to be replaced by the bossy Persson, known to friends and enemies alike as HSB – short for *han som bestämmer*, "he who decides". As the new millennium approached, the Swedish government concentrated its efforts on turning the economy round and experts argue this quiet period was necessary to muster strength to face the challenges to come.

Sweden today

Sweden's export-led **economy** has rendered the country extremely susceptible to changes in world finances. As globalization has gathered momentum since the turn of the millennium, Sweden has faced a number of difficult choices which would have been unthinkable during the heady days of Social Democracy. Privatizations, mergers and general cost-cutting measures within the much-cherished welfare state have brought Sweden more into line with countries that went through equally painful economic change decades ago. Some economists argue it is this enforced shaking up of the business environment from outside, rather than any direct government measures, that is responsible for Sweden's improved economic fortunes since 1998 – although **unemployment** remains stubbornly above government targets.

Since 2010, Sweden has found itself at the centre of the scandal surrounding **Julian Assange** – founder of the media website, Wikileaks – who was wanted for questioning by Swedish police over sexual assault charges. A court ruling in 2011 cleared the way for his extradition to Sweden, but since 2012 Assange has sought asylum inside the Ecuadorian embassy in London. In October 2016 he was set to be interviewed by an Ecuadorian prosecutor in the presence of Swedish officials. The case has brought the Swedish legal system to the world's attention amid claims that Sweden's rape laws would not hold water in an international court of law.

In 2015 Sweden implemented far-reaching changes to its generous **immigration policy**. Unable to cope with the influx of 163,000 people who claimed asylum that year, notably from Syria, the government substantially reduced the number of asylum seekers Sweden would accept. In late 2015 passport and border controls were introduced at ports and **border crossings**, and from summer 2016 the payment of accommodation and daily allowance for refugees served with expulsion orders was

2006	2009	2015
Deep cuts to Sweden's extensive welfare state to boost economy	Sale of Volvo to Chinese confirmed	Sweden starts to clamp down on its immigration policy amid Syrian refugee crisis

stopped. Under the tough new laws, it has become considerably more difficult for refugees to gain residency on grounds of distressing circumstances in their country of origin. In May 2017 it was reported that the temporary border controls introduced in 2015 ended.

In 2017 the Swedish government decided to reactivate military conscription (this was inactivated in the period from 2010–2017), in 2018 the first men and women were called up for service.

In 2018, IKEA founder Ingvar Kamprad (91) died at his home in Smaland. He founded the company on the family farm when he was 17 years old.

2017	2018	2018
End of border controls	IKEA founder Ingvar Kamprad (91) dies at his home in Smaland	Military conscription is reinstated

Swedish architecture

The all-encompassing Swedish preoccupation with design and the importance attached to the way buildings interact with their wider environment have provided Sweden with a remarkable wealth of buildings, both domestic and commercial, during the past century. Despite this, planning for a perceived shortage of affordable housing has also meant that almost every town of any size is blighted with a plethora of faceless postwar apartment blocks which can look more Soviet than Scandinavian. To get the most out of Sweden's hugely rich architectural history, it's invariably worth seeking out the historic heart of a settlement – from small country towns to larger commercial cities.

There are rich pickings in terms of **Romanesque** and **Gothic** buildings, particularly ecclesiastical and royal ones, and the number of **Renaissance** and **Baroque** buildings is quite remarkable. But Sweden's architectural heritage is not always so grand; the more vernacular constructions – from rural cottages to fishermen's homes – provide a fascinating insight into how Swedes have lived and worked for centuries.

Prehistoric buildings

Discussion of **prehistoric** buildings in Sweden is mostly a matter of conjecture, for the only structures to have survived from before 1100 are ruined or fragmentary. The most impressive structures of **Bronze Age** Sweden are the numerous grassy burial barrows and the coastal burial sites (particularly apparent on the island of Gotland) that feature huge boulders cut into the shapes of a prow and stern. One of the best known of the latter type is at **Ales Stennar** on the south Skåne coast – a Swedish Stonehenge set above windy cliffs.

More substantial are the **Iron Age** dwellings from the **Celtic** period (c. 500 BC to 800 AD). The best example of a fortification from this era is at **Ismantorp** on the Baltic island of Öland. Dating from the fifth century AD, this remarkable site has limestone walls up to fifteen feet high and some eighty foundations arranged into quarters, with streets radiating like spokes of a wheel.

From the remnants of pre-Christian-era houses, a number of dwelling types can be identified. The open-hearth hall, for example, was a square house with an opening in the roof ridge by which light entered and smoke exited. The two-storey gallery house had an open upper loft reached via an exterior stair, while the post larder was a house on stilts allowing for ventilation and protection from vermin.

Romanesque to Gothic

The Christianization of Sweden is dated from 1008, the year St Sigfrid is said to have baptized King Olof. In the eleventh and twelfth centuries the Church and the monastic orders were the driving force behind the most significant building projects, with the most splendid example of Romanesque architecture being **Lund cathedral**. Consecrated in 1145, when Lund was the largest town in Scandinavia and the archiepiscopal see, this monumental building was designed as a basilica with twin western towers, and boasts some tremendously rich carvings in the apsidal choir and vast crypt. The chief centre of Romanesque church building, however, was the royal town of **Sigtuna** to the northwest of Stockholm. Apart from boasting Sweden's oldest street, Sigtuna has

GOTLAND GOTHIC

The most rewarding place to explore Sweden's Gothic architecture is **Gotland** – the countryside is peppered with almost one hundred richly sculpted medieval churches, while the island's capital, the magnificently preserved Hanseatic seat of **Visby**, is replete with excellent domestic as well as ecclesiastical Gothic.

the ruins of three eleventh-century churches – one of which, St Peter's, features the country's oldest groin vault.

Round arches, a distinctive feature of Romanesque architecture, flourished wherever limestone and sandstone were found – principally in regions of southern and central Sweden, such as Västergötland, Östergötland and Närke, as well as Skåne. An easy supply of both types of stone was to be found on the Baltic island of Gotland, from where numerous baptismal fonts and richly carved sandstone decorations were exported to the mainland both to the west (Sweden proper) and the east (Swedish-controlled Finland).

Of the great monastic ruins from this period, the finest is the **Alvastra monastery** (1143), just south of Vadstena near the eastern shores of Lake Vättern. A portion of the huge barrel-vaults can still be seen, though much of the graceful structure was carted off by Vasa to build his castle at Vadstena.

Gothic architecture emerged in the thirteenth century, one of the finest early examples being the **Mariakyrkan** in Sigtuna (1237), which with its red-brick step gables is markedly unlike the austere grey-stone churches of a century earlier. The cathedral at **Strängnäs**, due east of Stockholm, is another superb piece of Gothic brick architecture, while in Malmö, the German-inspired **St Petri kryka** survives as a fine example of brick Gothic, a style often known as the Hanseatic Style. The cathedral at Uppsala (the largest in Scandinavia) is another intriguing specimen, designed to a French High Gothic plan by Parisian builders as a limestone structure, but eventually built in brick in a simpler, **Baltic Gothic** form. A good example of late Gothic is **Vadstena convent church**; begun in 1384, this austere limestone and brick hall was built exactly as decreed by St Birgitta, the founder of the church.

Few examples of the castles and fortifications of this period exist today. One of the best examples, **Varberg fortress** in Halland, just south of Gothenburg, was built by the Danes, while the best Swedish-built medieval fortifications are in Finland, a Swedish province until the early nineteenth century. One stark and beautifully unmolested example of a fortification in Danish-controlled Skåne is the castle of Glimmingehus; dating from around 1500, it was built by Adam van Duren, who also supervised the completion of the cathedral of Lund.

Renaissance and Baroque architecture

Gustav Vasa (ruled 1523–60) could not have had a more pronounced effect on Swedish architecture. In 1527, with his reformation of the Church, Catholic properties were confiscated, and in many instances the fabric of monasteries and churches was used to build and convert castles into resplendent palaces. Wonderful examples of such Renaissance palaces are **Kalmar castle**, in the south of Småland, and **Vadstena castle** – though, unlike Kalmar, the latter's interior has been stripped of its original furnishings. Another magnificent Vasa palace, a glorious ruin since a nineteenth-century fire, is **Borgholm castle** on the Baltic island of Öland.

While few churches built in this period enjoyed much prominence, one of outstanding elegance is the **Trefaldighetskyrkan** (Trinity church) in Kristianstad, Danish king Christian IV's model Renaissance city in Skåne. With its tall windows, slender granite pillars and square bays, it is the epitome of sophistication and simplicity.

BAROQUE BEAUTY

The most glorious of palatial buildings from the Baroque era is **Drottningholm** outside Stockholm, a masterpiece created by Tessin the Elder for Dowager Queen Hedvig Eleonora. Tessin's other great creation was **Kalmar cathedral**, the finest church of the era and a truly beautiful vision of Italian Baroque. Nicodemus Tessin the Younger followed his father as court architect and continued his style. He designed the new **Royal Palace at Stockholm** following the city's great fire of 1697 and the two contrasting **Karlskrona** churches: the domed rotunda of the Trefaldighetskyrkan (Trinity church) and the barrel-vaulted basilica of the Fredrikskyrkan (Fredrik's church). Karlskrona, like **Gothenburg**, is a fine example of regulated town planning, a discipline that came into being during this era.

By the time Gustav II Adolf ascended the throne in 1611, a greater opulence was becoming prevalent in domestic architecture. This tendency became even more marked in the **Baroque** area, which in Sweden commenced with the reign of Queen Kristina, the art-loving and extravagant daughter of Gustav II Adolf. The first wave of Baroque was largely introduced by the German Nicodemus Tessin the Elder, who had spent much time in Italy.

The eighteenth century

In the eighteenth century **Rococo** emerged as the style favoured by the increasingly affluent Swedish middle class, who looked to France for their models. This lightening of architectural style paved the way for the Neoclassical elegance which would follow with the reign of Gustav III, who was greatly impressed by the architecture of Classical antiquity. Good examples of this clear Neoclassical mode are the **Inventariekammaren** (Inventory Chambers) at Karlskrona, and the **King's Pavilion at Haga**, designed for Gustav III by Olof Temelman, complete with Pompeiian interiors by the painter Louis Masreliez.

Another, and quite distinct aspect of late eighteenth-century taste, was the fascination with **chinoiserie**, due in large measure to the power and influence of the Gothenburg-based Swedish East India Company, founded in 1731. The culmination of this trend was the **Kina Slott** (Chinese Pavilion) at Drottningholm, a tiny Palladian villa built in 1763 and now beautifully restored.

The nineteenth century

Two vast projects dominated the Swedish architectural scene at the beginning of the nineteenth century: the remarkable **Göta Canal**, a 190-kilometre waterway linking the great lakes of Vänern and Vättern, Gothenburg and the Baltic; and the **Karlsborg fortress** on the western shores of Vättern, designed to be an inland retreat for the royal family and the gold stocks, but abandoned ninety years later in 1909.

By the mid-nineteenth century, a new style was emerging, based on Neoclassicism but flavoured by the French-born king's taste. This **Empire Style** (sometimes referred to as the Karl Johan Style) is most closely associated with the architect **Fredrik Blom** of Karlskrona, whose most famous building is the elegant pleasure palace **Rosendal** on Djurgården, Stockholm.

During the reign of Oscar I (1844–59), while the buildings of Britain's manufacturing centres provided models for Sweden's industrial towns, the styles of the past couple of centuries began to reappear, particularly Renaissance and Gothic. One of the most glamorous examples of late nineteenth-century neo-Gothic splendour is **Helsingborg town hall**, built around 1890 as a riot of fairy tale red-brick detail. The names which crop up most often in this era include Fredrik Scholander, who designed the elaborate **Stockholm synagogue** in 1861, and Helgo Zetterwall, whose churches of the 1870s and 1880s bear a resemblance to neo-Gothic buildings in Britain and Germany.

The twentieth century to the present

Some of the most gorgeous buildings in Sweden's cities are the result of a movement which germinated in the final, resurgent years of the nineteenth century – **National Romanticism**, which set out to simplify architecture and use local materials to create a distinctive Swedish style. Its finest example, which was much influenced by the Arts and Crafts movement in Britain, is Stockholm's **Stadshuset**, built in 1923 from plain brick, dressed stone and rustic timber. Another luscious example is Lars Israel Wahlmann's **Tjolöholm castle**, just south of Gothenburg – a city in which some of the finest apartment buildings are those produced in the associated Art Nouveau style, known in Sweden as **Jugendstil**. One beautifully renovated building in full *Jugendstil* form is the theatre in Tivoli Park in **Kristianstad**, a town otherwise known for its Renaissance buildings. Stockholm's 1910-built *Hotel Esplanade* is a fine example, though the cities of Gothenburg, Malmö and Lund amongst others are rich in the heritage. The small town of Hjö on the western shores of Lake Vättern has a fine clutch of *Jugendstil* houses.

In the second quarter of the century a new movement – **Functionalism** – burst onto the scene, making great use of "industrial" materials such as stainless steel and concrete. The leading architect of his generation was **Gunnar Asplund**, famed for Stockholm City Library (mid-1920s) and his contribution to many other buildings – his interior of the law courts in **Gothenburg's Rådhus** is a favourite among architecture students and enthusiasts today.

The creation of the welfare state went hand in hand with the ascendancy of a functionalist approach to architecture, which rejected many of the individualistic features of traditional Swedish design. By the 1960s, the faceless **International Style** had gained dominance in Sweden, as town planning gave way to insensitive clearance of old houses and their replacement with bland high-rises.

The late 1980s and early 1990s saw restoration becoming the order of the day with areas that had been left to decay – such as the old working-class neighbourhood of **Haga** in Gothenburg – gently gentrified and preserved. More recently the emphasis has shifted towards environmentally sympathetic architecture. Intrinsically Nordic in their tone, these new buildings are often low-level structures constructed from locally sourced wood, with vast areas of glass capitalizing on natural light.

A little further south, in Gothenburg, the natural science museum, **Universeum** is a splendidly organic building – all rough-hewn wood, glass and concrete reflecting in the pools of water outside. One of the highest-profile projects of the twenty years is the **Moderna Muséet** and **Arkitektur och Designcentrum** on the island of Skeppsholm, in Stockholm harbour. Designed by the Spaniard **Rafael Moneo**, the building eloquently complements the diverse structures of the city's waterfront without trying to overshadow them.

JUGENDSTIL – SWEDISH STYLE

Forget any notion of **Swedish design** and style consisting solely of IKEA flat-packs and stripped-pine simplicity. One of the country's most splendid periods for architecture and design was the end of the nineteenth century and the first decade of the twentieth – the era of Art Nouveau or **Jugendstil**.

This free-flowing style was employed to decorate the facades of urban landscapes across Europe, but the luxuriant curves and organic shapes were never so resonant as in nature-loving Sweden. Towns across the country still boast a wealth of beautiful examples from this elegant era: Stockholm's Östermalm area is rich in *Jugendstil*, while in Gothenburg, the curves and curls are most apparent in Vasastan. In Malmö, Helsingborg and Lund the best houses – often cream-stuccoed with green paintwork – are peppered with images of quirky faces, rising suns and stylized flowers.

Geography

Sweden is known above all else for its forests and lakes, yet the sheer diversity of its terrain is less familiar. While there are indeed a vast number of lakes – the largest of them Vättern and Vänern – and swathes of forest blanket vast tracts of the country, the southern shores of Sweden are fringed with sandy beaches, and the east and west coasts are a myriad of rocky islands forming archipelagos. The Baltic islands of Gotland and Öland provide an entirely different habitat to anywhere on mainland Sweden, with limestone plateaus, dramatic sea-stacks and a variety of flora found nowhere else in Scandinavia.

The appearance of Sweden's terrain owes most to the last **Ice Age**, which chafed the landscape for 80,000 years before the ice finally melted away 9000 years ago. Grinding ice masses polished the mountains to their present form, a process particularly evident in scooped-out U-shaped mountain valleys such as **Lapporten** near Abisko, in the extreme north of the country. Subsequent to the thaw, the landmass rose, so that former coastlines are now many kilometres inland, manifested in the form of huge plains of rubble, while the plains of Sweden were created by the deposition of vast quantities of silt by the meltwater.

The northwest of the country is dominated by **mountains**, which rise well above the timber line. Deciduous trees are most prevalent, except in the most southerly regions, where coniferous forest predominates.

Sweden also boasts some of Europe's most impressive **archipelagos**, such as the dramatically rugged Bohuslän coast on the west, and Stockholm's own archipelago of 24,000 islands, many covered in meadows and forest, on the east.

The country is also known for its **lakes**, which number more than 100,000. These support rich aquatic life, mostly salmon and salmon trout, although the coastlines are where most of the country's fishing takes place.

The north

Sweden's mountainous north is home to many of the country's national parks. The mountains here are part of the **Caledonian range**, the remains of which are also to be found further south in Europe, notably in Scotland and Ireland. Formed around 400 million years ago, the range is at its highest at **Kebnekaise** and **Sarek**, both above 2000m, in the extreme northwest of Sweden. Ancient spruce, pine and birch forest extends continuously along most of the 1000km range, providing an unspoilt habitat for birds such as the golden eagle. The treeline here lies at around 800m above sea level; higher up are great expanses of bare rockface and heathland, the latter often covered in wild orchids.

Central Sweden

The most extensive of Sweden's plains is in the **central Swedish lowlands**, a broad belt spanning from the Bohuslän coast in the west to Uppland and Södermanland in the east. Divided by steep ridges of rock, this former seabed was transformed by volcanic eruptions that created rocky plateaus such as Ålleberg and **Kinnekulle** (Flowering Mountain) to the west of Lidköping. The latter is Sweden's most varied natural site, comprising deciduous and evergreen woodland, meadows and pastures, and treeless limestone flats. Particularly notable among the flora here are cowslips, lady's-slipper orchids, wild cherry trees and, in early summer, the unusual and intensely fragrant bear-garlic.

Stretching some 160km north from Gothenburg up to the Norwegian border, the rough and windswept **Bohuslän coast** possesses a considerable **archipelago** of around three thousand islands. Most of these are devoid of trees – any which existed were cut down to make into boats and houses during the great fishing era of the eighteenth century. This low coastal landscape is peppered with deeply indented bays and fjords, interspersed with islands and peninsulas. To the north of the region, the waves have weathered the pink and reddish granite, and the resulting large, smooth stone slabs with their distinctive cracks are characteristic of the province. Inland from this stretch of coast are steep hills and plateaus which are separated from one another by deep valleys, the inland continuations of the fjords. Long, narrow lakes have developed here, the Bullaren lakes being the largest.

One of the region's most splendid areas of virgin forest is **Tiveden National Park**, around 50km northeast of Karlsborg and just to the northwest of **Lake Vättern**, one of the two enormous lakes in this part of Sweden, the other being **Vänern**. Fishing being a major sport in Sweden, Vänern and Vättern attract thousands each year who wish to try their luck. Around 1300 tonnes of fish are taken from Vänern alone each year, with commercial fisheries accounting for around eighty percent of the catch. The lake's waters were once the most productive for salmon in Sweden, but the construction of hydroelectric dams ruined the spawning grounds, and by the 1970s salmon was almost extinct here. In an effort to complement natural reproduction, salmon and brown trout have been raised in hatcheries and released into the lake with considerable success.

The south

The southernmost third of Sweden, the country's most highly populated and industrialized region, is a mixture of highlands (in the north), forests, lakes and cultivated plains. In southeastern Sweden, the forests of **Småland** have kept the furnaces of the province's glass factories alight since the seventeenth century. In the south, where the highlands give way to a gently undulating landscape, the combination of pastures and fields of rape and poppy makes for some glorious summertime scenery in **Skåne**. Though this province has a reputation for being monotonous and agricultural (true of much of its southwest), it also boasts tracts of conifers, a spectacular coastline and lush forests of beech, best seen in the first weeks of May. The province also boasts dramatic natural rock formations at **Hovs Hallar**, a stunning castellation of red-rock sea stacks on the northern coast of the Bjäre peninsula.

To the east of Skåne, the **Stenshuvud National Park** has rocky coastal hills surrounded by woods of hornbeam and alder and moorlands full of juniper. Animals untypical of Sweden live here, such as tree frogs, sand lizards and dormice.

Öland and Gotland

Sweden's two largest islands, **Gotland** and **Öland**, lying in the Baltic Sea to the east of the mainland, have excited botanists and geologists for centuries. When Carl von Linné first arrived in Öland in the mid-eighteenth century, he noted that the terrain was "of an entirely different countenance" to the rest of the country, and indeed the island's limestone plateaus – known as **alvar** – are unique in Sweden. In southern Öland, **Stora Alvaret** (Great Limestone Plain) is a thin-soiled heathland with vividly colourful flora in spring and summer.

Gotland is the more dramatic of the two great islands, thanks to its tall sea stacks (*raukar*), the remains of old coral reefs which loom like craggy ghosts along the island's shoreline. Like Öland, Gotland sustains rich floral life, including at least 35 species of orchid.

Books

English-language books on Sweden are remarkably scant. Although Swedish publishing houses are producing quality titles – particularly fiction – surprisingly few find their way into English. Books marked ★ are particularly recommended.

HISTORY AND POLITICS

Sheri Berman *The Social Democrat Movement*. A comparison between the Swedish and German social democratic systems between World War I and World War II. Whilst Sweden placed itself at the forefront of the drive for democratization after the Great Depression, Germany lacked direction and opted for Hitler.

H.R. Ellis Davidson *The Gods and Myths of Northern Europe*. This "Who's Who" of Norse mythology, which includes some useful profiles of the more obscure gods, displaces the classical deities and their world as the most relevant mythological framework for northern and western European culture.

Eric Elstob *Sweden: A Traveller's History*. An introduction to Swedish history from the year dot to the twentieth century, with useful chapters on art, architecture and cultural life.

Lee Miles *Sweden and European Integration*. A political history of Sweden comparing the period 1950–66 with the accession to the European Union in 1995.

Bridget Morris *St Birgitta of Sweden*. A comprehensive and intelligently researched book offering a rounded perspective on Sweden's first female saint and her extraordinary life. Accessible and educational without being over-academic in approach.

Michael Roberts *The Early Vasas: A History of Sweden 1523–1611*. A clear account of the period. Complements the same author's *Gustavus Adolphus and the Rise of Sweden* and *The Age of Liberty: Sweden 1719–1772*, which, more briefly and enthusiastically, covers the period from 1612 to Gustav's death in 1632.

Franklin Daniel Scott *Sweden, The Nation's History*. A good all-round account of Sweden's history from a poor, backward warrior nation to the prosperous modern one of today.

Jan-Öjvind Swahn *Maypole, Crayfish and Lucia – Swedish Holidays and Traditions*. This little publication is superbly written and informative about how and why Swedish traditions have evolved. In contrast to the pictures, the prose is historically accurate and both entertaining and frank about what makes Sweden tick.

ART, ARCHITECTURE AND DESIGN

★ **Henrik O. Andersson and Fredric Bedoire** *Swedish Architecture 1640–1970*. With superb colour plates, this is the definitive survey of the subject, with parallel English/Swedish text.

Katrin Cargill *Creating the Look: Swedish Style*. A great book to help you create cheerful Swedish peasant interiors. Includes lots of evocative photographs by Christopher Drake and a long list of stockists of the materials you'll need. A practical guide, the book includes some background information to place the designs in context.

Görel Cavalli-Björkman and Bo Lindwall *The World of Carl Larsson*. A charming and brilliantly illustrated volume, charting the life and work of one of Sweden's most admired painters.

Barbro Klein and Mats Widbom *Swedish Folk Art*. A lavishly illustrated and richly documented history of its subject, relating ancient crafts to modern-day design ideas.

Mereth Lindgren, Louise Lyberg, Birgitta Sandström and Anna Greta Wahlberg *A History of Swedish Art*. A fine overview of Swedish painting, sculpture and, to a lesser extent, architecture, from the Stone Age to the present. Clear text and good, mostly monochrome, illustrations.

★ **Nils-Olof Olsson** *Skåne Through The Artist's Eye*. A likeable, cleverly balanced illustrated book encompassing everything from the prehistoric to the present day in its coverage of the country's southernmost province. Steering clear of the usual demarcations in art history, it shows how much contemporary artwork can help with our understanding of history.

★ **Håkan Sandbring and Martin Borg** *Skåne – Wide Horizons*. A glorious visual study of Skåne – the ultimate coffee-table tome for anyone who loves the sort of beauty at which Sweden excels. From country scenes to urban visions and all the quirks of Swedish life in between, these brilliantly hued photographs will keep you absorbed for hours.

Lars Sjöberg and Ursula Sjöberg *The Swedish Room*. An exceptionally well-documented journey through developments in the design of Swedish homes, covering the period from 1640 through to the nineteenth century (stopping short of National Romanticism, Art Nouveau and Functionalism). The book sets design patterns in their historical and political context, and includes beautiful photographs by Ingalill Snitt. There's also a section on achieving classic Swedish decor effects, and a good list of suppliers of decorative materials, though without exception all are in America.

LITERATURE

★ **Hugh Beach** *A Year in Lapland*. As a young man, Beach went to live with the *Sámi* reindeer herders of Jokkmokk. In later life he returns to the Arctic Circle to chart the fascinating changes that have occurred to northern Sweden and its traditionally nomadic inhabitants.

Frans G. Bengtsson *The Long Ships: A Saga of the Viking Age*. A real gem of historical fiction, bringing the Viking world vividly alive with solid background on arcane Norse traditions such as "trollcraft", "gold-luck" and "the Ale-death". This marvellously pacy adventure story is literally laugh-out-loud funny.

★ **Andrew Brown** *Fishing in Utopia: Sweden and the future that disappeared*. After living in Sweden in his 20s, the author returns to the country in later life to explore his relationship with it in general, and social democracy in particular.

Marikka Cobbold *Frozen Music*. Cobbold – who is herself Swedish, though lives in England – paints a very true-to-life picture of Swedish mannerisms and way of life. This novel about the relationship between a Swedish architect and an English woman is set on a very well-drawn Swedish island.

Stig Dagerman *A Burnt Child*. One of the author's best works, this intense short narrative concerns the reactions of a Stockholm family to the death of the mother. A prolific young writer, Dagerman had written short stories, travel sketches, four novels and four plays by the time he was 26; he committed suicide in 1954 at the age of 31.

★ **Kerstin Ekman** *Blackwater*. A tightly written thriller by one of Sweden's most highly rated novelists. Set in the forests of northern Sweden, the plot concerns a woman whose lover is murdered; years later, she sees her daughter in the arms of the suspect.

★ **Kerstin Ekman** *Under the Snow*. In a remote Lapland village, a police constable investigates the death of a teacher following a drunken brawl. The dark deeds of winter finally come to light under the relentless summer sun.

Robert Fulton *Preparations for Flight*. Eight Swedish short stories from the last 25 years, including two rare prose outings by the poet Niklas Rådström.

Pers Christian Jersild *A Living Soul*. The work of one of Sweden's best novelists, this is a social satire based around the "experiences" of an artificially produced, bodyless human brain floating in liquid. Entertaining, provocative reading.

Selma Lagerlöf *The Wonderful Adventures of Nils*. Lagerlöf is Sweden's best-loved children's writer. The tales of Nils Holgren, a little boy who flies all over the country on the back of a magic goose, are continued in *The Further Adventures of Nils*.

Stieg Larsson *The Girl with the Dragon Tattoo*. The gripping international bestseller which charts the efforts by Lisbet Salander and Michael Blomkvist to discover why Harriet Vanger disappeared over forty years earlier.

Sara Lidman *Naboth's Stone*. A novel set in 1880s Västerbotten, in Sweden's far north, charting the lives of settlers and farmers as the industrial age – and the railway – approaches.

Torgney Lindgren *Merab's Beauty*. Short stories capturing the distinctive flavour of family life in northern Sweden.

Ivar Lo-Johansson & Rochelle Wright *Peddling My Wares*. An intriguing exploration of life for a young, self-educated Swede. This autobiographical tale is written by the last surviving member of the "Thirties Generation" and is as popular today in Sweden as when it appeared in 1953.

★ **Vilhelm Moberg** *The Emigrants*. From one of Sweden's greatest twentieth-century writers, this is one of four novels depicting Karl Oskar and Christina Nilsson as they struggle their way from Småland to Minnesota. It's a highly poignant story dealing with the emigration of Swedes to the US.

★ **Michael Niemi** *Popular Music*. The enchanting tale of two boys, Matti and Niila, growing up in Pajala in northern Sweden in the 1960s and 1970s. Dreaming of an unknown world beyond the Torne Valley, they use their fantasy to help take them there. Winner of the August Prize for Sweden's best novel in 2000.

Agneta Pleijel *The Dog Star*. By one of Sweden's leading writers, *The Dog Star* is the powerful tale of a young girl's approach to puberty. Pleijel's finest novel yet, full of fantasy and emotion.

Clive Sinclair *Augustus Rex*. August Strindberg dies in 1912 – and is then brought back to life by the Devil in 1960s Stockholm. Bawdy, imaginative and very funny treatment of Strindberg's well-documented neuroses.

Hjalmar Söderberg *Short Stories*. Twenty-six short stories from the stylish pen of Söderberg (1869–1941). Brief, ironic and eminently suited to dipping into.

August Strindberg *Plays: One (The Father, Miss Julie and The Ghost Sonata); Plays: Two (The Dance of Death, A Dream Play and The Stronger)*. The major plays by the country's most provocative and influential playwright, analysing the roles of the sexes both in and out of marriage. Only a fraction of Strindberg's huge output has been translated into English.

Swedish language

For most foreigners, Swedish is nothing more than an obscure, if somewhat exotic, language spoken by a few million people on the fringe of Europe. Many travellers take their flirtation with the odd hurdy-gurdy sounds of the language no further than that, since there is no need whatsoever to speak Swedish to enjoy a visit to Sweden – recent surveys have shown that 95 percent of Swedes speak English to some degree. However, Swedish deserves closer inspection, and if you master even a couple of phrases you'll meet with nothing but words of encouragement.

Despite what you might think, Swedish is one of the easiest languages for English-speakers to pick up; its grammar has developed along similar lines to that of English and therefore has no case system to speak of (unlike German). Many everyday words are common to both English and Swedish, having been brought over to Britain by the Vikings, and anyone with a knowledge of northern English or lowland Scottish dialects will already be familiar with a good number of Swedish words and phrases. Your biggest problem is likely to be perfecting the "tones", different rising and falling accents which Swedish uses (the hurdy-gurdy sounds you're no doubt already familiar with).

Swedish is a Germanic language and, as such, related to English in much the same way as French is related to Italian. However, its closest cousins are fellow members of the North Germanic group of tongues: Danish, Faroese, Icelandic, Norwegian. Within that subgroup, Swedish is most closely linked to Danish and Norwegian, and the languages are mutually intelligible to quite an extent. A knowledge of Swedish will therefore open up the rest of Scandinavia to you; in fact Swedish is the second official language of Finland. Unlike Danish, for example, Swedish spelling closely resembles pronunciation, which means you stand a sporting chance of being able to read words and make yourself understood.

Basics

Swedish **nouns** can have one of two **genders**: common or neuter. The good news is that three out of four nouns have the common gender. The **indefinite article** precedes the noun, and is *en* for common nouns, and *ett* for neuter nouns. The **definite** article, as in all the other Scandinavian languages, is suffixed to the noun, for example, *en katt*, a cat, but *katten*, the cat; *ett hus*, a house, but *huset*, the house. The same principle applies in the plural: *katter*, cats, but *katterna*, the cats; *hus*, houses, but *husen*, the houses. The plural definite article suffix is therefore *-na* for common nouns and *-en* for neuter nouns (and confusingly identical with the definite article suffix for common nouns).

Forming **plurals** is possibly the most complicated feature of Swedish. Regular plurals take one of the following endings: *-or*, *-ar*, *-er*, *-r*, *-n*, or no ending at all. Issues like the gender of a word, whether its final letter is a vowel or a consonant, and stress can all affect which plural ending is used. You should learn each noun with its plural, but to be honest, the chances are you'll forget the plural ending and get it wrong. Swedes have no apparent difficulty in forming plurals and can't understand why you find it so hard. Show them the plurals section in any grammar and savour their reaction.

Adjectives cause few problems. They generally precede the noun they qualify and agree in gender and number with it; *en ung flicka*, a young girl (ie no ending on the adjective); *ett stort hus*, a big house; *fina böcker*, fine books. The *-a* ending is also used after the definite article, irrespective of number, *det stora huset*, the big house, *de fina* *böckerna*, the fine books; and also after a possessive, once again irrespective of number, *min stora trädgård*, my big garden, or *stadens vackra gator*, the town's beautiful streets.

Verbs are something of a mixed blessing. There is only one form for all persons, singular and plural, in all tenses, which means there are no irksome endings to remember: *jag är* – I am, *du är* – you (singular) are, *ni är* – you (plural) are, *han/vi är* – we are, *de är* – they are. All verbs take the auxiliary *att ha* (to have) in the perfect and pluperfect tenses (eg *jag har gått* – I have gone, *jag har talat* – I have spoken; *jag hade gått* – I had gone, *jag hade talat* – I had spoken). The price for this simplicity is unfortunately four different conjugations which are distinguished by the way they form their past tense. Verbs are always found as the second idea in any Swedish sentence, as in German, which can often lead to the inversion of verb and subject. However, in Swedish, there are no "verb scarers" which are responsible for the suicidal pile-up of verbs which often occurs at the end of German sentences.

Pronunciation

Rest assured – you're never going to sound Swedish, for not only can **pronunciation** be difficult, but the sing-song **melody** of the language is beyond the reach of most outsiders. Swedish uses two quite different **tones** on words of two or more syllables – one rises throughout the entire word, while the other falls in the middle before peaking at the end of the word. It's this second down-then-up accent which gives Swedish its distinctive melody. Unfortunately, identical words can have two different meanings depending on which tone is used. For example, *fem ton* with a rising accent throughout each word means "five tons", whereas *femton* where the accent dips during the *fem-* and rises throughout the *-ton* means "fifteen". Equally, *komma* with a rising tone throughout means "comma", whereas *komma* with a falling tone followed by a rising tone is the verb "to come". In short, try your best, but don't worry if you get it wrong. Swedes are used to foreigners saying one word but meaning another and will generally understand what you're trying to say.

Vowels can be either long (when followed by one consonant or at the end of a word) or short (when followed by two consonants). Unfamiliar or unusually spelt vowels are as follows:

ej as in m**ate**

y as in **ewe**

å when short, as in h**o**t; when long, sort of as in r**aw**

ä as in g**e**t

ö as in f**ur**

Consonants are pronounced approximately as in English except:

g before e, i, y, ä or ö as in **yet**; before a, o, u, å as in **gate**; sometimes silent

j, dj, gj, lj as in **yet**

k before e, i, y, ä or ö approximately as in **shut** and similar to German **ch** in "ich", otherwise hard

qu as in **kv**

rs as in **shut** (also when one word ends in r and the next begins with s, for example *för stor*, pronounced "fur shtoor")

s as in **so** (never as English **z**)

sj, skj, stj approximately as in **shut** (different from soft **k** sound and more like a sh-sound made through the teeth but with rounded lips – this sound takes much practice; see below)

tj approximately as in **shut** and with same value as a soft **k**

z as in **so** (never as in **zoo**)

The soft sound produced by **sj**, **skj** and **stj** is known as the **sj-sound** and is a peculiarity of Swedish. Unfortunately it appears widely and its pronunciation varies with dialect and individual speakers. To confuse matters further there are two variants, a back sj-sound formed by raising the back of the tongue and a front sj-sound formed by raising the middle or front of the tongue. Gain instant respect by mastering this Swedish tongue twister: *sjuttiosju sjuksköterskor skötte sju sjösjuka sjömän på skeppet till Shangai*, meaning "seventy-seven nurses nursed seven seasick sailors on the ship to Shanghai".

Books

Swedes are always keen to practise their English, so if you're intent on learning Swedish, perseverance is the name of the game. The excellent *Colloquial Swedish* by Philip Holmes and Gunilla Serin (published by Routledge) is the best **textbook** around and should be your starting point.

Of the handful of **grammars** available, by far the most useful is the six-hundred-page *Swedish: A Comprehensive Grammar* by Philip Holmes and Ian Hinchliffe (Routledge), which is head and shoulders above anything else on the market. Good bookshops can supply the *Collins Gem Swedish Dictionary*, perfect for checking basic words whilst travelling around. It's also available in Sweden under the title *Norstedts engelska fickordbok*. Of the **phrasebooks**, the most useful is *Swedish Phrase Book and Dictionary* (Berlitz).

USEFUL WORDS AND PHRASES

BASIC PHRASES

yes/no ja/nej
hello hej/tjänare
good morning god morgon
good afternoon god middag
good night god natt
today/tomorrow idag/imorgon
please tack/var så god
here you are/you're welcome var så god
thank you (very much) tack (så mycket)
where?/when? var?/när/hur dags?
what?/why? vad?/varför?
how (much)? hur (mycket)?
I don't know jag vet inte
do you know? (a fact) vet du…?
could you…? skulle du kunna…?
sorry/excuse me förlåt/ursäkta
here/there här/där
near/far nära/avlägsen
this/that det här/det där
now/later nu/senare
more/less mera/mindre
big/little stor/liten
open/closed öppet/stängt
women/men kvinnor/män
toilet toalett
bank/change bank/växel
post office posten
stamp(s) frimärke(n)
where are you from? varifrån kommer du?
I'm English jag är engelsman/engelska
…Scottish …skotte
…Welsh …walesare
…Irish …irländare
…American …amerikan
…Canadian …kanadensare
…Australian …australier
…a New Zealander …nyzeeländare
what's your name? vad heter du?

what's this called in Swedish? vad heter det här på svenska?
do you speak English? talar du engelska?
I don't understand jag förstår inte
you're speaking too fast du talar för snabbt
how much is it? hur mycket kostar det?

GETTING AROUND

how do I get to…? hur kommer jag till…?
left/right till vänster/till höger
straight ahead rakt fram
where is the bus station? var ligger busstationen?
the bus stop for… busshållplatsen till…
train station järnvägsstationen/centralen
where does the bus to… leave from? varifrån går bussen till…?
is this the train for Gothenburg? åker detta tåg till Göteborg?
what time does it leave? hur dags går det?
what time does it arrive in…? hur dags är det framme i…?
which is the road to…? vilken är vägen till…?
where are you going? vart går du?
I'm going to… jag går till… …
that's great, thanks a lot jättebra, tack så mycket
stop here please stanna här, tack
ticket to… biljett till…
return ticket tur och retur

ACCOMMODATION

where's the youth hostel? var ligger vandrarhemmet?
is there a hotel round here? finns det något hotell i närheten?
I'd like a single/double room jag skulle vilja ha ett enkelrum/dubbelrum
can I see it? får jag se det?
how much is it a night? hur mycket kostar det per natt?
I'll take it jag tar det

it's too expensive, I don't want it now det är för mycket, jag tar det inte
can I/we leave the bags here until...? kan jag/vi få lämna väskorna här till... ...?
have you got har du något
...anything cheaper? ...billigare?
...with a shower? ...med dusch?
can I/we camp here? får jag/vi tälta här?

DAYS AND MONTHS
Monday måndag
Tuesday tisdag
Wednesday onsdag
Thursday torsdag
Friday fredag
Saturday lördag
Sunday söndag
January januari
February februari
March mars
April april
May maj
June juni
July juli
August augusti
September september
October oktober
November november
December december

THE TIME
what time is it? vad är klockan?
it's... den/hon är... ...
at what time...? hur dags...?
at... klockan...
midnight midnatt
one in the morning klockan ett på - natten
ten past one tio över ett
one fifteen kvart över ett
one twenty-five fem i halv två
one thirty halv två
one thirty-five fem över halv två
one forty tjugo i två
one forty-five kvart i två
one fifty-five fem i två

two o'clock klockan två
noon klockan tolv
in the morning på morgonen
in the afternoon på eftermiddagen
in the evening på kvällen
in ten minutes om tio minuter
ten minutes ago för tio minuter sedan

NUMBERS
1 ett
2 två
3 tre
4 fyra
5 fem
6 sex
7 sjö
8 åtta
9 nio
10 tio
11 elva
12 tolv
13 tretton
14 fjorton
15 femton
16 sexton
17 sjutton
18 arton
19 nitton
20 tjugo
21 tjugoett
22 tjugotvå
30 trettio
40 fyrtio
50 femtio
60 sextio
70 sjuttio
80 åttio
90 nittio
100 hundra
101 hundraett
200 två hundra
500 fem hundra
1000 tusen
10,000 tio tusen

FOOD AND DRINK TERMS

BASICS AND SNACKS
ägg egg
bröd bread
bulle bun
glass ice cream
grädde cream

gräddfil sour cream
gröt porridge
kaka cake
keks biscuits
knäckebröd crispbread
olja oil

omelett omelette
ost cheese
pastej paté
peppar pepper
pommes fries
ris rice
senap mustard
småkakor biscuits
smör butter
smörgås sandwich
socker sugar
sylt jam
tårta cake
vinäger vinegar
våffla waffle

MEAT (KÖTT)
älg elk
biff beef
fläsk pork
hjort venison
kalvkött veal
korv sausage
kotlett cutlet/chop
köttbullar meatballs
kyckling chicken
lammkött lamb
lever liver
oxstek roast beef
rådjursstek roast venison
renstek roast reindeer
skinka ham

FISH (FISK)
ål eel
ansjovis anchovies
blåmusslor mussels
fiskbullar fishballs
forell trout
hummer lobster
kaviar caviar
krabba crab
kräftor freshwater crayfish
lax salmon
makrill mackerel
räkor shrimps/prawns
röding arctic char
rödspätta plaice
sardiner sardines
sik whitefish
sill herring
sjötunga sole
strömming Baltic herring
torsk cod

VEGETABLES (GRÖNSAKER)
ärtor peas
blomkål cauliflower
bönor beans
brysselkål Brussels sprouts
gurka cucumber
lök onion
morötter carrots
potatis potatoes
rödkål red cabbage
sallad lettuce/salad
spenat spinach
svamp mushrooms
tomater tomatoes
vitkål white cabbage
vitlök garlic

FRUIT (FRUKT)
ananas pineapple
apelsin orange
äpple apple
aprikos apricot
banan banana
citron lemon
hallon raspberry
hjortron cloudberry
jordgubbar strawberries
lingon lingonberry/red whortleberry
päron pear
persika peach
vindruvor grapes

CULINARY TERMS
ångkokt steamed
blodig rare
filé fillet
friterad deep fried
genomstekt well done
gravad cured
grillat/halstrat grilled
kall cold
kokt boiled
lagom medium
pocherad poached
rökt smoked
stekt fried
ungstekt roasted/ baked
varm hot

DRINKS
apelsinjuice orange juice
chocklad hot chocolate
citron lemon
fruktjuice fruit juice

grädde cream
kaffe coffee
lättöl light beer
mellanöl medium-strong beer
mineralvatten mineral water
mjölk milk
öl beer
rödvin red wine
saft juice
skål cheers!
starköl strong beer
storstark large strong beer
te tea
vatten water
vin wine
vitt vin white wine

SWEDISH SPECIALITIES

ål eel, smoked and served with creamed potatoes or
   scrambled eggs (äggröra)
ärtsoppa yellow pea soup with pork, spiced with
   thyme and marjoram; a winter dish traditionally eaten
   on Thursdays
biff à la Lindström meat patties with beetroot and capers
biff Rydberg sautéed chunks of beef served with fried
   potatoes, onions and mustard
filmjölk soured milk
fisksoppa fish soup usually including several sorts of
   fish, prawns and dill
getost goat's cheese
glögg mulled wine, usually fortified with spirits to keep
   out the cold, and drunk at Christmas
gravad lax salmon marinated in dill, sugar and
   seasoning; served with mustard sauce and lemon
hjortron a wild, orange-coloured berry (the
   cloudberry), served with fresh cream and/or ice cream
   or made into jam

Janssons frestelse köttbullar potato and anchovy
   meatballs served with a brown creamy sauce and
   lingonberries
kräftor crayfish
lingon lingonberry (sometimes known as red whortle-
   berries), a red berry made into a kind of jam and
   served with meat dishes as well as on pancakes and in
   puddings, eaten at Christmas
långfil a special type of soured milk from northern
   Sweden
lövbiff sliced, fried beef with onions
matjessill sweet-pickled herring
pepparkakor thin, spiced gingerbread biscuits popular
   at Christmas
plättar thin pancakes, often served with pea soup
potatissallad potato salad, often flavoured with dill
   or chives
pytt i panna cubes of meat and fried potatoes with a
   fried egg and beetroot
raggmunk potato pancakes
semla sweet bun with almond paste and whipped
   cream; associated with Lent
sillbricka various cured and marinated herring dishes;
   often appears as a first course in restaurants at
   lunchtime
sjömansbiff sailors' beef casserole: thin slices of beef
   baked in the oven with potatoes and onions, topped
   with parsley
smultron wild strawberries, known for their
   concentrated taste
strömming Baltic herring
surströmming Baltic herring fermented for months
   until it's rotten and the tin it's in buckles – very smelly
   and eaten in very, very small quantities. Not for the
   faint-hearted!
Wallenbergare burgers made of minced veal mixed
   with cream and egg yolks

Glossary

älg elk
ångbåt steamboat
ankommande arriving
ankomst arrival
avgående departing
avgång departure
bad swimming (pool)
bastu sauna
båt boat/ferry
berg mountain
biljett ticket
bio cinema
björn bear
bokhandel bookshop
bro bridge
brygga jetty/pier
cyckelstig cycle path
dagens rätt dish of the day
domkyrka cathedral
drottning queen
ej inträde no entrance
extrapris special offer
färja ferry
gamla old
gamla stan old town
gata (g.) street
gränd alley
hamn harbour
hantverk handicrafts
hembygdsgård homestead museum
hiss lift
järnvägsstation train station
kapell chapel
kåta traditional *Sámi* hut
klockan (kl.) o'clock
kyrka church

lilla little
loppis flea market
muséet museum
nakenbad naturist beach
öppet open
öppettider opening hours
pressbyrå newsagent
rabatt discount
rådhuset town hall
rea sale
ren reindeer
restaurang restaurant
rökning förbjuden no smoking
simhall swimming pool
sjö lake
skog forest
slott palace/castle
smörgåsbord spread of different dishes
sovvagn sleeping car
spår track
stadshus city hall
stängt closed
stora big
storstark strong beer
strand beach
stuga cottage
systembolaget alcohol store
tåg train
tältplats campsite
torg square/market place
tunnelbana underground (metro)
turistbyrå tourist office
universitet university
väg (v.) road
vandrarhem hostel

Small print and index

A ROUGH GUIDE TO ROUGH GUIDES

Published in 1982, the first Rough Guide – to Greece – was a student scheme that became a publishing phenomenon. Mark Ellingham, a recent graduate in English from Bristol University, had been travelling in Greece the previous summer and couldn't find the right guidebook. With a small group of friends he wrote his own guide, combining a contemporary, journalistic style with a thoroughly practical approach to travellers' needs.

The immediate success of the book spawned a series that rapidly covered dozens of destinations. And, in addition to impecunious backpackers, Rough Guides soon acquired a much broader readership that relished the guides' wit and inquisitiveness as much as their enthusiastic, critical approach and value-for-money ethos. These days, Rough Guides include recommendations from budget to luxury and cover more than 120 destinations around the globe, from Amsterdam to Zanzibar, all regularly updated by our team of roaming writers.

Browse all our latest guides, read inspirational features and book your trip at **roughguides.com**.

Rough Guide credits

Editor: Zara Sekhavati
Authors: James Proctor & Steve Vickers
Updater: Lise Jacobs
Cartography: Ed Wright
Managing editor: Rachel Lawrence

Picture editor: Aude Vauconsant
Cover photo research: Aude Vauconsant
Senior DTP coordinator: Dan May
Head of DTP and Pre-Press: Rebeka Davies

Publishing information

Eighth edition 2020

Distribution
UK, Ireland and Europe
Apa Publications (UK) Ltd; sales@roughguides.com
United States and Canada
Ingram Publisher Services; ips@ingramcontent.com
Australia and New Zealand
Woodslane; info@woodslane.com.au
Southeast Asia
Apa Publications (SN) Pte; sales@roughguides.com
Worldwide
Apa Publications (UK) Ltd; sales@roughguides.com
Special Sales, Content Licensing and CoPublishing
Rough Guides can be purchased in bulk quantities
at discounted prices. We can create special editions,
personalised jackets and corporate imprints tailored to
your needs. sales@roughguides.com.

Help us update

We've gone to a lot of effort to ensure that this edition of
The Rough Guide to Sweden is accurate and up-to-date.
However, things change – places get "discovered", opening
hours are notoriously fickle, restaurants and rooms raise
prices or lower standards. If you feel we've got it wrong
or left something out, we'd like to know, and if you can
remember the address, the price, the hours, the phone
number, so much the better.

Please send your comments with the subject line
"Rough Guide Sweden Update" to mail@uk.roughguides.
com. We'll credit all contributions and send a copy of the
next edition (or any other Rough Guide if you prefer) for
the very best emails.

Photo credits
(Key: T-top; C-centre; B-bottom; L-left; R-right)

Index

Map symbols

The symbols below are used on maps throughout the book

▬ ▪ ▪	International boundary	⊙	Statue	⊞	Hospital
▬ ▪ ▪	State/province boundary	◆	Point of interest	☀	Viewpoint
▬ ▬ ▬	Chapter division boundary	★	Bus/taxi	≍	Bridge
	Pedestrian street	🏛	Stately home	⌣	Swimming pool/area
	Motorway	ⓘ	Information office	⚓	Church (regional maps)
	Street	Ⓣ	T-bana station	⛴	Boat
- - - -	Footpath	@	Internet café/access	◯	Stadium
▬◼▬	Railway	⁚⁚	Ruin	⊡	Church
	Coastline	♖	Castle		Building
— —	Ferry route	☧	Lighthouse	☐	Park
	National park boundary	⊠	Gateway	☐	Beach
▬▬▬	Wall	⚚	Waterfall	⊓	Christian cemetery
✈	Airport	⌂	Lodge		
▲	Mountain peak	🏖	Beach		

Listings key

■ Accommodation

● Eating

■ Drinking, nightlife & live music